DAVID BOWIE

ALSO BY DYLAN JONES

London Sartorial

Manxiety

London Rules

Mr. Mojo

Elvis Has Left the Building: The Day the King Died

The Eighties: One Day, One Decade

From the Ground Up

When Ziggy Played Guitar: David Bowie and Four Minutes That Shook the World

The Biographical Dictionary of Popular Music

British Heroes in Afghanistan (with David Bailey)

Cameron On Cameron: Conversations with Dylan Jones

Mr. Jones' Rules for The Modern Man

iPod Therefore I Am: A Personal Journey Through Music

Meaty Beaty Big & Bouncy

Sex, Power & Travel

Ultra Lounge

Paul Smith: True Brit

Jim Morrison: Dark Star

Haircults

DAVID BOWIE

A LIFE

DYLAN
JONES

CROWN
ARCHETYPE
NEW YORK

Published in the United States by Crown Archetype, an imprint of the Crown Publishing Group, a division of Penguin Random House LLC, New York.
crownpublishing.com

Crown Archetype and colophon is a registered trademark of Penguin Random House LLC.

Library of Congress Cataloging-in-Publication Data is available upon request.

ISBN 978-0-451-49783-3
Ebook ISBN 978-0-451-49785-7

Printed in the United States of America

Book design by Anna Thompson
Jacket design by Rachel Willey
Jacket photograph by Mirrorpix/Getty Images

10 9 8 7 6 5 4 3 2 1

First Edition

For my Stargirls, Sarah, Edie & Georgia

CONTENTS

PREFACE

On October 31, 2016, as the rest of London was being swamped by hordes of drunken roisterers in nylon skeleton costumes and Donald Trump Halloween masks, many carrying neon pumpkins and covered in fake blood and blankets of spooky cobweb spray, Sotheby's in Bond Street was an oasis of old-school gentility. All day the art handlers in the Mayfair auction house had been putting the finishing touches to the *Bowie/Collector* public preview, straightening up the Graham Sutherlands and the Damien Hirsts and struggling to reposition a gigantic Ettore Sottsass sideboard. Tonight there was going to be a private opening dinner for one hundred lucky people, and the exhibition needed to be inch perfect. By 7:45, the gallery was almost full as the likes of Tracey Emin, Keith Tyson, Elisabeth Murdoch, Robert Fox, Jasper Conran, Nick Grimshaw, Sam Smith, Saffron Aldridge, Alexander McQueen's Sarah Burton, U2's Adam Clayton, Bowie's art consultant Kate Chertavian, and dozens of other luminaries from the worlds of art, music, and publishing made their way slowly through the halls—many taking selfies in front of a wall-sized blow-up of the *"Heroes"* album cover, some mimicking Bowie's famous Erich Heckel hand gesture.

His greatest hits playing at entry-level volume, anecdotes were shared, conversations remembered, and even more imagined. Some of Bowie's friends were there, as well as many people who had worked with him. There was even the odd journalist or two. There were people there who shouldn't have been there, and many who weren't who ought to have been, but then such is the nature of the London society dinner.

The artworks themselves seemed to glisten like evidence, every one of them a pit stop in Bowie's life, each purchase a punctuation mark, a story. Standing in these rooms, looking at David Bowie's extraordinary art collection (most of which had been in storage for years, and included examples of outsider art, surrealism, and contemporary African art, as well as two hundred works by many of the most important British artists of the twentieth century, including Frank Auerbach—"I want to sound like that looks," Bowie once said about one of the artist's swollen oil paintings), it was impossible not to feel his significance, as if any of us needed any more proof, because as a collector he suddenly seemed more important than any of the trinkets in the room. Here was a man who hadn't just inhabited the verge of greatness, he had stood in its very middle. An autodidact who tried to map his own cultural life, and who ended up creating one of the most important cultural lives of the last fifty years, David Bowie was his very own creation, his very own work of art.

As we sat down to eat, a carefully placed book about an alcoholic San Franciscan dentist stared up at me. In September 2013, to mark the Canadian opening of the *David Bowie Is* exhibition at the Art Gallery of Ontario, the curators, Geoffrey Marsh and Victoria Broackes, released a list of Bowie's hundred favorite books. And at Sotheby's I found one of them on my plate: *McTeague*, Frank Norris's graphic portrayal of the seamy side of survival in turn-of-the-century urban America, first published in 1899, and first read by David Bowie sometime toward the end of the '60s.

Each of the hundred dinner guests had been given one of Bowie's favorite books—my neighbors had been given *The Outsider* and *The Sailor Who Fell from Grace with the Sea*—an unexpectedly delightful touch to celebrate the opening of the show. As the guests worked their way through caviar salt and gin-cured salmon, followed by salt-marsh lamb rack and Wellington, you could tell some of them were trying to work out if there was a reason they had been given their particular book. Tracey Emin got *A Confederacy of Dunces* by John Kennedy Toole ("A funny, slapstick one," she said); film producer Paul McGuinness got *Earthly Powers* by Anthony Burgess; and the chairman of HSBC got *Madame Bovary*.

There were many speeches that night, all of which mentioned Bowie's profound curiosity and passionate espousal of the artists he collected. Simon Hucker, Sotheby's senior specialist in modern and postwar British art, spoke, as did the auction house's Frances Christie and Oliver Barker. In the flurry of activity preceding the auction, Beth Greenacre, the curator of Bowie's art collection since the turn of the century, said that many of the artists "challenged the past and its established orthodoxies," artists who were intent on creating a new language. "He allowed us to look at the world in a new way and the artists he collected are absolutely doing that," she said. A few weeks earlier she had told the *Financial Times*, "There is something very English about [the work], and that is what David was: he retained his passport, no matter where he lived. And these pictures form a narrative about him, and his interests. He was an observer, and he was a historian. He really looked back at history to understand his current position, and that is what these artists were doing too."

Quoted in the *Guardian* around the same time, Simon Hucker said that Bowie had been attracted to artists with whom he saw a connection—often outsiders or cultural refugees trying to break with their own history. This was the boy from postwar Brixton with his sights set on the world. "It comes back to him being really interested in who he was," said Hucker, "the culture he grew up in, the world of his parents, the world of his childhood."

This was a sentiment echoed at Sotheby's. "It's so weird, so strange," said a friend of mine. "Looking at all the stuff on these walls, it's like he's been everywhere, but also like he never left. His whole life is here."

I make it a thing, when I gazelle onstage to believe in myself,

I make it a thing, to glance in window panes and look pleased with myself.

—DAVID BOWIE, "CANDIDATE" (ALT. VERSION), 1974

ACKNOWLEDGMENTS

First of all, I would like to personally thank the 182 people who agreed to be interviewed for, or contributed to, this book. This book is their book, as it contains their testimonies, their own stories. I hope they feel I've done them all justice. I spoke to people all over the world, in London, Paris, Milan, Miami, Los Angeles, New York, Chicago, Arizona, Cardiff, Sussex, Montreal, Essex, Sydney, Brixton, Bromley, Beckenham, Cambridge, Hay-on-Wye, Ipswich, Woodbridge . . . everybody talk about, pop music!

Obviously the Bowie book industry is operating on something of a different scale than it was when he was still alive. Since his enforced retirement midway through the Noughties the books started to come out on an almost six-monthly basis, but since his death there has been a tsunami. Many of the books written about Bowie are biographies of the metaphor that we have come to know as "Bowie"; I wanted to write about the man, the person himself. Of course, there are many who oversee their very own Bowie industries, and many more who have taken the opportunity to tell their stories in long form—and who can blame them? For this book I wanted to cast the net as wide as possible, and as well as focusing on the many tall poppies who knew and worked with David over the years, I also spoke to the raft of people who perhaps previously hadn't had the opportunity to tell their stories with as much encouragement or fanfare, people who had been involved with him before he was a star, in his pomp, and during the long stretches of post-imperial fame. I'd like to thank them all—the musicians who worked with Bowie, the family friends, professional friends, childhood acquaintances, lovers, actors, producers, directors, stylists, artists, curators, journalists, photographers, promoters, art directors, publishers, publicists, authors, designers, comedians, fans, boldface names, everyone. As a form of history, the oral biography has the capacity to be more honest than others, and the lack of subjectivity employed by the editor should enable the truth to shine through. But then, who ever remembers an event in precisely the same way? As Bertrand Russell said, "When a man tells you he knows about anything, you are safe in inferring he is an inexact man." Yet the recollections contained here, many of which include minor contradictions, have produced a fascinating prism of whatever the truth actually is. A few of the testimonies have had to come from sources outside of my own work, as some of the significant people who came into contact with Bowie have long since passed on (John Lennon, Mick Ronson, Luther Vandross, Tony Scott, Ron Asheton, and so on), while there were others, such as Iman Mohamed Abdulmajid and Coco Schwab, for instance, who were impossible for me to pin down. These other sources include BBC Radio 2, *The Black Collegian Magazine*, Bowiewonderworld.com, the British Library Archives, the *Daily Mail*, Davidbowie.com, *Empire*, *Entertainment Weekly*, the *Guardian*, *LA Record*, the journalist Legs McNeil, *Mojo*, *Musician*, *Music Scene*, National Public Radio, the *New York Times*, *Nineteen*, *NME*, Oocities.org, *Reflex*, Francis Schoenberger, the *Sunday Times*, and *Uncut*.

All of the quotes from David Bowie himself are taken from the seven formal interviews I conducted with him over the years, along with some quotes from an interview commissioned for *i-D* back in 1987 when I was still the editor (and for which I wrote many of the questions), used with the kind permission of Tricia Jones (who conducted the interview), plus one quote from a BBC Radio series, *Bowie Verbatim*, another from a speech Bowie gave to the Berklee College of Music in 1999, and one from Hugh Thomson's interview with him for *Five Years*. After his death, Bowie's interviews started to take on a new poignancy, something I started to see myself when I looked back through my own interviews with him. Things

I skipped over, or took for granted at the time, now seemed strangely loaded, heavy with meaning. They certainly helped me frame this book.

David Bowie never forgot to connect. Having struggled for a decade to make it in an industry that he often thought was collectively conspiring against him, little was left to chance, and the ruthlessness with which he assaulted his audience when he finally did become successful was only matched by the extraordinary quality of the material, and the stagecraft, that he used as ammunition. Whereas in the '60s Bowie was always slightly behind the curve, as the '70s clicked in, he inched ahead of it, peering at the future through a Manichean viewfinder. He showed that what he was doing was not a trend, but rather a direction, one that would change on a whim, or indeed with the wind. He excelled at the art of individualism, rarely tacking toward the center, and relentlessly moving forward. In this age when there is indiscriminate access to almost everything, it would have been difficult for Bowie to operate so successfully, but back in the '70s he was a divining rod, his own as well as ours. His talent was so immense it was often bewildering. But then he'd learned how to use what "little" talent (his term) he had to its fullest effect. Bowie often said that God's cruelest gift was bestowing only a modicum of talent on a person, and yet he exploited what he had in a way that was all-consuming. He was a fascinating fusion of ambition and craft, coupled with an innate charm, and—after that first unsuccessful decade—an often unerring sense of timing.

He also deployed his curiosity as an analytical torch, repurposing in completely original ways, rarely embarrassed to claim something as his own. In that first, formative decade of his career, Bowie's work bore a relation to many forebears, and it was only with "Space Oddity" that he showed that he had a mind of his own, and genuine human purpose. (Having said that, at the time this was considered to be something of a novelty record, and it could have simply been regarded in the years afterward as nothing more important than "Rock Me Amadeus" by Falco, for instance, a novelty tie-in from a different era.) There are many who think that Bowie was unrelentingly calculating, carefully building his personae and his records like a bomb-squad technician, deciding which color wire to snip, petrified that a mistake would end his seemingly inexorable righteous passage. In reality he just mixed things up as he went, using bits and pieces he'd collected along the way. And boy did he collect. The world of pop has always been prey to cryptomnesia, the psychological condition of "creating" something already experienced, the accidental copying of something unknowingly overheard (the most famous example is George Harrison's appropriation of the Chiffons' "He's So Fine" for "My Sweet Lord," which even the judge believed had been unintentional—even though he found him guilty). Bowie wasn't unaware when he lifted something; he knew.

"There was always an exchange of information within our friendship," said Mick Jagger, after Bowie died. "And I suppose there was always an element of competition between us, but it never felt overwhelming. When he would see me, he'd give me a hug, and I could feel him going up behind the collar of my shirt to see what I was wearing. He used to copy me sometimes, but he'd be very honest about it. If he took one of your moves, he'd say, 'That's one of yours—I just tried it.' I didn't mind sharing things with him, because he would share so much with me—it was a two-way street."

He had undergone an apotheosis long before he died, but there is still an urgency about Bowie's music, an urgency that makes it difficult to simply consign that music to the realm of myth and legend. It is unique. As Oliver Sacks wrote, in his beautiful little book *Gratitude*, "There will be no one like us when we are gone, but then there is no one like anyone else, ever. When people die, they cannot be replaced. They leave holes that cannot be filled, for it is the fate—the genetic and neural fate—of every human being to be a unique individual, to find his own path, to live his own life, to die his own death."

Bowie's ability to connect was something felt by everyone who fell under his spell. It somehow seemed that he was talking to us all individually, and so consequently we tended to feel extremely protective of him, each of us imagining that we were the only person who really "got" him. I was a highly impressionable twelve-year-old in the summer of 1972, and I too thought I might be the only person to "get" David Bowie, little knowing that *Top of the Pops* had probably been seen by something like twelve and a half million people. Still, my interest was piqued, and in many ways I stayed interested for the rest of his life. The first thing I did—apart from unsuccessfully attempt to ape the Ziggy haircut—was start to collect anything and everything I could that was Bowie-related. But then I was always a terrible hoarder.

So many people felt they had a personal connection with David Bowie, and this became more than apparent when he died. As soon as he passed away, not only were all the social media channels full of music-related images, eulogies, and mini-blogs, but every national newspaper in the world had—seemingly in cahoots—decided to clear their front pages and carry a version of Brian Duffy's genuinely iconic *Aladdin Sane* image. Bowie died during a period when the media was controlled by people who had grown up with him, whether they owned an iPhone 6 or edited a broadsheet. Everyone had a story to tell. The British fashion designer Pam Hogg, for instance, whose work often references Bowie, and who would go on to design the outfits worn onstage during the Bowie tribute at the Brits a month later, wrote this on her Instagram feed: "Always meet your heroes. Blitz club 1979 . . . I hear all this screaming. I thought it was a fight. A few mins later I literally bumped into someone on the dancefloor . . . near died when I realised it was David Bowie . . . we automatically laughed and danced . . . it was about 30 secs . . . a memory for a lifetime . . ."*

So many memories, so many stories. Like I say, I'd like to thank everyone who agreed to speak with me for this project, while I am especially indebted to Alan Edwards, who went out of his way to facilitate many of the interviews, continually espousing my good intentions. I really can't thank him enough; he had no commercial incentive, and no reason to be so helpful, other than a sense of friendship (to me) and loyalty (to David). By which I mean that Alan wanted to help me get the story as "right" as possible. I would also like to thank Kevin Doughten (for commissioning the book and for being such a collaborative, gifted, and resolute editor; editors hate being edited, but you've made the book better in the process), Ed Victor (for brokering the deal), as well as Sarah Walter, Edie Walter Jones, and Georgia Sydney Jones, along with the wonderful Eleanor Halls, whose dedication, enthusiasm, and ability to charm

* There would be so many tributes that after a while they ceased to have meaning. As the *Guardian* said about yet another posthumous fandango, "It was almost unsurprising when the Bowie prom was announced, promising Bowie with a twist—but who really wants Bowie with a twist? Bowie was the twist."

all conspired to make this a much better book than it would have been had she not been involved. She is a great journalist. Particular thanks are also due to Iman, Bill Zysblat ("[David was] the rarest combination of genius and graciousness. I miss him every day. [He] was a quick study, from the first online fan club to the first securitization of royalties, David completely understood the underpinnings of the deals"), Rob Stringer, Tricia Jones, Trevor Dolby, Mark Russell, Alice Rawsthorne, Rosie Boycott, Chris Keskie, Mark Richardson, Matthew Hobbs, Nicky and Rob Carter, Rosie Goldsmith, Hanif Kureishi, John Pearson, Chris Charlesworth, Lottie Stanners, Linda Davis, Maria Padget, Robert Chalmers, Jonathan Heaf, Margot Farnham, Fiona Dealey, Julian Stockton, Olivia Cole, Anna Ford, Emma Reeves, and Francine Stock. I am particularly indebted to Paul Gorman, Dorian Lynsky, Jason Heller, Michael Kaplan, Tony Oursler, and Alexis Petridis for allowing me to quote substantially from their pieces. Thank you also to the lovely Clare Shenstone (the inspiration for "Heroes," and whose dream about swimming with dolphins is so central to the song), whom I spoke to at length about her connection with David, her time with him in Berlin, and the peripatetic nature of their relationship; in the end she decided she didn't want her story told, however our own connection more than compensated for my initial disappointment at this. Thanks also to Jeffrey Morgan, and to *Creem*. All William Boyd's quotes are copyright © William Boyd 2016. Erin Kean's article first appeared on Salon.com at http://www.Salon.com. An online version remains in the Salon archives. Reprinted with permission.

Finally, I'd like to save the biggest thanks to my agent, Ed Victor, who died earlier in the year. Ed was my agent for fourteen of my books, but more importantly, he was a dear friend of mine—not just a huge literary figure but a man you could count on when the going got tough. I miss him terribly.

INTRODUCTION

"It is indeed true," said someone from his management office when I contacted them that morning. "We found out about an hour ago, and we're finding it very difficult to function. He really is gone." It was 6:40 in the morning, but I know I wasn't the first person to call. Oddly, I heard myself through that by now rather old-fashioned form of communication, email, as various friends and colleagues sent messages, both from the UK and the US. I checked my Instagram feed, and saw a flurry of posts, iconic images accompanied by heartfelt commiserations, and distress.

A few minutes later, requests to write obituaries followed.

All of which obviously swirled around the shocking news itself. When people die, especially significant people, others can busy themselves, freely expressing emotion, offering professional consolation. With Bowie, it was different, as I know so few people whose lives were unaffected by him.

For me and members of my generation, the Bowie generation, his death was more momentous than John Lennon's. Of course, it would be invidious to compare the two, but it is still difficult even now for me to grasp just how much he meant to me. I was a teenager when he emerged, and was one of the many people who saw his performance of "Starman" on Top of the Pops *in the summer of*

1972, one of the many millions whose lives were altered at such an impressionable age.

For my generation, it is difficult to overemphasize just how important David Bowie was to us, not just in terms of music and fashion, but also in terms of how we carried—and continue to carry—ourselves in the world. I remember exactly where I was when I heard about Lennon's death, but Bowie's passing will stay with me in a more permanent way.

On the day Bowie's death was announced, I was in the middle of Men's Fashion Week at Victoria House in Holborn, and there wasn't a dry eye in the house. It would be a cliché to say that everyone felt numb, but then clichés are clichés for a reason, because they're true. Almost everyone in the building appeared to be moved. Some had fallen in love with him when they were teenagers, others had only come to him recently, discovering him as a heritage artist; but nearly all of them had a relationship with him and his music. Almost every show I saw that day made some kind of nod toward Bowie's passing, and when I walked into the Burberry show in Kensington Gardens a few hours later, "Where Are You Now?," his melancholic comeback single from 2013, was blasting across the park. As I sat waiting for the show to start, I got an email from a famous musician, one for whom Bowie had been a huge influence: "What is extraordinary and wonderful and a measure of the man is that the very last song David gave to us all is up there with some of his greatest tunes," he wrote, referring to a song on his final album, Blackstar*—released the previous week, on his birthday. "He placed what is probably the best song on* Blackstar *(with its now poignant widow's weeds of a cover) last. 'I Can't Give Everything Away,' he sings. An artist to the last. We are all David Bowie."*

I knew Bowie a little, and unlike many famous people who can have some of the sheen rubbed off them when you meet them, Bowie became even more intriguing when I did, because his curiosity, his obsession for "the new," appeared to be genuinely innate. The first time I met him, in 1982, he asked me for a light for his Marlboro. I was an extra on the dreadful vampire movie The Hunger, *in which Bowie was starring with Catherine Deneuve. It was my job to walk up and down the metal stairs in Heaven, the gay nightclub underneath the arches in the Strand, in London, as "Bela Lugosi's Dead" by Bauhaus blared out of the speakers. For a twenty-one-year-old Bowie obsessive this was a dream come true, a day that turned into an anecdote that would eventually kick-start a very odd relationship, one that continued for over thirty years. My last brush with Bowie happened the summer before he died, although it was merely a chance encounter with the landlords of the hotel Bowie had stayed in when he was building his house in upstate New York. It would be betraying a confidence to tell anyone what they told me, but it seems Bowie had not lost his ability to charm.*

He was as important to the '70s as the Beatles were to the '60s, and yet his reach and his influence continues today in a way that we have yet to quantify, try as we might.

I knew he had been ill—many did—but I had no idea it was critical. Having been in touch for several decades, when he became sick around a decade ago—caused initially by a series of heart attacks—he disappeared from view. I knew he had bought a huge apartment complex in downtown New York, I knew the people who sold him his house in Woodstock, and I knew his personal publicist and management company extremely well. Yet recently every communication had been through a third party, almost as though he was pushing himself away from the world.

Like everyone who grew up with the man, Bowie would confound, annoy, and occasionally disappoint me, but I never found him less than fascinating.

In a way he was my own personal fascination, and maybe yours too.

Even when he became ill, he kept an almost obsessive eye on those in his orbit, especially if they were writing about him. A few years ago I wrote a book about Bowie's performance on Top of the Pops *in 1972, an extended essay that tried to form an opinion about the '70s from those four short minutes on a television program. I needed various permissions from Bowie to use certain photographs in the book, and over a period of a few weeks he eventually agreed to me using them. However, I also included several facts in the book that I knew to be wrong—some descriptions of the BBC dressing room, some quotes, and some outfit changes that I knew to be inventions (as I had actually invented them). I did this as I hoped he might contradict me, and actually give me some more material for the book. Perhaps this was conceited, expecting him to actually read the manuscript, but then I also knew that he had the power to not release the pictures I needed. But Bowie remained mute: even though he had tacitly endorsed the book, he would rather I print the myth.*

That was Bowie all over.

In fact, his entire professional career was one of myth, legend, and invention. Brilliantly so.

When I was writing my first Bowie book, as I was finishing the final chapters, I went to visit my father in Cheltenham, in his flat in the shadow of GCHQ (this turned out to be the last significant time I saw him before he died). He asked me what I was working on, and I told him that I was writing a book about Bowie's extraordinary performance on TOTP, *and how he influenced an entire generation of future music and fashion obsessives. When he asked me why, I reeled off the various elements of his performance that had been so challenging, so inspiring, and so transgressive. I described the way in which Bowie had toyed sexually with his guitarist Mick Ronson, the way in which he had dressed like a pansexual spaceman, the way he sashayed across the screen like a 1920s film star, and, saliently, the way in which his flame-red hair, his Day-Glo jumpsuit, and the general glam color fest had almost colonized the program. I explained that this was the moment when the '70s finally outgrew the '60s, when the monochrome world of boring, boring southeast England had exploded in a fiesta of color.*

My father looked at the floor, took a moment, and then said, very quietly: "You know we had a black-and-white television, don't you?"

1

LIVING IN LIES BY THE RAILWAY LINE

1947–1969

He was a postwar baby, born in London in 1947. He was part of the new world, two years after the end of the old. A London baby. He went to school in Brixton before being cast out to the suburbs. Even when he was young he knew he wanted to be bigger than he was, wanted to be a bigger man. When he started to work in advertising he thought he'd broken through, but he had no idea what was to come. In the beginning, he was feeling his way—he was in the Kon-Rads, the King Bees, the Mannish Boys, David Jones and the Buzz, Davey Jones and the Lower Third, Feathers, the Hype—but he had no idea who he was going to be when he'd finished.

David Jones was born on January 8, 1947, at 40 Stansfield Road, Brixton, the son of a cinema usherette and a promotions officer for Barnardo's. He lived there until he was six, when his family moved farther out to Bromley in Kent. While his father was middle class, his mother came from a poor, working-class family. David used to say that there was a dark cloud over her side of the family, as it was full of mental instability. When he let his guard down, or when he wanted to amplify that side of his upbringing, he would say that "tragically" two or three of his aunts committed suicide. He would say that this seemed to be something he would hear constantly while growing up: How so-and-so has left us now. He said once, "I guess most of us have battled with reality and something else all of our lives. I think [my elder half-brother] Terry probably gave me the greatest, serviceable education that I ever could have had. He just introduced me to the outside things. The first real major event for me was when he passed Jack Kerouac's On the Road *on to me, which really changed my life. He also introduced me to people like John Coltrane, which was way above my head, but I saw the magic and I caught the enthusiasm for it because of his enthusiasm for it. And I kinda wanted to be like him." Terry—the savant of cool jazz—would adumbrate his life as a sort of ticking clock of impending, accelerated mortality. As for his mother's sisters, his aunt Vivienne was diagnosed with schizophrenia, his aunt Una died in her late thirties having experienced periods in a mental institution as well as electric shock treatment, while Aunt Nora actually had a lobotomy because of her "bad nerves."*

DAVID BOWIE: I had a very happy childhood, seriously nothing wrong with it. I was lonely but I never really wanted and certainly never went hungry, but I obviously saw people deprived around me and kids going to school with their shoes falling apart and kids looking like urchins. It left an impression on me that I never ever wanted to be hungry, or at the wrong end of society.

KRISTINA AMADEUS (DAVID'S COUSIN): David's parents, especially his father, "John" Jones, encouraged him from the time he was a toddler. His mother, Peggy, spoke often of our deceased grandfather, who was a bandmaster in the army and played many wind instruments. David's first instruments, a plastic saxophone, a tin guitar, and a xylophone, were given to him before he was an adolescent. He also owned a record player when few children had one. When he was eleven we danced like possessed elves to the records of Bill Haley, Fats Domino, and Elvis Presley. David's father took him to meet singers and other performers preparing for the Royal Variety Performance. I remember one afternoon in the late '50s when David was introduced to Dave King, Alma Cogan, and Tommy Steele. "My son is going to be an entertainer too," he said. "Aren't you, David?" "Yes, Daddy," David squeaked in his childish high-pitched voice, his face flushed and beaming with pride. Although Uncle John never lived to see David's huge success, he was convinced it would become a reality.

WENDY LEIGH (BIOGRAPHER): David grew up petted and privileged. He wasn't a working-class hero by any stretch. It was actually quite a suburban life, even though it was in south London, in Brixton. His father was the number-one PR at Dr. Barnardo's, so David was immersed in the idea of presentation from a very young age. He was taken to all the shows by his father, introduced to celebrities, and he learned how to promote, how to sell himself. No one ever talks about the fact that he was incredibly influenced by his father, who had access to this exciting outside world. Every performer needs to be a great seducer, and David learned that from an early age. His father showed him a lot of love. He showed him how to get on, how to charm, and how to practice the art of being nice.

GEORGE UNDERWOOD (CHILDHOOD FRIEND): His dad was lovely, a really nice gentle man. His mum, well, even David didn't like his mum. She wasn't an easy person to get on with. She was very cold. Very insular. I think that's why he liked coming round to my house, because my parents were totally different. "Hello, David, want a cup of tea, David?" My parents were very welcoming, but this wasn't what would happen round at his house. Mrs. Jones would hardly ever say anything to me. I'm not sure what it was, but she was never happy. She always gave David such a hard time.

DAVID ARDEN (MANAGER): I was brought up in Brixton around the same time as David Bowie, and everyone thinks it was a tough place, but it was actually rather nice and full of variety artists. Half the houses were owned by [Trinidadian pianist] Winifred Atwell, who had bought them for investment purposes, and she used to rent them out to music-hall acts and light entertainers. John Major lived a few streets away from me, and his dad was an acrobat and juggler. It later turned into a rougher neighborhood, but at the time we were brought up there it was very arty-crafty. If you were an artist in London, in music hall or variety, or in showbiz of one kind or another, that's where you lived. So Bowie was surrounded by this extremely artistic community. It was vibrant in that way. He wasn't just a performer, wasn't just a singer-songwriter, he was an artist, and he got that because of where he was brought up. I'd go into the arcade in Brixton, under the railway arches, and buy my reggae and jazz records there, and

David would do the same thing. We had local people round to dinner all the time, and they were all in the business, people like Dickie Henderson. There were also lots of places to go and see acts too, as the area fed off the people who lived there. So it's no surprise he turned out the way he did.

ANNE BRIGGS (NEIGHBOR): For a time as children we lived at Clapham in South London and were regular visitors to Brixton Market. There were all manner of traders, hawkers, stalls selling anything—Technicolor clothing which only the new residents of Brixton would wear, fruit piled up on shiny green fake grass cloths, vegetables of all kinds, and barrow boys with such constant and witty sales patter that people would gather round to listen and heckle. There were the West Indian traders with their Caribbean vegetables and lilting speech encouraging passersby to try their vegetables and fruit. Then there were buskers, always with their promoters, either providing music or awe-inspiring feats of physical flexibility, juggling or occasionally sword swallowers, all with their constant conversation attracting the crowd. Tanks of writhing eels in slightly murky water alongside stalls shrouded in white selling the little pots of jellied eels—no doubt to emphasize their freshness . . . cockles, winkles and shrimps were measured in old half pint and pint tankards. Pills and potions offering miracle cures of some sort or another—if we hovered to try and read the packets we were whisked away.

GEOFF MACCORMACK (CHILDHOOD FRIEND): I first met David when I was seven, at Burnt Ash Primary School, when he moved to Bromley—we had little brown uniforms. I'd already met George Underwood when I was four, at the local church school, St. Mary's. I was in the cubs with David, in the choir together. We bonded over music, and both loved rock and roll, and as we grew older loved Little Richard. The Britain we grew up in was really quite grubby. There were still rations until the '50s, and you'd walk to school via bomb sites. The music was bad, there was no decent food, and everything was gray, so when American music came along it completely changed everything. David's father used to fund-raise with the stars of the day, people like Dickie Henderson and Tommy Steele.

I initially thought David was an only child, as he was only ever the only child in the house. I only found out much later that he had a brother.

We never discussed it. I think it was a mutual understanding, as I had a brother who left home early to join the forces. He moved abroad and he wasn't in my life either. So it was almost a mirror thing. David had a good relationship with his father, and he was always quite generous. He would always buy him records, and he got a lot of records through work. His father used to get American music that we'd never heard before and most of the country have never heard before. Most of the rock and roll we heard in this country was rerecorded by British artists for labels like Embassy that we used to buy in Woolworths. So to hear the real thing was quite rare and a real treat. David had Fats Domino's "Blueberry Hill" when that came out, "Hound Dog" by Elvis Presley. He also had "I Put a Spell on You" by Screamin' Jay Hawkins, although David's mother wouldn't let him play it in the house as she thought it was the devil's music, which I suppose it was in a way. Our favorite was Frankie Lymon & the Teenagers, "I'm Not a Juvenile Delinquent." When he did *The Next Day*, I told him I loved it, and he actually said, "It's not 'I'm Not a Juvenile Delinquent,' but it'll do." I remember him lending me a couple of records and I left them on the windowsill in the breakfast room at home, and they melted in the sun. It was really upsetting to him when I gave them back to him. About seven years ago I came across a bunch of 78s, including Frankie Lymon and "Hound Dog," and I had a case made and sent them to him.

We had an upbeat relationship that was based around stupidity and silliness. It was always like that, and that's what we provided, fun in each other's lives. So it never occurred to me to ask questions about his family, as it seemed intrusive. And not what we were about. He never asked me about family life either. Everything was at face value. But David was a born performer. That was the drive, the ambition. He wanted to express himself. We drifted apart for a while when we went to different schools. George and David were art school boys, whereas I went to a secondary modern. I was a mod. I would go up to the West End, get some purple hearts, go to the Scene, the Flamingo, Discotheque. Whereas George and David were on the fringes, going to jazz clubs. We always stayed in contact but then reconnected when we were living in the same area around South Kensington in the '60s. I suppose we were pseudo-French then, trousers with turn-ups, brogues, and bikes with an engine on the front wheel.

DAVID BOWIE: My cousin Kristina was a huge Fats Domino fan and had "Blueberry Hill" and I had Elvis Presley's "Hound Dog" and we did a trade because I preferred the sound of that. What I liked about it was that I couldn't understand the lyrics and that really made an impression on me—there was some secret information there that I didn't have. I think that's been something that's been important to me ever since. It was [Little Richard's] sax lineup he had behind him that impressed me more than anything else, because I'd only heard the saxophone through my brother's records as being a jazz thing and that was too complicated for me. I was always very vain. I always liked clothes a lot, I guess it was my way of confirming I had a personality, not really being sure if I did or didn't. If you wore clothes of a certain nature you automatically were a personality because clothes maketh men, but going up [to London] on the train there was a guy with makeup on and he was a mod. He wore eye shadow and he looked rather peculiar and I thought he looked rather good. One of my keenest memories of the Marquee club in the mid-'60s is having a permanent erection because there were so many fantastic girls coming over from Europe. All these Swedish girls were flocking to London to come and get an R&B star, so you grew your hair really long and hoped that they recognized you as [the Yardbirds'] Keith Relf—I made a better Keith Relf than Brian Jones. Anyway I hung out with Jonesy a few times and he was too short and fat.

KRISTINA AMADEUS: I don't remember him being worried about being lower middle class. His father was from a very affluent family who were partners in the Public Benefit Boot Company. He went to a good public school and inherited money when he came of age. David's grandfather was killed at the end of World War I and his wife died the following year, so John inherited from both his parents and his own grandfather. But David did, like Jagger, adopt an almost Cockney accent for a while because it was trendy.

DAVID BOWIE: Elvis had the choreography, he had a way of looking at the world that was totally original, totally naïve, and totally available as a blueprint. Who wouldn't want to copy Elvis? Elvis had it all. It wasn't just the music that was interesting, it was everything else. And he had a lot of everything else. (There was once talk between our offices that I should be introduced to Elvis and maybe start working with him in a production-writer capacity, but it never came to pass. I would have loved working with him. God, I would have adored it. He did send me a note once: "All the best and have a great tour.")

GEORGE UNDERWOOD: I was nine at the time, and I was enrolling for the cub scouts in Bromley, the 18th Bromley Cub Pack, and David was enrolling on the same day. He'd lived in Brixton, near Stockwell, until he was six, so had only been in the area a few years. We immediately started talking, and the subject was mostly music—what we were listening to on the radio, how much we liked Lonnie Donegan, et cetera. We went to Bognor Regis camping with the cubs, and then when we went to the Isle of Wight David took a tea-chest bass and I took a ukulele. That was our first public performance, round the campfire. There was a café not too far away, with a jukebox, and "Tom Hark," which was number one at the time, and "All I Have to Do Is Dream" by the Everly Brothers were both on the jukebox and I remember us harmonizing to them. Then we both went to Bromley Technical High School, after we did our eleven plus. One day David asked me if I wanted to see the Cisco Kid. His father organized celebrities to entertain the kids, and he'd arranged for the Cisco Kid to come and perform for them. At the time he was quite a popular TV cowboy, and of course he was from America, which gave him a lot of kudos. Both David and I loved anything from America, especially the music. So we went down to see him, and there he was in all his regalia, in his black-and-silver suit. His real name was Duncan Ronaldo, and he had this short, stubby guy who used to follow him around, a sidekick who was about twenty years older than him called Pancho, played by Leo Carrillo. And after we'd chatted to the Cisco Kid for a while, he leaned in and whispered to us, and, in a strong Mexican accent, said, "He is the real Cisco Kid." We all thought he was a fictional character, but it stuck with us. David actually wrote to the American embassy, saying how much he loved American culture and American football and could they let him know if anything interesting was going on in London. He really loved American football. David could become an expert on something very quickly and then turn round and dismiss it a couple of weeks later. So they invited him to go up to the embassy and he asked me to go with him. They presented him with a set of shoulder pads, a helmet, and a ball. We were photographed for the *Bromley & Kentish Times.* David loved all that. We also joined the Bluejays, which was a baseball team who played in Beckenham Place Park. He loved all the paraphernalia, all the dressing up. David was a faddist, and that was another one of his fads.

My first gig was Buddy Holly and the Crickets at the Elephant & Castle Trocadero. It was the first gig of his UK tour, March 1, 1958, in the largest cinema in Britain, and I think David was a bit jealous that I'd gone. I got his autograph, and the rest of the band, and I came to school the next day and I was really proud of it, but David didn't like it. He was more of a Little Richard fan, but he didn't like the fact I'd got there first. I remember coming home and telling my mum it was the best day of my life. And she said, "Do you wanna cup of tea before you go to bed?" When Buddy Holly died the following February, I didn't want to go to school, as I was so upset. David and a guy called Peter Hamilton clubbed together to buy me a bar of chocolate to try and make me feel better.

A little bit later we went to see Little Richard together, at the Woolwich Granada I think, and Sam Cooke was on the same bill. In the audience was Gene Vincent, who wasn't allowed onstage because of some contractual agreement. Sounds Incorporated were backing everyone, and at one point the emcee came out and said, "We've got an unexpected guest who's going to come out and do a number for us now, so please welcome Mr. Gene Vincent!" So he stood on the side of the stage and performed "Be-Bop-a-Lula." When Little Richard was performing, we thought he'd had a heart attack. We were only six or seven rows back from the stage and saw everything really close up. He did this amazing thing where he stood on this white grand piano, and then started to make groaning sounds and holding his heart. David and I both looked at each other and wondered what was going on, and thought we were about to watch Little Richard die. David was always prone to exaggeration, and he started saying that Little Richard was going to die. So he fell onto the stage, lying there with the microphone right by his side. Then the emcee came on and asked if there was a doctor in the house, and then we noticed that all of the musicians had started to go back to their instruments, and all of a sudden Little Richard lifted his head up and shouted "Awopbopaloobop Alopbamboom!" and the crowd went mad. David was flabbergasted, and he obviously never forgot it. What stagecraft. David loved oddities, loved people who were somehow different. Who else would champion the Legendary Stardust Cowboy?

I bought an electric guitar and started to play it, and I was in a little band in Orpington with the son of a friend of my dad's. And then David started to take an interest, as we talked about it all the time. We were always singing at school, doing harmonies and whatnot. Whenever there was a wet break—when it was raining and you weren't allowed to go outside—we'd get our guitars out and start singing. Peter Frampton would join in too. He was only in the first year and we were in the fifth, but he was good. This is when I hit David in the eye. It was coming up to David's fifteenth birthday, and we both sort of liked the same girl, Carol Goldsmith. I invited her to a party, and David got absolutely drunk, but I stayed sober and asked Carol out, and she said, "Yes, next Wednesday at the youth club." David was a competitive sort, and he was furious. On the day, he phoned me and said, "She doesn't want to go out with you; she asked me to tell you." I thought, Oh well, but went out anyway, and another friend said, "You're late. Carol waited and then left." David's call was complete rubbish, and when I later heard him boasting about how he'd got off with her, I saw red. I hit him. I didn't know until a week later that he'd been rushed to hospital, so I went to see him and said, "It's not worth it over a girl," and we stayed friends. Just before we left school, a career person came along, and we'd line up and [she'd] ask us what we wanted to be when we left. People said, well, I'm going to work in my dad's firm, or I want to be a bus driver or whatever. And then there's David, who's right in front of me in the queue, and said to this woman, "I want to be a saxophonist in a modern jazz quartet." And I burst out laughing.

DAVID BOWIE: Some of the earliest music that I remember having an effect on me was ska and Blue Beat, those kind of musics. I had a brother, a half-brother, Terry, who was a jazz and soul fan and he would bring home albums by Tony Bennett, he was his favorite. He always thought Tony Bennett was better than Frank Sinatra; I think he was probably right actually. Looking back I think Bennett was actually quite a master. [Rock and roll] definitely represented a lifestyle, along with the celluloid images of people like James Dean and Monty Clift and Brando and clothes that had flecks in the material; we didn't have much of that in England. It was a new kind of language or culture and the only way that you could really receive it at the time was either Radio Luxembourg or the American Forces Network, which was sort of one of those under the sheets and listening to the top ten once a week. It was doled out in such small doses it seems to me unless you found a café with a jukebox. When you feel that you are privy to secret information it always becomes so much more personalized. So Little Richard was really the one because he was the first one that I actually saw perform. My mother took me to see, at my insistence, *Jukebox Jamboree* it was called over here. He had one song in that and then he had another in *Rock! Rock! Rock!*, and it was the sax lineup that he had behind him which impressed me more than anything else because I had only heard the saxophone through my brother's records as being a sort of jazz thing, and it was too complicated for me. I didn't get it, but hearing it pump just sort of . . . well it made me ask my father if he'd loan me the money to buy a saxophone—he bought me a saxophone and I paid him back with pocket money from a meat round that I had to get on Saturdays so I could afford to pay him back, which I did reluctantly eventually.

PETER FRAMPTON (CHILDHOOD FRIEND): I actually saw Dave about a year before I went to Bromley Technical High School, in 1961. He was in a band called the Kon-Rads at that stage, playing sax and singing, basically the front man. They were doing low-level gigs, like playing at schools and open-air fetes, raising money for the school, or the RSPCA, or whatever. I first saw him on the steps of the school. My dad and mum took me there on the weekend, and this band were playing at the entrance, the Kon-Rads. Dave was singing everything from Elvis Presley songs to playing instrumentals on the sax. Dave was great. I soon got to know him and his closest friend, George Underwood. They were very close. I got to know them through my dad, because before I went to the school I asked him who was into rock and roll, and who played guitar. And my dad said, "Well, I think that Jones and Underwood are pretty much into that." So I made a beeline for both of them, and ended up jamming with them on the art block stairs. My dad would hide the guitars in the office that we'd brought to school, and at lunchtime we'd get them out and that was when

I learned my first Eddie Cochran song, "C'mon Everybody," which was taught to me by David.

HANIF KUREISHI (AUTHOR AND PLAYWRIGHT): David started to explore London, traveling all over the city, and became great friends with Marc Bolan, even though they came from different parts of the city. As well as stealing clothes from Carnaby Street they used to do painting and decorating together.

RICHARD YOUNG (PHOTOGRAPHER): I grew up in Stamford Hill in north London, and went to a really rough, tumbly secondary modern school in Stoke Newington High Street called William Wordsworth. It was horrible. My best friend at school was Mark Feld, and we were inseparable. We used to sit next to each other, play together, bunk off school together. He used to come to school in handmade suits, handmade shoes, handmade shirts. This was 1961, '62. I knew he was going to be famous, and he did, when he became Marc Bolan. We both got expelled on the same day for the same reason. We both got caught for the umpteenth time on a Friday afternoon because we didn't want to go and play with the other haddocks—that's what Mark called the other kids at the school—on a really muddy playing field in Dagenham. There was a really long coach drive to Dagenham, and we'd shoot off into Soho instead. At the time Mark and I started going to a club in Princes Street, just off Regent Street called Le Bataclan, where all the French au pair girls went to, all the ones who worked for the nice Jewish families in St. John's Wood and Swiss Cottage. They played the most incredible music, all soul and R&B. And one night I was down there I met this guy called Geoff MacCormack, and we were both into the same kind of music—blues, soul, early Motown, Mary Wells, James Brown, things like that. He was a very good-looking boy. And his friend was this guy called David, who was also into the music, really into it. He was always dancing with the au pair girls, who always took us back to their houses because they were empty, because the families who owned them had other houses elsewhere in the country, elsewhere in the world, maybe in the Caribbean come wintertime. Geoff lived with his mum down in Blackheath, and I used to go down there some Sunday afternoons to listen to records—Stax, Chess, blues, and soul. And

David used to join us. We used to sit on the carpet together, eating cheese sandwiches and cakes and tea or coffee, whatever Geoff's mum was making. David was already trying to be a singer, but he usually just sat there listening to the records.

Mark, myself, and David were all the same age. Mark once told me that the name Bolan came from two names: "Bo" for Bowie, and "lan" from Dylan. I'm not sure if this is true, but after all Bowie was the godfather of Marc's son Rolan. They were very competitive but they were very good friends to each other. He wasn't like Marc in those days, who always had a great dress sense. Marc was in *Man About Town* magazine, and was always considered to be a bit of a face, in three-piece suits and leather waistcoats. With Bowie you could tell that all he was interested in was music and fashion, music and fashion. He was in [the boutiques] John Michael, then John Stephen, then Vince, then Hung On You. He'd go to the Giaconda Coffee Bar, the Ship, the Edwardian pub. Both Marc and David would pick up rubbish bags of clothes behind the shops in Carnaby Street.

DAVID BOWIE: There were two sets of mods in England, there were the mods that happened around '61 out of the modernists who were the spin-off from the Kennedy thing. That was really the first teenage fashion that was relevant to my lot—the Kennedy look, and from that developed this Italian thing with the shorter hair and the Italian suits, mods with their fluorescent socks and their ankle swingers [trousers that] came about three inches above the ankle. And short jackets that were worn about fourteen to fifteen inches from the nape of the neck to the small of the back, and again I got my father to advance me the money to buy a suit from Burtons. I chose a very nice dark-green tweed with the fourteen-inch bum-freezer jacket. Going to work when I first left school, I worked in an advertising agency in London. I was what was called pompously a Junior Visualizer, which meant in between making the tea I would do paste-up jobs for adverts for the newspapers. One of our products was AYDS Slimming Biscuit. Going up on the train [to London] there was a guy that had makeup on, I think his name was Michael, and he was a mod. I'd never seen that before; I'd seen the clothes, but he wore eye shadow and I thought that was really peculiar and I thought it looked rather good. Then I found out that up in London all the mods wore makeup. This is the first bunch of mods. Later on of course they became the mods that wore the anoraks and had the Lambrettas, but I was no longer a mod by then.

[When you come from] suburbia you find yourself in the middle of two worlds. There's the extreme values of people who grow up in the countryside and the very urban feel of the city, and in suburbia you're given the impression that nothing culturally belongs to you, that you are sort of in this wasteland. I think there is a passion for most people, a sort of curiosity about them to escape and get out and try and find who one is and find some kind of roots, and both of us got out for the same reasons, exactly that, the desperation and exhaustion with the blandness of where we grew up. So many of the people that I knew at the time were either artists [who became] musicians, or musicians who became artists. Everybody went to St. Martins or Sidcup or something and my stream at school went to this place called Bromley Tech. We were lucky enough to have a master called Owen Frampton, who was Peter Frampton's father, and . . . he was quite an innovative guy inasmuch as he developed the first art course for ten-year-olds upwards, so it was sort of pre–art school art school, so the bulk of our day was preparing us for the art world. Some of us who were greedier than others like myself went straight from school to a job rather than go to art school because we wanted to get the readies as fast as possible. The trouble is you ended up in an agency.

Anyway, in the evening I was playing also with several bands playing saxophone. I found that I could make just about the same amount of money by playing sax in the evening as I was getting during the day.

PETER FRAMPTON: When I went to Bromley Tech in 1962, I realized how well loved my father was as a teacher. And David loved my dad's course. I'm not privy to the relationship that David had with his own father, but I don't think it was that great. That's all I know. But I know that he kinda had more of a relationship with my dad. They had a very strong relationship. He looked up to him, respected him.

MARY LOVETT (TEENAGE FRIEND): David was just always a part of our group somehow. I grew up in West Wickham, so I hung around in Bromley and Beckenham, and my first husband was Peter Frampton. Peter and I used to meet after school. So, David was always a part of his history, and mine. He and his friend George Underwood were just always there somehow. Beckenham was very affluent; it had been built as an upper Victorian suburb I believe, and a lot of the roads were still unmade-up as they would have been for horses and carriages. In fact, the road that David lived on was unmade-up. The house that he lived in was one of those huge, old, redbrick houses. Beckenham was still quite upper class, I suppose, in a way, but Bromley was very working class.

My lovely father-in-law, Owen Frampton, although he had a wicked sense of humor, was rather strict in a way—quite military. It's funny to even imagine him teaching David, but Owen obviously sensed a talent and had a sense of humor about his students. He was the one who told Peter about David and kind of put them together. There were a lot of little bands in that area at that time and they were kind of school bands. There was a sort of circuit of gigs in our area and amazing people played them and I know that David played them too. There was a little church hall on my road, Gates Green Road, called the Assembly Rooms, where we had our Youth Fellowship and I know David played there. And another church hall called Justin Hall in West Wickham, which almost all the bands played. The Beatles were responsible for so many people's lives changing and they certainly were for mine. When I was at Beckenham Grammar School, I started listening to Radio Luxembourg and heard the Beatles, Buddy Holly, and everyone else. I started meeting local musicians, and one of them was Peter Frampton. He was fourteen when we met. He was at school with David, although he had to change schools because his father taught there, and it was too uncomfortable for him. So, David lived in Bromley and there was a really good gig called Bromley Court Hotel that everyone played at, including Jimi Hendrix and Spencer Davis, the Yardbirds and Graham Bond. Really amazing bands. So good, and it had a stage that was about this high off the ground, so you were standing so close. Peter and I would go there a lot. It was fantastic and I just became completely enthralled with the music scene and it was amazing in that area. Then Peter joined the Herd, and David was on the periphery for a while, until Peter formed Humble Pie and David started opening the show for them. David was very arty at the time, like Marc Bolan, and I'm not sure any of us quite understood what he was doing.

OWEN FRAMPTON (TEACHER): Whatever the necessary ingredients are to produce vintage school years, they must have been mixed in exactly the right proportions in the years 1960–66. He [Bowie] was quite unpredictable. He was completely misunderstood by most of my teaching colleagues, but in those days cults were unfashionable and David, by the age of fourteen, was already a cult figure. At this point in my teaching career, I was thoroughly used to individualistic pupils and was rarely surprised by anything that happened. Even when David varied the color of his hair or cropped it short, or plucked his eyebrows, I accepted his actions as a means of projecting his personality, and of that he had plenty!

HANIF KUREISHI: I went to Bromley Tech, seven years behind David, from 1966 to 1970. It was during a time of the so-called Bromley contingent, along with Billy Idol and Siouxsie Sioux. We were really influenced by semi-decadent things like *Cabaret*, and Bowie was this ruling god. He was a figurehead for us. He was feminine, extreme, dressed-up. He was a local hero, and played some of the local pubs and clubs, and was a really big deal to us. There was a picture of him in school, and the teachers would say, "If you don't behave yourself, Kureishi, you'll end up like him." He liberated all suburban teenagers. So I think he knew about publicity and PR and how he appeared when he was dressing up and being photographed and all that. He looked great with his hair and suit on and all that. He always had a strong sense of that. It was a standard shit school and we were considered to be no-hopers—we were bums. We were lucky if we got a job in the civil service or in insurance—we were lower middle class, H. G. Wells clerks. But the idea that someone like us from round the corner could become a rock star was very inspirational. It was quite creative down there in Bromley, despite the utter boredom and awfulness of the suburbs. It was Sunday night in the rain waiting at the bus stop. But actually everyone had underground records, they had clothes.

PETER FRAMPTON: When you're three years apart in your very early teens, twelve and fifteen, it might as well be "I'm two and he's sixty." Because you usually hang with your age group. But the thing that kept us close together was the music. Anything at the school that was to do with music,

I was part of, as was David. My father encouraged us. At the end of my only year at the school, we grew closer because my dad put on an end-of-year concert for the school and another for the parents, so there was a show during the day and one at night. There were a lot of different performers on the show, and the headline act was George and the Dragons, which was George Underwood and Dave and a drummer and possibly a keyboard player. They didn't have a bass player and my band—the Little Ravens, named after Ravens Wood School—didn't have a drummer, so we shared. We were the support act, although I even played with the lost property lady; we sang "There's a Hole in My Bucket."

GEORGE UNDERWOOD: When I got a job as a singer with the Kon-Rads, I'd go to school with big black rings under my eyes because I hadn't got to bed before two or three o'clock in the morning. I was only fifteen. David had just started to play the sax, so I asked him to come along and meet the guys. So he joined the Kon-Rads and I left soon after, even though they still had my amplifier.

David always used to get these fabulous records from Dobell's on the Charing Cross Road. There was a guy at David's agency who was a bit of muso who used to ask David to go and get records for him, and David was like a kid in a sweet shop. Dr. John. Charlie Mingus. Bob Dylan. And then John Lee Hooker. He had a great style. Quite simple, not too many changes, but really raw. Authentic. We both tried so hard to emulate his sound, and after a while we thought we should try and play it live. So we found a drummer, and performed under the name the Hooker Brothers. I think we only did two gigs, and one was at the Bromley Court Hotel, in the interval between Mike Cotton Sounds' set. And Mike Cotton came up to us afterwards and said, "That's brave." Very unusual, anyway, two young white kids singing about the blues. We didn't know. Then we had a few more stabs at groups before David found something in the classified section of the *Melody Maker*, where you went if you were looking for singers or musicians. He'd been looking in the paper, and had seen an ad for a band who were looking for a singer, and they were based in Fulham. Which was a long way from Bromley. So he asked me to go with him. It turned out to be the King Bees, and we started rehearsing together. I was still at the art school and David was still at the ad agency, although David started saying that he wanted to pursue music, that music was going to be his thing. He wanted to be professional. The dynamic in the King Bees was fine, but it turned into David and me against the others, because I don't think they were into the blues as much as we were. Everyone was into the blues at that time, I know, but the lead guitarist was a bit too Chet Atkins; it wasn't raw enough.

David wrote to the entrepreneur John Bloom, who was the Alan Sugar of his day, and in the letter—which David's father helped write—David said, "Brian Epstein's got the Beatles, you need us . . ." or something precocious like that. And lo and behold a few days later we got a telegram asking us to go to a meeting with a show-business manager called Leslie Conn, who Bloom had passed the letter on to. So we went down to see him in this little office in Soho, and we took our equipment and played "Got My Mojo Workin'." I don't think he was into the music but he thought there was something there, and asked us to come round and play at a friend's flat and do the same sort of thing again. It was an opulent house somewhere in Golders Green. Then we played at John Bloom's wedding anniversary in the basement of a restaurant in Soho. A group called the Naturals were also playing, and they were like a Beatles tribute band, and the crowd thought they were very acceptable. But then we came on with our scruffy jeans and long hair and they didn't like us too much. I remember Adam Faith was in the crowd, as well as Shirley Bassey, Roger Moore, and Vera Lynn. We played "Got My Mojo Workin'" and various other Muddy Waters songs and we came off with our tails between our legs. David actually burst out crying. That was his first professional disappointment. After that we did *Ready Steady Go*, and I remember dancing with Patti Boyd. That was the night the Animals played "House of the Rising Sun" live, because up until that night everyone had been miming. Lo and behold the band in the next dressing room to us was the Crickets, who had just come off a plane from the US. And then next door to them was John Lee Hooker. David came in and said, "You'll never believe who's down the corridor!" He told me to go and look at his hands, and so I did. And they were amazing. He used to work in a steel mill, and they were very long and elegant, worn, and he had this amazing technique where his little finger would almost go down the fret board. He had a huge span. Only David would have noticed that. He was always good at finding things. People say he was a magpie, and he was, but he always made that thing he stole his own.

DANA GILLESPIE (GIRLFRIEND): When I was thirteen or fourteen I discovered the joys of the blues, and so would regularly go down to the Marquee in Soho whenever someone interesting was playing. It was easy to get in in those days. I saw the High Numbers, who later became the Who, the Yardbirds, anyone playing blues or R&B. One night the King Bees were playing, and David came onstage looking like Robin Hood, with thigh-length suede fringed boots, and flowing lemon-yellow hair. It was the first time I'd see them. After the set, I was standing at the back of the club brushing my hair, and this guy came up from behind and took the hairbrush and started brushing it for me. And then he asked if he could come home with me. So, one thing led to another and I said yes, and we walked home. Of course I soon realized that one of the reasons he wanted to come and stay was that the trains didn't run all the way to Bromley that night. . . . My quarters were on the top floor, so I brought him up to the top floor. . . . I don't need to tell you what went on that night, but we were very young. The next morning I had to take him downstairs and he met my parents on the landing because their bedroom was two floors below. And my father said that he thought it was a girl coming down from the top floor. Because in those days no one had seen such long hair. From then on he would come round all the time, and he would stay over and creep upstairs past my parents' bedroom.

Bowie's determination to flout convention, even the relatively recent convention of the pop orthodoxy, was evident even then. Stella Patton, one of the Kon-Rads' backing singers, says, "I could always remember David as being difficult. The band all wore the same clothes, but he didn't like that. He always had an exercise book with him and he would always be scribbling, writing down lyrics." His sexuality, at least his interpretation of it, started to manifest itself too. "I remember him saying he was bisexual," says Kon-Rads' guitarist Alan Dodds. "But I have to say there was absolutely no evidence for that. I think he was just up for anything that was a bit different." It was a perception that was to stick. "We thought Marc Bolan was gay, we thought David Bowie was gay," the Who's Pete Townshend said once. "We thought all the cool people were gay."

GEORGE UNDERWOOD: The King Bees ended when David turned up one day and said he'd got another band. He'd been rehearsing with another band and had decided it was time to move on. I'd heard that [the producer] Mickie Most was looking for a solo artist, and he recorded me under the name Calvin James, as Calvin was the name of his new son. When David found out, he was really pissed off that I'd jumped through all the hoops and somehow got a record deal. He thought it should have been his. Suddenly I was at the top, and this was the thing he was desperate to do. He said it was unfair as I always had my art to fall back on, yet for him it was everything. Anyway we had a huge row and we didn't see each other for a while. As it was it didn't work out and I did go back to my art. David went on to the Mannish Boys, the Lower Third, and the rest. The next time I saw him was at the Dominion when he was doing all the mime stuff, and he was great. By that time he had hooked up with his manager Ken Pitt, and had started to become very effeminate. I thought he'd turned slightly. He was mixing with very theatrical people at the time. He was fine with me because as he was very competitive, he liked the fact I was no longer in the business. I wouldn't say he was ambitious so much, he just had this zest for life, a zest for music. It was like a worm, an itch you have to scratch. When he joined the Kon-Rads I could tell that he was determined. I think he almost dreamed it before he did it. It was a dream that came true. And as he went on, everything he did had roots back to the '60s.

PAUL REEVES (CHILDHOOD FRIEND): I knew him as Bromley Dave, as that is where we were both from. I first met him in 1965, when we all used to congregate in the record store inside Medhurst's, the department store in Bromley. I always liked him and knew he had talent, but I have to say we all thought that George Underwood was the one who was going to be the big rock star. I thought David was a bit of a dilettante, dabbling in any kind of pop that came along. He was interested in being a crooner, an entertainer, and you could tell that when he started making records like

"The Laughing Gnome." George was my friend, and he was sulkingly good-looking, and when he got signed by Mickie Most we all thought that George would be the one that would really make it big.

NICK KENT (JOURNALIST): The first time I ever saw Bowie was in 1964, when he was the leader of the longhair brigade. I must have been thirteen years old, and he was seventeen. Bowie was the founder of "The Society of the Prevention of Cruelty to Long-Haired Men" and he was on the *Tonight* show on television to argue his case to a presenter who had suggested that longhaired men looked just like women. He was funny. He said, "For the last two years we've had comments like 'Darlin'!' and 'Can I carry your handbag?' thrown at us." You could tell it was a bit of a put-on, but I remember thinking, Now, this fellow we'll probably be seeing again. It wasn't a good show and he was rather shallow, and it wasn't a great first introduction to David Bowie, but that's where it started. Then you started to read about him in the music press, throughout the '60s. David Bowie was always going to be the next big thing. At the end of every year, all the music papers would make their predictions for the coming year, and they invariably said that next year was going to be David Bowie's year, and it never was. They said he was just too talented and too good-looking not to make it. So he became a known quantity. He was someone who was very promising.

BERNARD GLAZIER (NEIGHBOR): In 1964, I was living at Grove Park and had recently started working in advertising. One morning this lad about my age got in my carriage at Grove Park station, two stops up-line from Bromley North. His name was David Jones. He was carrying what looked like a saxophone case, and I had a guitar with me—so we talked about music and the world of design and advertising in which he was also employed as a junior. We met quite a few times like that—he seemed a rather quiet, enigmatic lad. One morning, three lads I vaguely knew from the Downham estate got into our carriage and started to take the piss out of David's somewhat "gentle" appearance. After a bit of persuasion, I managed to convince them he was "OK" and they backed off. They were not nice people. Shortly after that I moved and no longer used that train. I forgot all about David Jones.

DANA GILLESPIE: I went once to his parents' place, as he asked me to go there and meet them, in Bromley. I was thirteen or fourteen, just after we met. And I go there and they're in this tiny little working-class house, and I've never seen a house like this before. I walk in and the parents are sitting there and there's a television blasting away in the corner, and nobody spoke. I think we had little tuna sandwiches. I came from a house where everyone chatted away and had a lot of social intercourse, but his parents didn't say anything. It was a really cold house, a very chilly atmosphere. It was a tiny little house, the smallest I'd ever been in. Our house in South Kensington was enormous, but this looked like everything had been squeezed into it. I could immediately tell that David didn't really like living at home. He was uncomfortable during the entire visit. When his parents went out, David said to me, "I want to get out of here. I have to get out of here. I want to go up in the world." So he went up in the world. . . . He was ambitious from an early age, but then he had the talent. He had great interest in so many things.

MICK ROCK (PHOTOGRAPHER): David didn't really talk about his brother. You could say that he went through life looking for people to replace his brother, although he probably knew he couldn't really replace him. He obviously loved him. But David was light, not dark. He was so, so positive.

CHRIS CHARLESWORTH (JOURNALIST): There were always rumors about David's half-brother, but the truth didn't really come out until the Peter and Leni Gillman *Alias* book was published in the mid-'80s. It gave a detailed account of the schizophrenia in the family, and David absolutely hated that book. He thought it was all behind him, but they dredged everything up.

HUGH PADGHAM (PRODUCER): I think he was embarrassed by his brother.

MICK GARSON (PIANIST): He talked about his brother a little, as he was worried that he might have that potential gene, and that he could go off the rails the same way. Maybe it was true, but he just channeled whatever it was into a different direction. He probably had a genetic disposition. But he loved his brother. He expressed guilt, but he didn't go into it in any great detail. You could just tell that it was hurting him. It was delicate. He talked to me, as I had my own spiritual pursuit. Kindness, connection. He said that in this lifetime he wasn't going to pursue that spirituality, as his life—this life—was based on his fame and his career and he was going to see it out. He absolutely knew he had more than one life.

DAVID BOWIE: One puts oneself through such psychological damage trying to avoid the threat of insanity, you start to approach the very thing that you're scared of. Because of the tragedy inflicted, especially on my mother's side of the family, there were too many suicides for my liking—that was something I was terribly fearful of. I felt I was the lucky one because I was an artist and it would never happen to me because I could put all my psychological excesses into my music and then I could always be throwing it off.

OLIVER JAMES (PSYCHOLOGIST): His mother's curse was part of the family folklore, like we all have folklore in our family, and Margaret used to talk about it all the time. It even had a name: Margaret's curse. But what interested me about the relationship between [his brother] Terry and Margaret and Bowie's father was that he was such a good example of how schizophrenia is caused without anyone being actually sexually abused or physically abused, although he was a little bit, but primarily *emotionally* abused. It is fair to say that Margaret was good with babies, and she couldn't stand them after that. Simply put, David developed differently than his brother because he was nurtured as a child, whereas Terry wasn't.

He possibly had guilt about not making more of an effort to protect Terry. Later in life, when Terry was incarcerated in Cane Hill, he didn't go to the hospital to meet him until his mother grassed him up. Terry was an important person, there's not a question about that, in his childhood, and in his teenage years, and he was a very cool guy. Him being cool helped Bowie to develop his own cool. I guess he would have felt guilt about the favoritism from his father, because as Terry had a different father, David's father didn't want Terry in the house. David was certainly the chosen one. So he must have felt guilt, as he was treated better, he was loved, and he appeared to have some control over his life, at least to a certain extent. His mother was vain and she encouraged the same in him. He was very preoccupied with his looks from a young age, and you can see he got that from his mother. But I wonder how much he knew about his mother's past. She messed around, and I wonder how much she told him about that. He presumably knew about Terry's father at some point because Terry had a picture of him. Maybe she used to brag, maybe she wanted to show Bowie what a goer she'd been in her youth. Either way, David's father was horrid to Terry because he represented Jack Rosenberg, his father.

David was someone who was capable of presenting tremendous charm, and it's absolutely staggering that long before he was famous, people would get the impression of meeting someone very, very special, someone with a very special connection. And he could only have achieved that by putting on a face, which is something he learned to do as a child, at home. He presented himself as someone feeling different emotions to the emotions he actually was feeling. He obviously got a great deal of pleasure from his sex life, and he wanted to have a relationship with each individual woman; he didn't just want to have sex with them. I think he enjoyed the experience of seduction. My friend who did the V&A exhibition, Victoria Broakes, said that after meeting him she couldn't remember anything he said, so in a way he trained himself to be effectively invisible.

HANIF KUREISHI: He talked about his brother quite a lot. He was really quite interested in that side of the family, the schizophrenic side, and the fact that his mum had had two previous children. He'd obviously had quite a strange life as a child because his mother had had two previous children who she had in a sense lost. She was living with David and his dad. And his dad worked for an organization that looked after lost children. I often wonder what it was like. Terry had quite an influence on him in terms of things like he gave him books and introduced him to American culture and jazz and the Beats. It must have been very puzzling for David as a child, having this mad brother and the lost sister. I remember him talking about being introduced at a young age to [John] Coltrane by his brother, and not understanding it but thinking it was something good to know. I always got the sense that he couldn't quite work out the Terry element of his life. He found it confusing. He would talk about how awkward it was in the house for his mother and father when Terry was around, how difficult and disturbing it was. And I've often wondered if the whole alien thing didn't come from that. Someone who is sort of slightly to one side who doesn't quite get what's going on. He always wrote in character, even in the early days. He wasn't a great polemicist. There weren't narratives. Sometimes when I spoke to him on the phone, I got the sense you have with some psychotic people when they're just talking to themselves. It's just a monologue, and he is just sharing with you what's going round and round in his head. You probably wouldn't call that madness really, but there's a sense of sort of solipsism. But as you know on the other hand he was incredibly together, organized, busy, interested . . . so you wouldn't say that he was psychotic or disturbed in any way that disabled him. His mother must have been quite disturbed, to have lost two children, and one of them's schizophrenic. She's going to be quite creeped out, isn't she? He said he came from a cold family and yet he did have that feeling of specialness about himself. Of being a very loved child. He didn't seem like an unloved child to me. You didn't think, Oh, he's been pissed about by his parents.

DANA GILLESPIE: People would say to me, "Ooh, you're dating David Bowie!" But it wasn't just the sex, we were just really good friends, and it was more of a musical relationship. He would play my guitar, or listen to my songs, and play me his. I was also learning the drums then. I went to a very upmarket day school in Sloane Square, and he'd come to pick me up and walk me home, carrying my ballet pumps for me. He did the same thing when I moved to a stage school, the Arts Educational, at Hyde Park Corner. I used to go with him to *Ready Steady Go*, where we'd hang out in the green room. They had dancers on the show, so we used to do that too. When I started getting serious about recording, he suggested a song called "Love Is Strange" by Mickey and Sylvia, and sang the bass line—I'll always remember that. I never thought that we were just boy- and girlfriend and that we were going out. From an early age I never felt that musicians kind of fit into normal boy/girl relationships, especially not the young ones. Fidelity is not the type of thing you would expect from a musician, especially from a front man or a male lead guitarist. It goes with the territory. So I came into the relationship with my eyes open, even at that young age.

PAUL SMITH (FASHION DESIGNER): When I was eighteen I got myself a car, a 1945 Morris Minor, and I started driving down to London at the weekends. I don't know how, but I got to know a lot of interesting people quite quickly. It was a very exciting time. I met Tommy Roberts and Eric Clapton, Rod Stewart and Jimmy Page, all these amazing people in the early stages of their career. We'd drive down to Soho, and Bowie was always around. He was everywhere. There were a lot of scene-y people, and there were still a lot of mods about, but Bowie was everywhere. There was always a group of people who never rated him because of his interest in dressing up. He was a bit theatrical for everyday guys. They had mixed feelings about the theatrical aspect. They liked the music very much, but a lot of people who were more about blues thought it was not about the music, it was something else, but of course it was. It was self-expression.

DAVID BOWIE: I don't think I would have had the strength of mind at the time to want to go out and just sing my songs straight off. For me, it was always about developing an interesting character.

SIMON NAPIER-BELL (MANAGER): Since the mid-'60s I'd been aware of a chap called David Jones who was hustling round town trying to find the right group and image for himself. He had an unsuccessful single out, "The Laughing Gnome." Then he started studying mime with Lindsay Kemp and changed his name from Jones to Bowie, on one occasion appearing as a mime act supporting Marc Bolan when Marc was still performing acoustically as Tyrannosaurus Rex. But to me David was just someone on the scene rather than an actual pop star. I was phoned one day by someone I didn't know, who introduced himself as a manager with a hot act. This was Ralph Horton, who was managing David Bowie and the Lower Third. Horton said he needed an established co-manager to work with him to realize the act's potential. I went to meet him at his flat in Pimlico. In the corner of the room there was a not particularly attractive young man who I'd never seen before. Ralph introduced him as David and said he was going to be a superstar. He said if I agreed to jointly manage, I could have sex with him. The sheer sleaziness of the proposal (not to mention the grubbiness of the flat in which the proposal was being made) was enough to make me run—which I did. As far as I was concerned, I was never offered a 50 percent share of Bowie's management (nor a taste of his sexual favors) but simply asked to take on a total unknown (called David Jones) whose current manager seemed to be little more than a pimp. Later, of course, Bowie moved his management to Ken Pitt. I often wondered if Horton made the same offer to him, and whether that was the basis for the change of management. When Ralph Horton suggested the deal, Bowie didn't exactly interrupt to stop him. So presumably he was in on what was being offered.

DAVID ARDEN: My family used to make fun of everyone at the time—cripples, Jews, everybody, that's just the way we were. We were in the music business. It was protection in a way. And the Old Man [Don Arden] always used to call Ken Pitt the accountant, because that's what he was like, very straight. He wasn't rock and roll at all, he wasn't even music hall. He was the accountant, a bit of a makeweight, an average man.

DAVID BOWIE: Even when I was struggling in the '60s, before I had any success, even before I had had a hit record, I wanted to chop and change and do different things. In those days I was trying to find a voice, trying to find something that worked with people who were buying records, but it was always about change. I wanted to express myself, and who can express themselves if they just do the same thing all the time? Everyone back then was trying to do something different, so why would you want to do something different and then just repeat it, because then you'd be just like everyone else. And I never wanted to be like everyone else. I think back to some of the material I recorded before "Space Oddity" and I know it doesn't fit in with the whole narrative of what I do, but if you look at it through my eyes then it absolutely does, because I was exploring a mainstream, almost music-hall stream of work. I was being a song-and-dance man, and I wanted to compete with the Sinatras and the Anthony Newleys of this world. I covered a lot of standards at the time because I wanted to learn how I could do it better than anyone else.

TIM HOLLIER (MUSICIAN): Eventually David needed a manager that would take him to the next level, and so he hired Ken Pitt, who was very old-school. He moved into Pitt's flat in Manchester Street in June 1967, and started writing novelty songs about bombardiers and gnomes. David used to say to me, "I've got to go and see David Essex tonight, even though I don't want to, I've got to. And I've got to see Cliff Richard. . . ." Ken Pitt was sending him to these shows to learn the trade, to learn the stagecraft. So he spent six months just concentrating on what he was going to do next, independently of Ken Pitt. I respected the fact Ken was trying to make David a performer, but David didn't like doing it.

KEN PITT (BOWIE'S MANAGER): Initially I thought that David was someone who could be groomed. I first saw him down the Marquee, and just loved the way he moved onstage. His songs were actually very good, really outstanding for someone of his age.

WENDY LEIGH: Ken Pitt was in love with David. I don't think the affair was ever consummated, and Ken never said it was, but Ken was madly in love with him and David used that. David could make people fall in love with him. David used to walk around naked in front of Ken when they were living together, so he was almost goading him. The persona that David liked to adopt was the Artful Dodger from *Oliver Twist*, with a little bit of little boy lost. He did have an amazing body, very lithe with these amazing hips, and incredible skin, and David worked it. David was Ken's boy, or at least he always thought so. David even went to see Ken just before Ken died. I would be very surprised if he didn't help Ken financially. He only walked away from people when it was cold-blooded professionalism, but he didn't walk away from people he liked. The only one he really walked away from is Mick Ronson. David was a bit sociopathic, but then aren't all stars?

HARVEY GOLDSMITH (PROMOTER): Ken Pitt was quite a character. He was flamboyant, an old-fashioned showbiz character, a bit vicious when he needed to be. Essentially he was in the crossover theatrical world. He and Ken Pitt were like chalk and cheese. He wanted to turn Bowie into a light entertainer, as he didn't really know anything else, and didn't understand the rock and roll world. He could handle Manfred Mann or Tommy Steele, Anthony Newley or Cliff Richard, but not someone like David Bowie.

WENDY LEIGH: Bowie was a voiceprint of Anthony Newley, Anthony Newley's double really. And Newley was furious.

SIMON NAPIER-BELL: Ken Pitt wasn't exactly a white-hot manipulator, but he was a pleasant enough man, and had managed a hit act before [Manfred Mann]. He knew about PR and probably taught Bowie a bit, and maybe helped him financially too. But Bowie was always going to be the type of artist who moved from person to person to get what he needed most at any one time. At the time he moved to Ken Pitt, Pitt was obviously a step up the ladder from Ralph Horton, his previous manager.

KEN PITT: My mind naturally keeps going back to that time in the Marquee club when I saw this David Jones and his band the Lower Third—and you find the dreams getting all mixed up with the hard facts.

When I started with him he knew nothing about the media. He's got to take the credit because he had a lot of natural charm. One lady who fell for him was Penny Valentine, and also George Tremlett [both journalists]. It got around amongst journalists that he was a very bright boy, a lot of fun to interview. I certainly gave him advice from the very beginning. He was anxious about what to say. I would tell him exactly what the interviewer's interests were, and I told him that whatever you do, don't argue, don't get into a heated conversation. I never put him up to saying anything that wasn't true. I told him you've got to try to anticipate the interviewer, tell him or her what they want to hear, and adopt a different style according to the different types of media. I would never sit in on an interview. He's interesting to talk to and he gives interesting answers to questions. I think the reason why David managed to maintain a good relationship with the media was his ability to reinvent himself. He was never boring.

PETER FRAMPTON: By 1966, I was in the Herd, just starting out. And I remember David saying that he was watching *Top of the Pops* one evening and did a double-take—"Hold on, that's Peter! And why isn't he at school?" So in that respect I beat him on TV, whereas George Underwood beat us both as he was on *Thank Your Lucky Stars*, produced by Mickie Most, when he was only fifteen. David at that point was still doing Davy Jones and the Night Timers, and Davy Jones and the Lower Third, and then as soon as Davy Jones and the Monkees came out, he changed his name to David Bowie.

TOMMY HILFIGER (FASHION DESIGNER): He told me that the real reason he changed his name to David Bowie wasn't anything to do with Davy Jones. He said it was the *New Musical Express* starting to call Mick "Jagger Dagger." He said if he can be Jagger Dagger then I can be David Bowie, like the Bowie knife.

DAVID BOWIE: There is an energy about London that never died away, something about the extraordinary mix of people here. I felt it growing up, especially in the '60s, when I was trying to get a foothold as a performer, and I feel it whenever I perform here. London is in a perpetual cycle of reinvention, which means as an artist you can never take it for granted, as the people who like you can be very demanding. When I was writing about the London experience, it was easy to hold a mirror up to what was going on, as I was there myself, trying to get involved.

DANA GILLESPIE: He would go down to Carnaby Street and get himself kitted out in a fancy outfit, because he was very into his image. You would never see him walking around like a slob. He didn't do slob. We would sit in the Gioconda café in Tin Pan Alley, Denmark Street, having a cup of tea or showing off. That was the place you would go if you wanted something like a backing singer or a bass guitarist. One time he rushed in and grabbed me by the hand and took me round the corner to Francis Day and Hunter, which was a music store back then, grabbed me into a tiny booth and said, "Listen to this, it's my first single." And of course it was "I Pity the Fool," which I really liked, and then on the flip side "Take My Tip." Because I lived in the same place for so many years, David used to often come over. One night he rang up and said, "I've just written a song, I'm coming over in half an hour." And half an hour later he was at my front door, and I was there with the photographer Gered Mankowitz, and Gered and I listened to him sing the first version of "Space Oddity." In the early days, before "The Laughing Gnome" or "Space Oddity," he had been very theatrical, especially when he was with Lindsay Kemp. I couldn't have said he was a great lead guitarist because he wasn't, but he was a good strummer, and things went on in his head that he was able to articulate to people around him. And that is an art in itself. Because he knew exactly what he wanted. He was a great leader.

JULIEN TEMPLE (DIRECTOR): The '60s were a very difficult time for David because he was in the middle of all this frenetic activity, yet he wasn't part of it. It was as though his face was pushed up against the glass, and he could see what was going on but couldn't join in. He saw it all happening right before his eyes but he wasn't there. It was a decade of constant frustration for him as nothing he tried, worked. He was reinventing himself every eighteen months in an attempt to get some attention and yet nothing he did appeared to work in any meaningful way. He was an artist, only one who hadn't yet found the right way to express himself.

JASON HELLER (WRITER AT *PITCHFORK*): Science-fiction legend Robert Heinlein's *Starman Jones* was published in 1953, when Jones was six years old, and the sci-fi-loving English lad who would grow up to become David Bowie considered it a favorite. Surely he was captivated by the fact that the story's astronautical hero shared his last name—and that, with a bit of imagination, he might someday become his own kind of Starman Jones.

During the formative years of the mid-'60s, Bowie was the front man of a short-lived group named the Lower Third. And that rock band incorporated an odd choice of song into their repertoire: "Mars, the Bringer of War," a movement from *The Planets*, the orchestral suite by the English composer Gustav Holst. The suite was known to British audiences of Bowie's generation primarily from its use as the theme to the popular *Quatermass* science-fiction serials produced by the BBC in the '50s. Bowie was a huge fan of *Quatermass*, once admitting that as a boy he would watch it "from behind the sofa when my parents thought I had gone to bed. After each episode I would tiptoe back to my bedroom rigid with fear, so powerful did the action seem to me."

As the amphetamine-fueled mod scene morphed into the acid-fueled psychedelic scene, London became the laboratory in which Bowie began conducting experiments of his own—ones that sought to transmute science fiction and fantasy into the sounds of popular music. Like most of his pre–"Space Oddity" output, Bowie's 1967 song "Karma Man" made little impact on the public consciousness. The song, however, vividly depicts a tattooed man whose elaborate body art tells wondrous and hideous tales. . . . Nineteen sixty-seven also saw the release of "The Laughing Gnome," a novelty single that's been dismissed by many Bowie fans as fluff. It's a curious song, a pastiche of singer Anthony Newley's silly, music-hall style, sped-up voices, and a bizarre, retro-Victorian vibe. But it also taps into a newfound cultural fascination with mythic creatures like gnomes, elves, and goblins, thanks in large part to a late-'60s resurgence of interest in J.R.R. Tolkien's *The Lord of the Rings* trilogy, originally published in the mid-'50s, as well as its predecessor, 1937's *The Hobbit*. But unlike the earnest appropriation of hobbits and elves that had begun to pop up in folk and progressive rock in the late '60s, Bowie's emerging style pointed more toward the future rather than the past. And not in an optimistic way.

PAUL MCCARTNEY (MUSICIAN): I have fond memories of David in the '60s where I used to live in London, and still live actually. And I was bachelor free then. And it was a bit like a salon in my house; anyone could drop in. Just to hang out. Anyway there was this young boy lying about, hanging around outside, and I said, "Come on in then." I invited everyone in. And it was a guy in a floppy cap, with curly hair. And I said who are you, and he said David Jones, Davy Jones. And he had a demo for me. He played me the demo, and I thought, That's really good. I must admit I thought his voice was a little like Anthony Newley, with the same kind of similarities, you know. But I thought he was great—a very personable, cool guy. I wished him well.

BOB HARRIS (DJ): I had moved to London in 1966, as I was absolutely fascinated by the whole atmosphere of the city at that time, and the whole counterculture, as it was bursting into color. By 1968 I was an aspiring broadcaster and journalist, and along with Tony Elliott had just launched *Time Out* magazine. At the weekend I was also going regularly to an underground venue called Middle Earth in Covent Garden. This was an all-nighter, and was the first time I saw David perform, in a mixed-media group called Feathers, with Hermione Farthingale and Tony Hutchinson. I think Marc Bolan introduced us, as I was hanging out with Marc a lot at the time at Trident Studios, where Tony Visconti was producing

Tyrannosaurus Rex. David of course then began to work with Visconti, which is where I started seeing him. David was around a lot, and we started spending so much time together that my first wife and I invited him over to our flat for supper. And he came over, but as he had been working on a film [*Virgin Soldiers*], he'd just had a short back and sides. It really did look so funny seeing him at the time, because the whole fashion was for long hair. He was charming, very polite, and very English. Very gentlemanly. One of the common ground points for us was Anthony Newley, because Newley was such a hero of David's. And those records that Newley was making in the early '60s, like "Strawberry Fair," were incredibly influential for David. He really loved the theatrical aspect of "What Kind of Fool Am I" and the novelty of "That Noise," which was a single of Newley's that was a big hit. But you listen to those records, and you compare them to, say, "The Laughing Gnome," and you can draw an absolute straight line from one to the other. I remember those early conversations with David, exploring our record collections, and of course Newley was writ large.

As Terry was eleven years older than his half-brother, he would show David around London—when he was around himself, that is—introducing him to the dive bars and flesh pots of the West End, immersing him in the world of jazz. He wasn't around much, but when he was, he was the dominant sibling. As a way to reciprocate, in February 1967, Bowie took Terry to his first rock concert, to see Cream at the Bromel Club in Bromley. The rock world was alien to Terry, and the gig had a colossal effect on him. They were walking home and suddenly Terry started behaving in an extremely strange fashion; it was as though he were having a vision. He saw the road opening up. He saw fire in the cracks in the road, and he went down onto all fours, trying to hold the road, saying that he was being sucked off into the skies from the Earth. Bowie had never seen anyone in that kind of metaphysical change before, and it scared the hell out of him.

These attacks would happen again. Chislehurst Caves are not far from Bromley. Cut from Cretaceous chalk, they were apparently built by the Druids, at least according to legend. During the First World War they were used to store ammunition, and during the Second World War used as an air-raid shelter—a big one. By the '60s, bands had started performing there, flattered by the fact that they were actually "underground." Siouxsie Sioux, who hailed from Bromley, said they used to freak her out. "They were very dangerous," she says. "They used to cordon off bits you couldn't go down. Kids would sometimes go down there and get caved in." This is where Terry Burns ended up one day in 1967, when he turned up at his aunt Pat's house in Bromley, where he was living, only to find that they'd suddenly moved to Australia. As he tended to go AWOL, Pat and her husband had no way of letting him know. So he went wandering, ending up in the caves, where he stayed for eight days straight. When the police eventually found him he was taken briefly to David's home before being taken back to Cane Hill Asylum, a place that would become something of a home away from home.

TONY VISCONTI (PRODUCER): The first time I met David was late in 1967 and he was a young songwriter signed to the publishing company that I worked for in London. My boss, David Platz [who ran an independent production company], said you seem to have a knack for working with weird artists . . . and he used that word exactly . . . "weird." And he said, I'll play another artist you might enjoy working with, and then he played me some music by a twenty-year-old David Bowie. He played me the first album David had just made for Deram—there was a song on there called "Uncle Arthur" and another called "Mr. Gravedigger"—they all had very silly titles, but it was really cool and I said he's great. I said he's really talented but he's all over the place, he doesn't write in any particular style. And my boss said that's the problem. "If you work with him, could you get him to write in one style?" I said I would have a go, as I really liked him. David was actually in the next room, and so my boss opened the door and there was the young twenty-year-old David Bowie. He knew all about me and he was prepared to meet me, so we had a lovely first meeting. We spoke for hours in the office and then spent the day together. We talked about his music and what we liked, and we were both drawn towards the same artists at the time, underground music like Frank Zappa. . . . We were both big Zappa fans and we were talking about films that we liked, and anything that was from far away and anything that was black and white and made in France or Czechoslovakia or Germany and all that, so we had a lot in common. The office closed, and it was a beautiful autumn day so we decided to go for a walk. We walked from Oxford Street to the King's Road. It was quite a long walk, and then we saw that the cinema there was playing the latest Roman Polanski film, *Knife in the*

Water, and we went in and watched it. First day. So it ended at like nine in the evening. We said good night to each other, and we became good friends immediately. We really enjoyed each other's company.

LINDSAY KEMP (MIME ARTIST): It was 1967. I was performing in a show called *Clowns* at a little theater, sadly no longer here, off St. Martins Lane in Covent Garden. It could only fit about fifty but we squeezed about a hundred in. We did very good business. My agency used to get me the occasional gig as a warm-up mime act to rock bands at the time. They were also helping David find some work, and one of the girls in the office said I should listen to his record. So they gave me a copy of his first LP [*David Bowie*]. I took it home and fell in love with him before I'd even met him. He looked very nice on the cover. Very pretty, very lovely. The next night I played one of the tracks on the record, "When I Live My Dream," before the show started, and that night the secretary actually brought David along to see the show. She was a mutual friend but I think he was probably going out with her. He went out with most people. And she said to him, "You're going to love Lindsay Kemp." He was pleased to hear his record played, as very few people had heard it; no one was buying his music at that time. And of course David loved me too. It was love at first sight really. He came backstage after the show and was enchanted by it, by my world, by the Pierrot Harlequin, the backstage dramas that the show was about. It was a commedia dell'arte musical, a sort of backstage circus with songs. The show was very much inspired by Picasso's early paintings of the blue and pink period, of the hungry harlequins and Pierrot and their families and so on. When he knocked on my dressing-room door it was like the archangel Gabriel standing there. He was in a beam of light, glowing, I mean beautiful. It was love at first sight. I can see him standing there now, shining. I was like the Virgin Mary. I didn't fall onto my knees at that time; the dressing room was too crowded. He asked if he could come and study with me. That's all we talked about. In a few words, he just asked if I could teach him. I said yes of course, let's talk about it, come and see me tomorrow. So he visited me at my flat in Bateman Street in Soho. We chatted about our mutual passions for the musical and certain singers and music and so on. Jacques Brel, French singers like Catherine Sauvage, the theatre. The next day he began doing classes with me at the Covent Garden Dance Centre. He was a very promising student, very diligent. Much fancied by all the women in the class, especially when doing the improvisations. They took every opportunity to jump on him and start rolling around with him on the floor. He was attractive to men and women. He was charming, and beautiful on the outside. He was very charismatic and very humorous. I think his humor as well as his beauty attracted so many people to him. In those classes I can say that I taught him to dance and I taught him how to communicate, how to express himself through his body, mostly through improvisations. Then within hours after the class we spent that evening together in my flat in Soho and we mucked about a little. That's when we consummated our relationship. If David was nineteen when I met him, I was nine years older. He was considering giving up music altogether and going out to a monastery on the borders of Scotland. He had been studying Buddhism very seriously for a few years. He really thought that music had given him up. He wasn't getting anywhere when I met him. He was working in an advertising office doing mostly photocopying. He became my muse. For Pierrot in *Turquoise* he was very beautiful. He played a balladeer called Cloud. So he drifted on and off the stage like he drifted in and out of my flat on Bateman Street. He drifted in and out of different rows in that little show. He was a great inspiration. I don't think his love was as deep as mine. We split for a few months while he went on to do various gigs organized by Ken Pitt, but we continued to meet up. He stayed over occasionally in Soho and we created this little Pierrot show in December 1967 at the Oxford Playhouse, which then went on to the Mercury Theatre in London. It was a very big success.

There were always lots of other women. He was very sneaky. He was even having an affair with a girl called Natasha, who was one of my costume designers that I didn't find out about for ages. I really don't blame him for that, for having others on the side. He made no commitment to me; we weren't married or engaged. We were once at this little theater in Whitehaven, and we had beautiful rooms in a farm near the theater. We nicknamed it Jollity Farm but it turned out to be far from jolly, needless to say. I climbed into my four-poster bed whilst David was having a shower and I waited and waited. And I thought, What is he up to? And so reluctantly I fell asleep. Then I woke up and I heard noises, coming through the walls. Oh! Groans! Sighs! Oh God, I thought I would die. From the room of my best friend Natasha! I hovered outside her door for a few moments. Oh, it was awful. It was the most painful experience of my life. I wanted to end it. We had the premiere of the show the following evening. I couldn't bear it, I didn't want to live. So I ran out into the freezing cold weather and I decided I wanted to run out into the sea. The sea was too far away, however. So I thought, OK I'll get a bicycle and I'll bicycle into the sea. But it was hell, it was so cold. I had seen this in a movie, in *The 400 Blows* or something. I thought, Oh, that's a lovely way to end it . . . to bicycle into the sea and disappear forever. But I didn't have a bicycle and it was too cold and the tide was out. So instead I scratched my wrist. But not very deeply and I was found later that morning slumped on the floor of my dressing room. I remember coming round and hearing sacred music and thinking: "I've made it!" But then I realized it was the piano at the start of the show. I was taken to Whitehaven Hospital, where the doctors gave me a plaster and they told me not to be so daft. The show opened that night and the plaster came unstuck from my wrist and the blood started seeping into the white silk of my Pierrot costume. It was all very, very dramatic. That night David couldn't go to my room, and Natasha was rattling a bottle of sleeping pills and so the poor fellow ended up sleeping in a chair in a freezing cold hallway.

PETER FRAMPTON: When I left the Herd I joined Humble Pie with Steve Marriott, as we both wanted to be in a band where we played music, rather than just being screamed at. Humble Pie's first package tour was called *Changes '69*, and our special guest was David, and while we were on the tour, he suddenly became famous, as "Space Oddity" went to number one, and "Natural Born Boogie," our record, was number two. We were traveling in Andrew Oldham's Rolls-Royce Phantom 5, and unfortunately they all smoked hash, and I didn't, at that point. I caught up later. I'd done it a couple of times and it made me feel sick. One day we're driving up to a gig in Birmingham, and they're all smoking and I'm going green in the backseat. So when we arrived at the venue I was just about to pass out, and I remember David saying, "What the hell have you done to him?" I passed out in Dana Gillespie's breasts. David was always looking after me, and he became my elder brother at that point. He was like my stepbrother. I remember the day I showed my dad the cover of *Hunky Dory*, and he just went, “Oh my God.” He didn’t quite get it, but he respected him for doing it. We would crisscross the globe and bump into each other during the ’70s. I bumped into David when I was making my first solo album, *Wind of Change*, in 1972, at Olympic Studios in Barnes, while he was there producing “All The Young Dudes” for Mott the Hoople, and we would speak on the phone a lot. I was in Australia after my car accident in 1978 [Frampton was nearly killed when he was involved in a crash in the Bahamas], and I wanted to get out onto the road to prove that I could still do it, which was obviously a down period for me. David was there at the same time, and reached out to me, coming to see me at the hotel in Sydney. He said that I shouldn’t be on the road yet, and that I should still be recuperating. He was always looking after me, always wanted to know how my family was doing, how my dad was.

2

COMMENCING COUNTDOWN ENGINES ON

1969–1970

ROY PIKE (ANTIQUES DEALER): Beckenham was like a village back in the '60s, it was a lovely little place. Everyone knew each other, and nowadays I don't know the people three doors down. When I moved in with my wife, a lady in Victorian dress came round with a welcome basket, just to say hello. We'd never met the woman and never saw her again, but she just appeared, like an apparition, to welcome us to Beckenham. That's what it was like back then, friendly. There were a lot of big Victorian houses, with staff, and lots of unmade roads. You felt as though you were on the outskirts of something, in a nice way. Most of the shops were local. We had a butcher's, Tucker's, where you could buy a whole sheep if you wanted to, or half a pig. A greengrocers, dress shops, a printing works. There was a bandstand too—David played on it once. Everyone was pleasant, and you could have real conversations with the people who ran the shops. There was a café serving teacakes, a sports shop, Dunn's, the big local shop, Duncan's the family builders. I remember a shop tried to open called Bottoms Up, but the council wouldn't stand for it, so they had to change the name. There was a camera shop too, and years after David moved away they found an uncollected box of negatives he'd obviously taken at some point. I think people who didn't live in the area thought that everyone who lived in Beckenham was well off, but we all had mortgages. It was just a nice place to live.

ROY DALLEY (NEIGHBOR): Beckenham was like the '70s sitcom *The Good Life*, and there were lots of Margot Leadbetter types around. It was quite posh. The high street had this wonderful old Sainsbury's that was furnished with dark wood and had a dark wooden floor. There were some beautiful properties in Beckenham, and it wasn't like Bromley or Lewisham. Bowie shocked a lot of people when he moved in. It was suburbia.

MARY FINNIGAN (LANDLADY, LOVER): In 1969 I lived in a very ugly, crumbling Victorian house in Beckenham. It had been divided into four flats and I had the biggest ground-floor flat. I moved there from Cheshire in the '60s, and at that time I wasn't working full-time, I had really dropped out. I was separated from my husband, living on benefits, and I had two children.

David was friends with my upstairs neighbors Barry and Christina Jackson, who were the same sort of people as me. One day I was lying in my garden and I heard this beautiful music coming out of their open window, and it was a nice sunny April morning. It was confident, personal, and melodious. This, I thought, is not your average wannabe rock star. This is something special. I called up and said, "Who's playing?" and this head popped up out of the window; he had pale blond hair, a thin face, and a runny nose. He said, "Hello, I'm David, who are you?" and I said, "I'm Mary. Would you like to come downstairs and sample a tincture of cannabis and have a cup of tea?" I had been legally supplied tincture of cannabis by one of several hip doctors who prescribed it privately; as a consequence, everybody worked out that you could get the extract from which the tincture was made, which came in a little pot which was dark, green, and gooey, and all you had to do was tip your little finger into it.

So, I invited him down, and we had teaspoonfuls each of the tincture, and cups of tea, and we grazed through the fridge, and my kids came home. He seemed to like them, and after they had tea and went to bed, we carried on, and seemed to have an instant rapport. We just talked about all sorts of things: life experience; cultural, political, historical perspectives; and all sorts of stuff like that. He had a very eclectic view of life in general, but he was not at all narrow-focused. People tended to be a bit insular, thinking if we were going to change the world this was the way it was going to be. David wasn't like that at all, he said that you have to be inclusive and share with everyone, and that was really his pitch from the word go. We tended to agree on almost everything, and at some point in this conversation, I said, "I've got a spare room, would you like to be my lodger?" He said, "Yes, please," because he was living with his parents in Bromley, and was not at all happy. David told me he'd been in the music business for several years and had already released an album, which was not promoted and didn't sell. He told me he saw himself as a radical singer-songwriter. He was broke, and he didn't like his manager, Ken Pitt, who wanted to turn him into a Cliff Richard figure. He'd split up with his girlfriend Hermione, and was flat broke. At that time he was being a folkie, working in a duo with John Hutchinson.

So a few days later, he turns up on the doorstep with a small suitcase and a twelve-string Gibson, which is what he'd been playing when I first heard him. And my instincts about his creativity were absolutely right, because when he arrived, the kids were already home from school, Carolyn was ten and Richard was eight at the time. And he said, "Can I play you a song?" and we were all sitting in the kitchen, and he perched himself on the stool, and he took out this little long box, a little amp. And he played us "Space Oddity." He hadn't recorded it at that point, and it was written as a duet for him and Hutch. Me and the kids said, "This is a wonderful song, it's got to be a hit, it's fantastic!" The song triggered Richard's imagination, and he disappeared off to the kids' room, and came back with a drawing of a spaceman in his capsule, surrounded by the moon, planet Earth, and various other extraterrestrial phenomena.

So David moved in, and a few days later, his kit came with him. He told me he was going to need his kit, but I had no knowledge of what this represented. One morning quite early, there was a knock on the door and a van parked outside, and this guy said, "I've got David's kit," and he unloaded it. By the time he finished unloading it, you couldn't get in the children's room or my room at the end of the corridor, because it was completely blocked with assorted speakers, amplifiers, tape recorders, leads, and microphones.

By this time, David and I had become lovers. I have to say I was spellbound by his charisma, his charm, and his talent. He set up a very elegant seduction. David was not the most domesticated person in the world, and he was not really interested in food or cooking. On this occasion however, I came back home late, and the flat was very tidy, there was really nice cooking smells and the kids had been put to bed. And so he fed me with a candlelit dinner and a nice bottle of wine. Then we went into his room and he made a little nest on the floor, with cushions and great big speakers on either side, and played me his favorite music. Jimi Hendrix—that was the first time I heard stereo phasing—and Pink Floyd, Jacques Brel, some baroque music, probably Monteverdi, and some arcane ones I can't remember. And we were lying there together and of course one thing led to another. David was very apologetic about the fact that there was so much clutter in the house, but was adamant that it had to stay. He was seven years younger than me, and actually very sexually sophisticated.

KEITH CHRISTMAS (SINGER/SONGWRITER): It was not uncommon for us all to pack into a small room at the Troubadour in Bristol, or Les Cousins in Soho to hear artists like Bert Jansch or John Renbourn play with no PA to an utterly silent audience, but it was because of Mary Finnigan that I started guesting at the Three Tuns. I hadn't heard of David, as he was not playing the same sort of gigs as me. But the Three Tuns was his place, his residency. David never seemed very confident in his abilities, but he was definitely driven. He gave his all when he played without ever seeming to believe he was going to hit the big-time. He had a pretty droll sense of humor. David was starting to experiment with a more visual performance style towards the end of that summer and he was being strongly influenced by Lindsay Kemp. At the start of that year he was a folkie looking for a niche and by the end of it he was looking seriously exotic.

BERNARD GLAZIER: Around 1968 or 1969, my band was looking for performance opportunities and I responded to an ad in the local paper from a chap called David Bowie, about a new club, the Beckenham Arts Lab. He was out when I rang and I spoke to his mother. He rang back and we made an appointment. On the allotted evening I got a surprise. A knock on the front door of my flat in Bromley and there was David with his American girlfriend, Angie. I didn't have a clue who David Bowie was, but standing in front of me was David Jones, who I used to meet on the train from Bromley North when we were kids traveling into work. We got our guitars out, and I showed him some of my special tunings—one particular sequence later found its way into "Andy Warhol."

MARY FINNIGAN: "Space Oddity" had been written as a duet, but Hutch was in a terrible state of indecision, with his wife demanding he go back to Scarborough to be with her and the baby. Hutch was a cool guitar player and a member of a mime and music threesome called Feathers. The third member was David's ex-girlfriend, Hermione Farthingale. Feathers disbanded after a short life-span when David and Hermione split up. And David was saying, "Let's put our careers together and work as a duo." Eventually, Mrs. Hutch won out, so David was left with a solo career and a song written for two people. He got round that in performance by playing along to a tape. He used this strange instrument called a Stylophone, a battery-powered electronic device with a keyboard played with a stylus. It sounded like a cross between an organ and a jet plane.

As for us, our lifestyle was unsustainable because there wasn't enough money coming in. So one day David said, "I think we should go down Beckenham High Street and see if we can find a place to set up a folk club." David used to go to London at least once a week, even twice, and stay over. He said he was staying with my friend Calvin Mark Lee, who was then an A&R man for Mercury Records, and had spotted David's talent, and was helpful and supportive. I was so naïve, and believed David was in a monogamous relationship with me. I didn't know at the time; it was a long time before I found out that in fact that he had been bisexually multi-timing for the entire duration. Calvin was bisexual and, I discovered later, involved with David. David also told me about his relationship with mime artist Lindsay Kemp. Lindsay was David's mime and stagecraft guru for a while and was also his lover—but again I didn't find out about the physical aspect until much later. Plus, the whole time he was with me, David was also with Angie in London. I knew nothing of this; I was the little woman back in the suburbs. At the time I wasn't really aware of him with other men. There was only one point it crossed my mind, when Lionel Bart came to visit. I was excited because he was very famous at the time, and he turned up in a white top head Roller. I sort of hung about while he was there, and he was obviously trying to get rid of me! So eventually, he threw the keys of the Roller at me and said, "Go away and play," so I drove off in his white Rolls-Royce and left him and David alone. So it was pretty obvious with hindsight what was going on, but I didn't clock it at the time. I was very naïve.

So, we went down Beckenham High Street, and we alighted on the Three Tuns. And the landlord said, "Yes, you can have the back room, and no you don't need to pay for it, I'll make my money on drinks' sales." It was as dingy as any run-down pub could be, it had yellowy walls, it smelt of tobacco and stale beer, it was not very clean and it was very shabby. We thought, Yeah, it's the right size and the right location, and what can we do about the décor? I said to David, "Leave it to me, I know exactly what to do to turn this into a nice, appealing place that has actually got something in common with the prevailing Zeitgeist." I collected a whole bunch of cushions from the flat, I got a lot of Indian bedspreads, I got San Francisco and Indian posters, and I borrowed a light projector from a friend of mine in London. I had white sheets to project onto. So I turned a back room in a pub in Beckenham into a sort of mini Haight-Ashbury. The first night, David took care of the music, and he did it totally professionally and very methodically. He had Tony Visconti and his friend Ricky playing with him. It turned out he knew a lot of people on the folk circuit, because he went to London looking for gigs. The first night we had about twenty-five people, we did it with Barry and Christina from upstairs; they manned the door, and took the entry money, five shillings. The next Sunday we had about eighty, and thereafter it just exploded. We never had less than a hundred. It was jam-packed, and people came from far and wide, from all over South London. A psychedelic happening in the back room of a pub, where it cost five shillings to get in. David wrote a new song every week, he was very productive. The whole of his second album was written when he was living with us in Foxgrove Road, and he got a lot of very good people playing for him as a main act. He wrote one new song after another, scribbling lyrics in a notebook and figuring out tunes on the Gibson. When he felt OK about a song, he would say, very politely, "What do you think of this?" On warm afternoons he would sit on the swing in the garden, working on words and music, usually with one or both of the children messing about around him. "Wild Eyed Boy from

Freecloud" came about during one of those sessions, inspired by Richard's games. He even started working on a song called "The Circling Sponge," especially for Richard.

He always did a long set at the pub, and he compered every night. People like Keith Christmas, the Strawbs, Peter Frampton, Rick Wakeman, Amory Kane. It was really very good. The interesting thing was that the people we attracted were all very creative in their own spheres. And we realized that they didn't want to just be entertained, they wanted to participate. We had both been to the Drury Lane Arts Lab, and at that time arts labs were moving out from London right across the UK, and springing up everywhere. We both alighted on the idea simultaneously, "Shall we turn the folk club into an arts lab?" So David proposed the idea next Sunday, and the whole room cheered. So the Beckenham Arts Lab was created, and at that point everybody's creativity was part of what happened on Sundays. There were puppet shows, book readings, visual art, and the conservatory at the back was open in the summer. There were posters, print makers, so the conservatory became a marketplace. Calvin bought some psychedelic posters back from San Francisco and it was absolutely thriving. On a Sunday night, the music, but more than anything else the energy, spilled out onto Beckenham High Street, and everybody was captivated by it and the whole of that boring dormitory suburb came to life, and it was absolutely fizzing with energy.

AMORY KANE (MUSICIAN): In 1969, I had a residency at this little basement club called Bunjies in Litchfield Street, just off Tin Pan Alley, a folk cellar—it used to flood a lot—where Eric Clapton played, along with Paul Simon, Gerry Rafferty, Tom Paxton, and Bert Jansch. Even Bob Dylan. Al Stewart actually gave me the gig, as I replaced him. Every couple of weeks this lovely guy with yellow hair and a big red Gibson guitar would come down and play, and bring his wife, Angela, with him. Then he'd invite me down to the Three Tuns, where he had his own residency, and later we played the Beckenham Free Festival. The thing that he gave me was his interest in yoga, as he mentored me in the field of Pranayama yoga. He was a dedicated practitioner of yoga when I knew him, and that's the reason he had the body of a god. He'd already worn a space suit for a performance we did at the Wigmore Hall, peeling off parts of the suit and throwing them at the audience as part of a ballet, but when he played me "Space Oddity" at the club one night I said, "That's amazing, and I'm not even going to know you in a year."

DAVE WALKING (NEIGHBOR): I was hanging about in Beckenham, and one day somebody said this guy called David Bowie had started a folk club. He'd made a record called "The Laughing Gnome." So we went to see him and he was rather good. He played "Amsterdam" by Jacques Brel, and the best thing about him was he didn't sing with an American accent, which everyone else did. He was quite good friends with Marc Bolan, and a lot of what David did next was a bit like Bolan for adults. He also loved Charlie Mingus, especially "Oh Yeah," one of the greatest jazz records of all time. He liked Ornette Coleman, who used to play a plastic saxophone, and David had one too.

BILL LIESEGANG (MUSICIAN): I used to live in Beckenham, with a band. My best friend, who was the singer, Neil Holmes, he got to know David through the Arts Lab. We were both sixteen. I had moved out of the area, but I kept coming back at the weekends to do gigs. Neil took me down to David's place in Foxdale [*sic*] Road, Beckenham, where he was staying with Mary Finnigan. He was a perfect gentleman, a really funny guy. We were talking about the revolution and stuff. He was a bit older than us, so he used to tell us stories, about what he was up to, which was fascinating, because we were new. I remember having a little jam with him, he had his twelve-string guitar, and he was busy writing a song. He came across as this slightly eccentric, creative guy. Very energetic, full of ideas. He was basically the archetypal hippie, with long hair, and he had just started to do his "Space Oddity" poem thing. He was pretty poor, he didn't have any money, just a load of amplifiers, keyboards, and PA speakers around his flat. He was always with Mary. We used to see him at the Prompt coffee bar on Beckenham High Street, talking about street theatre and *The Lord of the Rings*. That was the thing to have—and a little shoulder bag. Beckenham seemed to be a magnet, and there were all these people with long hair getting chucked out of their homes. The parks were full of these longhaired kids round about my age all smoking dope, and then they would all assemble on the Arts Lab on Sunday night.

TIM HOLLIER (MUSICIAN): I knew David in a period when he knew he was going to do something very important, during a year we spent together largely in the King's Road. Because it was never about Carnaby Street, always the King's Road, hanging around in the Chelsea Arts Club. There was Nick Drake, Peter Sarstedt, Roy Harper, and all these different singer-songwriters who lived and played around the area, but David was different, there was no question. There was a lot of marijuana around at the time, and the memories are hazy, but David was always the one to watch. I remember he had a manager, quite an enigmatic character called Calvin Mark Lee, who I met through Mary Finnigan. Calvin had a flat in Sloane Street, and I used to hang out there with my then wife, Wendy, David, and Rory Fellowes, Julian Fellowes's brother. Julian was still at Ampleforth in short pants, while we were classically trying to be the beautiful people in the King's Road. David accepted that Wendy, who was your classic English blonde, and I were heterosexual, as far as anyone was in the '60s, but he was starting to experiment in other areas with Calvin, who was an incredibly elegant American Filipino with very long hair. We were all playing together in various folk clubs in London such as the Troubadour, and after a while we started going down to Beckenham, using the Three Tuns as a base. David asked me to be his first guest there, although he was the amazing one. He had been working with Lindsay Kemp and he had started to have real stage presence. Sometimes he would simply set his guitar down and just sing an unaccompanied song. I remember him singing one he appeared to have just made up on the spot called "When I'm Five I Will Catch a Butterfly in My Hand." And then at the end of this little song, he would accidentally crush the butterfly in his hand. And he would lift it up. And the whole place was quiet, you know, fifty or sixty people all silent. He had presence, and few people had presence in the '60s.

JACKIE HOMEWOOD (NEIGHBOR): I went to see David every Sunday at the Three Tuns. I was fifteen and a half and there was no control at all about getting into pubs. It was the place where everyone went at the time.

There was an R&B night during the week, but Sunday was the best night. I'm not sure that David Bowie was initially the draw, but he happened to be playing every Sunday, and then gradually we all went to hear him play. Pubs shut at 10:30 on a Sunday so you had to rush off afterwards and catch a bus home. There wasn't a stage, so he just stood by himself in the corner playing. When he met Angie she would be sitting near him, but usually it was just him. He had all these long blond curls, dressed like a quintessential hippie with flares and a tight-fitting denim jacket. He got better every week. At the beginning you just thought it was a local person playing in a pub, but when he first played "Space Oddity" you knew that things were changing. He made the record, it was a hit, and he stopped coming because he was becoming famous. And when he stopped playing we stopped going.

ANGIE BOWIE (EX-WIFE): It was at the Roundhouse. That was the first time I met David. I was there with Mercury Records, with Calvin Mark Lee and Lou Reizner, who were running the [A&R department]. David had a band called Feathers who were performing. The Who were the top of the bill, then Scaffold, then Feathers. Calvin and I had a mission. We were trying to get Lou Reizner to record "Space Oddity." I'd heard the demo, and hearing Feathers perform it that night was the endorsement. David was charming, and we met his girlfriend Hermione, who was absolutely lovely. They were all fabulous. So, you know, we chatted, and then off we went. The thing I took away from the evening was that live, David was very exciting, and so I had to turn that into a persuasive tool to get Lou Reizner to stop raising all these obstacles. It was a £400 deal for a single, I mean, it was so ludicrous. It was one of those off chances that might do well or might not. I thought, Take a shot, why not do it. That's the way I pitched it to Irving Green, who was the president of Mercury. The next time I met David, the deal had been done for the single, and Calvin had arranged that I had to talk to Irving Green about it. And I said it seemed ridiculous to have done all this negotiating and not get an album out of it. I mean, what if it does well? So Irving said it was a good idea, and they put a caveat in it, which said they could pick up an album if they wanted to. So the next time I saw David, they had started recording the album; they had got a little activity in England for "Space Oddity," but nothing in America. They were nervous as could be. Then Calvin took us both out to dinner. David had broken up with Hermione and he was nursing a broken heart. He wasn't really doing what Calvin needed, as Calvin needed him to be out promoting. So Calvin wanted me to cheer him up, to help him out. We hit it off and had a great time. We had dinner at the Dumpling Inn, and then we went on to the Speakeasy and King Crimson were there. They had a party for their album, which was debuting that week. We danced, we jived, there were all kinds of wonderful dance music. He was very forward. He was just a confident person. He didn't take liberties but he had an opinion about things and he was articulate. He was very capable of expressing himself on many different subjects. I knew he had not been to college, apart from some time at art college, but he was very well read, and I found out later that that whole demeanor was as a result of his father's personable demeanor as a PR representative for Barnardo's. His half-brother, Terry, happened to be a beatnik aficionado and had read William Burroughs, and was generally on top of things regarding the Beat Generation. So David was lucky because he had those two influences at home, and then he had all his friends in the music business and people in the publishing business. So the polish was there, but he was between a rock and a hard place, as the Mercury album wasn't going to happen unless "Space Oddity" was a big hit. He needed some help, a marketer. A promoter. That was what became very apparent to me. We stayed together for a couple of days and then he went back to Beckenham, because he had a show at the Arts Lab to do. He did the show but got sick, and as Mary Finnigan, his landlady, was out of town, he asked me to come down to stay with him. I'm sure they were together; he just hadn't told her [about me]. She wasn't there so I didn't know. I had no idea who she was. I didn't even know who he was. All I knew was that this was an artist that we were trying to get signed to Mercury. And we had done that. So when we went out for dinner with Calvin, I became interested on a girlfriend/boyfriend level. I thought, Oh well, he's kind of fun, I like him. I thought this would be a good way of proving what I could do as a marketer. Because having seen him live and how he performed onstage, and having already heard the Deram album and the new songs for the *Space Oddity* album, I knew he was very capable as a writer. There was no issue.

GLENN GORING (MUSICIAN): David and Angie had rented a large ground-floor flat in Haddon Hall, Southend Road, Beckenham. It was pretty much an open house. You didn't have to make an appointment or anything formal like that to visit, which I often did. At that time Zowie [Duncan] Bowie was an infant. So you would have this nappy-changing, toy-rattling, baby-crying family environment woven into this bohemian, slightly crazy atmosphere. I first met them in the spring of 1969 when Comus, the band in which I played guitar, performed at the Three Tuns. The first time we played there, I remember David sitting cross-legged on the floor just a few feet away from my barstool. He was rocking backwards and forwards, a big grin on his face, enthralled. I was really struck when, sitting on the same barstool I'd just vacated, David produced the famous Stylophone and performed "Major Tom." The Stylophone was seen at the time as a kind of toy made famous by Rolf Harris. It was not taken seriously as a musical instrument in its own right. It looked so insignificant resting on David's knees as he began to slide the small, plastic stylus across the metallic "keyboard." But suddenly, hearing those warbling notes booming out of the PA transformed this toy into something totally unique, a strange mixture of the cheap-and-nasty and something much more haunting and profound.

Bowie was quite serious about Buddhism, and his interest was something he kept up throughout his life. It might have been easy to assume this was just another affectation, but he subscribed completely to the Buddhist ideas of "self-empty" and ascetic withdrawal. Intellectually, it all made sense to him, and Buddhism, and in particular the Mayahana branch, would occupy him for the rest of his life, and indeed right up until his death. "Bowie said that 'the idea of transience' never left him: the self as a figment, a will-o'-the-wisp illusion, the thinnest of membranes masking a profound emptiness," says the writer Simon Reynolds. "But in Buddhism this interior void is not troubling or nihilistic: the true self is the no-self, a positive emptiness that is distinguished from the puffed-up 'substance' of the public persona. Reality, the world of appearances, is Maya, a word that means variously illusion, magic and dream. But in Mayahana, the self too is a 'magic show,' a trick done with mirrors." He would begin to take succor from the fact that all images, public personae, and characters were fake. This not only helped him contextualize all the previous permutations of himself—in the Kon-Rads, the Mannish Boys, the Buzz, etc.—it started to shape his future. "It's much more a realism for me to think that this (clothes, hair, gestures, the room) is all me, that there's nothing else in here," said Bowie. "It's all outside. I prefer that way of existence."

MARY FINNIGAN: When you look back in hindsight and see Beckenham the way it is now, it has that legacy, so there's a little bit more substance to the place because of Bowie. We did street theatre on the Saturday morning down the High Street, and then the Bromley Arts Centre asked if we would do some gigs there, in a very posh detached house. There was a nonstop party at my flat, and after the Three Tuns, everyone would come back to the flat. It had to be quiet and acoustic because of the kids and neighbors, but the party would go on until the wee small hours. People fucked by rote. Endless cups of tea and spliffs, no alcohol. So at the Bromley Arts Centre, we decided to put on this Tibetan lama, called Chime Rinpoche, who was David's guru. He was one of only four Tibetan lamas in the UK in 1969, and he was a monk in maroon robes, although in common with many lamas who migrated to the West, he disrobed soon afterwards when the temptations of the flesh became too much. David was very much into Buddhism at this time, and he actually introduced me to it. I learned to meditate, and because of this a lot of us decided we would have to stop doing psychedelics. It seemed a logical extension of the deep introspection of taking LSD. You had to get to grips with finding that experience through your own psychometric emotions. David was scared of LSD and he hinted that he found the prospect of losing control during the psychedelic experience terrifying. He talked about his half-brother Terry's mental illness. "He's schizophrenic and it probably runs in the family," he said.

David talked a lot about Chime, and was on the verge of becoming a monk, because whatever David did he did 100 percent. But he couldn't get the music out of his head, and realized that he had to pursue that because it was integral to his being. At a certain point in Los Angeles, when he had this hideous cocaine habit, and was drinking himself to death, he rang Chime and said, "I'm desperate, I need your help." Well, lamas of Chime's stature don't go; you go to them. So he didn't, and went to Berlin instead, where I think he and Iggy dried out together. The way he lived his life, on the stage, there was no separation, until he settled down with Iman. All of those shape-shifting personalities were rooted in his experience on the cushion in my flat, because the first thing that you get to, when you make a breakthrough in your Buddhist practice, is that there is no such thing as a separate self. You get a holistic perspective, the interconnectedness of all things. For a time he was very ego driven but I think he got past that, I think Buddhism had a lot to do with that.

I came home one day and the flat was immaculate, and usually after coming home I would have to clean up because David never cleaned up after himself. He never washed up, never cleaned; usually the place was very untidy and messy, guitar strings all over the place. But this time it was immaculate. There was a sort of whiff of Chanel, and I crept into David's room, very carefully, and it was empty. There was a kimono draped over the chair, and a notebook with a song written in it, and the song was called "Beautiful Angie." I went to bed, woke up a few hours later, and could smell cooking. There was this American voice coming from the kitchen, and David strumming some chords. I got up, and there was this woman who turned around and greeted me: "Hello Mary, how wonderful to meet you, David's told me so much about you!" It was Angie. She was nineteen, but streetwise, beautiful, and terribly and completely at ease. I had no idea at the time. What do you do when you're living as lovers, and then you coolly bring the replacement into the house and expect to get away with it? With hindsight I look back on it and think, "I absolutely do not know why I allowed this to happen."

This went on for months. It ended up being quite fun actually, because I got over it eventually. Angie and I got along together quite well, but the thing about Angie was that although she seemed to be very assured, she was neurotic as hell. She had to be the center of attention. David eventually described living with her as "like living with a blowtorch" and I called her part angel, part hellcat; she had many qualities, and did more than her share of domestic chores, was wonderful with the kids. But also extremely turbulent, very disturbed, very spoilt. Nowadays I think Angie is her own worst enemy.

ANGIE BOWIE: I had worked with a lot of artists at Mercury, and David had more panache than all of them. He had star quality. But I kept thinking to myself that he shouldn't be beholden to someone, staying at somebody else's house. Because a young man who hasn't got his own house is really somebody's boyfriend or somebody's son. He's not an individual yet. It became apparent to me that what I needed to do was to find him a place for us to live once we were going out all the time. I started looking, and within two or three months I found a place on Southend Road. It came to be known as Haddon Hall. It was a great place. A strange shape. It was the central nervous system of an old Victorian mansion built for the Crystal Palace exhibition. And so it was pre-built for the summer months, when the exhibition was on. It had balconies all the way around it, and the front was on Southend Road but it backed onto a huge golf course. It was totally rural and quite charming and quite lovely with a huge garden at the back. I found it, as David was dealing with the death of his father at the time. That was not something that we could do together. He was very excited and looking forward to it. But I had to persuade Mr. Hoy to let us live there. Mr. Hoy was the gardener, who had been left the house because the man who owned it couldn't stand his own children. So Mr. Hoy divided it into seven apartments. When I went to look at it, there were two professors from City College in London, one of science and one of math, a marvelous lady and a marvelous old gentleman, who had twenty-eight cats! Twenty-eight cats! And the entire house, because of this huge stained-glass window which was at the top of the stairs, was like a solarium. They had it full of plants, and the cats thought they were outside, and I think you can imagine what I am insinuating. But it didn't alter the fact that it was exquisite. Two very old professors, twenty-eight cats, and none of it made any difference. I boshed straight in and I just kept meeting [Mr. Hoy]. I kept saying, "Oh please, come on, I've chosen the curtains." Because he was worried we wouldn't be able to afford the curtains because they were big long twelve-foot ceilings. I said, "My mum and dad gave me some money to get married, which is enough for the curtains and the carpets." Haddon Hall was fourteen pounds a month, and we had a year's lease. And so we moved in! And before we moved in—I mean, eighteen buckets of bleach later, the cats had been removed!

BILL LIESEGANG: Angie was quite brash compared to us English people. David was pretty laid back in his attitude so I think all of Angie's PR experience was incredibly useful to him, especially where Ziggy Stardust is concerned. I think if he hadn't met Angie, David might have continued as a sort of Bob Dylan type. He was in awe of Humble Pie's Steve Marriott, who was also from Bromley. I remember he was also moaning about Marc Bolan becoming commercial and selling out. David had got a lot of publicity, but he was still David Bowie in his dress with his curly perm. He did this street theatre thing when he got everyone to walk down the road with bowler hats and giant penises on their heads.

ANGIE BOWIE: David and his half-brother were very close as well. I had Terry at Haddon Hall for a while, as I brought him from Cane Hill to live with us for six months. Why not? Why should he be at Cane Hill when he could be at home with us? They gave him drugs which they said were going to manage him as best as possible, and David felt so guilty. I said don't feel guilty, get Terry to come and spend some time with him and it will change everything. And it did. A lot of his music afterwards, where he deals with insanity and madness, his understanding of why it's so cutting edge and why one is so much always on that edge, I think had a lot to do with the fact that he had a chance to spend time with Terry and talk to him. And the worst part of it was that Terry started to feel so much better, that of course he didn't want to continue taking his medication anymore. It's a good thing on the one hand, but not a good thing on the other. And as he wanted to get married to a girl he had met at the asylum in Cane Hill, David and I kind of wanted to talk him into at least taking enough of his medication that he could manage himself. We kept saying to him, You know if you don't take it, are you going to be all right? Married? We weren't exactly sure how it would work. Well, before we had a chance to even say anything, they took her away and sterilized her. Because that's what they did in England at that time if you were in an asylum and you were a woman. They sterilized you so you couldn't give birth. So anyway they were married and it was OK. Everything seemed to be fine for two or three years, and then, I guess it wasn't going so well. I wasn't there because I had already been seconded to New York and LA. I would come back and try and find out what was going on, after David and I parted. Two or three years later I heard that Terry had walked in front of a train. He never had any alarming episodes when he was with us; I never saw his schizophrenia. He was wonderful. But of course that's another bad thing. When you haven't seen a person having a fit or being restrained, or maybe accidentally hitting someone who tried to help them . . . I've always felt that I was making out that it was less than it was. And I knew that was wrong. I always tried to stop myself. David was better than I was with that. He said, "Angie, we're fighting a losing battle because we can't watch him twenty-four hours a day." We couldn't do that; he was a grown-up. It's embarrassing, you can't do that to someone. You can only suggest it. We weren't putting the same constraints on him like an institution would. The whole point was that he would have some peace and quiet and solitude and talk to his brother and play with the baby [Zowie, born in 1971]. But I loved Terry, because I loved David and I wanted to do everything I could possibly do to help his family and to help him be happy.

JAYNE COUNTY (PERFORMER): As far as David's brother Terry we were told to *never* bring it up, so we didn't dare.

Future Spider Woody Woodmansey says that Terry's schizophrenia manifested itself in his total lack of filter. Woody would be having Sunday lunch at Haddon Hall, along with the rest of the band, plowing through a meal cooked jointly by Angie and Peggy, when Terry would suddenly arrive. "You'd ask, 'What have you been up to, Terry?' And he'd reply, 'I've been wanking.' His mother would say, 'I don't think people want to hear about that at the dinner table.'"

MARY FINNIGAN: Before they moved to Haddon Hall we decided to hold a free festival. The idea just emerged from a lab meeting, because we wanted to raise some money to get some premises. There had only been Woodstock so far, so we decided to put on a free festival at Croydon Road Recreation Ground, on the sixteenth of August. David was away, he was doing some song festivals, and while he was away Angie and I were running the Arts Lab, and David's dad rang up. He sounded a bit rough, and said, "When David gets back, can you tell him to call me?" So, Sunday night, David came back, and I told him to call his father. He rushed off but a few days later his dad died of pneumonia. David blamed me for the fact that he didn't know, but as far as I was concerned I told him as soon as I could. When the festival happened, David was devastated, in absolute grief. So, Angie and I did 90 percent of the organization, although David did the music. Lots of people had a wonderful afternoon, except for David, who was snarling and snapping at everybody. Afterwards, when we totted up what we had earned, we had made about £600, because of all the stuff we sold. David was supported by Bridget St. John, Keith Christmas, Tony Visconti, and John Peel. Calvin Mark Lee had brought a huge collection of psychedelic posters. Angie made burgers all day, somebody else did candy floss, somebody else drinks. When I came back to the flat, David and Angie were ready to move out, Angie having found Haddon Hall, and I got my home back.

ANGIE BOWIE: As for David's mother, well, losing her husband was bad enough. That was tragic. He was young; it wasn't his time to go. He had pneumonia, he was overtired, he couldn't reach the oxygen upstairs; he should have been in the hospital. She wasn't particularly informed or aware of how sick he really was. The doctors didn't help her. David had no idea either, as he was out of the country at the Maltese song festival. We got on the bus to go to the airport, and David went back to London and I went to Cyprus to see my parents, and his father was dead when he got back to London. So I got a phone call from him. He talked to my father to ask him to send me back. I wasn't close to David's mother at first, as she was a strange lady. I later became very fond of her, but she was as difficult as she could possibly be at the beginning. She was one of the first girls to wear trousers in Tunbridge Wells, she had two children out of wedlock, and she had an audacity and a judgmental attitude that did not go well with her past. And I was not very shy about saying that, you know, she needed to lighten up. I confronted her on many occasions. On many occasions she would call up screaming, insulting me down the phone. So I said to David, look, I'm out of here. So I went back to my parents in Cyprus. I said, you know, I didn't need this crap. She used to insult me because we were living out of wedlock! It was so tired and so old, it was boring to the extreme. I was like, Oh please, have you got nothing else? I suppose she judged me on her own sins. We were both Catholic. So I guess she had some sort of hold over my conscience through that. But all she did was irritate me. I was so unlike what she imagined. The only thing I was interested in was being able to market David's work. So finally I packed her up and I took her to Cyprus! I took her to stay with my parents. She was there for six months; she had a blast! She just needed to be with people who were her age and who were nice, you know what I mean? I think trying to fit in all the time, trying to see David's shows, without her husband, it made her feel lonelier. It made her sound off. I couldn't be angry with her, how could I, it was his mother for crying out loud. And she had just lost her husband and I was just heartbroken for her.

I had met them both only ten days before, and he was fine. They were going to visit Terry. I came back three weeks later and he was dead. And she was unlike the lady I had met before. It was just like night and day. Now, don't misunderstand me, she wasn't outgoing, or voluble, or particularly pleasant before, but afterwards, she was really unpleasant. She kind of grew into the fact that she was now a spinster.

She wasn't protective of David, she never got like that. She had no input whatsoever. David's father was his parent. He and his father were just joined at the knee, like total best friends. He was involved in show business, he signed for all the stuff for when he was in the Mannish Boys and the Lower Third and they had to get a PA and all that. So they were thick as thieves.

GLENN GORING: I bumped into David one afternoon on a bus, a 194 heading in the direction of West Wickham. I got on and saw David sitting toward the back on the left, alone, staring out the window. I caught his eye and we exchanged nods, but he didn't smile, as he normally would have. He turned back to the window, apparently distracted by the passing world. When I sat next to him, he didn't look up. It was obvious he wasn't in the mood for conversation. Eventually I broke the silence and asked him how he was. Then, with a hint of anger and bitterness in his voice, he came straight out with it: "My father's just died."

ROY PIKE: I remember when David first came into the shop; he was incredibly charming. He just appeared one day, and then suddenly he was here all the time. He was a lovely young man. David wore this big floppy hat, and had long hair, which wasn't really fashionable at the time, because the hippies hadn't come in yet. He wore a big casual jacket, flared trousers, and always wore this long Afghan coat. He lived in that coat, and never seemed to take it off, even in summer. He certainly stood out, that's for sure. But he was very polite, always very respectful, called me Mr. Pike, never Roy, even after we'd known each other for years. He had very good manners. I remember my wife saying it was the first time in her life she'd ever seen a man with a shoulder bag. It looked odd, but he carried it off. Then of course there were his eyes, which were different, and which made him stand out, made him noticeable.

He started coming in once or twice a week, just to browse, and started buying the odd thing from us, which I'd take down to Haddon Hall for him. Angie used to come in too, although we never cared for her that much, and strangely they would never come in together, only separately. We sold him a cabinet, a chest of drawers, tables, lots of things. Always looking for things that were out of the ordinary, he was. He lived on the ground floor there, with a long winding staircase and all the windows on the first floor were sealed up. But I was always taking things up there. There was a chap opposite Haddon Hall who was trying to get rid of a black grand piano—I can't remember the make—and so I told David, who bought it for fifty quid, and we both dragged it over to the Hall. The chap wanted me to sell it for him, but I couldn't have moved it, so David took it, and starting writing songs on it. He stopped working on the guitar and started on the piano. I remember once delivering something and Zowie had just been born, and I cuddled him. He was only born a day or two before, and was so quiet. I used to pop in all the time, and I remember being quite shocked one day when I went in and saw David standing on the piano painting the ceiling. He had paint on his shoes and that became his style, always with paint on his shoes. I carpeted his mother's flat once, but I could never get paid, so David paid instead. I sold him a Malaysian sideboard once, which he painted white, and a treadle organ with foot pumps that he covered in Perspex and used to use in performance.

There wasn't really a bohemian scene here, just David's little group. Nice people. David was always having problems with his manager, Ken Pitt, and was always complaining about him. He wanted to get out of his contract, as he felt he was being pushed in the wrong direction. I think at one point he even got some advice from Lionel Bart. It was Lionel Bart or someone like that. Angie was always a bit of a nutter, though, a bit of a fruitcake. When she moved out she moved into Foxgrove Road, and there were always lots of men around. She had a good upbringing—her father was an ambassador or something—but she was very loud and showy. She put herself about a bit when she split up with David. She was always over the top, always talking loudly. She once asked me what something was in the shop, and it was a collection of small bollards that I'd bought from a decommissioned ship, and whenever she used to come in she'd shout, "Bollards, Mr. Pike!" She used to think that was very funny.

TONY VISCONTI: So we started recording *Space Oddity.* There were so many things that I loved about recording with David. Number one, he had a great voice—it was theatrical and I could hear that he could do tricks with it. Singing came very easy to him; it wasn't a struggle. Shortly after I met him and I heard his songs—which were folk rock, which "Space Oddity" came out of, that strumming his twelve-string guitar—I knew he could sing rock. The other thing that struck me was his lyrics. No one apart from Bob Dylan and a few others, Roy Harper and the serious folkies, were writing very political or very metaphysical lyrics that made you scratch your head and say I don't exactly know what they're saying but it sounds deep. David definitely came from that school—his lyrics were very, very impressive, and as a record producer when a person writes lyrics that well, you don't want to cover it up with overproduction. So it's very, very appealing when you meet someone like that. So I tailored my production techniques to him immediately. What we tried for the first album—the *Space Oddity* album—which was not quite successful, but wasn't bad, was that he needed a band. Normally if there is a soloist, you get session musicians who are much older and who get paid by the hour. Sometimes they can be a bit indifferent but at least they play perfectly. I thought David needed people his own age, that really got him. He was definitely a generational artist, but he spoke to his generation. And I didn't want to get some fifty-year-old drummer in there who might play impeccably, but who also might be looking at the *Daily Mirror* in the breaks, which they do. So I hired a band that I was working with called Junior's Eyes. They were all David's age and really great musicians and they made the album. They were really sympathetic and listened carefully to the lyrics and they played very well, but folk rock wasn't his style and that was evident when we finished the album. He needed to drop that twelve-string for a bit and we needed to find a powerhouse band for him. And that happened in the form of Mick Ronson.

RICK WAKEMAN (PIANIST): I did a session for Tony Visconti in 1968 for a band called Junior's Eyes. There was a Mellotron in the studio, and they were very new at the time, so I played around with it for a couple of hours. I knew about the problems they had keeping them in tune but after a while I found a way you could cheat to keep it in tune; it was a mixture of doing arpeggios with your fingers, making sure there's always two notes being held down at the same time, and playing with a pitch control. Then when David started recording "Space Oddity," he wanted a Mellotron mixed in with everything else, but couldn't keep the thing in tune. That's when Tony Visconti called me. After that we recorded "Wild Eyed Boy from Freecloud" and "Memory of a Free Festival" and a couple of other things.

KEITH CHRISTMAS: David was very nervous at the recording of *Space Oddity*. We sat in this massive studio in Hyde Park and he played me some songs. He cried when he heard the playback to "God Knows I'm Good," so it must have meant a lot to him and it showed a very emotional side of his character.

RICK WAKEMAN: David Bowie is far and away the cleverest man I've ever worked with. An absolute walking genius to work with. I did about two thousand sessions in four years, and of all those sessions the person I learned more from was David. He was so far ahead of the game. He absolutely listened to nobody who he felt didn't have anything worth listening to. He wasn't into listening to managers and record-company executives. 'Cause his argument was: "If they want to be musicians, let them go and make a record, don't tell me what to do." And it was a wonderful attitude.

I remember going into the studio [for "Space Oddity"], and we recorded it, did my Mellotron bits, and walked up the stairs to go into the control room. And he was in there having a blazing row with the guy from Phillips, the record company guy. Because he wanted the single to be in stereo. And there weren't stereo singles then.

The guy said, "No, we don't do stereo singles. Jukeboxes are in mono, everything's mono."

And David said, "I don't give a damn, this is stereo. In a little while, everything's going to be in stereo. There's going to be stereo jukeboxes. Everybody's going to have stereo at home, this has to be in stereo."

He was dead right and it's reputed to be one of the first, if not the first, stereo single. If you can find the Phillips one, it's as rare as rockets. I used to have one but four marriages have gotten rid of that.

He was always incredibly prepared in the studio. He said to me: "Never waste time in the studio. Studio time's really precious. Whilst you might have the money to waste in the studio now, there might be in years to come a time when you might wish you had that money. You'll look back at the time you wasted."

He never wrote in the studio; everything was already done. He was always what he called "75 percent prepared." You go in and he'd get the piece that far, and then the studio would take it that extra 25 percent. He respected the studio, and I think that's the one thing he taught me more than anything else: respect the studio. It's not a plaything.

Amazing character. Amazing man.

BOB HARRIS: I was now spending a lot of time at David's recording sessions as well as Marc Bolan's, and in fact I appear on "Memory of a Free Festival" on his second album, the *David Bowie* album that became *Space Oddity*. My first wife, Sue; and our friend Tony Walcott, who subsequently became vice president of Columbia Records; and Marc Bolan had called in to Trident to see David. He and Tony Visconti were just about to record "Festival," so David, Tony, me, Sue, Marc Bolan, and Tony Wolcott all sat on the studio floor singing "The sun machine is going down and we're going to have a party." Visconti kept re-recording, building up a Phil Spector–like wall of sound, to sound like a festival crowd. And then at the end we all whooped and hollered and whistled and shouted, and that's what you hear on the fade.

VAL PORTELLI (FRIEND): I went to Raglan Infants' School from 1953 until 1955, which is when David was there. I remember him from that time but he was just another kid. I didn't really get to know him until he went to the local technical college, when he started putting together a band with a few friends, including George Underwood. We were in the same classes for years, until I left to work in Lloyds Bank in Beckenham High Street. In those days, when you opened an account, you needed a letter from somebody respectful to introduce you. David came in with a letter from his father, who had an account there, to say he was a respectable, decent sort of person. I noticed him because every other man had short hair and a suit, but he came in wearing a blue dressing gown and makeup. He would have been about eighteen. I could hear some of the old ladies in the queue whispering, "What is the world coming to?" Some of them didn't know whether he was a girl or a boy. As I say, he stood out. He was so different, almost starting a new idea, a new convention. I remember when he came in, he'd just had a hit with "Space Oddity" and instead of saying, "Could you sign the checkbook request?" I said, "Can I have your autograph, please?" And he was really embarrassed. Around the same time, Mick Jagger actually came into the branch, as he had met David at a concert in Richmond. He didn't have an account there, but I think David said, "Go up to my branch, and they'll help you cash some money." When he came in, there was a woman in her forties on the desk, and because his account wasn't there, she asked him for some identification. And we girls were at the back saying, "That's Mick Jagger!" and all getting excited. And of course this lady, this supervisor, she said, "OK, I will cash a check for you, but can I have some identification?" And Mick Jagger just turned sideways and said, "My face." Which is something David would never have done. His mother also had an account there, and as he started getting famous, she always wanted to talk about him. Angie used to come into the bank too, but to be honest I couldn't stand her. She was a snotty bitch.

BOB HARRIS: It is easy to say in hindsight, but you could emphatically tell that David was going to be a star. He wanted it. There were several things that came together that made success inevitable. He had this lovely way about him, he had almost a kind of dreamy look in his eyes. Plus of course his eyes were particularly fascinating. He was very driven: you got the sense that although he didn't know completely where he was going, he knew he had to go there. We had already seen the multilayers of his self-expression, because in Feathers you had mixed media, and he'd been very influenced by Lindsay Kemp. This is why *Time Out* got behind David, because I just felt David was so charismatic, you just knew he was going to be a star.

TONY ELLIOTT (*TIME OUT* PUBLISHER): In 1969, I trekked down to Beckenham with Bob Harris, who was involved then with *Time Out* and who was embarking on his career as a DJ. Bob had been booked to play in a school hall and David Bowie, with very long, perfect hair nearly down to his waist and wearing a floor-length dress, was the live act. Just him and a guitar. The audience was tiny but very engaged. Afterwards he was very quiet and hard to talk to. The music at this gig was quite restrained and very tasteful and did not leave much of an impression. I remember thinking, "Oh just another folk singer."

BOB HARRIS: I was also DJing at the time, and I was renting a flat in Blackheath from a guy who owned a mobile disco. And he double-booked himself on this particular weekend, and obviously he couldn't be in two places at the same time, so he asked me if I would fill in for him. It was a college in the east end, a Saturday evening, and I was there to floor fill basically. I mean, it was just dancing, a student night, crazy, with lots of beer and everybody getting incredibly drunk. I played Motown, and Stones, and Stax records, but I mentioned to David that I was doing this gig, and said why don't you come? It was one of his very first dates with Angie, because I remember she was sitting at the side of the stage with her legs dangling over, and David bought with him a little sort of speaker cum amplifier, with a cassette slot, to play the music. And he had the backtrack of "Space Oddity" on the cassette, so I said why don't you do a couple of numbers in the middle of the evening? So the dance floor was full, and I said, "This guy is coming on, he's got a new single coming out, and here to play it for you is David Bowie." His equipment wasn't plugged into the main speakers so there was very little volume from the unit he bought, and as he got going with "Space Oddity," all the kids started wondering what was going on. And all the dancing stopped, they couldn't hear him anyway, so they started booing and shouting, until they hounded him off. I got angry, grabbed the microphone, and said, "How could you boo this guy offstage? He's absolutely brilliant, and mark my words, remember the name David Bowie, as he's going to be a star."

By this time I'm working at Radio 1, and start to get David in to do sessions. I was still hanging out a lot with both him and Marc Bolan, and while there was quite a lot made in the press of the two being in competition with each other, in my experience that actually wasn't the case. They were actually encouraging each other—Marc even played guitar on "The Prettiest Star," and had started to wear ballet pumps and silver jackets. The two in a sense were validating each other. Marc was very rooted in rock and roll, but there were so many other aspects to the visual side of the way David wanted to present himself, and when Ziggy arrived, all the preparation for it had been going on in David's head for years.

On March 19, 1970, David and Angie turned up at the Bedford Square apartment of the painter Clare Shenstone and announced that they were getting married tomorrow, and asked her if she would be a witness. Bowie had been coming up to town by himself, taking Clare to nightclubs and occasionally staying over. David and Angie were married the next day at Bromley Register Office, in front of Shenstone and two other friends, John Cambridge and Roger Fry, as well as an uninvited Peggy Jones. It was a mutually beneficial arrangement, as it meant Angie could stay in the country, and facilitated Bowie's Green Card. He was twenty-three; she was twenty.

MARY FINNIGAN: At the beginning of 1970, I went to India for six months, and I left the kids with a couple who knew David and Angie. When I got back, we stayed friends, partying at each other's homes. I was always round at Haddon Hall as they had so many parties. Tony Visconti lived with them for a while, but Angie didn't get on with him, and Mick Ronson came along too. What a beauty, what a sweetie. He was not articulate, but he was a musician of great skill and enormous quality, and he had learnt to read scores and arrange. He was the technical genius behind the whole Ziggy phenomenon; David had the ideas, the tunes, the lyrics, the concept, but Mick put it into a workable form. He was beautiful to look at and had the most wonderful sweet nature.

They managed to dump Ken Pitt, and replace him with Tony Defries, who initially didn't do much for David. It only started when "The Prettiest Star" was a hit, and the whole vibe changed completely; it became very showbiz, very camp. It didn't feel right; I was uncomfortable about it. Haddon Hall became a very odd place, and there was an atmosphere of decadence. Angie started patronizing me, so I didn't like being there much anymore, and all these showbiz people were brittle, superficial. Then Ziggy happened, and everything exploded; every time I went there, there was a gaggle of teenyboppers sitting outside, and their private life disappeared. Angie was gracious with them, but they had to move. They went to Maida Vale and then to Oakley Street in Chelsea. I visited there once, and Angie had surrounded herself with unsavory characters. She seemed to have made every mistake in the book.

CAROL BARETT (FAN): I used to live at 29 Southend Road, which was opposite Haddon Hall. I used to escape from the garden as a child and go and knock on David Bowie's door, and nose around to see who was around and what cars were there. I was eight or nine, and I loved the people who used to visit. There was a black lady with bright-yellow canary hair, with Zowie in her arms. She used to come to the door sometimes; sometimes it was Angie. And Angie fascinated me, I really thought she was an angel with her white hair and her paleness, I remember that. And how nice everybody was to me. Never told me to go away! There were mad people going in and out—some of the men I saw near Haddon Hall wore handbags.

LINDSAY KEMP: I didn't see him for a while until he came up to Edinburgh, where I was living, to participate in a film called *The Looking Glass Murders*. My contribution was very naïve, but David was more sophisticated than me. Certainly his songs and his music and his lyrics and his poetry. And he was beautiful. We rehearsed and then filmed it all in one day in Edinburgh. He and Angela had just got married. We shared a mattress on the floor of my apartment on my floor in Edinburgh, the three of us. David was in the middle, she was on the edge of the mattress. She knew we were lovers. Anyway, we were like Jules and Jim; it was a very lovely relationship. I loved her also. Not in a physical way . . . we were just great friends. But David was incredibly physical. He was delicious.

I liked Angela very much, as we were close friends. I wasn't jealous because their marriage was very open, and David and I continued to be lovers. It was a very bohemian relationship. In fact, David claims it was my bohemianism that was one of my attractions. He loved my Soho lifestyle, but I don't think I influenced him as much as he said I did. But having read so many interviews where David says I was one of the greatest influencers in his life, I've started to think again. I influenced the way he walked, the way he spoke, the way he moved, the way he dressed. I introduced him to the avant-garde theatre and the theatre in Japan, the Kabuki. He was a great mimic. Not a great mime, a terrible mime actually, but he would mimic people like Stan Laurel brilliantly.

BOBBIE WATSON (MUSICIAN): Glenn Goring and I were having a relationship at that time, and at some point David asked Glenn and I to go for a meal at Haddon Hall. Angie cooked, Woody Woodmansey was there by then, and Mick Ronson, and Zowie was playing around. Different people were starting to pop up. They were in the process of doing the place up, and they had done one room where it was a Chinese sort of style, carpets that were dark blue and cream. The wood floor was covered with Chinese artifacts and pottery. The Spiders from Mars had just recorded an early version of "Queen Bitch," and it sounded amazing, although I'm not sure they were the Spiders yet. At this point Woody looked more like a pop star, while David still had his curls, although as he had already had a hit record with "Space Oddity," you could tell that more and more he expected to be the center of attention. Angie spent most of her time in the kitchen, although she was one of those people who think, Ah, my husband is a fantastic rock star. David never seemed happy around her. I think she liked him for the kudos, I might be wrong. I think she was a bit grabby. There were spliffs after dinner, I think. It was all about weed then, with maybe a bit of acid thrown in. It's odd, but I got the impression he thought he was going to be famous.

NICK KENT: "Space Oddity" was a significant record. When I was seventeen I was living in Horsham, which is, like, thirty miles outside of London, a whistle-stop commuter town, and the only place where young people could congregate was a coffee bar, and people would sit in that coffee bar in 1969 and play "Space Oddity" over and over again. It was a record that absolutely nailed a moment. Obviously there was the moon landing, but the song hit the moment. What a great song. This is where Bowie arrives. Whenever I spoke to Iggy Pop about David Bowie he would always say, "That guy is a white hot talent." Everyone I knew spoke about Bowie as a talent, apart from Roxy Music. They might not have liked him and they might not have liked what he represented. They may have been threatened by him, they may have been intimidated by him, and made to feel insecure by his talent, but there was always that respect. Whether it was the New York Dolls, Mick Jagger, or Marc Bolan.

Of course, you're talking about very bitchy times. It was all about "Who is the fairest in the land?" Glam rock was vanity-driven, as one would imagine it to be. It was very much like that Bowie song "Queen Bitch"—*I could do better than that.* People would be standing there at gigs saying, "Impress me." At the Roundhouse, every Sunday between three o'clock and eleven o'clock there would be a gathering of the London music underground, the tribes. Syd Barrett would be there, Kevin Ayers would be there. You'd see all of these people who could have been David Bowie. Syd Barrett could have been David Bowie but he didn't have the ambition or the basic sanity. Back in 1970, if you'd have asked around, people would have said, "The Beatles have broken up, Bob Dylan's in semi-retirement, so who's going to fill the hole?" And people thought it was going to be Syd. Or Kevin Ayers, a very pretty guy from Soft Machine. But he didn't really have the talent or the ambition. These guys' idea of a good time was sleeping off a hangover, not focusing on the next career move. David Bowie was focusing on the next career move. He was one of the first people from the '60s to cut through to the '70s, along with Elton John, Rod Stewart, people who had been around in the '60s and had made a little bit of a name for themselves, but hadn't really punched through to mainstream success. Cat Stevens was another one, a guy who had had a couple of hit records in 1967, but now in 1970 had reinvented himself as a kind of James Taylor mystic poet–type guy. Bowie's dread at that time was being a one-hit wonder.

If you listen to the *Space Oddity* album you can hear the sound of a guy who is still a work in progress. There's two really good songs on *Space Oddity*, there's "Letter to Hermione" and "Space Oddity" itself. The rest of it is a little bit overachieving, not quite sure what it is. This is the trouble with Bowie in the '60s, as he can't focus on any particular thing. He's interested in being a mod, but he's also interested in being a rhythm and blues singer. He wants to be Little Richard and he wants to be James Brown. He wants to be Jacques Brel as well. And then he wants to be Bob Dylan, like everybody else did at the time, briefly, and then he hears Simon and Garfunkel and he becomes a duo. This guy was pinballing all over the music culture. Then he was obsessed with Scott Walker, and started working in the Scott Walker mold. All of these things would fascinate Bowie and he would leap into them. He had a wide canvas. When you dealt with Lou Reed and Iggy Pop, they had a very narrow canvas, and when they talked about other music that they liked, and what they thought of as good authentic rock and roll. They liked early rock, Jerry Lee Lewis, Chuck Berry, et cetera, and a lot of areas of contemporary rock they thought of as absolutely bogus. Totally inauthentic. Bowie didn't give a fuck about authenticity. He was like a magpie. If something looked good, he'd take it. If something sounded good, he'd have it. I like it, I don't care about the context, I'm not interested in whether you think it's good or not, I think it looks good and it makes me stand out.

VAL PORTELLI: I remember finding out that his half-brother had gone to a mental asylum. I thought he lost his brother when they were young, but he had just been away. Whenever he came back he then went away again. I know there was a history of mental problems in the family, but David didn't really mention it. It wasn't the kind of thing people talked about. He seemed determined to make it, almost as though he wanted to do it for his brother. There was a sense that if you could break Beckenham you could break anywhere. It was the opposite of the bohemian Soho. If you were in Soho, it was known for the artists and experimental people, you would be in the comfort zone. But Beckenham, because of its respectability, it would be more difficult than Soho or the Left Bank in Paris. So, perhaps because Beckenham was more respectable, it made him work harder to break through.

DANA GILLESPIE: He always said what he needed was a really good manager, which was true, as at the time he didn't have one. One day he rang me up and invited me down to Haddon Hall to meet a new friend of his. He had found Tony Defries, and he was very excited by it. He said he'd finally found someone who was going to turn him into a star. He said that he'd be good to manage me, too. I saw this fuzzy-haired guy with a beard smoking a big fat cigar. Tony Defries was an extraordinary man, even though at the end there was lots of acrimony between him and David, I never saw any of that. I thought he was great, and he was very helpful in the early days; we had amazing times when I was signed to MainMan. By this time I was playing Mary Magdalene in *Jesus Christ Superstar*, but I was still going out working as I needed gigs to get paid. Bowie and I had both auditioned for *Hair* and got turned down, but *Superstar* was great because it was a job, and in those days a job was a job. So I'd work in the West End and then go down to Haddon Hall at the weekends and just hang the whole day with them. Defries would drive. Lots of ideas were hatched at Haddon Hall, and that's when obviously Ronno [Mick Ronson] first turned up with the other two, Woody and Trevor, although I was never that close to them. I was closer with Ronno because we started working on my *Weren't Born a Man* album. I was around at a lot of the sessions David was doing, hence me singing background vocals on "It Ain't Easy." And he made quite sure I was on that John Peel session—I sang on "Andy Warhol" as well as "It Ain't Easy." David said he wrote "Andy Warhol" for me, although to this day I don't know why, except the cover of my second album for MainMan was the picture of me with Warhol-style silkscreen printing. David was meant to produce my first album but by then he was fast becoming famous, so Ronno ended up doing it instead.

JAYNE COUNTY: At one time I think some people thought Tony Defries was a bully and he was working David to death, like a workhorse plowing a field of rocks. But in the beginning people just didn't want to know about this so-called glitter freak and this new music that the press had labeled glam rock. Except for a few adventurous rock fans here and there, people were basically scared shitless of this new movement in music. It was considered decadent and deviant. At first the press just didn't know what to make of it, and began making up names for it, like drag rock, and the singers were called gender benders and sex swappers! It was a hoot. The reason Defries worked David so hard is because he had to get David's name out there as a genuine musical artist and not just some sex freak. People were eager to write David off as a freak show with no real musical talent, and Tony had to show that David actually was a highly talented artist with vision and staying power. It also kept David out of trouble, because he had to concentrate on what he was doing, so Defries did him a big favor.

Tony Defries was seen as both protector and thief, and while there would be the inevitable squabbles—major squabbles—about misappropriation of funds, he had an extraordinarily effective strategy for turning his client into a genuine star, both in a micro and macro way. Not only would he start to make it more difficult for anyone, especially journalists, to get close to Bowie (creating a sense that not only was he far too busy to interact with mere civilians, but also exacerbating the feeling that because he was speaking publicly a lot less than he used to, when he did, by dint of this, what he said was to be taken a lot more seriously), but he also encouraged his charge to act in a more imperious, almost regal fashion: what Defries did was to encourage Bowie not to open doors for himself, not to pick up anything if he dropped it, and not to offer to help, or pass anything. By ignoring door handles, he semaphored that he expected others to open doors for him. At the very end of 1971 he invited the young Welsh journalist Dai Davies down to Haddon Hall for dinner, as he had recently been hired by Defries to be Bowie's press secretary, and during dinner he painstakingly explained how he was going to handle people in the future. "After that dinner it was if he didn't notice a door had been opened," says Davies. "Whether he was with a man or a woman, I never saw him open a door for himself again." The putative Ziggy had become royal.

MICK ROCK: Tony Defries was both a force for good and bad, and I know what David would say, but Tony was not an honest soul. He was obviously a difficult person. I do remember being in his office and there was a secretary there and Tony gave her some paperwork. He said, "Take this to David and make him sign it." He said, "It won't take long, David will sign anything." And I told this to David a few years later and he said, "It's true, I would sign anything." You could argue that his manipulation made David a star, his machinations did get David into a situation where he blew up. You've got to give him the credit for maneuvering into a position where RCA gave David all that money to sign him. Tony used to say to me, "David is a very strange fellow," and I'd think to myself, You're a pretty strange person yourself.

HARVEY GOLDSMITH: Tony Defries was a completely different kind of animal. He really was an animal. If anything put David Bowie off touring it would have been Tony Defries, because he used to drive him nuts. He was very tough, and very on the edge.

CHRIS CHARLESWORTH: David was very friendly towards *Melody Maker*, at least at the beginning, and we were very supportive of him. We used to see him at La Chasse on Wardour Street, the place a few doors up from the Marquee that musicians and music people used to go to. Keith Moon once arrived at La Chasse by the fire escape after having climbed over the rooftops from the Who's offices in Old Compton Street. It started when the Marquee was dry, when you could only get soft drinks there, so people would nip up there between sets. It was a tiny little room, smaller than most people's living room, and you couldn't fit more than thirty people in. I first met Bowie there in about 1970–71. He hadn't quite adopted the Ziggy look yet, as his hair was blond, not carrot red. The whole paper liked him—me, Michael Watts, Roy Hollingsworth. The only one who didn't was Richard Williams. So we used to see him around the place, at clubs, gigs, after parties, record launches, he was always around. Until, that is, Tony Defries put a block on him, and started keeping him out of sight, treating him like a star even though he hadn't really had a hit yet, creating the star persona. And David totally went along with this.

GEOFF MACCORMACK: He changed his ideas so much, and he was like someone trying to escape something and finding different ways of going out and finding his vehicle to entertain. I was surprised it took him so long to become successful, and it didn't happen until he was managed as a star, which is all down to Tony Defries. Regardless of what he did on the books, David knew Defries was getting him exposure, knew he was going somewhere. Defries gave him support, and David could see a way through the wall. He had a different vision. He could visualize things.

KEN SCOTT (PRODUCER): Tony told David that he was going to make him a star. And he did it by encouraging David to become quite distant from everyone around him, by acting as though he was already famous. I've seen lots of people do this since, but David was the first time I'd seen this process in action. It was fascinating to watch. Defries was doing things in order to make David a star that no one had done before, and he was very aggressive, and because it worked then I think David became more and more under his control. I think he believed other things that Defries said that weren't necessarily true, or helpful, such as his insistence that Bowie separate himself from the rest of the band. I could never work out if the personality change was because he was adopting the Ziggy persona, or whether it was the result of becoming successful. Success changes everyone. The whole thing became intertwined. He basically became more distant, which was a huge issue with the band. It's difficult to overestimate just how much he changed during that short period of time. What you have to remember is that when the band got together, even though it was David who was steering them, they were very much a band, very much a group of lads, but as soon as the success happened, David's ascendancy was almost vertical. Up and up he went.

3

SO I TURNED MYSELF TO FACE ME

1970–1972

Having spent eight years trying to make his way in the music industry via the Kon-Rads, the Kings Bees, the Mannish Boys, the Lower Third, the Buzz, Turquoise, and Feathers etc., as well as a spell as himself—reimagined as David Bowie—at the beginning of 1970 he formed yet another group, this one called the Hype. The band's first gig was supporting Country Joe and the Fish at the Roundhouse on February 22, 1970, and was the first dawn of glam rock. Bassist Tony Visconti wore a white leotard, silver crocheted briefs, and a green cape. John Cambridge, the drummer, wore a pirate outfit complete with an eye patch, while Mick Ronson was dressed as a cartoon gangster, wearing a gold lame suit with matching fedora. Bowie was Rainbow Man, wearing diaphanous scarves and a bodysuit. The costumes were designed by Angie and Visconti's girlfriend, Liz Hartley, and while they were really only worthy of a school play, they helped Bowie move from subaltern status to rock-star status. He disbanded the Hype almost immediately, and focused instead on a new idea, the Spiders from Mars.

MICK RONSON (GUITARIST): I mean, it was David's gig: he got it all together. But I did help. We worked really well together, onstage and in the studio. I was always musical. When I was very little I started playing piano, then later, I learned the violin. I started off as a blues guitarist in Hull in a band called the Rats. We were into all-night blues sessions. Jeff

Beck was my idol. I used to copy everything he did. Woody Woodmansey was in the Rats and, later on, Trevor Bolder. When I first came to London, I couldn't get enough musical work to support myself. One day I was mowing a lawn, when Rick Kemp [who originally played in the Rats before joining folk band Steeleye Span] came along. He was on his way to play on Mike Chapman's *Fully Qualified Survivor* album. Anyway, he took me with him and it was on that session that Tony Visconti first heard me. He introduced me to Dave. One day I was round at Dave's and John Peel called up to ask him to do his show. Dave asked me if I felt like helping out. I didn't know any of the numbers, because I'd never played with him before. I just filled in around what Dave was doing. And we kept working together on and off until the Spiders were formed. It felt funny at first dressing up and all that, then gradually it became part of me.

RICK WAKEMAN: He sat me down and said he was forming a band called the Spiders from Mars, and asked me if I wanted to run it. That afternoon I'd just been asked to join Yes, so this was a very weird day. I said I'd think about it and call him tomorrow. I've often said that if it had been the day before I would have said yes, but while there was no doubt that David was one of the most influential people I'd ever worked with—I loved his music, I loved his songs, I loved the way he treated musicians—obviously the Spiders from Mars would be playing David's music, and I actually wanted to contribute musically myself. So I told him. He actually said, "I think you've made absolutely the right decision, in every respect."

MICK RONSON: It took a bit of a struggle to make up my mind when David asked me to join him, because I was in debt and Dave wasn't doing very much. But there was some kind of special excitement. We did a few live gigs with Tony on bass and Woody on drums. Then we had a crazy time recording *The Man Who Sold the World.* I don't think [my parents] always understood what [I'd] been up to, but they never interfered. I think it used to be a bit difficult when all the Bowie thing was going on. I know people used to stop my sister on the street and say, "Is that Mick of yours a poof?" That was all really David's image. I never got involved with all those queens who used to hang out around David. I just used to get on with my work and have a few drinks, but David felt he had to play his image to the hilt. He always found it difficult relating to regular people and especially to the rest of the band. I was the link.

CHARLES SHAAR MURRAY (JOURNALIST): I hadn't interviewed Bowie before because I was a kid writing for little magazines like *Oz*. Richard Neville took me to see him at the Roundhouse—it was one of two Roundhouse shows he did, but not the one where everybody wore costumes—and I remember he came out and did the beginning of the set solo and acoustic, and then brought the band on. I remember him doing Van Morrison's "Madame George" and also that he had a harmonica holder, and as these gadgets are prone to occasionally do, it was coming loose. Every time he attempted to play the harp, it would move further away, and he was having to crane his neck. When you're playing solo you can't stop and readjust it, because then you have to take your hands off the guitar and stop in the middle of the song. In retrospect it was an endearing sign of human frailty. For some reason I remember that Mick Ronson had his hair dyed black rather than bleached platinum. But I definitely remember that he was peeling off a lot of Jeff Beck runs.

TONY VISCONTI: When we met Mick Ronson, it turned our world over. We knew David had the talent to be successful, and I knew that he could make a great art rock album like Led Zeppelin or Jimi Hendrix. He had it in him, but Mick Ronson was the missing piece. After Mick had played five notes I knew he was the one. David and I looked at each other and we couldn't stop smiling. Mick at the time was like Jeff Beck, Eric Clapton, and Jimi Hendrix all rolled up in one person. He was our age and we were the generation right after the Beatles so he simulated all those magic guitar styles from British rock guitarists. He had it all and his technique was phenomenal, as were his sensibilities. He knew the right notes to play, the right way to play a song. Give him a song for ten minutes and he was there—he just played all the right things. It's great when you don't have to spend half your life explaining something to a musician.

MICK ROCK: Mick was a Northern lad who didn't quite know what was going on. He was such a great arranger, though, and a really accomplished musician.

DANA GILLESPIE: Ronno was such a simple guy in a way. He had that accent which I can't do, and a very serious face, but when he smiled it was like the sun came out. He was very sparkly, and had twinkly eyes with the longest eyelashes you've ever seen, the sort of thing that make women think it's unfair that men get them. He wasn't keen on all the dressing-up lark, but he did it because it was part of the gig. I often felt that being down on his knees in front of David was probably not his idea of fun, but it was showmanship.

MICK RONSON: He was just beginning to try things, but he always liked to dress. He was the local freak, you know. He was always a bit outrageous. He used to say, "Let's go out and look at some antique shops," which really didn't interest me. I was never interested in antiques myself. He used to come back and say, "Look at this I've just bought, isn't it wonderful?"

TONY VISCONTI: With *The Man Who Sold the World* we tried something different, something harder. It was our second album and I was already playing live shows with David on the bass. And then Mick got his friend Woody Woodmansey down from Hull to be the drummer. And this was the core group that became the Spiders from Mars. So we made *The Man Who Sold the World* with Mick and Woody and myself. And of course David was the lead singer; we had plans to go on the road and promote David and even open up for him. We would be the opening act as well as his own band. The album is my favorite album I've ever produced. It's adventurous, we broke all the rules; we just threw caution to the wind. There was no single on the album for a start. "The Man Who Sold the World" became a single for Lulu eventually, but we didn't write it with a single in mind. We wanted to make an art rock album. It had to be seen by our peers as a work of art rather than just a pop album, along the lines of a Frank Zappa album, as David and I were into the idea of a concept album. A few years earlier the Beatles had made *Sergeant Pepper* and so we wanted to do a concept album too. We thought *The Man Who Sold the World* would be it. The single went out of favor for a while because the likes of Led Zeppelin and Yes were making albums that were outselling singles for the first time in history. We wanted to be seen as a great album group. When we started rehearsing, all of us lived in Haddon Hall in Beckenham. And we cleaned up an old wine cellar and put up eight crates on the wall as soundproofing—to this day I don't think those crates ever worked. We got a lot of complaints from the neighbors, as we spent weeks down there, all day long, because we made this album our job and it was conceived right from the beginning as a concept album. And we were working on the sound. This is what we couldn't quite do for the *Space Oddity* album—there was no David Bowie sound yet, and so we were concentrating on that very earnestly for that second album. By the time we got into the studio we were actually very well rehearsed and it was just a matter of putting all the tracks down and recording it. I think we had a four-week budget, which was not a lot at the time, but we made a few mistakes that we just had to let go. But it's a great album really, and we felt so satisfied afterwards.

I felt like I had learned something, too, by being self-focused and trying new techniques that I had never tried before. There are a lot of backwards echoes on it that are really difficult to do, as you have to record something then turn the tape over and then apply the echo when the tape is running backwards and then flip it back over again. Then if it doesn't work out you have to flip back again and try it another way. So we wanted to make startling new sounds that could only exist in the studio, because the Beatles had told us the studio is a musical instrument. That's because when they started doing "Strawberry Fields Forever" they said they could never perform this song live—it was all the same thing, flipping the tape over and chopping the tape up and all that stuff. So we were on a mission to do something completely original. I knew how to do most of these things, and if I didn't know how to do it I would figure them out on the spot. David was a cheerleader, and if I managed to pull one of these effects off he would be so grateful. That was always the basis of our relationship: He would think of something and then he would present me with a challenge. And if I did it then he would get really happy. Mick Ronson was the same way too, when he wanted effects on his guitar that he heard on other records.

GLENN GORING: One night David asked if I'd like to hear *The Man Who Sold the World*, which hadn't been released yet. I thought he was going to put the album on but he sat down crossed-legged and played it on his guitar. I sat there while he performed the entire album. Every now and again he would ask me what I thought about this or that song. And I had to ask myself, what the hell was my opinion worth at this moment? Some pieces were certainly more melodic than others and I hoped my muttered approvals were understood for what they were. In all honesty I was not a huge fan of David's music at that particular period of his career. I remember thinking as I watched his chord positions played close-up, and his right hand churning over the strings, that he wasn't a great guitarist. But for David Bowie, what the hell did that matter?

TONY VISCONTI: There were inevitably aspects of Marc Bolan's work that seeped into David's. I would discover one thing and then perhaps incorporate it into someone else's record. Some special effects I used cinematically. Some special effects might be perfect for one song but you just couldn't throw it on another song just because it's a special effect—it had to be the right one. But definitely Marc Bolan and I were up to the same kind of trickery as well in the studio, which started around the same time because, when I was doing *The Man Who Sold the World* I was still working with Marc. In the studio, Marc was all about Marc, whereas David was more generous. However it was always David's record—his name is the biggest name on the cover, not mine. But here's what it is: David was always tenacious with an idea and he would not let it go. He would switch very rapidly, he would listen to your idea and he would give you very little time to develop it, no more than five minutes, maybe twenty. If it wasn't working he would say, "Well, try this, I know what it is now," and then he would not let go of his own idea. I don't think there's anything wrong with that, because even if someone played on his album and they were the bass player or a guitarist, it was still a David Bowie album. If they had any ideas that were overlooked or slighted in any way they should have just kept those ideas and made their own album. There's a joke in the business, that if you don't like something you go, "I like what you just played but you can save that for your own album."

WOODY WOODMANSEY (MUSICIAN): Coming from Yorkshire, we were musician-musicians. We didn't dress up. Meeting David it was like, this guy dresses up! Even for breakfast! When I first met him he had a rainbow T-shirt on, hair down his back, bangles on, red corduroy trousers. Shoes with red stars painted on them. I thought, bloomin' 'eck, he's more dressed up than my girlfriend. But we chatted for a few hours and he played stuff, and we thought this guy can write, and he means it. Mick and I had never really met anyone that determined. He was assuming he'd made it already. That was something we were still going for. We were wondering what you need to make it, what's the missing ingredient. We thought you'd do it, and someone would tell you you'd made it. We'd got it the wrong way round.

ANGIE BOWIE: I just happened to see these dresses at Mr. Fish. I saw them and picked them up, and David said, "Oh look at that!" And I said yep, try them on. And we did a deal with Mr. Fish and we walked away with both gowns. Both gowns were incredible, and David took them with him on the 1971 tour of the United States. He did New York and Boston and then he went to the West Coast, and he played songs from *Space Oddity* without a band. He only had a guitar. He had those gowns with him, and he played to people at Rodney Bingenheimer's house and people at Tim Fowley's house. He did the rounds and got to know folks, and it was a great thing because all of those people talked about David Bowie when he was gone. They said how interesting he was, how amazing he was, and then they would play his music. By the time we came back, although we didn't have enough people in the audiences—because no one had actually spent enough money in advertising it—there were hardcore fans. They were so devoted and so into the music and into the different subjects that David was talking about, that they really were the backbone of his audience. They brought more and more people. So after three or four years of very light attendance, we were able to fill Universal Amphitheatre six nights in a row, or Radio City Hall three or four nights in a row. It took a while but we kept going.

DAVID BOWIE: The trip to America in January 1971 changed how I felt about what I was doing, as it opened up so many new doors for me. The country was still alien, and the music that was coming out of the cities was far more urban than it was in Britain. The whole scene with Andy

Warhol, the Velvet Underground, Ultra Violet, Moondog, the Stooges, it was all fascinating, and I have to admit that I was swept up in it. Obviously it was during this trip that the whole Ziggy Stardust thing began to gel. I couldn't believe the country could be so free, so intoxicating, and so dangerous. It suddenly made Beckenham seem very small, very timid, and very English. I needed to get out of that whole British sensibility, and that's what I did with Ziggy Stardust.

What isn't discussed as much as it should be in regard to the origination of Ziggy Stardust is Bowie's slightly embarrassing meeting after a Velvet Underground gig at the Electric Circus in New York in January 1971. After the show, Bowie showered Lou Reed with praise, only to be informed that the man being showered wasn't Reed at all, but rather John Cale's replacement in the band, Doug Yule. As Reed had since left the band too, Yule was the focal point, the cause of Bowie's embarrassment.

To his credit, Bowie thought the whole thing rather funny, although as he left the venue that night, he started ruminating on the idea that perhaps he could do the same thing, impersonate someone onstage. Such was his confidence that it didn't appear to concern him that, unlike Lou Reed, Bowie wasn't famous, so how would anyone know he wasn't real?

It should also be noted that Ziggy appeared during a period when many other glam stars pretended to be other people when they were onstage, notably Alice Cooper, Gary Glitter, and to a certain extent Bryan Ferry. Bowie's extra gear was pretending to be Ziggy offstage too.

DAVID BOWIE: The first time I went to America there was a wonderful writer who lived in Greenwich Village. The first thing he did within a couple of days of me getting there was play me *Loaded* by the Velvet Underground and this was like the new release. I thought, Wow, I'm in America, I'm in Greenwich Village and there's this guy playing me *Loaded*—this is heaven and I've brought a dress with me. In New York I was very impressed by transvestites; they were kind of pre-Raphaelite, there was something about the Edward Burne-Jones/Rossetti thing that I thought was a purist new energizing of the British spirit. I had long hair at the time and it looked like something interesting—so I wore that around for a bit.

TONY ZANETTA (ACTOR, PORK; WARHOL ACOLYTE): The big thing in Los Angeles was Rodney Bingenheimer. If I was the guy in New York, Rodney was the guy in L.A. They flip-flopped about him—they liked him, they didn't like him. But he made David on the West Coast.

RODNEY BINGENHEIMER (DJ): I had been Davy Jones's stand-in on *The Monkees* TV show, and then got a job as DJ at KROQ. I was also doing FM promotions for Mercury Records, and my job was to take the artists round to different radio stations. I had a friend at the time called Al Hernandez, who had seen David play back in London in 1969 and he told me about him, so when he came into L.A. in February 1971, I took him around all the studios. I picked him up from the airport in a friend's Cadillac. He was all by himself, dressed in these loose black clothes, looking like a ghost. He was great, as he was into the Stooges, Velvet Underground, all that stuff that most people had never heard of at the time. I took him everywhere—we saw Marlon Brando, Gene Vincent, Elton John. I took him to record stores, clubs. We walked by Hollywood High one day and the kids were all outside playing ball and they went mad when they saw him because he looked like an old Hollywood film star, like Veronica Lake. This was just after I spent two weeks taking Rod Stewart around. But David was different because he was just out there—long dresses, a floppy hat, colored hair, he looked incredible. I'd never seen anyone look like that, and at the same time he was very friendly, real funny, very positive. He was quite shy. If he needed to go to the bathroom he would always ask so politely. I took him out to some stations in Orange County, and people just couldn't cope with him putting on his makeup in the booth. I'd take him to parties up in the Hills, out in the Valley, over in Brentwood—he'd sit on the floor and cross his legs and play songs for people; he played a version of "Hang On to Yourself" cross-legged on a waterbed, acoustic, before it ever appeared on record. I saw him write the lyrics on some Holiday Inn napkins. He was talking a lot about this creation he was thinking of writing songs for, an alter ego, Ziggy Stardust. Rod Stewart was more of an outspoken, aggressive guy. He wanted to go out all the time, whereas David was far more shy.

Later I also had this place called Rodney Bingenheimer's E Club on Sunset Strip near the Chateau Marmont, which David actually came to after his concert at Santa Monica Civic. I was playing Elvis Presley records, and David was dancing with himself in front of the mirror. And then I opened this club playing British music, the English Disco, on December 15, 1972, my birthday. David encouraged me to open it, in fact he suggested it. I had been to London to see my girlfriend, Melanie McDonald—who later married Tony Defries—and David had told me to look him up, so I spent a lot of time at the *Hunky Dory* sessions at Trident Studios. In the evenings I went out to all these pubs and clubs and went to this club called the Cellar, where they were playing Roxy Music, T. Rex, Slade, all that stuff, and I really liked it. So David said I should play this music in L.A. So I bought a bunch of records in London, came back, and found a place. We put up all these posters of David, T. Rex, Suzi Quatro, it was like a David Bowie cathedral. Everyone came—Led Zeppelin, the New York Dolls, Iggy Pop, Mott the Hoople, Kim Fowley, everyone. Everyone who came looked like a miniature rock star. It ran for three years. There wasn't much going on in L.A. at the beginning of the '70s. Everything had kinda stopped at the end of the '60s. So whenever bands came to town they came to the English Disco—they came for the girls, the beer, and the steak-and-kidney pies. I wanted to bring a little piece of London back to L.A., and people went crazy for it. They would be dressed up like David, or the Sweet, in red snakeskin platform boots, feather boas, dyed hair, crazy-colored dresses. Women wore tube tops, guys wore leather, shirts covered in stars, glitter makeup . . .

For visiting Anglo rock stars, Bingenheimer soon became a conduit of quite epic proportions. He seemed to have access to an apparently limitless supply of young girls eager to hang out with emerging British rockers. "If you were given the blessing of Rodney Bingenheimer, then your week at the Whisky a Go Go was like a pussy parade of girls wearing three sequins at most," says Michael Des Barres, who at the time was singing with the band Silverhead. "He was the guy. He met us at LAX Airport when we first arrived in '72, with a cavalcade of rich girls from Pacific Palisades."

ANGIE BOWIE: I would say that for quite a long time David had a sex addiction. Even when he was in the Mannish Boys he was obsessed with sex. Dana [Gillespie] said that back then the band used to have a hearse, which was basically their booty buggy, you know. So yes, there was probably a sex addiction. We had an open relationship. That was a very "said" agreement. We talked about it a lot, and publicly. People always asked us. Once I had been in the *Daily Express*, and then I talked to *Woman's Own* about it. I did this magazine and that magazine and before I knew it, it was well documented. The open marriage was a part of it, bisexuality was a part of it. You must understand, I was expelled from the College of Connecticut for Women. They expelled me because I was having an affair with a girl. They tried to lock me up in the infirmary and they were not amused. I said, "Do you know what, I need a pen and a pencil in my jacket pocket, can you get me my clothes?" So she got me my clothes, and I got dressed. I opened the window. It was the second floor, but it was a rolling lawn out. So I did a dive, and tumbled out of the window. I ran across the whole campus, got to Scott Catherine Blunt dorm, went upstairs, packed my stuff, and in an hour and a half I was out of there and on the road to New York to the airport to get on the plane. That's how fast I left. Because before I left Cyprus, my father said, "Don't ever let them tell you that they're going to give you anything but an aspirin for a cold. Anything else that they try and give you, they're trying to lock you up and trying to make you a part of their health system." He said, run. And I did. I was totally devoted, from fifteen years of age, to LGBT rights. I was totally and utterly convinced that anyone who had any other idea about how society should be was depraved. These people were not people I wanted to be around. But yes, David was bisexual, I was bisexual. I wouldn't have had any use for David if he hadn't been bisexual. Being bisexual obviously helped his image; of course it did! How could you go to a dance club, and not understand or appreciate all the fabulous alternative society people who love your music! So it was very planned. I didn't manufacture his image though, I didn't have to! He was a mod! And then he went through a hippie stage. He was doing the unwashed and slightly dazed look.

Then we went dancing at the Sombrero [actually called Yours or Mine] on Kensington High Street one night, and there, in this fabulous '50s beautiful vintage nightclub was this guy—God, he was gorgeous. He was more handsome than anyone I've ever seen in my life, and it turned out it was Freddie Burretti. And Freddie was wearing hot pants, a shirt with short sleeves, and this long hair that was curled and practically went down his back. And he was so handsome and Scandinavian-looking, he was divine. David couldn't believe his eyes—he kept saying, just look at that guy! And I was saying, I know! And look at that gal with him! And there was this precious person! This little amazing Indian girl, with platinum short tiny hair. She looked like a negative! Her hair was white and she was just the most beautiful golden brown, and maybe five foot four. And she wore really high heels, so now she was like five-ten. And skinny, and beautiful. And she was crazy about Freddie. She had a friend who was always with her, another beautiful girl, a gorgeous girl, who was just lovely. Then there was Michael, who was another friend of theirs. And we met them all. And it turned out that Freddie was a tailor, and he made everything he was wearing. David looked at me and I said, "Well! It looks like we found a little more than we were looking for when we went dancing!" Freddie and his friends Daniella and Antonella, who was a marvelous hairdresser, all came down to Haddon Hall. And Freddie started working on costumes for Mick and the boys. We started what was basically a design studio at Haddon Hall. Me, Freddie, Daniella, Antonella. I had done eight years of couture at school, so I was definitely a seamstress, and so was Daniella. And Antonella was used to having to help Freddie at the last minute, so we were all seconded. In the meantime, Tony Visconti and the boys had built a rehearsal room downstairs, and we were upstairs doing the costumes. It was really like an arts lab. So David had graduated from the Arts Lab on a Sunday evening at the Three Tuns, to an arts lab at his own home, which was putting together what would be the staging of Ziggy Stardust. Freddie made the clothes for David, Ronno, Woody.

LEE SCRIVEN (FILMMAKER): I used to be a musician in Bletchley, and one of the guys I played with said he grew up with this boy named Freddie Burretti, who went on to make David Bowie's clothes. I started investigating his life, as we both had a very similar upbringing, moving out from London's East End to Bletchley. He was a curiosity as it was unusual for someone from my hometown to have had such an impact; by the time I finished I realized it was more than an impact. The reason they clicked is because they were both mods. Freddie had an absolute obsession with clothes, as did Mr. Bowie. The other thing was that he was a fantastic dancer, which compounded the sense of one-upmanship. He could also box, so he had a lot of self-confidence, and if you put those three factors together, that's one powerful character. He was actually very humble, and knowing his brother like I do, and having a sense of what his father was like, I think they were a very humble family—very old-fashioned, East End, don't be too flash, don't be too garish, and if you're good at something just pull something back a little.

The infamous meeting between Freddie and Mr. Bowie happened in the Sombrero in 1971. Freddie was the star of the club, and the clientele waited to see what he would be wearing, and what dance routines he had worked out. It was a massive theater for Freddie, and he was the star of the show in front of a lot of TV personalities, and general eclectic London people. It had a *Saturday Night Fever*–style dance floor, with segments instead of squares. It seemed to be a magnet for the weird and wonderful, which Freddie obviously loved. It was a gay club and Freddie must have been so liberated to leave a town like Bletchley. But even in those days you couldn't be too flamboyant when you left the club.

Mr. Bowie was very astute, and he could see that Freddie was already a star. It was Angie who came over to talk to Freddie, but he thought twice about going over to talk to Mr. Bowie because he's dressed to the nines and Mr. Bowie's in a Mr. Fish dress with long hair. I think it was Angie's forcefulness and probably a bottle of Champagne that convinced Freddie to go over. Anyway, they seemed to click immediately, which, as I said, had to do with their mod ethics. He was absolutely fixated by Freddie's clothes, especially when Freddie said he'd made them all himself (he used to get suits off the peg, and then unstitch them and make them up again). Bowie hadn't had a big hit for a long time, and was just quietly sitting in the corner. I think he had self-belief, but he wasn't full of a lot of self-confidence, and there's a difference. And there's this kid, who's just wowing people with his presence, and so Mr. Bowie thinks maybe he can get him to sing his songs. Although obviously after a while he started to think that he could do it himself, with Ziggy Stardust, rather than rely on Freddie. He made so many clothes for him, for *Pin Ups*, *Diamond Dogs*, for all the tours. At one point both Paul McCartney and Elton John wanted him to make clothes for them too, but Mr. Bowie's management put their foot down.

TONY ZANETTA: It was May 1971. We were doing Andy Warhol's play *Pork* in New York, and there was an article about David in *Rolling Stone*. David has just done his Mercury promotional tour, and there was a little article with a picture of him. Of course this captured our attention, as he was the man in the dress. It was intriguing. We liked that. In New York, *Pork* was known as an Actors' Equity showcase, which meant that you could only do twelve performances, which we did at La MaMa. And during those twelve performances, a guy named Ira Gale, who was one of Andy's art dealers in London, saw the play and wanted to bring it to London. He probably wasn't the ideal candidate, because he was not a producer. Warhol wanted the show to go to Broadway, but there wasn't anybody interested in doing that. The only person interested in it was Ira Gale. The thing that appealed to Andy was that it would keep the play alive for the summer, and they might have more of a chance of getting a Broadway producer, which they never did. So we decamped to London in June, for the run of *Pork* at the Roundhouse. The first part of the process was getting English understudies, and one of the people who auditioned was Dana Gillespie. We think she stole a script and gave it to David Bowie, which is where the song "Andy Warhol" comes from.

We opened at the beginning of August, which is when I met David. I didn't go to the Country Club show that Jayne County, Cherry Vanilla, and Leee Childers went to. I met him when he came to see the play. He came backstage afterwards with Angie and Dana Gillespie and Tony Defries and maybe Mick Ronson. He wasn't at all what I had expected. I mean, he was this married bloke, number one. He was very nice, kinda sweet, but kinda shy and quiet, and not particularly engaging-looking. He had long, mousy stringy hair and was dressed very tamely. Angie on the other hand was very extrovert and flamboyant. We used to go to the Sombrero. Angie was a lot of fun, and we hung out all night. David didn't really engage too much; he was sitting at a table, talking. Angie was more playful. She asked me if I wanted to come the next day to have Sunday lunch with them. She said they'd send a car for me, which I thought was odd.

So they did. A little old lady came to pick me up in a minicab. I got into this car and didn't know where I was going, I was just putting myself in their hands, or in this lady's hands. I was going off on this adventure, and that's literally what I did. And never came back. It wasn't until I got to their house in Beckenham that I began to connect with him. Once I got to their house their roles kind of shifted. He wasn't extroverted, but just very engaging. David had this ability to turn the charm on and off. You could be in a crowded room with him and you wouldn't even be able to find him, because he could just totally turn it off and disappear. Or it would be like this blinding light was suddenly shining on him. He really had that ability.

That day in Beckenham I could tell that he was very intelligent, we shared a lot of interests, he was interested in theatre and theatricality. We talked about Lindsay Kemp and mime and I shared my experiences of the Playhouse of the Ridiculous and *Pork*. We had a shared love of Hollywood and stardom. And of course he played me a lot of music. He had a sense of destiny. He was very quietly determined. He was very young, very bright-eyed about the future, with great optimism. I'd never really met anyone who had it to the degree he did. He had a sense of destiny and what he was going to accomplish. But mainly what he wanted to accomplish was bringing the idea of theatre to music, dressing up rock and roll and having some fun with it. He wasn't wildly extroverted.

LEEE BLACK CHILDERS (PHOTOGRAPHER): We had brought *Pork* to London. Cherry Vanilla was in the title role. I was the assistant director. Cherry was still very much a groupie, and I was trying to get ahead with my rock and roll photography. So we pretended we were working for *Circus* magazine in America, which we weren't. But in those days it was easy to pretend. So we called up these record companies and pretended we were in town. And we got in to see everyone; Rod Stewart, Marc Bolan—we were really having a wonderful time in the rock and roll scene of the very early '70s. And I saw an advert for David Bowie, even though he was very unknown at this point, and I had read a little thing about him wearing dresses and stuff. I said, "Cherry, let's go and see this person; he wears dresses!" Except he wasn't wearing a dress when we saw him so we were very disappointed. He was very thrilled with us working for Andy Warhol and everything, so he came again and again many times to see the show, with his wife, Angela.

JAYNE COUNTY: My first impression of David was one of confusion. He just looked so womanly. I thought he must be transsexual, because he looked totally feminine! Very long hair, baggy girly-style clothes, a big hat! Looked like he was wearing makeup base. He was squatting on the floor singing acoustic songs along with Mick Ronson. They looked like they just stepped off the love train on the way to Woodstock! Tony Defries later hired us all to work for him and David at MainMan, David's management agency. MainMan was basically the cast from *Pork*.

CHERRY VANILLA (ACTRESS): Andy wanted a different feel for London. The girl who played the lead was a trained Broadway actress, and in Andy's mind he wanted someone more raw. I auditioned for him, which is how I got the part. In London our apartment was nicknamed Pig Mansion. People were as titillated as they were repulsed and disgusted by us. We went with the strength of a group. We felt like Warhol's stars in London. The first time I met David was when I went with Leee Black Childers and Jayne County to see him at the Country Club on the outskirts of London. Leee knew about him because David had apparently done a radio-promo tour of America a year before. We introduced ourselves to Angie, who introduced us to David, and we all became friends. We all recognized something in each other. I think he saw the roles we could play for him. It was organic. We started playing our roles for him almost immediately. We weren't servants, but we wanted to tell the world how fabulous he was. Everything was sexual in those days. Time was going fast and we were going to have a good time. You just wanted to accomplish something and also have as much fun, and as much sex, as you could. We were all in love with him. We had to be, to be the way we were. He was our mission. We were in love with our discovery, and in love with the idea of everyone else falling in love with him. We took on subservient postures. But then we were going out and having sex with him, so how subservient is that? We just wanted to end up in bed with him at the end of a working day. The sexual attraction was immediate. He was married, but we knew he had an open marriage. At first I was mostly attracted to Mick Ronson, because he was the shy lead guitarist, which is like a groupie dream come true. Blond, shy, and a musical genius. I just adored Mick. He was straight and apparently not tied up with a girlfriend or a wife, as David was. But I was also attracted to David and Angie, obviously. He was basically a straight man who had no problem with homosexuality. He dabbled a little, had some experimentation. But just think what he did for homosexual boys. That's so giving and beautiful and fearless. The same goes for geek boys, who weren't interested in sports. Socially, what he did was incredibly generous. If I had to choose a word to describe him in those early days it would be "focused." He was always incredibly focused, always working.

Thursday, June 3, 1971, was the first time the Spiders from Mars actually played together. Mick Ronson had been with Bowie for a while, and drummer Woody Woodmansey for a year, with bassist Trevor Bolder being the new recruit. The session took place at the BBC's Paris Studios in Regent Street, a recording for John Peel's radio show, In Concert. *When Bolder made a mistake in "Song for Bob Dylan," Bowie shouted at him. Suddenly Ronno, Weird (Bolder), and Gilly (Woodmansey) were all on the good ship* Ziggy.

TREVOR BOLDER (MUSICIAN): We were a gang, I suppose, me, Mick, and Woody. But by the time we started in the Spiders we'd been together for a couple of years, playing together, all from Hull and we'd known each other for years and years, since we were kids really. And I think David was quite lucky to get us as a band, really, in that we slotted quite quickly into being the Spiders and it worked so well. I don't know if he'd have got that with individual musicians. I think he tried it with individual musicians earlier on but it didn't work. But we'd been playing together as a band, we were all best friends; I mean Mick Ronson was the best man at my wedding. And me and Woody were great friends, and I think that's why we were like a gang.

JULIEN TEMPLE: My father is from the Glastonbury area, so in 1971 I skipped school in order to go down to the festival. I was probably sixteen. These days of course people go prepared with washing machines and catering but back then it was extremely primitive. You were barefoot, and there was no fence, no ticket. But along with that there was a certain sense of chaos, I guess. At the time David wasn't on anyone's radar, as we thought of him as a novelty artist with just one hit, "Space Oddity." I think the big attraction on the night he was due to play was Traffic, and things inevitably went off-schedule, so he got shunted off the Pyramid Stage. Everyone crashed out after Traffic but then as dawn broke people started running around, waking you up, saying you've got to come and listen to this amazing guy, as David had just started his set. He was in full *Hunky Dory* mode—long hair, a dress, and just his guitar, playing the dawn chorus. It was a breathtaking performance, quite spectral, and you realized immediately just how powerful all this creativity was. I'd seen David and Tony Visconti in *Hype* at the Roundhouse a little earlier, but this was just amazing, and five thousand people were just hypnotized by him. We knew instantly that here was a major talent.

The actress Julie Christie was at Glastonbury, accompanying Nic Roeg, who was making a film of the festival. She describes it that year as a huge exotic town straight out of a sci-fi story—a town vibrating with sexuality. She remembers an entire naked family sitting on the back of a gigantic carthorse, and a naked motorcyclist with his penis laid out tidily in front of him on the fuel tank. She also remembers David Bowie, "because his music was wonderful and, like so many of the boys, he looked like a girl."

DAVID HEPWORTH (JOURNALIST): In Glastonbury's chaotic fields—among the head bangers, tribal drummers, mud sliders, face painters, geodesic dome dwellers, exotic religionists, naked exhibitionists, boy mystics in patent-leather shoes, bewildered children, pert-nippled girls rehearsing their music and movement lessons in the open air, ravishing film superstars like Julie Christie, rake-thin models rarely seen more than a few yards from the Chelsea drugstore, and puzzled musicians surveying the bobbing heads of gibbering loons, their brains fried with acid—here, in one week in June 1971, were born many things. Acts like Fairport Convention, Family, Traffic, and Terry Reid played that week, the latter two at the peak of their powers. But more significantly, this was the week when David Bowie ceased his eight years of merely dabbling in music and got serious. His stock had been rising since his return from the United States in February. He'd appeared on *Top of the Pops* the week before Glastonbury, miming the piano part on Peter Noone's hit recording of his song "Oh! You Pretty Things" and had recorded an *In Concert* for BBC radio, where he appeared in public for the first time with Mick Ronson, Woody Woodmansey, and Trevor Bolder. Bolder, having only previously seen him as a normal bloke in shirt and jeans and assuming him to be just another bandleader, had been amazed to see Bowie get changed into a gown before the show. Bolder came from Hull, where such sights were rare.

Bowie and Angie, who had evidently found someone on whom to park three-week-old Zowie, made their way to Glastonbury by train, alighting at a remote country station and then attempting to walk to the festival site. This was made more difficult by the costume he had decided on for the day, which was Oxford bags [trousers], unsuitable shoes, and a Three Musketeers hat. He was supposed to go on in the early evening of Tuesday, June 22, but delays and the organizers' fear of the neighbors complaining about noise meant that he didn't appear until dawn the following day. He performed as a duet with Ronson, unveiling most of the songs from *Hunky Dory* for the first time. He had already started recording this at Trident Studios in Soho. He played the song that was a hit for Peter Noone; "Kooks," the song inspired by the birth of the child they had left behind; "Changes"; "Song for Bob Dylan"; and "Memory of a Free Festival." That Sunday evening as he was traveling back by train, Radio One broadcast the *In Concert* show he had recorded the week before. It felt to Bowie and his retinue, which included Dana Gillespie, Tony Defries, and his publisher Bob Grace, as though things might be finally falling into place.

KEN SCOTT: We recorded *Hunky Dory* that summer, and it was a great experience. I would say that in all the time I recorded and produced David, his vocals were pitch-perfect 95 percent of the time. Considering that I worked on six of his albums, that is an incredibly high success rate. He really was the very best vocalist I ever worked with, and I worked with John Lennon and Paul McCartney. He was an average musician, and he could strum along to whatever was needed, but then he didn't micromanage. He knew what he wanted and he was able to get other people to get it for him. But as a singer he was beyond compare, literally. He was the very best. The way he allowed Rick Wakeman to become a virtuoso on *Hunky Dory* was masterful. Other people would have smothered him. David knew what was best for him.

RICK WAKEMAN: David used to call Haddon Hall "Beckenham Palace." The minstrel's gallery was bigger than my entire house. He also had a grand piano, which was unusual in those days. He asked me to sit down, took out this battered old twelve-string guitar and said, "I want you to listen to these songs." And then he played "Life on Mars?" and it was fantastic. It ticked every box. Great melody. Great chords, surprises, and then when you thought it was going to go a certain place it went somewhere else. He was very good at that. When I asked him why he was playing his songs on a tatty old twelve-string guitar, he said, "If it sounds good on this, think about what it will sound like with good musicians on good instruments." He said that too many people fool themselves by playing on great instruments, but it's actually the great sound that they're listening to. He also said that if a song works on a piano, it will work on anything. He also had a great voice. I did some stuff with Cat Stevens around the same time, and before he did his vocals he would go out and smoke a packet of cigarettes. David didn't need to do that.

I remember leaving St. Anne's Court, Trident Studios, and coming home and saying to a couple of friends I met that evening in the local pub, that I'd just played on what I considered to be the best song I'd ever had the privilege to work on. ["Life on Mars?"] had every single ingredient. The great thing about David was, he was a wonderful melody man, but it wasn't just the melodies—he had great ideas for chord structures, and would always throw in the odd surprise when you were least expecting it. And that was what was so great about playing his stuff. He'd be teaching you a song, and you'd be going along and thinking, I know how this is going to go, and then he would change. A very clever guy.

TREVOR BOLDER: I suppose we were recording *Hunky Dory* and *Ziggy Stardust* at the same time, as David already knew what direction he wanted to go in. As soon as we recorded "Moonage Daydream" I knew something was going to happen. After listening to the guitar solo, I just thought, This is going to be amazing, this is going to go somewhere. This is special. And then it did, you know. That was the point when I knew, Hang on, there's something special here. This is going to be really, *really* good.

ROY DALLEY: I lived on a council estate on Beckenham Hill Road, which was half a mile from Haddon Hall. The estate had been built for people with trades, and my father was a carpenter. It was really quite beautiful there, with very mature oak trees, but I guess we were scruffy South London council-house kids. I was ten years old at the time, and when my friends and I discovered that David Bowie lived down the road we'd go down there and hang out. We soon found out which house was the house of the weird pop star because Haddon Hall was really quite unlike anything else along that road—it was a kind of dark, almost scary-looking place from the outside. It was also very beautiful in an elegantly wasted kind of way. We knocked on the door at least six different times before anyone answered. One day Angie answered the door, and after that she always did. She was incredibly generous with her time chatting to us all. She was unlike anybody I'd ever come across up to that point. She had a larger-than-life personality, but there was no sourness or bitterness within her—she was very boisterous. Her hair was some kind of tone between sky blue and turquoise, and cut in the same style as Bowie's. We would always be asking her what Bowie was up to, and she went through a period of saying that what she was really excited about was a song on his new LP, "Life on Mars?" All she could talk about was *Hunky Dory.* She said that this was going to be the one that made people sit up and listen. Bowie himself would always be in the background. We saw him once, sitting at the window, with the bright-red hair, but as soon as he saw us turning into his drive he just shot away. Angie came to the door one day in a trouser skirt thing and then all of a sudden from between her legs almost like between stage curtains appeared her son, Zowie. He was just a toddler, and while he didn't break into song he reveled in being the center of attention. [Bowie's] producer Tony Visconti lived there too, and I distinctly remember seeing chocolate-colored people walking up and down in pastel-colored bikinis and pastel-colored afro wigs. I'm not sure what gender they were. It was a very theatrical twenty-four-hour lifestyle they all had. You'd also see other kids hanging around, as he was becoming famous by then. We weren't rude, we were just wide-eyed kind of kids going to see the weird pop star who lived up the road.

BOY GEORGE (SINGER): Angie had opened the window at Haddon Hall when we were kids and shouted, "Why don't you all just fuck off?" We were delighted—it was an acknowledgment of sorts. We adored Angie just as much as we adored David.

CHERRY VANILLA: When I first met him he didn't take many drugs, maybe a diet pill every now and then and a glass of white wine to get himself tipsy. He didn't really get high until he started getting into cocaine, which I actually helped him get into. He went into cocaine really fast, but then he came out of it quite quickly too. I helped him get the very best cocaine when he was doing it, but he only did it for eighteen months or two years tops. I think it was just cocaine, and not aware of him doing anything else. He only really liked cocaine.

JULIEN TEMPLE: A few months after Glastonbury I saw David again, this time at a screening of Fritz Lang's *Metropolis* at the Everyman Cinema in Hampstead. The Everyman was a very small cinema, and so you had David and his entourage walking in and creating havoc just because of the way they looked—very exotic, very alien, very colorful. Suddenly the place shrunk. They were all incredibly charismatic and it was just a buzz to have them in the theater. He had red hair and looked extraordinary. I'd never seen anything like it. He was a man transformed, and I was blown away by his look, and by his entourage, who were all suitably cartoon-like. It was as though the party had arrived, and as soon as they swept into the cinema, you spent your time watching the film, then swiveling around to see what they were doing themselves, what Cherry Vanilla was up to, what David was doing. It was already theatre. Even then, and this was probably late 1971 or early 1972, he looked extraordinary, and was already having so much influence on people that those around him had started to copy the way he looked. It was visually stimulating, as you had all these automatons onscreen, this wild pack in the audience, and an incredible flickering light. *Metropolis* was quite a big film for him.

DAVE STEWART (MUSICIAN): As a musician, when you first heard his records, you knew how complex they were. Structurally he was astonishing, as you never knew where a song was going to go. His melodies don't go where they are meant to go. It was like he had some dough or some clay and he could make anything. *Hunky Dory* just blew me away, especially the work that Rick Wakeman did on it. I learned every song on the album, because they were so instructive. I learned so much from copying those songs.

KEN SCOTT: The five of us started on *Hunky Dory*, and got so close that we could almost finish each other's sentences. It had almost reached that point. We were making records for ourselves, and if other people happened to like them then that was great. For me the transformation happened over a period of time, so it wasn't any great surprise. I didn't really notice as it was going on, because it was so gradual. I was seeing David fairly regularly, and the character just got further and further evolved. It's like your kids: when you see them every day you don't really think they're changing; you don't realize how much they've grown until their grandparents come over and say, "Oh God, they got so big." It was that kind of situation.

The thing that surprised me most about *Ziggy* originally was the fact that David thought I wouldn't like it. We'd finished *Hunky Dory*, and it was only a very short time later that I saw David and he said we've got to start making another record. *Hunky Dory* hadn't even come out yet, but his management wanted him to do another album, so that's what we did. And he said, "Although I don't think you're going to like this one. It's going to be a lot more rock and roll." I can't remember if he said it was going to sound like the Velvet Underground or Iggy Pop, but as I didn't know of either band at the time, it didn't really make much difference. And he was completely wrong. I loved every second of the album. I think my greatest achievement with the record was making an album that the five of us were happy with. It was the perfect team, and there was a great sense of camaraderie when we were making the record.

NICK KENT: *Hunky Dory* is up there with *Revolver*. If you're talking about great records then *Hunky Dory* is a great record.

ALAN YENTOB (FILMMAKER): *Hunky Dory* is one of the great albums of all time.

DANA GILLESPIE: The songs he wrote around the Haddon Hall times, things like "Kooks," "Oh! You Pretty Things," and "Changes," they were very much a part of him. He hadn't really traveled the world that much. So they were from the heart. When he started moving around, to America and Berlin and Paris, his mind filled with other thoughts, but the *Hunky Dory* songs were all him. Those early songs just came from within and the only outside influence one could get in those days was whatever record you could find or the odd thing on your black-and-white television. So they came from within. I remember we used to all be sitting in Haddon Hall and he would say, "Quick, there's Kabuki on!" and we would all stare at Kabuki on television. Or it would be, "Listen to this" and he would play something weird and wonderful on the guitar. He was mad about Anthony Newley in *Gurney Slade*, mad about anything that he felt was different. Although he played blues on the very first night that I heard him, he never really did it after that. My theory is that so many musicians and rock and roll bands, Beatles or Stones, all started with forms of blues because they're so easy with their three chords and twelve bars. So it's a great beginner style for a musician to get going with. But he went beyond the blues, David; he just used it as a foundation. Then he started experimenting with interesting chord progressions, and I've always so admired that in his songs. They go to places where you don't expect them to go. But then so did his mind and so did his lifestyle for quite a while. *Hunky Dory* was the record that changed him.

Woody Woodmansey thought Bowie was bisected, like his brother Terry, and said he seemed like an artist in preparation—adopting a Yorkshire accent if a Yorkshireman was present, and doing the same for Cockneys, Mancunians, or Australians. He said he seemed to be able to take on a new persona and then write songs better than that person themselves, in a "truly authentic, unforced way." The one thing Bowie and Woodmansey argued about was, typically, clothes; on one occasion when Bowie had asked him to wear something, Woody point-blank refused, adding that he thought he looked like a cross between Lurch from The Addams Family, *and a deck chair.*

As Bowie morphed increasingly into Ziggy, his tolerance for those strands that connected him to his past was evaporating, and he let many relationships slip through his fingers like boat ties. When Terry turned up at Bowie's aunt Pat's house one day, having spent a week sleeping rough, she took him round to Haddon Hall to see if his brother could put him up. When Angie opened the door, Bowie apparently simply said, "Sorry, we're busy."

TONY ZANETTA: At that moment I was his key to the Warholian world. Little did he know that I really had very little to do with the Warholian world. He was definitely more interested in me than I was in him. But his career was about to take off and he knew it. He had been with Tony Defries for a while, they had been shopping for a record deal, and they were about to do big things. Everything was percolating. David and Angie came to the final performance of *Pork* and by this time we had bonded and I kind of felt responsible for them. That night I took them to the Hard Rock Café, which is where everyone was going that summer. But David wasn't really comfortable in that kind of environment. He wasn't someone who wanted to go to the cool, trendy place. Because he wasn't David Bowie yet. He wasn't comfortable being someone on the sidelines. He was not an aggressively flamboyant person. He was calm. Then I went back to New York, and a few weeks later they came to New York to sign the deal with RCA. In September 1971 he signed with RCA. I was there. I was the New York friend. That week Tony Defries, David, Angie, and Mick all stayed at the Warwick Hotel—why? Because the Beatles had stayed there! I spent the whole week with them. All this was done through Gem, Lawrence Myers's company, as MainMan didn't exist yet.

I also spent a lot of time with Tony Defries. First of all, you have to understand that he was only, like, a couple of years older than we were—David and I were pretty much the same age. But he seemed like ten or twenty years older, because of his personality and his manner. He had a very measured way of speaking. He was a very calm, focused person. When Tony Defries was in the world you just knew that everything was going to be OK. He was very intelligent. He wasn't a child of the '60s, and there was nothing hippie or trendy about him. He was very grandiose. He dreamed big, real big. It felt very good to be in a room with Tony Defries, because you suddenly became a part of that grandiosity, that big dream. David had exactly the same quality but in a different way. They were both extremely ambitious and extremely focused. They really made a good match. They were going to conquer the world. There was no doubt when you were in the room with them. It was Kismet when they came together, because Defries was the perfect partner for him. They were so alike it was comical. David didn't have a lot of shelf life left, and I don't know if he would have found someone else to look after him like he did. We toured all over the city, visited everywhere that week. I remember being outside Radio City and

David very casually saying he was going to play there. It wasn't even a rock and roll venue, but within eighteen months he did play there.

I took them to the Factory to meet Andy, and that was interesting. One of the main impetuses of going to the Factory was so that Tony Defries could meet Paul Morrissey and talk about representing Factory Films in Europe. He thought he could solve all their problems. There was Andy Warhol, and there's me, who played Andy in Andy Warhol's play. There's Allen Midgette, the guy who played Andy on the college circuit when Andy sent an impersonator out instead of doing it himself. Then there's also David Bowie, who played Warhol in the film *Basquiat*. It wasn't an excruciating meeting, but it wasn't great. The meeting was kind of tense because Warhol was not a great talker, and neither was David. It was awkward. Nobody was really taking this conversation and running with it. So they were circling each other and then David gave him a copy of *Hunky Dory* and played "Andy Warhol," which Andy hated. Which didn't help the meeting.

He also met Lou Reed and Iggy Pop that week. Lisa and Richard Robinson introduced David to Lou Reed. Richard worked at RCA in the A&R department, and that week he had a party and invited Lou and David along. RCA also threw a dinner on the day David signed, at the Ginger Man restaurant. After that dinner I took David to Max's Kansas City, bumped into Danny Fields, who called up Iggy to come down and meet David. When Iggy met David he basically never went away again. David was magnetic. He had charisma, and was seductive more than sexy. At the time the English were very different sexually from Americans, because even though we were fucking everything in sight, we were still very repressed. The English weren't. They were easier with it, and bisexuality wasn't a big deal. A lot of couples would occasionally have a threesome with a man or a woman, and so what? It wasn't earth-shattering. You didn't have to brand yourself. You were just sexual. That certainly applied to David and Angie. David wasn't a sex hunter; he wasn't going out looking for sex all the time. But sex was always a little part of the equation. A lot of people might've ended up in bed with him because he was so seductive. Whether he needed to be adored, or whether he was just adored, it would always surface. He was the adored one.

DANNY FIELDS (MANAGER, PUBLICIST, AND AUTHOR): One night in September 1971, Richard and Lisa Robinson called me and asked if Iggy was still staying at my apartment, which he was. We had both fallen asleep watching television. She said she was with David Bowie, they'd just had dinner with Lou Reed at the Ginger Man, and now they were on their way to Max's Kansas City and wanted to know if we were coming down. David really wanted to meet Iggy. So I woke him up, and told him that the person who had been so nice about him in *Melody Maker*—he'd voted him as vocalist of the year or something—was down at Max's and wanted to meet him. We thought it was astonishing that someone in the UK knew who Iggy was. I was de facto managing Iggy then, and I thought it would be a good idea if they met, as Iggy was at a loose stage of his career. Professionally, prospects were not too promising. So we walked down from Twentieth Street and Fifth Avenue, where I lived, to Eighteenth Street and Park Avenue. Five short city blocks. We walked into the back room at Max's, which was kind of empty, but then it was two thirty in the morning. They were introduced and immediately began talking about music. I made my excuses and went to sit elsewhere, as I didn't know anything about music, and have always found it difficult to talk about it intelligently. And that was the beginning of their relationship. They were off and running. David was very good at spotting talent more cosmic than his own, and very good at flattering people. And Iggy knew that David had more money, more resources, and more credibility. They worked it out between them, and we have the records to prove it. But both Lou and Iggy were a little bit closer to heaven. David was a vampire, but a good vampire, he did something good with the blood. He shared the nutrients.

KRIS NEEDS (JOURNALIST): When Bowie made his first appearance at Friars Aylesbury on September 25, 1971, as he told me at the time, its success created the path he should now take. At that time, Friars was already one of the coolest clubs on the circuit. It was only an hour from London, and regularly hosted the likes of Mott the Hoople and Genesis. It was a warm club, as were the audience. It was a benign place, and you knew you would get a good reception there. In 1971, the promoter David Stopps phoned me to discuss some prospective bookings, and he mentioned that he'd been offered David Bowie. At that time, Bowie was only really known for "Space Oddity," but he had also been dabbling with some Velvet Underground songs, and as I really liked them I was intrigued. I recommended he hire Bowie, so Stopps paid Tony Defries £150 for Bowie to test his new band at Friars on September 25. This was the first proper performance by the Spiders, and I designed the flyer for it. There was already a bit of an Aylesbury connection as Bowie had given a song he had written, "Star," to a local musician called Les Payne, who had often appeared at Friars with his band, Chameleon. He liked Aylesbury. The "market square" in the opening line of "Five Years" is actually the clock tower in front of Friars.

On the day of the gig, Bowie turned up, and was both amazingly shy and amazingly charming. He was such a sweet man. He still had long blond hair, and had a big black hat, sort of baggy black culottes, red platforms, and a beige jacket. Oh, and no shirt. He looked cold and asked if we had a heater. The hall was only half full, even though it was only 50p a ticket, and he was supported by the band America, who had just had a hit with "A Horse with No Name." I stood on the side of the stage, just behind Mick Ronson's amp. David said "We're gonna start slowly till we get the hang of it," and then they played "Fill Your Heart" from *Hunky Dory* and "Buzz the Fuzz" by American singer-songwriter Biff Rose to warm up, so the gig sort of started slowly, quietly. It got rowdier as the band played "Queen Bitch" and Chuck Berry's "Around and Around," which I think he said was going to be the title of his next album. They did "I'm Waiting for the Man" as an encore, and then I went backstage. He was really pleased that it had gone so well. He said that he really wanted to come back and play later in the year, but that when he did, he was going to be completely different. He actually said that he was going to be a huge rock star. You could tell that he was on the verge of something. There was a unique, wired euphoria around those early Ziggy gigs which I've never encountered anywhere else, but was probably similar to the time Jimi Hendrix first played in London.

CHRISTOPHER ZARA (JOURNALIST): Suzi Ronson was a restless youth. As a twenty-one-year-old hairdresser in the early '70s, she worked at a neighborhood hair salon in Bromley, but she had her sights on bigger things. Fate intervened in late 1971 in the form of Peggy Jones, one of

Ronson's regular customers, whose son David was a local musician in need of a hairstylist. At the request of Bowie's wife, Ronson (then Suzi Fussey) visited the Bowies' home in Beckenham to have a go at Bowie's locks. "We looked through magazines, talked about hair and style and everything, and I ended up cutting his hair off." And then dyeing it bright red. "We were still lingering in hippiedom here," Ronson says. "Marc Bolan was definitely a change—he put a little glitter on his cheeks and started wearing makeup. But David took it to a completely different level."

The Ziggy haircut was inspired by a magazine photo featuring a model at a photo shoot by Kansai Yamamoto, the designer who would eventually create costumes for Bowie. As Ronson tells it, Bowie was searching intently for something different, an entirely new look. Although the haircut would be a drastic departure from the long hair most rock stars wore at the time, Ronson said she knew instantly that Bowie could pull it off. "I was completely excited about it," she says. "Remember, I'm looking at a tall, thin man, with a long neck, white skin, blue eyes, and very androgynous-looking. He was the perfect person to do this kind of style."

The hairstyle took a little time to perfect, however. After the initial cut, Ronson took samples of Bowie's hair back to her salon to experiment with color treatments before settling on the flame red. And getting it to stick up was no easy task. Ronson ultimately discovered that a product called Gard, an anti-dandruff treatment, helped to stiffen his hair if it were properly set and dried. "If you look at the *Ziggy Stardust* album cover, it's not really sticking up because I hadn't really figured out the setting lotion yet." Ronson skillfully parlayed the Ziggy Stardust haircut into a full-time job as the band's hairstylist and wardrobe assistant. It was no accident the look required constant maintenance, making Ronson an invaluable asset once the album became a runaway success. "I knew if I created something that needed touching up every two or three weeks, I was in. I would go with them on tour. I saw the danger of being someone's wife or girlfriend. They got left behind. I wanted to be on the bus, not waving at it."

London in 1972 was like the Bakerloo Line—all brown and Bakelite and dark even when lit. Decimalization, which was meant to hint at the white heat of modernization, had only encouraged Londoners to think that they were all slightly worse off than they'd been before it was introduced the previous year.

A gallon of petrol was 35p, a pint of beer 13p—figures that were still new to people. A pensioner interviewed on the BBC News *couldn't understand "why they didn't wait for us old people to die out" before changing the currency.*

It wouldn't be enough to say that every day in London in the early '70s was like Sunday; specifically they were like any Sunday in November between the hours of four and five o'clock in the afternoon. It was almost as if the country had been brushed with a charcoal wash. On small black-and-white televisions, in overinked black-and-white newspapers, in magazines that only sparingly used color, the world was held at a safe monochromatic distance. As the writer Chris Bohn pointed out in the New Musical Express, *when looking back at 1972, "Psychedelic color had fast faded into uniform blue denim and fledgling heavy metal; love and peace had come to stand for passiveness and eventual apathy; the spirit of '68 was doused once it was channeled into the conventional left."*

Yet if one put his ear to the ground, or had his finger on the pulse, he might be able to tell that change was afoot. "What makes 1972 special goes beyond folk memories of a glorious summer lived out to the sound of a then-hip Rod Stewart singing 'You Wear It Well,'" wrote David Lister in the Independent *not so long ago. "What makes that year special is that it marked a borderline between the Sixties—the years of affluence, experiment, sex and drugs, and hippie, idealistic, and, yes, flaky politics—and the real Seventies, the years of inflation, unemployment, changing attitudes to gender and sexuality, radicalisation and the first mentions of words that were much later to become commonplace: terrorism and terror."*

This is the world that Ziggy Stardust landed in, beamed down to a sullen, punitive, disgruntled gray country, a so-called Great Britain that hadn't been Great for some time, full of sullen, disgruntled people who by rights shouldn't have taken too kindly to a pipe-cleaner-thin pop singer dressed up as a gay alien in a quilted jumpsuit. But take to him is exactly what they did.

KRIS NEEDS: He came back to play Friars with the proper Ziggy look in January 1972. He had completely altered his persona, and having told so many people that the new stage show was going to be outrageous, the place was buzzing. Everyone was so excited. I was backstage before the gig and remember Mick Ronson being very unhappy that he was being asked to wear his gold jumpsuit. After a really long wait, the lights went down and we heard "Ode to Joy" from *A Clockwork Orange* over the PA, as a load of strobes filled the hall. Then they all came on and they looked amazing, with Bowie wearing these red wrestling boots. The shock of seeing Ziggy Stardust live for the first time remains a major turning point of my life. I've said it many times, but for me that night just kick-started the '70s. In the dressing room afterwards, Bowie just looked at me and shouted, "I told you!" When I got home that night, I wrote in my diary, "Met David Bowie again tonight. I can't believe how nice he is."

TREVOR BOLDER: In January 1972 we did a run-through of the Ziggy show at the Friars Club in Aylesbury, and it went down an absolute storm. The time we'd played it before we had been doing all the *Hunky Dory* stuff and the folk stuff, and it was a folk audience. And when we went back we thought we were going to get the same people again, but they were different. We all looked at each other and it was like, Jesus, this is going to work. . . .

HARVEY GOLDSMITH: I came across Bowie because I read about him. I was running a series of shows at Hemel Hempstead Pavilion, and in January 1972 Bowie played at the Assembly Rooms in Aylesbury. Having seen him, I booked him to play in Hemel Hempstead that May. Both concerts were extraordinary. He had this manager called Tony Defries, who had started a management company called MainMan. He came up to Hemel Hempstead, and before David had gone onstage, Defries gave me a lecture on how David was going to become the single most important artist in the world, the best artist, and this, that, and the other, and I should really get involved with him. Then David Bowie went onstage with a pretty amazing band, the Spiders, and they just nailed it. The audience went nuts. When he came offstage, I remember Tony Defries just laying into me, telling me once again just how big and how important David was going to be. And he was right. My acid test with artists is always the stage, because the edge of the stage is the dividing line between the business and the real world, and if an artist can get across that barrier, the edge of the stage, and the audience connects with them, then you know you've got a winner. So many times bands play and the audience watches, but they're talking, they're drinking, they're not engaged. That didn't happen with

Bowie. He was so different. At the start of the '70s, everyone was coming out of the woodwork, but Bowie was better than all of them. Bolan had the talent but he didn't have the stamina. So I did this show with Bowie, it was a big success and everybody was talking about it.

On January 22, 1972, on the cusp of fame, Bowie told Melody Maker*'s Michael Watts he was "gay, and always have been."*

LEE SCRIVEN: Looking back on it, I like to think that Freddie Burretti being gay encouraged Bowie to make his coming-out statement to *Melody Maker.* It happened at the high of their friendship and closeness, as Freddie was sort of living at Haddon Hall and looking after Zowie, so I think he did it for Freddie. If you've got a very close friend who's homosexual and always felt oppressed, I think you'd have to wear the badge of honor to say something about this in a roundabout way.

MICHAEL WATTS (JOURNALIST): I think he did it deliberately. He definitely felt it would be good copy. He was certainly aware of the impact it would make. I think he'd had a relationship with a man at some point in his life. I think it was something [his manager Tony Defries] encouraged. He understood the news value of something like that. I was aware of a changed mood towards gay people, not just in rock, but in culture as a whole. Bowie was very alluring. You couldn't help but feel he had a hell of a lot of magnetism. It was a mixture of film-star and rock-star appeal—he was so much better-looking than other rock stars. We met in his publisher's office, in Regent Street. He was dolled-up as Ziggy—skintight pantsuit; big hair; huge, red plastic boots—dazzling. Only recently had he stopped wearing a dress—"a man's dress," he elaborated. He was slightly flirtatious, and made me uncomfortable with myself. "Camp as a row of tents," I wrote. Soon he was coming out to me. "I'm gay," he said, "and always have been, even when I was David Jones."

KEN PITT: I wasn't at all happy when the "I'm gay" interview appeared. It wasn't the kind of thing I would have advised him to do. I had been observing what was going on in San Francisco, how gays were creating comfortable housing out of slums, designing clothes, going into business, and flourishing. I could see how the gay scene was changing and I realized it would happen here eventually. And I knew that if the right kind of artist was to talk about this with great sincerity it would break down all the barriers. That's why we did the interview with *Jeremy*, a dreadful magazine. I was horrified by the Michael Watts interview, and the fact that it was repeated in the *Evening Standard* that night.

JOHN LYDON (SINGER): Around *Ziggy Stardust*, Dave Bowie was an absolute full-on "I'm a homosexual." That was his image. And it was as challenging to the world as you could ever hope to be at this point, and that was a damn brave statement to make. And yobs, hooligans, basically working-class guys really liked him for the bravery, for the front of it. It was taking on the world, going, *That's what I am and fuck you!* A very, very good thing.

JAYNE COUNTY: I always thought David and Angie's marriage was kind of for show, really. They were more like friends. They would often pick up tricks and bring them back for all sorts of carrying on.

PAUL REEVES (FASHION DESIGNER): He would not have made it without Angie. In essence David was actually quite shy and retiring, and it was Angie who was the pushy one. She had the vision. When he suddenly announced he was gay, that was Angie. That was her doing. She styled him, she put him in women's clothes, she was the one who understood androgyny. By this time I was designing clothes, and had a shop in Fulham called the Universal Witness. Both of them used to come in, and that's when they started buying women's clothes for him. I made the big floppy hat he wore for the *Hunky Dory* sessions, the one he wore at Glastonbury, and I remember an electric-blue fake fur women's coat he used to like. They both bought a lot of Oxford bags at the time, and knitted Lurex off-the-shoulder jumpers and things like that. They were both very good at interpreting the right vibe of the time; the Ziggy hairdo, which everyone thought was amazing, was actually based on a haircut that lots of us were wearing at the time, who hennaed their hair and brushed it up. But he was a very effective sponge at absorbing the influence into his own look.

HARVEY GOLDSMITH: Angie was hard work, a flower child gone wrong. Angie was a nutcase, completely wild. She was always a car crash.

NICK KENT: Angie Bowie was the original Nancy Spungen, the original Courtney Love, and her downfall was that she wanted to be a star. But she didn't have the skills; she didn't have *any* skills. She was too top heavy as a personality. She didn't so much light up a room as detonate it. She had to be the center of attention.

CHARLES SHAAR MURRAY: Angie was very high energy, very much Hollywood diva in training mode. She had Warhol-y fabulosity. It was thanks to Angie and Tony Zanetta and Leee Childers that the word "faaaabulous" spelled with at least four *a*'s became *NME* currency. You had to say it in a bored, monotone voice. A Lou Reed drone.

RICK WAKEMAN: When I knew Angie quite well in the early days, they were very happy and she was very supportive of anything he wanted to do. There's no doubt that she helped him enormously. The thing is, half of anything to do with fashion, like anything, is having the courage to do it. And David had the courage. David was ahead of everything, but no one was really quite ready for David. I think David could tap into his female side and his male side and an out-there side whenever he wanted to do . . . and was like, Well, if you don't like it, I don't care.

CHERRY VANILLA: I was a nymphomaniac at the time, and I suppose Bowie was a sex addict. He just had a good time. He may have intellectualized it, but it was really just sex. Lots of sex. You have to remember we were living through a sexual revolution. To me it seemed natural to me to have as much sex as possible. We didn't go to gyms so dancing and sex were our exercise. You could fuck your fat off. Sex was an act of rebellion at the time—fuck the Church, fuck the establishment. Let's fuck.

WENDY LEIGH: Of course David was bisexual, but only when he chose to be. He obviously had an affair with Lionel Bart, but only because it was expedient to do so. David went to Lionel for business advice, and I think he was fully prepared to swap sexual favors for financial advice. David was also very influenced by Lionel. If you listen to his wonderful song from *Oliver!*, "As Long as He Needs Me," it has this wonderful chord change in it, where it goes one way when you're expecting it to go another. Then listen to "Life on Mars?" straight afterwards and there it is again, the chord change going in the other direction. So I've always wondered how much Lionel Bart had to do with "Life on Mars?"—maybe more than we think. David was eager to learn from people, but eager to steal too. His relationship wasn't just an affair, it wasn't just sexual. David went to visit Lionel when he was in hospital after an accident, and they were actually very close. I suspect that Lionel was more than a mentor for David. One of David's talents was he knew who to use. He used his bisexuality. As one acquaintance from the time said, "I said he would either be a gigantic star or make a lot of money in the Piccadilly men's loo." There were certainly times when it seemed as though David were available if the deal was right. He used his appeal to get what he wanted, whether it was sexual or not. It was all about David in bed, and with men I don't think he ever had sex unless it was a means to an end. It was a bisexuality of ambition. I actually think it's very refreshing that he used the casting couch; after all, it's usually women who get accused of that.

LINDSAY KEMP: When Angie married David I think there was an arrangement whereby they would be free. She got a bit fed up in the end and left him because he was slightly overdoing his freedom I think, so it wasn't really a marriage at all. It was really a business relationship. But he made that clear to her before he married her, you know. They had a great relationship during the time that Angie, David, and I were together; it was a lot of fun. And of course she pushed him. She was the power behind the throne, she was the Lady Macbeth.

CHARLES SHAAR MURRAY: I don't think we felt that the *NME* owned Bowie, as that would have been really presumptuous. Maybe Tony Parsons felt he owned the Clash, but we weren't proprietorial about Bowie. We didn't have a hissy fit if he talked to *Melody Maker.* The journalists at the *NME* were youthful obsessives on drugs who didn't have much of a life outside of our bubble. We used to end up after work or gigs at each other's houses and flats, and we'd sit up all night with a bunch of new albums, a few bottles of wine, and a bunch of drugs and we would listen to important new stuff—Oh, there's a new Wailers album, a new Roxy album, Bowie's new record—and we would stay up all night arguing and debating. This stuff mattered to us, and we thought we were being read by people who also thought it mattered. We felt that we were taking on the music business in defense of the musicians, or taking on the musicians in defense of the audience, or taking on the audience in defense of the art. We loved it when one of our favorites did something really good, and we got really upset if we thought they'd made a dumb or lazy record. We took it as a personal insult.

TREVOR BOLDER: The *Old Grey Whistle Test* performance in February 1972 we did in an afternoon, in a ridiculously tiny studio, so small we couldn't move. It looks intense when you look at it now, but we literally didn't have anywhere to move. This was our first big thing with the BBC, and we couldn't wait to see it. It was broadcast the following week and we all watched it at Haddon Hall, the whole band, and we crawled around the TV to watch it, slapping ourselves on the back for finally being on TV.

NICK KENT: I saw the first official Spiders from Mars gig in London in February 1972. He had done the infamous interview with Michael Watts and he'd cut his hair. He no longer looked like Veronica Lake. So on Wednesday that copy of *Melody Maker* went on the stands, and on the Saturday he played his first gig in London, at Imperial College, and I was there. Just a week before I started writing for the *NME*. Bowie came onstage with Mick Ronson, Trevor Bolder, and Woody Woodmansey, and they hit the first chord of "Hang On to Yourself," and after four bars the PA just stopped. Silence. They're all dressed up to the nines and then nothing, just silence. This terrible silence. All the hype of the week had been this performance at Imperial College, and this was his showcase. In London, in front of everyone important in the industry, and after sixty seconds onstage, silence. The sound had gone, which is every performer's nightmare. And so Bowie was standing there, and for a split second, you could see panic in his eyes, thinking, What the fuck am I going to do? And what he did was put his guitar down, put his hands on his hips in this really camp way, and proceeded to give us all a run-down of what he was wearing. OK, boots Anello and Davide, trousers Freddie Burretti . . . He just did this camp routine, and then after about a minute the sound came back on. In that minute, Ziggy Stardust's destiny was manifest. If he'd walked offstage, as 90 percent of performers would have done, sloping offstage in a Spinal Tap way, he would have been over. But Bowie stood there, brazen, and won the audience over. There were a lot of potentially hostile elements in the audience, and he totally won them over. We were all going, OK, you've made us look at you, now impress us. But the show was great, and you could see that this was one step on from Marc Bolan. At that moment there was T. Rexstasy in the UK, and Marc Bolan was bigger than Jesus. But people with sophisticated ears could see that Bolan didn't have the talent to carry on. He had had a two-year stint of golden hits, and those singles were very good, but he did not have the ability to develop.

David had spent the '60s developing. He'd learnt all the chords. He'd spent hours, days, weeks, months, learning to play. He did the work. Whenever Rick Wakeman talks about Bowie, he talks about this guy who was a total professional. If it was ten o'clock in the morning and he had a recording session, even if he didn't have a song ready, he was there. He'd go in. He wouldn't sit there and read a newspaper while someone spent seven hours getting the right drum sound, he'd go in and start work. He'd be at the piano or the guitar and he'd start writing lyrics, and by midday he'd have a backing track, probably with a bunch of people he'd never worked with before, and by four o'clock he'd have a finished demo. That's how he did it. You don't spend fourteen years making an album, you don't spend four years making an album. You'd go in and do it. He did everything in two takes, no messing around.

Before the *NME* I worked at *Frendz*, and someone on the magazine knew someone at MainMan, and so I was trying to get an interview with him. I realized that he was going to be the big figure and I wanted to talk to him. I used to call up three or four times a week trying to get an interview, and I would always be told that he was busy. I was even told he was at the dentist once, which, considering how much work he had on his teeth during the Ziggy time, I could believe. But he was always busy. Tony Defries had made David unavailable. He was doing the Greta Garbo, Elvis Presley thing of keeping away from the press, trying to make him as distant and as exotic as possible. Defries made a lot of enemies, although I don't think Bowie knew what he was doing in his name. When I toured with the Rolling Stones in late 1973, months earlier several of the road crew had worked on the Ziggy farewell tour, and according to these guys, and there was more than one of them, they'd gone to Defries for their money and been told they weren't going to get paid. He said the very fact that you've worked with a superstar of the caliber of David Bowie is recompense enough. You can put that on your CV now. And you'll get work. And you don't do that to roadies. But Tony Defries did that. I don't believe Bowie knew. Bowie had a generosity towards people. MainMan was a shambles. There were people doing nothing drawing huge salaries. And Trevor Bolder and Woody Woodmansey were on a basic wage.

MICK ROCK: I was vaguely aware of David in my last year at Cambridge in 1969, with "Space Oddity," but it was treated more as a gimmick record than anything else. Then, about three years later I used to have access to the *Oz* offices, as they had a darkroom there. Felix Dennis was the only one who ever appeared to be there, and the other two—Richard Neville and Jim Anderson—I never saw. God knows what they were up to. Felix always had a huge pile of promo LPs, and one night he said I should help myself. So I picked up a copy of *Hunky Dory*, took it home, and fell in love with "Life on Mars?" I'd already started working as a photographer, and had worked for Rory Gallagher and Syd Barrett. I think it was my relationship with Syd that later cemented my relationship with David, as he idolized him. That, and what Tony Defries would always say to me, that "David says you see him the way he does himself." I went up to see him play one of the first Ziggy gigs at Birmingham Town Hall on March 17, 1972, with David's plugger. There were only about four hundred people there. I was writing as well as taking pictures, so I could do both. The very first pictures I have of him I took backstage, and then I started shooting him all the time. One of the first sessions was for the men's magazine *Club International.* He was a very gracious man. When I saw him perform in Birmingham, even though his outfits and the makeup weren't as exotic as they later became, the rudiments were there and the performance above all was mesmerizing. I think I was kind of hypnotized by him. We laughed about our names, admired them, because my name was real, and his was made up, although they were both very good rock and roll names. We had some silly little banter about that. That show was primitive, but it still had power. The way he projected himself it was as though he was playing to a much bigger audience. We started hanging out, and he loved hearing all my stories about Syd Barrett. But then I loved hearing all his stories about Lou Reed and Iggy Pop. He took me down to Kensington High Street, to the Sombrero, where there were all these amazing characters. It was a revolutionary little place, full of all these androgynous people. It was all about dancing. Older gentlemen, younger girls; older gentlemen, younger boys.

TREVOR BOLDER: Even Noddy Holder's sideburns weren't as long as mine. Mine started out as [part of] a full beard. When I joined Bowie, I was in the Rats, with the rest of the Spiders, and because of the Beatles I'd grown a full beard. And I looked really odd compared to Mick and Woody, because they were clean-shaven. So when we started to put the Spiders show together I looked really strange. So I thought, Well, I can't go on with a full beard, it looks really odd. So I shaved the middle out, so I had a 'tache and sideburns. And then I thought, Well that looks really odd as well. So I shaved the 'tache off, and I was just about to shave the sideburns off when Angie Bowie said, "Don't you dare shave them off, that'll be part of your image." So it was her decision that I kept them, otherwise they would have gone as well. And then of course she decided that she wanted to spray them silver. Which is exactly what she did. David took a lot from Marc Bolan, because Marc had got there just before him.

WOODY WOODMANSEY: Bass drum skins had to have the name of the band on them back then. I had a blank one, and I said, no, I'm not having that, so I took it off and wrote "The Spiders" on it. Bowie came in and looked at it for two minutes. I thought, well, he's either gonna like this or not, and he looked at me. No expression. And then went, "OK, what's the first number we're doing?" So it passed the audition. It was Ziggy and the Spiders from then on.

MICK ROCK: The fellatio picture is one of the most striking images from the Ziggy period. A few days after the release of *Ziggy Stardust*, there were a thousand people—his biggest audience to date—at Oxford Town Hall, and I was shooting the show from the front, because I had the access. I wanted a different view so I went to the side, and that's when it happened. David said he wasn't trying to look as though he was going down on Mick, and if you look at the picture you can see that he's not actually on his knees. He's chomping on Mick's guitar but his feet are splayed. He was hugging Mick's buttocks in a cute way, but he only did that because of the way Mick was swinging his guitar around. He said, "I was simply trying to bite Mick's guitar." He was playing a passive role to Mick's macho role. The crowd certainly had never seen anything like that before. I remember him rushing offstage afterwards and he said, "Mick, did you get it? Did you get it?" And I'm thinking to myself, Well, I think I did. I'm not sure. It happened so fast. Everything happened so fast in those days. So the next day I got up really early, processed the film, saw the shot, blew it up, and then brought it in to show David and Tony Defries, who both loved it. This was proper shock value, like Jimi Hendrix setting light to his guitar, or Pete Townshend smashing up his. This had gay overtones as well, which was still quite shocking in 1972. The rock industry had never seen anything like it. It was mad. Rock photographers were fairly low down on the rungs at the time, but that picture really set me up. And he knew that. David was a very fast read, and he would pick up on things very quickly and absorb them. Then he would make them his. David was a complex person, there was no doubt about it. Complicated, a true artist. I didn't realize until much later how hard he had worked to get where he was. He had had time to evolve, which is what made him so good. He had time to marinate.

TREVOR BOLDER: Well, you got accused of being the same as Bowie, which was unfair, because we weren't. We were just a band going along with his idea of how to be big. I mean, it was a big issue for Mick, because Mick being the blond guitar player, he was like David's sidekick, I suppose he got more people thinking he was like David than we got. But it was a bit of an issue when you came back to Hull. Because people get jealous, don't they? So you'd come back to your hometown and all the people who were your mates, or you thought were your mates, turned out to be not your mates, because they put you down all the time. We didn't get a lot of it, but you did get that sort of thing happening just because you were associated with David.

When he wanted to describe exactly how he wanted us to look, he took us to see *A Clockwork Orange*. A lot of people thought it was *Star Trek* but it wasn't, it was totally based on the characters in *A Clockwork Orange*. And we just dressed up. It was the makeup thing that was the big deal; I remember that. Ronson was definitely against it, but then when we started using it, it wasn't that bad because we didn't use that much. It was more theatre makeup than anything glammy or anything. He just wanted us to stand out. Whereas if you go onstage and you look normal, there's nothing different. So he wanted us to wear this makeup, which wasn't a lot but it made your features and your face look different, and it made you stand out. We went along with it; of course everybody took to that, and all the girls liked [it], so it was all right after that. It was good. I am enormously proud of what Bowie achieved on our behalf, as it was like reaching the summit of Everest. If he'd pushed it at us, we might have pulled away, thinking, What's he trying to do? He just slowly did it for us.

MICK ROCK: I mean, he wanted it. He was extremely ambitious and in the early days of Ziggy he could taste it. He knew it was about to happen and that made him an invigorating person to be around. He was hip too, because much as everyone knows about the Velvet Underground and Iggy Pop these days, no one knew about them back then. But I did, and he did. We thought we were very hip. I'd taken a lot of LSD at Cambridge and thought I was pretty experienced. He trusted me though, as he knew I was capturing something that was evolving. He was very open and relaxed with me. He wanted me to take the pictures that were going to get him noticed. He mixed a lot of elements—it was the shaved eyebrows, it was the wild hairdo, the color, the outfits. He needed an official photographer, and I suppose that's what I became. I shot him so many times, and while I shot Iggy and Lou and Debbie Harry and Freddie Mercury, my bond with David was really strong. The thing about David was that he knew what he was doing. He wasn't a dark soul, not like Iggy, and certainly not like Lou. He had the ability to generate all this positive energy. Ironically Iggy was the one we all thought would go first, but he's a tough little bugger.

ROBIN DERRICK (ART DIRECTOR): I distinctly remember my older brother bringing the *Ziggy Stardust* album home for the first time. I remember staring for hours at that image of him on the back cover, and reading the TO BE PLAYED AT MAXIMUM VOLUME line and thinking it was so otherworldly. To be sitting on a sofa in my parents' house in Keynsham and being transported like that, it was quite extraordinary. Also the way in which the lyrics applied to both Bowie and Ziggy, the whole thing was fascinating. Up until then you had a singer and you had songs, simple as that. *Ziggy* was such an extraordinary record, and it influenced an entire generation, whether we knew it at the time or not.

KEN SCOTT: RCA had said they needed a single, so we went and made one. "Starman." It was as simple as that. I like it, and it's a cute record. I didn't notice the Judy Garland reference [the song was thought to sound a lot like "Over the Rainbow"] at the time, but when I made "My Sweet Lord" for George Harrison I didn't realize that it sounded a bit like "He's So Fine" by the Chiffons. When you're working on records you just don't hear anything other than what you're making at the time.

Much later, after Bowie died, I appeared on a panel with Ken Scott at an Advertising Week *conference. At the end of the discussion, Ken played the vocal track from "Five Years," which was a revelation to everyone in the room who wasn't Ken. As the song reaches a climax, Bowie starts crying. He is so moved by his own lyrics, and involved in the song that he actually cracks up crying. You can't hear it on the finished record, but it's there, and now I've heard it I hear it every time I play the song. This performance makes a mockery of those who say that this was Bowie's "insincere" period. He is so distraught, so moved by his own lyrics.*

TREVOR BOLDER: The bass line on "Starman" was very simple, and we recorded it very quickly. Everything we did with David was, like, one take. He learnt it and away we went, and that was the finished product. But it's a pretty simple bass line to play. I just used to play whatever came into my head that felt good, really.

BONO (SINGER): There was a huge influence of chanson tradition in his work. Now it's so obvious to me. I completely missed it, in my teens, but if you listen to "Five Years," and put on a funny French accent, it's "*Five years! Ra ta-ta-ta!*"; as well as being a kind of brand-new sound, it completely has its roots in deep traditions like the chanson. We came across Brecht through him, and one of the famous lyricists of all time, the great Belgian, Jacques Brel! He opened up all that for us. Coming from North Dublin, to be a fan of David Bowie wasn't just to be a fan of David Bowie. He was a portal into all kinds of other worlds. You have to understand, after the war, going through the rubble of that destruction became the antidote to a hateful world. And it was this love and peace and feminizing of culture. And he represented that. And you're like, "Wow!" Punk made it male again, but that was an amazing thing. If you look back at the postwar period, you think, How did that happen? There was a period there where in the Western world, it was really OK to be feminine; that had its origins in the rubble of the Second World War.

DAVID BAILEY (PHOTOGRAPHER): I took my first pictures of Bowie for *Vogue* in 1972. He came in full *Ziggy Stardust* costume. Acting already. I said to him, "Who are you today? Lassie or fucking Hamlet?" But right then, right at that moment, he was Ziggy Stardust, and there was nothing I could do about it. You never know who you're getting when you photograph an actor, and he was always an actor. In some ways he was easy to photograph because he laid it all on for you, but you didn't really know what was going on behind all the fancy dress. You would see him around London before that, at parties, always on the fringe of things, but he was around. I remember seeing him at a party in Sloane Square around this time, with Mick [Jagger], and I remember how they both looked the same, because they were whippet thin and not that tall. They were like two Giacomettis standing next to each other, two skinny pop stars. You always look tall when you're skinny. He was always asking questions about art, seemed to love art.

The ad for Ziggy *that appeared in* Zigzag *magazine has him sitting on a stool, wearing wrestling boots and the same haircut he wore on* The Old Grey Whistle Test. *The copy line reads: "Can a young guy who went through truly incredible 'Changes' and made it all 'Hunky Dory' ever find true happiness as a 'Starman'?" Ziggy Stardust was the first pop star with built-in obsolescence, a self-willed creation, and Bowie's ambidextrous android was the forerunner of punk's glam savages. If Bowie was Pygmalion, then Ziggy was his Galatea. It's easy to forget just how important the* Ziggy Stardust *album was at the time, as this was an album that was genuinely appreciated—loved, in fact—by those who bought singles, who bought into fame, and those who bought albums, and who bought into integrity. The* Ziggy Stardust *album had a weird, broad appeal (unsurprisingly, perhaps, as it had been based on* Sgt. Pepper's Lonely Hearts Club Band*). Then, just at the time when Bowie needed to start consolidating his success, building on all the momentum of the last few months, he gave away the greatest, most commercial song he had written so far. Having heard that Mott the Hoople, a rather orthodox rock band from Herefordshire, were on the verge of splitting up, he gave them a new song he'd written, "All The Young Dudes." "Everyone in Mott knew right away that it was a hit," said Ian Hunter, the band's lead singer. "I would never have given that song away to anybody. I got the feeling he'd tried and tried, with his own version, and got bored with it. But once he was in the studio with us, he knew exactly what sound he wanted." It was an extraordinarily successful hit, the lyrics peppered with references to some of the night owls he and Angie had been hanging out with at the Sombrero. When Bowie wrote, "And Freddy's got spots from ripping off the stars/From his face/ Funky little boat race," he was referring to Freddie Burretti.*

Still, even if he had just given away his most commercial song, he was gradually replacing Marc Bolan as the love object of the nation's teenage girls. "Bolan was someone that girls wanted to mother, rather than the person they wanted to be fucked by," says T. Rex's former manager Peter Jenner. Bowie had exactly the opposite effect.

GEORGE UNDERWOOD: Marc Bolan became very unpleasant towards the end. He could see how successful David was becoming and he hated it. I did a bit of work for him and I would go round to his flat and it would look like a bomb had hit it. He used to say he'd had "a bit of session." He was full of self-loathing, and used to sit around watching videos of himself when he was younger, and thinner. Drinking too much, too many drugs. Wasn't in a good frame of mind. When David wrote "All The Young Dudes" for Mott the Hoople, it mentions T. Rex, and I think Marc thought he was having a dig, but he wasn't. David always had time for Marc, was always singing his praises.

TONY ZANETTA: David came back to New York in June 1972 to see Elvis at Madison Square Garden, which was the last time David flew. He was suddenly Ziggy Stardust. He didn't look like the same person. He'd been working pretty much nonstop from January to June, doing gigs in England. He was more tense, and wasn't really quite the same person, because I think he was really beginning to rev up. They were making plans to come to the US that fall, which is when Tony Defries created MainMan properly, and that's when it became formal that I was working for them. It was more like Angie saying, "Oh darling, we're going on tour in the fall, and you must come with us." It didn't make any sense, because I wasn't a guitar player, but then things started happening really fast. I had $5,000 that I could tap, finding an apartment for Tony, buying clothes for David and Angie, passing out photos of David. You couldn't focus, you didn't know where to look. It was bizarre, like a three-ring circus. It was kinda awful, not focused. It was distracting. Suddenly it was the Ziggy circus, and the next stop was America.

SIMON NAPIER-BELL: From *Ziggy Stardust* onwards it would have been difficult not to find him interesting. When the album first came out I had to make a trip from London to Zurich, alone, driving. On the ferry from Calais I looked for some cassettes to play on the way but I couldn't find any, except in the tobacconist. When I asked if he had any he said no, he didn't stock them. "But you can have this one," he said, handing me *Ziggy Stardust.* "Someone left it on the counter. It's crap." I played it from Calais to Zurich, nonstop, eleven hours driving in all, so I listened to it right through more than twenty times. "Space Oddity" was extraordinary in both its content and production. And that gave Bowie an instant appeal. And by the time *Ziggy Stardust* came three years later, he had become a complete self-contained package—theatrics, music, image, and perfect press controversies. To anyone who managed acts he had to be appealing. He had it all.

4

JAMMING GOOD WITH WEIRD AND GILLY

1972–1973

CHARLES SHAAR MURRAY: I first met him in July 1972, the Dorchester interview for the *NME*. I'd seen him before that, but that was the first time we were actually face-to-face. I thought he was very intelligent, and seemed to be less overwhelmed with all the flamboyance around him and emanating from him than everybody else was. He seemed much more relaxed than I would have expected him to be. Here was a guy who had been bouncing around the music business for ten years, since his mid-teens. I was twenty-one and he was twenty-five, and he was getting very close to what he had been working towards since he was fourteen or fifteen. And he didn't seem carried away with it. He'd not just prepared for it by mastering his craft, or rather by mastering all the different dimensions of craft that he brought to the table, but it's almost as if he'd become spiritually prepared for what he was doing. Alternatively, maybe he was retreating behind the mask of Ziggy, and feeling that he wasn't really involved, and that it was just the character doing it. Which is a method of operation he found harder and harder to maintain over the following few years.

NICK RHODES (MUSICIAN): *Ziggy Stardust* was the first album I ever bought, and the whole period still has enormous significance for me, in particular Bowie's performance on *Top of the Pops*, and before that *Lift Off with Ayshea*. I saw *Lift Off* at my parents' bungalow in suburban Hollywood, on the outskirts of Birmingham, the same town that [Duran Duran's] bassist John Taylor, grew up in. I was ten years old and besotted. I was sitting in the living room, which was very *Abigail's Party*, with a little more sophistication, but not that much. The furniture was brown, with a round glass G-Plan table in the middle of the room, with a huge color television with the smallest of screens. My parents had bought it for the moon landings, failing to realize that all the transmissions would be in black and white. Thinking back now the TV looked like a piece of conceptual art. It was just this enormous cathode-ray monstrosity, but it did the trick because David Bowie pumped out of it.

Hosted by the singer Ayshea Brough (along with an owl puppet called Ollie Beak), the show that week featured Tony Christie, Hello, and a South African performer called Emil Dean Zoghby, as well as Bowie. *Lift Off* was a teatime show, and we watched it when we got home from school. She was a groovy-looking chick in white zippy outfits and there was always music on it. That night Bowie was wearing the jumpsuit he would wear on *Top of the Pops* a few days later, but played an ordinary, unlacquered acoustic guitar. Woody Woodmansey had yet to bleach his hair. We already knew who Bowie was, because we liked the record as we'd heard it on the radio, [people at school] were talking about him, and we'd seen his pictures in magazines. So we raced home from school that day, as we knew he was on. He was a phenomenon in the same way the Sex Pistols were a few years later.

At school the next day nobody talked about anything else. The approach, the look, the sound of him, the excitement that he was singing about aliens. At that point most people were still singing dull old love songs, and Bowie really came from such an obtuse angle, visually, conceptually, lyrically. He was unique. For me, at that time of my life, when I was just discovering music, it was so magnetic, and he was genuinely exciting.

My parents would often watch *Top of the Pops* with me, as they were quite turned on by knowing what was going on in the charts, and I remember they actually liked him. They liked Bowie so much they took me to see Bowie when he played the Empire Pool in Wembley in London in 1976, on the *Station to Station* tour, not once but twice. I'd become such a fan and he had become such a focus of what I thought I wanted to do with my life at the time. They were very indulgent of Bowie because this was the person who inspired me and the rest of Duran Duran and most of the rest of the British music industry that exists now to do what we all chose to do. I told my parents when I was ten that I wanted to be a rock star when I grew up, which they laughed off and said, "Yes, well that's very nice darling, but let's not talk about it now." But when I was still saying it at fourteen it was a little more worrisome for them. At fifteen I could play guitar, and a year later, formed a band. I wore huge, wide trousers, bum-freezer jackets with wide lapels covered in Anabass badges, and shirts with unforgivably large collars. I accessorized and adapted everything. I remember during punk I would pin my tie back with paper clips to make it look thinner. You just adapted whatever you had. I remember in assembly at school, the headmaster announcing that, "Just because Nicholas Rhodes is doing this to his clothes doesn't mean all of you have to do it."

One of the most embarrassing moments of my life was when I had just moved into a new house in London, and had a surprise visit from Bowie and Iman. They just happened to be in London, and popped round on the off chance I was in. They both looked immaculate, but my house was full of boxes and piles of books and delivery cartons. There were no chairs, it was a complete mess, and there was junk everywhere. Anyway, my dad is there, painting one of the rooms, and when I introduced him to David and Iman, he put down his brush and said, "Hello David, could you give us a quick rendition of Major Tom, then?" At that moment I wanted the floor to open, but David took it in good grace.

The thing about David Bowie is that he totally changed the whole game at that point. There were lots of other people who were equally as innovative at the time, some people maybe even further ahead—you look at Lou Reed, Iggy Pop, Bryan Ferry and Roxy Music, Eno, there were lots of people with progressive ideas—but it was David who managed to focus that '70s energy into something that was irresistible. You bought into the whole thing. You didn't just buy into how great the songs were, or how strange the lyrics were, you bought into him being different, and it rubber-stamped you as being someone who thought about life in a different way. I was an incredibly young adopter, but having said that most of my friends at the time were fifteen or sixteen. Bowie bonded a generation.

TREVOR BOLDER: I suppose the greatest part was in the very early days, before we made it, when we all lived at Haddon Hall with David and we were putting it all together. It was so much fun, you know? Writing the songs up and going in the studio together, it was real fun. That's my fondest memory, even though there are great memories from after, when we made it really big, but it was the early days of no pressure on us. We just had a lot of fun. We went down the pub together; nobody knew who we were. We went into the studio and there was no pressure. David wrote his songs and we played along, and then they were put together. *Top of the Pops* changed all that.

It was seven thirty p.m. on July 6, 1972, and I was sitting by myself watching Top of the Pops *in our semi in Deal, Kent, and couldn't quite believe my eyes. Back then, the show was regularly watched by 12 to 13 million people every week, almost a quarter of the population. A large percentage of viewers were teenagers, like me, who—having David Bowie strut about in his space-age onesie singing his new single, "Starman"—thought he was talking directly to them from the BBC studios. He was wearing a multicolored jumpsuit and playing a blue acoustic guitar, and he looked scary. Essentially, he looked carefree in a way that no pop star had ever looked before. It was colorful, risqué, transgressive, and very, very appealing to an impressionable twelve-year-old. Previously, my pop consumption had been based around one-hit wonders and odd T. Rex records. Bowie, to me, was a complete revelation. For me, he kick-started the '70s, as the decade turned from black and white to color overnight.*

TREVOR BOLDER: Tony Defries had been trying to get us on *Top of the Pops* for ages, encouraging the producers to come down and see us, but then we did a gig at the Croydon Greyhound and the BBC crew all came down, along with the producer, and that's when we were offered the show. We had already done a TV spot or two, but this was the big one, this was the show that everybody watched.

NICHOLAS COLERIDGE (JOURNALIST): Doesn't everyone remember where they were when they first saw David Bowie? For me, it was on television in the back room of the Eton college tuck shop, Rowlands, and he was performing "Starman" on *Top of the Pops*; shocking-red Ziggy haircut, Rainbow zigzag jumpsuit, hips gyrating, electrifyingly alien and disconcertingly sexy. It must have been the first or second Thursday of July, 1972, "Starman" having just charted. Bowie's audience in the squalid, testosterone-rich Eton dive was largely unimpressed. Probably a hundred pupils were hanging out around the TV, with plates of chips and saucers of ketchup and there were catcalls of derision. "Pooftah." It was summer term and the room was packed with boys in cricket and rowing kit, and these sporty pupils with their ketchup-dunked chips staring indignantly up at the screen. It was all so provocatively . . . queer.

TREVOR BOLDER: On July 5, the day of the *Top of the Pops* recording, the entire band felt elated. By eleven o'clock, as we climbed into the limo outside Haddon Hall—the management had decided that we should do the trip in style—it was already a hot day. Our stage clothes were all on hangers laid out in the boot, along with two bags of shoes. It wasn't quite the hottest day of the month, but it was hot enough for us to pile into the car in our shirtsleeves, with no jackets. From being kids we'd all watched *Top of the Pops*, and seen all these monstrously successful bands on the show and never really thought we'd get there. To actually be there and play on it was a thrill. I actually achieved a goal in that way. As we were miming, we were a lot more nervous than we ought to have been. I always remember standing at the side of the stage when Status Quo were going on and thinking that this wasn't somehow real, as they had had quite a few hits by then so it really felt like the big-time. It was just before midday when we arrived, the time we'd been told to turn up. We climbed out of the limo, and then ambled into the Stage Door reception, all the while being monitored by the crowd of young autograph hunters lying in wait in the lobby. We walked by the famous sculpture of Helios, across the lobby, past Security, past the marble-set lifts and into Studio 8. First right, then right again, and then left under the stairs, and there it was, just fifty yards from the reception. We arrived at the studio around twelve fifteen, went to our dressing room, hung around for a bit, playing cards and gossiping about the other acts on the show, and then went to the BBC bar. Then we did the dress rehearsal, a nonstop run-through, as if they were doing the show live. And then we had another break, and then about six o'clock they brought in the audience. Then we did it live, straight through, and then went off to the BBC bar again. In the bar people kept coming up to us and asking if we were in *Doctor Who*.

TRACEY EMIN (ARTIST): He had such a huge influence on me as a child. I saw him on *The Old Grey Whistle Test* in the green jumpsuit when I was about eleven, but it was the *Top of the Pops* performance that really got to me. I couldn't believe someone could be so sexy. But it wasn't like I projected my sexuality onto him, like a crush or fantasy or whatever. He made me feel sexy, and that's how it worked. He made every outsider feel like they were an insider, feel like they're doing the right thing. For all his glam rock, he wasn't glam rock; he looked like the real thing. Ziggy Stardust was so immaculately well done, and not embarrassing. How could he look like that, and it not be embarrassing? He pulled it all off, and I think it's because of the sincerity of it. It wasn't like, "Oh, who shall I be today? How shall I get my next number-one hit?" I loved that side of it, but what I was really into was more mature, un-aggressive poetry, geography, music, and cut-outs. And he was into that too. It's because of David Bowie that I got into Egon Schiele. Because of him that I started exploring art that I wasn't really sure of.

NICK RHODES: I think people have forgotten the significance *Top of the Pops* had throughout the '70s. It really focused the entire nation, every Thursday night for half an hour, on music, on what was going on. Sometimes the groups could be absolutely horrendous, and other times they were just brilliant. It didn't matter if you had to watch a lot of gimmick acts as you knew you were going to get Roxy Music, or David Bowie or Cockney Rebel or Sparks, or any other number of oddities. Everybody watched it. It was a family event.

TONY BLACKBURN (*TOP OF THE POPS* PRESENTER): There were no autocues in those days; at least, I didn't use them. I was a bingo caller more than anything. I just had to introduce the acts. You had to try and make sure that everything was perfect, because if you had to do a retake, it cost so much money. I loved the glam-rock era because it was so much fun, what with everyone dressing up. It was a real performance. All of the acts could be guaranteed to put on a show. It was almost like music hall. I met Bowie after presenting *Top of the Pops* that night and I told him that I loved "The Laughing Gnome," not meaning anything by it, and he turned and very gently said, "Oh, that's not me," and walked off.

TONY PARSONS (JOURNALIST): I watched it at home in Billericay. Missing *Top of the Pops* would have been like missing church on Sundays—you just didn't do it. As soon as I saw him I knew it was my thing. Pop culture was still pushing at the frontiers, still pushing west, and Bowie was an extension of that. My dad would have been watching it with a tray on his lap, having just come back from work. He was the type of man who would leave the room when [drag artist] Danny La Rue came on the TV, so he can't have been impressed with Bowie. I was though.

The sexual ambiguity was there for all to see, but it wasn't threatening, it was only like Jagger wearing his hair over his collar. It felt inclusive. You've always had these guys like Marc Bolan or Mick Jagger or Russell Brand, who play with their sexuality, and they're always the ones getting all the girls. Plus you had Mick Ronson, who was clearly a brickie from Hull, so that was OK.

Surrounding Bowie you had the likes of Sweet, Mud, and the Glitter Band, and they were oh so obviously geezers, even if they were wearing Christmas baubles on their ears. David Bowie wasn't a geezer. He wasn't overly concerned with socioeconomic politics either, and was far more interested in the way that cultural touchstones influenced the Zeitgeist. This was only a few years after the first moon landing, when space travel was suddenly no longer exotic, when the expectations amongst all of us was that trips to the moon would soon be as common as taking a Number 19 [bus] up to the Arsenal. You couldn't watch the moon landing and not imagine that we would all soon be bouncing around between the planets.

NEIL TENNANT (MUSICIAN): [As] I'd already seen Bowie play in Newcastle the previous month, it wasn't some sort of epiphany for me watching the *Top of the Pops* performance, exciting though it was. I was already obsessed with Bowie and so were my friends. It was *The Old Grey Whistle Test* performance in February of that year that made the big impact on me, the camera so close on Bowie's face at the beginning of "Five Years." The

Top of the Pops appearance just confirmed that the public was catching up and that Bowie finally had a hit. It was also rather thrilling that Bowie was so daringly "camp" on TV.

The thing that really did it for us was the advert for "John, I'm Only Dancing"—the picture where he's got his arm outstretched. It was a bit of a classic glam-era image, that! I had a Ziggy haircut—dyed red as well. I did get his autograph in 1972, at the Newcastle City Hall in June, which I have to say was over half-empty! During "Suffragette City," when he sang "Wham, bam, thank you ma'am," they showered the audience with pictures of David as Ziggy Stardust, which was just about to come out. And I got him to sign one of those on his way out, which I still have funnily enough. My brother Simon and I used to tape [his BBC Radio sessions] and by the time *Ziggy Stardust* came out we knew almost every song on it already. "Hang onto Yourself," "Moonage Daydream," "Ziggy Stardust"—I'd all taped off the radio. "Starman" had been the single. I remember initially preferring those radio recordings. One actually forgets that "Starman" wasn't a particularly big hit. David didn't have a top-three single until "The Jean Genie," and it seemed rather frustrating at the time. We did have *Ziggy Stardust* the week before it came out though, because RCA's records were produced in County Durham and I had a friend whose father worked at the factory there.

IAIN R. WEBB (FASHION JOURNALIST): That edition of *Top of the Pops* was the night before my fourteenth birthday. What a gift. After that first sighting, a pair of girls' lace-up platform shoes were duly purchased from the small ads at the back of the *NME*, while the Ziggy Stardust cropped pedal-pusher trousers were copied in part from the fashion favored by Smoothies [teens who were followers of the TV show *Budgie*, featuring a cheeky chancer portrayed by actor Adam Faith]. I cut my hair at the kitchen sink into a very bad approximation of his spiky hairdo and wore Antique Green nail polish. One Saturday, my mum returned from her regular shopping trip to the nearby town carrying a brown paper bag. It contained a secondhand fox fur, which I draped over my shoulder when watching *Match of the Day* with my dad. As Bowie went from snug, bum-freezer jackets to swimming in roomy demob suits, my own version came from the back of my dad's wardrobe. I wore this with a trilby and a pair of Mary Jane shoes.

Poor Dad. Bowie was all the things my life in a West Country village was not: extraordinary, exotic, and exciting. From that moment on, I devoted all my waking hours to lovingly documenting his every move in scrapbook after scrapbook (a dozen in all) and spent art class at school painting his portrait, mostly wearing outlandish new outfits designed by yours truly. I even fashioned a clay bust of him in pottery class.

MARK COOPER (BBC PRODUCER): The thing that interests me is intentionality. I might be completely wrong, and I know that Bowie was a careerist and capable of being completely calculated about these things—and I always thought the moment he told Michael Watts he was gay was calculated—but there's something completely natural about the way he puts his arm around Mick Ronson's shoulders. In hindsight we assume that a lot of this stuff is intentional, but a lot are just happy accidents. When he does it, it doesn't look as though he's doing it for the first time, or for effect. It's also a generational thing. I think Jagger could have done what Bowie did, quite naturally, sidling up to Keith and throwing his arm around him onstage. But no one cared about Jagger, as he was an old man. The notion of a singer interplaying with their guitarist was not necessarily a new thing. It was generationally new. Plus Bowie was one of the few artists [along with Roxy Music and Elton John] to play both *The Old Grey Whistle Test* and *Top of the Pops*—he was both rock and pop, and so he straddled those two worlds too.

TREVOR BOLDER: It all happened after that night. We went out on the road and did a British tour, and where we'd been playing to maybe fifty, sixty people a night in small venues, we were selling places out. Friars in Aylesbury was the big one [July 15], as that's where we tested everything out. That was sold out, and then everything started to go. . . . Everybody wanted to see the band. So that was when we realized it was taking off.

PETER YORK (CULTURAL COMMENTATOR): Suddenly we all sort of registered it at the same time. We knew he was important, after all he was a pop singer who wore clothes by Kansai Yamamoto. I had a friend called Mick Rock at the time, and he was always around. The thing I remember most was the Friends of the Earth/Save the Whale benefit concert on

July 8, 1972, a few days after the *Top of the Pops* thing. People were dressed up like mad, and some of them got it right, and some got it wrong. But it was wonderful to look at. Everyone dressing up, the design, the spectacle, the sexual energy, lots of gay kids doing a bit of early venturing. You could enjoy it on so many different levels. And then we started seeing him all the time. I loved him, and if you were a *Pure Pop for Now People* person, and you opened the *NME*, say, and it was all about King Crimson, you'd close it tight, as they were absolute mastodons of ghastliness. And then triumphantly glam rock arrived, and the things that we liked the most were obviously Bowie and Roxy Music. I had dinner with Bryan [Ferry] about three years ago, and he was being quite snotty about David, the idea that he was such a plagiarist, and I was thinking, You've got spot-on taste and perfect pitch but you're not quite right there. You've allowed a few things to cloud your judgment. I call it picking up, not plagiarism. People of advanced taste would say the [competition] was Bryan and David, and of course David appeared to be operating on a bigger scale, and had more international traction and hit a bigger nerve. He was marvelously pretentious, with lots of allusions to . . . stuff. He read bits of books. A bit Continental. Drawing on Andyland. He distilled it all, and we loved it. It was a kind of composite motivation. The sex, the clothes, the design, the intellectualism.

NICHOLAS COLERIDGE: How rapidly obsessive fandom takes root. Within a day of hearing "Starman" on *Top of the Pops*, I'd gathered the backlist, just four albums at that point: *David Bowie: London Boy, Space Oddity, The Man Who Sold the World,* and *Hunky Dory,* and then the one that sealed the deal, *The Rise and Fall of Ziggy Stardust and the Spiders from Mars*, released on 6 June that year. I can't pretend my devotion differed in any important respect from that of any other fifteen-year-old Bowie fan. I confess that, in those barely liberated days, I preferred evidence that my bisexual hero was more straight than gay. So it was good news he was married to Angie, less good they'd reportedly first met when sleeping with the same guy. And the album cover of *The Man Who Sold the World*, showing Bowie wearing a Michael Fish "man dress," was uncomfortable. His voice, with its range, passion, and yearning, had a spooky Dalek quality and the lyrics felt like poetry to my teenage ear.

KRIS NEEDS: Bowie returned to Friars for a third performance on July 15, I think primarily as a showcase for a planeload of American journalists and record company execs. Tony Defries knew a Friars show would guarantee the right kind of reception. The guest list included Lisa Robinson, Lenny Kaye, and *Creem*'s Dave Marsh. Though I managed to see the sound check in the afternoon, I couldn't get to Bowie. Tony Defries had put a barrier up, refusing all interviews, and it was impossible to get through to him. When I tried to make my way up the staircase to the dressing rooms, my path was blocked by Stuey George, Bowie's new bodyguard, who informed me that I would get to see David "over my dead body." So I didn't see him again until he came back with Iggy Pop in 1977.

GEORGE UNDERWOOD: The success of Ziggy changed everything, because as soon as David started to get a little bit of success he was the happiest man in the world. All he ever wanted was success. And as success bred success, he was off. Beckenham, the Arts Lab, "Space Oddity," then he was off. I spent so much time at Haddon Hall, nearly as much time as David had spent at my house in Bromley when we were younger. I met Tony Visconti, all the Spiders, it was all coming together here. I remember being at Haddon Hall when he first played "Suffragette City." And at the end of the performance—he just played it on twelve-string—I shouted out, "Wham-bam, thank you, ma'am!" which was a song from a Charlie Mingus album, *Oh Yeah.* And it obviously ended up on the record. After Ziggy started working, he took real pleasure in molding his success.

LINDSAY KEMP: It was Angela who first got me involved with Ziggy. She played me the record and said, the name might not be very you and the music is very different from the old days, with their beautiful ballads and musical influenced songs and so on. Some of the music was quite heavy, but it was thrilling. And she said she wanted me to stage a production based on these songs. For the big Ziggy concert at the Rainbow, Angela was great fun and so helpful. She would take me on shopping trips and buy makeup boxes and costumes. It was a dream for me because I had never had any money to spend on a production before. I only had things I had before, things I had made with crepe paper. Here I was, holding all these fabulous fabrics and having this great theater, the Rainbow.

TREVOR BOLDER: Everybody always wants to talk to me about the Spiders, and they want to know what Bowie was like, and what it was like going out on the road together. It was a magical time for us, for the band, but it's obviously become an incredibly special period for people who like the music, especially those people who weren't there at the time, or who weren't even born. When [I was] out on the road with [Uriah] Heep I met loads of people who are Spiders fans. My daughter went to see Moby and she went backstage a couple of years ago, and he wrote a song called "Bring Back the Spiders from Mars," and he was doing the "I am not worthy" routine to her. It's bonkers. No matter where I go in the world, or who I meet, as soon as they discover I was in the Spiders, they want to talk about it. I'm not sure we realized that this was going to be the case all those years ago. Sure, we knew it was an important period for Bowie, and we knew it was an important period for us, but I don't think any of us understood just how important the whole thing was going to be in the history of rock music. The Spiders from Mars are almost a mythical band nowadays, a mythical band who happened to be real.

NICK KENT: Bowie was viewed at the *NME* as the main guy, the center of the '70s rock world, the absolute center. Myself, Charlie, and Ian MacDonald all had huge respect for him. At the *NME* when there was a new Bowie album we would all sit round and listen to it and debate it—what is David saying? In the way that we once would have done about Bob Dylan. You don't do that with Coldplay. What Coldplay are saying on their new album is, Well, the last album sold 7 million so we're giving you more of the same because we know you like that kind of thing. David often wrote lyrics that were meaninglessness selling itself as abstraction, but usually there was real depth.

DAVID BAILEY: He wasn't my kind of man, as I found him too affected. I knew what he was all about because the beatniks used to do what he did in Paris in the '50s, putting a grid over a book and then drawing round it and picking out words as though they were meaningful. That's how he wrote, using found words, just like William Burroughs used to do. So I got it. Just didn't think it was particularly interesting, as it had been done before. You can come up with things that are totally ridiculous and yet they're meant to be laden with meaning. Silly. He was always onstage, always playing David Bowie, always being what you wanted him to be. So I found it impossible to connect with him, as he was controlling everything. He was the personification of an actor actually. He always took things very seriously, which I don't. If I found something serious then you probably wouldn't know, but if he did then you absolutely would. That's the difference in personalities. I don't think I ever got him, not in a picture. I might have got a good picture of Ziggy Stardust, or Ciggy Stardust, but I don't think I ever got a good picture of David Bowie. He was just one of those guys who didn't like to give anything away. He was a bit like a woman because he liked dressing up so much. Very theatrical. Very Marcel Marceau. But he was always on time.

In September 1972, the Ziggy *tour went to the United States. The US tour was wild, although perhaps no wilder than any other grade-A rock and roll tour of the time. What made it different was David and Angie's very public codependent relationship. For a while on the tour David was seeing the soon-to-be-infamous groupie Cyrinda Foxe, who would go on to marry Steven Tyler, the singer in Aerosmith. His affair with her was apparently just as fluid as his marriage.*

CYRINDA FOXE (GROUPIE): He once called me into the room [from the bathroom] to talk to him while he fucked a girl, and he needed someone to talk to, and that was me. I'd be watching the TV and talking with David, and he'd be screwing the groupie. Very nonchalant. [I saw Angie] crawling around on her hands and knees after having sex with a bodyguard, because it was so intense that she couldn't walk afterwards. David would be in one room with me, and we'd be making love or we'd be talking while he was doing it with another girl . . . and Angie would be in the other room making the walls shake.

GEORGE UNDERWOOD: We were on the Greyhound bus on the US tour of 1972, and there was a little pig-nosed amp and an electric guitar at the back, just there for our entertainment. So I started playing, trying to do an old John Lee Hooker song, which almost sounded like a bass line. And it's going on for a while and David asked for the guitar and starts playing the riff for "Jean Genie." Based completely on a John Lee Hooker riff. This was David's first US tour, and he had invited someone to come on tour with him, maybe Dana Gillespie. Because he wanted someone as a companion who wasn't in the business. I got a call from David asking if I'd like to go to the States. I had only been married a year, and so we both went, my wife and me. He said a car would come and pick me up two weeks later. Two weeks later it turns up and drives us down to Southampton, where we board the *QE2*, first class. Five days later we're in New York. It was so funny being on that boat, and he kept us entertained for most of the journey. He came down to dinner on the first night in one of his Ziggy outfits, a white dress version of something he wore onstage, complete with big wings on the shoulders. Everyone turns around and is literally coughing up their soup. After he didn't come down for dinner anymore, as everyone was staring at him. I said, "What did you expect?" We were there for two weeks, and when Tony Defries looked at how much everything was costing, he said the Underwoods hadn't cost him any money. And that's because I was paying out of my own pocket. I took all the money I had in the bank and paid for every meal, everything we did. I didn't want to be a hanger-on. David was cross, but he wanted me to stay, so he said that maybe I could do an album cover for him or something. We discussed me doing a cover for the rerelease of *The Man Who Sold the World*, but by the time we got to New York they'd already gone with the picture of him kicking his leg up in the air. So I ended up staying for three months.

The audiences on the *Ziggy* tour of the US just couldn't believe their eyes. Every night was a sensation. The audience was brutalized, and had never seen anything like it. We went most places by Amtrak, which is a great way to see the country. He was high rolling on that tour. Every night was a party. We were talking one night in his hotel suite, and he disappeared into his bathroom and came out with his eyebrows shaved off. The phone never stopped ringing. People everywhere. That tour was bonkers, exhilarating but mad. It was a rock and roll circus. Angie was obviously there, running around. For all her faults as a mother, Angie was instrumental in getting Ziggy up and running. Getting fabrics, designing costumes. Her enthusiasm was second to none, and she was a huge help to David at the time, as was Tony Defries. David didn't seem to care about anything other than making it work. In the US he was treated as a star and he really wasn't one. He wanted me to go on to Japan with him, but I had to go home so he asked Geoff MacCormack to go with him.

LINDSAY KEMP: David was selfish, but he wasn't nasty. Fame didn't make him that way, as he was selfish from the start. He wasn't very greedy. He lived an instinctive life. We didn't talk about philosophical things. We talked about people like Jean Genet, Antonin Artaud, the theatre of cruelty; the avant-garde. I was planning on dramatizing Jean Genet's novel *Le Notre-Dame des Fleurs*, which became *Flowers*. It put me on the map and brought me fame and fortune and took me round the world a couple times. We talked a lot about Genet and a particular piece I was working on, and I hoped he would perform in it one day. But of course he did go away and wrote "The Jean Genie."

WENDY LEIGH: One of the ways in which David made it in America was by being very English and having these wonderful manners. Let's not forget, he wasn't a working-class hero, in the same way that Mick Jagger wasn't. He was middle class to the core, and in the States he used to play on his Englishness. He would romance women, sing to them, properly seduce them. He would talk and talk and talk until they were desperate to sleep with him. After a concert in Los Angeles in October 1972, the DJ Wolfman Jack threw a party at his home, with Bowie as the guest of honor. He spied a girl on the dance floor who was dancing with Kim Fowley, who knew everyone. David asked Fowley if she was with him, and when Fowley said no, he walked across to her, and said, "My name is David Bowie. Would you like to accompany me to the bathroom?" When they eventually came out, he kissed the girl on the cheek, shook her hand, and said, "Thank you." He played the English gentleman to the hilt. He did it with a lot of class and a lot of elegance. I don't think he stepped on people's faces in order to go to bed with them. He did it all with great style.

JOSETTE CARUSO (GROUPIE): I'm a New Jersey girl, and I knew lots of rock stars at the time. I was a groupie, a groupie girl. I was nineteen, and had been seeing rock stars since I was sixteen. I went on tour with

Jimmy Page and Led Zeppelin, and I knew Jeff Beck very well. I knew Deep Purple, the Kinks, Ten Years After. I was living with my mother when I left to go on the road with Led Zeppelin. I was sixteen, and my mother wasn't happy. I knew that she would be worried out of her mind. So I called her and I just said, "I'm with Jimmy Page and I'm not coming home," and I hung up. I just went from one band to another. I was having fun, and I wasn't looking to settle down with anyone or looking for a relationship. I realized straight off that these guys weren't looking for a relationship, they were just looking to have some fun, and so was I. I wasn't a runaway, I just went from band to band to band and had a great time. After a while the bodyguards got to know me, and knew that I wasn't going to steal anything. I was getting what I wanted, with the limousines and the concerts and the backstage and the shows and knowing all the other girls wanted to be with them. But I was going to be the one sleeping with them afterwards. It was an ego thing, I won't deny that. I didn't fool myself into thinking there was any emotional involvement. I loved all these guys but none of them were like David Bowie.

BEBE BUELL (MODEL, SINGER): He came walking into Max's Kansas City in that blue suit and that red carrot hair, no eyebrows. I mean he truly looked like he landed in his spaceship and parked it outside. We were all pretty blown away. So he got my phone number from someone, and then called me. I was only nineteen, so he asked me if I wanted to go sightseeing. He told me he was a little embarrassed to ask me. He said these mega-cool people found him foolish, and would I find him foolish? And I said no! Where do you want to go?! I thought it was delightful and there was no sexual vibe to it. He was just like a child who wanted to go see the Empire State Building and go see the Rockettes at Radio City. He wanted to go to the museum, he wanted to see the giant whale. So we went to see the Rockettes. He had the biggest smile on his face the entire time, cheering and clapping and he was just mesmerized. He told me, this is like the Mary Poppins version of a crazy-horse saloon in Paris. I thought that was kind of the perfect description. Do you know when we went on top of the Empire State Building he kept running around in a circle? Because he couldn't believe the view and he just thought it was beautiful. He just couldn't get over the view, and the wind was hitting his face, and he had that smile, and he didn't smoke a cigarette for about an hour. That was a record for him, I think!

I took him to see Bruce Springsteen when he did a show upstairs in Max's, where he was playing the piano and singing these songs. David had heard he was special and gifted and wanted to see him. I know that David was one of the earliest fans of Bruce Springsteen, that I can assure you. Bruce was singing his heart out at Max's, and there were very few people up there other than David and I, and David kept leaning over to me and saying, "Can you believe his lyrics?" and he was just blown away by them. I remember him asking me, "Where is Asbury Park?" as he didn't quite understand some of the portraits that Bruce was painting because it was all about the Jersey Shore. I drove him to the Jersey Shore one day, and he was really blown away by that, by where Bruce had grown up and where he got all his songs from. And I think he wanted to get a corndog or something, traditional beach fare. I couldn't eat meat so I just ate a candy apple. He was worrying that I was going to pull my teeth out. I said my teeth are real, they can handle it! And then I took him back to the city. You know, I think we even took the Staten Island Ferry. He wanted to go on the boat, he wanted to do all these things.

No one recognized him, as he wasn't huge yet. There was a time in New York where there was no paparazzi, and the only people that got chased by the paparazzi were the likes of Jackie Kennedy. I didn't get introduced to the volume of the paparazzi till I dated Rod Stewart many years later and then I learned what it's like to be chased around by them, but when I hung around with David Bowie or Mick Jagger, those guys took taxis and were very discreet. They didn't go looking for the picture to be taken like a lot of people do today. They had a lot of class and decorum and David actually had a limousine. I think he was trying to give everybody an image, you know what I mean? He wanted it to look already like he was a rich, successful rock star. But the thing is he did stay at a smaller hotel, at the Gramercy Park, which is a lovely, enchanting hotel. I adore it but he wasn't uptown at The Plaza or where the Stones or Marc Bolan would stay.

Whenever I would hang out with him or have tea or whatever, there was a lot of chaos. There was Mick Ronson, his girlfriend Suzy; there was a lot of movement, clothing being constructed, makeup all over the desktops and lots of contemplating what style was going to be worn. We went to see the New York Dolls one night, I remember doing that with him. He wanted to go see Bette Midler at the baths, so I took him to that. I know that everybody assumed we were lovers and we really weren't and I always try to clarify that. There was kissing and canoodling and an attempt to make love but it ended up in a heap of laughter if you really want to know. I would come over and the women would be coming in and out. There was so much traffic coming in and out of his bedroom. I remember I came over and saw three women and he says, "I'm having an amazing time. There are so many beautiful women in New York, Bebe." All we did was play with makeup. In a way he was a character actor. He invented so many enchanting characters, he was like Willy Wonka. Angela was never around at that point. She had her own world and her own life, and I always assumed that she preferred women.

I was living with Todd Rundgren but we were not married. I don't think Todd minded me hanging out; well, I think he did a little bit because of the artistic thing that men have. Todd admired his music as we would both lay on our waterbed and listen to Bowie and so I think that when he saw that Bowie and I had become close, he became very curious. David really wanted to go see him in concert and so I remember taking him with me to see Todd at Carnegie Hall. Todd had a pretty prestigious show and he was dressed quite flamboyantly. David had a suit that looked like one Todd wore. Todd didn't nick it, maybe their minds were thinking alike, I don't know. But I took David to that concert and I remember he sat and watched very attentively.

There was a time when I leapt out of bed at three o'clock in the morning because David called and he was in tears having some emotional crisis. So I went. What he liked about being with me was that I didn't put any pressure on him. I didn't expect him to perform or blow my mind sexually or anything. I was a very young girl who totally appreciated and understood the complexity of his personality but I had a little experience, as I was living with a mad genius at the time too.

TREVOR BOLDER: We lived and breathed the Spiders. Of course, it was a performance, but when we started the tour we weren't really the Spiders from Mars. As the tour went on we took the name and we actually became the characters, to go along with the whole Ziggy thing. So we tried to live up to people's expectations of us when we came offstage. When we were in America we had all this gear, and of course the Americans went over the top for that sort of stuff. They thought we were really decadent, really out there. But once we'd finished performing we just used to put our jeans and T-shirts back on and we went back to street clothes. We did a show in L.A., and we all went back to the Beverly Hills Hotel, and there was a knock on the door, and all these kids were there dressed up in these weird outfits and stuff. And of course we were in jeans and T-shirts and these kids said, "Jeez, you guys are really weird." And we thought, *Have you looked in the mirror?* Because they were living what we were doing onstage, but we were walking away from it once we'd finished. We were different to what was going on at that particular time. A lot of other groups didn't really understand what we were up to, because we looked so odd. They were going, "What's going on here?" Because they were used to seeing bands like Fleetwood Mac, who didn't make any attempt to dress up.

MIKE GARSON (MUSICIAN): I was surprised when I was approached to work with him back in 1972, because I didn't know who he was. He could have been anyone because I didn't know who I was going to audition for. I had just finished a series of jazz concerts, and the one just before the night he called was in Manhattan around Sixty-Ninth Street and Broadway. I was playing with a sax player who had played with Miles Davis, just one of the greatest jazz musicians in the world. I'd been practicing eight hours a day for the previous ten years to get where I was. I looked at my family that night and said, "This won't work." I was living in Brooklyn in an apartment that cost $150 a month, but when you're earning $5 a night that's difficult money to find. Tongue in cheek: "I think I need to go out with a famous rock star." Those were my exact words. But interestingly enough, they say that if you can think it in your mind you might be able to manifest it, and the next day I got a call from Woody Herman. But I also got a call from David Bowie. I think it was Tony Defries. He got a real kick out of me saying, "Who is he?" So that day I went from Brooklyn into New York City, walked into RCA Studios, and these guys were wild. Red hair, funny clothes. In the booth were David, Trevor, and Woody. At the piano, greeting me very warmly, was Mick Ronson. The sheet music was "Changes," which meant nothing to me, but having played a thousand weddings and bar mitzvahs in New York I could read anything. So I played it. And I swear within seven seconds Mick said, "You have the gig." Everyone else was smiling. They hired me for eight weeks and they couldn't get rid of me. In the first two years David must have fired five bands and I was the only one who stayed. He kept changing styles, but because I had a fairly broad spectrum, having played so much classic and jazz and pop and gospel, I could play with anyone. He was the best casting director there ever was, better even than Miles Davis. Everyone he ever chose had a purpose. He got everything out of me that I'd ever learned. He would open up to me late at night because I had nothing to do with his world. He loved that I knew nothing about rock. I still don't. He was just fascinated with my lifestyle as a jazz musician, and I was fascinated with his brilliance. In 1972 I would sneak out into the audience to watch the show because I only played on half the songs. I was mesmerized. My jazz buddies thought I'd sold out. I actually thought they were not furthering the music, as they were just regurgitating Charlie Parker. The next thing after the audition, I'm in Cleveland rehearsing. I'm sitting at the piano, and I look to my right and I see this stack of speakers, and said to David, "The PA is facing the wrong way." And he smiled and said that's your monitor system, that's just for you. I had to readjust. I got the idea that Tony Defries was trying to build something big here, what with the no-interview thing, and the way in which everything was controlled. Everyone had such style; everyone was exquisite. Platform shoes. The lot.

JOSETTE CARUSO: I went to see Bowie at Carnegie Hall in September 1972 and it was unlike anything I had ever seen before. The show itself was insane, as everybody just dressed up beyond belief to see him. It was a real party, and New York had never seen anything like it. Oh it was all feathers and glitter and the highest heels and the reddest lipstick, everyone dressed up as if they were going to an extravagant rock opera–type event. At the concerts I usually went to with the groupies, we always used to dress up, whether it was wanted or not. But with him it was different in that everybody was dressed up, it wasn't just the groupies. The guys were all wearing makeup, they had their hair all teased up. I had never seen anything like this before, not even at a New York Dolls concert. So I was backstage after the gig, and David's bodyguard invited me to go back to the Plaza Hotel. So I go, and was standing around in this amazing silver sequinned mirrored dress when David walks up to me and says, "I can see me in you . . ." Which was the most flirtatious thing to say. But that was very David. Very polite, very flirtatious. Anyway, we were talking and making out and then he whispered that Angie was starting to look at me and was probably going to throw a plate of cakes at me. So David invites me to the next gig, which was in Philadelphia. I didn't go to the show; I went straight up to his suite at the Benjamin Franklin Hotel and waited for him. When he turned up he really turned it on. He properly seduced me. I remember we talked a lot about *The Catcher in the Rye*, as he seemed to identify with the book's protagonist, Holden Caulfield. We talked about Nietzsche, Freud, Picasso, pedophiles, so many different things. He appeared to really want to talk. I was impressed at how well read he was. He spoke about the books that he was reading and asked for my opinions on them. He was also impressed that I knew somebody who worked with Picasso. He looked so thin, and so fit. His skin was so white and translucent, and there was this complete contrast with his makeup as he still had his rouge on. We sat drinking very good red wine and he started serenading me with "Walk on the Wild Side." He was obsessed with Jeff Beck, and kept asking me about him because he knew I knew him very well. He said that he would have loved to have Jeff Beck on guitar rather than Mick Ronson, and described how he bent notes with his fingers, and how he had this amazing way of playing. He was really concerned that people might think Mick was ripping off Jeff Beck. We spoke for over an hour, as though he was actually trying to woo me. And then all this conversation obviously led into bed, where he was wonderful. I mean, just terrific. He was very well endowed—I mean, absolutely—and really knew how to fuck. He didn't appear to be on drugs, but he really knew his way around a woman's body. He was an English gentleman, and it wasn't just about him. He took control in bed, and he was very considerate, and very focused on making love, on fucking me. He was very intense—lots of kissing, lots of hugging, lots of fucking. The sex was wonderful, I mean he was the ultimate rock and roll lover.

Something weird happened later that night in Philadelphia. Something really chilling. At one point there was a knock on the door, and, after a while, one of his bodyguards went to answer it, and then called for David. So David went off and came back a few minutes later white as a sheet. He was visibly shocked. Someone had just turned up and offered him a warm, dead body for David to have sex with. The town had never seen anything like David before, and he obviously looked like such a freak that some sick people thought he might be into necrophilia. That was the perception of Ziggy, and that's how crazy that tour was, that's how decadent it was. David was completely horrified. He said, "Who on Earth do they think I am? Why would they think I'd be interested in something like that? Why would I be interested in fucking a dead body?" It took him a while to calm down, but once it was over he just moved right past it. If he had been into that I would have left immediately.

NICK KENT: I was never one of his intimates because he was wary of me. I'm a very particular kind of journalist and I wouldn't have given him safe passage. It wouldn't have been in his interest to embrace me. Iggy Pop was ideal for me because his life is an open book, and those were the kind of people I was better at writing about. I respect people's privacy and I don't like getting into people's sex lives for instance, but I was interested in their drug life because it usually had such a dramatic effect on their music.

JOSETTE CARUSO: I was introduced to Trevor Bolder at the Carnegie Hall concert on Thursday, September 28, 1972, and all he could talk about was losing his job. He was concerned about being booted off the tour and asking if I thought that was going to happen and what might happen to him after there was no more Ziggy. I told him that he was a great bass player and I was sure he would find other work, but he was concerned about the expiration time coming up. It was sad in a way because he knew that it was coming to an end.

MICK ROCK: David was very charming, and very friendly. It was never difficult being around David. He was amazingly self-disciplined, and he was always very careful in how he approached things. He didn't micromanage, but he liked to surround himself with people he could trust, who knew what they were doing, even if they weren't sure they could do it themselves. That's sort of what happened to me, as he gave me the confidence to just go for it. Somehow I was at the right place at the right time with the right instincts. Through him I met Lou Reed, Iggy Pop, Mott the Hoople, and I shot all of them. All these people had been dropped, they were failures, and yet David was trying to resurrect them all. He waved his magic wand, and I got a little touch of that too. It was like a rising tide, as all the boats went up.

NICK KENT: Lou Reed and Iggy Pop were two of the most maniacal, ego-driven people you could ever hope to meet. They were control freaks. So the very fact that they would acquiesce to Bowie tinkering with their music was a major thing. They saw Bowie in conflicted ways. They could see that he was using them to a certain degree, but you have to remember that they were marginal characters. Nowadays people claim that the Velvet Underground and Lou Reed had amazing cachet back in the early '70s, but they were the cult of cults. It's true that if you went round to someone's house and they had a Velvet Underground record then you thought that this person was worth talking to. But maybe one thousand people in Great Britain owned Velvet Underground records. Maybe five hundred people owned Stooges records. Maybe. So he may have been using them, but it wasn't as though he was glomming on to the Rolling Stones or Rod Stewart.

He chose Iggy Pop and Lou Reed because he knew that the '60s were dead. He understood that since the Beatles had broken up, the decade was over. No one else understood that. He realized that his future lay in articulating a new sensibility that could be aligned to the '70s. The pendulum was swinging. It wasn't about big guys with beards playing mandolins anymore. The Band were over. Nineteen seventy was all about clean-shaven men singing about science fiction. It was a 180-degree swing. Bowie understood the pendulum swings because he'd been through all of this in the '60s. One month he was in a rhythm and blues group, the next month a mod group, then a freak-out group. He knew how things changed, and how you could become obsolete in the blink of an eye. He made it his business to stamp his personality on that decade. And he knew that Lou Reed and Iggy Pop were both ahead of their time. And those were the guys to be with. He wasn't going to sell more records, but his work was going to be informed by these guys, and he could align himself with them. It was cachet. He wanted to learn from them.

Two months after the Imperial College gig the Spiders from Mars played the Polytechnic of Central London, and the Stooges, Lou Reed, and Mott the Hoople were all in the audience. This is the first time that I met Ron Asheton from the Stooges. And all these guys are standing around thinking we're here because we have to be, because Bowie is now our patron. The Stooges were like a motorcycle gang, and they're thinking, What is this shit? They're not usually impressed. Bowie knows that they're all there and at the end of his set he turns to Iggy in the audience and he performs "Sex Machine" by James Brown, which is the only time he ever played it. And he did it for Iggy, as if to say, *OK, you think you're the James Brown of garage rock, and you might think I'm camp, and you might think I'm fake, but I can do James Brown as well as you can.* And he did. That was how Bowie got people's respect. And Iggy respected him. Bowie tried to copy Iggy, and he did some of it successfully, but not the stage diving, as you can't stand up on an audience if you're wearing platform boots. I remember Mick Jagger telling me that the only person he had respect for as a performer was Bowie. He knew he had to be on top of his game. . . .

HANIF KUREISHI: He was very disappointed in his relationship with Lou Reed because Lou Reed was such a cunt. However, I remember him talking to me about being at Lou Reed's apartment and finding all these Andy Warhol things. He had such huge admiration for Warhol because of Warhol's ability to change, to steal. And to not worry about being original. Bowie *loved* that.

LOU REED: The whole glam thing was great for me. This was something I had already seen with Warhol, but I hadn't *done* that thing. The '70s was a chance for me to get in on it, and since no one knew me from Adam particularly, I could say I was anything. I had learned that from Andy: Nobody knows. You could be anything.

HARVEY GOLDSMITH: Everyone said he was a nightmare but Lou Reed and I actually became quite good friends. I found him funny, and he was a really nice guy. Whenever I was in New York he would take me down to the Mineshaft, this members-only gay club on Washington Street in the Meatpacking District. He had a sailor for a boyfriend called Rachel. Whenever I went he would take me to one weird and wonderful place or another. I think he was trying to turn me at one point! Publicly Lou and David got on extremely well, fed off each other, although privately I think there was a lot of rivalry. I suppose he could think that he'd been conned by Bowie, and there are a lot of casualties that Bowie has left along the way. I don't think Lou had any resentment that I was aware of, but I can't be sure.

BOB HARRIS: Mick Ronson was fantastic in the studio, and while I know that David gets the production credit for Lou Reed's *Transformer*, the hub of it was Mick. But because Mick was a modest sort of guy, really, despite the showmanship, he never really wanted to push anybody else out of the spotlight and claim it for himself. You can't overestimate Mick's contribution to the sound, the look, and the image of Ziggy Stardust. Much later I spent some time with him in Woodstock while he was hanging out at Bearsville Studios, and I got the sense that he felt very sad and disillusioned by the fact that David had moved on from him so comprehensively. I just felt he had this sadness about him, I think he found it very difficult.

NICK KENT: *Raw Power* was a touchy point for both of them because Iggy was not happy with Bowie's mix of the record. But Iggy and James Williamson had not previously done themselves any favors, because their idea of recording was putting everything into the red as far as possible. That was the Stooges' idea of recording, just bleeding everything right into the red. It was the opposite to good sound. Bowie tried his best with them, but there was only so much he could do with their way of recording.

CHARLES SHAAR MURRAY: Did Bowie rip off Iggy Pop and Lou Reed? Maybe. He ripped people off, put them on the shelf, and then would maybe come back for them. Maybe not. Lou Reed did feel used. Lou's biggest ever hit was the *Transformer* album, and that was Bowie and Ronno. The only two songs that civilians are aware of are "Walk on the Wild Side" and "Perfect Day." Art rock geeks will be able to argue for hours over which of the two live versions of "Waiting for the Man" is definitive. But civilians just know those two songs. Lou wrote them but it was David and Mick who crafted the arrangements and made them popular. Just as I think David had something to prove on *Diamond Dogs*—that he didn't need Ronno—so was Lou miffed that people might think he needed David Bowie. David wanted to work with Lou again, but Lou was notoriously stingy about sharing credits, let alone royalties, and he didn't want to write with him again. He had an auteur complex, and Bowie didn't fit into that. Lou was also a prime member of the awkward squad. He could lose a charm competition with Van Morrison.

LOU REED (MUSICIAN): He's very clever. We found we had a lot of things in common. David learned how to be hip. Associating with me brought his name out to a lot more people too. He's very good in the studio. In a manner of speaking he produced an album for me.

NICK KENT: Lou Reed viewed Bowie as Bette Davis viewed Eve in *All About Eve.* Lou Reed even referred to Bowie as Eve on several occasions. But once they'd worked together he realized that Bowie had skills that he didn't have. The thing is, Bowie got Lou Reed hits, he got Iggy hits. Up until Bowie they hadn't had any hits.

RON ASHETON (MUSICIAN): One day in 1972 I got a call from Iggy, and it was perfect Iggy, because he said, "Well, we auditioned a hundred bass players and drummers and we can't find anybody good, so do you guys wanna come over to London and play on the new album?" My first thought was, *Yeah, thanks a lot, asshole.* The first time I met David Bowie was the first day I arrived in London to work on the *Raw Power* album. Bowie was drunk, and he brought two Jamaican girls with identical, carrot-top David Bowie hairdos with him. They went down the basement to the kitchen, or the dining-room area, and drank wine and stuff, and I didn't really participate a bunch with them. Then Bowie got kinda disorientated in the house. I showed him the front door, and he grabbed my ass and kissed me. I went to coldcock him, but then I thought, Huh? Whoa, it's David Bowie! So I didn't do it, but then he didn't really want to talk to us anymore.

Scott Asheton (the musician and Ron's younger brother) says that the first time he met Bowie was in Seymour Walk in South Kensington, arriving with two women, one black, one white. Scott thought that Bowie was freaked out by the Ashetons' appearance. "We were all sitting around smoking hash, drinking some wine and just relaxing. And Bowie, he came in like a wild animal in a cage, just totally flipping out! Really, really nervous—and later we found out that he was afraid of us, ha-ha-ha!"

RON ASHETON: When Bowie was rehearsing for his show at the Rainbow, we went to the rehearsal. We were watching these guys get ready for their first, big Spiders from Mars show. So we were at the show and we'd gotten prime seats and he was playing, and the place was packed, and my brother and me were going, "Ah, we already seen this shit, let's go get a beer!" We went to the bar, and there was Lou Reed. He was drunk and on pills, so he gave us each a Mandrax [Quaalude]. The next day I got a phone call to come down to the MainMan office. Bowie's manager Tony chewed me out for getting up in the middle of David's show and walking out. He was furious. I was like, "Fuck you, man. I mean, every seat was full, and I just didn't wanna be there!" But when we went over to London to work with Bowie, it was a good situation. It was all top-notch stuff. We had a mews house with four stories and a driver. MainMan, at that time, was just top notch. I must say, Bowie helped Iggy every step of the way. I don't know how many fucking times Bowie got him deals. If it wasn't for Bowie, Iggy would be dead. The only reason Iggy is playing music today is because of Bowie. I mean, Bowie admired Iggy—and in a way, he wanted to be like him.

NICHOLAS COLERIDGE: One afternoon, my school friend the satirist Craig Brown announced he had two tickets to see Bowie at the Rainbow, Finsbury Park, during the Christmas holidays, and would I like to go? We took the train up from Sussex and at some point must have changed into Bowie gear. (Where? The train loo, presumably.) Is it really conceivable I wore a striped matelot T-shirt under a denim shirt with silver nylon lamé sleeves? Half the audience had enviable Ziggy haircuts. Sunday, December 24, 1972: my first Bowie concert, seats in the third row of the dress circle, and the man did not disappoint. All that remains is a memory of fuzzy orange light and loudness, a cover version of the Stones' "Let's

Spend the Night Together," "Rock 'n' Roll Suicide" as the finale, "*Give me your hands . . . 'cause yer won-der-ful*," please God, let this concert never end. During the long cab ride home, I sensed that Craig had not bought into the universal truth behind Bowie's towering genius and lyrics to the same degree I had. He had reservations, even dared mock. Well, some people exist on a less sensitive plane and just can't get it.

BOB HARRIS: And then suddenly it was over. I lost contact with Marc Bolan and David around the same time. I had known Marc for about five or six years, since 1967, and when the *Born to Boogie* film with Ringo Starr came out, we lost touch. He was off. I compered the 1972 UK T. Rex tour, but then he's off to America, and I just don't see him anymore. And it was exactly the same with David. I was the compere on the early gigs of the *Ziggy Stardust* tour, but because I was now on the radio, there was a limit to how much free time I had, and then: Boom!—I didn't see David anymore either. At the end of 1972 he just disappeared on me completely. John Peel had a similar experience with David, and a similar one with Marc Bolan, although that was as a direct result of John giving Marc a stinging review. He had a column in *Disc & Music Echo*, and he used it to review the T. Rex single "Get It On." John had not liked the curve that Marc had taken from T. Rex into electric pop; in fact, he really disapproved of it. And he wrote this terrible review, saying the only redeeming factor of the single was on the fade when Marc says, "Well, meanwhile, I am still thinking," which was a throwback to Chuck Berry. Well, Marc read this, and he was mortified, and vowed never to speak to John again. Whereas with Bowie, even though he had been through various reincarnations and tried stylistic guises to be famous, when he eventually became famous, there wasn't a sense that he was selling out, it just seemed to be another sort of stage persona. With David you really got the sense that new chapters arrived all the time, as people came and went all the time. They were steps along the way.

GEOFF MACCORMACK: I went on tour with him for three years and it was a three-year party. I got a call from him while I was at work asking me if I wanted to go on tour with him as a backing singer, so I said yes! I did three tours and six albums with him. I wasn't sure I was entitled to be there, but we had fun. And of course in the early days he wouldn't fly, so we traveled everywhere by boat. We boarded the SS *Canberra* on January 24, 1973, and had a great time. He obviously preferred to travel with me, the lighthearted silly friend. There were big things happening; he needed to relax. We developed these personas for the boat, and it got quite silly. I think that was his downtime, that was his time to recharge. We'd kind of playact. He became Oscar at that point, which was my pet name for him. He was Oscar because he had this definite Oscar Wilde thing about him, you know. At dinner I would say, "Oscar . . . more vegetables?" And he would say, "I find vegetables so very vulgar." During the day we'd talking about afternoon tea being a big event. Coming back we came by train, the Trans-Siberian Railway, and traveled through Russia, went via the Berlin Wall. All those experiences contributed to *Diamond Dogs*, I'm sure.

COCO SCHWAB (BOWIE'S ASSISTANT): I first met David at a welcome-home party at Haddon Hall in 1973. He and Geoffrey [MacCormack] had just arrived back from Japan on the *Trans-Siberian Express*. My first impression was how tired and skinny he seemed. The famous red hair was a bit crumpled, but his essence, the warmth and kind gentleness, was there (through that worldly weariness) and he hugged Andrea [the Bowie fan club assistant] and me and made us feel welcome. Andrea and I had only been working at MainMan for several months and had not actually met him yet.

I got started working with David by answering an ad in *The Evening Standard* in London asking for "Girl Friday needed for busy office." I had run my finger down the page and stopped there in totally arbitrary fashion. I needed a job to earn expense money for a trip my photographer friend and I were planning to take. We had a magazine interested in us to do a story of two girls on a Greyhound bus tour of America, kind of Jack Kerouac *On the Road*–style, but two girls as opposed to two guys. They were only willing to pay a certain amount up front and we thought to save a bit more we'd get short-term jobs.

When I was due to leave MainMan six months later, David called and asked me why I was leaving. I explained about this Greyhound bus tour of America thing. He paused for a minute and said, "How about a limousine tour of America?" I paused for about a nanosecond and said something like, "Uh, OK." Needless to say, I don't think my photographer friend ever truly forgave me.

SIMON NAPIER-BELL: All artists are deadly rivals even when they're pretending not to be. Bowie and Bolan were no different. And of course, when Bowie happened in the USA, Marc was insanely jealous. Both of them had the measure of the press. They knew how to manipulate journalists and create stories out of nothing—keep them endlessly in the public eye. When I first saw Bowie emerge in public as a mime artist I would have been most surprised then to have known how successful he would become later. But once Ziggy Stardust was out and happening, there seemed no reason why Bowie wouldn't go on and create more and even better things in the future.

Kansai Yamamoto said he actually had no idea who David Bowie was until he saw him wearing his clothes onstage at Radio City Music Hall in New York in February 1973. Yasuko Hayashi, his stylist, was doing work for Bowie and had given him some of his clothes. This was the first time Yamamoto had ever met an artist who was wearing his designs. "Before then, I didn't know how immensely talented he was," he says. "At the time, David Bowie was all about transcending gender. I didn't know anything about concepts like that, so I remember thinking: Whoa, when I saw him wearing clothes I had designed for women. The clothes were influenced by hikinuki, *the method of changing costumes quickly in Kabuki. The audience in New York saw the costumes transform a few times during the show. I realized I had done something really cool when everyone in the audience got on their feet and clapped."*

IAIN R. WEBB: While flicking through glossy fashion magazines, Bowie discovered Japanese designer Kansai Yamamoto, who unveiled his designs in London in 1971 in a show that featured several of the outfits later worn by the singer. It also included some influential theatrics, such as the use of *kuroko*, traditional kabuki stagehands, for a series of quick-change outfits. Not only did Bowie commission Yamamoto to design the costumes for his *Aladdin Sane* tour (these included a unitard, a satin cape printed with Japanese script, and a skimpy all-in-one decorated with frolicking woodland creatures), he also lifted the spiky hairdo that the models sported, along with their red-and-black wedge boots. Apparently, Bowie balked at shelling out the equally high-rise designer price tag and had PVC copies made. Yamamoto also fashioned glittering ensembles for the singer that were part samurai, part sci-fi hero.

LEEE BLACK CHILDERS: I went back to America and got a job for *Sixteen* magazine, working for the glorious, brilliant Gloria Stavers, who taught Jim Morrison to shove his cock down the side of his leather pants so it looked big and bulging. She taught him that trick, so she was a star maker. And then the call came from David Bowie. He had become this huge sensation, and wanted us to work for him. Because the last time we went to see him it was at this little club and there were only, like, ten people there. He'd become a huge sensation and he was going to do an American tour, but he didn't want business-type people working for him, more arty-type people.

Typical of us we just said yes, OK, even though we didn't know anything about the music business. So Tony Zanetta, the guy who had played Andy Warhol, became the president of the company, I was vice president, and Cherry was secretary. So over he came to do the tour. Now of course we had read that interview in which he says he's bisexual. That had preceded him of course. Now, to most of America bisexual just means gay. It's queer. So there was a lot of backlash against that and everything. They launched a protest against him performing. And Cherry Vanilla had gotten on the radio the week before to do pre-publicity, and not only said that David was gay, but she also said that he was a Communist, somehow. So suddenly it was like this gay Communist is coming to the South to perform to their children! So the Ku Klux Klan turned out in a huge number. I was the road manager for the tour, and when we get to a town that no one had been to before, David would say, "Well, Leee, get out your guide—where are we going?" And you would look at the list of gay bars and go to a gay bar, because even though it wasn't necessarily for any gay purpose, a gay bar is just somewhere you can be more comfortable, if you're acting like David did then, as Ziggy Stardust—so that's how we did the whole tour. We never had any trouble except once in Seattle, Washington. We looked up a bar in the gay guide and went to it, and it was some sort of vocal power dance of some kind, and everyone in the whole bar was in drag. Everyone was stoned. You know, there were nuns, drag nuns. It was a totally wild night. The next morning I wake up with the phone ringing, and it's Tony Zanetta saying, Is David with you? I said no; someone was, but it wasn't David! He said, We can't find David, he's disappeared. So we spent four hours in total panic because we had to get on a plane that afternoon to fly to Arizona for the next gig. No David.

Suddenly the phone rang and it was David. And we said, David, where are you? And he said, I don't know! I don't know where I am and there are all these people. Everyone was so crazy and now I'm in the middle of a house and when I look out of the window all I see is trees—I think I'm in the middle of a forest somewhere. So I went and got a bellboy from the hotel and asked him if he knew anything about the area, the geography. And he was a groupie, so he got on the phone with David for about ten minutes, and managed to work out where he was. So we were able to go and get him. But that was the most of any trouble we'd ever had.

I remember an episode about gayness in Memphis, Tennessee, with the promoter who was promoting David's show. And he had a side line in running a male brothel. Not really a brothel but like a call-boy service. And I went down to make sure the hall was all right promotionally, ahead of time. And of course the first question he asked me was, "Is David really gay?" I found something like that really quite impertinent. David really sings, and he really writes his own songs, but whether or not he sucks cocks is really none of the promoter's business. So I said, "Really, this is not what we're here for." And it took me a really long time for me to convince him that I was serious. Because if he was gay, and I was gay, and anyone else in the entourage was gay, then he'd supply us for our whole stay at Memphis with gorgeous escorts, as all part of the service. And of course once I found out that that was what he was on about, then naturally I was totally thrilled. This guy was so beautiful. And then we were met, with David, at the station. We were met by the Memphis police, and were escorted through town with a motorcycle escort, stopping all traffic as we went through in a limousine. And the police walked right through into the hotel, where the big hospitality suite had been, and all these gorgeous rent boys were just standing there waiting for us, and all the police were with us too, and it was all just like, "Cool!" No one had any problems at all with anything, it was really weird. It was like something out of an old polyamory-type novel.

NICK KENT: I met Bowie in 1973 in Detroit. I was with BP Fallon, who was Marc Bolan's publicist at the time, who was a crazy guy. He didn't know Bowie but he knew he was in town playing a gig, so he called up the hotel and tried to arrange a meeting. We went down to the hotel, and talked to Bowie's bodyguard, and we were told to come back after the gig. So we went to the gig, which was extraordinary, and if you think the Ziggy shows in Britain were decadent, you should have been on the US tour. They were wild. In Detroit and Michigan, which were unhinged rock cities, a lot of people were taking drugs at gigs. Those gigs were like Fellini's *Satyricon*. If you went into the toilets people were openly having sex, everyone was taking Quaaludes or cocaine; it was mad, completely mad. People would go to David Bowie concerts in London and they'd turn up as peacocks, it was very much a fashion show, as though you were in Paris. In America it was like, How fucked up can we get? That was Bowie's audience, as somehow it was more radical to be sexually ambiguous in America.

So we went back to the hotel after the gig, and Bowie was very composed, wearing these pristine Oxford bags and a mauve shirt, and he looked incredibly androgynous. He was in full makeup. This was the *Aladdin Sane* tour, although the record hadn't been released yet. He had an acetate of the album, and he played us the first side, saying he couldn't play us the second side in case Tony Defries found out. What really struck me was how he looked at me. This was the first time we had had eye-to-eye contact, and I remember him looking at me and checking me out. He was like a robot—he was working out exactly what I was worth to him. And he was working out exactly what persona he was going to show to me: *I'm going to humor you, but I have to watch out for you, (a) because you're a journalist, and (b) because you're a bit of a loose cannon because you're dressed up like Siegfried and Roy*. You could see him computing all this. He was very friendly, courteous, but he wasn't going to let anything slip. I asked him for an interview and he said we'd do it in Los Angeles at the end of the tour, although I could tell that he was thinking he was going to stick with Charlie Murray, as he was his outlet at the *NME*. We went back the second night and the atmosphere was very different because he'd decided to have a party, and as the word had got out, the suite was full of a whole bunch of Detroit street life. There were a lot of really messed up people in that room, and Bowie was kind of alarmed. He couldn't escape. He wasn't on drugs and he looked completely straight. There were a couple of girls who tried rolling a joint and they were kicked out. He was very paranoid about anything to do with drugs, as he didn't want to get busted. He also didn't like anything to do with marijuana, and he was alarmed by people's behavior at this party. It was in his personal suite and he couldn't leave, which was a mistake. He looked out of control.

WENDY LEIGH: David used sex right from the very beginning to get what he wanted. He was obviously genetically blessed, and didn't mind who knew it. He used it shamelessly. David did in a way what Freud did: he paved the way for people who perhaps had frustrating sex lives, who were not heterosexual, who didn't just want a life spent in the missionary position, who perhaps felt alone, who maybe felt embarrassed about wanting more out of their sex lives. He freed people from the prison of their sexual desires, anyone who wasn't mainstream. He said it's all right to dress up as a woman, he said it's all right to be gay, bisexual, trisexual, it's all all right.

MICHAEL KAPLAN (JOURNALIST): In the early '70s, the Sunset Strip was a magnet for rock stars: Bowie, Zeppelin, Iggy Pop, Mott the Hoople, the Who. They all hung out in the VIP rooms of louche L.A. nightclubs like E Club, the Rainbow, and Rodney Bingenheimer's English Disco. And with them, of course, came groupies. Scantily clad fourteen- and fifteen-year-olds like Sable Starr and Lynn "Queenie" Koenigsaecker sipped cherry cola, dropped pills, and evolved into pubescent dream girls for the platform-shoed rockers who could get anything and anyone they desired.

TONY ZANETTA: Rodney got all these kids worked up about David so much that when he arrived he arrived a star because he had all these new fans. Those little girls were charming; they were twelve, thirteen, fourteen fifteen years old, those groupies. But they were lovely. So adorable. Lori Lightning and Sable Starr were the most documented ones.

LORI MATTIX (AKA LORI LIGHTNING; FORMER GROUPIE): What I remember most about the E Club was Bowie. I met him when he was doing the Spiders from Mars Tour. I had not yet turned fifteen and he wanted to take me to his hotel room. I was still a virgin and terrified. He had hair the color of carrots, no eyebrows, and the whitest skin imaginable. I grabbed on to [DJ and club co-owner] Rodney Bingenheimer and said I was with him. So we all just hung out and talked. I had probably kissed boys by that point, but I wasn't ready for David Bowie.

Next time Bowie was in town, though, maybe five months later, I got a call at home from his bodyguard, a huge black guy named Stuey. He told me that David wanted to take me to dinner. Obviously, I had no homework that night. Fuck homework. I wasn't spending a lot of time at school anyway. I said that I would like to go but that I wanted to bring my friend Sable. She was dying to fuck Bowie. I figured that she would sleep with him while I got to hang out and have fun. At the time, Sable and her sister Coral were up in Laurel Canyon. People there were so high all the time—Quaaludes, heroin, whatever . . .

We got to the Beverly Hilton and all went up to Bowie's enormous suite. I found myself more and more fascinated by him. He was beautiful and clever and poised. I was incredibly turned on. Bowie excused himself and left us in this big living room with white shag carpeting and floor-to-ceiling windows. Stuey brought out Champagne and hash. We were getting stoned when, all of a sudden, the bedroom door opens and there is Bowie in this fucking beautiful red and orange and yellow kimono.

He focused his famously two-colored eyes on me and said, "Lori, darling, can you come with me?" Sable looked like she wanted to murder me. He walked me through his bedroom and into the bathroom, where he dropped his kimono. He got into the tub, already filled with water, and asked me to wash him. Of course I did. Then he escorted me into the bedroom, gently took off my clothes, and de-virginized me.

Two hours later, I went to check on Sable. She was all fucked up in the living room, walking around, fogging up windows and writing, "I want to fuck David." I told him what she was doing and that I felt so bad. Bowie said, "Well, darling, bring her in." That night I lost my virginity and had my first threesome. The next morning, there was banging on the door and it was fucking [Bowie's wife] Angie. I was terrified of her. David said not to worry about it. They were already at the point where they had separate rooms.

TONY ZANETTA: No one talked about the age of the girls at the time, and it wasn't an issue at all. You can't judge 1972 by 2017 standards. There was a magazine called *Star* that was completely devoted to these girls, prepubescent groupies. It was as common as mud and nobody batted an eye.

LORI MATTIX: You need to understand that I didn't think of myself as underage. I was a model. That time of my life was so much fun. It was a period in which everything seemed possible.

HANIF KUREISHI: He loved black women. He really had a thing about black women.

AVA CHERRY (SINGER): It was 1973, and I was living in New York working as a model. And my manager at the time handed me this album, *Ziggy Stardust.* And I looked at it and thought, he's cute, but he had green hair. And I go, "Who's this?" When I took the album home I loved it. He could sing as well as being cute. I was friends with Stevie Wonder, and he was doing a show at Carnegie Hall. He says to me, "Ava, I know you know all the places around, where can we have the after party after Carnegie Hall?" So I suggested Genesis, where I was working as a waitress, which was an upscale disco owned by Hiroaki Aoki, who launched Benihana. So Stevie has his after-party there, with Lou Reed, Bill Cosby, Aretha Franklin, and everyone, and it was *amazing.* My manager comes up and goes: "You know that guy whose record I gave you, David Bowie? I invited him to the party." Apparently he had just played Radio City. I'm singing to myself, and David comes over to me, introduces himself to me and says, "Oh, are you a singer?" His hair was red and mine was blond, and he says, "Wow, I really love your look!" So we sit and talk, and he mentions his new album, *Aladdin Sane*, and this tour he's got coming up in Japan. He asks if I want to go to Japan with him, as a singer in the band, and tells me he'll meet me at RCA the next day and introduce me to his manager. So the next day I meet Tony Defries, I audition for Mick, Trevor, and Woody, and I'm given all his records and an itinerary for the tour—and then David takes me to dinner, at the Gramercy Park Hotel, where he was staying. We had a wonderful dinner and then went to see Charlie Mingus. I really didn't love Charlie Mingus but he did, so we went, and he was really nice and I felt as though he was a perfect gentleman. David was a really smart man and I was very taken with him. I was really falling for him. He obviously felt the same so he invited me back to the Gramercy Park Hotel, where we had some drinks, listened to *Aladdin Sane* and then one thing led to another. It was so romantic, and felt like magic to me. I'd never met anyone like him before, and had never slept with a foreigner. But then next morning the doorbell rings and it was Angie. She was very bombastic, like "Hello, darling!" I was a kid, feeling that I was being blown into a little bit of a riot, but I didn't know how much of a riot. I said, "Who is this?" And she said, "Oh, I'm David's wife! I'm Angie!" So I tried very hard to keep my facial expressions from going, *Huh?* Because I had really fallen for this guy. Then she goes just as quickly as she arrived—"Goodbye, see you!" Just like it was nothing. David sees the look on my face and then tells me they have an open marriage. When I ask what that means he says she's free to sleep with whoever she wants to and so am I. I said, "That's kind of messy though, huh?" And he said, "No it works out quite well because most of the time she's on the other side of the world in France and I'm over here and when I'm over there she's over here." He told me to just stop worrying. I had all these questions as I'd completely fallen in love with him and I just wanted it to be the way he said that it was going to be. So I thought if his wife is telling me that they have an open marriage and he's telling me that it's OK then maybe it is. I really wasn't trying to hurt anybody. They were so busy trying to convince me that everything was cool. So that's how I ended up dealing with it.

He said we were going to go on tour together, and that we were going to have a great time, and he was going to send me the tickets. So I said I was going to go to Chicago to say goodbye to my parents and that he could send the tickets there. I quit my job, my apartment, and when I got to Chicago I got a telegram that says, "Dear Ava, so sorry but the tour's been cancelled." Something to do with him being sick. I wanted to die. I was like, "Huh?" So anyway, I'd already met this older guy, who had invited me to spend the summer with him in Monaco. I didn't really like him, but now I had nothing to do and nowhere to live, so I said yes. I was delusional. I thought to myself I'm going to go to Europe and find this David Bowie and tell him what I think of him. I mean, I didn't want to leave it like this. So I fly into Monaco and it is the most incredible landscape. I'd never been to Europe before and I felt like Cinderella. He picks me up and takes me to his beautiful apartment. I still didn't want to be with him and I was kind of just grinning and bearing it, but OK, I was in Europe and that was my main goal. I went out to parties, and met people like Omar Sharif, but every day I'd been playing *Ziggy Stardust* at the house. He'd come into my room and I'd be playing this record and he'd go, "Why are you playing this guy's record over and over?" I told him I wanted to go and find David, and then he realized that I didn't want to be with him. So he gave me some money, and I went to Paris. I spent eight months there, working as a model, going back and forth between Spain and England and wherever. And I was doing pretty well. But I was still looking for David Bowie.

After eight months, I'm in this bar and I hear someone say his name. So my ears prick up. I go running down to the end; "*Excusez-moi, savez-vous David Bowie?*" And this guy says he's in Castel, the famous club, right now. So I run over. I looked nice, but I wasn't dressed for Castel. Anyway, I run down the stairs and bump into his bodyguard, Stuey. A Cockney lad. He sees me and says, "Ava, Ava what are you doing here? The guvner's going to be shocked when he sees you!" And I was like, "Yeah, I bet he is." So he takes my hand and takes me over to him. He was sitting with this woman who was dripping in diamonds and pearls and all that, but he looks at me, says, "Let's go" and off we go. Anyway, we make up, he says he's going to get me a job in London, and then nothing happens. So I find out he's recording at the Château d'Hérouville and I take a train to find him. And then we were together for the next four years.

MICK ROCK: The 1973 American tour blew him up. Everything he did blew him up just a little bit more.

TONY ZANETTA: The US tour was a circus, but there was never any money. The advances were not big, and the gigs weren't generating money. Tony Defries just made it work. He was insistent that David wouldn't open for anybody; he had to headline. He was going to tour in the US as a star. Limos, first-class hotels, no interviews. But there was no money. Everything was charged to RCA. I literally had a bag full of petty cash. If you wanted cigarettes you came to me and I'd give you some money. It was a random tour anyway because none of it was planned, and further complicated because David wouldn't fly, so we had to work out how to get from point A to point B. In a week you would normally play six or seven gigs to make the money, but because David wouldn't fly we would do three, two, sometimes only one gig a week. We went from Arizona to Florida for one gig. Madness. RCA had an in-house travel bureau, so everything was booked through them. Tony was meant to pay them but of course he never did. From September to December we spent $400,000, and we brought in about $100,000. Defries wasn't squirreling money away, he was using whatever money he could find in order to move this machine.

CHRIS O'LEARY (BLOGGER): Bowie was scared of airplanes, so he took a ship, the RHMS *Ellinis*, home to Britain in mid-December 1972. During the trip he read Evelyn Waugh's *Vile Bodies* and found, he thought, similarities between the novel (completed months before the 1929 crash, and whose narrative ends in a near-future with World War Two already under way) and his own times. He soon got a song out of it.

At a London press conference in the summer of 1972, just as *Ziggy Stardust* broke, Bowie seemed unnerved by his success, though he had been trying to be a pop star for nearly a decade. Something disturbed him about his rise, he said, along with Lou Reed's new prominence ("Walk on the Wild Side" would hit the top ten) and the glam boom. Once there had been well-groomed boys in matching suits on *Top of the Pops*. Now there was Roxy Music, who looked like extraterrestrials in a witness relocation program, or Slade and Roy Wood, hill trolls in Halloween costumes, or the Sweet, a bubblegum group who leered at their audience and seemed to be sharing a private joke. It was a sign that modern civilization had reached the point of absurdity—its entertainments had become bizarre and sordid, even menacing.

In Waugh's novel, ridiculous young people dress up in costumes, sleep with each other, have treasure hunts on city streets at midnight, drink and drug themselves to oblivion; it ends on a battlefield. "Aladdin Sane" was Bowie's parallel sequel: a premature epitaph for his own lost generation. Though this time the party would end with a nuclear holocaust (hence the song's "(1913–1938–197?)" subhead—Bowie seemed to really think that the world would end before 1980).

There's a sadness and frailty to "Aladdin Sane," set in B minor, with its lyric a meager collection of fragmented images—glissando strings, bouquets of faded roses. It's as though Bowie realized the decadence of Waugh's era had a panache his own time lacked. Bowie had just come off a months-long rock tour of America in 1972, and had endured/enjoyed the debauchery, the loud fashions, the noise, the bad food. It was a fly-blown existence and Bowie wanted a nobler victim: in "Aladdin Sane" he invented a more glittering world to snuff out.

DAVID BOWIE: *Aladdin Sane* was a very schizoid record, a very paranoid record made during a period when I really wasn't myself. Honestly I wasn't really sure who I was, as the whole Ziggy Stardust phenomenon was getting out of control. I was becoming ludicrously successful, but I was starting to be surrounded by very strange people, the kind that attach themselves to you when you become famous. There were some very mixed-up people on that tour, including myself, and I didn't like myself very much at the time. In all honesty I had pretty much exhausted everything I wanted to do with strict rock and roll, as it had all come to a head with *Ziggy Stardust*. *Aladdin Sane* was really just Ziggy in America.

MIKE GARSON: By the time we started recording *Aladdin Sane* I couldn't do any wrong, but I learned a lot. I wanted to learn everything about the rock and roll world. Ken Scott was fabulous and really knew his stuff.

KEN SCOTT: All our ears and minds had changed, and we were looking for different things. The drum sound was much more live than it had been before. With David's arrangements—he threw a lot more in than he did in *Ziggy*. And then there was the addition of Mike Garson. There had been acoustic piano before, which Ronno or Bowie had done, but they're not the greatest keyboard players in the world, and Mike made a big difference. On *Ziggy* it was all very sparse—there had been two bits of synth, that was it. Now on *Aladdin Sane* there were a lot more keyboards, Mellotrons, a Moog synthesizer, as well as acoustic piano.

MIKE GARSON: On the solo on "Aladdin Sane" he was encouraging me to go back to playing more free-form jazz. There were these two chords that were quite simple, and because they were so simple I thought they called for some bluesy playing. So I played a blues solo first. And he said, "No." I played a Latin solo. He said, "No." He wanted something avant-garde. So I did it in one take. It was he who pulled it out of me, because it wasn't my first choice. Now, once he said that, it was a take one, but it wasn't my choice to go there, so I give him big kudos for that. And everybody always wants to talk about that one track; they all want to talk about that one solo. He was the best producer I ever worked with, because he gave me so much. In truth the notes found me as much as I found them, and the solo seemed to come out of nowhere, although I am asked to replicate it all the time. I've played on maybe three thousand albums, every fucking day there's at least five emails connected with "Aladdin Sane" from someone somewhere in the world, that specific track, and I don't understand. I'm not resentful, I'm just baffled, because even though I've done all this other stuff, I'll probably go down in history known only for this, and if that's the way it is, that's the way it is.

BRIAN DUFFY (PHOTOGRAPHER): Tony [Defries] realized that in order to get the record company really going, you had to get them up to their neck in debt, which was of course a masterstroke. He wanted to make the most expensive cover he possibly could get a record company to pay for, because he realized that if it cost £5,000, the record company were going to pay attention. Tony said, "Can you make it expensive?" No problem. One: dye transfer, a genius method of being able to spend the most amount of money to get a reproduction from a color transparency onto a piece of paper. Two: get the plate made in Switzerland—the most expensive place in the world to get plates made. Then to employ me to design it and create it—even better, more wasteful. Then we went to Conways, who were the most expensive typographical house—more money.

At the cover shoot, Duffy decided to photograph Bowie naked. He had also been making various doodles of a lightning bolt, inspired by the ones he'd seen at a Ziggy Stardust concert (which Bowie had borrowed from the Elvis Presley "Taking Care of Business" lightning flash). However, it was Bowie himself who came up with the idea of the lightning flash as a cover motif, and then the makeup artist Pierre Laroche (the "Picasso of Pan Stik") suggested putting it across his face. But when Duffy saw it he said, "No, not fucking like that, like this," and drew a much bigger flash right across Bowie's face. Then he said to Pierre, "Now, fill that in." Which he did. The red flash is so shiny, so glacé, because it was actually filled in with lipstick.

NICHOLAS COLERIDGE: My early hero worship took many avenues, and bordered on stalking. Reading that he'd studied mime with Lindsay Kemp, I took mime classes with Kemp myself in a church hall in Battersea, vainly hoping Bowie might drop by for a refresher lesson. One wet evening, I located that sacred site, 23 Heddon Street in London's Soho, where the Brian Ward portrait was snapped for the *Ziggy Stardust* album sleeve, with the famous red telephone kiosk. There wasn't a lot to see, frankly, but it made a connection. Having started a club with Craig Brown to invite celebrities down to lecture at school, an early guest after Elton John and Brian Eno was Angie Bowie, who ate spears of asparagus in an excitingly suggestive way over dinner, and satisfied our craving for Bowie info at one degree of separation. (She had arrived with Bowie's personal photographer, Leee Black Childers—yes, three *e*'s, this was the '70s—and we quizzed them both forensically: "Where do you and David live?"—Oakley Street, Chelsea—"Do you share makeup tips?"—Sure we do.)

MARY FINNIGAN: In 1973 there was a Ziggy performance at Earls Court, and David had given us very good seats. Afterwards they threw a party, and I took Caroline, my daughter. After the party, David came up to me, wearing his Ziggy outfit, he put his arm round my shoulders and walked me to the door, and he said, "Mary Finnigan you're a wonderful woman and I will never forget you," and I never saw him again.

OLIVER JAMES: It must have been strange for him, not knowing if he was going to die at a young age, but the reason he moved on from people so often was probably because of his very early experiences of being let down by Peggy, which I think would have been very likely. Peggy would have been quite self-orientated in caring for him as a baby and would have shut him out. Also, his narcissism came from his father's favoritism of him. He was really loved by his father, and continually celebrated. He thought he was entitled, and often talked about being a leader, having grandiose plans for people. He sings about it too, discussing his feelings about becoming more important than anyone else—and so on a practical level, he worked out which people could be useful to him, and which he could afford to lose. "Thank you very much and goodbye." After all those years faffing about with different groups, he learnt how to be pretty ruthless. He was a control freak, and because of how he was treated by his mother when he was small, he was needy, he got bored quickly, and needed new experiences every day.

NICK KENT: I lambasted him for the Earls Court gig, which he never forgave me for. In one of his last interviews before his forced retirement, he was asked if there was any criticism which still stung and he mentioned the Earls Court review. Earls Court held fourteen thousand people and was a huge place. It was a mistake by Tony Defries because he was greedy, and the place wasn't soundproofed. The sound went everywhere. Big halls often didn't carry music, and if you were Pink Floyd, Led Zeppelin, or David Bowie you needed to play big halls. Earls Court was a disaster. I genuinely regret some of the things I wrote about him in that piece, particularly about the theatricality, which I initially didn't like. Talking about it now it just sounds ridiculous, but there were issues of authenticity with Bowie. To the rock critic of the time, Iggy Pop was authentic and Bowie was a mime artist. Lester Bangs didn't like the theatricality either. But then it was over almost as soon as it had started, when Ziggy went to Hammersmith.

MIKE GARSON: It was terrible when the band found out how much money I was making. I was just on the plane one evening, and Woody asked me how much I was making a week on the tour. I said, "I was embarrassed to tell you, because I know you guys are making three times more." So I said I was making $800 a week and his face turned white. He said they were making $80. So on the next tour I got reduced to $500, and they went up to $500, but it was a horrible moment. But it soon didn't matter.

NICHOLAS COLERIDGE: It didn't occur to us devoted fans that the Ziggy era would not continue forever. So it came as a devastating shock when, on July 3, 1973, a year almost to the day when he'd first appeared in my life on the tuck-shop TV, he announced at a Hammersmith Odeon gig that, "Not only is this the last show of the tour, but it's the last show that we'll ever do. Thank you." "Tears as Bowie Bows Out," reported the *London Evening Standard*, which was where I first spotted the shattering news. A period of mourning ensued. But gradually it emerged that it was not David Bowie who would never perform again, but only his alter ego, Ziggy.

DENIS O'REGAN (PHOTOGRAPHER): A friend asked me to go with him to see the Ziggy Stardust show at Hammersmith Odeon, and I went along expecting to see just a rock star, and I had never seen anything like it—it was rock music, theatre, mime, it was just way beyond anything I had ever expected to see at a rock concert. So I borrowed a camera, although I couldn't really use it, and all I really got when I did use it was shots of knickers being waved. But the real disappointment was the next day when I saw the headlines and it said David Bowie had retired. I didn't believe it at the time, but it really affected me. When I eventually got to know David, and started shooting him regularly, he got really specific about what I did and didn't photograph. One day, David said, disarmingly, "So what are you doing with all the pictures you don't show me?" So I said, I put them in my bin. He said, "In your room?" And I said, "In the waste-paper bin." And he didn't say, "Get out of my sight," but it was something like that. He was really, really angry, because he said the cleaner could pick up those pictures and get them all published. He took complete ownership of his image, and hated seeing things that he hadn't sanctioned. He could really lose his rag.

CHARLES SHAAR MURRAY: At the *NME* we weren't kingmakers, but for a brief period I was a conduit. I started to suspect this when people started to get a bit snarky, saying that I was [Bowie's] "representative on Earth."

One thing I became aware of quite quickly was that a lot of journalists he'd dealt with in earlier stages of his career, some of whom had actually been very supportive of him, were suddenly not flavor of the month and he wouldn't talk to them anymore. With each phase he wanted to deal with a new bunch of writers who wouldn't necessarily have firsthand recollection of the last round. He didn't want people writing, "Oh I knew him when he was a hippie with ratty hair and holes in his jeans." So the likes of Penny Valentine and Chris Welch didn't get to talk to him anymore. He was talking to me. Then the lazy Susan rotated a bit more and it was different people again. But each time he wanted to be able to present himself as a new person. Then of course sometimes he wouldn't talk. I remember being flown out to Fort Lauderdale at the tail end of 1972 to see him do a Spiders show, and he said hello and traded a bit of small talk but he wouldn't sit for a full interview. It was all pretty rationed. I was flattered by the attention, but remember I was a young naïve kid from the provinces, and the whole thing was a novelty. Getting published was a novelty. Getting free stuff was a novelty. Suddenly you're moving in the world you've only read about.

For a certain period, I was the person he spoke to. An example of this is his retirement concert at Hammersmith Odeon. The week of the Hammersmith concerts, I had a week's holiday booked in Cornwall with my then girlfriend. I'd seen several shows on that tour, so I thought, I know it's the end of the tour, but it's just another show. I've seen it. I've got this holiday booked, I'm a bit knackered and I've seen a lot of his gigs. A few days beforehand Jeff Beck's girlfriend had rung me up and said that Jeff would quite like to go to this show, and I'd called Bowie's office and asked them to sort it. They said of course, because he was Mick Ronson's idol. Then when I was on the phone, they said, "Hold on, David wants to talk to you." He came on the phone and said, "Look, I'm knocking it on the head after the final show. Don't tell anyone apart from the people in the office because even the band don't know yet." He said he wanted the story on the front of the *NME* the day after the final gig. He knew when we went to press, and as the gig was on the Tuesday, there was just enough time to do it. The paper was on the streets in London on the Wednesday, and on the Thursday in the rest of the country. I went and told Nick Logan [the editor], I gave him the quotes and we put the front page together, and the front page was actually coming off the presses before Bowie had actually announced onstage that he was killing off Ziggy Stardust. The only other weekly music paper that had the news was *Record Mirror*, and that was only because they went to press a day after us. *Sounds* and *Melody Maker* were well pissed off, as they were caught with their Kansai Yamamoto strides down.

ANGIE BOWIE: The boys were unceremoniously dismissed, without my prior knowledge. I guess David was informed by Defries. Because they asked for money and Defries didn't want to pay. David and I were still thinking Ziggy Stardust and the Spiders from Mars, but Defries wanted to make him start thinking of David Bowie as a solo artist and then hiring other people. But we weren't ready. I wasn't prepared, and David wasn't in a way either. Because you know, it was a bit quick.

TREVOR BOLDER: We didn't know anything about it beforehand. I was a bit like, "What the hell's he on about?" Woody thought about walking offstage before we did "Rock 'n' Roll Suicide." He told me later that if he'd known beforehand, he wouldn't have done the gig. That's why they didn't tell us. They couldn't take the risk we'd say "Up yours!" and walk. Everybody else knew. Mick Ronson knew. They just kept it from me and Woody.

It started out as a band, really, and we were all in it together. Like the Musketeers. He asked us to join him and we said OK, because we were on a record deal at the time and we gave that up to be with him. We were promised the same share of everything if we would do this, and it was, like, David Bowie and the Spiders from Mars, or Ziggy Stardust and the Spiders from Mars. We started out playing in clubs in London and, as a band, we went to all the gigs together in a car, but the bigger he got—and the band would go wherever he'd go—the less we actually saw him. We only saw him as we walked onstage. He separated himself from us towards the end; he was like a solo artist that didn't need us, while in the beginning he definitely needed us.

We just sort of floated along with it. It didn't intimidate me, as I was married with two children and I had to get on with that side of life as well. So I really enjoyed what we did, I really enjoyed playing. We didn't have the sort of pressure that David had. He had all the interviews, and everything was on his shoulders and we were the band behind it all. We just got on and did what we always wanted to do since we first started playing as kids.

DAVID BOWIE: Ziggy was a monster but he was my monster. My very own monster, ha!

MARY LOVETT: The Hammersmith Odeon show was extraordinary. Peter [Frampton] was on tour with Humble Pie, so I went with our good friend Terry Doran, who worked at Apple and looked after George Harrison. The show was particular for many reasons, not least the fact that everyone was dressed up. Not just some of them, but everyone, as they felt they could be. David really legitimized everyone who wanted to feel as though they could express themselves. The Hammersmith Odeon was like a huge fancy dress party. Terry and I also went to the party afterwards at the Café Royal. It was an outrageous party. David and Angie were there, obviously, along with Mick and Bianca Jagger, Lou Reed, everyone. I remember Angie finally arrived, walking through the room like an empress, arm in arm with Bianca, who was carrying a riding whip and wearing a headdress. A very interesting costume. You could tell by the people at the concert and the party afterwards that he was embracing a lot of outside people who were finding a home with him. So I realized that was really different and unusual. He was touching a lot of people who needed a place to go. I didn't really know how he was doing it but I thought it was pretty amazing. He touched so many people. When he announced he was retiring Ziggy we were all so shocked, as it was such a brave thing to do. The Café Royal party was like a court, almost a court of clowns and jesters in fancy costumes who were sort of flaunting about.

TREVOR BOLDER: As David got bigger, so the Spiders were pushed to the margins. I've got mixed memories about that time, really. There are really bad memories towards the end, when he changed as a person, and that was difficult to cope with at the time, because we were friends. He was really nice until then, just a regular sort of folk, but the bigger he got, the bigger his head got, and the less important we were to him. From all the stories I've heard, with all the musicians that were with him, speaking to lots of them who have worked with him over the years, he trod that thin line: when he didn't need you, he'd discard you, but while he needed you, he was very friendly towards you. I saw him do it to a few people as well—they used to do shows with him, and once he finished using them, he didn't want to see them again, and if they came to gigs, he wouldn't let them in. They tried to see him play, and he'd be like, "I don't want them here tonight, I don't want them here!" That's just the way he worked. He took the best bits from people and then discarded the rest.

But the worst point was when it all finished—being out of work, being penniless: in the end, we had no money, and I had a family, and Bowie didn't really care about that. I'll never forget what he did then. He just didn't want to know, and me and Woody and Mick were really pissed off. Honestly, who wouldn't be? But it was a shame really, a shame that we sort of drifted apart.

I think we could have gone another year. I think Bowie knew that as well; I think later on he thought it could have gone that bit further. And I always thought that the Spiders, with Mick, should have gone on as a band on its own, and done something as well. But it was all broken up and separated by the management, because they didn't want that. They didn't want the Spiders to be out on the road as a band, because they thought it might have taken away from David. They just wanted to give Mick his solo album, and me and Woody were left in the lurch, and we didn't know where to go or what to do. So we sort of floundered around with no money.

ROBIN DERRICK: When I was at *Arena* [magazine] in the early '90s, we did a Bowie special, and I arranged for the magazine to get permission to photograph all Bowie's old Ziggy costumes. I flew to Lausanne, Bowie's home in Switzerland. Almost all of the clothes from his tours from the last twenty years were stored and archived there, and the day after arriving, having hired a watch photographer's studio half an hour away, Coco Schwab, Bowie's long-term assistant, turned up in a van with dozens of outfits, all hung perfectly and draped in cellophane. Bowie had put the outfits together himself. There was the kabuki kimono, the pale blue suit from the "Life on Mars?" video, the circuit-board jumpsuit Bowie wore on *The Old Grey Whistle Test*, and the quilted one he wore on *Top of the Pops.* Two things were remarkable about the outfits, the first being that this was exactly what they were, outfits, not street clothes. The red boots copied from Kansai Yamamoto were literally held together with tape. I always imagined that the outfits would look more like the things you'd find in stores, but all of them looked like stage costumes. Reinforcing the idea that Ziggy wasn't Bowie, he was an act. When I looked through the costumes, some hadn't been touched since they were last worn, and there was even a beer stain on one of the kimonos. The second thing that shocked me was how small the clothes were: I was able to wrap my hands around most of the waists. They were absolutely tiny. When we photographed some of the clothes again ten years later, when I was working for *Vogue*, we got Kate Moss to model them. But she couldn't get into them, so we had to call up Bowie and ask if he minded if we let them out. He didn't mind.

PAUL MORLEY (JOURNALIST): He played with the idea of being a rock star but he was very good at sabotaging that role. And at the moment when he looked like he might become Billy Joel or Elton John—that moment when you get accepted and therefore you are fixed, he walked away. He had to work out: How can I be famous; how can I be that star that I want to be, but also be able to keep changing? Because of course the very consequences often of keeping changing is that you ruin your popularity because those that love you want you to be the same. So he managed to be absolutely the same all the time, always David Bowie, by constantly changing.

5

BATTLE CRIES AND CHAMPAGNE

1973–1974

TONY ZANETTA: The retirement happened for a variety of reasons. Number one: we couldn't get the dates for tour three. Number two: everybody was exhausted, shattered. Number three: the publishing glitch, and David not wanting to give any more money away. He was already starting to have problems with Tony Defries, and he wasn't sure what he was going to do next. Which is why he did *Pin Ups*, which had no original songs on it. So it was a perfect time to take a break and regroup.

TONY PARSONS: I think he stopped Ziggy when he did because the reality of fame was more than he could handle. He had wanted it all his life, and had tried to get it for over a decade, but when it finally came it frightened the living daylights out of him. I remember the Earls Court gig, when he came out in the Japanese robe as the music from *A Clockwork Orange* came blasting out, there were all these Australians taking their clothes off and getting in fights and vomiting on girls in the front row—[this was when Australians could still afford to live in Earls Court, that is]. And the reality for Bowie was that he couldn't contain it anymore. He was owned by everyone. You always see that, when it's not your private property anymore, when suddenly you've seen the Jam on *Top of the Pops*, or the Clash play in a stadium, or David Bowie at Earls Court, it's not him talking to you in your bedroom anymore, it's an industry.

And I think he recoiled from that. Because he was big, a big star, and people were ready for something new, ready for the new thing, and he was so flash—everything was choreographed, everything was thought about, everything looked great and the songs were great, and he looked great. And so it went into the mainstream, and he had an aversion to the mainstream. He'd been poor, and he'd been ripped off, and he wanted to be successful, but the reality was too much for him. He was a very astute businessman at the end, and I think that was very important to him; he saw that as an expression of love, making money for your family and providing for them after you've gone. He was like Sinatra, in that he was an artist, but he knew when he needed to replenish the coffers. I think a lot of the gigs that I really loved were when he needed the money. When he wanted hit records, he got in Nile Rodgers, and said, "I want you to do what you do." And Nile said, "I'm going to make that funky," and Bowie'd say, "No, make hits." He knew he wanted hits, he knew he needed hits. And I think because Bowie had been so badly managed, he managed his own career brilliantly, he knew the moves he had to make. These very high-end compilations, his hands are all over them. So I think he liked success, but he didn't like the dumbness.

CHARLES SHAAR MURRAY: The retirement wasn't a real retirement, because he went straight off to France to cut *Pin Ups*, and then he did the *1984 Floor Show*. The reason he got rid of the Spiders was because he was going in a soul direction and he didn't think they would be comfortable with it.

With *Diamond Dogs* it was almost him saying I can make a rough rocking guitar album without Ronno. Mick felt he'd been betrayed and hung out to dry with the solo thing, which he didn't want to do. It wasn't really his idea. It wasn't that he couldn't cope with the musical challenges, but psychologically Mick was totally unsuited to that role. He was one of the greatest second bananas in the business. He was a great problem solver. Bowie decides at eleven p.m. that he wants a string quartet on a particular song the next day in the studio, and so Mick stays up all night with a bottle of wine and some spliff and does the charts for the arrangement. He was always throwing his coat over puddles. A genuinely sweet man. But the retirement was all about a new chapter.

JUSTIN DE VILLENEUVE (MANAGER): Twiggy and I were no longer a couple but I was still managing her. We were staying in the Hotel Bel-Air in L.A., as we were in California talking to studios and agents and having a high old time. Peter Frampton, who I had known for ages, asked me if I'd heard *Aladdin Sane* by David Bowie. I wasn't really aware of his music at the time, but he'd referred to Twiggy as "Twig the Wonder Kid" on the album, and as soon as I heard it I knew he was something special. You could tell immediately that he was at the top of his game.

Bowie wanted to meet Twiggy, and we wanted to meet him, so I arranged for them to see each other. Bowie really wanted to be on the cover of *Vogue*, as it was one of the magazine covers he hadn't appeared on. *Vogue* had never had a man and a woman on the cover before and I thought it would be a great coup to have both him and Twiggy on the cover. I knew Bea Miller, the editor, and Barney Wan, the art director, so I called them up and off we went. I wasn't strictly a photographer, in fact at that time I wasn't a photographer at all, but I'd seen a lot of snappers take pictures of Twigs, and I thought it couldn't actually be that difficult. And it wasn't.

Twigs and I flew to Paris because Bowie was in France, at the Château d'Hérouville, the Honky Chateau, recording *Pin Ups*. *Vogue* booked the studio, and all of us converged there. We had a huge entourage—I even had a butler at the time, I'm ashamed to say, as did Bowie. The thing is, Twiggy and I had just come back from a holiday in Bermuda, and so we were both incredibly tanned. And so the picture looked ridiculous, as Twiggy was completely brown, brown as a berry, and he was snow white, deathly white. When he took his shirt off I was actually quite taken aback by how pale he was. He was like a sheet. He really was the Thin White Duke. So the lovely Pierre La Roche worked wonders. I'd always been obsessed by masks, as people do interesting things when they have a mask on. So I asked Pierre to give them both masks, and it was perfect. They both look oddly enigmatic. The cover picture was actually the very first frame I took. I did a couple of Polaroids and then just stormed into it. They got on brilliantly, and it clicked. Thing is, it wasn't until I looked at Bowie through the lens that I realized he had different colored eyes. He did have an aura about him, something you could never quite put your finger on. He was always surrounded by lovely-looking girls, wherever you saw him. Girls everywhere. That always made me very intrigued.

I knew *Vogue* was going to love the picture, but a few days after the shoot Bowie called up and asked if he could use it for his album cover. I asked him how much it was going to sell, and he thought about it for a while and then said, "Well, probably about a million." So I said to Twigs, "Well, I think he can have it then." *Vogue* was furious, and Barney didn't talk to me for ages. In fact no one from *Vogue* ever talked to me again. Twiggy and I were in L.A. a few months later and we were driving down Sunset Boulevard and we saw the cover on a huge billboard, and I turned to Twiggy and said, I think we made the right decision. It sounds silly but I have to say it was one of the most glorious moments of my career.

To this day, so many people think it's Angie on the cover. The first pressing of the album had a beautiful inner sleeve with all the credits on, which I thought was very slick at the time, but every pressing after that was just a plain inner sleeve, and as they didn't reprint the cover, there were no credits on it. So not only did they not know I'd taken the photograph, but no one knew it was Twiggy either. But the cover made perfect sense as *Pin Ups* was an homage to the '60s, all David's favorite records from '64 to '67, and Twiggy was the face of the '60s. Bowie looked brilliant at the time, as he got all his clothes from City Lights, which was run by my old friend Tommy Roberts. It's a shame that we didn't get the *Vogue* cover, but years later I saw a copy with Ryan O'Neal and Marisa Berenson on the cover, so they got their double act after all.

TOMMY ROBERTS (DESIGNER): City Lights Studio in Covent Garden was always my favorite shop, more so than Mr. Freedom or Practical Styling, my other shops, because I actually liked the clothes. It never made any money but all the pop stars at the time came in—Bryan Ferry, Bowie. Angela Bowie started coming in before her husband, and she was always picking out things for him as well as stuff for herself. She'd always pick up a suit or jacket for him. The suit he wore on the cover of *Pin Ups* was one of ours, and when people got wind that we'd made it, all these kids started coming into the shop. After that, whenever any of them pointed to something and asked if Bowie had worn it I automatically said yes. Why wouldn't I? By then he was already a cult.

CHARLES SHAAR MURRAY: Bowie championed the power of the imagination in rock music, and almost gave his audiences permission to unleash their own imaginations. Not in the same way as the Beatles in their psychedelic phase, or Dylan with his literary influences, that weird mixture of French symbolist poets and dustbowl folkies. Bowie championed the power of the imagination. He took his time, he tried a lot of different things, and flitted from one thing to another, but he always picked something up and took it with him to his next destination. He had a lot of resources, almost handpicked from all the places he'd visited. Even "The Laughing Gnome," which everyone laughs at, quite rightly, because it's not nearly as good a kid's song as "Yellow Submarine," had vari-speed voices, which he would use to far more serious and chilling effect in things like "The Bewlay Brothers" or "Fame." On the version of "See Emily Play" on *Pin Ups* he uses vari-speed voices incredibly impressively. I actually saw him putting down the backing vocals in the studio. He sang one part, and the engineer Ken Scott asked if he wanted to hear it back and he said, "No, just set me up another track." And then he put another vocal down. And then he said, "I want this to be speeded up." And then he sang the third track and asked for it to be slowed down a certain amount, and then he sang the fourth one. He sang all four parts without hearing any of it back and then said, "Right, play them back to me." And it was absolutely perfect. He was an absolute maestro in the studio, both as a singer and as a producer, and also as a visionary who obviously had to imagine it and hear it in his head before any of it was actually put down on tape. It was just bam, bam, bam, bam. Perfect. No fucking about, boy, it was there. The man knew what he was doing. Remember the coke blowout was still a year or two away, and all he seemed to be doing at this time was having a couple of drinks and the odd spliff. There was no serious dopery going on.

MARIANNE FAITHFULL (SINGER): He was actually on the first tour I did, in 1965. He was called David Jones then and he was at the bottom of the bill. I remember the Hollies and Freddie and the Dreamers and all sorts of other funny people, but I don't remember David at all. I only really became aware of him when he did *Pin Ups*. I got rather interested in him then because he did some beautiful versions of a lot of '60s songs. That's when I got to know him, and I liked him very much, I could see how clever he was. When we did *The 1980 Floor Show*, I thought the costumes were amazing but I thought it was all a bit frightening in all honesty. I thought it was very sweet of him to ask me to be on the show, and I was happy to be there, and to be doing it with him, but I just found it a bit weird. I think he just liked me, and I certainly liked him. I first met him in a very sort of non-weird place in the studio when he was making *Pin Ups*. He was just very good, very professional, beautiful, very good voice I thought. He actually had lots of different voices. I liked the voice he used on "Sorrow"—which was just gorgeous—not the Anthony Newley voice. In the studio I just watched him work, as I didn't think it was appropriate for me to say anything. Then we slowly became friends. In the beginning I went for lunch with him and his wife Angela, which was frightening as they were both putting on an act, and putting on the style, as you might say. I went with [old boyfriend] Oliver Musker, just the four of us, with them putting on an act. That's what they did, especially Angela. I think they both decided to sort of be like that. It must have worked, but it didn't really work on me. David wasn't being himself. Certainly Angela wasn't being herself, whatever herself is I have no idea. [With them] it was that sort of first love, and they seemed very close but their relationship obviously did deteriorate, because of infidelity and drugs and orgies, things like that. I didn't want anything to do with all that. I kind of stayed out of it. I'd had enough of that kind of shit in the '60s. I didn't like it in the '60s and I wasn't going to start liking it then. We sort of lost contact after Oakley Street. I expect I was sort of getting into drugs too, you know, and he was, and maybe I don't really remember. I'm not sure if my drug thing really coincided with his. You know, he didn't want me around anyway in that period. I didn't fit in. He was on his trip, with all his friends. Angela wasn't really my cup of tea, and as for the androgynous thing, it wasn't a new thing at all. It was just like Keith [Richards] wearing eye makeup and Brian [Jones] dressing up like Anita [Pallenberg].

In her autobiography, Marianne says she and Musker spent a lot of time with David and Angie at this point, especially in Oakley Street. "One night we were all a bit drunk at David's house and David began coming on to me. We went into the corridor. I unzipped his trousers. I was trying to give him a blow job, but David was scared to death of Oliver." So scared that he couldn't perform.

CHARLES SHAAR MURRAY: On October 20, 1973, I was at the taping of *The 1980 Floor Show* at the Marquee, and I remember marveling at Bowie's ability to switch his charisma on and off: he could enter a crowded room, full of people for whom he was the focus of attention, and not be noticed until he was ready to be noticed. A little while later I was attending an industry lunch at which Bowie was being presented with about a zillion gold and silver discs, and ended up at the house he was then renting in Cheyne Walk, a few doors down from Mick Jagger's place, where Bowie played me some extracts from his current work-in-progress, which turned out to be *Diamond Dogs*. I was wearing a promo T-shirt for one of Bowie's contemporaries, and Bowie was mildly offended. "He's a real cunt," he said, "and one day I'll tell you why."

AVA CHERRY: All his team thought that I was going to be someone that he's having a fling with and it would be over in a couple of weeks. Everybody underestimated me. Angie obviously didn't like the fact that I was sticking around. After I moved into Oakley Street she used to scream, "I don't want her in my house, I don't want her in my house!" He was giving me a lot of attention and affection but she should never have agreed to me staying in her house. It just seemed so stupid to me. But she was so sure that I was just going to be a flash in the pan that that's what she did. Mick Jagger knew David, and I was friends with both of them. So all three of us used to hang out a lot, and yes we did have some fun together. We were staying at the Sherry-Netherland one night in New York, where David had given a party for Rudolph Nureyev. At the end of the party, everyone was gone apart from me and David and Mick, so it just ended up with the three of us sleeping together. That was it. And we had a wonderful time, and we had a lot of fun.

NINA SIMONE (MUSICIAN): [When we met in New York in July 1974] he said, "The first thing I want you to know is that you're not crazy—don't let anybody tell you you're crazy, because where you're coming from, there are very few of us out there." He looked just like Charlie Chaplin, a clown suit, a big black hat. He told me that he was not a gifted singer and he knew it. He said, "What's wrong with you is you were gifted—you have to play. Your genius overshadows the money, and you don't know what to do to get your money, whereas I wasn't a genius, but I planned, I wanted to be a rock and roll singer and I just got the right formula." He [had] more sense than anybody I've ever known. It's not human—David [wasn't] from here.

KEVIN ARMSTRONG (MUSICIAN): Tony Defries I think did a lot of damage with Bowie's finances. He was a sort of bloodsucker.

CHARLES SHAAR MURRAY: Bowie had everything under control apart from the fact that he had the worst deal in the world with his manager Defries. The deal was reportedly, we split everything fifty-fifty. Even by the standards of independent black record companies of the '40s and '50s, that's outrageous. It shows you how desperate Bowie was to make it, and how confident he was that he was going to make it this time, that he accepted the terms. He was prepared to sign away virtually all of the income from what he was doing in order to get over and make the impact.

SIMON NAPIER-BELL: Bowie and Tony Defries obviously helped each other move up a step in the industry, but Defries would never have become a top manager without Bowie, whereas Bowie obviously had the thrust and ruthlessness to keep pushing his way to the top one way or another. I would say Tony Defries's success was all down to Bowie.

NICK KENT: Lou Reed, Iggy Pop, and Mott the Hoople were all signed to MainMan, and they realized quite quickly that Tony Defries was only interested in Bowie, and while he may have been ostensibly looking after them, through MainMan, he was only interested in protecting Bowie. He saw Bowie as his Elvis and just saw the others as afterthoughts, as Carl Perkins. Bowie was the only star. Bowie had cracked the mainstream, and Iggy and Lou Reed never did. There were times when Iggy was in a bad way and he would reach out to Bowie, and there was always a connection between them, a respect and genuine affection. Bowie didn't have that for other people. Bowie genuinely loved Iggy, but then Iggy is very lovable. He had an unlovable side, but he was lovable too. When Iggy was in the Stooges he was the general of his own army, but when he went to work for David Bowie he was the lone soldier on the hill, standing with mercenaries.

WENDY LEIGH: Tony Defries was very good for David. He really moved him on. David learned a lot from Defries.

TONY ZANETTA: Defries was a real businessman, whereas David didn't know a thing about it. It was all Chinese to David. Tony Defries was totally a force for good, he was fantastic. He had told David not to worry about money. He might also have said sign on the dotted line, but the dotted line wasn't that different from what a lot of other artists signed with a lot of other managers. He said, don't worry, you don't have to have a side job, I'll pay your bills, and I'm going to get you a fantastic record deal and make you a star. If you had that kind of ambition and someone came along and told you that, you'd think, Oh, that sounds good. Someone who was interested in your every move, who discussed every move you made, who never got bored with any of your nonsense or personal problems or overdraft, and who was always there for you. This was who Tony Defries was. They discussed every part of David's career step by step by step. Nothing was not discussed to the nth degree. This is what I stepped into. Tony Defries started coming to New York by himself. As David wasn't signed to RCA UK but RCA global, it gave Defries more leverage. He was signed to the mother company. And every time he came to New York he called me. You know, to basically do errands. We became closer and closer and closer, and I looked forward to his visits. I could always do with the hundred or two hundred bucks he would throw my way. He would also listen to what I had to say, which no one had ever done before.

In the beginning David talked about his brother a lot. In the early days of the Warwick Hotel in New York he talked about his family, as his cousin Kristina was living there. She was a little older. Her mother I think had been institutionalized. They were close because they had been close as children. She was his main link to the family. According to him everyone was schizophrenic—the sisters, the aunts were crazy; the brother was schizophrenic; there was a lot of madness in the family. The undercurrent to that was, I'm mad, I'm insane, and this is my way out of it. After a while it wasn't really spoken of, so much, but it was always there. His personality definitely became erratic as the Ziggy thing took over him and it took over all of us. In some way we all became Ziggy, even after

David dropped him. It was kinda neurotic. We started to treat him like an object, not like David Bowie the person. He was David the star, and his peculiarities were definitely indulged. So he could be tense, he could be this, that, or the other thing, and it was just part of the package. David was really wild at the time.

ANGIE BOWIE: The orgies we had in London tended to be just me, David, and one other person. The most charming orgy description I've ever had was by Lindsay Kemp. "I seem to remember that I was the ham in that sandwich!"

WENDY LEIGH: I knew Angie and I didn't like Angie. I thought she was a confection. She was too much, and perhaps too little as well. She was always very mannered, always doing a bad am-dram performance, always needing to be the center of attention, always needing everyone in the room to take notice of her. She was frightfully self-inflated. I had lunch with Angie and her friend Vicki Hodge in Casserole in the Kings Road one day in 1974 and went back to their house in Oakley Street for coffee. I was interviewing her for a book I was writing called *Speaking Frankly*, about what really happens in bed, and she was telling me about how much sex she was having. She was brazen about it. I remember thinking at the time that anyone who married Angie was going through the door to a place near the wilder shores of sexual experimentation. David definitely fell into bad hands. I'm sure she taught him a trick or two, but she was too much, too flamboyant.

David and Angie presided over her own personal Sodom and Gomorrah, the focal point of which was "The Pit," a fur-covered bed in the sitting room, where, in front of a series of audiences, who generally ended up participating themselves, everyone had sex. Seriously, it was like a sexual cocoon. Vicki said that David and Angie used to have the most amazing orgies at Oakley Street. She even told me that her boyfriend, the gangster John Bindon, saw Mick Jagger having sex with Angie while David watched. Bindon was later employed as security on one of David's tours, but at this pit he was treated like a freak because of his huge member. Angie gave a very good impression of proudly saying that they were both in an open marriage, but secretly she was incredibly jealous of all the people David was sleeping with. She was possessive and she didn't actually want to be in that situation. She just went along with it.

A bodyguard, small-time actor, and sometime gangster, Bindon became notorious not just for his antics (in 1978 he was famously acquitted of the brutal murder of underworld figure John Darke at the Ranelagh Yacht Club, in Fulham, even though Bindon had administered the stabbing), but also for his affair with Princess Margaret, a shocking liaison that would have serious ramifications for both of them. But while his film parts are largely forgotten, and his thuggery appreciated only by his biographers, it's his prowess in the bedroom that still captures people's imagination. Two things set Bindon apart from your average petty criminal. The first was his ability to ingratiate himself with pretty much anyone he met and, rather more impressively, his twelve-inch penis. His member was almost certainly what made him attractive to Princess Margaret, who used to "entertain" Bindon both at her home in Kensington Palace in London, and also at her holiday home in Mustique (he was photographed with her on a beach there wearing a T-shirt bearing the slogan "Enjoy Cocaine").

Angie Bowie also allegedly fell under Bindon's spell, and was apparently so enamored with his johnson (she christened it "The Mighty Marrow") that as well as enjoying it herself, once got five of her friends to sleep with him at the same time, apparently while she watched. Around this time, in the early '70s, Bindon was also something of a stud for hire, hired by frustrated middle-aged women, often while their husbands watched.

In 1979, when Bowie went to visit Iggy Pop at Rockfield Studios in Wales, when he was recording the follow-up to his New Values *album, Bowie tried to cheer his friend up by regaling him with stories about the gangster-turned-penis (or penis-turned-gangster); bizarrely, the pair of them turned Bowie's monologue into "Play It Safe," a song that would appear on Iggy's next LP,* Soldier. *By the time the album was released, a chorus referencing Princess Margaret had been excised.*

PETER YORK: There was a really beautiful mixed-race girl who stalked Bowie when he moved to Oakley Street from Haddon Hall [via a brief sojourn in Maida Vale]. She was literally the girl who came in through the bathroom window. In the early '70s she went to a provincial Bowie gig—

Reading, let's say—climbed in through a window, found his dressing room, and then demanded David have his wicked way with her. Which he did. Thereafter she pursued him everywhere, and her main concern in life was to stalk David Bowie. To the vast irritation of Angie she had gone to Oakley Street dozens of times, and clearly it had all ended up very, very badly. She ended up throwing milk bottles into the basement. She took stalking to new heights. She was extraordinary, and frightening, too. Years later she rang me once from Geneva, saying she'd just been to the house and been told he wasn't there. At some level I think he quite liked the flattery and the attention. He was the lance of love, and she was utterly obsessed with him. At one point she had been referred to an NHS shrink and unsuccessfully tried to have an affair with him. As he wasn't coming across she threatened to report him to the authorities.

MICK RONSON: I never really left. David stopped working on the road and wanted to sit down for a little rest, so if I had stayed with him I would have sat down and done nothing. I didn't know how long he was gonna stop for—as far as I was concerned he was stopping, that was it. Then David got the itch and so I went back on the road with him for *Diamond Dogs*. Then they arranged for me to do one or two concerts [on my own], and then it started getting good so I decided to carry on and do a bit more. When David was getting back to going on the road again, I was busy doing my own thing so I never went with him on the road again.

In an interview for the Mail on Sunday *in 2008 to accompany a Bowie cover-mounted CD, Bowie told me that the* Diamond Dogs *"Sweet Thing" medley was originally written for his aborted musical* 1984.

DAVID BOWIE: I'd failed to obtain the theatrical rights from George Orwell's widow, and having written three or more songs for it already, I did a fast about-face and recobbled the idea into *Diamond Dogs*: teen punks on rusty skates living on the roofs of the dystopian Hunger City; a post-apocalyptic landscape. A centerpiece for this would-be stage production was to be "Sweet Thing/Candidate/Sweet Thing," which I wrote using William Burroughs's cut-up method. You write down a paragraph or two describing several different subjects creating a kind of story ingredients list, I suppose, and then cut the sentences into four or five-word sections; mix 'em up and reconnect them. You can get some pretty interesting idea combinations like this. You can use them as-is or, if you have a craven need to not lose control, bounce off these ideas and write whole new sections.

I was looking to create a profligate world that could have been inhabited by characters from Kurt Weill or John Rechy—that sort of atmosphere. A bridge between Enid Blyton's Beckenham and the Velvet Underground's New York. Without Noddy, though. I thought it evocative to wander between the melodramatic "Sweet Thing" croon into the dirty sound of "Candidate" and back again. For no clear reason (what's new?) I stopped singing this song around the mid-'70s. Though I've never had the patience or discipline to get down to finishing a musical theatre idea other than the rock shows I'm known for, I know what I'd try to produce if I did. I've never been keen on traditional musicals. I find it awfully hard to suspend my disbelief when dialogue is suddenly sung. I suppose one of the few people who can make this work is Stephen Sondheim with works such as *Assassins*. I much prefer through-sung pieces where there is little if any dialogue at all. *Sweeney Todd* is a good example, of course. *Peter Grimes* and *The Turn of the Screw*, both operas by Benjamin Britten, and *The Rise and Fall of the City of Mahagonny* by Weill. How fantastic to be able to create something like that.

GUY PEELLAERT (ARTIST): I had this idea to adapt Nik Cohn's book *Awopbopaloobop Alopbamboom* into a series of small films. I wanted to invent little animated scenarios involving real pop stars. One idea was to have Elvis or Johnny Cash and Jerry Lee Lewis as truckers. But I couldn't make it work, so I called Nik, went to meet him, and we decided to make a book together, *Rock Dreams*. I wanted the book to be full of myths and legends, and although it was thought to be a cynical book, it was full of love, full of affection for the music and the people who made it. *Rock Dreams* was always meant to be a monument to a dream, a monument to a myth. For *Diamond Dogs*, Bowie wanted something futuristic but something sensual. He had seen the work I was doing for *Rock Dreams* and he had obviously liked it, although I think far more important to him was the knowledge that Mick Jagger had asked me to do the cover of *It's Only Rock 'n Roll*. He managed to get his record out first and he liked to say that Jagger didn't speak to him for ages because of it. For a while the *Diamond Dogs* cover became the thing that I was known for, especially because there was a real sensation about the original version, the banned version, with Bowie's cock. He loved the idea but I think he also knew that the record company wouldn't be happy. And when they saw it they weren't happy. *Rock Dreams* was all about the extremes of possibility, the flash and fire of pop music, and you have to have that excitement or else it's not working. *Diamond Dogs* was meant to be flashy, over the top, extreme, a freak show.

OLIVER JAMES: *Space Oddity*, *The Man Who Sold the World*, and *Hunky Dory* were all about him being scared of becoming insane. *Hunky Dory* is very clever in the way it conceals the fact that it is all about madness. Those records are about him saying, "I'm not scared of you, I'm going to take you on." He was confronting his madness, and turning it into art. By the time he got to *Ziggy Stardust*, *Aladdin Sane*, and *Diamond Dogs* he was worried about being driven insane because he was having a huge amount of sex, a huge amount of drugs, and becoming famous. By this point he'd run to the end of his runway, he'd taken too many drugs, he'd had too much sex.

DAVID BOWIE: *Diamond Dogs* scared me because I was mutating into something I just didn't believe in anymore, and the dreadful thing was, it was so easy. The *Diamond Dogs* period was just an extension of *Aladdin Sane*, which in itself was just an extrapolation of *Ziggy Stardust*. But by the time of *Diamond Dogs* that persona had started to feel claustrophobic, and I needed a change. I had spent most of the '60s trying to get a break, trying to find a hit in amongst all the material I had written, but when "Space Oddity" came around then I knew that this new persona was going to work. I believe passionately in the creative spark, although judging by how long it took me to find something that worked, I'm not sure I used it properly initially. *Diamond Dogs* was making me sick, both physically and creatively, and I was shifting into melodrama.

ORSON PEELLAERT (CURATOR): My father was a living mystery, as he would get up at five in the morning, go down to his studio by 5:10, come back up in the evening for dinner, and then go back again. He was the cliché of the artist, and was immersed in his world. My father definitely had the time-intensive side of the work. He had three assistants working on the images day and night because they were so complex. This was Photoshop before Photoshop existed. He couldn't afford permission fees, and so had to distort images while finding ones with the exact angles. He took hundreds of Polaroids of source material. People have no idea how much work he put into these—every image is like a Stanley Kubrick movie. People take images for granted these days, but this whole project was so labor intensive. It was hyperreal, which at the time was not considered to be art. These images played with reality and there was an incredible tension between fantasy and reality.

The whole story of how my father got to work with Bowie was a trick. Mick Jagger had already commissioned my father to produce the cover of *It's Only Rock 'n Roll*, and had invited my father to spend some time on the European leg of the 1974 tour in order for him to collect imagery. He shot lots of pictures backstage for source material for the project. When he returned he didn't hear back from Jagger, so he thought he was behaving like a rock-star diva. And then there was an exhibition of my father's work at Biba in London, which is when Bowie approached him about *Diamond Dogs.* Bowie had already been introduced to his work by Jagger, and he made it a mission to outsmart Jagger and get him to produce something first. On the day of the shoot with the dog and Terry O'Neill, Bowie invited my father to breakfast, as he was in town for the Biba show. And then Bowie asked him to come with him to the shoot, and very quickly my father realized it was a trick, and he ended up art directing that shoot, even though the images were only going to be used as the source material for his paintings for the album cover. He didn't put up much resistance as he admired Bowie. Then when *Diamond Dogs* came out, Jagger was furious, and said that in future he would never show anything to Bowie, as he would make it his own and make it better. David had the original of the *Diamond Dogs* cover as he lent it to the V&A for the exhibition, and I think Jagger has the original of *It's Only Rock 'n Roll* somewhere too.

TERRY O'NEILL (PHOTOGRAPHER): The first time I photographed Bowie I was completely enchanted. He didn't say very much but you sort of gravitated towards him. This was 1972 and I was photographing him and Angie for the fashion editor Felicity Green at the *Daily Mirror.* Angie ran the session—do this, do that. David just stood there in different outfits. She was incredibly bossy. So I became friendly with Tony Defries, who used to call me up from time to time whenever he wanted something done. And one of the jobs was to shoot the art for the *Diamond Dogs* album cover. The idea was that they'd bring a Great Dane to the studio, along with Bowie, and then I'd shoot the dog, and David would copy them. I showed all the Polaroids to David, then he posed like the dog, and I shot him like the dog. Then all the art was given to Guy Peellaert, who drew the album cover. He wasn't on the shoot, I just gave it to Tony Defries. When we'd finished I just said, "Let's do a couple of shots with the dog," and David's sitting there and suddenly this dog leaps up in the air, trying to bite the strobe light. Every time the strobe went off, the dog jumped up. It was supposed to just sit at David's feet obediently, but the strobe lights going off freaked the animal out, and suddenly it leapt up on his hind legs, barking loud enough to wake the devil. Everybody scarpered as the dog ran around the studio—everyone apart from me and David that is. I was behind the camera and a photographer always feels more remote and disconnected when he's looking through the lens—and thank God I had a wide-angle lens on. As for David, he didn't move at all. He was completely focused.

David Bowie didn't do sequels. On the 1974 Diamond Dogs *tour of Canada and North America—which began in Montreal on June 14—his fans went berserk. He hadn't appeared live in the country since the previous March, and in that time had become the kind of pop star who attracted limpet-like adoration. The concertgoers on the* Diamond Dogs *tour seemed obsessed. Having not toured the United States for over a year, his followers were expecting him to turn up onstage wearing his Ziggy clothes; instead he appeared wearing baggy pleated trousers, suspenders, a white cotton shirt, and black ballet pumps, with his hair slicked back. During the show's intermission—a convention borrowed from the theatre—the more heavily made up audience members could be seen heading for the bathrooms, where they would wet down their spiky hair, rub off the lightning bolts from their faces, and alter their clothing. The obsessives would stalk him at the hotels on the tour, hanging out in the lobby, forcing themselves into the elevators and stealing David's hairs from the backseat of his limos parked outside, and occasionally emptying his cigarette butts from the car ashtrays. If they couldn't sleep with him, other souvenirs would have to do.*

EARL SLICK (GUITARIST): I met David somewhere around spring in 1974. It was an audition for the *Diamond Dogs* tour. I was the replacement for Mick Ronson. I knew about his work, and I damn well knew David was a very big star, but at the time I wasn't all that knowledgeable about him because I was in the blues world. At heart I'm a blues guitar player. Which I think he liked, but then he must have, or else he wouldn't have hired me. My friend Michael Kamen had mentioned my name to him, which is how I got my shot at the audition. I was twenty-one, and I figured this was a great opportunity. I purposefully didn't tell anyone about it in case I didn't get it. The actual audition has to be the weirdest experience I've had in my entire career. I got a call from Coco Schwab, and turned up at RCA Studios in New York City, where they were mixing *Diamond Dogs*. She brought me into the main studio. There was the amp I'd requested, a hundred-watt Marshall, and I'd brought a guitar with me. I put these headphones on and a voice came over and said, "Hello." I couldn't see the control room as they blacked it out. They asked me to play along with the stuff, and they played some tracks from *Diamond Dogs*, and I just played along. This went on for twenty minutes. And then David came in the room, we sat down and played some guitars and bullshitted for a while, and that was that. It was weird. I thought there'd be a band, but there was nothing.

Next day I get the call and I'm in. I went up to the Sherry-Netherland Hotel, and hung out for a while. The disparity between the blues world and David's world was quite extensive. I would have been more shocked at his world if I hadn't already have played in the backup band for *Hair*. Talk about fucking weird. I'd already been exposed to way stranger than David. The only thing that was odd was that the guy had no eyebrows, which was kind of weird. When I got talking to him he was down-to-earth as hell. Totally fucking down-to-earth. Not what you would expect. Focused. He was picking my brain, sizing me up, but then I was doing the same thing.

He wasn't focused on the tour though. He was focused most of the time, but not all of the time. There were times when he was not just there. There's no doubt about that. No way. I don't polish shit over. I tell the truth. Trust me, I was no angel, and I had serious fucking drug and alcohol problems myself. But I do have enough memory to know that there were some nights when he was just not there. It didn't make for a functioning band relationship. I know that drug [cocaine] very well, and what will happen is the drug just makes you isolate yourself emotionally from everybody. He wasn't as forthcoming as he could be, couldn't engage in conversations. He was completely isolated from the rest of the band before the shows, after the shows. It was like him and then it was us. It was not a band by any stretch. Except onstage, which was scripted. And that was mostly with the dogs [backing singers], Gui Andrisano and Warren Peace, Geoffrey.

Diamond Dogs was a weird period, because everything that David had done up to that point suddenly exploded. It was like a nuclear explosion. Ziggy, the retirement, this, all of a sudden David skyrocketed. It was Bowiemania. I was grooving like hell, man, I was twenty-one years old! What do you think I was doing? All of a sudden I'm this little rock-star guy, you know? Then he decided to just abandon the whole thing. *Diamond Dogs* is probably one of the most iconic things he did in his entire career, but it wasn't that long, it didn't even make the West Coast. He went straight into the Philly Soul period, when we did *Young Americans.*

I was in Glasgow in May 2016 with Lulu to film a digital James Corden–style car karaoke short for a car company. One of the sections was devoted to her relationship with David Bowie, a relationship which resulted in one of her biggest hits, a saxophone-driven cover of "The Man Who Sold the World" in 1974. She was sitting in a hotel lobby in Sheffield, discussing a forthcoming TV series when in walked "this stick-insect man with a white face and orange hair, not red, but bright orange." He invited her to his gig that night, one thing led to another, and soon they were lovers. "He was lovely, although my mum and dad thought he was a bit odd. He could be very funny and down-to-earth, but he was also extraordinarily beautiful, which was quite disconcerting." He also suggested that they record together, although Lulu didn't believe it at first: "I thought, yeah right, I'll believe that when I see it, but he came through. We recorded 'The Man Who Sold the World' and 'Watch That Man' but I don't think they're great versions. I got a hit, but I'm not so sure they were that great." Bowie also encouraged her to lose weight, and told her that smoking would improve her voice—"He never stopped, always smoking Disque Bleu or Gitanes." They later recorded a song that he had written specifically for her, "Can You Hear Me," which would later appear on Young Americans. *"He was having terrible problems with his record company at the time, and the record stayed unreleased. It's probably in a vault somewhere."*

TONI BASIL (CHOREOGRAPHER): We launched the Lockers in 1973, which was the first American street dance group to ever break through into the mainstream. We did TV specials, we opened up for Sinatra at Carnegie Hall, we opened up for Funkadelic at Radio City. So we had a wide audience. Bowie had the same agent we did, and Angie was in America and saw what was happening. They also knew that I had a history of choreography, working for Dick Clark and the *T.A.M.I. Show.* So Bowie asked me to go to London for a meeting. I knew about Ziggy, and had seen the Pennebaker film about him. When I saw the film I thought to myself, Oh my God, he's straight. He had this androgynous approach, which gave him a style of moment that people had never seen before. I met Bowie, met his management—who appeared to be spending a lot of David's money on their own dinners and their own wine—and he sent me to see Tim Curry in *The Rocky Horror Show*, because it had just opened in the West End and it was the hot thing. Then when I got back to L.A., I got a call from my agency asking if I wanted to go to New York and choreograph the opening number of the *Diamond Dogs* show. I said, "Make a good deal because I'm gonna do the whole show." I knew it, I just knew it. I knew his aesthetics and mine were really similar, and even though he was British and I was American, we both came from a background of research. I came from a showbiz family and had stood on the side of the stage all my life. I knew that what I had, he didn't, and what he had, I didn't. I met him in his hotel and brought this drawing of a silhouette of a body looming over a city. It was based on a Man Ray. That's how we opened the show. Originally his backup singers were going to be the *Diamond Dogs* on leashes, and Michael Bennett, who was involved with the choreography, was uncomfortable with that. I didn't see it that way. I remember him screaming into another room: "Coco, the dogs are back in the show!" When you could get past him being so drop-dead gorgeous—he was always the most beautiful thing in the room, male or female, children or whatever—he was alluring, elegant, never raised his voice. He was *wow.* And fantastic to work with. Because we were alone together working a lot, I really had to do my homework. I always came in armed with more than one idea, because he knew the music back and forth and he was armed with a jillion ideas. He taught me so much. I saw him come up with the boxing gloves and rope routine for "Panic in Detroit" in the space of a minute. I wanted so badly to make a proper exchange. This was taking rock to theatre and taking theatre to rock. I do know that I walked into our first New York meeting with peg pants, and when I told him they were from Jenny Waterbags, we went down there immediately and bought a pair. That became his look for the tour.

The show changed my career, as suddenly a lot of people starting taking an interest in my work, including *After Dark* magazine. They ended up putting me on the cover, which was copied by David for the cover of *Young Americans.* He used the same photographer—Eric Jacobs—and the same concept. But then he made me co-director of the show, which was a gift he didn't have to give.

GEOFF MACCORMACK: Toni Basil was a ballsy lady. She had a dance group called the Lockers, who did street dance, and they were amazing. David was always after her. I don't know whether he got her, but he was always after her, always grabbing hold of her during rehearsals.

GEORGE UNDERWOOD: I remember at the height of it all in the '70s, he said to me, "You know what? I might not see you for ten years. But it doesn't matter. I'm going off on this journey, but it doesn't matter because we'll still be the same when we see each other." It was almost as if he was saying goodbye. But of course we did see each other. He could cut people. He could be backstage, walking down to the stage, and people would come up to him and say, "Hi, David, remember me?" and he would have his face on and he'd just walk straight past them. I would always try and make them feel better by telling them he was in the zone. But then at the height of the Ziggy thing his personality was completely taken over by this new persona.

CHERRY VANILLA: When I worked for MainMan I suppose our relationship was a bit more formalized, but all it really meant is that I saw him more. I was getting $100 a week and my rent paid just to tell people they couldn't speak with David. We had charge accounts at Max's Kansas City and a limo service. But now we were promoting David Bowie. MainMan was the first time in the history of rock that the office help had a following just like David had a following, because the magazines wrote about us. They knew all about us and what we were doing, who we were having sex with. I know I used the line at the time as it was sassy and generated column inches, but I didn't really trade blowjobs for record plays. I had sex with DJs who became important or were important, but that was before David. And on the road, promoting him, there was one DJ I had sex with, but he was already a David Bowie fan. I was like a sacrificial whore for David, and I didn't care, because playing a sacrificial whore was a role I liked. It opened doors for other sacrificial whores. I was in love with him. And the only person I really wanted to have sex with at the time was David Bowie. Then there was the moment when that was really the most convenient thing for both of us. It happened a few times, and sometimes during his druggie days. But that was that. It was efficient, and fabulous, because he was great sex. I hope I was for him as well.

AMANDA LEAR (SINGER): Well, personally I owe a lot to David because he was the first one to insist that I should become a singer. When I first met him I was a fashion model working for Ossie Clark, Mary Quant . . . and just being a model wasn't very satisfying, but I had no other possibilities to express myself and David was the first one to say, "Why don't you sing?" He actually paid for my first singing lessons, with Florence Norberg. He also put me on a contract and made me sign with Tony Defries and MainMan, and wrote my very first recording, "Star." MainMan were paying my rent and flying me to New York. On the side, of course, I was also having an affair with David, with the blessing of his wife, Angie. Their marriage was not very, I don't think, happy towards the end. Angie was a very busy girl. She desperately wanted to make a career for herself. She wanted to get into everything and organize everyone's life.

I remember little Zowie playing on my knee. At the time we lived right next to each other in Chelsea. I lived in Glebe Place in a flat with Susannah York, and David was just in Oakley Street. You could see into my flat from his house. We met through Marianne Faithfull. She called me one night and said, "David is madly in love with you and is dying to meet you."

The first image he saw of me was the cover of the Roxy Music album, the picture of me with Bryan Ferry [*For Your Pleasure*]. He thought to himself, I like the look of this girl. I must say, Antony Price did this incredible styling, and it was new. In those days we had British girls with long hair. And then suddenly here comes this incredible woman, clad in black leather, stiletto heels, all very Hitchcock. So David saw the photograph, loved it, and wanted to meet the girl, which was me. But of course he expected me to be exactly like the girl in the picture. There was a big misunderstanding right from the start. He fell in love with a photograph, not a person. He expected me to be dominating. But I was completely the opposite. When I finally came out with my album I called it *I am a Photograph*, because I realized that being a fashion model, I was not a person. I was an illusion. And that was because of David.

When Marianne called I said, "It's two o'clock in the morning, and I'm actually sleeping," but then she put him on the phone. It was a bit rotten to do this because I was half asleep, but he was asking me to come over. He sent his car for me, and even though he had a cold—he had a red nose, and looked absolutely terrible—we decided to go to Tramp. We spent the whole night with Mick Jagger and Bianca. He wasn't very attractive, as he was very pale, very white with red hair and no eyebrows. Honestly that wasn't my type of boy. . . . I was going out with Bryan Ferry at the time and I was going out with good-looking boys and Bowie was very peculiar. But he had something absolutely fascinating and we spent the whole night talking and talking and talking. . . . I realized that there was something missing in his education because he didn't go much to school and there was a lot of things he was dying to learn. He knew about me and Salvador Dalí so he wanted to know all about Dalí and Surrealism, which he didn't know much about. Then it was like that all the time. I remember on his birthday in January, I said, "Look, for your birthday I've got a present for you, I'm gonna take you to a little cinema in North London to see *Metropolis* by Fritz Lang." And David Bowie had no idea what German Expressionism was and had never heard of *Metropolis*, had never heard of Fritz Lang. That was it, the next day he was straight into Fritz Lang and wanted to know all about this black-and-white German thing. And immediately he decided to change the set for his new tour. All the stage, the décor of the stage, he wanted to turn into German Expressionism. Every time you would mention something to him he would immediately jump—there was no cell phone and no Google, but that's what he would've done, look up everything immediately. For example, when I mentioned William Burroughs, he'd never heard of him, and so the next day he rushed out to buy *Naked Lunch*. He was a man who wanted to learn and I liked that very much because most people, the musicians and the rock stars that I had been out with, were only interested in their own music. They would listen to music endlessly morning to night, talk about recording, but that's it; they were not interested in anything else to do with geography, history, antiquity, or whatever. Bowie was different; he really had this great passion to learn things and to progress. He was not just a copycat, you see. I also turned him onto *Barbarella*, and all those sexy cartoons. There was one called *Octobriana*, a Russian cartoon about a crazy woman who could fly, who could do everything that people in Russia couldn't do at the time—so Octobriana was saving the world, she was jumping into a volcano. She was sort of a Lara Croft superwoman, and Bowie got really interested in these drawings—this very sexy woman—and decided to produce a movie based on the story of Octobriana.

So we started seeing each other quite a lot and he was sleeping most of the time in my place and I had Angie calling first thing in the morning saying, "Can I speak to my husband," which was very peculiar. Angie was very understanding and she knew that David was in love and she wanted me to please him. We went shopping together, and she would buy me lovely things, like lovely silky underwear from Janet Reger. She'd say, "You must wear this because David will like it." Even when I said I didn't like it, she'd say that David would, and, "I'm buying it for you, to seduce him." It was very weird, although he was a nice romantic sometimes. He would surprise me with flowers or something, or an amazing present. He was lovely. But I must say he spent a lot of time on his career. He spent a long time in the studio, a long time preparing his tour. We discussed *Diamond Dogs* because he was preparing the *Diamond Dogs* tour and he spoke to this French Belgian cartoon artist called Guy Peellaert and he had made cartoons like *Barbarella*. And he was quite clever in the way he was doing it. And Guy Peellaert did the cover of *Diamond Dogs.* So I introduced them both, yes. David was very selfish. All musicians are selfish and surrounded by secretaries and managers. They're not like everyone else.

CHERRY VANILLA: We were planning an album together called *Electric Beatnik*, which was going to be a mix of his synthesizer music and my poetry. We talked about it a lot on the phone, and in person in Canada, and then a friend was throwing a cocaine party for him in New York, and we were both there. I mentioned the album to him, he said something to me in German and walked away. And that's the last time I spoke to him. The last time I saw him was in the '80s when he was going out with Susan Sarandon. They were both at this charity event in New York. There was a receiving line. Artists move on.

6

GEE MY LIFE'S A FUNNY THING

1974–1976

DANA GILLESPIE: Tony Defries would always say to us that really you can't do anything unless you move to America. All of us. David, Angie, Ronno, me, everyone. He started to say if you want to go through life first class, you must live first class. So once David was up and running with the big RCA deal, MainMan opened its Park Avenue offices, and we all had secretaries and 24/7 limos and it was quite a wild time to be swanning around. Lots of coke, lots of sex. When we first went to New York, David and Angie would be in the Sherry-Netherland hotel, hanging out with Mick Jagger, behaving badly. We'd already had fun times when he had the house in Chelsea in Oakley Street, but New York was something else—life lived on the edge. When MainMan was up and running in New York I would see him on the odd days off but I wasn't initially aware of the breakdown between him and Defries. He was having his wild period of life, and as I was friendly with Angie I could see the marriage breaking down and what had been a fantastic happy family became a disaster.

AMANDA LEAR: I followed David to New York, where MainMan decided to launch my career. They gave a great big lunch at the Four Seasons in New York, but the record never came out. They were too preoccupied with *Young Americans*, so in the end I got fed up, I split from them and I went to Munich, where I got signed by another label. When I went to Germany he was into his American trip and I didn't really like what he became afterwards. He changed his look, got into drugs, left his wife. I dunno, he lived a strange life, always hiding away. I cherished these couple of years we were together because it was the days of Ziggy Stardust, he was this really weird person, and I admired him so much. I was very sorry that most of my friends didn't like him at all. They hated him, thought he was too weird and that he was using me and even Salvador Dalí. I said to Dalí one time in New York, "Let's go see David Bowie, I'll introduce you to him, because he's really great." And Dalí didn't like him at all, he thought he looked ridiculous with his sort of outfit that was made for him. And he was just, jealous I think.

David lived a very secluded life. He never went out in the day. Forget shopping or restaurants, he would only go out at night. So one weekend I took him to stay with some friends living in Sussex, and it was a nightmare, a disaster. I said to him, "You're going to see cows, and fields and trees and green and flowers. Nature!" And he didn't set foot out of the house all weekend. He stayed in and watched TV. I was so angry. What is the point? But he said he liked to stay in because the house was full of books. He loved all the pictures, and the TV. And he just stayed in his room. He didn't want to go for a walk. He didn't care about flowers or any of that. That really annoyed me. Perhaps he changed. He must have, because he spent some time in Switzerland. But in those days he wasn't into nature.

JAYNE COUNTY: As a person I thought David was very mysterious, as if he was always keeping some dark secret or as if he was hiding something from you. We got along OK but no deep bond developed, that's for sure. He was kind of hard to really get to know on many emotional and business levels, especially during the *Diamond Dogs* period. He loved my songwriting and he was amazed that I could pop them out like a ball out of a cannon. I gave him quite a few ideas. He was always on the prowl for new ideas, as he drew energy and brain waves from everyone around him, that's why he loved being surrounded by talented, creative people. He had quite a selection of radical freaks around him at MainMan. Someone was always coming up with a new idea for him to try.

I remember once he seemed eager to find out what I thought of his heart-shaped shaved pubic hair, almost like a little boy trying to impress his favorite schoolteacher. It was at the refrigerator, while I was looking for some ice to go in my drink. It was in David's hotel suite with just a few people over for a drink and a bump or two. He unzipped his pants, right there at the opened fridge door. I looked down and sure enough his pubic hairs were heart-shaped and dyed a bright pink. I said something lame like, "Wow that is so cool," and his pants were slipping lower and lower and it became obvious that he was flirting with me. I could see the top of his Oscar Mayer. I made some excuse as I had absolutely no interest in David sexually at all and I think that that was one reason he turned against me.

It was pretty obvious that David was taking coke. He became very skeletal in his appearance and began rattling off speeches that sounded meaningless to the rest of us—strange things about witchcraft, demons, and sexual prostitution in ancient times, the Holy Prostitutes of Tyre and Sex Temples, weird things that made everyone nervous. He began to get paranoid and accusing people of ripping him off and stealing his drugs. He was always ranting about people's teeth and dental bills! One night at Max's he went into a rage that Marc Bolan was stealing songs from him. Finally, people began to be scared of him. One day it got out at MainMan that David was on his way there and he was raving about Leee Black Childers's dental bills again and we all ran out of the building and went into hiding for the rest of the day. He had to have cartilage removed from one part of his body and put in his nose because the coke had eaten his nose cartilage away.

KEN SCOTT: When we were recording *Diamond Dogs* we worked on the song "1984," and he was already referencing Barry White. He wanted the hi-hat and the strings to sound like they would on a Barry White record. He was already anticipating the sound of *Young Americans.* He had already moved on.

KEITH CHRISTMAS: In 1974, I got a phone call in a London flat owned by a French lady I was staying with. She said, "There ees someone on the phone oo sez 'is name ees Davvid Boweee." I thought it was a wind-up from one of the London liggers I knew, so I said, "Tell him to fuck off."

She came back very insistent so I took the call and this distinctive voice asked me to fly to New York to try out as a guitar player for the *Diamond Dogs* tour. So I flew to the US on the last of the old Boeing 707s, which was more like a Cold War bomber than an airliner. I arrived in New York with just under £2 in my pocket and was met by an enormous African American man in a chauffeur's uniform to get driven to a hotel in a limo. Next day I had to ask for an audience with Tony Defries, who was very unimpressed with me asking him for some expenses. When I met David it was like seeing a person transformed. He was absolutely fine to me, but it was like being in the presence of a sultan. I sat in the lounge of his suite of rooms, with David Cassidy and his girlfriend sitting there waiting to be taken to speak to him about the possibility of Bowie writing a song for him. They didn't speak to me and they both seemed very nervous. I don't know what came of it but the meeting didn't last long. While they were in the other room I was chatting to an African American lady who was extremely feminine and buxom. That evening we were in a limo going to a club and David told me from the backseat that the lady was a man. He explained her figure as being down to large amounts of hormone treatment. He smiled and said, "They can be a lot of fun." I didn't get the job, but I was really pleased to get to visit New York.

GLENN HUGHES (MUSICIAN): In the summer of 1974 I was staying at the Beverly Wilshire Hotel, as I was in L.A. making *Stormbringer* with Deep Purple. I was in my room with Ron Wood one night, and I get a call from Angela Bowie, who I had never met. She said, "My husband would really like to meet you." I said "I'm in my hotel," and she said, "I know, we're on the floor above!" So I went up there with Ron and was blown away by how Bowie looked. Here I was in my bellbottoms and long hair, and there he is in a mustard-colored suit, pink shirt, and red hair. David was very tiny and very fragile, probably no more than ninety-six pounds. He came up to hug me and there was nothing to him. We sat down to talk, and all he wanted to talk about was R&B. He was about to record his blue-eyed soul record, *Young Americans*, and was getting a new band together around him, Ava Cherry, Luther Vandross, et cetera. He had seen me singing on TV and knew that really I was a black white man. He was fascinated by that. He was a great conversationalist, and after a while there was the two of us. We talked till about two in the morning, and he made me feel very comfortable. He was seven or eight years older than I was. I went to my room and tried to get to sleep but I was so blown away. I woke up midafternoon and he called me up and asked if I wanted to come and see his *Diamond Dogs* show tonight, which was extraordinary, full of costume changes, a real Broadway production. We soon became inseparable, and I hung out with him during the day and went to see the show four or five times straight. He would come to the studio and watch me record, sitting by me in the studio, not in the control room. A couple of my band mates didn't appreciate that I was hanging out with David because they didn't think it was right for us. We were seen together all the time, and they were worried this would be sending out the wrong signal. I was recording in the day with Deep Purple, finishing around seven, and would then go to the gig, sometimes with Iggy Pop. There were often other people around but we were with each other. I started to feel comfortable around him by night three or four. We just did coke. In fact my whole time with David was that way. He wanted me to sing on *Young Americans*, but after some rehearsals with Ava Cherry, Deep Purple had to go to Hawaii, so it never happened.

We never slept in the same bed, as we never slept. The love was what spurred us on, the love for music, and the love of drugs. Then when we were alone, we did become addicts. Cocaine is a demonic drug, although we did not need cocaine to have fun however. We argued like man and wife. About everything. He was *very* confrontational. He wasn't physical but he was verbal. He was fucking smart, had incredible wit. But he was self-righteous and he was driven at the time by an obsession with the Third Reich, and he was viewing that shit at my house. He was so into the narcissism of Hitler. He didn't want to be him, but he was fascinated by the Nazi movement. When you do cocaine it makes you very, very energetic. I would get out of the room when he would do this. You go into a trance on cocaine, and he would just watch reels and reels of film about the Nazis. He never did the arm-lifting thing, he was just fascinated.

He was also fascinated by black American music and the devil. He felt the pool in his L.A. home was haunted. He felt the devil was in the pool. We had been up for a couple of days, and the wind must have been howling because the water started to bubble in the pool. It bubbled like it was a Jacuzzi, and it was just me and him and I swear to you, I have a pool, and

I've never seen it bubble before. But that fucking pool was bubbling. You might think, oh my God, these two fucking nincompoops. But on coke you could talk yourself into seeing anything. Do yourself a favor. Stay up for seventy-two hours and you will see shit move. You'll see a box fall off your table, you'll hear things. We were just so damn high.

We loved each other and we kissed on the neck, we held hands, we loved it. I didn't even know David was bi; I didn't know until about 1978. I wasn't convinced. My dad was down the coal mine, I was from Staffordshire, I was as straightlaced as you could fucking get. I was a pub-going guy. David loved the fact that he was hanging out with what he called "a bigger star" than he was. That made me howl.

CHRIS CHARLESWORTH: On the 1975 tour I went to Detroit to interview him. Bowie would exaggerate situations to create headlines, and had become fabulous at manipulating the media. On this occasion he told me he was running out of money and the only reason he was on the road was to generate income because of his deal with Tony Defries. I didn't know whether this was true or not but I printed it because it was a good story, just like when he told Michael Watts he was gay. At the time we all thought this was a bit rum because he had a wife and a son, and he was an incredible womanizer. He always had a different girl on his arm, and there was a girl at MainMan in New York who had a brief fling with him only to find out that he had slept with every other girl in the office. And I don't mean that as a vague euphemism; he actually slept with every other girl who worked for the company. In New York he had a torrid affair with Cyrinda Foxe, a party girl who eventually married David Johansen from the New York Dolls and Steven Tyler from Aerosmith. She worked as a publicist for MainMan in New York and actually appeared in the "Jean Genie" video. She's the "Lorraine" that Bowie mentions in "Watch That Man." Anyway, we were in Detroit when he told me he was broke and that Tony Defries had stolen all his money, and that John Lennon had advised him to manage himself.

I was the American editor of *Melody Maker*, living in New York, and then I was offered a job working as a publicist for RCA. David used to joke that I now had to do as he said. As soon as I started working for the label, whenever I organized an interview with David, I noticed that he would ask the interviewer questions, acting as though he was actually interested in what they had to say. He'd ask if they had read any good books lately or seen any films or theatre or art exhibitions. He wanted to get to know who was interviewing him and figure out if they were an interesting person, and whether or not he should be wasting any time on them. If he thought they were smart he would give a much better interview. He could be incredibly loquacious. The thing was, he said he was broke yet had this huge stretch Mercedes 600 luxury sedan humming on the street outside. It was obvious he was on coke, as he was ridiculously thin, and quite distracted. Iggy was on tour with him, although just as a guest, and when he wanted to talk he just sort of dismissed Iggy, and told him to come back in an hour or two, so Iggy went wandering off. He was never aloof in person, only by reputation.

TONY ZANETTA: We toured nonstop for a year, and Defries was busy planning the third tour, which he wanted to be a 90-10 deal, with 90 percent going to the artist, and 10 percent going to the promoter, which was unheard-of at the time. He also wanted the expenses deducted from the promoter's 10 percent. It was a greedy deal. You might have been able to do that with Elvis Presley, but not with someone of the stature of David Bowie, who still hadn't sold any records. So Defries could not get anywhere with this tour.

The money didn't really start coming in until the *Diamond Dogs/Young Americans* tour, and when it did, it all fell apart. These two men who were really quite different but who shared this common ambition accomplished the first stage of their ambition. Then they took a step back and looked at each other and decided they didn't want to be with each other anymore. David didn't really need Tony anymore. He took the stance that he had been ripped off, but actually there was a misunderstanding of the deal, where David thought he owned 50 percent of the company but actually owned 50 percent of himself. The deal hadn't been besmirched. They'd split everything fifty-fifty after expenses, but they'd split fifty-fifty of David Bowie's income after expenses. David didn't have any right to any of Iggy's income, or Mott's income. But he was the only one who had any income and he was supporting a company that was out of control. They should have got an accountant.

David had moved out of Haddon Hall, moved to Maida Vale and then ended up in Cheyne Walk. He had been working nonstop for a year. And now he's a rock star, hanging out at the Speakeasy with Mick, and this one and that one. Defries is now the successful mogul living in New York. He had got rid of our meager office in the little apartment in East Fifty-Eighth Street, and now had a suite of offices on Park Avenue. He had a driver to take him to a new rental mansion in Greenwich, Connecticut. He had become the mogul he always wanted to be, and David had become the rock star he'd always dreamt of being. And they're not even in the same country. They talked on the phone but less and less. This is when Corinne Schwab was hired to work in the Gunter Grove MainMan office, as Tony couldn't care less who he owed money to there. She spent all day fending off creditors. And David still had to ask MainMan for money. He also found out that this state of affairs was going to last until 1982, when the Defries contract ran out.

David came to New York in April 1974, ostensibly to put the *Diamond Dogs* tour together—which we called tour four even though tour three hadn't happened. And he saw all this money being spent and he didn't like it. So he starts planning the *Diamond Dogs* tour. This was going to be the next stage, something very formally theatrical. We brought in some Broadway people to help with the show but they were actually a lot less experienced than the rock and roll people. And the show was too much, a little too ill conceived. Expensive, expensive to put up, and a lot of technical parts that didn't work. And Tony is not around. MainMan had Ava Cherry, Amanda Lear, Iggy, Freddie Burretti, Dana Gillespie, Wayne [Jayne] County, Mick Ronson, Mott the Hoople, a whole stable of stuff. Dana was actually taking a lot of Tony's time, as she was his favorite. He certainly isn't devoting 100 percent of his time to David Bowie. He is running his empire, he is fritting about with the other artists, and at the same time David is putting together this massive tour, which is out of control from the beginning. David is staying at the Sherry-Netherland hotel, spending thousands of dollars a week on room service, having to organize this tour by himself. Everything was very professional, with a real tour manager, and proper support, but as Tony isn't there, everyone goes to David with their problems, and he's pissed off. Also, David's doing coke like there's no tomorrow. He had not been involved in drugs before, but now he's up for three days at a time doing coke. Coke does a couple of things: apart from ruining your body, it makes you feel omnipotent, like you're the smartest person in the world. Defries, who barely drank a glass of wine, loathed drugs, and he loathed David on drugs, as then there was no chance of any communication at all. So in June, after the Madison Square Garden show, which was a huge success, I went out on the road with him to try and hold his hand. I ended up as a Ping-Pong ball between the two of them. Then, after the Universal Amphitheatre show in Los Angeles, David decides he doesn't want the set anymore, and it morphs into the *Young Americans* tour. Defries was furious when he did this. This was what some people called the Black Show, with Luther Vandross and Carlos Alomar. It was a minstrel show, with David as a black man. Some people called it the White Show because the set was just a plain white background. It was a brilliant show, but from a manager's point of view it was a disaster because Defries was still trying to establish David, and you had Ziggy Stardust turning into a black guy. It was like a really weird career move to make. In Tony's mind David is completely out of control, and in Bowie's mind Defries is totally useless. He didn't need them anymore.

My last official encounter with David was on the last date of the tour, in Atlanta. Thanksgiving. To commemorate this I wanted to throw a little party for the band and the crew, a family party. We were staying at the Continental Hyatt House, but when I tried to book a room for the party I was told that everything was full because of the Thanksgiving weekend. I should have known right then that something was weird. They said we could have the party in a suite instead. We had every room on the floor, we had this extra suite in the corner, and David was in a suite on another floor. The only room we didn't have was a suite right next to the one I had hired. I got a call from the front desk asking us to turn the music down, even though we only had a boom box. Soon there was a knock on the door, and all these vice squad cops burst out of the suite next to us. Everyone threw their drugs on the floor, and David even tried to get them to arrest him, but it was me they took, for possession of cocaine and six other charges. The charges were eventually dropped, but this was the last time I worked for MainMan. A short time later I went to visit him at his house on West Twentieth Street in Manhattan, where he was living with Ava Cherry; the baby, Zowie; and a bunch of others. I used to drink a lot back then, and had had a lot of brandies, but it ended ugly, and that was the end of it. I was also close to Angie, and toyed with the idea of managing her, even though she was totally unmanageable. I was marked by the Ziggy Stardust experience, and in a way we all were. He became a star, Tony became a mogul, and here I was, with nothing.

TOMMY HILFIGER: I saw him in the back room at Max's Kansas City, back in the '70s, 1974 I think. He was with Lou Reed and David Johansen from the New York Dolls, and it was a scene. Max's was a real scene then, but it was a scene every night. You couldn't move for people around him. He was like the king. Glam rock was at its height, and there was a scent of punk in the air. People wore velvet suits, snakeskin boots, shag haircuts, glitter. Hippies had cleaned up and gotten dressed up. And everything came from London. The bells were wider, the jackets were more fitted, with higher shoulders, the lapels were more rounded. The shirts were either floral or printed. Or shiny. Guys were wearing eye shadow, sequins. Dangling earrings, a real femininity and androgyny about the place. And David was leading the charge.

ANGIE BOWIE: David and I were happy for about eight or nine years. We became unhappy, or I did, when I thought that the areas of his life that he was not sharing with me were not joyous. They were drug-orientated. I was called out on many occasions across the world. I mean, four or five planes later I would get somewhere and have to deal with many situations, which were very worrying. And I thought I was not equipped to deal with him. They were all to do with madness, craziness, and paranoia. I worried for him. It was a situation where you really are not equipped. I think the reason now why there are so many drug counselors around is that so many people went through it, and the only way they survived was that these people who they talked to all became drug counselors themselves. I mean, I don't know what else it could possibly be. It was almost like, if you haven't been there, you can't bring someone back. I took drugs sometimes but I didn't have an addictive personality like he had. And David would never persuade me to take stuff. It was the privacy of it that made me fear the danger. There was nothing sociable about it—this was a deep, dark pit.

Late 1974 was a tumultuous period for both Bowie and Iggy Pop. Not only was cocaine having a more than corrosive effect on Bowie's psyche, but Iggy was so out of his mind that, following an altercation with the LAPD in which he was barely ambulatory, he had been admitted to the UCLA Neuropsychiatric Institute.

MICK ROCK: David got Iggy out of the loony bin in L.A. He was very compassionate. As much as he had to be self-consumed, he was very alert to what was happening to his friends and associates. He empathized with people.

NICK KENT: On *The Dick Cavett Show* he looked like a man who had taken a lot of cocaine. The paranoid eyes, the chewing, the hollowed-out cheekbones. He was the same on *The Russell Harty Show*. He had been cocained.

DICK CAVETT: [David was] nervous before the show. It was a little off-putting, and I got a lot of credit for getting through that interview, but he got better, and he settled a bit. He had a bit of the sniffles, as hip people pointed out, but he's a great, great artist, and that made it a happy experience.

ANGIE BOWIE: Our marriage was a partnership to accomplish making David a worldwide star. In the meantime, we also had a love affair which was very nice, and a child, which was even better. So that's what we did. I fell in love with him but I fell out of love with him and became more business orientated after about 1975. I think for a while he was tortured. I think he was trying to figure out what it was. I watched a lot of people take advantage of him and it hurt me, but I also didn't want to be a part of it. We had done a deal originally, when we got together. Not only that we would have an open marriage but that first we would work on his career and then we would work on mine. And that when we had finished those two jobs, we would both be successful and we would both be satisfied that we had done the best for each other. So I worked very hard on his career. Then at a certain point I said I'm going to do this, I'm going to take risks, I'm going to go to these classes. And he was fine, no problem whatsoever.

But another point I said OK, well now, I need to actually perform. And I did *The Mike Douglas Show*, singing "I've Got a Crush on You." And David was so astonished that he wrote "Golden Years." But nothing happened. By the time we had helped everyone else, he didn't have any time for my career. He had forgotten those promises. It wasn't his job, it was my job to do on my own. It really pissed me off. Oh it got me so angry. I wasn't in it because I needed to be recognized as some strange intergalactic star. I just needed to be allowed to write.

Tony Defries tried to get MainMan employees like Tony Zanetta and Cherry Vanilla to devise a way to get David to divorce me. It was just awful. Ten executives! There were ten of them and he said find a way to get David to divorce her. He couldn't handle me, and he knew I could see right through him. And I hated that he made David work like a dog. He wasn't scared of me though; he wasn't scared of anyone. But David did get rid of him. David said to me, "You're right, he's gotta go." Otherwise he was working to support an entire entourage. David didn't like confrontation. He didn't care for it at all; he would always rather leave. It was pointless trying to fight with him, as it was like fighting with a blancmange. There was no resistance. You felt like you were torturing a child. But I said to him, I think that you're being taken for a ride by all these people that you've been supporting. And I said, when I ask you for something, I feel like I'm in a long line of people with their hands out. I said we shouldn't feel like that. So that was my appeal to him to save himself from being worked to death.

David took so many drugs because he was working too hard. David was supporting the entire MainMan company that Tony Defries had set up in New York. But there were 100 or 150 people living off David's sweat. Even the most chilled person would have turned to some sort of relief. He got better, you know, he fired Defries, he changed his tune, he said he was going to move, he said he was going to divorce me. I got out of the picture, and he was still not completely better until well into the '80s. He was still wrestling with his demons.

DANA GILLESPIE: MainMan ended badly, as I think we all knew it would. There was a very strange atmosphere towards the end, as bills weren't being paid, telephone calls weren't returned, it was odd. Now, I had started going to Mustique again as I had been I going there when I was younger with my parents. I introduced Tony Defries to the island, and this was back when there were only a few houses on the island, and long before Mick Jagger coerced David into buying a house there. In those days, and this is 1975 remember, you had to plan a phone call two days in advance, actually book it. And I was with Defries on the island, and he was saying that he was going to have to have this difficult call with David. And I was there when Defries ended it. I was sitting outside but I could hear everything through the slatted windows. He told David that he couldn't continue to be involved, and that he didn't want to work with him anymore. It was a very heavy conversation. I distinctly remember him saying, "It's over." It was the end of a chapter. I moved back to England when MainMan collapsed, but I couldn't record for anyone else for five years because of all the contractual disputes. It was very raw. I continued to see Angie, but I didn't see David again. Everyone was frozen out, something that I know Ronno took very badly.

CHRIS CHARLESWORTH: When Defries locked up all his money, shall we say, Bowie went pleading to Ken Glancey, who was the president of RCA, and begged for a loan. So RCA bankrolled him to the tune of half a million dollars.

TERRY O'NEILL: I didn't really like his music as I was more of a jazz fan, but he had a great mind and was really good company. He was always polite, and it was a pleasure to work with him, as opposed to the lads from Liverpool or the Stones from South London. So I'd always be willing to do jobs for him because he was so nice. A year after *Diamond Dogs* I was in L.A. and Tony Defries asked me to come and photograph the show. The next day I get a call from Elizabeth Taylor, who I'd got to know, and she said, I'd love to meet David Bowie. She wanted to cast him in this film *Blue Bird* she was making. She asked me to invite him to her house in Beverly Hills on Sunday, as she was having lunch with George Cukor, who was going to direct it. So I did. I turned up on the day, and Bowie hadn't arrived. Then it's two o'clock, then three, then four, and he still hadn't arrived. Five o'clock comes and there's still no Bowie. This was crazy because it was usually the other way round, as Elizabeth had a habit of keeping everyone else waiting. So we're just about to pack up and go home when he arrived with Cherry Vanilla, who he was seeing at the time. In fact it was probably Cherry Vanilla's fault that he didn't turn up. He was very fond of her. He charmed everyone, and we started taking some pictures, and Elizabeth and him got on great. But he was out of it. No one had ever made Elizabeth Taylor wait for five hours before, but he was quite wasted when he pitched up. Tony Defries later asked me to shoot him with William Burroughs too. I also shot him at Peter Sellers's birthday party in L.A., when he played saxophone in an impromptu band with Bill Wyman, Keith Moon, Ronnie Wood, and Joe Cocker. He was like David Niven.

ALAN YENTOB: David had seen a small documentary I'd made for the BBC in 1974 called *Profile of a Monster*, a parody of how people make profiles on television. I got a call from Tony Defries who said that David had liked it, and so I went to New York to meet him. And David boldly said, "Would you like to make a film about me?" So I did. I was surprised by the calculated side of him. He was about go on tour with the *Diamond Dogs* show, and as it was this extraordinary spectacle, he wanted it documented. The next time I met him was in L.A. I decided I was going to call the film *The Collector*, because David was a person who collected characters, and also because he was sort of propelled by curiosity. In his early life he didn't quite know what he was going to be, and he was pursuing all kinds of things. He painted, he sang, he danced. He had collected all of these characters and he was going through a period where he was disposing of them—Ziggy Stardust, Aladdin Sane. So I wanted to make a film about his personality through the songs.

The first thing I asked him to do was to make a death mask, which is the first scene in the film, and surprisingly he did. He was obviously preoccupied with these notions of mortality, as so many of his songs were about that—"Rock 'n' Roll Suicide," "Aladdin Sane," Jacques Brel's "My Death." He had suicide in his family, he had a schizophrenic half-brother, he was surrounded by trauma, and so this side of life was something he was well aware of. But he had this imaginative gift, so every minute he had he wanted to use effectively, creatively. He was interested in visual representation, in mime, in theatricality. You could tell by his tone of voice that he was preoccupied with these things. I went and found a cameraman in L.A., as I didn't know how long the film was going to take, I didn't know what time of day or night I was going to be shooting. I actually found the cameraman in Malibu, and when I went to his front door I was greeted by this completely naked man, as he had just got out of the swimming pool. It was already a weird trip. From then on we just went on the road, and it got weirder and weirder.

I was surprised by the amount of access I got, and I was surprised by how open he was with me, and how he talked to me in confidence. I had to pinch myself sometimes. We didn't share cocaine, but when you see him in the back of the car, or being interviewed, you can tell what condition he was in. He was very thin, eating very little. And he had a very demanding show to do night after night. There was a scene where he was clearly being followed by a police car, and you can see that he's worried. He's talking about arriving in L.A. when there's an earthquake, and he was on edge, worried that the police were going to catch up with him and say that he'd taken some cocaine. He was pretty fragile at that time. He later told me that at the time he was "so blocked, so stoned, it was quite a casualty case, and when I see that film now I cannot believe I survived it."

With the film he wanted to put on record what he was doing. The point about the *Diamond Dogs* tour was that it was very extravagant; every sequence was different, every character was reimagined and developed, so it wasn't like a normal concert. He didn't sit there and sing the *Hunky Dory* numbers, he reenacted them. That was what was so special about the show. So my view is that he didn't want me to capture his collapse or his psychological state, he wanted me to capture the stage show. He felt the show was saying goodbye to all these characters and he wanted it to be put on record. But what emerged was something else, as at the time he was this very troubled, very fragile guy who was rethinking his career and where he was going. And going through a difficult period.

So most of the interviews were either in the backs of cars in the early hours of the morning, or very late at night. There is that line in the film where he says that he never wanted to be a rock and roll star, "Really guv, I never did . . ." He was conflicted. What's unusual about the film is that it's only him and the fans, no one else. It's entirely about the songs. What I loved about it was when you listen to those songs, whether it's "Changes" or "Life on Mars?" or "Oh! You Pretty Things" or "Space Oddity" for that matter, they're all about vulnerabilities, they're all about these kids who might identify with him because they come from a similar kind of background, who come from a provincial place who don't quite know what they're going to do with their lives. He was brought up in a place that wasn't quite inside the city. The fans aren't necessarily talking sense, but they have been given this lifeline by him and his songs. They were offered an escape, an escape into imagination and other places. He was in a continual conversation with them. He had a psychological insight into people's moods, aspirations, and vulnerabilities, which all came from his childhood.

He was clearly thinking about the next stage in his life, Philadelphia, Carlos Alomar, Luther Vandross. He was about to become a soul singer. He was on a transformative journey. By the time he got to Philadelphia he was far more up, as was the music. He'd already moved on.

EARL SLICK: Being a blues player, and having to make a living in New York City, I was already doing Sam and Dave, James Brown, Wilson Pickett, and all that shit, I was playing the real thing. So *Young Americans* wasn't a stretch for me. But he'd brought Carlos Alomar in, who was more from the pop R&B area. I was more of the Memphis shit. So the album was more of a Carlos thing, rightfully so, for what David needed. He was ruthless with people, especially musicians, and I was surprised I was kept. What happened was, when we finished *Diamond Dogs*, there was a break, and during that break, I was told that David had got another guitar player and that I was out of the picture. So I just went about my business. I was a little pissed off, because of the way it was done, and then out of nowhere I get a phone call: can you fly to L.A., like, now? So I was back. That was when we did a kind of a hybrid of the end of the *Diamond Dogs* tour going into the next phase, so this is September 1974. But by then Carlos was the musical director so I was a guitar for hire. We went from doing a lot of stuff from *Ziggy*, *Aladdin Sane*, and *Diamond Dogs* to doing versions that were less rock and roll, and went through a few different rhythm sections in the interim. We were also starting the *Young Americans* record, so it didn't feel that great. I have to be honest with you, it really didn't. Everything was disjointed. But *Young Americans* was a Carlos record and he did a great job.

CARLOS ALOMAR (GUITARIST): He came to America after doing the Spiders from Mars, and during that time it seems that he had contracted this situation with Lulu, to do some tracks, including "The Man Who Sold the World." I was a session musician working at RCA, working in Studio A, Elvis Presley's studio. Tony Silvester, who was one of the singers of the Main Ingredient, told me there was a shot at this gig. I really wanted to meet Lulu. I'd seen *To Sir with Love*, and she was this blue-eyed soul singer, I said, "Yeah!" But when I turned up at the session, she wasn't there. Who was there? David Bowie. He was using words like "Hey man," and "That's cool," these phrases that were typically American, but sounded so weird coming from a Brit. Brits used to study Americans, and they knew their Bo Diddleys and their Chuck Berrys. He was such a sweet guy. He had a vast knowledge of African American music, R&B music. I cut the gig, my guitar playing was very good, and he was impressed with that. But then I told him, I said, "Man, you look terrible. You look like shit, you need to eat some fucking food." Those were my actual words. I was always very forward with David. I said he needed to eat, and so he came in his limousine to visit me and my wife, Robin, in our house in Queens.

I offered to take him to the Apollo Theater, where I was playing with the Main Ingredient. I also played in the house band there. He'd always wanted to go, and loved it. He had this orange hair and his big-rimmed fedora hat and he was not only the only white person there, he was whiter than white. He is probably the whitest white guy I have ever seen. Imagine stepping out of a limousine looking like that and walking into the Apollo Theater in front of a line of black people all lining up, waiting to come in. He just strolls right in and gets a front-row seat, he was in the lap of luxury. I introduced him to Richard Pryor that night, who couldn't make him out at all. He said, "What's this white dude doing in my dressing room?" David was fearless, he didn't care. I'm a Latin guy, Puerto Rican, although everyone thought I was black, so I took him to all the Latin clubs, and we hung out. He tried to hire me three times before he could afford me. I was already married to Robin, so I was already answering to a higher power. So *Young Americans*, here we come! That album, self-labeled in his own right as plastic soul. I defy that and say that it was a true, authentic soul record; he had the formula 100 percent. You'll hear a lot of people try and sing "Fame" and "Young Americans," but when it comes to the other songs on the record, they can't touch him. He had falsetto on top, and massive bottom on the bottom. I had been working with the O'Jays, the Ohio Players, so I knew. He knew exactly when he heard what he wanted, that Harold Melvin and the Blue Notes thing that he knew. He knew when he heard the Wes Montgomery guitar sound that he wanted, and when Luther started singing those background vocals, this became a real album. We did one song a day. Boom. Sometimes we did two songs a day, and David didn't even have the words written. He had to run home and stay up for four or five days just to match the moment.

Ultimately, as a man's man, you've got to have a sense of humor and you've got to be who you are from the beginning. I'm not one to kowtow, I'm not one to kiss ass, I'm not that kind of guy, and David Bowie respected men who knew what the hell they were doing. I'm a minister's son, and all I want to do is have a good time and hold on to my happiness. When you are a musician, you have to develop a great personality, a great disposition, or else why would anyone want to go on tour with you? I think that's why we clicked. I'm the guy that never brings problems. I ran a very tight ship, and he knew he could count on me. This is how we had a relationship that lasted all those decades.

MIKE GARSON: When we were recording *Young Americans* he couldn't really get his creative thing going until two or three in the morning, until the cocaine arrived. So consequently I'd be the only one awake, as I never used any drugs in my life. At six in the morning he'd be very wide-eyed and on top of things. It didn't matter what state he was in, we never argued; in fact in thirty years we didn't argue once. He was always so focused, always professional, always smiling. He relied a lot on David Sanborn and Luther Vandross on that record, because so much of the structures were complex, and the vocals were incredibly complicated. My continual joke was, when is it my turn [to get fired], because I managed to stay the course, whereas everyone else eventually got fired. But then he made *The Man Who Fell to Earth* and he didn't need me anymore. We're in the Plaza Hotel in New York, around Christmas time in 1975, and he turns to me and says, "Mike, you're going to be with me for the next twenty years." And the phone rang approximately twenty years later, asking me if I could be in New York the next day. I think he may have called me a little earlier if he had known that I had quit Scientology in 1982, but there we are. He used to call me Garson the Parson.

Scientology had a terrible reputation in Britain, and it had big problems in the psychiatric world, and his brother Terry obviously had a lot of problems. So David already had a very bad opinion of the subject. At the time I was drinking the Kool-Aid. I later changed my mind, but at the time I thought there were certain things about Scientology that worked. I was good at differentiation and I could take that 10 percent that I thought was very powerful and use it. But there were lots of things on the organizational front that didn't feel good to me, so I eventually left. I actually got Woody [Woodmansey] into Scientology, so when I left in 1982 he stopped talking to me, and we were best friends at the same time. And he hasn't talked to me since.

AVA CHERRY: Paul McCartney was staying at the Plaza in New York, and David and I went up to see him. Linda McCartney opened the door and we said hello, but Paul was not really friendly. So we sat down across from them on opposite couches. And I could tell David felt a little uncomfortable. They offered a drink and I had some water or something. But they just sat looking at us like we were under a microscope. Paul was staring at David and didn't say anything. So David said: "Paul, I met with John," and started talking about John, but when he asked Paul a question he didn't answer. Linda answered instead. Then he looked at Paul again and said something else to him and she answered the second time. So David got angry and said, "Paul you can't answer your own questions? You can't speak yourself?" Paul said something smart, and so David looked at me and said, "We're going." And we got up and walked out. And that was it. It was really bizarre. I remember another time we were at this party with Bob Dylan, Ronnie Wood, all these stars, and they were all being a bit frosty to David. We walked in and there was a very chilly atmosphere, like: Who is this glam-rock guy? Bob Dylan said, "Who does this guy think he is?" And David said to me, "Who do I think I am?" They tried to make fun of him, and seemed like they were jealous of him. There were lots of people like that. At a party at David's apartment once in New York, Jimmy Page spilled something on one of the silk pillows. And when David saw it he wanted to know who had done it. He thought I had done it. He stood there chastising me about the pillows. So finally someone says it was Jimmy. So he looks over at Jimmy and says, "You had me blame Ava for this? And you didn't say anything?" Then they exchanged a few negative words and Jimmy said, "Well, I'm going to leave," and David said, "Why don't you take the window?" I think the reason Jimmy Page was there was because David was obsessed with Aleister Crowley, and so was he.

When Bowie moved to the United States, he had initially stayed in a variety of hotels before renting apartments on West Seventeenth Street and West Twentieth Street. In March 1975 he swapped coasts and moved his base to L.A., while his cocaine addiction coarsened into an inevitable chore. Having stayed with Glenn Hughes at his house in Los Feliz, he then lived with his manager Michael Lippman for a brief period in Hollywood, before renting a bungalow with an indoor swimming pool at 637 North Doheny Drive, on the perimeter of Beverly Hills, and just around the corner from the Troubadour, and then a much larger house on Stone Canyon Road in the woods above Bel-Air.

AVA CHERRY: There was so much going on at that time. When David realized that he had had so much money stolen from him he just collapsed. His management company were basically spending all his money, taking trips back and forth to Paris and staying in the most expensive hotels, and just doing stuff and spending the money. I was living with a friend in Laurel Canyon, and David had just moved to Doheny Drive. I called him up when I moved there and an hour later he was at my door with a suitcase. He was not in a good way. Then we lived together in Century City for a while. L.A. was his next big adventure. David was the kind of person that when he was ready to go to the next experience, that was it, he was off. And L.A. was like that for him. Maybe you might be put on the shelf for a later date like Iggy or somebody like that, but if it was time for you to dissolve in that moment then he'd finish with you. I saw him a couple of times over at Herbie Hancock's, as Herbie was a Buddhist at the time. And then there was one time where he was staying in Marilyn Monroe's house. He told me it was haunted. Things were so awful during that drug period. I saw a little bit of it but not too much. It was devastating for him. I tried to stay out of it, because it made me feel depressed. When he was with me it was controlled to a certain point and then when he went off on his own it became something totally different. I still loved him and cared about what happened. I did find consolation in friends like Mick Jagger and Keith Richards. They tried to make me feel better about what was going on.

HARRY MASLIN (PRODUCER): When I first met David, I suppose I was a bit of an outsider. I was called in as the engineer on *Young Americans*, and then took over the production when David started working with John Lennon [Tony Visconti had already been released from the project]. It was rather bizarre for me, as I came into a scene I wasn't used to and I had people like Mick Jagger hanging out in the studio, and John Lennon in the control room, looking at what I was doing. It was a little disconcerting for the first week or so. I was at home having a traditional Thanksgiving dinner with friends, blasted out of my mind—on alcohol, nothing heavier—when I got a phone call. It was David, and he said, "You have to do me a favor, my booking is up at Record Plant and I need additional time to continue my work." I replied by assuring him that I would do my best to get the additional time. He then hit me with the zinger: "You have to do me another favor, you have to produce the rest of *Young Americans*." And I kind of took the phone away from my ear and thought, Oh really? A favor? I said, "Well, David I think I can do you this favor." The original reason why the Record Plant—where I was working at the time—put me on his project was because I was kinda the R&B guy, and *Young Americans* was an R&B-influenced album, so we started on the new songs, and he took me into the inner circle, so to speak. He was very kind. He knew that I was still walking on eggshells a little bit, but he also trusted me and my musical intent and my engineering prowess, for lack of a better word. I remember specifically mixing "Fame" and being completely paranoid after the first mix, thinking that I could do a better one than the one I turned in to RCA, but then I had people like Carlos Alomar come up to me and tell me what a wonderful job I did on the mix, and I started to calm down a little bit.

AVA CHERRY: *Young Americans* was amazing because at that time David was one of the first white artists they'd recorded at Sigma Sound Studios in Philadelphia. David was immediately accepted by the black community. Before he arrived I'd heard that some people were sniping about him coming to the city, but I never saw anything like that. I heard there were some players who didn't want to be on the record because David was white, but I don't believe that. David had already mapped exactly how he wanted to do it. He had met Carlos Alomar, and he didn't really care if there was a stigma. We went in there and just played away. David was very detailed about everything that he wanted to do. He would be writing it down and he would write in a diary and write different things every day, all the time. He knew exactly what he wanted to do and was not ruffled by any of those things. We went in and it was great. He also did a show at the Tower Theater in Philly, and that was a huge thing for the city. That's where he recorded *David Live.* It was great singing with Luther Vandross, as he was such a great singer, such an accomplished arranger, and our voices melded together like magic and butter.

LUTHER VANDROSS (SINGER): My friend Carlos [Alomar], whom I had grown up with, got a job playing guitar for David Bowie. Carlos invited me to the studio. He and his wife, Robin, had gotten married a couple of years before and she is also a singer. As a matter of fact, Robin is one of the girls with whom I used to sing in the hallway. I stated making little vocal arrangements and showing them to Robin. I didn't know that Bowie had overheard all this. He was sitting right behind me at the board, and he said, "That's a great idea. Put that down." So I put it down and next thing you know one thing led to another, and I was doing the vocal arrangements for the whole album. I wrote one of the songs on the album. Bowie overheard it and said, "I want to record that. Do you mind?" When I did it, it was called "Funky Music." Bowie changed it to "Fascination." He said he didn't want to be so presumptuous as to say "funky music," since he was a rock artist. He said, "Do you mind?" And I said, "You're David Bowie, I live at home with my mother, you can do what you like."

AVA CHERRY: I was there the day David brought John Lennon into the studio. He actually wrote a diary entry that day where he says, "January 30th, introduced Ava to a Beatle." We were going in that day to record "Fame," and before the session David was freaking out because he was so nervous. He really admired John Lennon, and that day David was like a little kid. And then John comes in the door and John had those granny glasses on, right? And David looks and me and says, "He really does wear those granny glasses!" He really liked the fact that Lennon had the whole Lennon look. What you imagine John to be is exactly how he was: charming, funny, and they both hit it off immediately. They became really, really good friends. It was only me, Carlos, John, and David in the studio—and I think Geoffrey [MacCormack] might have been there. Yoko came and brought us some sushi and then she left. She was very sweet. I liked her. She was not how I imagined her and how the Beatles said she was. John was sitting there at one point with his twelve-string getting ready to play "Across the Universe," and he looks up and says, "Are we having a good time?" We were all so happy that John Lennon was so relaxed. David was just over the moon. He drew David a caricature of himself. And David put it in this solid gold frame. He really loved it. I didn't think "Fame" would turn out the way it did. I thought because John Lennon was on it that he was going to get lots of critical acclaim, but it was just a James Brown groove at one point.

DAVID BOWIE: I spent quite a lot of time getting to know Lennon, and I do remember we went to a lot of bars together. We spent hours and hours discussing fame, and what you had to do to get it, to get there. If I'm honest it was his fame we were discussing, because he was so much more famous than anyone who had been before. I remember that Carlos and I were working on this riff, and I remember than it was John who started riffing on "Fame," screaming at the top of his voice in the studio. He was screaming, I was writing the lyrics, and Carlos was crashing through the riff. It all came together so quickly and so brilliantly. It was an incredibly intoxicating time and I can't quite believe that we didn't try and write more things together, because just being around him was breathtaking. He had all this energy, which I suppose I didn't expect when I first met him.

HARRY MASLIN: John happened to be in the studio [Record Plant] with me one day as I was working on "Fame." I decided to start the record off with a backward piano chord leading into the downbeat of the song. Without telling him my motive, I asked John if he would be so kind as to go out to the piano and just hit one chord when given the appropriate cue. He agreed and sat himself down at the grand piano. In preparation, I proceeded to take the multitrack tape I was recording on and give it a backward/upside-down wind, my usual technique of recording something backwards. I recorded some snare rim hits as a cue for John. He was waiting patiently through all of this but as I got on the studio talkback to explain what I needed him to do, he gave me a bit of a puzzled look. John hit the chord perfectly (of course) and it came off exactly as planned. He came back into the control room and as I was turning the tape over to hear the desired effect for the first time, his curiosity got the best of him and he asked me what I was doing. I then explained to him what I was trying to achieve. He followed up with a statement that could have been devastating to me had it not been that I knew he meant no harm. "The Beatles never did it that way," he said. Crushing! Trying to save myself from humiliation I said in a bit of a sarcastic, mimicking voice, "OK John, how did the Beatles [with emphasis] do it?" He told me that the Beatles would have just recorded the chord directly to a piece of quarter-inch tape in a normal manner, given that tape a backward wind and then "fly" it on the multitrack, which would be running in the normal direction. Trying to save my ass and professional self-esteem (and with a smile) I told him that of course I had considered that technique but due to the precise timing I was looking for, had chosen the alternate method.

So we did well with the album, although at that point I didn't know if I was ever going to hear from David again.

JOHN LENNON (BEATLE): [*Rolling Stone* said I was "playing second fiddle . . ." but] that's garbage. What second fiddle? I'm not playing second fiddle to Ringo when I play rhythm guitar. It's all right for me to play rhythm guitar in back of Ringo's record, but if I play rhythm guitar in back of Elton's record, or in back of David Bowie's somehow I'm lowering myself. . . . I think they are good artists. And they are friends of mine, and they asked me to go and play. It's like in the old days. Like Brian Jones is on a track of the Beatles years ago. And he played saxophone. In those days you weren't allowed to say, the record companies wouldn't allow it. So it was never mentioned. Everybody used to play on each other's sessions, but nobody ever said anything. Nowadays it's always said. And Elton asked me to play on "Lucy." He said, "I'm gonna do this song. I'd love it if you came and played." He was too shy to ask me. He got a friend that we both have to ask me . . . and I said, "Sure I'll come." So I went to play and sang chorus or some garbage. Why is it not belittling for Mick Jagger to sing in back of Carly Simon? Why am I some kind of god that isn't allowed to do anything?? It's bullshit.

DAVID BOWIE: I guess he [John Lennon] defined for me, at any rate, how one could twist and turn the fabric of pop and imbue it with elements from other art forms, often producing something extremely beautiful, very powerful, and imbued with strangeness. Also, uninvited, John would wax on endlessly about any topic under the sun and was over-endowed with opinions. I immediately felt empathy with that.

The seductive thing about John was his sense of humor. Surrealistically enough, we were first introduced in about 1974 by Elizabeth Taylor. Miss Taylor had been trying to get me to make a movie with her. It involved going to Russia and wearing something red, gold, and diaphanous. Not terribly encouraging, really. I can't remember what it was called—it wasn't *On the Waterfront* anyway, I know that.

We were in L.A., and one night she had a party to which both John and I had been invited. I think we were polite with each other, in that kind of older-younger way. Although there were only a few years between us, in rock and roll that's a generation, you know? Oh boy, is it ever.

So John was sort of [in Liverpool accent], "Oh, here comes another new one." And I was sort of, "It's John Lennon! I don't know what to say. Don't mention the Beatles, you'll look really stupid."

And he said, "Hello, Dave." And I said, "I've got everything you've made—except the Beatles."

A couple of nights later we found ourselves backstage at the Grammys where I had to present "the thing" to Aretha Franklin. Before the show I'd been telling John that I didn't think America really got what I did, that I was misunderstood. Remember that I was in my twenties and out of my head.

So the big moment came and I ripped open the envelope and announced, "The winner is Aretha Franklin." Aretha steps forward, and with not so much as a glance in my direction, snatches the trophy out of my hands and says, "Thank you everybody. I'm so happy I could even kiss

David Bowie." Which she didn't! And she promptly spun around and swanned off, stage right. So I slunk off, stage left.

And John bounds over and gives me a theatrical kiss and a hug and says, "See, Dave. America loves ya."

We pretty much got on like a house on fire after that.

He once famously described glam rock as just rock and roll with lipstick on. He was wrong of course, but it was very funny.

Towards the end of the '70s, a group of us went off to Hong Kong on a holiday and John was in, sort of, house-husband mode and wanted to show Sean the world. And during one of our expeditions on the back streets a kid comes running up to him and says, "Are you John Lennon?" And he said, "No, but I wish I had his money." Which I promptly stole for myself.

It's brilliant. It was such a wonderful thing to say. The kid said, "Oh, sorry. Of course you aren't," and ran off. I thought, "This is the most effective device I've heard."

I was back in New York a couple of months later in Soho, downtown, and a voice pipes up in my ear, "Are you David Bowie?" And I said, "No, but I wish I had his money."

"You lying bastard. You wish you had my money." It was John Lennon.

BOB HARRIS: I interviewed John Lennon in 1975 and he went into great details about the recording process of "Fame." He said that it developed from a simple riff, layering up and up in the studio, really building up from nothing. He said that as he was always in New York, and rarely left it, when the British guys came into town, they called him up and asked him to show them around. I remember John saying, "They don't need me, but it's nice to hang out." David had done the same thing, coercing Lennon into the studio to try and work on some tracks. "We were in the studio, and this riff started coming out, and we worked on it for three or four hours until the song was written." And it sounds like that, as it has that lovely loose spontaneity to it. And that was what John said: "It just sparked."

JOHN LENNON: [How do I feel about people like Elton and Bowie doing covers of all those old Beatles songs?] I love it. I was thrilled he [Elton] was doing it. People are afraid of Beatle music. They are still afraid of my songs. Because they got that big image thing: You can't do a Beatle number. . . . You can't touch a Lennon song; only Lennon can do it. . . . It's garbage! Anybody can do anything.

DAVID BOWIE: John Lennon was good at telling people off, but not me.

OLIVER JAMES: Bowie didn't do narrative like Lennon. He wasn't explicit. Bowie was genuinely an artist who wanted to get to the truth, but through the manner of the expression of what he was trying to communicate. He was making art, not telling a story. It's like Nic Roeg, and him and Nic were like the perfect match I suppose. I said to Nic once, "Why don't you make documentaries?" And he said, "Oh no I couldn't do that, I couldn't reveal that much about myself." As though his films hadn't done that already! The reason why art is so great is because it's not just describing the problems that the art is trying to express, it becomes art in the process of creating it, and then producing it. David was reaching out to the truth, but there was obviously a part of him that didn't want to confront the truth, which was his family.

PAUL DU NOYER (JOURNALIST): Bruce Springsteen wrote "It's Hard to Be a Saint in the City" when he was unknown; it became the closing track of his 1973 debut, *Greetings from Asbury Park, N.J.* Though its hoodlum street-poetry sounds overripe, it impressed David Bowie. He'd already seen Springsteen play a New York club. Now, in the first flush of fame, he recognized the Jersey kid as a contender. Perhaps Bowie liked the urban dread: "After I heard this track," he said later, "I never rode the subway again. . . . That really scared the living ones out of me." I think there is an echo of it in Bowie's apocalyptic *Diamond Dogs*. Bowie attempted "It's Hard to Be a Saint" in 1974, while recording *Young Americans* in Philadelphia. And Springsteen dropped by the studio. The pair got along OK, but they were not soul mates. Besides, Bowie at that point was fundamentally off his cake. (Keepin' it real, Bruce wore a dirty leather jacket and arrived by public transport. Bowie, on the other hand, wore a bright-red beret and yapped about UFOs.) The track was abandoned, then revived a year later when Bowie was making *Station to Station*. Once again it failed to make the cut and has only appeared, since then, as a bonus outtake on sundry CDs. (He also tried Springsteen's "Growin' Up," and ditched that too.) From that point on their styles diverged entirely: Springsteen went from Byronic grease monkey to plain-speaking Everyman. Bowie's next stop was austere European art-noise.

DAVID BOWIE: I was in Hong Kong on holiday with John Lennon in the late '70s. We'd been drinking and we were trying to find a place to eat monkeys' brains. We actually found a place, but fortunately it was closed. However, we saw the tables with the holes in them—they put the monkey through the hole, whip its skull off, and eat it like an egg. But we both lingered and a couple of guys recognized Lennon. They took him in a back room, and he came out and said, "God, I'm high as a kite." They'd made him drink the blood of a snake. I guess it was a Triad thing, but it made him very stoned. Anyway, he went off and then came rushing down the road a few minutes later saying, "Open your mouth!" And he shoved this thing in my mouth—it was ghastly. I asked him what it was and he said, "Swallow it." So I did. And he said, "That's a thousand-day-old egg cooked in horse piss." I said, "You bastard!" They cook it in horse urine, then cover it in layers of different kinds of manures, and bury it in the ground. I think they probably bury it only for a few days, but they call it a thousand-day-old egg. They dig it up again and then you eat it. It was horrible.

Most people think that Lennon was trapped in America during that time, but it's not true. He used to carry a briefcase with just his wallet and a T-shirt in it, and he used to travel like that all the time. When he got to a new place and his T-shirt needed washing, he'd give it to the waiter or the bellboy. He'd sign it for them and then buy another one on the street. He'd get everything else from the hotel—a razor or whatever he needed. He would say, "That's how you travel." I suppose the period when he was going abroad a bit was when he had that strange thing going, when he wasn't really with Yoko. But his son Sean was with him. He took a nanny with him as well, but John was with Sean an awful lot in Hong Kong—except we used to go out at night and get raving drunk. One time we ended up at a strip club where beers were served at a round table, with a naked girl sitting in the middle of it and spinning around slowly. John was getting quite verbose because he had really put away quite a few, and the owner of the club asked us to leave. So we were thrown out by these, presumably, lesser Triad members. We're on the sidewalk, and John is frothing at the mouth and shouting, "Let us back in! We've paid our money, we want to come in and finish our drinks!" And they said, "No, you fuck off." And he said, "Do you know who I am? I'm a fucking Beatle!" I said, "I don't believe that. Say it again." He said, "I'm a fucking Beatle. I'm a fucking Beatle!" and we started laughing. We were just on the floor, it was so funny. And then we went to a street market and they were selling Beatle jackets, and I got him to put one on. I took a little Polaroid. It's so lovely. Just John and his Beatle jacket. "I'm a fucking Beatle!"

CARLOS ALOMAR: When we first went out on tour, I wasn't just going on tour with David Bowie, I was going on tour with my wife, with my best friend, with my cousin who worked in the wardrobe department, with the people who were already in my band. I gave him my whole life and then we all went on tour. It was a lot of fun. I was twenty-two years old! He was breaking out into a whole different David. He'd finally kicked off Ziggy. He was finally breaking, he was doing "Young Americans," he was on *Soul Train*, he was representing.

DAVID BOWIE: My Young American was plastic, deliberately so, and it worked in a way I hadn't really expected, inasmuch that it really made me a star in America, which is the most ironic, ridiculous part of the equation. Because while my invention was more plastic than anyone else's, it obviously had some resonance. Plastic soul for anyone who wants it. We really worked hard to make that record come alive.

Psychologically, this was the start of Bowie's very worst period, a time when his cocaine psychosis affected everything he did. He never looked less than extraordinary, though. He was invited to the Academy Awards in 1975, and could not have looked more strange. He was wearing a huge Spanish black hat, a cape, and carrying a cane. His old friend Gus Dudgeon was there, the man who produced "Space Oddity," and he couldn't believe his eyes: "He looks fucking dramatic, like the ultimate gigolo. He's surrounded by eight tons of charisma and everyone is gasping." Dudgeon hadn't seen him for six years, but when David sees him he walks over, the mask drops and he says, "God, bloody hell, how are you?" Gus says, "The Thin White Duke disappears and a completely different bloke appears. He gives us a hug and a kiss, sits and talks animated for fifteen minutes, and when he gets up to leave, on goes the hat, here comes the charisma and he's immediately the Thin White Duke again. What a star!"

GLENN HUGHES: This was his dark year. Everyone in L.A. did coke at the time but he did more than most. He did more than anyone. It was the year that cocaine damn near killed him. And it was the year pretty much spent with me. I saw him go through so many paranoiac moments. My house was literally half a mile away from some of the Manson murders, and one night David came to me in the middle of the night and said, "Where are your guns and knives?" I wasn't going to tell him where my guns were because they were really hidden, because when you're doing that much cocaine, you become extremely paranoid. You think someone's going to come and shoot you. It wasn't my gun, it was left by one of my close friends whose dad was in the mafia, and I hid it. But David went into the kitchen and got all the sharp steak knives and the butcher knives, and he hid them. When I came down in the morning I said where are all the knives? And he said it's just in case the Manson family—who by now were all in jail—came to get him. He was ninety-five pounds, and he was doing mass quantities of cocaine. I would say we were probably both doing seven grams a day each. And that is a lot of cocaine to snort. And we had an endless supply of cocaine. Knowing now what I know about cocaine, one of us should have died.

There was no security in the rooms with us. It was me, him, a keyboard, a book. He was making *Station to Station*, and he was writing the lyrics at my home. He wrote that album totally addicted. I was watching him going about the writing process. He was cutting and pasting his lyrics, he would write lyrics out and then cut the lines up and then jumble them up. Line one, two, three, four. He would have made line five, line two, and line seven, line three. That happened on two or three of his songs and it worked incredibly well. And he was drawing, with magic markers. He was about to start *The Man Who Fell to Earth*, and as he was getting into this role, he's drawing stars falling from the sky and humans falling from the sky and I'm thinking, "Am I going crazy? Or am I going to sit back and watch the show?" So I did watch it but it did freak me out. At the time he thought he was possessed by the devil. But when you stay up for three days straight, you're going to start seeing things. We stayed up almost four days without sleep. I had the intercom outside my house and I had it on twenty-four hours a day. One day it was pretty windy and he and I were sitting in the middle of my house and I could swear somebody was calling us. Or maybe he was hearing it. He was hearing "Glenn, Glenn" from this bloody speaker. He got me convinced that someone was outside calling us, and that's when I got the gun out. I got the gun, and David said, "What the fuck is that?" and I go outside, it's dawn, and the guy living above me was an elderly actor from the '20s, and I'm thinking, he's going to call the cops. He couldn't see the gun as it was in my underpants. You gotta laugh, because David is in a kimono, I'm in my underpants. Now, the sun is coming up, and I'm on the roof, David's freaking out. I could hear the police sirens coming up the hill, and I'm going, "Oh my fucking god." We had been up for like eighty-four hours.

If you listen to "Station to Station," and the line, "It's not the side effects of the cocaine . . ." he was always talking about the side effects of the cocaine. Sometimes we would have limos and go downtown and hang out and we'd end up in some strange places, and feel weird after an hour and leave and end up going home. He talked and talked and talked. I never ever saw David sleep. Ever. I never saw David eat much; he just drank a lot of milk. And after spending some time at my house, he found a home in L.A. two miles from my house. He moved there and I would go over there and hang out with Corinne Schwab. Without Corinne, David would have not been alive in the last ten or twenty years. She warded off all the wrong people. And you know, David and I were toxic. Cocaine is the devil's drug. There was a moment when we were getting high, and David started to bleed from his eye, actually bleeding. It was getting really bad, and then he went off to Mexico to shoot *The Man Who Fell to Earth.*

ALAN YENTOB: When he's in the back of the limo in *Cracked Actor* he says this line that many people now know off by heart. In fact, I remember Kate Moss repeating it to me word for word. These were also the lines that appealed to Nic Roeg, who got in touch with me after the film was screened. Bowie is drinking from a carton of a milk, and when I ask him about being in America and soaking up all the idioms and culture there, he says, "There's a fly floating around in my milk. There's a foreign body in it, you see? And it's getting a lot of milk. That's kind of how I felt. A foreign body. And I couldn't help but soak it up. I hated it when I first came here, I couldn't see any of it. Look, there's a wax museum! Fancy having a wax museum out in the middle of a bleeding desert. Think it would melt, wouldn't you?" That was basically his screen test for *The Man Who Fell to Earth.* The notion of this Martian let loose in America is of course what Nic Roeg was thinking of as well. This enigmatic figure wearing a big hat in the back of a car is where he got that idea from. *The Man Who Fell to Earth* is almost a documentary. It was a big risk that Nic took, and he obviously needed to sell him to the studios, as no one had ever heard of him. He was an unknown, and certainly hadn't acted before. But Nic liked the sense of isolation, the fragility and the way in which he was like a stranger in a strange land, and that all convinced him that he was the right person. It was a very intriguing film. Bowie was never an actor per se, but because he inhabited the role himself, it worked.

PAUL MAYERSBERG (SCRIPTWRITER): I had worked with Nic Roeg on a couple of scripts which didn't get made, and *The Man Who Fell to Earth* was the third one. It was given to him by David Cammell, the brother of Donald, and had previously been optioned by a company called Canon. They were going to make a TV series like *The Fugitive* or *The Invader,* one of those things where he comes back every week. And in this series he was an alien from outer space, who turns up in America and every week nearly gets discovered and has to run away. But the series never got made and it got picked up by Columbia in Hollywood. After the success of *Don't Look Now,* Nic was offered a three-picture deal at Columbia, and one of these films was *The Man Who Fell to Earth.* That's how it started, and I wrote that with him in 1974/75. In my first draft I had used some lyrics from "Space Oddity," "Changes," and so forth, almost as an accompaniment to the script. The last scene had "Rocket Man" by Elton John, "Till touchdown brings me down." So there was a pop aspect to it. In a way it was natural that Bowie got involved.

We wanted to cast someone who could conceivably not be of this Earth, who wasn't a known actor, which is why we thought of Michael Crichton.

He is very tall, almost seven foot, so he might have looked like someone from outer space. But I think that was a passing fancy, not a real casting idea. We had some trouble persuading people about Bowie. The producer Michael Deeley had some trouble with it because he doesn't sing in the film. And also, how do we know he can act? In America, Columbia, who eventually passed on the film, couldn't understand the script. Also, as Bowie didn't sing and it wasn't a musical, they thought, what's the point? It wasn't an expensive film, maybe one million, but even so, it was a question of what we could afford. We'd seen *Cracked Actor*, which alerted us to Bowie, but I wasn't worried anyway—because a performer is a performer is a performer. That's it. Anyway, it wasn't my decision, but it never struck me as a worry in any way. David wasn't a great actor; he was an extremely talented amateur. Film isn't undermined by that, just look at Mick Jagger, and Nic was always very keen on using people who could perform, whether it was Mick in *Performance* or Art Garfunkel in *Bad Timing*.

The filming actually happened very quickly. After being stopped and stymied, it then gathered speed and the money came quite quickly. I made various changes to the script when we were in New Mexico, but I didn't change one line for Bowie, not one word, and he didn't change anything either. He never changed his movements, and was almost like an automaton. I think he was probably afraid to do anything differently. He improvised absolutely nothing. Would never think of it. There were scenes when he would do things three or four times exactly the same for retakes. He was quite remarkable in that way. He was very keen to put himself in Nic's hands. He was having a lot of difficulty with MainMan at the time, and that was a real worry for him. So I think the film became a relaxation, and also I think he was pleased to be away from England. That's the impression I got. He seemed to me to be in a transitional state, but then maybe David was always in a transitional state, I don't know. He was away from home, and curiously was quite similar to the character in the film; in other words he'd come to a strange place.

In his music I liked the fact that he seemed happy with a state of unease. That was unusual. They were unresolved stories, and he didn't seem to mind that. There was a search for something. And the sort of weird ecstatic calling, like a preacher or a bird. Looking for ecstasy, looking for something really wonderful. We first screened it, for friends, at British

Lion, or maybe it was Shepperton, but it was not received with thrilling admiration, by any means. Even at the press screenings there was quite a lot of doubt about its ability to be successful. It opened the same week as *The Slipper and the Rose*, directed by Bryan Forbes, and that got the lead reviews everywhere. And in America it was a disaster, completely recut.

NIC ROEG (DIRECTOR): I saw Alan Yentob's film *Cracked Actor.* Casting is strange. Usually an actor comes for a part but on other occasions the part seems to just go towards one actor. That was the case with David and *The Man Who Fell to Earth.* I went to see him in New York. Our appointment was for seven in the evening. He eventually turned up at four in the morning. We only talked for about fifteen minutes. He didn't fuck around with compliments. He said, "I'll be there." I said, "You have to let me have more than that—for producers, for the studio." He said, "I'll be there." Some people doubted him because he was from the music business, but he was very professional. Peculiarly prepared. He arrived on location in New Mexico two days before we needed him and he was always very pleasant to the cast and crew. But in the evening he always went off alone. What had appealed to me about him was that he never really consolidated a position where people could put him in a box. He couldn't be pigeonholed. What I found difficult was that he was so hard to reach—not emotionally but on a purely physical level. There are barriers, a filter system, around every star, of course, but they seemed particularly strong around Bowie. I told him that it would take him a long time to get over the film. Originally he was going to do the soundtrack as well, but it proved too difficult. We all had pressures, deadlines. Eventually we brought in John Phillips to do the score. Then six months later David sent me a copy of *Low* with a note that said, "This is what I wanted to do for the soundtrack." It would have been a wonderful score.

CANDY CLARK (ACTRESS): I was part of the casting process. Nic Roeg and I went over to [Bowie's] house, a rental on Doheny Drive, and he was very agreeable, he wanted to do the film. It was a huge part, and who wouldn't? He accepted it right there and then. He wanted to be in the film. I was pleased, as he certainly looked the part. So when I met him it wasn't like I was a super fan, we were just going to make this movie. I wasn't apprehensive about the movie, as I knew he could do it. He didn't show any apprehension. He promised Nic Roeg he wasn't going to do drugs on the movie, and he seemed sober to me. When you look at him in the movie, his eyes are soft, he's paying attention, he can hear you. He wasn't congested. He seemed like a man of his word. He wasn't jittery like he was on some of those chat shows. He was always on time, always available to run lines, and I attribute that to being a musician and always rehearsing and playing the same songs. A lot of actors don't enjoy the repetition of running lines, but he loved it. There was a lot of dialogue and it was good dialogue so you didn't want to be winging it. He came to New Mexico with a trunk full of books—he really read a lot.

But then he had an entourage to keep him clean and pressed. He lived in a house, while the rest of us lived in a hotel. He had a few keepers, including a lady called Coco. I never got invited out to the house. Once shooting was finished, his driver Tony would take him home. After he was done for the day there seemed to be a veil of other people in the way. It was strictly a business relationship. He wasn't the life of the party on the set. He was great in the role, and I could see it right in front of me. He could act. Very accomplished, full of empathy.

DAVID BOWIE: I'm surprised how good *The Man Who Fell to Earth* is still, it really stands up. Nic Roeg was a master, and I feel extraordinarily privileged that I got the role. It's hazy, but I think he was about to cast Peter O'Toole, but then he saw me in the *Omnibus* documentary on the BBC [*Cracked Actor*] and obviously changed his mind. I think there was some sort of audition or meeting in New York, which I was probably late for. But he was very determined, very patient, and obviously a very good director, to be able to get that performance out of me.

CANDY CLARK: The Christmas after the movie came out, my doorbell rang at my little house in Los Angeles and David was at the door. There was a limousine waiting outside, and he had bought me a little rhinestone pin. It was so unexpected. How did he even get my address? In England they ran the director's cut in the theaters, but in the US they got a commercials editor to take twenty-three minutes out of it so it didn't make any sense and didn't make any money. I was meant to go out and support it but I just couldn't do it because the distributors had ruined it.

CHARLES SHAAR MURRAY: I saw him in L.A. once when he was recording *Soul Train* and the Cher show, and I've never met anyone who hated the city more. He was very open about his absolute loathing for Los Angeles. Also, Bowie was trying to manage himself at the time, but he wasn't very good at it. While Jagger can spend the whole day negotiating with people, having people come up and ask for decisions, and then go on and do his show, David couldn't do that. He didn't delegate enough.

TRACEY EMIN: I once asked him what it was like making *The Man Who Fell to Earth* and it turned out he didn't remember most of it. I quoted the line where he says to his driver, "Slow down, Arthur," and he said there was a time when he had no recollection of saying it. At the time he was on uppers, downers, a concoction of drugs just to keep going. When I asked him if being "out of it" adds to the creative process—Van Gogh and absinthe, Victorian writers and opium, rock stars and cocaine—he said "having experienced drugs, the work is never the same again. *Station to Station* was a drug album. *Low* and *Heroes* were not. *Never Let Me Down* was. It's all contradictory."

DAVID BOWIE: I've never really thought about whether or not a person can be too thin. Well, I certainly was at one point, back in the '70s, when I just ate peppers and drank milk. I have various photographs of me looking skeletal, which remind me how badly behaved I was back in the '70s. They're Polaroids as well, which makes it even worse because they're badly lit. I occasionally look at them and think, "How did I ever get to that state? How did I ever survive it?" So yeah, you can be too thin! I know some of those outfits, and some of those characters were iconic, and I know the image was enhanced by my skeletal nature, but I wouldn't recommend it as a process, I wouldn't recommend it as a career template.

HARRY MASLIN: David was managed at this point by Michael Lippman, and one day I got a call from Michael saying that David would like me to work on the next album. I was surprised and happy and shocked and said sure.

I was still in New York at the time, so I flew out to California just to scout out studios, and wound up at Cherokee Recording Studios. Cherokee was a very new studio at the time. They hadn't had any big hits to my knowledge, and were still trying to figure out who they were. But I chose it because it was quiet and because it was new. I felt we would get less paparazzi and less glamor from the media and I think I was right.

BRUCE ROBB (CHEROKEE STUDIOS): We had established ourselves as a studio out in the country, in Chatsworth, working with everyone from Little Richard to Steely Dan, and then we moved into Los Angeles, on Fairfax Avenue, to the old MGM studio. This was in 1974. One day in 1975 I was in one of the smaller studios and I get a call from the front desk. "David Bowie is here and he'd like to see Studio 1." He walked around the studio, which was a big beautiful studio full of colored lights, and then walked over to the piano, played one note, and said, "So this is Cherokee. I'd like to do my record here." And I thought, That was quick! You could tell that he was a serious musician, he was proper. You wouldn't start an album with a song like "Station to Station" if you weren't serious.

HARRY MASLIN: So after selecting Cherokee, we planned some instrumental rehearsal time, and David and I ran through the tracks just to get the basics down, just getting the feels together. Most of the lyrics hadn't been written yet. Some of the music hadn't been written yet either. It was kind of expected that David would come through by the time we got in the recording studio. Which he did. He was famous for going into the corner or going into the men's room and writing some lyrics, which is what he did on "Golden Years." He literally went to the bathroom and came back with the lyric, went to the mike, and did the song in one take. I was blown away. He told me that he didn't consider himself to be a vocalist, but I told him that that was one of the most amazing performances I had ever seen.

CARLOS ALOMAR: There are not that many songs on *Station to Station*, and the intro to "Station to Station" itself is over three minutes long. We mashed all these songs together. It's not really a rock and roll record. "Golden Years" was kind of David's version of "On Broadway," but I told him he had to be careful, so I came up with a new riff for it. Earl Slick and I work in different ways, and while I would record something and just put a holding part in, he would then come in and make it all his own. My line was the inspirational line, his was the real line. His sound was very close to Mick Ronson, which David loved, and he was able to create a link. Sure, "Station to Station" and "Stay" are experimental records, but the rest of the album is medium poppy. David was *on* it. If you need to have fifteen cups of coffee, or whether you want to buzz around on coke, people do what they have to do. I do not condone being so out of it that you don't remember anything, but the fact that you are able to rise to the challenge at the moment, that's the challenge.

BRUCE ROBB: He was partying, having fun, but then during that period everybody was doing coke. It was unbelievable. He wasn't close to the worst of the lot. I mean, I worked with Harry Nilsson for thirteen months, and that was tough. He was just doing what everybody else was doing. He was such a gentleman. He'd even pick up the trash after his sessions, which I've never seen another artist do, especially one of David Bowie's stature. He would say it was his session so he should clear it up. He'd send Christmas cards every year, which looked like he'd made them himself.

HARRY MASLIN: He was doing a lot of drugs at that time. As he said himself, he was very much dependent on cocaine at the time. And at times, it was difficult to deal with it. Not that he lost his charm or his ability to be gracious or polite, but being so out there on another planet sometimes, it was a job to bring him back down. It was also my job to keep up with him, so I'm in a very precarious situation here; I've got to do a little cocaine just to stay up with him. If you're working with somebody who wants to work eighteen hours a day, there's not much else you can do other than caffeine pills to keep yourself up. David was in a situation at that time because of who he was; he didn't have to seek the drugs, he would have people who would come over and want to be part of the crew. Some of whom were doctors or dentists. And he would be supplied lots of pharmaceutical cocaine: pure, crystal, in a bottle, sealed. Which probably was the best thing he could be doing if he was going to do cocaine. At least he knew that it wasn't cut with anything that was dangerous. And I felt the same way about that.

On the other hand, it was so readily available that he overindulged. And there would be times where he would not show up, and I would get very irritated. Mostly because it was my responsibility to [control] the budget. So if I had a studio that I was paying maybe a couple grand a day for, and my artist didn't show up, it went against me. So I had talks with David about being responsible and showing up. There was one time where he didn't show up for about a day and a half, and I actually went up to Stone Canyon and started banging on the door. I was worried about him too and wanted to wake him up and make sure he was OK. He opened the door and he was a little out of it and tired more than anything else. I said this can't go on. I can't be responsible for this situation. And of course David being David, we agreed, but while it carried on to a certain extent, I don't think I ever had to go up to the house again. There remained times in the studio however where he'd be so out he'd be seeing colors and talking about his son and how his son also sees colors and talks in colors and he was just really out there. He was very frail, he had been up for a couple days, Angie was in the outer studio, and I remember going up to her and saying, "You have to get him out of here. He is completely dependent, he is somebody else, he is so out [of it]." I was very worried that we might lose him, to be completely honest with you. I certainly didn't want to be the one that was responsible or held responsible for the situation, and I was a little forceful with Angie because she was basically scared of him. Angie didn't know how to handle him either. I forced her to take him out of the studio, and they called a car and got him out.

CARLOS ALOMAR: A man is the architect of his own design and the architect of his own demise. What I did know was that he rose to the challenge regardless of what state he was in and for that you have to respect the man. Many situations that we deal with allow us to see, like a Billie Holiday situation—we know you're on drugs, but damn can you play! Miles Davis—dabble if you want to, but damn can you play! I've noticed in my history [of] R&B and jazz, and the other things I grew up with, you could see anything from a junkie to a pimp to anything. It didn't really surprise me. I wasn't there to judge him; I was there to support him. And as long as I supported him, as long as he didn't fall, he was handling it and anything I could do to help him, that's what I was there for. I remember a lot of it was basically, "Do you ever eat? I'd go to his room and see a lot of food but I'd also see a lot of uneaten food. Many times he'd say, "Don't ask me, Carlos, I don't remember anything."

BRUCE ROBB: The sessions went so smoothly and so quickly. It was a very friendly studio, and people used to walk in and out of the rooms; Jeff Beck would come in and do a solo, Bonnie Raitt would be sitting out on the back stairs because nobody would hire her. A while after Bowie started, Sinatra's people came in and said that Frank was going to come in and record, as the arranger Don Costa had originally used one of the studios as Frank's strings room. Don said he was going to bring Frank in, but that we weren't to talk to him, and that we had to call him Mr. Sinatra and don't ask him to do a mike check.

Sinatra had a reputation but I think he just liked to fuck with people, he liked to fuck with what he called the establishment. When he was amongst other musicians he was a musician. A singer. And there were so many similarities between him and David. They were inquisitive about one another, and they were intrigued. One night Sinatra said, "You've got this Bowie guy in here. How is he?" And we told him he was really good. Then Bowie would say, "Oh my God, Sinatra's here. I'd love to meet him." So we set up a dinner with the two of them. Sinatra had an Italian restaurant he liked up near Robertson and Beverly, so we booked them a table there. They came back to the studio in Sinatra's limo and at that point it was pretty obvious that they were becoming fast friends. There was a good deal of respect. Sinatra expected that kind of respect, because he was one of our first musical superstars. He didn't know who David was, but after meeting him, they got on. They visited each other's sessions. He heard some of the *Station to Station* playbacks, and he liked Bowie's version of the Dimitri Tiomkin and Ned Washington song "Wild Is the Wind." David even sang a harmony part on one of Sinatra's songs. It was a Christmas album. So it went on that way and they became kindred spirits. Way apart in years, but that hardly mattered.

HARRY MASLIN: The best thing about working with David for me, apart from all the negative stuff with the cocaine, was that David was a true artist. He would be willing to try anything. Many artists you have to convince to try a particular part, a part on the piano, a string part, a vocal part, whatever. David would try anything without question. He would not necessarily approve of everything or like everything but he would give it a go. In fact at the beginning of "Golden Years" there's this harmonium thing that starts off with just three notes. And he played it and played it out of time. And he said, "Oh, should I do that again?" And I said no. It's perfectly out of time. I told him to trust me on this one. And we left it like it is and to this day it's one of my favorite things.

EARL SLICK: *Station to Station* is undoubtedly his best record. There were very few of us in the studio. There was me, David, Carlos, George Murray, Dennis Davis, and I brought in Roy Bittan, who happened to be staying in the same hotel as me, and who was playing with Bruce [Springsteen] at the time. For some reason Michael Garson was out of the picture at the time. On that record I spent a lot of time with David. We were really out of it, but for some reason communicating really well, probably because we were both in exactly the same mind space. He was able to drag some stuff out of me. He was in a worse state than he was on the *Diamond Dogs* tour, and I don't know how he was functioning, but he was. I don't know how any of us were. Maybe it's because we were in our twenties, I don't know. Don't try this at home, kids, but I think had we not been in that state of mind, that record would have never sounded like that. Staying up for two days at a time, and half out of our minds, just loosened us up to the point that we would do or try anything. We were focused as shit. I love that record. There were things that I could do that I didn't know I could do that David knew I could do, and he figured out how to drag that out of me. It took over two months to record, which was a long time in those days. And then I quit.

HARRY MASLIN: *Station to Station* was a big "mix" album. After we got the basic tracks it was up to me to put the thing together. A song like "TVC15" was recorded in many sections, and so after the recording he basically wiped his hands of the album and started painting up in the hills in his house, and sent me back to New York to mix the album.

I brought it back for David to approve, and I went up to the house, and he was actually painting whilst we listened to the final mix. When I asked him what he thought, he just said, "Good job! You did great." Jumping back a little bit, we had all the guys from RCA come down to Cherokee to hear the album for the first time and it was quite an experience because they were all basically suits at the time, I knew they weren't going to understand what they were going to hear. Because it was quite different from *Young Americans*, and it was quite different from what had gone before. And they sat on this couch in front of the console, said "That's just marvelous." They didn't know what else to say. They knew that "Golden Years" was a potential single, but I don't think they understood or appreciated anything else.

At the time we were making *Station to Station* I was living at the Hyatt House on Sunset, or the Riot House as it became known, the rock and roll hotel. I had one groupie come to my room one day, and she just knocked on the door, and when I opened it she said, "Are you anybody?" And I said, "Well, I think I'm somebody, but maybe not the person you're looking for." That was the sign of a true groupie hotel. But as I said, I had to go back to New York at the end of the album and do the mixing at the Hit Factory. I was actually a bit shocked at the time, as I recall it, David didn't want to be involved at all. Because with *Young Americans* when we mixed it, David literally had his hands on the console, I had to slap his hands a couple of time and be like, "Get off the console, David!" When you listen to "Fame" and you hear the reverb go up on it in different places, that's David cranking it up. And I'm like, "Get away from that!"

When David wasn't there I did a little bit of everything. Working with Slick or working with Carlos or doing the percussion stuff that I wanted to do. But David was involved pretty much on a daily basis. It was rare that he wasn't there. We worked together in collaboration. "TVC15" has the both of us playing saxophone on it; he played tenor and I played baritone.

BRUCE ROBB: David was after feel, and sometimes he would spend a whole day doing finger snaps, just to get what he wanted. Dressed in his linen shirts and his baggy pants. Sometimes it happened quickly, and sometimes it took a while, but it was all about feel. He could hear what wasn't there.

HARRY MASLIN: It's such a diverse record. With "Wild is the Wind," for me that really did come out of complete nowhere. I was surprised rather than shocked that he wanted to do it, so I was like, Let's do it! And actually that is one song which I did do a technical fuck-up when I had some of his vocal leaking into the main acoustic guitar track, which is a real no-no. But when I put it together for the mix, it actually added to his vocal sound, and I thought, You know what, I'm not gonna fix any of this because it sounds really cool. So I just left it as it is and people loved the sound of it and I was quite pleased that they did. There were times though when he was doing so much cocaine that he would come into the control room, and he'd have a bottle of pharmaceutical coke with him, and he'd pour out a pile, on my side of the console, then he would pour out a pile on his side of the console, then he would go out to the piano and pour out a pile, then he would go to the music stand where the vocal mike was hanging and pour out a pile, so he never had to move to take another bump or another hit of cocaine. And we're talking piles, we're not talking lines. And again I was very, very careful not to do what he was doing because I had to be in charge. The only time I would do some was when I had to literally keep up with him in the sense that I didn't want to go to sleep. That's how crazy it was. But we made a great, great record, and one that I am enormously proud of.

Musically, David allowed me a lot of freedom. As an example, I wanted to put some percussion on one or two of the songs. Well in those days, the electronic drum machines were very new and very limited as to what they could do. The main drum machine had a mono output, which to me was very limiting. It meant I would have to do twelve takes if I wanted to do a part. So I took the thing into the shop and I ripped it apart, and I made it into a multiple-output machine, and we did all this percussion stuff and David was cheering me on about it and saying it was great. At the beginning of the song "Station to Station" there is a lot of Earl Slick feedback, and Slick was out there with the amps and the guitar, and David was out there with him, and I was egging David on, and David was egging Slick on, and we got what we were looking for. Slick was looking at both of us like we were out of our minds. But Slick is a very underrated guitar player, he's very creative and he would do whatever we wanted to do, but in that instance he probably just thought we were crazy.

I really don't remember ever thinking, We have to make this album a particular way, and that's why the songs are so different. We didn't try and keep consistency. *Young Americans* demanded consistency, and it had a very R&B feel and we wanted to maintain that throughout with the mixing and whatever else we did. But with *Station to Station* he was open to suggestion and experimentation. I think that's how we approached it, musically. David would play a feel that he had, and they'd run through it, and Carlos would help and everyone would contribute, which is how it would usually work. And I would oversee the whole thing, and give any suggestions about the feel and whatever. But nothing was honed to perfection in SRI, it was all honed to perfection in Cherokee.

I thought David was an extremely complicated person. Usually, people in the arts are either visual or aural, and David was both. He saw things differently from most people. Obviously one can see that from the personas he had at the beginning of his career. And we dealt with that in the studio. That duality of visual and aural, I think you can see it in something like "TVC15" for instance, and even "Station to Station," where he wanted the train sound at the beginning. He said, "Wouldn't it be great if it moved?" That to me is all visual. Even the feedback to me is more visual than it is aural. He's seeing that sound. It may sound crazy but I truly believe he's seeing the sound.

I can't speak for the other people, but with me, he was always extremely open. I mean, I'm not somebody who sits back and doesn't put my input. I suggest constantly whether it's technically or musically, as I grew up being a musician and a technical person simultaneously. And that's why I think we came out with a unique album. It was a collaboration. And that interchange between energies and imagination was wonderful.

NICK KENT: Bowie was red hot up until *Station to Station*, and then he became white hot. It's his most fucked-up record in terms of his personal lifestyle, but it's fantastic.

When Elvis Presley died in August 1977, Bowie briefly considered recording a tribute album, arranging classic Elvis songs for Iggy Pop to sing. He had been a fan all his life. Bowie's first performance, aged eleven, was an Elvis impersonation for an audience of Boy Scouts in Bromley. Years later, he would paint Elvis's TCB ("Takin' care of business") lightning bolt logo onto his face on the cover of Aladdin Sane. *His Ziggy Stardust concerts usually closed with the melodramatic "Rock 'n' Roll Suicide," which Bowie sang wearing an Elvis-style jumpsuit—copied by Bowie's designer friend Freddie Burretti from one of the King's—before departing the stage. This was immediately followed by the announcement, "David Bowie has left the building."*

A year earlier, Bowie had even tried to get Elvis to record "Golden Years," only to have it turned down. Bowie was so keen for Elvis to record the song he even sang a little like him on the verses, pitching his voice as close to the King's as he could ("channeling the spirit"). For Bowie, Elvis was the consummate blueprint. Bowie himself has said that his debut album "seemed to have its roots all over the place, in rock and vaudeville and music hall. I didn't know if I was Max Miller or Elvis Presley."

When he was quizzed back in 1972 about the number of glitter-eyed young boys who were seen at T. Rex concerts dancing with each other in the aisles, Bowie said, "What about Elvis Presley? If his image wasn't bisexual then I don't know what is. People talk about fag rock, but that's an unwieldy term at the best of times."

HANIF KUREISHI: He said that during his cocaine period in L.A. he nearly died several times. Your blood pressure drops terribly. Once he overdosed and only survived because someone put him in a warm bath.

GEOFF MACCORMACK: L.A. at that point was a strange place, especially when you think to walk anywhere was considered weird at that time. The first thing that happened when you met someone was not a handshake but a spoon in your nose; it was a very different place. The situation was unreal so our existence was unreal. I think David actually wanted to experiment, he wanted to be weird. I don't think it was a suicide run, he just wanted to see what it was like. He was a bit of a playactor, and used to do things for effect, that was part of him. One night in his house on Doheny Drive we were both pretty wired, and we came up with this game where we had to list three objects that weren't in the house, a kind of extrasensory perception test using me as the medium. I came up with a list: pyramid, windows, children. Then we went through the house looking for them, and obviously couldn't find anything. In the last drawer we looked in was an old Christmas card in the shape of a pyramid covered with little windows and the faces of some children. Weird, really weird.

That night we were listening to a DJ on the radio called the Shadow, who was playing the Goons and Monty Python records and talking about Shakespeare's birthday. So we found a book on quantum mechanics or something, and re-covered it and called it *The Complete Works of Shakespeare.* We drove down to the studio to give him the book, at around five thirty in the morning, when there was nobody up but Mexican gardeners, and as we got out of the car, the DJ was playing "Young Americans." He couldn't believe it. We gave him the book and it freaked him out. He went back on the radio to say, "You will not believe this. Ladies and gentlemen, David Bowie has just walked into my studio and given me a book on William Shakespeare . . ." And of course no one believed him. That's the kind of thing we did. That was our own black magic. He looked his absolute best when he was taking too many drugs, but he was still taking too many drugs.

GLENN HUGHES: At the time he fired Tony Defries, Tony was still hanging around and David was freaking out paranoid. In the spring of 1975 I get a call from David, and he said, "Glenn, I gotta escape my manager, Defries, I got to get away from him. I'm going to come to you on the train." Not only did David never travel on planes, but he never got in elevators. He hated tall buildings and had terrible vertigo. I once got him to come with me to the Rainbow Room in New York to go to a party and he was scared to death because it was on the nineteenth floor. So he wanted to change his management but he didn't know how to do it. He came to me because he was looking for shelter, someone trustworthy. He knew that I was loyal.

Sex was his great escape. I know that he had sex with as many women as I've known. It was nonstop. Probably in the thousands. There was every color: Japanese, Chinese, Americans, black girls, Greeks, girls, girls, girls. There were girls going in and out all the time. Dozens of them. I saw a lot of gay guys hitting on him too. I think behind closed doors he was pretty fucking wild. He was sexually draining. There were so many girls coming and going one by one, nonstop. He was almost like a vampire looking for . . . not blood but sex. I think he had a sex problem, and he may have had a disease caused by cocaine addiction that was turning into a sex problem. The amount of sex he had increased in accordance with his cocaine addiction. I knew the girls he was having sex with. In hindsight I think he would have liked me to have been involved. I mean he loved me. He genuinely loved me. I'm not saying he wanted to be with me, but I know that he loved me and he held my hand . . . we were very close. We were very sensual guys. I'm not bi, I'm not gay, but we would walk around kissing and holding hands. He would call me "Old Bighead." I have a very big feminine side, and that's what Bowie loved. He threw away all of my bellbottoms, all of my high-heeled shoes, all of my rock-star clothes. He cut my hair. He said, "This has got to stop, you have to change, you can't follow what everybody else is doing." In 1974 I looked like a girl, with long hair. He had no problem walking around in the nude in front of me. Oh, I was so damn naïve! David and I fell in love because of music but then we found out we were both addicted. It was Romeo and Juliet. We were dying. It was amorous. I loved him, not sexually, but I adored him.

NICK KENT: There was a ritual when Bowie took cocaine, as he liked to use the cover of the first Average White Band album, which was completely white. He would snort the coke from this cover. This would be how the evening would progress.

GLENN HUGHES: Oh my, the orgies. Back in London I had two rooms at the Hyde Park Hotel. I had a room with Angie there, and I also had a room with David. Bowie had a mansion on the heath, I stayed there too. So one of the nights I decide to leave Bowie at the house and go and stay with Angie instead. I have a key to the room and I go inside and I kid you not, there were at least seven or eight couples, going at it. All having sex. And Angie wants me to come in and join them. And this is the only time she really tried to get me involved with others. Now I wasn't angry, I kind of felt hurt in a way. She wasn't my girl, she wasn't mine, but I felt hurt.

It wasn't just a ménage a trois, it was like a fucking gang bang for god's sake. They were all fucking going at it. I couldn't stay in that suite, not with that going on.

HARVEY GOLDSMITH: He was quiet, considered, and didn't have any airs and graces. There was never any fuss, that's just how he was. Even when he was strung out he was polite. But then he was shielded from a lot. Coco was always very protective of him, and he relied on her for everything. Before Iman she was his rock, although she could go over the top sometimes. I remember backstage at the Empire Pool gigs in 1976, everyone came to see him—Eric Clapton, Mick Jagger, Pete Townshend, George Harrison—but Coco had given instructions that no one was allowed to go backstage, and so nobody was. I went backstage after the gig, and the corridor outside his room was like a morgue. He asked me if there was anyone in the audience that he knew, as he was surprised that nobody had come back to say hello, and I told him that the biggest stars in the world had dutifully lined up to pay homage, but that they weren't allowed to see him. He went ballistic.

HUGH PADGHAM (PRODUCER): Coco used to tell us stories of David's bad coke years in L.A., when she used to go round to check on him, and he would be lying on the floor. She would get the coke mirror and hold it up to his nose to see if he was still breathing. I think David was the love of Coco's life and she never got over it. She was resigned to the fact that she could be with him, but only as a PA. There were times when she seemed like a bit of a Yoko, a bit of a pain, but I remember her quite fondly.

CHARLES SHAAR MURRAY: One day in 1976 Bowie's mother called the *NME* and said she wanted to speak to someone. Now, I would never ever have thought of originating something like that, we didn't call her, she simply called the paper and said she wanted to talk to somebody about her son, said she had some things she wanted to get off her chest, wanted to get a message out to David's fans, blah, blah, blah. I told Nick Logan and said I felt a bit weird about it but he said I had to go down and see her. She still lived in Bromley I think. She didn't really have anything to say other than that she felt lonely and neglected by her son. I sort of felt I'd been suckered into it. I didn't want to write it up but Nick insisted. We used this satirical headline, "A Mother's Anguish," which of course everybody took totally seriously. David was a bit pissed off but I think he eventually forgave me. You expect to be manipulated by people in the industry, but not by somebody's mother.

7

SIT IN BACK ROWS OF CITY LIMITS

1976–1979

CHALKIE DAVIES (PHOTOGRAPHER): I was at Victoria Station when David returned to Britain and there was the incident with the supposed Nazi salute. But it wasn't a Nazi salute at all. In May 1976 he arrived back in London on the *Orient Express*, he was met at Victoria by a chauffeur driving his newly acquired black open-top Mercedes. He stood up in the back of the car and waved to the crowd for about fifteen seconds. I got a picture of him doing this, but it was out of focus because his hand was moving. Back in those days, if they wanted a white background on an *NME* cover they literally painted the photograph white, and so somebody decided to put a hand where the withery hand was, but that made it look too much like a salute. The *NME* came out on a Wednesday and then the papers picked it up and decided it was a Nazi salute. It was taken completely out of context. Then I think someone found some quotes about fascism that he did in an interview in Amsterdam and it got blown beyond all proportion.

JULIEN TEMPLE: David kept up with everything, and he was especially intrigued by punk. In a way I think he felt as though he was somehow partly responsible. They were his children in a sense. He kept up, always kept up. When Iggy played the Rainbow in Finsbury Park in 1977, when David was playing keyboards for him, I went along with John [Lydon] and Sid [Vicious], and went backstage afterwards. There was already a tremendous rivalry between the old guard and the new, and there was a party going on somewhere afterwards, and I remember vividly that John and Sid really didn't want Iggy and David to come to this party. So we arranged to go in convoy, and there was this farcical car chase across London, with John and Sid deliberately trying to lose Iggy and David. It was comical, but we lost them eventually.

SIOUXSIE SIOUX (PUNK ICON): I was fifteen when I first saw David Bowie. He was singing "Starman" on *Top of the Pops*, and I was in hospital recovering from a serious illness. I just couldn't believe how striking he was. That ambiguous sexuality was so bold and futuristic that it made the traditional male/female role-play thing seem so outdated. Besides, I'd lost so much weight and had got so skinny that Bowie actually made me look cool! He was tearing down all the old clichés, but he was also having a lot of fun doing it. Bowie was well into clothes and dressing up, and that had a lot of resonance with me, although I was never a Bowie lookalike. A few years later, when he began to withdraw from it all, it really felt like there was something missing. Until then, his albums had been eagerly anticipated. But by the mid '70s there was a vacuum. It was no coincidence that so many people involved in punk at the beginning had been inspired by him. Bowie was the catalyst who'd brought a lot of us, the so-called Bromley Contingent, together. And out of that really small group of people, a lot happened, including Siouxsie and the Banshees.

LEGS MCNEIL (JOURNALIST): "Never wear a new pair of shoes in front of him," said Mick Jagger about Bowie. Jagger's implication was either that Bowie was a notorious thief (of ideas, trends, or the latest fashions), or that he'd run right out and get it in order to claim ultra-hipper-than-thou trendsetting status.

I had a run-in with Bowie at Andy Warhol's Factory back in 1976 or early 1977 that proved Jagger's quip.

I forget who told me Bowie was going to be at the Factory, but when John Holmstrom, the editor-in-chief of *Punk*, heard the news, he packed me off with a cheap cassette recorder and told me not to come back to our cavelike offices at Tenth Avenue and Thirtieth Street without a Bowie interview. What I didn't know was that this was Bowie's second summit meeting with Warhol, after their disastrous first meeting in 1971. He'd played Warhol his new song "Andy Warhol," and Andy said absolutely nothing. He just pulled out his Polaroid camera and said, "I really like your shoes!"

David was crushed. But that day at the Factory in the mid-'70s, Bowie was a genuine rock and roll star. He'd proved himself to be a viable commercial entity of comparable status with Warhol, an equal. There was a crowd of people surrounding Bowie when he walked through the Factory to the back room, where Andy was waiting for him, surrounded by his own coterie of supporters. It was more like a gang war than a private meeting. All the hangers-on were topping themselves with one-liners, vying to be noticed for the history books. I'm sure Andy was relieved to have so many people around because he seldom had much to say, ever.

I waited by the receptionist's desk, for forty-five minutes to an hour, for Bowie to re-emerge so I could ask him for the interview and be on my way. It was excruciatingly boring, as all the gay guys who worked for Andy were too important to talk to me. Real fucking snobs. I tried hitting on the only girl in the place, Katherine Guinness, the heiress to the Guinness beer fortune, who was mildly amused by my efforts but wasn't interested.

Anyway, Bowie finally came out of the backroom surrounded by his minions, who seemed to have doubled in size behind the closed door. As he was bidding Andy a fond farewell, I slipped over to him and said, "Mr. Bowie, I was wondering if you'd be willing to do an interview for *Punk* . . ."

Without speaking, Bowie grabbed the Suicide record out of my hands and his entourage swept him down the hall, into the elevator, and outside to a waiting limo, which presumably swept him off to the next fabulous event. I didn't even have time to say, "Hey, you fucking pooftah, gimme back my fucking Suicide record!"

I did get back at Bowie though. A few weeks later he came to CBGB with Bianca Jagger, which wasn't that strange. What was strange was that it was on some off night in the middle of the week when some shitty band was playing and the only people there were me, Joey Ramone, and some diehard drunks. Ha, you ain't at Studio 54 now, asshole, I thought as I watched David and Bianca traverse the piles of dog shit on the floor that

Hilly Krystal's Salukis had deposited. Then I went outside and stole the hubcaps off his limousine. I fucked that up though, and read in the *New York Post* the next day that their limo got a flat tire on the way home.

TONY PARSONS: Bowie was the one person who was always there, even during punk. I saw him with my very first girlfriend, Kim, at Earls Court, in 1973 on the *Aladdin Sane* tour, and I remember being on the *NME* and going to see the Berlin tour he did when he didn't have any money, and flying up to Newcastle to see that. I remember being that young, single parent, and not being able to get a babysitter for my kid, and taking my kid to see him when Bobby was about seven, in Birmingham. And he was just always there, he was really always there. So, for me, for someone who was a child in the '60s, and grew up aware of all that great music in the '60s, but not really a participant because I was too young, he was the person who unlocked the '70s. The moribund, early-'70s rock music, the thing that punk rebelled against and revolted against, he really seemed an antidote to all that and he seemed authentic in a way that a lot of the glam stars weren't. He just felt like our thing. In the '60s the scene was just about a few people around Chelsea in London. In the '70s it was everybody, all the suburban kids like me, with a cheap *Aladdin Sane* haircut from Basildon.

I used to go to funk clubs more than I went to rock concerts; I'd go and watch the Faces, and go and watch the Who, but I'd [go] down to the Goldmine in Canvey Island, listening to the Gap Band and Kool and the Gang. And Bowie seemed to get that, he seemed to have that ability, which really only the greatest have got, of breaking down barriers. Elvis did it. Rock music was really white, it had reached the end of all that promise, all that brightness, all that excitement that I felt as a kid, listening to the Beatles and the Stones; it had all come to the end. And he was the antidote to all that, it just kind of struck home. And it was a time when we thought that rock music would always reinvent itself, we thought there would always be another new thing coming down the road. Nobody ever thought it was going to become museum culture, a dead art form, which is what it became. And he clearly wanted it. I always thought he was an artist who wanted to be a star, and a star who wanted to be an artist. He was genuinely passionate about his craft and what he did, but also he wanted to be famous.

HANIF KUREISHI: I knew the Bromley contingent, just before punk, and my mates used to wear pins and nappies and bondage trousers and things like that. I just felt a bit embarrassed about it, I have to say. But I used to go to the Roebuck in King's Road, the Water Rat and Chelsea Potter, the punk pubs. And there was a mixture of Chelsea playboys with their shirts open and their medallions and their cars outside. And I used to see all my lot in Bromley. They got quite nasty, and some of them were into prostitution, a lot of heroin. But I didn't want to take heroin. I wanted to be a writer by then. I was much more interested in the Royal Court, which was at the other end of the King's Road, than I was in becoming a junkie. Bromley was very middle class though. Johnny Rotten and Glen Matlock . . . they came from council flats and had much more violent backgrounds. Billy Idol, William Broad, he was very middle class, and wasn't like Sid Vicious at all, and it was all about dressing up, so I was a bit puzzled by that. I liked punk, but I'd much rather go home and listen to Marvin Gaye or Patti Smith. But we all loved David Bowie. He was the bridge between the old and the new.

TONY PARSONS: I was a Bowie fan when I joined the *NME*, and it wasn't like I had a relationship with him, it wasn't like David was coming round to my flat to listen to soul music. When I joined the *NME* in 1977 he was the only person I was in awe of meeting because I had been a fan, it wasn't like the bands that I hung out with and wrote about. The Clash, the Pistols, the Talking Heads, these were my contemporaries, but Bowie was my hero. I was going out interviewing bands, staying up for three days and nights straight, which was really the high point of rock and roll excess, and Bowie's music just sounded fantastically moving, and fantastically human. Although it was numbed by experience, numbed by chemicals, even now I'm shocked when I listen to the love songs on *Station to Station*, I'm shocked how moving I find them. For me, he subtracted rock music with *Low*, when he was in Berlin. It was a really radical, artistic move, not a gesture. And for me, it mirrored what the drugs had done to him, what the drugs had done to everyone. It was music of exhaustion. By the time *Low* came out, I knew people who were very serious heroin addicts, I knew people who were dying, who were killing themselves, I knew people that would be lucky to come out of the drug experience undamaged, myself included. And that music reflected that. And it was always a part; he was always separate from the rest of it, he really did create his own agenda, and that was what was unique about him. We became genuine friends later, but at that time I was just a fan. I loved his music right throughout punk. I loved *Station to Station*, and the White Light [Isolar] Tour, one of the greatest gigs I've ever seen in my life. For me it was just such a fantastic performance, just so brilliant. Very plain setting, just chuck up a few sixty-watt lightbulbs and put on some baggy white trousers! That was the time of the famous RCA campaign: There's old wave, there's new wave, and there's David Bowie.

NICK KENT: Iggy respected Bowie's privacy. He saw Bowie as a patron and he wanted to protect that relationship, just in case he needed him again. He also owed him a hell of a lot as Bowie gave him his solo career, first of all by writing the songs on *The Idiot* and *Lust for Life*, then playing the instruments, paying for the sessions, and going out on tour with him. The thing with Iggy was that in the Stooges he always gave 100 percent, and when you do that you blow your voice out. There are certain professional things you need to do as a singer and one of those is to protect your voice, and Iggy never did that. He'd just lost control. Bowie was telling him that he needed to take care of his voice. So he sat him down and got him to develop the baritone voice that you hear on *The Idiot* and *Lust for Life*, and he wrote songs for that voice. "Sister Midnight" was written for Iggy's new voice, and it worked perfectly. "Funtime." All of them. So that Iggy could go onstage and not burn himself out after ten minutes, which was often the case with the Stooges. Their shows only lasted half an hour because they were just carnage. He showed Iggy how to become a professional performer, someone who could go onstage and perform for an hour and a half, someone who could keep the energy going and not blow his voice. So he was a mentor.

Iggy was also following him around on the *Station to Station* tour, as he had nothing better to do and no money. It must have been incredibly frustrating for him, as he had no money, no band of his own, and he was a pariah in the music industry because he had fucked up so many times. And David Bowie was looking after him. Bowie was also staying up for three or four nights at a time, behaving in a somewhat skittish way. If you were working for Bowie at the time you would have been somewhat stressed. He also had lots of other side projects. He was working with Ava Cherry, his girlfriend at the time, who he was recording with. He was making records with his friend Geoff MacCormack, also known as Warren Peace. So there was also no job security, as Bowie would spend a few days recording with Iggy and then go off and do something else for a while. It was Bowie's largesse that kept everything going. Bowie liked having him around because Iggy is very good company. He's very witty, well read, a quick thinker.

And Bowie needed quick thinkers, which is why Bowie got Brian Eno involved later on. He didn't need Brian Eno. Eno brought considerable influence to *Low* and *"Heroes,"* but Bowie could have made those records himself. But he was using Eno. Brian used to live near me in Maida Vale, and I saw him one day when he came back from recording *"Heroes."* I asked him how it had gone and he said it had been extremely difficult—"challenging" was how he put it. The problem was that Eno liked to work during the day, and Bowie liked to work at night. He would be in the studio at six in the morning, while Bowie would turn up at six in the evening. He was still on the night shift. So what Eno would do during the day was record all those instrumentals that you hear on the records. Then Bowie would come in and say, yeah I like that, and maybe add something to them. So that's why a lot of those instrumentals are on the records, because Bowie was asleep. Brian Eno is someone else who uses opportunities to their maximum effect. There were problems because at the time Bowie wasn't as straight as he would like us to believe. He later claimed that *Low* and *"Heroes"* were made in a cocaine-free environment, but I'm not sure that's strictly true. He was using less cocaine than he had used during the *Station to Station* period, but he was still using, plus of course he was still on coffee and nicotine. Those were his most constant drugs, and perhaps some of his later health problems were brought about by his nicotine and coffee problems rather than anything else. The chain smoking and the coffee, one espresso after another.

GEOFF MACCORMACK: [In Berlin] I knew Iggy because he was so stoned, so I used to pinch his girlfriends. Once David, me, and Iggy, we went to the studio and I sat on the piano and started playing these chords, Iggy started singing and so I kind of left them to it and I went outside and there was this really attractive girl waiting to see Iggy and I convinced her that he was really busy and he was just creating art and shouldn't really be disturbed again. The song was "Turn Blue."

TONY PARSONS: Iggy Pop gave me a book once that Bowie had given him, and it was the letters of the Van Gogh brothers, Theo and Vincent. That's how they saw themselves in Berlin, one genius artist and one perhaps not quite the genius.

IGGY POP (SINGER): He'd always marvel at what a dick I was—how awkward I was in social situations and in all the things that you can do to make your career go better. So finally he said, "Look, we're going to call this album *The Idiot*." I took it as a challenge: OK, I'll show you. We had a good friction in our working relationship. He's the kind of guy who had obviously read *The Idiot* by Dostoyevsky, which I hadn't, and he probably saw all the resonance of the term and its possibilities. But I think his basic thrust, when he suggested it, was just to insult me—"You fucking idiot."

The friendship was basically that this guy salvaged me from certain professional and maybe personal annihilation—simple as that. A lot of people were curious about me, but only he was the one who had enough truly in common with me, and who actually really liked what I did and could get on board with it, and who also had decent enough intentions to help me out. He did a good thing. He resurrected me. He was more of a benefactor than a friend in a way most people think of friendship. He went a bit out of his way to bestow some good karma on me.

DAVID BOWIE: I wanted to find some kind of satisfaction in life rather than this desperate kind of searching. I just did too much and I came close several times to overdose. It was really graphically clear; it was like being in a car where the steering had gone out of control and it was going towards the edge of the cliff. I was very worried for my life, so I ended up in

Berlin, the smack capital of Europe. I didn't have any idea until I got there until I found out that's what it was, and who did I take with me? Iggy Pop, who was trying to get off smack. Surviving all that and realizing you don't have to be a casualty was like being reborn. I think that throughout the '60s and '70s I was driven by lust. As much as anything it's a great creative force that in turn is replaced by anger when you ask where the money is, then you get depression, and then you go to Berlin and write really moody instrumental stuff.

BRIAN ENO (MUSICIAN): I knew he liked [my] *Another Green World* a lot, and he must have realized that there were these two parallel streams of working going on in what I was doing, and when you find someone with the same problems you tend to become more friendly with them. He said that when he first heard [my] *Discreet Music* he could imagine in the future that you would go into the supermarket and there would be a rack of "ambience" records, all in very similar covers. They would have titles like *Sparkling* or *Nostalgic* or *Melancholy* or *Sombre.* They would be mood titles and so very cheap to buy you could chuck them away when you didn't want them anymore.

TONY VISCONTI: *Low* wasn't a difficult album to make, we were freewheeling, making our own rules. But David was going through a difficult period professionally and personally. To his credit, he didn't put on a brave face. His music said that he was "low." I find "Warszawa" very uplifting. Despite a few really bad days we had quite a lot of fun making *Low*, especially when all the radical ideas were making sense and things were starting to click. I remember after a couple of weeks of recording I made a rough mix of the entire album so far and handed a cassette of it to David. He left the control room waving the cassette over his head and grinned ecstatically saying, "We've got an album, we've got an album." I have to qualify that statement by saying that at the beginning, the three of us agreed to record with no promise that *Low* would ever be released. David had asked me if I didn't mind wasting a month of my life on this experiment if it didn't go well. Hey, we were in a French chateau for the month of August and the weather was great!

BRIAN ENO: We slipped into Peter Cook and Dudley Moore characters. Bowie was Pete and I was Dud, and for the whole time we stayed in character. "Ooh, I dunno about that synthesizer part, Dud." The way he worked impressed me a lot. Because it reminds me of me. He'd go out into the studio to do something, and he'd just come back hopping up and down with joy. And whenever I see someone doing that I just trust that reaction. It means that they really are surprising themselves.

JON SAVAGE (JOURNALIST): I think *Low* is a perfect record. The lyrics were very jumpy and autistic, just images flashing without much logic, but side two was a complete revelation. A big turning point, it was the secret sound of 1977, the soundtrack to taking amphetamines and feeling alienated. "Weeping Wall" is very light and spacey, with shimmering marimbas: it's tied into the exploration of space and synthetic textures that later fed into electronic disco. The second side of *"Heroes"* develops the ideas on *Low*. "Moss Garden" is just extraordinary: ambient music before the genre. It's Bowie going beyond again. This really haunted my dreams in late 1977: that was around the time that I stopped listening to punk and began to think synthesizer music was the future. That's what Bowie did. Like the Beatles in the '60s, he signaled cultural shifts. He's the '70s Beatles, in that respect.

RICKY GARDINER (GUITARIST): Coco had called me and asked if I could go to the Château [d'Hérouville] to work on David's new album. When I arrived I met Iggy, and that was good, although I didn't know who he was of course. I had no idea, I thought he was a roadie or something. He said, "This my new album [*The Idiot*], do you like it?" and this awful mono cassette machine was pushed into my face and it sounded terrible and I said, "Oh yes, great." David was going through a divorce and separating from his management and wasn't all together. That's why his album must have been called *Low*, I think. *Low* was basically a prog album, although I think David was slightly late in the prog department, as prog had been replaced by punk. He looked decidedly disheveled, poor thing. The wee boy Zowie was there; he was six. It was all a bit sad really. David seemed preoccupied, and he was just watching the speakers and looking into space.

He was unshaven. However, I liked Angie, and she was a tidy specimen. And she worked hard, Angie did. David's first gigs as David Bowie, when he had stopped doing his Johnny Ray impressions, and started using his Cockney accent, she made his costumes out of the curtains on the stage. She was a great support to David.

[He then invited me to] his flat in Paris to look at some of his paintings, and was much livelier. One painting was dappled, what you might imagine Impressionism to be. And there was a boat emerging from the water and I immediately thought of water as being emotion, and that he was emerging from some emotional conundrum or other. And he wanted my opinion. So I told him emergence, it's about emergence, but I couldn't care what he thought of what I said, really. I refused to be star-struck. We were contemporaries, and nice enough as he was, and correct as we say, he was fine. He was a Capricorn and he wanted to be successful. He needed to be, I think. We got on well. All stars are overrated. They're people. I think some of them crave it when they're young because along with that comes money but ultimately they want peace. It wears a bit thin. He wasn't difficult to work with, not with me anyway. But then again, he wanted to crack Germany and we were fairly popular in Germany. He'd come from L.A. and he'd landed in Berlin and fair enough he wanted to do some stuff. He was a big star then.

Together David and Iggy were a pair of naughty boys really. They explored Berlin and the clubs and quite frankly they were dreadful. People talk about Berlin as if it were marvelous, but frankly it was just weird. They had a cabaret which was sexually deviant, and I just didn't need this. But David wasn't deviant, anything but. During the tour in America for example there were no boys outside these hotel rooms, just black girls he had a thing for. Both of them were pretty normal. I remember we were in some hotel in the US, and David and Iggy came knocking at our door, asking my wife, Virginia, to go and play! I don't know where they thought I was. So I said, "Hello, David," and they scampered off. Nothing was ever said after that.

David never spoke about his family, although I remember when he did the tour with Iggy, when he played keyboards. I think his mother came to a gig in London, and he wasn't pleased. I think Stuey George looked after her. David was uncomfortable about the approach. Bless her, she thought, Oh look, David! Oh I must go up and see David. But Stuey was kind and said, No, you can't go up there. David didn't want her to come up.

IGGY POP: He subsumed my personality, lyrically, on that first album. At times it was like having Professor Higgins say to you, "Young man, please, you are from the Detroit area. I think you should write a song about mass production." He wrote a chord progression on a ukulele and said, "Call it 'Lust for Life.' Write something up." He saw me sometimes, when he wanted to voice it that way, as a modern Beat or a modern Dostoyevsky character or a modern van Gogh. But he also knew I'm a hick from the sticks at heart.

David was worldly. I learned things that I still use today. I met the Beatles and the Stones, and this one and that one, and this actress and this actor and all these powerful people through him. And I watched. And every once in a while, now at least, I'm a little less rustic when I have to deal with those people. He came to my parents' trailer in Detroit, and the neighbors were so frightened of the car and the bodyguard they called the police. My father's a very wonderful man, and he said, "Thank you for what you're doing for my son." I thought, Shut up, Dad. You're making me look uncool.

HANIF KUREISHI: Why the fuck would you do all that for Iggy Pop? I guess for David, Iggy Pop was just Terry, wasn't he? He was his brother, his long-lost brother. I remember Bowie saying—if you love Iggy Pop there must be something wrong with you. Iggy Pop was really, really crazy, compared to Bowie who was much more centered. Maybe he was just Terry.

CARLOS ALOMAR: Making *The Idiot* was great, because I met Jimmy Osterberg, rather than Iggy Pop, this cat that came around to hang out with his friend David, and he was just a lovely sweet man. He is the kind of guy who reads the newspaper and looks over his glasses at you and says, "Good morning." Then onstage his alter ego comes out and you think, Fuck me, who is that? When David asked me to do the album, it was like primal scream therapy. Iggy just came in and started singing about his mom, and how she stepped on his heart, and we're thinking, This is serious stuff! David also told me this: If you see something, write; if you feel something, write. Write, write, write. David did a tour with Iggy as a keyboard player, and he tried to undermine his situation by saying I'm not David Bowie, I'm a keyboard player. Yeah, right! But that tour was the craziest, most awesome thing I ever did. We were on the front line, and the first two shows we did, there was this angry mob. What did I do wrong? They're throwing beer at me! Welcome to punk music and Iggy Pop, you stupid fuck. I learned how to kick a fucker in the face in a minute. Once he spit at me, whether they were a guy or a girl, I'd kick them in the face. I just didn't understand the world I had been thrown into.

JOHN GIDDINGS (PROMOTER): I first met David when he was Iggy Pop's piano player, at Friars Aylesbury in 1977. Iggy said that David was the most expensive musician he'd ever worked with, and David said he never got paid! That was the first time I helped promote a "David Bowie" show, and I went on to promote him for the rest of his career. It came down to trust in the end, as all David wanted was to be able to walk out onstage, in London, Moscow, New York, wherever, and know that nothing was going to go wrong, that everything was going to be perfect. He didn't want to know how you did it, but once he trusted you, that was it as far as he was concerned. He didn't interfere. People are famous until you get to know them, and once you got to know David you realized that he was an incredibly smart, funny guy. Jim and David would sit around and talk about everything—art, music, politics, theatre—but never about their own work or careers. They weren't obsessive about it in the way that many musicians are, didn't need to show off about it.

I remember once being in a restaurant with them in Berlin, and the table was covered with all these glasses full of wine and water, with different amounts in each. And they both started hitting them with knives and forks, making up a song, a good song, on the spot. They were full of creativity but they didn't brag about it. They thought it was silly when people talked about the problems of fame, as they knew they could both walk around unrecognized if they wanted to. It was all a matter of how you carried yourself. David was special. I've promoted everyone in the business, but David is the only person I've ever wanted to ask for an autograph, not that I ever did, obviously. There was no one to touch him. Freddie Mercury was in a band, Mick Jagger was in a band, Bono was in a band. David was all alone. The Stones were a blues band, U2 were a folk band, but David was David. And yet he was always a Bromley boy at heart.

NICK KENT: Bowie and Iggy went to see a screening of *Taxi Driver* in Berlin, and Iggy was so knocked out by the film that he immediately went and got a Mohawk, a Travis Bickle Mohawk. And Bowie went and saw a bunch of Fassbinder films and decided to grow a mustache. They were creating new identities for themselves, pretending they weren't rock stars, but rather reluctant émigrés. The *NME* got wind that Bowie had grown a mustache, and we printed this in our gossip column. On the day this issue hit the streets, I was in the office waiting for a phone call while everyone else was out at lunch. So every time the phone rang I had to pick it up, and I got a series of calls from hysterical, obviously gay young men asking me if this was true, that he'd grown a mustache. They were all flabbergasted. Why had he done it? Was it really true? Did we have photographs? People were incensed. A lot of these people were from the north, and I always imagine they were Holly Johnson [from Frankie Goes to Hollywood] and Steven Morrissey. It gave me an insight into how extreme Bowie's influence on his audience was.

DEBORAH HARRY (SINGER): The first time we met David Bowie was when we supported him on *The Idiot* tour for Iggy Pop, in 1977. We were all star-struck. How could you not be? He was David Bowie. We were obviously very pleased to be doing the tour, and it was a momentous occasion when they casually walked out onstage together when we were doing our sound check. We already knew that he was due to perform with Iggy, but it was still a thrill seeing him. On a couple of the other tours we had done, it was very competitive, and they tried to make the opening band look very insignificant, but David and Iggy took care of us. They wanted us to put on a good show. I don't think we had full sound and lights, but they were, you know, encouraging. He was very generous, and gave me pointers about how to interact with the crowd. It was more like tech support rather than creative stuff, working the stage, working the lights. I guess I was pretty dull at that point.

He was intriguing, as you could see that he had a process in the way he metamorphosed. I couldn't say what that process was, but it certainly involved exploration, which was one of the reasons he was so interested in us. I remember him talking about Japan and how infatuated and inspired he was by Japanese culture and costume, which was very clear by looking at a lot of the things he ended up doing. On this tour he was totally not in the front at all, and he was off to the side, focusing on playing. It was a tough bunch of guys, you know, really seasoned, strong musicians making this crunchy sound. It was really gutsy, and very good for Iggy. I think he did it out of love for Iggy, paying Iggy back in a way for being an inspiration to him.

I was complaining about being recognized, saying that it was getting difficult to walk around, and he said, "Oh, I always walk around." And when I asked Bowie how he did it he said that he changed it up a little bit, wore a hat, put a pair of glasses on, and he would just vanish into anonymity. He could turn it on and off.

CHRIS STEIN (GUITARIST): They were waiting for us in the hallway when we arrived. This was in Massey Hall in Toronto. He was always the consummate professional. He obviously wanted to find out what was happening, and he was interested in what was happening in the whole new wave thing. He seemed obsessed with Television and Tom Verlaine's hair, which I could never understand. I thought it would have been Richard Hell's hair, as he had the quintessential cut, but he was always going on about Tom Verlaine's hair. Maybe he was jealous. Maybe there was hair rivalry. But he was asking us all about what was going on in the New York scene. I'm sure he wanted to put the moves on Debbie. But the time wasn't right, apparently! He wanted to know about the downtown scene. He wanted to maintain his relevance. I don't know if he was too worried, but who knows. But he was aware of Iggy's role as this seminal punk figure. He had a great time doing those shows too, as they were a really loud band, a massive sound, and he was really enjoying himself. There was a lot less pressure on him not being the front man too. Iggy went out with us more than he did. David was a little more reclusive. There was a moment when we were in Seattle and Iggy and me and Clem [Burke] and Gary [Valentine], I guess, went to the local punk house and did an impromptu show in a room in this house, and for years after that, every time we were back in Seattle someone would go, "I was at that legendary thing . . . !"

David could turn his charisma on and off. There's this story about Marilyn Monroe walking down the street with the daughter of Lee Strasberg, Susan Strasberg, and Susan says that nobody was noticing her [Marilyn] at all. And then Marilyn says, "You wanna see something?" And she changes her demeanor a little bit, and all of a sudden everybody in the street was buzzing because it was her. Bowie could do that kind of thing too. That was his chameleon nature. He came over to our house on Fifty-Eighth Street a couple of times. We got stoned together. We had this fancy townhouse for a while when we had more money, and he fucking showed up in the middle of the night with Mick Jagger, just us and them and Ava Cherry and Jerry Hall. I got to sit on a coach with Mick Jagger and smoke a joint. That was cool.

CARLOS ALOMAR: When we were making *Low*, *"Heroes"*, and *Lodger*, David and I had the privilege of working with George Murray and Dennis Davies. We were the Damn Trio, and we had the ability to exemplify every thought David had. We could flip anything around, kick out arrangements, time signatures, three-quarter time here, four-quarter time, a half bar here, we could do anything.

TONY VISCONTI: When we were recording *Low* we would vacillate between being really chatty for about an hour, and then very studious. We both really loved Peter Cook and Dudley Moore and a lot of other British comedians, but then all of a sudden we would just snap into hard work without a cue. Because we were friends we would just chat about things. But he would never crack the whip, nor would I—we just had so many past experiences to base our work on.

ROY YOUNG (MUSICIAN): I came in around *Low*. I was a regular at the Speakeasy, in London's West End, which is where all the musicians went after a gig, no matter where they were playing. It was just around the corner from the BBC, and was definitely the "in" club. Everyone that was in there was a name, you know. It was quite interesting. I used to play there, and would rub shoulders with Rod Stewart, Eric Clapton, Elton John, all the names that we know. We all mingled together because we'd all worked together. David used to come in, and he was like a Jekyll and Hyde, I think, and you never knew which one you were going to get. He had that quality to be able to be a different person every time you saw him. I thought it was quite neat actually. Whatever he carried, he carried it quite well. I remember one night he turned up as Ziggy Stardust, and the next minute everyone is rushing around trying to look like him. It was all the glamor and glitter, and the next day people were running out and buying gear down Oxford Street [to] buy the stuff to compete with David. The funny thing was, after a while it just looked so funny because everywhere you looked there was David Bowie. Then David started wearing a white shirt and a pair of blue flannel pants and the next thing was, all the people ran out and bought white shirts and blue flannel pants. I was playing at the Speakeasy when David called me to ask me to work with him on *Low*.

When we were recording *Low* at the Château, it transpired that we both liked to fish. Very odd, as you wouldn't imagine he would like to fish. Art, he was very much on top of all that, I felt. He spoke about the horn players with Little Richard. He loved the saxophone. He was fanatical about Little Richard, Fats Domino. When we were recording he was very good at just letting you take the reins. That was interesting because it could've happened that we weren't quite getting the effect that was needed for the album and so therefore, they let it go and go and it got more and more interesting as it went along.

I used to drink a lot of gin and tonics while I recorded, and one night David said, "Give me one of those gin and tonics." So I gave him one, and he kept asking for more, and clinking his glass on the microphone. Every time he wanted another gin and tonic he'd clink his glass on the mike. He got so hammered that he fell asleep at the board. Tony Visconti kept recording, but David was fast asleep, snoring. Tony kept asking him what he thought and all you could hear was this snoring. So Tony started mimicking it, saying. "What do you think of that, David?" and then mimicking his snoring. We eventually had to take him to bed, carrying him up these winding stairs to his bedroom at the top, but then he fell all the way down the stairs. And I mean all of them. The next day at breakfast he lifted up his shirt and showed us all the marks on his back. Tony Visconti gave me such shit for the gin and tonics, I was nearly banned from the sessions. It was a very depressing album, anyway. He talked about fame a lot. He was very affected by the fact that he wanted to be famous, to be the guy running down the street and everyone chasing him and wanting to touch his body and girls screaming. But then when he got it he didn't like it, said he couldn't walk down the street anymore.

His son, Zowie, was traveling with us, and he was always impeccable, always impeccably dressed.

PAUL WELLER (MUSICIAN): I was in Dingwalls sometime in '76, maybe '77, with Joe Strummer when "Sound and Vision" came on, and we couldn't fucking believe the drum sound. Neither of us had heard anything like it. I loved that, and I loved the barroom piano on "Be My Wife," and all the crazy instrumentals. My recent records have been far more experimental, and while a lot of the influences come from psychedelia, a lot of them come from mid-period Bowie. I went through a spell of not really liking him, as I thought he'd gone off, but I have to admit I bought all of Bowie's records from *Hunky Dory* onwards, right up until *Lodger* and *Scary Monsters*. All of his stuff back then was really groundbreaking. I never liked all the music, but it was always different, always pushing forward. Everyone in some way has been influenced by him. I've recently become much more of a fan, due to my missus, although *Low* is probably actually my favorite record of all time.

CHARLES SHAAR MURRAY: My problem with *Low* was that I'd basically just crawled out of a deep hole, a mini breakdown caused by several years of acute amphetamine addiction, and *Low* reminded me of everything I'd just crawled out of. And when I interviewed Bowie the following year, I told him that *Low* appeared to be an actual sonic incarnation of post-speed addiction breakdown, and he said that's exactly what it was. He said he made that record because he'd just been through something similar, and wanted to get it out of his system. He wasn't glorifying psychotic withdrawal, as I initially thought he was, he was actually exorcising it. And then we were all chums again. We'd both been through the wars in our different ways, to different degrees in the intervening years. Him being a rich rock star who got drastically fucked on coke, me as an impoverished journo who got drastically fucked on speed. He may have been wearing a carefully chosen outfit from the normal-bloke section of his wardrobe, but he seemed like he was back on the straight and narrow, and had discarded a lot of baggage during that time. *"Heroes"* was an album about triumphing over a state of mind that *Low* seemed to be wallowing in.

Stuey George was David's bodyguard, and his jokes—benign though they were—tended to be at his boss's expense. "A Starman that won't fly," he used to say, whenever mention was made of Bowie's reluctance to board a plane. In Berlin there were no birds in the sky, just taxis and lots of walking, irregular working hours and lots of beer and coffee. When Bowie had been living in L.A. the year before, he had hardly left his house, but here he was in Berlin, trying to replicate the dark, solitary psychosis of drug-addled Los Angeles. Lyrically Low *was fueled by his L.A. diary, while musically it was basically upside down R&B*—blue, blue, electric blue. *Bowie designed to unnerve and disconcert.* Low *was a comedown album.*

JAYNE COUNTY: Around the time of *Low*, and having moved to Berlin, he had a torrid affair with Romy Haag, and they were quite an item for a while, much to Angie's disdain. Romy flew into a rage one night and threw David out in the street because she said he was stealing her ideas from her show at her club. He took all the images, gestures, and staging from her act and Romy was furious. I know he was also influenced by a few of the demos I was sending him. He went crazy and called everyone saying that he loved my songs and that I was a fantastic songwriter. He was supposed to produce an album for me but nothing ever came of that except some of my ideas began popping up on his songs. I don't think it was intentional, I mean he wasn't being evil or anything. I think he listened to my songs then went about his business, then when he started writing new songs some of my ideas unintentionally, subconsciously, made their way into some of his material. It was mostly the subject matter, not the actual sound of the songs. I'm not resentful now. I got over it. I'm now very flattered indeed. David was always a nice lad but he was easily influenced by others. For instance his sound changed immediately when he went to see the Human League one night at CBGBs. He was like that.

TONY VISCONTI: Working with Bowie was much more than going to a studio. It was a social event too. We would eat together, go to shows together, go to clubs together, and really soak in the local culture. That was always his way of working, and Berlin was perfect for him in terms of what he wanted at that time. It was a stark, scary place, yet it had a very exciting nightlife, with exotic locales such as the Turkish Quarter, and it was swarming with artists like Tangerine Dream, who were friends of ours. David was writing with Brian Eno back then, and the three of us got on really great. I think David just liked living in Berlin. There was so much of it, in those days, that was fantastic, fantasy-like, that didn't exist anywhere else in the world. The impending danger of the divided military zones, the bizarre nightlife, the extremely traditional restaurants with aproned servers, reminders of Hitler's not-too-distant presence, a recording studio five hundred yards from the Wall—you could've been on the set of *The Prisoner.* I got a real wonderful memory of that city. I know the wall had to come down, but in many ways, it was a much more romantic city with the wall around you. You felt like you were in a black-and-white film from the '40s. You were expecting Humphrey Bogart to walk down the street any minute.

It was a very bizarre situation. Every day we'd see military tanks in the street—really huge tanks that were almost fifteen to twenty feet high, with big gun turrets at the front—and black jeeps that weren't the standard military green. It was almost like being in a futuristic Arnold Schwarzenegger film, but this was happening in the '70s. The city was surrounded by a moat that was mined. So if you fancied swimming across from East to West Berlin, you'd probably be either caught in barbed wire or exploded. If you had a British or American passport you could go into East Berlin . . . and when you went into East Berlin you were going about thirty years into the past. Because it was a Communist territory there were no brand names but they had billboards with a picture of a fish saying, "Eat fish" [or a] picture of a milk bottle [that said] "Drink milk" in German. There were no products in a Communist country then. The women were dressed as if it were the '50s: they had narrow skirts, beehive hairdos, and stiletto heels. It was a most bizarre situation. David was parked one night on the west side and he was having a cigarette with a girl in his car and a Red Army guard knocked on his window and asked him for a light.

Now, this guy shouldn't have been in the west. Wacky stuff used to happen like this. He came under the river in a passage to ask him for a light. David was so freaked out. "You guys should be over there, on the other side." That's a lyric from "Heroes," actually.

ANGIE BOWIE: Berlin called to him in other ways. He chose to live in a section of the city as bleak, anonymous, and culturally lost as possible: Schöneberg, populated largely by Turkish immigrants. He took an apartment above an auto parts store and ate at the local workingmen's café. Talk about alienation.

IGGY POP: There's seven days in a week: two for bingeing, two for recovery, and three more for any other activity.

COCO SCHWAB: I loved how Jim [Iggy] would pick new neighborhoods in Berlin and then just go out and walk them. Then he'd come back and say, "Wanna go for a walk?" He'd show us from time to time what he found. It was always fun. I remember one elevated subway ride where you ride into East Berlin with no checkpoints and then back out with absinthe into the west. Trust Jim to find that one.

TONY VISCONTI: They use "Heroes" for every heroic event, although it's a song about alcoholics. We did it on twenty-four tracks in Hansa Studios in Berlin. With all of the backing vocals and instruments on it, we only had one track left for the vocal. So Bowie would do a take and listen to it and he'd say: "I think I've got one better." And I'd say, "Well, you know we can't keep that take." This was before digital recording. So he'd pull his socks up, take a deep breath, and go and do a better take than the one he did before. And that was it, it was gone, the previous vocal was gone. We kept doing that. Having experience in the studio, you have to know when to say, "I think we've got the take." There's no way of going back to take five or take two; they were gone, evaporated. I did a lot of records that way. That's when you work as a team, as a producer, coach, singer, artist. Everybody's on the same page and everyone is just hyped up with adrenaline.

BRIAN ENO: That time was really confused. It was much harder working on *"Heroes"* than *Low.* The whole thing, except "Sons of the Silent Age," which was written beforehand, was evolved on the spot in the studio. Not only that, everything on the album is a first take! I mean, we did the second takes but they weren't nearly as good. It was all done in a very casual kind [of way]. [However] Bowie was pretty much living at the edge of his nervous system . . . he was very, very upset. I felt desperately sorry for him going through that and trying to make a record. But as often happens, that translated into a sense of complete abandon in the work.

ALAN YENTOB: He was significantly different when I interviewed him in Berlin, as he had entered a different phase of his life. His interests were different, Berlin was a fascinating space to be in, electronic music was to the fore, he was learning new things. You could say that Brian Eno rescued him during this time, and he was very influential. Because the Berlin period was so different than what had come before it, it seems very calculated, in the sense that it was really about who he had come across. But then he was always like that. He was always picking up things and collecting thoughts and ideas from others. He assimilated them and then represented them.

HANIF KUREISHI: David could be funny with Brian Eno. He was very competitive with Bryan Ferry. He used to do a very funny imitation of Bryan Ferry in front of Bryan, who used to look rather embarrassed. He used to do his voice, his high voice. He was a great mimic, and used to do a very good Keith Richards. He used to play Trivial Pursuit with Keith.

PAUL MCGUINNESS (FILM PRODUCER, FORMER MANAGER OF U2): I remember Eno telling me that one time he was sharing an apartment with Bowie and Iggy Pop in Kreuzberg, and he says there were a lot of rows about what was in the fridge. "Who's taken my eggs?" He says they were like students—"Who took my socks, you bastard!" It was like *The Young Ones.*

ROBERT FRIPP (GUITARIST): In February 1977 I went to live in New York and in July, the telephone went at my apartment on the Lower East Side

and the voice came on and it said, "It's Brian, hello! I'm here with David, we're in Berlin, hang on I'll pass you over." So Eno passed the phone over to David and David said, "Hello, we're here in blah, blah, blah, do you think you can play some rock and roll guitar?" and I said, "Well, I don't know because I haven't really played for three years, but if you're prepared to take a risk, so am I." At that point at I had no intention ever of returning to the music industry, this festering pit of dishonesty, deception, theft, violation, greed and all the rest of it, but hey this was Brian calling, I'd done two albums with Brian, this was Bowie, a magnificent live act who'd written some of my favorite pop/rock songs, so yeah! Why not? By and large when I get calls from people, it's when they don't know what they want, but they know they want something.

A first-class plane ticket on Lufthansa to Frankfurt with connection to Berlin arrived shortly afterwards. Flying first class [for] the first time in my life, the Lufthansa stewardess leaned over and said while pouring Champagne and pretending to be pleased to see me, "First class is the only way to fly," and I believed her. On the in-flight sound system was "Sound and Vision" from *Low.*

So I landed in Frankfurt and had to make the connecting flight, carrying my Cornish pedal board, with fuzz, wah-wah, and volume pedals. At the time, 1977 in Germany, the Baader Meinhof Group were in active go mode and I remember the German security guard looking at my pedal board, wondering what on Earth I was trying to smuggle on board. So anyway I made the connection to Berlin, caught a taxi to my hotel, which I believe was the former SS headquarters, dumped my stuff, got myself together, and then went to Hansa Studios by the Wall for about quarter to six in the evening, jet-lagged, pretty sleepless, and said to David and Brian, "Well, would you like to play me some of the things you've been doing?" Eno said, "Why don't you plug in?" So I plugged into Eno's magic suitcase, his VCS3 synthy. They hit the Roll, Play button [makes drumming noises] and then on bar three [makes guitar noises] and skysaw guitars and that straight into "Beauty and the Beast." What you hear on the record, the first track of *"Heroes,"* is the first note I played on the session.

This was a time of change. David was clearly in transition personally and musically and Brian, well, Brian can no doubt speak for himself. So, here you have three men in their early thirties, in a changing time musically, a changing time in the world, in a city which was on the edge and Berlin at the time was on the front line. I toured in Germany with King Crimson in '73 and '74 and you were in no doubt that this was [the] front line in the Cold War. You would perhaps be sitting in your motel having breakfast and overhead there's the American Air Force patrolling the border. The liminal zone, the in-between place, is where creative artists go to work because it's on the edge, it's unsettled, it's not fixed. This is the place to be and the Hansa Studios by the Wall still was missing a roof. You looked at it and there was the Berlin Wall with the machine-gun turret, which from time to time would look into the control room in the studio. It was a time and place and at least two of the three characters there were on the edge and in a moving zone. It was a place that a creative artist would move to be.

In terms of *"Heroes,"* enough work had been done for me to work on top, but not enough to stop me playing on top. I didn't have very much in the way of guide vocals to work to. I had a few phrases but not much. It was very quick, very spontaneous, and the key to working both with David and with Brian was always "play." Very good professionals often forget to play. Both Bowie and Eno play. Working with them it's as if the only reason we're there is to have fun and let rip, see where it goes. So, my best hunch would be there was a framework, a map of the terrain, but it didn't tell you how you get from A to B. Working with Bowie and Eno, above anyone else I've ever worked with, they set up the situation for me to fly. Encouragement and support, without any reservation, constriction, editing—it was stunning. I was in Berlin for the total period of one week. The actual recording was two, three days.

Both Eno and Bowie were actually shrewd about not being governed by the rules of the marketplace. Professionals would take close care of what was possible in the marketplace and act accordingly. The other approach, the approach of the artist not the professional, is to produce the work and then see what you have to do to deliver it, knowing that the world will act against you.

BRIAN ENO: He got into a very peculiar state when he was working. It used to strike me as very paradoxical that two comparatively well-known people would be staggering home at six in the morning, and he'd break a raw egg into his mouth and that was his food for the day, virtually. It was really slummy. We'd sit around the kitchen table at dawn feeling a bit tired and a bit fed up—me with a bowl of crummy German cereal and him with albumen from the egg running down his shirt.

I was only involved in "Heroes" to do the backing track. He wrote the lyrics and the melody after I'd left—as he did for all the other tracks. And when I left, I already had a feeling about that track—it sounded grand and heroic. In fact, I had that very word in mind. And then David brought the finished album round to my place and that track came up and it said, "We can be heroes" and I was absolutely . . . it was such a strange feeling, you know. I just shivered. When you shiver, it's a fear reaction, isn't it? Well, we had all these backing tracks very suddenly—it seemed in about two days. And remember: this came after laboring for months and months on my record. And I thought, Shit, it can't be *this* easy. But gradually it began to hang together. Fripp did everything he did in about six hours—and that was straight off the plane from New York too! He arrived at the studio at about eleven p.m. and walked in and we said, "Do you fancy doing anything?" and he said, "Might as well hear what you've been doing." And while we were setting up the tapes, he got out his guitar and said, "Might as well try a few things." So I plugged him into the synthesizer for treatments and we just played virtually everything we'd done at him—and he'd just start up without even knowing the chord sequences. It was a very extraordinary performance. By the next day, he'd finished, packed up, and gone home.

David told me about this place in Kyoto called the Moss Garden and then we just started to work. And again, there was this very sloppy sort of technique—like, I was just playing around with this chord sequence on the Yamaha synthesizer and I said, "Give us a shout when you think it's long enough," you know, and sort of carried on. And then David looked at the clock and said, "Yeah, that'll probably do," and we stopped. And on the record, that's exactly where the piece ends.

The "Heroes" *cover was deliberately meant to ape punk. It may have looked as though it suddenly appeared in a vacuum, but the styling on the cover, the leather jacket and the monochromatic feel, were all meant to echo the iconography of punk. What seemed at the time indiscriminate and off-kilter was actually a parody. The cover photo by Masayoshi Sukita was inspired by the painting* Roquairol *by German artist Erich Heckel, in which the subject strikes a similar pose. The cover is also obviously a version of the cover of* The Idiot. *Bowie had initially been quite dismissive of punk, a form and an attitude that he felt was actually rather old-fashioned, and by dint of that, fundamentally retrogressive. He had been propelled in a pell-mell fashion toward his semi-exile in Berlin by a combination of curiosity, fear, and whim. This for him was new, unlike punk, which seemed reductive and possibly rotten. It was only when punk suddenly went mainstream that he thought he should reference it, and only then in a playful manner, on the cover of* "Heroes."

BILL PRINCE (JOURNALIST): Masayoshi Sukita was a commercial photographer working for an ad agency in Tokyo when he first visited New York in 1971, largely at the behest of a boyhood fascination with postwar American cinema and the cult of the "rebel" as expounded by Marlon Brando, James Dean, and Elvis Presley. The following year he went to London. "At the time there was very little information about David Bowie in Japan," he said. "When I arrived in London, I had never even heard his name before." A chance sighting of Brian Ward's high-kicking cover image for *The Man Who Sold the World*, advertising the singer's imminent shows at north London's Rainbow Theatre, changed all that. "I thought it was a sensational photo and an unusual image for a pop musician. And the concert itself was amazing. I quickly realized David Bowie wasn't a regular performer. I felt there was much more going on, so much more depth and imagination than from a regular musician." What he'd seen inspired Sukita to approach Bowie's management with the idea for a shoot, and their first session took place in August 1972. It was the beginning of what turned into a lifelong association—the photographer was there to meet Bowie as he arrived in Yokohama in April 1973, for his first Japanese tour, and was still taking pictures of him in 2009. "The *'Heroes'* photos were meant to have a 'punk' feel. The whole session was over in an hour. Afterwards, I selected about twenty photos to give to David-san, including the shot on the *'Heroes'* sleeve."

NICK KENT: The German records are among his very best. Bowie was obsessed with calling down the muse. With really creative people, and

Bowie was one of them, there is a sense of calling down the muse. And in Berlin he isn't just living with Iggy Pop, he's living with the muse. It's like Bob Dylan between 1963 and 1966; the muse moves in. The Rolling Stones between 1968 and 1971, the muse moves in. And then it leaves just as quickly and never comes back. And in the '70s, the muse was with Bowie all the time. Right there on his shoulder, whispering in his ear. Imagine having that talent, that amazing song craft. When Lou Reed wrote a song it was all on one level, and Bowie could do that with things like "Rebel Rebel," and he could do what Iggy Pop could do, but none of those guys could do what Bowie could do. He was like a musical chemist, a sonic chemist, like Miles Davis. Completely audacious.

On September 11, 1977, David recorded a song for Bing Crosby's Christmas special, Bing Crosby's Merrie Olde Christmas, *at Elstree Studios, with two of Crosby's children present. He did it as a favor to his mother. The crooner, who would die five weeks later, and the man with the burnt-apricot wedge swapped cheesy dialogue before singing an adaptation of "Little Drummer Boy," complete with a new musical counterpoint, "Peace on Earth," written by Larry Grossman.*

LARRY GROSSMAN: [We'd suggested they duet on "Little Drummer Boy"] but Bowie said, "I won't sing that song. I hate that song. . . . And if I have to do that song, I can't do the show. I'm doing this show because my mother loves Bing Crosby." [So we crafted a counter-melody that Bowie could sing.] It all happened rather rapidly. I would say within an hour, we had it written and were able to present it [to] him again.

MARY CROSBY: We were pretty young, but we knew that this was happening. That first moment when he walked in, it's etched in my memory. The doors opened and David walked in with his wife. They were both wearing full-length mink coats, they have matching full makeup, and their hair was bright red. We were thinking, Oh my God. But then they sat at the piano, and David was a little nervous, and he said, "Well, I only sing in this key."

NATHANIEL CROSBY: It almost didn't happen. You should have seen the way he was dressed in rehearsal. I think the producers told him to take the lipstick off and take the earring out. It was just incredible to see the contrast. But it happened.

TREVOR BOLDER: I don't think anyone has ever mentioned this, principally because I don't think anyone actually knows it, but Bowie tried to re-form the Spiders when he'd finished with the Berlin period. He rang me once, in 1978, at home, and he asked me would I go back and re-form with the Spiders. He said that he'd been away too long, doing whatever he was doing in Berlin with Brian Eno and Robert Fripp and all those people, and he wanted to know if I fancied going back out again. And I said, "Well, if you can get Mick to do it, we'll consider it." Bowie was having problems with America, I think; he'd done *Diamond Dogs* and all that but I don't think his career had gone how he thought it was going to. *Young Americans* had been a big hit for him there, but *Station to Station*, *Low*, and *"Heroes"* had been very European records, and he desperately wanted success in America. America was where he was focusing on at the time, and he thought he might stand a better chance at commercial success if he started doing some more orthodox rock music, and obviously by re-forming the band that had made him famous in the first place. If I'm honest I actually think he missed the band, in fact. He'd used other musicians but he missed the camaraderie of the band. He missed going out on the road and being one of the lads, even though he was never really one of the lads with us, not towards the end, anyway. But Mick wouldn't do it, as they weren't really speaking at the time, so it never happened. Mick was really annoyed that Bowie had shut down all communication, and didn't want to have anything to do with him. It could have been great, in fact it could have been amazing, but Mick just wasn't interested.

NICK RHODES: When I was asked to DJ at the Rum Rummer in Birmingham, I basically just played all my David Bowie records. This was in 1978, and we were just about to form Duran Duran, and all of us loved Bowie. Most of the other members of the band were working at the club in some capacity—cooking, cleaning, or washing up—but I actually got to play Bowie's records. Duran Duran had a single vision of what we wanted to do. We wanted to mix glam rock and punk rock with a little bit of disco, although the prime motivation for forming in the first place was

David Bowie. It always was. An entire generation of groups who formed in the late '70s or early '80s only happened because of David. He is basically responsible for British music in the first half of the '80s. There was decadence about him that was appealing, something dark, something German, but something very exciting.

In Bowie's world, everything at this time was about Germany. In 1978 Bowie starred in a West German film called Just a Gigolo, *directed by David Hemmings, and also featuring Kim Novak, Sydne Rome, and Marlene Dietrich. It was his first movie role since* The Man Who Fell to Earth, *and was an unmitigated disaster. So bad was it that Bowie said it was his "thirty-two Elvis movies rolled into one."*

RORY MACLEAN (TRAVEL WRITER): I was a wannabe film director, and was assisting David Hemmings. I was his dogsbody, his gofer, and I was the one who read all the scripts that came into the office. In the summer of 1977 this appalling script came in called *Just a Gigolo*, which was a knock-off German attempt at *Cabaret*, financed by German dentists' tax write-offs. The producer also made his money from soft-core porn films. David called his agent to let him know that he didn't want to do it, only to be told that both David Bowie and Marlene Dietrich had agreed to appear in it. So who cares if the script is awful?! So David Hemmings was persuaded. Apparently it took the producer six months to convince [Dietrich] to accept the role. Every time he telephoned her apartment, a woman would breathe into the receiver. "This is the maid. Madame is lunching in Versailles." The "maid" was obviously Dietrich.

I first met Bowie in Berlin in December that year. Hemmings and I had flown in to start the film, by which time Bowie had almost finished his Berlin phase, and was flitting between there, Lausanne, and Paris. At the time he was having all these custody battles over Zowie with Angie. I was a wet-behind-the-ears, naïve Canadian, but almost instantly Hemmings and Bowie became quite matey, in that quintessential English way. Bowie wanted to initiate us in the ways of the city, so invited me and Hemmings to his favorite transvestite club, the Lützower Lampe. The club's star, a sixty-year-old drag queen named Viola, sat on my knee and crooned German love songs in my ear: "*Schöner Gigolo, armer Gigolo, denke nicht mehr an die Zeiten . . .*" There were also more traditional females there that night, and Bowie didn't go home with one of the transvestites.

He was very relaxed in Berlin. He was really in himself, and while the normal man he appeared to be was maybe a persona too, it sure didn't feel like it. He was an ordinary exile. He was living a life away from the spotlight. Tartan shirt, baggy trousers, hanging out at the Exile restaurant. He seemed to be at peace with himself, and had spent a lot of time painting, having discovered German Expressionism. He had also just released "*Heroes*," so he knew that he had created something very special. We spent a great Christmas together, along with David Hemmings, and various partners and children. It was in a secluded restaurant in the Grunewald, the deep and dark urban forest that hugged the city's western fringe. We ate and drank too much and Bowie gave me a copy of Fritz Lang's biography. At the end of the happy evening I followed him downstairs to the huge, ceramic lavatory, where—as we stood before the urinals—we sang Buddy Holly songs together, and "Good Golly Miss Molly."

Coco was there all the time, and I had a lot of time for her. I remember Angie went into the apartment in Schöneberg and had gone into Coco's room and thrown all her clothes out into the street. Coco was extremely protective of him, and also such a facilitator. I don't know if there had been a sexual relationship, but she obviously loved him, really loved him, and would do anything to support him. Getting the canvases, getting the paints, finding apartments, getting him the books he wanted. Iggy was there too, and I first met him at David's birthday party in January 1978. We were in the first nouvelle cuisine restaurant in the city, and we all ate these immaculately produced minute dishes. Eno was there, Zowie with his nanny, Coco, Hemmings, me, and a bunch of other people. I remember Iggy getting outrageously drunk, and we all went off to Lützower Lampe. The birthday was a big affair, they even had matchbooks printed. Bowie hadn't completely reformed his north American habits, shall we say, and one night, Iggy sat in the passenger seat as Bowie rammed their car into their dealer's car again and again, for five long minutes. He then drove around their hotel's underground car park, pushing seventy miles per hour, screaming that he wanted to end it all by driving into a concrete wall . . . until the car ran out of fuel.

Berlin represented so much, that clash of twentieth-century opposites, being the clash of communism and fascism, and through David I fell in love with the place. There's a German word, *begeistert*—enthusiastic—and that's what I felt about Berlin. I had an academic interest in the place, an island of capitalism surrounded by communism, and three-quarters of a million Red Army soldiers. Bowie brought it to life, and his passion for it certainly inflamed mine. He was unduly influenced by his surroundings, and whereas all previous material had been bound up with persona, his new music was a direct result of his environment. If you look at "Warszawa" or "Neukoln" they all spun out of Berlin. The scars were all still there. There were so many playgrounds, but that's because they were destroyed buildings. In every street you could still find pockmarked walls, or houses full of bullet holes. The city was dying, and continually being squeezed by Khrushchev. He had this wonderful line: "If I ever want to make the West squeak, I squeeze its balls in West Berlin." That's what was happening. And there was something really attractive in that. The city was full of Wilmersdorf Widows, the war widows, and young anarchists. It was full of ghosts, full of darkness. We felt like exiles, cut off from the rest of the world. Everyone had a suitcase under the bed, just in case something happened. I think Bowie had a love/hate relationship with the place, because it was intoxicating, yet you were trapped.

On a film set, when you're shooting you become so involved, and so emotionally overwhelmed that you lose sight of the bigger picture. However when we finished we knew for sure that this was a flawed project. The great paradox is that both Bowie and Dietrich only agreed to appear in the film on the understanding that they would get to work together—these two twentieth-century legends having this unique opportunity to work together—which of course they never did. We filmed Bowie in Berlin, and then he went off to Texas to prepare for his 1978 tour, and then we filmed Dietrich in Paris for the same scene. Hemmings played the other character in both scenes, and when we were filming Dietrich, she said to him, "Do they pay you extra for this shit?" She was wonderfully pissed off.

DAVID BOWIE: I think we have to look back on *Just a Gigolo* with a certain amount of irony. I had a wonderful time making that movie because by the second week we looked around at each other and said, "This is a pile of shit, so let's have a good time!" So we had a good time. But it was an atrocious movie. I mean, it wasn't the end of the world or anything like that. When one starts out one's career with "The Laughing Gnome," it's very easy to put things down to experience.

RORY MACLEAN: After the end of *Just a Gigolo*, David Hemmings was asked if he wanted to direct the film of the Isolar Tour, but his heart was not really in it. He didn't really value the music. It was all paid for by Bowie, and I think the production budget was $100,000. We were going to film five or six concerts, including Earls Court and Bingley Hall in Stafford. But Hemmings was far too literal with the film, and when there were cutaways they were dreadful. When you hear trains on "Warszawa," he would cut to a stock shot of steam train going through a tunnel, and when David sang about the dolphins in "Heroes," there would literally be a cutaway to a dolphin. His concerts were more than adulation, they were about the thrill of the richness of celebration. But none of that was in Hemmings's film. It was a disaster. When Bowie saw it, he immediately took all the material, all the negs, all the material, the soundtrack, and sent everything to the vault in Elstree, where I think it still remains.

Every night in the audience there would be the Ziggy, there would be the Thin White Duke clones, and the Berliner clones, because there had already been some publicity stills released from *Just a Gigolo*. Bowie and I joked that there would soon be the Seven Ages of Bowie as opposed to the Seven Ages of Man. The thing that I found fascinating was the interval during the show, which happened after about seventy minutes. So how does a performer retain that energy during a twenty-to-thirty-minute break without resorting to drugs? What Bowie would do is go to the green room and sit down with a VHS and watch *Coronation Street*. Every night. I thought, This is glorious! He was sitting there in full costume as this occupied the front part of his brain. Seven-eighths of his brain were still in a tense state, ready to go back onstage, but the front part was watching *Coronation Street*.

MARK MOTHERSBAUGH (DEVO): Bowie showed up [to our show at Max's Kansas City] and he introduced us: "This is the band of the future! I am producing them in Tokyo this winter!" And we're like, That sounds good to us. Then afterwards he said, "I really want to produce you guys, the only thing is I'm up for this movie called *Just a Gigolo*, and if I get it I have to go to Berlin for a couple of months." The next week, we played again, and Robert Fripp and Brian Eno came. And they both said, "We would want to produce you guys if you were up for it." And we said, "Well, Brian, David Bowie last week said he was producing us in Tokyo." And Brian Eno starts going, "He's full of shit." At the time I didn't know that Eno was kinda pissed at Bowie because he felt he didn't get credited properly on *"Heroes"* and *Low*.

PAUL GORMAN (JOURNALIST): One morning in the early spring of 1979, Derek Boshier received a telephone call at his studio in Ladbroke Grove. On the line was the photographer Brian Duffy. "He was a bit mysterious that day. He told me that he wanted me to meet someone, a friend of his, and because he said, 'I think you two will really get on together,' I assumed he was fixing me up on a date." The blind date was arranged as a late-morning cup of tea at Duffy's studio in Swiss Cottage. In the meantime, Boshier paid a visit to one of his regular haunts, an art bookshop in Covent Garden. Here, he was informed in time-honored fashion ("You'll never guess who was in here asking about you") that no less than David Bowie had been browsing the shelves the previous day, hunting down catalogues and books featuring Boshier's work. Had Boshier paused to connect Bowie to Duffy (who had photographed the *Aladdin Sane* sleeve), he would have received less of a surprise when the star turned up at his studio a few days later. "So there was David," says Boshier. "He had just finished recording an LP and wanted to collaborate with me and Duffy on the cover design. From that moment we got on like a house on fire." Bowie explained that the album was to be called *Lodger*. Then, over tea and cigarettes, he and Boshier unraveled the various areas where their life and work intersected. Boshier is cut from similarly modest cloth to Brixton-born David Jones; brought up in Portsmouth, he was destined for a career as a butcher's boy when an art teacher intervened, recognized his talents, and propelled him onto the path to the Royal College of Art. Here, alongside classmates Peter Blake, David Hockney, Peter Phillips, and Pauline Boty, Boshier effectively minted British pop art with such paintings as 1962's *England's Glory* (the first artwork to incorporate an ironic representation of the Union Jack). As a result, Boshier appeared with all of the above in Ken Russell's BBC Brit-art documentary, *Pop Goes the Easel*, in which there is a section dedicated to him (and, with the gyrating Boty, he proves himself an exception among artists by pulling off a convincing turn of the twist in footage shot at a drunken RCA student party). Often—and significantly for Bowie—Boshier's paintings contained the recurring image of a plummeting naked "everyman" figure, either solo or as a collective cascade, as in the 1962 space-race peroration *Rethink/Re-Entry*. In the '60s, Boshier's pop-art canvases had formed the backdrop for fashion shoots by the British photographer Robert Freeman. He also undertook a riotous road trip across the States in a classic car with [David] Hockney and Ossie Clark, but split from them in New Orleans to explore the funky South, while they hightailed it to Los Angeles to hook up with Brian Epstein and the Fab Four. In fact the title of *Rethink/Re-Entry* was used a decade later by Bryan Ferry as the springboard for "Re-Make/Re-Model," the first song on the debut album by Roxy Music, which set out the group's art-directed futurism.

More than anyone who had tumbled through the heady pop-cultural wash of London in the '60s, Bowie homed in on the potency, the pathos, and humor inherent in Boshier's work, and in particular the falling-man motif. The artist had appropriated this figure from William Blake to express humanity's vulnerability, a move that resonated with the thoughtful rock star then attempting to come to terms with the mind-spinning trajectory of his career in the '70s. After all, hadn't he starred in *The Man Who Fell to Earth* just a couple of years before meeting Boshier? Meanwhile, a mutual respect had been manifested by Boshier's inclusion of Bowie as Ziggy Stardust in an untitled collage and also in the cut-up film installation *Change*, which pondered life's mutability in parallel fashion to *Hunky Dory*'s "Changes." And there was another link: mime. Though much derided, Bowie's use of physical adaptation in performance had been honed under the tutelage of Lindsay Kemp; and in his first year at the Royal College, Boshier was offered a free place for a term at mime master Marcel Marceau's school in Paris. At the time of Duffy's call, Boshier's practice could not have been more different from the pop-art moment; he'd forsworn the limitations of paint and dedicated himself to radical politics and all manner of alternative disciplines: 3-D sci-fi works in Perspex, film and photographic installations, collage, assemblages, and protest posters.

But it was his use of photographic augmentation which spurred Bowie and Duffy's interest in working with Boshier. That day in Swiss Cottage, the artist, the musician, and the photographer contemplated the themes of body posture, transformation, and descent, and arrived at—even by Bowie's standards—one of the most challenging record-sleeve packages of all time.

ADRIAN BELEW (GUITARIST): The first time I met David Bowie was when I was onstage in Berlin in 1978 when I was playing with Frank Zappa. There was a break in Frank's show where I would leave the stage for a few minutes, and as I walked over to the monitor mixer there was David Bowie standing with Iggy Pop. I walked over and shook his hand and thanked him for all the work he'd done, and told him I loved his music, and he said, "Great. How would you like to be in my band?" I motioned back towards Frank and said, "Well, I'm kind of playing with that guy, the one out onstage." David laughed and said, "Yes, I know, but when Frank's tour ends my tour starts two weeks later. Shall we talk about it over dinner?" So we agreed to meet after the show back at the hotel. When I went to the hotel, David was in the lobby with his assistant, Coco Schwab. As I walked past them they were being very spylike, very conspiratorial. He whispered to me, "Get into the elevator, go up to your room, then come back down in five minutes, and meet us outside, and we'll have a car waiting for you." It was very hush-hush. When I came back down and went outside there was a black limousine waiting. The driver opened the door and I got in the back with David and Coco. David immediately launched into all his ideas and thoughts about the next tour, where we would be playing, what material we might play, etc. He said he was going to take me to one of his favorite restaurants in Berlin, and as we walked in the first thing we saw was Frank Zappa and the rest of the band all sitting round this huge table. So what could we do? We sat down with them, and David tried to strike up a conversation with Frank, saying, "This is quite a guitar player you have here . . ." And Frank said, "Fuck you, Captain Tom." David persisted, and said, "Oh come on now, Frank, surely we can be gentlemen about this?" And Frank said, "Fuck you, Captain Tom." By this point it was getting a little embarrassing, so David said, "So you really have nothing to say?" To which Frank said, "Fuck you, Captain Tom." It was extremely awkward and yet David seemed to be fine. We agreed that we should probably go somewhere else to eat, and as we left the restaurant David said in his wonderfully British way, "I thought that went rather well, don't you?"

So Frank was going off to edit his movie *Baby Snakes*, and David's tour didn't look as though it was going to take that long, so I started in his band. But as soon as I started playing with David, Frank started a new band; which is just as well because David's tour eventually lasted a year. We obviously played things from *"Heroes,"* which had been the most recent album, but we were dipping back into things from *Low*, *Station to Station*, right back to early songs. I knew David was talking about doing a new record with Tony Visconti and Eno but at this point again it was very hush-hush. When I eventually arrived in Montreux to make the record, David told me it was probably going to be called *Planned Accidents*. It was a very curious idea.

The studio was a concrete bunker under a casino, because the previous building had burned down, oddly enough while Frank Zappa was playing there. This was where the song "Smoke on the Water" came from, as it was recorded there by Deep Purple. So when they rebuilt the studio they made it out of concrete so it couldn't happen again. The control room for the studio was on the first floor and you had to walk up some stairs to reach it. The actual studio was on the second floor, which is where the band would set up and record. There was a television camera in the studio so the control room could see us but we couldn't see them. The original idea with *Planned Accidents* was that they said there was about twenty tracks they'd already worked on, and they wanted me to go upstairs in the studio, put the headphones on, and start playing. And I said, "Playing what?" And they said, "No, you just start playing. You play what you like." I asked if I could hear the songs first and they said no. I was just given a tempo and time signature. They said they wanted to get my accidental responses. And I said, "What key?" And they said, "No . . . just go upstairs, put the headphones, and play along to the song." And they allowed me to do that twice for each song, no more. And then they'd take their favorite parts of the guitar tracks and cut them up, and string them into a composite guitar track. So all those guitar parts you hear on *Lodger* are things I made up on the spot to a song I'd never heard before. "Boys Keep

Swinging," "DJ," "Red Sails"—all made up on the spot. The guitar parts were meant to sound accidental and I think they kinda do. The whole thing took two days.

When I eventually heard the finished album, I recognized some of the songs but my parts were a complete surprise to me. It's a great record though, as it goes far afield, and there are so many different types of material on it. David gave me great encouragement and let me do what I wanted to do, within a framework of course! He used to say to me, "Just go wild, be as wild as you like. That's why you're here, and that's what I want you to add to the band." And when we played "Stay" or "Station to Station" onstage, as I was embarking on these huge guitar solos, he would never do anything but stand there, still, grinning from ear to ear.

PAUL GORMAN: While recording *Lodger*, Eno suggested they call it *Planned Accidents* as a reference to their experimental working methods. The decision to change the album title has been interpreted by some Bowiephiles as a reference to Roman Polanski's supremely creepy 1976 film *The Tenant*, in which the paranoid lead character, played by Polanski, hurls himself out of his apartment window. The similarity between Bowie's pose on the cover of *Lodger* and the figure outline in the poster for *The Tenant* has been seen to lend credence to this theory. But Boshier's work has never been concerned with providing pat solutions, relying instead on the creative definition that design provides answers while art poses questions. "To this day, I receive mail asking for the meaning of the cover," says Boshier. "While *The Tenant* may have been in David's mind, he never mentioned it. We wanted to create a scenario that would intrigue and at the same time draw on the areas of crossover between us."

And so the trio used the outer *Lodger* gatefold to actualize a planned accident. Bowie, with bandaged hand, disheveled suit, and the illusion of a broken nose created by stage makeup, was photographed by Duffy on a specially built trestle that lent discreet support in the depiction of him falling, or having fallen, calamitously backward against a tiled bathroom wall. Bowie's face was contorted by fishing lines stuck to his brow, chin, lips, and nose. These were tugged gently out of shot by his companion and manager, Coco, and makeup artist Antony Clavet. To enhance the immediacy of the image, Duffy used a Polaroid camera (the classic SX-70 favored by Ansel Adams and Andy Warhol). "I was blown away by David's commitment to the project and his ability to transform himself," says Boshier. "It was incredible to see the artwork take life." The photo shoot completed, Boshier set to preparing the design and realized a series of ink sketches as guides. The placement of Bowie's apparently broken body across the gatefold afforded another set of Boshier self-references; the title and credits were conveyed in a spiky hand-lettered font by a postcard-like panel, harkening back to the artist's use of Post Office symbols in such '60s works as *Postcard* and *SOS (Sunset On Stability)*. "Just before I started the final artwork, I mentioned that we hadn't talked about the design for the inner gatefold," said Boshier. "David replied, 'Do what you like,' so I chose the eternal themes: time, life, and death." Here, Boshier interpolated such images as Freddy Alborta's 1967 macabre photograph of Che Guevara's corpse, a framed card of fifteenth-century painter Andrea Mantegna's *Lamentation over the Dead Christ*, and an image of Bowie being made up for the cover shot lying on the specially designed trestle table.

But the deadline was tight and Bowie invited Boshier to deliver the finished artwork over lunch at his hideaway in Kreuzberg, Berlin's Turkish quarter. "David picked me up at the airport and drove me back to his amazing place," says Boshier. With Schwab, the pair of Brits reviewed the paste-ups in a small kitchen-dining area with a distinctly surreal atmosphere. "It had an inside/outside feel, like being in the open air but in an enclosed environment," says Boshier. "The walls were decorated with giant photo-murals of Alpine scenes, as if we were high up in a ski lodge." The rest of the residence consisted of high ceilinged rooms with Art Deco–framed windows. Bowie's eight-year-old son, Zowie, was living with him and occupied a typical child's bedroom, with toys, a bicycle, and walls decorated with crayon. In another room, Bowie had set up a painting studio with easels, canvases, and drying paintbrushes, along with books representing his abiding interest in such German Expressionists as Karl Schmidt-Rottluff, whose tortured faces likely influenced the performer's appearance on the sleeve of *Lodger*. As you'd expect from a rock star, one room served as a fully equipped recording studio. Like the others, it was decorated plainly, in white with simple blinds, but the last room Bowie showed Boshier offered a deep contrast: here were luxurious draped curtains, giant rugs on a wooden floor, leather couches, Tiffany lamps, and a roaring log fire, above which hung two small, traditional oil portraits, of a Teutonic matriarch and her pipe-smoking husband. "David told me that when his German friends visited, they felt immediately comfortable in that room," said Boshier. Later that day, Boshier asked Schwab if it had been preserved from the time of the previous occupants: "No, no," she laughed. "That's David's room. He invented that from scratch."

CARLOS ALOMAR: The trilogy—*Low*, *"Heroes," Lodger*—changed my life forever. In adjusting myself to the methodologies that were used, and the new form of freethinking and linear thinking that I was exposed to, it changed me. They taught me that every time I came back to David, I needed to change. He wanted R&B, rock and roll, electronic music, Emerson, Lake & Palmer, romantic music. Stir the pot and out comes the Thin White Duke. He was such a restless person. He didn't like being comfortable. Comfortable is genre-driven, and be careful, because it will outlive you and it will surpass you. David had a lovely saying, "Let go, or be dragged." He was David 2.0, 3.0. If I wanted five amplifiers, he'd get them for me, if I wanted to mike something differently, we'd do it. It was change, change, change. Bryan Ferry would introduce something and stay there. David would introduce something and leave it.

PAUL SMITH: I reconnected with David in 1979 in my shop in London. This is around the time of *Lodger.* I think he'd just moved back from Berlin. My studio used to be above the store in Covent Garden, and I'd often receive calls from staffers who'd whisper things like, "Jack Nicholson is in the shop! Harrison Ford is here!" My reply was usually, "Oh, that's lovely." But one day when they whispered, "David Bowie is downstairs," well, I went downstairs. I was acting all cool, pretending to be nonchalant, of course, and we began chatting. He was obviously quite an inquisitive person, and started talking about anything and everything, but interestingly not music. Technology, astrology, architecture, photography. And he started coming back all the time. As you know, he was someone who reinvented himself—so his stage wear and his music were very much part of a public persona. What was interesting to me, though, was his approach to his own personal style. As a designer, I've never really given things to people; I like people to wear my clothes because they enjoy them and not because they've been gifted them. And David would literally just come to the shop himself. No bodyguard, no stylist. He had a suit in Donegal tweed, and another in a houndstooth check, with a short jacket and a pleat trouser. We did a *GQ* shoot once with all Paul Smith clothes and he bought the whole lot. He once came into the Fifth Avenue shop and bought every shirt in his size.

When he came to my shop in Floral Street, he would say, "That book there, tell me about that book there." He was always interested in what was going on, interested in ordinary things. He used to love the fact that in the shop there'd be a ceramic next to a book next to a photograph. He was always searching for inspiration, picking up words in sentences. He would always say hello to whoever I was with, so I suppose he was a proper actor in that respect. Onstage he was a chameleon, but he never got it wrong, he always got it right. What I liked about it was how radical he was in terms of appearance, but it was never rude or bad mannered or incorrect, it was just a theatrical act. Sometimes people do things that are very extreme but you don't feel close to them for whatever reason, but he never felt that [way] to me. If he came in to see me now he'd say, "All right, Paul, can I have a cup of tea?" One time, a friend of mine's eighteen-year-old son needed a suit, so he brought him into the Floral Street store. The boy tried the suit on, came out of the changing room, and looked into the big mirror we had. At the same time, the door to one of the other changing rooms opened and out walked David. "Wow, you look great!" he said to the kid. "You look *really* great, man!" And this boy nearly passed out, he went pale white! Nearly fainted! That was just David. He seemed to pop up everywhere.

TIFFANY MURRAY (WRITER AND NOVELIST, AUTHOR OF *DIAMOND STAR HALO*): I was brought up at Rockfield Studios, just outside a village called Rockfield, near Monmouth in Wales. It was a farm owned by two brothers, Charles and Kingsley Ward, who were in skiffle bands in the '50s, who wanted to get into recording music. My stepdad, Fritz Fryer, was a musician in the '60s, in a Northern band called the Four Pennies. He then became a producer, and moved to Rockfield. My mother also opened a rehearsal space nearby, and bands like Queen, Led Zeppelin, and Black Sabbath came to play there before recording at Rockfield. So that was where I was brought up, and my earliest memories are of all these male musicians smelling of leather, dope, and alcohol looking after me when I wandered into the studio. Still to this day if I go to a heavy rock concert I fall asleep, because I find the music so comforting.

Iggy came to record *Soldier* in 1979, and Bowie came to visit him for a day, to lay down a couple of tracks for the album [singing backing vocals on "Play It Safe"]. He'd just finished *Lodger*, I think, and I was about ten. It was the only time in the studio's history that it was poshed-up, and all for Bowie's arrival. My mother said, "Well, it was David Bowie, darling." So she did an entire side of poached salmon with pickled cucumbers. David sat in the kitchen and worked his way through it, although Iggy wasn't really eating at the time. Iggy was probably having his head rubbed by one of the horses, whose heads stuck out of the stables in the quadrangle. He was the height of politeness, incredibly well behaved, meticulous. Salmon and a fag, salmon and a fag, sitting upright on this horrible leather sofa playing with [my brother] Jason. When *Scary Monsters* came out I remember thinking, I've met him, I've met him! I literally fed him salmon! But of course the reality is I didn't, but I thrived on that re-memory, which is what we all do with Bowie, as he is like this palimpsest that layers over bits of our lives.

JULIEN TEMPLE: When I'd finished editing *The Great Rock 'n' Roll Swindle* with the Sex Pistols, I did a formal screening, which was a censor's formality. In those days you had to put on a free screening so people could come and officially complain about it if they found it offensive. So obviously no one ever came to these things, although David managed to come to this one. It was in the Fox Theatre in Soho Square, and as soon as the lights went down I noticed a solitary figure slip in and sit at the back. And it was David, coming to see what all the fuss was about. And predictably, as soon as the film finished—whoosh!—he was gone, as though he'd never been there.

ALLAN JONES (JOURNALIST): This was 1979, and I'd gone to see Lou Reed at the Hammersmith Odeon, which even by Lou's standards was a pretty confrontational concert. By the end of the show most of the audience had left. People had been calling out for "Pale Blue Eyes," "Sweet

Jane," and "Heroin," and he was intent on playing his new album, *The Bells*, in its entirety. He also left the house lights on, which made the gig quite uncomfortable. The crowd continued calling out for his old songs, and so Lou eventually told us all to fuck off, so lo and behold a lot of people did. As soon as the audience had gone, and there were only a few of us left by then, he started playing "Heroin," "Waiting for the Man," and all the songs they'd been screaming for. The concert ended with his bass player, Ellard "Moose" Boles, singing a half-hour version of "You Keep Me Hanging On" by the Supremes, although he appeared to only know the chorus. The bass was so loud that it actually made my girlfriend physically sick. It was horrible. As we were leaving, a press officer from Arista Records asked if we wanted to go backstage and meet Lou, so we did. But by the time we got to the backstage bar, we were told that Lou and had left with Bowie, and would we like to join them for dinner.

So we went off to the Chelsea Rendezvous just off the Cromwell Road, along with a journalist from *Sounds*, Giovanni Dadomo and his wife. Lou and Bowie were sitting at the head of a long table in the basement, and we were shown to a smaller, adjacent table, along with some other people, including I think Jim Kerr from Simple Minds. Lou and Bowie appeared to be getting on really well, even though they'd had a falling-out a couple of years ago when Lou was recording *Sally Can't Dance*, and David had complained that his diction wasn't clear enough. So they were chatting away, dinner was served, and suddenly there was this kind of explosion, smashing glasses, and Lou was dragging Bowie across the table and bitch-slapping him across the face. He was screaming, "Don't you ever say that to me, don't you ever say that to me!" The minders didn't know what to do and just froze. Eventually they were separated and then just burst out laughing and hugged each other.

Five minutes later David was being dragged across the table again, with far more ferocity this time, with Lou screaming, "I told you not to say that!" This time he really went for it, and was raining blows on Bowie's head. At this point in his life Lou had been working out quite a lot and was actually quite a powerful man. He was eventually hustled out of the restaurant, while Bowie just sat at the table, head in his hands, elbows on the table, sobbing. I went over to ask him what happened and he started screaming at me, went berserk, and grabbed me. "You're a fucking journalist!" he shouted. So we ended up in a scuffle and it got really unpleasant. On each of the stairs out of the restaurant was a potted plant, and as he walked up them he kicked each one, and they all came flying back into the restaurant. He later went looking for Lou at his hotel, raging up and down the corridor calling Lou out. Apparently at dinner he had offered to produce another album for Lou as long as he got himself clean and straightened himself out. Which Lou obviously didn't like.

ANGIE BOWIE: The last time I saw him was in a coffee shop in Lausanne, outside the lawyers. We had coffee, we kissed, and we said goodbye . . . and I never saw him again. That was in 1979. We were divorced. It wasn't very happy. It was just final.

WENDY LEIGH: I wanted to interview Angie for something I was doing and although we'd had become sort of friends she wanted to charge me $500 for speaking to her. She was living in Atlanta at the time, and I FedExed her the check, and didn't hear anything. So I waited a week, called her up, and she said she didn't get it. I said, "You're joking, right?" And she said, "No, I'm not," and promptly put the phone down on me. I had said that I'd had proof of delivery from the post office, and she said, "I never go to a post office," in this terribly imperious way. And that was that.

8

PUT ON YOUR RED SHOES AND DANCE THE BLUES

1980–1985

DAVID MALLET (VIDEO DIRECTOR): I first met David when I was producing and directing *The Kenny Everett Show*, and we had him on the show performing a rehash of "Space Oddity." This must have been January 1980. He liked what I did for him and asked if I would make some videos. He was completely un-strange, highly intelligent . . . I think I would actually say that the biggest plus point was that he just wanted to collaborate. It started off as, I guess you could say, mutual suspicion. Rock and rollers aren't mad on television people, and television people are normally slightly in awe of, or, expecting the worst from, someone with his reputation. But everything I found was completely the opposite to what I would have expected. I probably learnt from him a lot of stagecraft and showmanship tricks, particularly stagecraft because he'd obviously learned from people like Lindsay Kemp. If he said, "Blah, blah, blah" and I said, "Oh bollocks, that won't work," he'd say, "Oh, all right then" and we'd come up with something else. We talked about old television a lot, ridiculous things, obscure British nostalgia. We had a little obsession with an English harp player called Shirley Abicair who was always on TV in the '50s. God knows what she was, just a ridiculous name that we both remembered from our childhood. Stupid things like that. In those days, video was regarded as the top form as opposed to a bit of wallpaper, which it is now, so you did your very best to make a film based on the record that was either to a lesser or greater extent illustrative of the song. On "Ashes to Ashes," David said he wanted to be a clown on a beach with a bonfire and wanted to include all the New Romantics, all these characters from the Blitz club. I said great, but I can improve on that, because I'd recently done something where I found a process which made the sky turn black and it made the whole thing look like some hallucinogenic dream. Great, says David, we'll do that. The norm for a video in those days was a day, but "Ashes to Ashes" broke the record at three. There was a beach, there was a studio, there was a building site, you know, on and on. It was epic.

The filming was interrupted at one point by an old man walking his dog, looking for driftwood. Mallet asked him if he wouldn't mind moving, and pointed out Bowie sitting outside the catering van. "Do you know who this is?" he asked. Sharp as a tack, the old man responded with, "Of course I do. It's some cunt in a clown suit." Sometime later, Bowie remembered, "That was a huge moment for me. It put me back in my place and made me realize, 'Yes, I'm just a cunt in a clown suit.'"

IAIN R. WEBB: In 1980, when Bowie planned to make a video to accompany "Ashes to Ashes," he visited the Blitz nightclub to handpick his costars, among them Steve Strange wearing designer Judith Frankland's black wedding dress. Frankland walked alongside Strange, behind Bowie, who was now dressed as a clown by longtime collaborator Natasha Korniloff [who had worked with Lindsay Kemp]. The Blitz's New Romantic crowd had started life at a Bowie night at Billy's nightclub in Soho in 1978. It was Bowie's original flamboyance that caught the imagination of the hardcore style snobs that formed the New Romantic scene, and what secured Bowie's credentials as a style icon was his elitist standpoint.

STEVE STRANGE (CLUB RUNNER): I was on the Blitz door and as usual we were up to full capacity when I saw a black stretch limo go round the corner three times. At the time we had already been given two warnings from the council over fire regulations and the number of people we had in the club. In fact the week before I had to turn Mick Jagger away because we were up to capacity. He was with Sabrina Guinness and Jagger said to me, "Don't you know who I am?" I said of course I do, please don't make this any harder than it is. Luckily I knew Sabrina and she calmed him down. So this time the limo pulls up and this really stroppy woman called Coco informed me, "I've got somebody very important in the back of that black limousine." Because she was so stroppy I gave her quite an arrogant answer. But when she said it was David Bowie I went into meltdown. I thought, Oh my God, what do I do now? If the kids queuing to get in the club even know he's in that limo outside, he'll be mobbed, so I went into overdrive thinking, How the hell are we going to get him into the building without causing too much of a fracas? I called security and we opened up the back level of the club, which was the fire exit, and got him upstairs and put him into what we thought was a quiet area, away from prying eyes. However, word spread from the queue and we had to get security downstairs to stop people coming upstairs. Everybody wanted to be near him. It got to a point where Coco came up to me and said, "David wants you on his table." I wasn't being arrogant but I said excuse me I have my job to do. I take my job very seriously. This is not a goldfish bowl; the kids that are in this club are here because they feel at home. My shift doesn't finish until one thirty a.m. When I finally went up to him he said to me, "I've been watching you and love what you've been doing and the sound that you're creating musically and I'd like you to be in my next video." He asked me to style and choose the extras for the video, which was "Ashes to Ashes." So four of us were told to meet outside the Hilton Hotel in London at six thirty in the morning and we were all thinking we're going somewhere fabulous, and then we're told we're going to Southend! They'd closed off the whole beach, but it was freezing. He came back to some of my other clubs, like the Camden Palace and the Café de Paris; in those days you had each other's home phone numbers, there was no changing your mobile phone like there is now. If you didn't move around too much you could stay in touch and we did.

ANGUS MACKINNON (JOURNALIST): So this was August 1980, and the *NME* had sent me to Chicago to see him in *The Elephant Man*, before it went to Broadway, and to interview him about *Scary Monsters (and Super Creeps)*. The show was excellent. A lot of people who saw it in both Chicago and New York said the Chicago cast, a rep cast, was actually a lot better. Relations with him and RCA were pretty difficult by then, and there was this woman in L.A. called Barbara Dewitt who would ring you up and shout down the phone, "You've only got half an hour!" I don't think he'd done an interview for some time, because I remember at the end he said something along the lines of, "I have to admit I wasn't looking forward to this at all, but it has actually gone pleasantly well."

One of the reasons I left Oxford without finishing my degree was because I'd seen the *Ziggy Stardust* tour, and wanted to find a way to write about it. I left to work in a record shop, and eighteen months later was working for *Sounds*. So I was a big fan. Bowie was by far the most fascinating person I met in the six or seven years of writing about such things. He had just divorced Angie and in our interview he was talking about everyday happiness, and he said that as far as someone like himself could ever be happy, "I am, and it's a real joy having my son." His self-analysis was lacerating. He talked a lot about his sense of self, and one of the things that came across, and this was not false modesty, was his constant anxiety that what he was doing wasn't quite interesting enough. Here was a person who seriously pushed himself, and constantly reevaluated his contribution, and he found himself lacking. Blessing and curse.

Another thing that struck me was how completely unto himself he was. Occasionally the persona would break and there would be this moment of real warmth, and he'd laugh in a particular way, or he'd be very jocular about something. You'd think, What percentage of this is the real life? But he gave you what you wanted. If you were in shades and tight black leather trousers he would give you the rock and roll interview, and if you were me, wearing drainpipe cords and a tweed jacket and the air of the rock pseudointellectual about you, he would give you that. He'd always been interested in Buddhism, and he said he often had a fantasy of retiring to a monastery on a misty mountain in Kyoto or somewhere, and he'd have his opium and eventually when he died he'd just disappear in a cloud of bliss. Even at the time I felt he really meant it. Fascinated though he was by the struggles of his own creativity, the appeal of this [disappearing] was huge. It must have been exhausting to be David Bowie. You could tell that it weighed heavily on him. The morning after our first interview, [photographer] Anton Corbijn and I met him again in this little bar a couple of blocks away [from the theater]. Coco and Anton then went off to scout for locations, and when Bowie and I emerged blinking into the sunlight, he jaywalked, looking the wrong way, as a large vehicle approached him, a truck I think, so I grabbed him and pulled him back onto the sidewalk. So you could say I saved his life!

JACK HOFSISS (DIRECTOR): I certainly saw David in *The Man Who Fell to Earth*, I mean, it was a major film at the time, and it was a major revelation that a rock star could create such a full character and be contained within the structure of a film. I didn't ever expect that our paths were going to intersect at any point, but a number of years later I was directing *The Elephant Man* on Broadway, and the lead actor was going off to tour with a national company that traveled around the United States. So we were looking for another actor to replace him. The play was very close to my heart and normally a director at that point might be just personally involved where he would approve of the actor [and] then stage managers would take the new actor and teach him the part. But as fate would have it I was at a club called Ross on West Sixty-Seventh Street, owned by a friend of mine. And during the course of that evening they introduced me to David, who happened to be there that night. He had just seen *The Elephant Man* and said he had liked it very much. And so that was that. In *The Man Who Fell to Earth* I saw primarily an ability to play a character who exists in isolation, and that was similar to the dilemma of the Elephant Man. The real John Merrick was locked up inside his grotesquery. So many people from rock and roll get by on playing a sort of persona but [here] was a real actor creating a [real] character. We all go through our lives with some sort of a limp, and we hide our limps very actively, so in a way the human being that you play who has a physiological limp is more human than others. It's the kind of stuff that actors love to do.

David did not need to be directed. I didn't really say that much about it, because it was unnecessary and the actor was right on the money. He kind of shamed the other actors of the company, who weren't nearly as disciplined as him quite frankly. There was a carefulness about David rehearsing the part. His performance was much more streetwise [than Philip Anglim's performance]. You really got the feeling that this man had been beaten around. And been through it. And therefore he was not gonna let people in until he knew them and was sure of their intentions. The central metaphor of the play was imagination, and the audience had to do the thinking. It was in part a mime role. There was a quality in the way he pitched his voice that made me [imagine] a little child, a little guy in there that had been knocked around the streets. I didn't know precisely if he came from a middle-class background or higher-class background, but he did know about that world.

David brought a level of truthful reality to the play. He knew these places that the play was set. He knew because it was his home. He knew London in a way that we who don't live there couldn't possibly. He felt like he had walked the streets and been looked at strangely. And he had synonymous relationships to the Elephant Man—I'm sure in his early days as a musician and certainly in his early days in the guises that he assumed in that part of his life. And if he took that on tour and walked the streets he would get looked at. That seemed particularly easy for David to access. You can tell when actors know something that's analogous to what the character's experiencing. And that's golden.

One time on a Wednesday afternoon we had a couple of David's fans sitting way down in the front, and there was this young guy who had a black leather jacket filled with little Christmas lights. And they were on. The jacket was all lit up. I remember I turned to the little usherette with the white bib and the flashlight and I said, "Excuse me, could you go down to Row B and ask that man to turn off his coat?" We gave new meaning to the word blue-haired matinee.

GIORGIO MORODER (PRODUCER): [In 1981] I was working on the movie *Cat People* and I was talking to the director Paul Schrader, and I said, "Who shall we take for the single? Who represents that weirdness of the movie?" And we immediately said David Bowie. So I wrote the song and I sent it to him. He loved it, he wrote the lyrics, we went to Montreux in Switzerland, where he lived at that time; we went to the studio owned by Queen, and we recorded it in less than an hour. He sang it twice, and it was done. It was absolutely professional. Obviously he knew the song because he wrote the lyrics. It was one of my easiest, fastest and greatest recordings ever.

TONY SCOTT (DIRECTOR): I'd been given *Flashdance* and it really was, "Fuck, what am I going to do with this?" Adrian Lyne had got *The Hunger* and was like, "What the fuck am I going to do with this?!" So we swapped scripts. A week after, he said, "My daughter's been watching this thing called MTV." He said, "I'm going to do an MTV movie of this piece of shit. . . ." [For *The Hunger*] I stole from Nic Roeg, for performance and for style, and I stole from Helmut Newton's erotica. His pictures tell a story. They're always erotic and sexy and perverse and strange and fucked-up. I showed the girls [Susan Sarandon and Catherine Deneuve] what I wanted. And they were a bit, erm, long faces. So I did a lot of body doubles. A lot of the sex in there is around the mouths and the faces. When you get down below it gets porno if you're not careful. I used a lot of smoke and so on. That was really the influence of my commercials. A lot of smoke, backlight, the occasional billowing curtain. Well, a lot of billowing curtain. It got slammed for being esoteric and artsy. It got fucking killed. It took me three more years to get another movie after it.

DAVID BAILEY: I shot David Bowie a lot over the years, and did some great pictures of him with Catherine Deneuve for their film *The Hunger*, in 1982, although he was always very reserved, and had a definite view of how he wanted to be portrayed. Which made it very difficult to take a picture of him if you were trying to be creative. In the early days it was easier to take a celebrity's photograph, because they didn't really know what to expect, but now they all know what they're going to get. The thing I hate is when someone phones and says, "I've got this great idea." I always say, "I've got a better idea. Why don't you come to the studio and I'll shoot you against a nice white background." Bowie always had very definite ideas about how he wanted to be photographed, which meant he should have been shot by someone else, not me. Actors are often hard to photograph because they never want to reveal who they are, and you don't know if you're going to get a character from a Chekhov play or a Polanski film. And in his heyday Bowie was a lot like an actor, always acting like someone else. They're always trying to put one over on you, because they want you to take a snapshot of their current version of themselves. It depends what mood they're in. It's always better to take a photograph of an actor when they're young, because as they get older they learn to disguise themselves. Bowie certainly knew how to disguise himself. But the difference between me and lots of portrait photographers is that I won't make people look like idiots. Photographing odd-looking people is a gift, because you've got such a lot to work from. But I don't like it when editors call me and ask me to make someone look aggressive, or sad, or powerful, or arrogant, or timid. That's unfair. It also becomes journalistic, and I'm not interested in journalism on that level. Why should you photograph powerful or rich people and make them look venal or corrupt? I photographed a series of powerful people once and I made them all smile, because that's not what you expect from a portrait of a powerful person. With Bowie I never knew what to do as he always had a preconceived idea of what he wanted to look like, which was of no interest to me.

JEREMY THOMAS (FILM PRODUCER): I was at the Cannes Film Festival in 1978 and at the awards ceremony I found myself sitting next to the director of *Empire of Passion*, Nagisa Oshima, who had won the Best Director award. He was one of my heroes, having directed classics such as *Death by Hanging*, *The Ceremony*, and *In the Realm of the Senses*. I adored his films. He was in a kimono, and I was just a young lad. We drank a lot of wine, exchanged business cards, and then a few years later a Japanese colleague came and said that Oshima wanted to know if I might be interested in making a film with him. It was based on the Laurens van der Post book *The Seed and the Sower*, about his experiences as a Japanese prisoner of war during World War Two. The screenplay was 250 pages long, impossible to make, but I said I was coming to Tokyo for the opening of *Bad Timing*, and could I bring [the screenwriter] Paul Mayersberg with me. He had written *The Man Who Fell to Earth* and at the time was working with me on *Eureka*. And so off we went, rewrote the script with Oshima, and then set about making *Merry Christmas, Mr. Lawrence*, a genuine co-production. Half the money was coming from Japan, and I said I'd find the rest. Looking back now I would say it's my perfect idea of a film, as it brought everything I love about cinema and culture together.

When we met Oshima he said that he saw Robert Redford in the role that David eventually played, so we attempted to get him, as it needed to be someone with blond hair and blue eyes, someone who could be so enchanting to a Japanese man. So then he started talking about

"Bowie-san." Through mutual friends I set up a meeting in Roland Gardens, near Blakes Hotel, one evening. Bowie was so smart, he knew exactly who Oshima was. He was cultivated. Liked Japanese culture a lot. We bonded over a love for William Burroughs, as at that time I wanted to make a movie of *Naked Lunch*. He loved Burroughs, loved J. G. Ballard, loved Brion Gysin, all the things I liked at the time. And he said he wanted to do it, immediately actually. From then on he was 100 percent committed, as committed as you'd want anyone to be on a project like this. He had a great spirit, and an acceptance of anything that might happen.

He had a real desire to be free on a desert island. We filmed it on Rarotonga—because of a New Zealand tax deal—where there were only a few hundred people, so David was free to roam around, ride his bicycle. There was no screen test, as Bowie had everything special that you needed—he was a very unique figure. Some of those images are still very powerful, especially the shot where he is buried in the sand, where the moth lands on his head, completely by chance. This was in the days before digital enhancement. David was completely involved in the film, and he had no issues with any hardships. He trusted his director, which is what you want from an actor. He enjoyed himself, and used it as a punctuation mark between what else he was doing. He used a lot of the people on the film when he was making some pop promos for *Let's Dance*.

The reason we cast him was a combination of his star power and his genuine ability to play the role. I've worked with lots of actors who are non-actors, but they're performers. And that was Bowie, the perfect performer. On that level he actually surpassed what I believed he could do with the film, and his strength and range were superb. The mime was all his idea, the shaving scene was all his idea. This was a film made by a Japanese master, and having David Bowie star in it helped give it context. David always wanted to be in the avant-garde, he wanted to be the first. He was a "before the others" kind of guy. He wasn't doing this film for the money. A rock star's life usually precludes them from significantly doing anything else, but not David. His river of life was the right one, he was a force for good. We showed the film on the Saturday night at Cannes, and this was the night the French medical students decided to riot, throwing condoms filled with blood everywhere. There was blood and tear gas all over the place.

PAUL MAYERSBERG: On *Merry Christmas, Mr. Lawrence* David was cast before I started writing, and it's the only time I had written something for an actor, and it was written specifically with him in mind. Oshima's original script was very long and not very good, so I came in to rewrite it. I met David in New York to talk about it, and although we were not close friends, we always got on very well. He was doing *The Elephant Man* just before. We talked about remorse, as that was the theme that we settled on, for the character, for Jack Celliers. I knew what he could do and what he couldn't do, so I made sure there were no long speeches. I made it as mimey as I could, so there's a lot of action, a lot of things for him to do. It was tailored for him. He looks beautiful in the film, like an angel.

The film was full of people who had never acted before. As far as I know, Ryuichi Sakamoto had never acted before, and he was quite a big star in the film. And Takeshi Kitano was like the Benny Hill of Japan. When I eventually saw the film, Bowie's performance was more spectral than I had written it, more ghostly. He had a strange quality in the film. Of course there are only men in the film, and I told Oshima I was worried about this. I was worried people might think it was a gay film. He said, "Oh no, don't be ridiculous." He denied this, and said that in war men have close relationships, not necessarily gay relationships. But I persisted, and wrote a few lines where the Japanese sergeant calls the English public schoolboys "faggots." I thought that would get rid of the idea, but come the opening in Cannes, I looked at the papers the morning after, and lo and behold, *Liberation* called it a gay film. At the press conference, some lady said it was the first film she could remember seeing which had an all-male cast, which in no way gave her a sense of aggression towards women. Bowie didn't strike me as being particularly gay; I think he just exaggerated all of that for the press. Essentially I think David did films as a sort of relaxation, where he didn't have to take charge of anything. He didn't have to be responsible. At all. He could put his life in the hands of the director, and I think he liked that. I don't remember him ever having an argument. Actually at the screening in Cannes, I asked him if he would ever be interested in doing a sequel to *The Man Who Fell to Earth*, which was an idea I had that would only have worked with Bowie. He said, "Oh, absolutely. Anytime I feel I need a nervous breakdown, I'll work with Nic Roeg." But I never saw that. Maybe he was joking.

SEAN DOYLE (BLOGGER): At some point in the early '80s, Bowie decided that he wanted to make one last, violent push for the global megastardom he'd been batting at since his first hit, and he set himself to the task with steadfast determination. He left his longtime label RCA, on the grounds that they'd failed to properly market his supremely unmarketable late '70s LPs. He dumped most of his regular collaborators and put together an expansive new team. He rudely brushed off producer Tony Visconti and hired Chic's Nile Rodgers. The result of all this was *Let's Dance*, the biggest commercial success of his career and the first album to win him a significant American audience. Longtime fans saw this as a kind of betrayal, and Bowie didn't help matters by adopting a brightly conservative new Reagan-era look and calling his former admissions of bisexuality "the biggest mistake I ever made."

NILE RODGERS (PRODUCER): I was turned on to David Bowie in a very unique situation. This was before Chic, and Bernard [Edwards] and I were in a band called New York City, and we were playing down in Miami Beach, and I met this girl at a nightclub and she invited me to spend the night with her on the beach. She was a photographer and she wanted to get naked under the stars. She brought her favorite music with her and it was *Ziggy Stardust*, and it was amazing. I'd never heard songs like that, never heard music like that before in my life, and I remember singing "Suffragette City" naked on Miami Beach. At the time I actually thought he was called Ziggy Stardust. That was a seriously great introduction to David Bowie, being naked on a beach listening to *Ziggy Stardust* for the first time. From that moment on I started devouring all of David's records, and I loved them. He had such *amazing* scope.

I first met David in an after-hours club called the Continental, in New York. I arrived at around five or six in the morning with a very drunk Billy Idol, and we both saw him at the same time. Billy said, "Fucking hell it's David Fucking *Booooowie*!" We were both pretty drunk. I went over to speak to him—I think Billy was starting to throw up at this point—and just started talking to him. All of my friends had been in the *Young Americans* band—Luther Vandross, Carlos Alomar, Dennis Davies. We all went to school together. So I thought we already had a connection. And we talked all night about music. He had a surprising amount of knowledge about R&B. That's why we got on so well, as he was shocked by what I knew, and I was shocked by what he knew. David was 180 degrees away from what I expected him to be like. I imagined him to be ultra-flamboyant, and more like the characters that he was playing. But in fact I was flamboyant compared to David. It was the '80s, so we all had foxtails hanging off our jackets, and David was sitting there dressed in a suit. No one dressed like that in those kinds of clubs. No one wore a suit! He was almost unrecognizable, sitting by himself, sipping orange juice, in one of the hottest clubs in New York.

Anyway, he said he was interested in me producing his next record, and we went from there. We did some demos in Switzerland, but to me the demos just felt like me auditioning, even though he had already chosen me. I guess he was just thinking, Let's see what this guy's going to do. . . .

"Let's Dance" was a folk song when I first heard it. David was playing it on a twelve-string guitar, which I found out he'd had for many years. He walked into my bedroom and started playing this strummy little song. Normally if it were folky and we hadn't had the kind of discussions as to what the album was going to be like, it probably wouldn't have bothered me, but he had painted such a clear picture for me as to what he wanted, not necessarily what the songs should sound like, but the effect they should have on people. That's what was cool. He showed me a picture of Little Richard wearing a red suit getting into a red Cadillac. And he said, "Nile darling, I want the album to sound like this." I saw the picture and I thought to myself, I get it. This picture looked like it could be from the future, but I knew it was from the past. I realized as soon as I saw the photo that he wanted a record that was evergreen, that would sound like a band could come out with it now and it still sound contemporary. David wanted hits.

Now, I'm not sure that I felt any pressure because of this, but I felt pressure because I was running away from hits. I was trying to be thought of as a more credible, serious record producer, and I wanted David to sort of propel me to the place where people could see that I could do jazz or classical or whatever. And that wasn't necessarily hit-orientated material. I wanted to do cerebral material, and if you luck out and get a hit, then it's cool. I suppose "Let's Dance" is sort of like that. If you listen to the full recording, the solo, the opening of the record with the pocket trumpet, and all that kind of thing, it was a more cerebral type of commercial record. But I couldn't have pulled that off with anyone else, and it was because it was Bowie that we could do a song like "Let's Dance," and it could be thought of as commercial. I knew the record was special but I had no idea it was going to be big. When I first worked on the arrangement with the band, we played it for David and he said, "Wow! Is this my song?" I remember the look on Stevie Ray Vaughan's face when he came up to play the solo, and he just heard the track and—again—he went, "Wow, what is this?" I could look at him and tell that he was feeling what I was feeling. I had never heard of Stevie Ray Vaughan at the time, and that was all David. He knew so much, had such varied interests, he was like the Picasso of rock and roll.

This was new territory, for all of us, for me, for David, for Stevie and for all the musicians on the record. There's only been a couple of times in my life when I knew the records I was making were going to be hits. "Le Freak" I knew right away, and I couldn't believe that the record company couldn't hear it. When we played it for them they hated it. We cleared out the conference room. They all went outside to figure out how to tell us it sucked. And that was the biggest-selling single in Atlantic's history, for thirty-three years until Flo Rida topped us a couple of years ago. We capped it, too, at 7 million. If we had let it go we don't know what it would have sold. I also knew "We Are Family" was going to be a hit. I knew that song was a monster. Not "Let's Dance."

NICK KENT: *Let's Dance* is his weakest record, it's his "I've got nothing to say and I'm saying it" record. "*Put on your red shoes and dance the blues.*" He's saying completely nothing. *I will be completely shallow and I will sell more records than ever. Just as a statement to you that I can jump from cultdom into the mainstream.* And that is why Bowie was unique, because he could do that. Elvis Presley couldn't do that. By 1975, Bowie had realized what being Elvis was really like, and he knew he was better than that. *I write my own songs. I don't need some big cigar-chomping manager running my life, I don't need that, I'm better than that.* Bowie was a class apart.

NILE RODGERS: *Let's Dance* is the easiest record I've ever made in my life. Seventeen days from start to finish. Mixed and delivered. When we finished the last track we never touched the record again. We were on a wavelength that was just spectacular, and we just clicked. "That is beautiful, Nile," David used to say, always so proper. He actually spent a lot of time sitting in the lounge watching TV and then he'd just come in and go "Wow!" and then he'd go back to the TV. And I'm actually thinking, "This is the highest form of respect that anyone has ever given to me." He didn't have a record deal at the time, and he paid for that record himself. So we had no one to answer to. I'm not sure that he normally thought like that anyway, but it just felt like me and David against the world.

I was just coming off of the whole "Disco Sucks" thing, so it wasn't like everybody in the world was trying to get me. In 1979, when the whole Disco Sucks thing had kicked in, even though I had had tons of hit records, and even though I had produced Diana Ross's biggest album—"I'm Coming Out," "Upside Down," and all that stuff—that was sort of the last hurrah for Chic. It was really toxic, and although I'd made all these records, there was a sense that we were a kind of novelty. I didn't have a hit after Diana Ross, not until *Let's Dance*, and even though it was only two years, to me it felt like an eternity. So we were both in a place where we were rescuing each other. It's like we were in a lifeboat together. He wasn't in such great spirits until he heard the musicians playing it, and that changed everything. He didn't know anyone on that record apart from Stevie, and everyone else was someone I knew. They were people who I could depend on, who I knew would bring a sort of funky element to avant-garde rock. I wanted to treat it like a jazz record, calling up a bunch of guys and having them come in and play. I was steering everything, and David really let me run with the ball. And we sold 11 million albums, the biggest hit of his career. Up until that moment he had been selling 3 million, maybe 4, but *Let's Dance* was a monster. It was scorchingly hot.

I was quite upset when the record came out because David hardly mentioned me. I think he was shocked by the success of *Let's Dance,* but it was such a departure from his normal style of music that I'm sure the journalists kept saying, "Nile Rodgers," and that probably pissed him off and made him feel uncomfortable. I'm guessing. He never told me that but I could just tell because the lack of credit was serious. When he was on the cover of *Time* magazine I'm not even sure I'm mentioned in the article.

That really sort of hurt. And I was vocal about it. And because of that, or maybe because he felt it was the right time, we kissed and made up. I was getting an award one night, and he gave me the award, and when he delivered his speech he said, "I am honored to give this award to Nile Rodgers, the only man who could make me start a song with a chorus."

Regardless of when you entered Bowie's world—or, perhaps more accurately, regardless of when you allowed him to enters yours—emotionally his work often had a way of moving backwards and forwards at the same time, not in the by-now old-fashioned retro-future sense first introduced by Roxy Music in 1971 as part of the necrophiliac economy, but in the sense that a lot of his best music manages to be both timeless and refreshing at the same time; I defy anyone to listen to "Let's Dance" and not experience both a wave of gilt-edged nostalgia, but also a feeling of slightly disturbing exhilaration, as though something rather wonderful is just about to happen. I remember just before "Let's Dance" was due to be released, in the spring of 1983, reading somewhere—in the NME *probably, when a rumor printed there was still assumed to have come from someone who knew what they were talking about—that Bowie was about to release a Philadelphia-inspired album, a modern, actually thoroughly postmodern take on his* Young Americans *volte-face. Me and my cronies sat around, slack-jawed, before proclaiming that Bowie had managed to fish out the Zeitgeist from the back of the sofa yet again; at the time we were all playing Gamble and Huff in the clubs we were notionally the custodians of, and we conceitedly congratulated ourselves on being as smart as Bowie was.*

But of course we were wrong. Bowie was a lot smarter than we were ever going to be. When we eventually heard "Let's Dance," predictably (or not) it was like nothing we'd ever heard before. It wasn't particularly novel, and nor was it especially difficult; far from it. The record was actually tremendously bold, almost unbelievably catchy, and borderline expedient. And yet it filled the room as no room had been filled before.

TONY MCGEE (PHOTOGRAPHER): In 1983 I was invited to a cocktail party in Chelsea given by Michael White, the impresario. He was the toast of London at the time, friends with Jack Nicholson, David Bailey, Nona Summers, and just about everyone else that ran around. And I had caught the attention of Michael and he thought it would be nice if I came over and had a few drinks and sat in the room and got to know a few people. At one point Jerry Hall came over and she said she wanted to introduce me to Coco Schwab. And I asked if she had anything to do with the pharmaceutical company in America, because I'd seen it all over L.A. and I thought it must be. And she said it is, she's the daughter. Then Coco came over and said that David was about to arrive, and I said, "David Bowie? You're not serious?" And within a minute he bounced into the room in a very good mood, feeling very much on top of his game, talking all about Serious Moonlight, all about *Let's Dance*, all about the anticipation of that. We sat and we chatted. What did we have in common? Well, I grew up next to the Tate Gallery in Victoria, and I spent most of my time there. I'd wander around. I loved the echoey halls and the cold floors and I loved the paintings most of all. I mentioned this to David and he said he would go there at least once a week. And I jokingly said, "I bet we walked past each other." We'd play this game in the gallery, running around, playing catch. This was 1963. And David said that he probably saw us, as he had played the same game. We both decided definitely we were already mates. Coco called me a few days later and said that David felt very comfortable with me and that something's going to happen. "I think you could do some interesting things," she said. She kept saying, "David is very comfortable with you." So we started shooting together. The first session we shot in my studio in Farringdon Road. He came in with Coco and he arrived with sacks of clothes—houndstooth check suits, Prince of Wales suits. I told him I was fascinated with his eyes, and he said his eyes were like my camera—I was using a Rolleiflex, which has a twin lens. He said one is for seeing, one is for taking. He said one is observing, one is recording. That was a lovely afternoon.

And then we were off. We suddenly became close. We were embarrassingly close. He was intense. An intense friendship for six weeks and then you wouldn't see him for six years. I really enjoyed the intensity I have to say. Whether or not it's necessary to sustain that, I'm not sure. I don't think it's important. What's really great is you have these periods in your life where, I don't know, you go on holiday somewhere and you meet a group of people and they feel very cool to be with when you're on the beach with them. And then there are tears at the end of August when you take the train home. And that's what it felt like. It was an intense August relationship.

JOHN MITCHINSON (HEAD OF RESEARCH FOR THE BRITISH TELEVISION PANEL GAME *QI* AND VICE PRESIDENT OF THE HAY FESTIVAL): I was working as the head barman in Legends in the West End in the mid-'80s, which at the time was a really hot club. One night, it had not been particularly busy, David Bowie walked in. He came into the bar and said, "Can I have a packet of Marlboro, please." He was blond, buff, in a suit. And I said, "Yeah . . . and thank you." He looked slightly embarrassed and I said, "I guess people say that to you all the time, but thank you, for everything . . ." And he said, "Thank you too. For the cigarettes."

HARVEY GOLDSMITH: Bowie was always an irregular performer, and he didn't perform to order. He had an internal clock, and he didn't do things until the alarm went off on his internal clock. But it wasn't like a normal clock; it was a David Bowie clock. I was never really sure if he ever actually liked touring. He was working in the early '70s with another promoter called Mel Bush, so I didn't work with him again until 1976, and the White Light Tour. He hadn't worked in London for three years, and he created one of the most spectacular shows I've ever seen, the Thin White Duke Tour. David and I seemed to get on quite well, so he left Mel Bush and came with me, and we did this series of shows at Wembley Arena. To this day they are some of the best shows I've ever seen, completely spectacular. The whole stage was just strips of fluorescent lighting. Then we did the Serious Moonlight Tour, when he decided to come back in a major way. We did three shows at Milton Keynes Bowl, we played Croker Park in Sunderland, we did Murrayfield, we did everywhere. These were big, big shows. These were the shows that made him a proper, global superstar, someone who could command a stadium, who had that genuine breadth of appeal. At this point in his career he could have done anything.

EARL SLICK: I arrived in Brussels in 1983, for the start of the Serious Moonlight Tour, and that was the first time I'd seen David since 1975. I checked into my room and literally two minutes later there's a knock on the door and it's David. We went out to a café as we had to clear the air. He told me his story, I told him mine, and we realized that each of us had gotten it wrong. The stories didn't match. We both got done. There had been lots of management issues at the time with Michael Lippman, who was managing us both, but we both got our feelings out of our system, so it was OK. He was a lot more lucid and a lot more approachable at that point. This time around we were doing stadiums, and in eight years he'd gone from doing twenty-thousand seaters to sixty-thousand seaters. We traveled in style, and everything was a lot easier. He had straightened his money out too, and Bill Zysblat was involved, and he was great to work with. The tour ended in Hong Kong on the anniversary of John Lennon's assassination. We played "Imagine" in his honor that night. He told me he was going to start another record at the beginning of the year, but I didn't get the call. So I guess I was out again.

BONO: I imagine I first met David in May 1983 at the US Festival, which was a giant event in the depths of California. Believe it or not, it was put on by Steve Jobs's [business] partner, Steve Wozniak, trying to throw a lot of money away. The Clash and Bowie and U2 were on, and I think it may have been there. He was probably the last rock star I could believe in, because after him came punk, and then we weren't allowed to believe in rock stars anymore. So he was the last one I gave myself permission to believe in. It's funny; my heroes become more so the more human they are. Getting to know David over the years as a person, he increased in stature for me, not decreased. Which I think is unusual. You know, when you find that they're not immortal. They're mortal and they smoke too many cigarettes, and they're a bit paranoid and a bit bitchy, and laugh a little loud. That just made me love him more. I wasn't expecting that sort of comeliness from the music. The otherworldliness was in the music, but the worldliness was in the man in person. And I find them to be very amusing.

We didn't discuss madness but we did discuss alienation, and he did it in a very wry way. He said, "Oh, the alienated love me!" He said, "Oh God, spare me from fucking alienation." He had this quite sparky personality, he was fun. And the darker side, which I did see, it was there, but he knew that he did alienation better than anyone. He also knew that for people who had difficulty forming, that he was often a role model, in his formlessness, in his shape-shifting self. People who had gone through difficult times in their teenage life, and it wasn't just sexuality, it was about anything, and he had this unbelievable ability to be inchoate, this sort of inchoate cry, saying it's OK to be lost. You can't underestimate that. Because being a songwriter you can sort of surrender to their melancholy, and you might too, but it's all a bit crying into your beer. But his was like, defiance, like it was OK. You can never deny what that meant to your life, having him in that very special defiant way. Not in that way like, "Oh you poor thing, you're going through something." Lots of songwriters have approached that, but his was like, "You're going to shine, you're going to be a star, you can do anything you want"—that sort of thing. It's amazing.

I spent a day with him backstage at his famous Milton Keynes concerts when he was promoting Let's Dance *in 1984, and then a few months later we ended up at the same party at the Notting Hill Carnival (at the home of a mutual friend, a Stiff Records alumnus called Cynthia Lole, who was about to start work on* Absolute Beginners*). The only details I can remember were that I had my head shaved after losing a bet with my friend Robin and that Bowie chain-smoked. I can't remember if he was still drinking at the time (I think not), but he smoked like a monkey in a glass box. Like many other journalists, I was flattered by his attention, and at one point even considered that we might actually be "friends." We weren't, and never would be, but I certainly got to know how his mind worked, and saw how he would size up people, situations, and culture—books, records, films—and analytically disassemble them for his own benefit. Bowie was the quintessential cultural magpie, and nothing was safe in his company. If it wasn't nailed down, he would have it. Metaphorically speaking, of course. He would make contact at the most inconvenient times, luring you into his web and making you feel as though you were the most important person in the world. You knew you were sort of being conned, but you didn't mind, as he was so unbelievably charming. He had the same thing George Martin had, an ability to talk to you for the first time and make you believe that not only had you suddenly bonded, but that everything you said was of paramount importance. Once, as we were chatting in the Halkin Hotel behind Buckingham Palace, we spent a good hour discussing exactly why Robbie Williams was famous. This would have been in about 2002, when Bowie was thinking of releasing an album* *called* Toy, *which was going to be made up of covers of some of the songs he'd released in the '60s. He seemed to be somewhat bewildered by Robbie's success, as to him he appeared to be little more than an exotically homespun old-school song-and-dance man. Bowie had spent most of his career following his instinct and hoping it would collide with public taste, and so when he was presented with a phenomenon that he didn't understand (like Robbie Williams), he wanted to get to the bottom of it. Bowie was mock-incensed that Robbie had co-opted so much of the John Barry Bond theme "You Only Live Twice" for his song "Millennium," and wondered how on Earth he had got away with it.*

DAVID BOWIE: I was never actually a material person. Ideas always meant a lot more to me. I never bought a big car. The company bought a big car for me to drive around in once. I had a limo in 1973 and '74 but I'm not a limo person. And I'm not a sports car person. Those kinds of things really aren't something I work for. All the money I've made has been since 1980, as everything before that just went. *Let's Dance* helped, and 1983 for me was like manna from heaven. All that money I'd gone through in the '70s suddenly came back to me, in almost a year. I'm not wealthy, I'm rich, and there's a difference. The rich know how much money they've got, and the wealthy don't.

CHARLES SHAAR MURRAY: I remember watching a mini documentary that was part of one of the videos of the Serious Moonlight Tour, and apart from the fact that he appeared to have a meringue on his head—and lots of people had meringues on their heads in the '80s—they showed him in Singapore being shown around a market, with his hands behind his back, and he'd become the dashing English gentleman about the arts. I thought, Bloody hell, he's turning into Prince Charles. It was almost, "Well, that's very interesting. What do you do?" as he was being wheeled about by these local dignitaries. I was expecting him to be quite remote when I first met him, and in a way he was being remote but behind a very cordial front. The thing about Bowie was, you might not see him for seven or eight years, but when you did he'd start talking as though you'd just seen each other the previous week. In those holy and less guarded days, I remember when we were doing the interviews at the Chateau for *Pin Ups*, Joe Stevens the *NME* photographer kept giving Bowie spliffs.

And he'd say he had to go in a few minutes, and then Joe would give him another joint and he'd stay another twenty minutes. He was matey when he wanted to be, and very good at being remote when he wanted to be, but David could have given charm lessons to Tony Blair and Mark Ellen.

ARTHUR FOGEL (PROMOTER): If you look at the bookends of his career, he was a left-of-center artist, and it was only with Serious Moonlight that he had this moment of great commercial success. There are different tribes of artists, and some are very much into the idea of making a record and then touring it, and reconnecting with their audience, not just for financial reasons, but for emotional ones. David wasn't that person. He enjoyed it, but he didn't enjoy it. The travel, the logistical stuff I don't think he liked. It wasn't the be-all and end-all, like it is for other artists. However, his instincts were second to none, and he was one of the greatest performers of them all. Sometimes I would watch him from the side of the stage and think he was the epitome of the quintessential rock god. He had the look, and the vibe, and the history. In some ways I think of him as that incredibly cool guy, maybe the coolest guy ever, in a suit. When the world was trying to be cool, he didn't really have to be. It was effortless. He was very comfortable with who he was, and his legacy. It became natural for him. I'm not sure there was any artist who had more influence among other artists, and what greater validation can you have?

HARVEY GOLDSMITH: Even when he was at the height of his drug addiction, it really wasn't that obvious. He was a bit distracted at times. When you were on the road with him you were aware that he was in a bit of a haze, but he was experimenting. He changed completely for the Serious Moonlight Tour, but then you have to appreciate that artists go through different periods all the time. He was extremely happy, possibly happier than he'd ever been before, but then he said creatively he was at his weakest.

DENIS O'REGAN: For the Serious Moonlight Tour, with that number of flights in such a short space of time, it was almost all private jets. So something was bound to happen. We were in the bar one night, with the pilot, the night before a flight. We were going to Berlin again. The next day we were inside the plane, sitting on a semicircle of seats. And it's the only time in my life I've ever seen a bunch of people turn completely white, because we all thought we were dying. There's a corridor out of West Berlin, and the pilot aborted the first take off, and the pilot said, "Ha-ha-ha . . ." and we all just thought, He's pissed! And he turned the plane round and took off, and when we reached that point where the plane leveled out, the plane dropped, and that's when we all thought we were dying. When we landed, David got out and fired the pilot, the air company, on the tarmac.

PAUL MCGUINNESS: I met him again in the '80s, when both he and U2 were on tour in Australia, and Bono and I met him one afternoon and went to a pool hall, where we played a lot of pool and drank a lot of beer. Bowie was incredibly maudlin. He really didn't look like the kind of person who had recently had the kind of extraordinary success that he'd just had with *Let's Dance.* I wouldn't say he was envious of U2, but he thought the world had overlooked him, he thought the world has passed him by. Of course, we thought that he'd had this incredible renaissance, as he had just had these huge global hits, with "Let's Dance" and "China Girl," but he didn't see it that way at all. He thought that he'd sold out, or somehow ruined whatever credibility he had. He may have just been drunk, but he was very unhappy that he wasn't taken seriously enough. Bono remonstrated with him and obviously told him that he was very highly regarded, and that after all he was David Bowie. But he didn't see it that way.

CHALKIE DAVIES: I don't think people realized that he lived in Australia for ten years on and off, as he had a place there in Sydney. It really helped him relax. In Switzerland I always felt he was living in a sad state of isolation. You could telex him but you couldn't call him, as he was sort of isolated by Coco. Just saying the words "Coco Schwab" could make an entire football stadium terrified, but in actual fact she was really quite sweet. The first time anyone knew he was spending time in Sydney was when he made the video for "Let's Dance" down there. He was an incredibly private man and yet had a network of hundreds of us who were told, if you see photographers, stylists, fashion designers, music, anything, keep me informed. People wonder how he always kept on top of things, but he kept on top because he had everybody telling him what was going on. Whenever I photographed him, I couldn't get more than five or six frames of any setup, as he always wanted to move on to the next thing. He'd be bored. He once threw a full-length coat up in the air, put his arms out, looked at the camera, and it's a perfect shot. Just one frame. Nobody moved like him, his movements were incredible. I used to ask him which frame he liked best, and he would say, "I have no idea. You pick." This was a man who looked in a mirror but didn't stare at himself in the mirror. He had absolutely no vanity. He also had a great way of putting people at ease, by going round the studio introducing himself. He knew the effect he had on people. At Julien Temple's wedding he went up to my assistant, who wasn't wearing a tie, and he said, "I'm so glad I'm not the only one not wearing a tie."

Having become a global superstar in the summer of 1983, with the release of Tonight *in September the following year, Bowie's seemingly innate sense of cool evaporated, almost instantly. It was as emphatic as it was temporary, and yet it seemed almost inevitable. After* Let's Dance, *Bowie was owned by everyone, and for a while there didn't appear to be anything special about him; so much so that I distinctly remember being in the* i-D *office in the spring of 1984 and being asked if I wanted to appear in the extended promo film Julien Temple was making to support the album,* Jazzin' for Blue Jean, *and rather snottily turning it down. Implausible, I know, and absurd to think of now, but that's how uncool we thought David Bowie was in 1984, when notions of cool were bestowed and terminated often within hours of each other. The album—which in general sounded like a collection of Thompson Twins outtakes (note: bad thing)—actually produced two Bowie classics, though: one singular and destined to become much loved, "Loving the Alien," and one that most people have probably forgotten, "Don't Look Down." A generic white reggae yacht rock cover of a song from Iggy Pop's 1979 album* New Values, *it nevertheless manages to capture completely the low-gear experience of walking along a Caribbean beach at sunset. It's not transgressive, not all that clever or very grown-up, but it proves that when he wanted to, Bowie could be as dismissively B+ as any other member of the rock aristocracy. "What I suppose I really wanted to do was to work with Iggy again," he said. "That's something I've not done for a long time—and Iggy wanted us to do something together. We worked very much the way that we did on* Lust for Life *and* The Idiot, *and I often gave him a few anchor images that I wanted him to play off—and he would take them away and start free-associating and I would then put that together in a way that I could sing. Rather than write straightforward songs, he would do collective imagery, and we'd rearrange things from there." He also said it gave him a chance to record some more covers, like* Pin Ups. *"'God Only Knows' I first did—or tried to do—with Ava Cherry and that crowd the Astronettes when I tried to develop them into a group. It sounded like such a good idea at the time and I never had the chance to do it with anybody else again, so I thought I'd do it myself. It might be a bit saccharine, I suppose."*

Bowie would sometimes subscribe to the maxim, "One for them, one for me." Tonight *was definitely one for them.*

SEAN DOYLE: Bowie followed *Let's Dance* with *Tonight*, a blatant cash-in filled with woeful covers and some of the worst material he'd ever recorded. There is no great story behind the album's creation: Bowie hadn't made a record for EMI for a while and they wanted him to make one. He scrapped together some new songs and began recording in Switzerland, doing little to flesh them out before piling them in gaudy production. Horns squawk, faceless backup singers croon, guitars wail stupidly, Mickey Rourke (of all people) pops into a song to assist some kind of rap verse (of all things). It's a laundry list of terrible decisions. *Tonight* is Bowie's true artistic low, particularly its hysterical, schlocky, sacrilegious version of "God Only Knows."

CARLOS ALOMAR: We were always trying to pluck songs from thin air. But in the '80s, the complaint was pretty obvious—the record company making you go back in the studio. And there were no new ideas. Not on *Tonight*. For "Loving the Alien" I wanted it to be like Phil Spector, so Arif Mardin could put strings on top, and then we had to make something work for Tina Turner. So we were thinking about the collaborators, not about the songs themselves. We were floundering. We had also gone through a period of Iggy Popism. David wanted to help Iggy with his career, and Iggy wanted to help David with his drug problem. And so the best way for that to be achieved was to work, work, work.

HUGH PADGHAM: A friend of mine called Bob Clearmountain, who engineered *Let's Dance*, had been asked to do *Tonight*, but he couldn't do it because he was already booked to do a Bruce Springsteen record, I think. He suggested me instead, which is how I got the call. I was just brought in as an engineer to start with, as Bowie had found this chap called Derek Bramble, an English guy, to produce it. David fell out with him halfway through the record I think, and we had a break, and then he rang up and asked me to finish the album. We were at this place called Le Studio in Morin Heights, a ski resort a hundred miles north of Montreal. I'd worked there before because I'd mixed the Police's *Synchronicity* there. But I don't think I was the one who suggested it; I think he just wanted to get on with it, as it was the equivalent of a residential studio, i.e. not in a city. Saying that, I think he got bored of being there, and I always got the feeling he'd almost given up finishing the album in the best way that he could, and he just wanted to finish it. Also, there was probably also an element of making sure David was hundreds of miles away from temptation, although there were various ladies who were chauffeured up from Montreal and New York. It was about six months before I was due to get married, and I remember he'd brought this girl up from somewhere, but she came with a friend, and the girl wouldn't come without her friend. So he was desperate for me to have the friend, but I couldn't.

It was very frustrating for me, because coming in halfway through, I just didn't get a lot of the music. Going back into the studio so soon after *Let's Dance* . . . [was maybe a mistake]. Because I'd been so busy myself—with engineering there is a huge amount of quite tedious stuff you need to do in the studio—I didn't realize that he hadn't had much time to prepare anything. He turned up with some demos, which Carlos said he'd never done before, but because he wanted to keep the momentum going, and probably because of pressure from the studio, he just wanted to get into the studio. Derek Bramble's forte was more soul-orientated, as he had been in Heatwave, which Rod Temperton was in, and who wrote for Michael Jackson. The thing is, he didn't have very much experience. For instance, when we were doing a vocal, he kept saying to David, "Do it again," and I'd look at David and mouth, "*Why?*" David is probably the best and quickest singer I ever worked with. He would just go into the studio and sing it twice, at the most, and it would be amazing. Literally faultless. He knew he didn't have to do it more than once or twice. David probably thought that he was the one who'd taken Nile Rodgers out of disco land, so he thought, I'll discover the next person. Secondly, there was a little bit of cheapskateness in there too—he probably thought that he gave away too much money on the last album, and thought he could get away with giving Derek half the number of points. Cynical, but maybe true.

I feel very privileged to have worked with David, but also slightly pissed off that it was on one of his worst records. We also had a lot of better tracks that he couldn't be bothered to finish as he just wanted to get out of there. I can't remember what they were, they were just called numbers 1, 2, and 3. I didn't really like "Blue Jean," as I thought it was really lightweight. I didn't like "Tonight," as I didn't like the faux reggae thing. And then I thought, David Bowie with Tina Turner? It was a bit like David doing "Dancing in the Street" with Mick Jagger; it debased him. There wasn't much original material on *Tonight*. And "God Only Knows" was a bit of a dodgy song to cover. I've never thought it was a good idea to cover a classic unless you have a fairly strong chance of improving it, which is unlikely, or subverting it in some way. When I was working with Phil Collins we decided to cover the Supremes' "You Can't Hurry Love," but it only really worked because he was a man, and so it was a completely different version. "God Only Knows" was bad judgment. My production had too much reverb and pomposity on it. Tina Turner was at the height of her fame then, and she was absolutely charming, but she was only there for a couple of days.

David's whole thing was vibing everybody up. He was a collaborator. He was fun, and had a great chuckle. Everybody got on. We lived in this little house about half a mile from the studio, and I always knew when it was time to get up, because whenever he woke up he would have this amazing coughing fit when he lit up his first fag. His voice was great, though—perfect, really. When we were recording "God Only Knows," he said, "My voice is actually a complete steal from Scott Walker and Anthony Newley."

DAVID BOWIE: My biggest mistake during the '80s was trying to anticipate what the audience wanted. On the one hand I was trying to shed this skin and on the other I was second-guessing the future. I *hated* myself during that time, but I probably hated myself more during the mid-'70s, during the drugs and what-have-you, but I suppose my depression and alienation were in keeping with the times. I had a very crystallized idea of where I was misguided and unfocused during both periods. I said to myself, "I don't wish to live my life like this; I have to change or else I will do something stupid." Strangely enough my ambition tends to come in moments of depression. I think it's always been this way, actually. Of course, it wasn't just the second-guessing of the audience that was a mistake during the '80s, creatively I allowed myself to go in a direction I shouldn't have gone. I was trying to be predictable, but nobody wanted predictable.

In terms of mistakes, there were a couple of albums that I rushed into, that I really should never have done. I was pressured by a record company, but not manipulated. I regret *Tonight* specifically, only because taken individually the tracks are quite good but it doesn't stand up as a cohesive album. That was my fault because I didn't think about it before I went into the studio. Everyone takes notice of some kind of criticism. You wouldn't be human if you didn't respond to how your own work is received. I won't mention who they are for obvious reasons, but there are two or three critics that I actually take great note of. A couple of times one particular guy has written things, and I've definitely taken note and thought, You know, he's actually hit it right on the head. Not that I would ever dream of telling him!

JULIEN TEMPLE: I was in L.A. when I got a call from someone who I soon found out was Coco asking me if I might be interested in working on a video with David, the film that eventually became *Jazzin' for Blue Jean*, which was the big marketing exercise for the *Tonight* album. So I flew back to London, we met, and what I remember is that I was completely surprised by how ordinary he was. I was expecting *The Man Who Fell to Earth*, someone otherworldly, and what I got was Cheeky Dave. I wasn't prepared for someone who was so matter-of-fact, and so straightforward. I had already had some experience of rock stars, and a lot of them appeared to be "on" all the time. Mick Jagger was always "on." But with David he appeared to be able to switch on and off. Whenever he wanted. He appeared to be able to summon whatever it was he needed, whenever he liked. So the first meeting was rather disorientating, although intellectually we clicked. We collaborated on what would become this twenty-minute film for "Blue Jean," and he was an absolute delight to work with. We even came up with the ending on the spot, when we'd run out of time and money, by feigning an argument between us and by breaking the fourth wall by having him yelling at me, the actor to director. He was very, very collaborative, and very keen that you got your point across. I think he felt that he was the casting director, and if he'd cast you properly, then he should just let you get on and do it. He wouldn't micromanage, he'd really want you to do what he'd hired you to do. If you watch that film now, I still maintain that the "ordinary" version of himself that he plays in the film is the closest approximation of what David was actually like. It's the nearest thing to the "real" David Bowie that's ever appeared onscreen. He wasn't exotic at all, he was just exotic when it suited him, or when it suited other people so much that he just did it to keep them happy. That was David. I actually think the exotic side of his character is based far more on his brother Terry. Terry was the mad one—literally. He was the wild one, the extrovert who devoured the underbelly of London. It wasn't David. Terry fed David all this fabulous stuff when David was still very young and impressionable, and he carried it with him throughout his life. You could see it in the way he paraded around Soho when we were looking for locations—he was channeling his brother. It was remarkable the number of people who appeared to already know him, and also appeared to already know Terry. It was almost as though Soho was his second home.

One night we all went to see *Purple Rain*, David, Mick Jagger, and myself, and both of them were incredibly jealous of what Prince had managed to achieve. Neither Mick nor David had really established themselves as actors, although David had certainly made more films than Mick, yet here he was the new kid on the block making a huge name for himself. David was actually quite irritated that the film was so good. Mick and David were both so competitive, but they'd both been beaten to the punch.

Looking back through old Bowie interviews, it is notable how often he mentions Mick Jagger. At one point in the '80s he told me: "I'm quite self-contained when I want to be. I like to get away from it all occasionally but I like a social life and I have a good one, so I'd miss that if I didn't have it. The people I see aren't usually involved in my particular career. They're not usually musicians—there's a few contemporaries, I guess, that I'm friendly with, like Iggy, naturally, and Mick Jagger. Everybody else is on a hello basis. I occasionally run into some of the newer guys. I got to know Nick Rhodes and Simon Le Bon from Duran Duran because we were in the same part of America together, and I really quite like them. They're nice lads."

CHRIS SULLIVAN (CLUB-RUNNER, DJ, JOURNALIST): You'd occasionally see him at the Sombrero in High Street Kensington at the end of the '70s, but I didn't actually meet him until he came down with Bianca Jagger to Hell one night, which was a one-nighter I was running in Soho in 1980. He had this soul-boy haircut, peg trousers, and a big brown tweed overcoat. It was early, empty, maybe only about six people there. My friend Christos [Tolera, the painter] went up to him and said, "Hello mate, how are you doing?" He thought he was an old soul boy he knew from Essex who used to go to the Lacey Lady. So Christos is asking him how he is and David Bowie doesn't really know what's going on, his eyes looking around the room. I think he may have been chemically enhanced at the time. Christos that is, not David Bowie. I think he went off that night with Helmut Newton. After he left, Christos came up to me and told me all about this guy he used to know and he was mortified when I told him he'd actually been talking to David Bowie for half an hour. I think Bowie was too polite to say anything. Christos said, "I thought there was something funny about him, because of his eyes. It must have been the drugs." I said, "The drugs he took, or the drugs you took?"

Bowie also turned up when Iggy Pop was staying at my house in Kentish Town, as he was seeing a girl I knew who was staying with me and my wife. He'd just done this concert in Marseilles where he'd said all French people were fags, and had had the shit kicked out of him, so he was holed up in Kentish Town with us, trying to keep a low profile and staying away from the press. All his gear was there, all his clothes, his bags, his toothbrush, his work, everything. The next morning a cab pulls up and it's David Bowie with Coco Schwab with Iggy's passport, off to take him away. He was like a minicab driver. A very polite minicab driver.

When we launched the Wag Club in Wardour Street in 1982, he started popping in a lot, often with Julien Temple. He seemed to like Soho, loved seeing what was going on, soaking everything up. I was called one day at home and asked if I wanted to be an extra in *Jazzin' for Blue Jean*, and when I turned up at six o'clock on the day of shooting they handed me a piece of paper and said, "These are your lines." They weren't the kind of lines I needed at six in the morning, let me tell you. For a person who runs a nightclub, six a.m. is like eight o'clock in the evening. Anyway, I had to do my thing as David Bowie is up a ladder, and I had to actually do some acting and I did it about six times and every time was worse than the last. He was very nice about it, and said it was the same for him on *The Man Who Fell to Earth*, which unsurprisingly didn't make me feel any better.

DAVID BOWIE: I always looked OK in clothes—I was kind of a target for designers, always. They sort of made a beeline for me and tried to get me to wear their things. But I guess it was up to me to choose which ones I would wear. The thing is, I always wore clothes for a reason, not to be fashionable. I've never seen the point of being fashionable, as then you obviously just look like everyone else. Which is the one thing I have never, ever wanted to be. It doesn't matter in what context you're talking about, I never ever wanted to be, or look remotely like, anyone else. Sometimes I was right in what I chose, sometimes I wasn't. I should never have touched the Culture Shock label in the early '80s.

CHRIS SULLIVAN: He knew people in Soho too. We went to dinner at l'Escargot one night and *everyone* knew him.

He then asked me to get some people involved in *Absolute Beginners*, so I helped him get Sade and Slim Gaillard, Eve Ferret, and lots of Soho faces. I loved working on that, as *Absolute Beginners* was one of the reasons I came to London in the first place. I'd spend a lot of time on set and would often babysit Duncan. He would have been twelve, thirteen at the time. He'd never heard a Welsh accent before, and I think he loved being there. He later told me it was those daily trips on set that made him want to become a film director. His dad would take him around, show him what was going on, introduce him to the cameramen. A proper dad. No wonder Duncan turned out to be so level-headed. Bowie was doing some filming at the Wag one day and because he was using my office as a dressing room he insisted on making me cups of tea. I said, "You don't have to do that," but he insisted. He'd never pass you in the street, always said hello. I'd bump into him in St. Martin's, Vogue House, anywhere, and he'd always say hello. He had a great ability to make people feel special. He was the most amazing man because you'd be chatting to him, and then he'd be called up for a take, and suddenly he'd turn into David Bowie. He'd just turn it on. Amazing. *Boom. Now I'll be David Bowie.* He'd come back and says, "How was that?" I mean, what do you say?

DUNCAN JONES (FILMMAKER): In many ways it was an incredible childhood. We traveled all over the world and we got to do some amazing things. I remember one time going to see a sumo wrestling show in Japan and being amazed. There were a lot of unique things that I got to do, and not a lot of people get to experience things like that. And I treasure those memories. But often I'd sit around being bored backstage at a concert. You know, it was like any kid going to watch his dad at work, no matter what they do. We were just waiting for the concert to be over so we could go home. I could hear the noise up front but I'd spend most of my time hanging out with the roadies and playing with them. You know those big crash cases that they put the equipment in? Big, thick metal boxes with foam padding—well, I'd stand inside one of them and get the roadies to push me around like I was in a go-cart. Every night when we'd leave I can remember the big hullabaloo—security guards and me being whisked into the car before my dad came out separately so that they couldn't get a picture of us together. The woman who was looking after me would have her arms wrapped around my head so that they couldn't get my photo. It was a big event just to get in the car and go home. It was the opposite for me when Dad was shooting a film. That was like going to Disneyland. I'd see the amazing sets being built, how the makeup worked. In *The Hunger*, Dad had to age at one point to become an old man and I remember him scaring the shit out of me. I hung out with him when he was doing *Labyrinth*. And I remember the amazing '50s Soho set on *Absolute Beginners*. All that made a huge impression on me.

I never learned to play an instrument. Dad tried to get me to learn the drums but I didn't want to. "The saxophone?" No. "Piano?" No. "Guitar?" No thanks! Bless him. He kept on trying and nothing was happening.

He really enjoyed introducing me to new things in literature, music, and films. When I was about seven we'd watch these adventure movies like *The Sea Hawk*, a pirate movie with Errol Flynn, or James Cagney movies on video. Dad introduced me to Fritz Lang's *Metropolis* and the original *Baron Munchausen*. He'd say, "You'll love this! It's amazing—you haven't seen anything like this before." I was eight when he showed me *A Clockwork Orange*. Around that time he showed me how to use an 8mm camera. It had the little Kodak cartridges that you stick in, and I remember it had the ability to shoot one-stop animation. I loved it and I'd take it with me when I went off on tour with him. I'd use my *Star Wars* figures and make these little animated films. He taught me, in a lovely way, the basics of making a movie, like how to do storyboards, write a script, do the lighting. He also taught me how to use a splicer—cutting the film and sticking it back together in the projector. I had this big blue box that was full of my storyboards and scripts. While Dad would go onstage, I'd be making my little movies.

CHARLES SHAAR MURRAY: I interviewed him when *Tonight* was coming out; in fact that was my last gasp as Bowie's representative on Earth, because it was arranged that I would more or less get an exclusive interview which would be syndicated around the world. I knew someone who had made £50,000 out of syndicating an interview with Paul McCartney so I was getting very excited. *Rolling Stone* took it, as did the *NME* obviously, although I had to lie to the new editor, Neil Spencer, and tell him that it was completely exclusive. I didn't tell him it was officially sanctioned and had actually been copyedited by Bowie himself. This was David at his most controlling, obsessive about the messages he was sending out. There was an editing session for the "Blue Jean" video with Julien Temple, and we all went and got drunk at Gaz's Rockin' Blues, a club deep in Soho, in Meard Street, near a knocking shop. That was fun because Bowie spent all night trying and failing to pull this beautiful black girl who worked on the door. He was a lad when he wanted to be. The rest of the night was spent swapping trivia about obscure R&B records, and he knew an awful lot about obscure R&B records. He could be a laugh could our Dave.

PAT METHENY (GUITARIST): I had written "This Is Not America" as the main theme for the score for *The Falcon and the Snowman*. After traveling to Mexico City, where the filming was taking place, and watching Sean

Penn and Timothy Hutton do a few scenes, I went back to my room and the whole piece came very quickly. Later while in London recording the score, John Schlesinger, the director of the film, suggested a collaboration with David Bowie for a version of the song to go over the final credits. Honestly, at that point in my life, I was focused on music that was creative in a different way and was really not that aware of Bowie in general. When Mr. Schlesinger suggested him, I went out and bought a few records and realized that actually I was a big fan, and I agreed he was absolutely the perfect person to sing that song. David came to a screening and I sat near him as he saw the picture for the first time. He was very nice and seemed quite aware of my thing, which kind of surprised me. My first impression was that he was incredibly smart and very alert. During the screening, he had a yellow legal pad on his lap and was writing constantly. At the end of the film, he had a list of maybe thirty (brilliant) song titles that he had thought of while watching. One of them was "This Is Not America," a line from the film.

By the time we went to Switzerland [to record with David], I had literally been up for three days straight finishing the score in London. It was one of those situations where they had added scenes, re-edited some cues, and generally wreaked havoc on what I had to deliver. And then, we had to go right from the studio to the airport to do this track for the final credits with David. I wish I had been a bit more rested to really enjoy it. Just watching him do his work was inspiring. He was just an excellent, amazing musician. After he had done the main vocal, he asked if any of us could sing, and as we couldn't, he did all the background vocals himself, kind of transforming into what seemed to be two or three different people as he did each part. That was pretty amazing. We were both just trying to get the music right. As I recall, we did talk a fair bit about Ornette Coleman.

9

WHO'S GONNA TELL YOU WHEN?

1985

When Bob Geldof first conceived of the idea of recording a charity single in aid of the Ethiopian famine victims, he had always wanted David to sing on it. As well as getting contemporary bands such as Duran Duran, the Police, Sade, Spandau Ballet, and Culture Club, he knew it was important to get what would soon become known as heritage acts involved—legacy performers who had a wide commercial and global appeal. Like Queen, Elton John, the Who, Status Quo, and the Rolling Stones, Bowie was obviously one of these. He had also recently been at his commercial peak with the whole Serious Moonlight Tour. So when Bowie was unable to sing on "Do They Know It's Christmas?," the Band Aid single that was released at the end of 1984, his lines were taken by Paul Young (who, it has to be said, did an admirable job), who at that time was one of the biggest stars in the world. But when it was time to put on the Live Aid event itself, Geldof knew that he had to get Bowie. When he eventually got him—and when he committed, he committed 100 percent—Bowie threw himself into the project. Bowie wanted it to be good, and he wanted his performance and his involvement to be intrinsic to the event's success. By securing David Bowie, Geldof raised the bar of the entire event. I wrote a book about the '80s a few years ago, using Live Aid as a pivot, and interviewed dozens of people for it. Everyone I spoke to mentioned how crucial Bowie was to the event—not just in terms of performance, but also how his involvement encouraged other artists to sign up.

BERNARD DOHERTY (LIVE AID PUBLICIST): It had initially been difficult to get a lot of the acts interested in performing, especially some of the Americans, but as soon as Bowie said he was in, it all started to roll. When Bowie said he'd do it, literally everyone said they'd do it. It shows you just how much influence Bowie still had. Everyone started taking our phone calls when David said he was in, which meant we got Queen, U2, Elton, the Who, Macca [Paul McCartney] . . . A lot of the bigger artists were wary of getting involved, as it was being organized at quite short notice, and it needed someone of David's stature to lend it credibility.

MIDGE URE (MUSICIAN): I first met David at a Kensington restaurant in the '80s. Bob Geldof asked if he'd present the Band Aid video for "Do They Know It's Christmas?" on TV, as the BBC had given us five minutes before *Top of the Pops* to air the single. (David had unfortunately been unable to take part in the recording of the song.) Bowie arrived fashionably late with his PA. As soon as everyone at the table—me, Bob, high-powered music biz managers, Band Aid trustees—saw him, we all stood up, as if the headmaster had arrived. Everyone turned into giggling fans, hanging on his every word. He readily agreed to introduce the single, even though he'd have to cut off the goatee he'd started growing to enable him to go out shopping in London without being recognized. The next summer David did Live Aid at Wembley—it wouldn't have been the same without him.

HARVEY GOLDSMITH: Bowie had originally intended doing something far more adventurous than just simply performing, which is why he hadn't put a band together earlier. He had originally intended to perform a reggae song with Mick Jagger, exploiting the half-a-second time delay between Wembley and Philadelphia, which is where the concerts were taking place. Their respective management teams organized a conference call that resulted in both of them singing in harmony down the telephone line with Bob Geldof. The idea was to have Mick in Philadelphia, and David in London, and they were going to sing a duet together. They chose a reggae idea, as they thought the loping beat would work with any delay. But as it was it didn't really work out like that.

BOB GELDOF (MUSICIAN): When we were exploring this idea, we had a few dummy runs. And they really were dummy runs, let me tell you. We got together in a room in Soho and we tried it out, seeing if it could work. I sang Bob Marley's "One Love" as an example. And then of course Jagger and Bowie joined in. I sang, "*One love, one heart, let's get together and feel all right.*" Then Bowie sang it. Then Jagger sang it. Then they sang it together. Verna [Live Aid's technical director] was somewhere in America listening to Bowie and Jagger crackling down the phone at him. It seemed unbelievable to me that I was sitting in a room with these two rock greats, working out a song, making suggestions to them, singing with them. *Singing* with them. Fuck me! It was so odd hearing their two familiar voices together in that tiny room. They were both desperately trying to outdo each other, and it suddenly struck me how competitive they were. Jagger was tilted back on his chair. Bowie sat beside me on the sofa. I started singing, "*One love, one heart,*" Jagger and Bowie harmonized on the last line, then David began in his low voice "*One love,*" and Jagger in a great blues shout repeated "*One love,*" then Bowie deep and sad "*One heart*"; Jagger like an old black woman "*One heart*" and then joyously together "*Let's get together and feel all right.*" It was a valiant attempt, but it was never going to work. We just didn't have the technology to make it work, although the amazing thing was watching the two of them try and outdo each other. Neither wanted to be the one to say that it couldn't be done, neither wanted to be the one who bailed out first, and so we kept going until it was obvious to everyone that it really wasn't going to happen.

HARVEY GOLDSMITH: After several attempts at working out a way to make it work, they eventually decided that this wasn't going to happen, and so we all went off to a nightclub together and they spent the evening trying to outdo each other on the dance floor. They were competitive even when they were dancing. Each of them was trying to attract the attention of all the girls in the club, but mostly they were competing with each other. This gave them the idea of recording a cover of "Dancing in the Street," to be broadcast at the Wembley event and released as a single. David also had another idea, this one involving a rocket ship, as Bowie wanted one of them to be inside a NASA Space Shuttle, doing a duet with the other on Earth. Seriously. I'm not making this up. At one point, just to try and move it on, and either get a green or a red light, I actually made a call to NASA. I asked them if they had a spare rocket that we could send Mick Jagger up in. I could tell they were thinking, Who is this nut case? In the end, as well as deciding to perform in their own special way—Mick with Tina Turner in Philadelphia and David in Wembley—they decided on an old-fashioned video, camping their way through a rather average version of the Motown classic by Martha and the Vandellas. It wasn't a great record, but the video was quite camp, quite fun, and it helped raise awareness as well as raising an awful lot of money.

KEVIN ARMSTRONG: In early 1985 I was given a tip-off by a friend of mine called Hugh Stanley Clarke at EMI who said I should turn up at Abbey Road with a guitar to meet a mystery artist and that I'd never regret it. So that's what I did and that turned out to be the demos for the *Absolute Beginners* sessions. David didn't turn up with the song fully formed, and I would go so far as to say I should have by rights had a co-writing credit on the song. We started work on the song "That's Motivation," which he did with Gil Evans on the soundtrack. And that's what we were there to demo ostensibly. Because we were so fast there was time left at the end of the session, and Bowie said, "Look, I've got this half an idea for another song. Can we try and throw it together?" I sat with him with a piece of paper and an acoustic guitar and helped him work it out. I think that's probably what led to the ten-year on-off association because I think at that point he realized I could work with him in some way. After working on the demo sessions, David phoned me and said he'd been asked to do this big charity thing with Geldof, and did I want to be involved? So I went to meet them in the middle of the night in a basement in Wardour Street to do some preliminary work. It was just him and Mick Jagger in a tiny room, and we all sat down and worked out "Dancing in the Street." It was a pretty pedestrian version, and neither of them thought it was brilliant, but we knew we had to get it done quickly. The record was fine but even then we knew the video was embarrassing. We were all invited down to the video shoot in Docklands after the session to watch the pair of them camping it up for the cameras, clowning about . . . The dynamic between them was interesting, as there was quite a lot of banter. David knew he had to work at performing, and he had obviously worked at it psychologically as well. He was not a natural performer, whereas with Jagger it seemed effortless. He could walk in with a toothpick and make it happen, whereas Bowie was much more studied. My fondest memory of David that day is the laughter. For somebody who's such an amazingly layered and sophisticated person, he could have been very intense and introverted. But there was a lot of laughter in him. A lot. During the working process, there was never a point where you thought, Oh, I'm treading on eggshells here. It was really fun. He was warm and charming and funny and there was this kind of crackling energy around him. That's something I felt upset about when he died. To have been close to that, that special energy that he had. You see it in very few people.

THOMAS DOLBY (MUSICIAN): That summer Bowie had been in the UK doing things like "Dancing in the Street." Kevin Armstrong and [bassist] Matthew Seligman played on "Absolute Beginners" and said Bowie was going to call me. He did, when I was at Olympic Studios, on a pay phone. He said his regular touring musicians were doing other tours so he asked me to put a band together to play at Live Aid. He was very busy because he was shooting *Labyrinth*, and he said he would come after shooting for an hour or two at night for three nights because that's all the time he could spare. His manner was very gentlemanlike, he was so grateful for everything. I thought I was talking to Edward Fox. If you had asked me what image popped into my head when I thought of Bowie I would have said the Thin White Duke, sitting in the back of a dream car looking at a fly in his milk, but he was the total opposite. He'd asked us to rehearse five or six songs, and so we had those ready for when he walked into the studio. When he arrived he just stood in the middle smiling and grinning and just turning around listening to what we were doing and made no comment at all. He just said it sounded lovely, just stood in the middle of the room and exuded, and it was very impressive. Most people would have tried to micromanage, feeling as though they should exert influence. But he just stood there, confident in the knowledge that he knew what he was doing. That was great. We were initially going to perform "Loving the Alien," but he soon realized that this wasn't an event to plug his new single, but an opportunity to make his appearance a churchlike moment. It needed to be classic Bowie, as we were all going to church.

CLIVE LANGER (PRODUCER): We first met at the St. James's Club. He asked us to go round, me and Alan [co-producer Winstanley]. He had already done a demo of "Absolute Beginners." The lift went up, straight into this apartment. And there he was. He had a bar there, so we had a beer and listened to the demo. The song was so good, it was like a gift really. They'd done the demo at Abbey Road studios, and, I mean he could have released that. But we worked quite hard on it and extended it and changed a few things, so it was worth doing. After that first meeting, I spent a lot of time of him. Not just recording. We would finish recording and just sit around and talk. His knowledge was massive. We were quite comfortable with each other. Coco once said to me that he liked me because I was normal. I don't know if that's boring, but maybe a lot of the people around him were trying too hard. We would go out for lunch around Notting Hill and people would take a double look and say, "No it can't be!" That was quite funny, experiencing the fame of David Bowie. We went to [the Notting Hill] Carnival with him and we were in a first-floor flat. He was sitting on the windowsill looking out at everyone, so whenever anyone looked up and saw him, he was quite pleased. He wasn't trying to hide at this point, wasn't trying to disguise himself. Wasn't trying to run away from fame. We went skiing that winter, and we were quite nearby to him so he invited us over. So we spent New Year's Eve with him in Gstaad. And Iggy was there, it was a small gathering. There were only about twelve of us in total, and we just sat around drinking Champagne. And when we walked into the house he made us each wear different hats. He gave me a magician's hat and Iggy had a Viking hat on. So we spent the evening talking to each other with these funny hats on. He wasn't drinking that much at the time. Coco was there at the time monitoring his drinking. We went skiing with him again at Easter. He liked watching old sitcoms on TV, he liked sitting around. We had a great laugh in the studio one time when we got him to sing "Absolute Beginners" as if he were different people, like Iggy or Lennon. He was a great mimic. His best was Anthony Newley, because obviously at the beginning of his career he really sounded like him.

HARVEY GOLDSMITH: Bowie and Bob were in my office trying to work on the reggae song when we started playing a lot of the videos that people had sent in for use in the show. The BBC had sent a lot in, and we had videos from all over the place. I had one of those pop-up televisions and we started working our way through the videos, looking for suitable material to play at Wembley. When that piece popped up, of all the terrible news footage, with the Cars' "Drive" already on it—["*Who's gonna drive you home tonight . . .*"]—we all looked at it and welled up immediately. And Dave immediately said, "Take one of my numbers off and put that up instead." That was another iconic part of the day. David Bowie actually gave up one of his songs—he was going to finish with "Five Years"—at one of the biggest concerts he'd ever done, in front of what was going to be the biggest TV audience ever, in order to play this video. We were all blown away by his generosity of spirit, as I'm not sure there were many performers who would have done that, or at least not volunteered to do so.

BOB GELDOF: I showed that film to David at Harvey Goldsmith's about seven thirty at night. Let's remember for a minute that Bowie is an absolute god. I got to know him when I was a kid. I hitchhiked to see him in Belgium on the *Station to Station* tour, told him I was in a band and showed him pictures of the Rats. I blagged backstage and he was so nice. Don't forget he launched Band Aid [by wearing] this lame T-shirt, FEED THE WORLD, and looked like a doofus. But he's the sweetest man. You just never think about David Bowie like that. We showed him the film, which was famine footage cut to the Cars' song "Drive." He sat there in tears and said, "Right, I'm giving up a song." I said, "Hang on . . ." I didn't want David Bowie giving up a fucking song. I mean, hello? But of course he was right. That was the moment that people said, Fuck everything, take whatever you want from me. And it took David Bowie to make that call. No one was going to suggest such a mad thing, but he suggested it himself.

KEVIN ARMSTRONG: We didn't have much time to prepare, just two days' rehearsal at Bray Studios in Berkshire, but we were ready. On the day, nobody could ignore the atmosphere that Queen created, as they had just been on before us, but it didn't seem in any way like, Oh, it's difficult to follow that. Because we were with David Bowie—we were going to walk on there and they were going to go nuts. And they did. By the time we hit the stage it was probably the best part of the day, the late afternoon. I'd never felt anything like that crowd. It did really seem to be like, you know, we're here to change the world.

Some artists arrived by car, others by helicopter (Elton John, David Bowie, Spandau Ballet, the Who, George Michael, and so forth). These were landing on a nearby cricket field, where a wedding reception was taking place; after various complaints from the father of the bride, David Bowie was dispatched to smooth things over, and—obviously—have his picture taken with the bride and groom. At the time, the music PR Gary Farrow was running his own agency, looking after the likes of Frankie Goes to Hollywood, Paula Yates, Wham!, and Heaven 17. A good friend of the Live Aid promoter Harvey Goldsmith, Farrow had been called by him to see if he could persuade some of his famous friends to let them use their helicopters for the day, to fly the performers into the stadium from the heliport in Battersea. Due to the number of acts on the bill, and the crowds, there was simply no other way to guarantee them arriving on time. And so Farrow rang the BBC presenter Noel Edmunds, along with some other owners, and they all agreed to supply them. They also arranged for the fuel to be donated, as well as the pilots' time. Because of the number of return flights needed, the operation was quickly labeled the biggest air-lift since the Falklands War. The helicopters were going to land on a makeshift landing strip, complete with wind sock and lights, on a cricket green behind the stadium, where a match was due to be played that day. It was agreed with the teams that the match wouldn't be canceled, but that they'd simply take the bales away whenever a heli needed to land. This went on all day. One of the security guards told Farrow that not even the pope had been able to land so close to the stadium. "That's because he didn't have a laminate," quipped Farrow. Bowie repeated this joke all day.

NOEL EDMUNDS (DJ): On the day it was the climax of their cricket tournament, and they wouldn't abandon their game for us so the umpires had whistles and when they saw a helicopter coming they blew the whistles and cleared the field for us to land. I seem to remember that David Bowie's management said he only flew in a blue helicopter—that's blue on the inside—and we managed to find one. I was killing time with him at Battersea before he flew in and I said, "Look at the inside of this helicopter!" He looked at me as if I were mad. He didn't give a shit what color the helicopter was.

PETE TOWNSHEND (MUSICIAN): Bowie had wheeled out a suit from his younger days and was delighted to explain to me how well it still fitted.

The band was practically new, having only played together three times previously, which is one of the reasons Bowie's set struck some as so flat. Thomas Dolby was playing keyboards, and was one of the few band members to enjoy it.

THOMAS DOLBY: To my astonishment, I felt like I was on a magic carpet ride. These songs were like our teenage anthems—my fingers just wafted along.

HARVEY GOLDSMITH: David and Freddie Mercury were actually quite similar, although Freddie was obviously more flamboyant onstage. Freddie crafted the science of getting to his audience, whereas David Bowie crafted the art of getting to his audience. David was a genuine enigma, as I don't think anyone really knew him, you knew what he decided you should know. That was David through and through, being an enigma that everyone thought they knew.

ALAN EDWARDS (PUBLICIST): It's always a little nerve-wracking when you are looking after your artist and doing two jobs at once. In my case, that day, I was doing about eighteen jobs. There wasn't much love lost between David and Elton—perhaps they'd fallen out at some point in the past—although the one musician David was genuinely pleased to see was Freddie [Mercury]. They really were delighted to be together again. They stood chatting, as if they'd only seen each other yesterday. The affection between them was tangible. David was wearing an amazing blue suit, and looked incredibly sharp and healthy. Just before David went on, Freddie winked at him and said, "If I didn't know you better, dear, I'd have to eat you." No wonder David went out onstage with such a big smile on his face.

Bowie had to follow Queen, although at the time I had no idea how he did it, as the Queen performance was extraordinary. It is quite rightly remembered as the greatest stadium performance ever, something that wasn't lost on the 80,000 people in the stadium, including me. As Queen left the stage after rocking Wembley's foundations with "We Will Rock You" and "We Are the Champions," I wondered why I hadn't been a Queen fan all my life, and felt rather embarrassed that I had treated them with such disdain. Like the other 79,999 people in the stadium on July 13, and the 1.9 billion watching on TV, I was completely won over. Their performance not only gave them a new lease on life, but they completely altered how many people viewed them. Their performance has since been voted by more than sixty artists, journalists, and music industry executives as the greatest live performance in rock (Jimi Hendrix's appearance at Woodstock in August 1969 came second, followed by the Sex Pistols' gig at Manchester Free Trade Hall in June 1976). And with good reason. On reaching his trailer, Mercury shouted, "Thank God that's over," and promptly downed a double vodka. Reaction to Queen's performance was predictable. In the stadium, the crowd was completely floored, as were the other acts, especially those who had yet to appear: Elton John rushed into their dressing room afterward, screaming that they had stolen the show. Next up was David Bowie, but how could he be anything other than anti-climactic? Seven-twenty should have been the perfect time for him to grab the audience, but Freddie Mercury's extraordinary performance made it impossible. I thought Bowie stood no chance, but he appeared to take it in his stride. By rights he should have been shell-shocked, but apparently not. The final song he sang was "Heroes," and he introduced it like this: "To my son, to all our children, and to the children of the world." With that, his pickup band started the song, and he managed to transcend himself.

THOMAS DOLBY: It was a gorgeous day. I lived down by the Thames and I went for a walk in the morning, and everybody had their windows open and you could hear everybody tuned to the same station; there was a whole community focused on the same thing. It was a bit like the moon landing. Because of the traffic I was instructed to go to Battersea Heliport, and Bowie was already there when I arrived, signing autographs and smiling in his blue suit. As soon as we got in the helicopter he changed. He was physically shaking, and started chain-smoking. The pilot kept telling him he couldn't smoke but he just ignored him, and kept asking how long it was going to take. He was a complete diva for these twenty minutes. He'd only recently started flying again, and I think this was his first helicopter trip. He was a complete bitch. I remember banking over the stadium and seeing the twin towers and seeing a giant screen with Freddie Mercury on it. When we got out of the helicopter, we were driven straight to the stadium, where we were surrounded by about two hundred photographers. As we got out of the car Bowie winked at me and said, "I love this bit." The personality transformation was really dramatic. There was no green room, and we were literally walked to the side of the stage, and then we went on.

We were mainly running on adrenaline, but as soon as we started rocking we went into this sort of more religious feeling, particularly when we played "Heroes." Then it was a mixture of euphoria and stage fright, because "Heroes" doesn't actually have that many changes in it. Simple songs are sometimes the easiest to mess up because you really have to concentrate; with more complicated songs the chord sequences keep you focused. But with "Heroes" you really had to know what was going on. Also, there are singers who have great dexterity, and singers who have great character, and Bowie had the ability to fuse the two. So I had also turned into a fanboy who was miraculously onstage with Bowie.

Afterwards, someone asked Bowie if he wanted to go to the Royal Box, so off we went. In front of us were Charles and Diana and they turned around and congratulated us and shook his hand. David said, "We're having a sort of sing-song at the end, do you think you will be up there?" And she said, "Well, I think I could manage the National Anthem."

KEVIN ARMSTRONG: It would be difficult to say that wasn't one of the highlights of my career. We weren't sure how good our performance was at the time, but the crowd seemed to love it, and the energy was indescribable.

BERNARD DOHERTY: Bowie was in floods of tears after his performance, blown over by the sheer force of emotion from the crowd. He was crying his eyes out. He couldn't cope with the enormity of it all, which was astonishing. This was David Bowie!

There was the obvious rivalry between Bowie and Queen, and although they were friends, each wanted to outdo the other. And while Bowie may have been smiling, he was worried inside. Like everyone else at Wembley that day, he knew Queen had stolen the show, and if truth be known, he was a little queasy.

Bowie and Mercury had worked together just a few years previously, when they had recorded the "Under Pressure" single in Montreux in 1981, and they got to see each other's foibles and predilections at close quarters. Bowie was living there, Queen was recording there, and it was suggested by a mutual colleague (the producer David Richards) that they meet. This resulted in a new composition, kick-started by John Deacon's bass line, and then accessorized by both Bowie and Mercury. Bowie originally called the song "People on Streets," but then settled on the slightly more abstract "Under Pressure."

"[Bowie] was quite difficult to work with," said Brian May, "because it was the meeting of two different methods of working. It was stimulating but, at the same time, almost impossible to resolve. We're very pigheaded and set in our ways and Mr. Bowie is too. In fact he's probably as pigheaded as the four of us put together. After 'Under Pressure' was done, there were continual disagreements about how it should be put out or if it should even be put out at all. David wanted to redo the whole thing."

ALAN EDWARDS: There was a sense of drama about the day, as the whole thing felt innovative, groundbreaking, fundamentally important, as though we all knew we wouldn't ever be at something like this again. I remember watching Bowie, and while he certainly wasn't overawed, you could tell that he was carefully watching people. You wanted to look around and remember things, as you knew it was a special day. There was a healthy competitive spirit backstage, although you also felt that everyone was involved for the common good. Every five minutes there was another surprise. Phil Collins getting on an airplane and playing in Philadelphia. I suppose it seems commonplace now, but as soon as that happened—and as soon as it happened everyone in the stadium knew about it—you knew you were a part of a truly global event. There was a sense of oneness, a feeling that the crowd and the performers were somehow all in it together. For one day. We all felt as though we were right at the center of the universe. This was before all the big global events, before the idea of global summits, or big charity events, or colossal fund-raisers. The G8 had started back in 1975 with the Group of Six, hosted by France with the UK, Germany, Italy, Japan, and the States, but it didn't have the resonance it would have after Live Aid. It fused politics and pop together, and made both seem far more important than they had been in the past, or at the very least gave both a different media perspective. Politics was immediately made popular in a way that appealed to a younger set of people, and pop was suddenly front-page news in a way it had never been before. In hindsight, none of the big events of the last twenty or thirty years would have happened without the ambition of Live Aid. Woodstock didn't really contain any politics, it was a just a big festival. Live Aid really meant something. And a lot of that was due to David Bowie.

MARK ELLEN (JOURNALIST): Before Live Aid certain people like Van Morrison and Rod Stewart or whatever were considered to be super antiquated. But when they saw Live Aid they saw a lot of bands that they hadn't heard of and they quite liked them. Also, people thought, I'd forgotten about all these bands, I'd forgotten that Dave Gilmour existed, I'd forgotten about Queen, I'd forgotten about David Bowie and I saw them and they were wonderful and actually the stadium experience looks very pleasant. Like it might be a worthwhile venture to go to see people in places like that. So this was the beginning of the heritage industry.

DAVID BAILEY: We built a studio backstage at Live Aid, and photographed everyone as they came offstage. That was a crazy experience, as it was so unreal. Everyone was famous, and it was like being at some sort of party that never ended. It was hectic. Everyone was great—Elton, Bowie, Paul McCartney, U2, everybody. Freddie Mercury was funny because he French kissed me quite aggressively—he came up and grabbed me, swung me round, and said, "I have to kiss you!"—and the only people who were a bit off were George Michael and Sade, who for some reason didn't want her picture taken. We auctioned off all the pictures afterwards. I loved it because I was one of only four people who had the magic pass, the pass where you could go everywhere.

GARY KEMP (GUITARIST AND SONGWRITER): What I thought was interesting about Live Aid itself was the way the hierarchy fell into place almost immediately. I had a particular moment when I arrived, when I saw my hero, David Bowie, at the bar wearing this beautiful suit. I made an approach, but he was talking to someone and I didn't quite get the connection that I would have liked to have got, so I rather secretly gathered myself and crawled away. I think a lot of us felt that we were in the room with our betters. And the '70s generation had never been better than they were that day, so I think a lot of the younger boys felt very much in their place.

BRIAN ARIS (PHOTOGRAPHER): One of the great things about Live Aid was the fact that while all these musicians had relationships with us, with photographers, they didn't really know each other, so there was this great curiosity on the day, as everyone started talking to each other. You couldn't separate Annie Lennox and David.

ROGER DALTREY (SINGER): I found Live Aid a very weird experience. It was just a series of dressing rooms. One minute you're sitting in a crowd and the next you're wheeled into what felt like a train station of people changing behind curtains. And we were only playing for fifteen minutes. It just seemed like the concourse of a train station, like Charing Cross, waiting to go home, or go onstage. One or the other. David was funny though. I knew David very well, and every time we met we used to laugh a hell of a lot together. After all, we were both London boys. In all of the photographs I've got of the two of us we are both cracking our sides. We didn't socialize a lot, but professionally we had a great relationship. I was a great admirer of his work, as he was a great inventor, a great pusher of boundaries, which I liked. He was fearless in that respect. This is very necessary in rock, and there was more weight to his music than most. But like I say, he was funny too.

Live Aid documentary producer Jill Sinclair was also producing a Christmas special that day for The Tube, *the Channel 4 early-evening pop show.*

JILL SINCLAIR (PRODUCER): The interviews were more like a gossip between old friends—what was it like and so on. In a break, Paula [Yates] and I sat down and tried to figure out some questions that would spark a different response. We came up with a list including, 'What are you going to do [right] now?' The first person we thought we'd try it on was David Bowie. I grabbed him and she asked him the new question. He looked at her, then straight at the camera, and said, 'I'm going to go home and I'm going to have a really good fuck.'"

10

I'VE NOTHING MUCH TO OFFER

1986–1989

JULIEN TEMPLE: You could tell that he really missed his brother. He wasn't in contact with him as much as he had been, and there was a sense that he found this extremely upsetting. They had been very close when they had been growing up, even though there was a substantial age gap, and he seemed to long for that companionship. This wasn't long before he killed himself.

When we were researching *Absolute Beginners* we would go and explore old Soho together, but this wasn't the Soho that was in the tourist guides, this was the grotty, debauched Soho, the one the tourists never see. It was almost as though he was treating me like his little brother, showing me the places where he'd met hookers, gangsters, drug dealers—all of these places he'd been shown by his brother back in the '60s. Terry had been instrumental in helping him grow up by showing him what really went on in London, what really happened away from the suburbs. It was Terry who taught him all about jazz, which was a passion for David throughout his life. It was Terry who turned him on to a world of possibilities that just wasn't available in Bromley. One of the worst things about being brought up in the suburbs was being so close to London but being so far away from it. The thing that astonished me was how familiar he was with everyone, because he really did know them, and he really had frequented all these dive bars and brothels. At the time we were filming, Soho was starting to become gentrified, and Bar Italia—the Italian coffee bar where I used to practically live—was thinking of having a complete refit in order to attract more customers. I told them that obviously they shouldn't do such a thing, and I said I'd bring my friend along tomorrow to tell them why. So the next day I came in with David and he told them that they were a fundamental part of Soho and that they should never, ever change. Of course they did as David said, and soon you couldn't move for the hundreds of people trying to get in there every night. I think the place had meant something to him way back when.

The important thing to realize about David is that he worried terribly about Terry, while at the same time being continually worried that he was going to fall victim to the same kind of schizophrenia. He absolutely idolized Terry, and in his eyes Terry was a hero. He really loved his brother, and hated the fact that he was incarcerated. One morning during the shoot for *Jazzin' for Blue Jean* I was late, and I'm never late, so I got up and rushed to the set but I was over ninety minutes late by the time I got there. But weirdly David wasn't there. He called me to apologize and then asked me to come round to this little hotel he was staying in, in Hans Crescent. He was sitting up in bed, in his little stripey blue-and-white pajamas, and he was crying his eyes out. I think something had happened to Terry. But that day I felt like his big brother. I think perhaps he looked for brother-type figures throughout his life.

I'd read Colin MacInnes's book *Absolute Beginners* as a teenager and wanted to turn it into a musical that tried to capture the dawn of the teen era in Britain. It was an incredibly ambitious, and perhaps foolhardy, venture. It was all about emerging teens, race riots in Notting Hill, the dawn of modern advertising, all told through the prism of the '80s. David got *Absolute Beginners* immediately, and said yes straightaway. He hadn't read the book, which surprised me, but he knew all about it, knew about Vance Packard and *The Hidden Persuaders.* I knew it would appeal to him as he had worked in a lowly capacity in the advertising industry back in the '60s, and I knew he would get all the references. Which he did. Advertising was so cynical in the '50s, as it was preparing young people to be consumers, training them to be teenagers who wanted consumer goods. I remember talking to Keith Richards and him telling me how disappointed he was by art school, as all they were doing was teaching you how to be designers, commercial artists, encouraging you to join a world of commerce. I thought David would get all that. He understood all the clothes, the cars, the needs for a mid-Atlantic accent, the need to disguise your way to the top.

PETER YORK: At the time I thought that Colin MacInnes was very important in the scheme of things, as was *Absolute Beginners.* I also discovered that to my complete amazement Julien didn't know anything about it. He had never read it—imagine! So I had a go at him about it, and told him it was a most marvelous book. I know much more about MacInnes now than I did then, as it turns out he was the uncle of a great friend of mine, and he wasn't terribly nice. But that didn't change the fact that as a middle-aged upper-middle-class predatory gay man he actually got inside all those new cultures of the '50s. So I'm partly responsible for a film that single-handedly ruined the British film industry, because it was disastrous. I tried telling myself that it was going to be very good, that it was our kind of film, but it was terrible.

When *Absolute Beginners* was released I'd just started writing for Tina Brown at *Vanity Fair,* and had been asked to write a piece on the film. I had an arrangement. But I failed to recognize the two crucial imperatives for her: (1) Her brother Chris Brown was the producer of the film, (2) A Bowie interview. She had to have a Bowie interview. So of course I rattled off something about the development of British juvenile life, and this wasn't what was wanted at all. Pump the film, get the Bowie interview. But Julien didn't deliver Bowie, which was a huge disappointment to Tina. So I think she got Philip Norman to write something instead.

It shows you how far Bowie's star had fallen by 1986, as when I suggested in The Face *offices that "Absolute Beginners" was an epic love song to rival "Heroes," I was laughed out of the building. I was right, but no one wanted to listen (to me or him).*

Decades later, various recordings began to leak online of Bowie recording the song at Westside Studios, singing over the top in a variety of voices: in the course of an hour he recorded uncanny impressions of Bruce Springsteen, Neil Young, Iggy Pop, Lou Reed, Van Morrison, Tom Waits, and Anthony Newley, and all were eerily accurate. The piece that Philip Norman eventually wrote for Vanity Fair *was breezy, but uncannily perceptive, inasmuch that Norman identified that Bowie had always been at home in Soho. "The pity of it is that no one managed to film Colin MacInnes's* Absolute Beginners *twenty years ago [in 1966]," he wrote. "Then there would have been only one choice to portray the novel's teenage hero, strutting the London streets in 'mock croc' shoes and Italian jacket, looking about him with eyes quick and bright as computer digits . . . Who else could it possibly have been but the teenage David Bowie?" Who indeed.*

JULIEN TEMPLE: David knew how to act, but he was too self-conscious to ever be a great actor, and he was nowhere near as good as all the wonderful manifestations of himself that he put into his music and that he used onstage. As a performer he was a person who could amplify his own personality through the creations he used to express himself, all these different versions of himself. He was very dedicated, and he could apply himself, but never without keeping himself in check. He could never really let go as an actor, as he was always too aware of what he was doing. He studied hard though, and he knew his stuff. He loved Buñuel, Cocteau, Fassbinder, but then he also loved Tony Hancock and the Ealing comedies. He could watch Tony Hancock's *The Rebel* on a weekly basis, and he would laugh and laugh and laugh. I always thought that was very telling. He was being taken seriously, and yet he would always worry that what he was doing wasn't quite good enough. But then he was an artist and he was meant to feel that way. David sang almost as though he was singing from another dimension, as he was an outsider who appealed to outsiders. He wanted people to challenge themselves, and to encourage themselves to explore their own minds, and not to settle for second best. He was convinced that everyone had potential and that all they needed to do was release it. In a way he was the patron saint of misfits, as he managed to personalize emotion without necessarily being didactic. His big thing was challenging people to explore to the full what they might be. He said, I've done it, so now it's your turn. You do it! People don't know what they want to be when they're young, and he said you should experience everything that you can, just in case you like it. There have been many people who have liberated us politically, but David liberated us emotionally, sexually. Ultimately, he wanted to set people free.

PATSY KENSIT (ACTRESS): I was sixteen when Julien first introduced me to Bowie on the set of *Absolute Beginners* at Shepperton Studios. Even though I knew I was going to be working with him I still didn't quite believe it. I thought we were going to become fast friends and he was going to fall in love with me in that idiotic way that teenage girls do. I was a stupid sixteen-year-old. He was very formal but gradually opened up as we worked together. He was very charming, but there were obviously boundaries, which I understood. But one day I was sitting having my makeup done and David walked in and picked up a hairbrush and started slowly brushing my hair. He didn't say a word, and he did it for about five minutes. And then he just left the room. I didn't really know what to do with myself after that.

When David was working, when he was on set, I've never seen so many crew. Everyone wanted to be on the set with him. Julien put him in a harness on top of this huge globe, and he was flying above it, and then he lands on top of the globe, and starts doing this dance. All the riggers, all the grizzled old lighting guys, everyone just had their mouths open. He was incredible. And a gentleman, but mysterious. He was intensely beautiful, stunning, and in incredible shape. I know it's a Liza Minnelli thing to say, but he was the consummate professional. He didn't have an entourage, only this woman called Coco, who was quite scary. *Absolute Beginners* is a much underrated film. It's flawed, but it was number one for six weeks in the UK, which must count for something.

Bowie sang the title theme for the film of Raymond Briggs's When the Wind Blows *in 1986, and also narrated the intro to* The Snowman. *Briggs was summoned, along with five other members of the production team, to a meeting where they were lined up to be introduced to the singer, "like royalty." Bowie said, "I admire your work." To which Briggs responded, "I wish I could say the same for you." He says he didn't actually know who he was. "He had bright pink shoes on, which was nice."*

BRIAN HENSON (PUPPETEER): I was the head puppeteer on *Labyrinth*, and was in my early twenties at the time. There may have been three names bandied about for the lead part of Jareth—Michael Jackson, Sting, and David Bowie. These were the only names my dad [Jim] was talking about, and I was a shameless supporter of David Bowie. I lobbied hard. I was just out of college, and Michael Jackson and David Bowie were controlling the industry, they were the biggest artists in America. But it was always Bowie. That's the one my dad wanted.

It started when my dad took me to see *The Elephant Man* in New York, and he turned to me and said, "You know what, he really has got his chops." That was his audition. In those days you did a lot of preproduction on a movie like this, so this was a good few years before we started shooting. So my dad met Bowie, and really liked him, and David really liked my dad. They connected. The movie was shot in London but David did his demo tracks in New York, and I remember hearing them and being blown away. My dad was used to hearing demo tracks from composers which would consist of one finger plunking away on a piano. But these were properly produced. He had strings, he had the Harlem Boys Choir, they were almost done, almost the finished article. I wasn't used to seeing my father impressed in this way.

David was at his most beautiful, and so he had a real presence when he walked into a room. Then he had this incredibly disarming smile, and was always telling jokes, and he loved to goof around, and always went to the pub at the end of the shoot. He had a drink with the crew pretty much every day. He was very hardworking, but never intense. He loved to laugh, as my dad did. He wanted Jareth, his character, to be the petulant rock star, which isn't really what David is, but that was the role, and he did it brilliantly. My dad was a little worried about the sexual connotations of the relationship between Jareth and Jennifer Connelly, but then that's what the movie's really about. I do know that David's codpiece had to be reduced as it was far too large originally. The whole movie is about the aggressive phallus, as Jareth represents male sexuality. The reviews were tough and the box office was a disappointment, but the movie has consistently sold since, and eventually went into profit. At the time my father was disappointed, but it came good in the end. . . . A lot of stars come in and don't care what's going on around them, but David came in and you could see immediately that he was thinking, Hey, this is a lot of work. . . . He was also comfortable with doing forty takes, which I have to say a lot of others aren't.

At one point David wanted to do a stage version of the movie. About ten years ago he called me and told me this. He said that out of all the things he'd done, *Labyrinth* was the one thing his daughter really loved. But he couldn't find a backer.

STEVE WHITMIRE (PUPPETEER): I think Jim Henson had also considered Sting for Jareth, but Bowie was always his first choice. I don't even think there was an audition, I just think we were elated that Bowie had agreed to do it. It was a really big deal for us for Bowie to want to make this film. We started filming in April 1985 in Elstree, where we had filmed *The Muppets*. A week before shooting we had a party at Jim's house in Hampstead, where we were all going to meet David for the first time. It was one of my more embarrassing moments because I think I probably gushed a little too much. I found out quickly that David could accept compliments well, but he really wasn't interested in hearing them particularly. He was glad that you were a fan, and he was thrilled that you liked what he was doing, but he was going to do it either way.

We shot for five months with David and these crazy puppets. There wasn't a lot of blue-screen stuff, it was just basic puppetry, with David on a three-foot riser, and us down in these pits in the floor. It was just like *The Muppets*. He was always intense in the performance, very focused on what he was doing, and then the minute Jim would cut, he would say something really silly. Which is what we do. The goblins were so ridiculous-looking that you had to laugh. It was camp and silly and we kind of played it that way.

There was a point during the film when David thought that his character should perhaps go a little further with the girl. His character is being pretty sexy, and he might have probably gone a bit further with that. I mean, his costar was a fourteen-year-old girl and there was some discussion about how far he should go. The decision was to keep it a little more metaphorical, rather than a coming-of-age, child-molester thing. . . . However, I know that there is some kind of online cult surrounding his "package," and my understanding is that David was not altogether happy with his costume choice. Regardless of whether or not he wanted to play a seductive character, I don't think he was crazy about his leotard. There are a couple of shots in that film that really focus on his groin, but they're actually focusing on characters next to him, and it just looks that way. They just happen to be only waist tall.

He arrived in a limo every morning, spent ages in makeup, worked hard, and then went home. He was a seriously disciplined guy. I know that his son, Duncan, worked in the creature department on that film, as a puppet builder. He was there for a few years. On its initial release I think the movie only made about half of its budget, and the reviews were mixed. But I know that Jim was aware of the cult following of the movie before he died in 1990.

GREG DAVIS (WARDROBE ASSISTANT): I was working with Ellis Flyte, who ran the costume department on *Labyrinth*, and we spent what seemed like an incredible amount of time working on David Bowie's codpiece. She asked me if I was interested in working on the film as I had already worked on *The Dark Crystal*, and to work with Bowie was such a dream. I had already met him once before at the Blitz club, when I drunkenly went up to him and told him how much I loved him, but I think everybody did that night. The original costume he was meant to be wearing wasn't actually that good, and was actually a bit naff, so Bowie spent quite some time working with us to make it more rock and roll, making it a lot cooler, although I have to say we spent so long on his codpiece, making it bigger, making it smaller—some days it was all we did. We were all a bit nervous working with him at first, but he was unbelievably charming. Even when he had had a late night, and there were quite a few of those, he never lost his temper or shouted. I remember one morning when he was late because he'd been out with Mick Jagger at some club the night before. He asked me if I had any drugs and the only thing I had on me was speed, so I gave him that. There was usually a lot of cocaine around, as it was the '80s and everyone was doing it, but that day speed seemed to do the trick for him. It certainly picked him up.

DAVID BOWIE: Having Joe changed my attitude immeasurably. But it grew slowly. I had the usual father thing—what's this funny little creature, wandering around, sort of gurgling. It wasn't until he started toddling that I realized what a ray of sunshine had come into my life. You must understand that my ex-wife and I only lived together for two years, even though we were married for such a long time. One day I suddenly knew something had to be done about Joe's life, because he wasn't being looked after in the way he should have been. I decided to take the reins, so I fought and won custody. As you probably know, it's a very unusual thing for a father to be given custody of his child, especially in Switzerland. Which, without having to say any more, indicates how the maternal side of his life was going. It was tragic. So I took full rein and ever since that time I've had to grow up with him, which has been so delightful and a source of reserve and discipline and energy. The single most important message I could give him still is: never even consider becoming involved with drugs. Something I could never underestimate the importance of. It's absolutely tragic, what it can do to you, and how it can screw you up. [In September 1987, before a PiL concert in Lausanne, at the Hot-Point festival, Bowie was confronted with his own personal legacy: Duncan, just turned sixteen, with recently dyed green-and-red hair. "You," said Bowie, "are not coming out with me looking like that."]

Bowie usually knew what was going on, even if he didn't always manage to connect with it. In 1986, knowing he needed to make another record, he contacted Jean-Paul Goude, the man who had turned Grace Jones—an exotic model with a so-so voice—into an icon of style. Bowie wanted Goude to direct a video for him, wanted him to bring his box of tricks and gift for reinvention to the party. Goude says he was charming, genuinely humble, and keen to collaborate (Bowie had traveled to Paris to meet him, "in his little tiny cap"). As was Goude, who knew that Bowie would help him continue on the journey that had been eased so much by his successful appropriation of Grace Jones ("I wanted to mythologize him again"). But one of Goude's agents got greedy, and asked for so much money that Bowie eventually ran scared. Consequently the video for "Day-In Day-Out," the dreadful lead-in single from Never Let Me Down, *was directed by Julien Temple, hitting a career low.*

SEAN DOYLE: While not quite as flat-sounding as his previous two albums, *Never Let Me Down* is still airless and crowded, produced to death. The extravagant production clashes sharply with the album's often socially minded lyrics, so much so that they become entirely flippant and insincere. The ugly bursts of brass and exchanges between Bowie and his exuberant backup singers don't really reflect the attempted urban grit of "Day-In Day-Out." In an almost mockingly cruel video, he croons and rollerblades past scenes of homelessness, prostitution, and police brutality. Of course, this isn't to say that there's much that's irredeemable—lyrically or melodically—under that mountain of terrible gimmicks. The title track is a halfway decent John Lennon impersonation featuring one of the album's most memorable melodies. "Time Will Crawl" is easily the best *Never Let Me Down* has to offer, a paranoid number inspired musically by Neil Young and lyrically by the Chernobyl disaster. He was recording in Switzerland when it happened and heard the first panicked reports of ominous nuclear clouds moving eastwards. Much of *Never Let Me Down*'s reputation as his definitive rock bottom comes from his own opinions of it, quoted frequently in the following years. He said in 1995: "My nadir was *Never Let Me Down*. I really shouldn't have even bothered going into the studio to record it."

CHARLES SHAAR MURRAY: I wouldn't have exactly predicted his success with *Let's Dance*, but I was actually glad to see him make a pop record. Although, I was worried about what kind of relationship would develop between him and this wonderful new audience. Would they demand too many compromises, and would they get them? Ultimately I thought *Tonight* was an album of classy filler with no center, while *Never Let Me Down* was just awful. With these records he wanted to reconnect without the responsibility. People started asking which is the real Bowie? But they all are, it just depends what time of day it is, what time of the month, what time of the year, what time of the decade. He was actually a lot more straightforward than people gave him credit for. He could be a space alien, or a slightly dodgy geezer from South London.

DAVID BOWIE: I made an awful lot of mistakes, and I did some good things as well. But I can't think in terms of editing it. It's just a bunch of stuff I did, and that's me. That's what I've done, all the goonisms as well as the nice bits. I guess, for my own absolution I would edit out me starting to take drugs—again it comes back to that, because so many bad things happened because of it. If I could have edited out that period, an awful lot of my life would have been absolutely different, and the next six years of putting it back together again would have changed. That's the other thing people don't realize—it's very hard to just give up. You go through a lot of dreadful things giving up. A lot of depression, a lot of switching addictions. In my case, I switched to alcohol. And it took an awful long time to shake that one off. It just goes on and on and it's really hard because your metabolism changes and it's been proven fairly well now that if you are addicted to any one thing, transferring to another is quite easy. It's pointless to try to switch people from heroin to a methadone treatment, because methadone is just as addictive as heroin. My problem was cocaine, and then I went from cocaine to alcohol, which is a natural course of events. You have to be lucky enough to have friends around you that want you to succeed. But you also want to have to stop yourself. You have to know in your own mind that you don't want to go on like that. That's the biggest hurdle. And if you can overcome that, then you're OK. 'Cause once you're addicted, you're addicted for life. It just takes one drink and he's gone again. He's out on a binge. For the rest of the weekend, bye-bye Bert. And he comes back on Monday full of remorse and guilt and everything. It's dreadful. You cannot take one drink.

TONI BASIL: I was asked to do the Serious Moonlight Tour but I couldn't because at the time I had a very brief career with my hit record, "Mickey." Glass Spider was fun, though. By this time street style had evolved, and we used that a lot in the show. There was also a lot of improv. David was different, but he was just as obsessive. He had everything and he knew how to put it all together.

PETER FRAMPTON: No one really knew what I looked like until *Frampton Comes Alive!*, and all the publicity that went with that, but by the '80s that was all over. The "big, huge, success and the world went crazy" period had completely died down, and the '80s were not a great period at all for me. I'd stopped touring, and was taking a break to try and work out what just happened. I had made an album, *Premonition*, my first one with Atlantic, in 1986, and David called me up and said he'd just heard it, and he said he loved what I was doing guitar-wise, and would I play on his next record. And I said, "Give me a second—yes!" We'd been on the same stage so many times, but never in the same band, and he was a mentor to me, so this was a dream for me. I think he'd looked at my career, and winced. He could see what I had been through. He could have had any guitarist in the world, but he chose me, and I think he did it to try and put right what had just gone wrong, even though I was partly to blame—taking my shirt off for *Rolling Stone* and allowing myself to be turned into a teen idol. That was the biggest gift he could have given me. I thanked him numerous times and I thanked him right until he died.

So he sends me a ticket, I went to Switzerland, and spent a couple of weeks there. We went out to dinner most nights, and one night he asked me what I'd say if he asked me to come out on the road, playing guitar with Carlos, and again I said, "Wait a minute—yes!" It was an enormous tour. We were into at least 30 or 40 trucks, 150 crew, it was like a travelling circus. I've never been involved in anything quite like that, before or after. It was extravagant. We announced the Glass Spider Tour at a club in London, and it was supposed to be just a press conference, but we actually played. My mum and dad came up for that, because I was playing with David. They came backstage afterwards, and the next thing I saw was my dad and David going off somewhere together. They had a great relationship, and it lasted till my father passed away in 2005. Dave called when he heard, and spoke to me and Mum.

The Glass Spider persona was as unfortunate as the album. At the press conference announcing his new EMI America deal, at the Players Theatre off the Strand, in March that year, Mockney Dave was to the fore, calling female journalists "love" and "dear" repeatedly. I remember feeling rather disappointed that he felt the need to treat the audience as though we were watching a late-night Channel 4 chat show. He said he'd like to make a movie with Kim Basinger—"'old on, I've got a list 'ere!"—and referred to his new band as "the lads." Here was the New Lad, exactly four years too soon.

CARLOS ALOMAR: The Glass Spider Tour was the Vegas tour, the greatest-hits tour, and you know what, I loved it.

MARTIN SCORSESE (DIRECTOR): I went to see his [Glass Spider] show in New York in 1987, when Squeeze opened for him, and this will give you an idea of his personality, I think—at least what I saw of it, what he allowed us to see. So, one of my closest friends is a man named Jay Cox, who wrote for *Time* magazine for many years. And Jay would come with me to all these different concerts, films, et cetera—it's been over forty-five years we've known each other and we're friends. He also writes with me, he wrote *The Age of Innocence* with me, he wrote lots of *Gangs of New York*, he's always with me. And David invited me to see the show, and said of course I could bring a friend, so I brought Jay. We arrived and there was a tent, which was sort of like the green room for visitors and we sat down at these tables and Debbie Harry was there with her manager. We talked for a little while and we got some food and David came out and said hello before the show. I introduced him to Jay and he was very pleasant—treating us fine—and he left us to start getting ready. And there had just been an article written, the cover story of *Time*, on David, and unbeknownst to me Jay had written it, and so after a few minutes, David comes rushing back in, and goes up close to Jay, takes his hand and says, "Are you the Jay Cox who wrote the article?" And Jay says, "Yes." And he looked at him, smiled, and said, "Really, really, really . . . scabrous," and Jay said, "Yes." And David said, "Congratulations," and then he stormed back out. I didn't know what to think, because I hadn't read the article. But [even] if he had been irritated by the article, what he did was come up to the person and smile and congratulate him and let him walk off, so that's interesting. They gave each other a look that was really low at certain points.

PAUL MCGUINNESS: The year of Glass Spider was the year U2 broke spectacularly, and when *The Joshua Tree* was successful all over the world. We converted a basic arena production into a stadium show, as the demand for tickets had been so huge, which was during the time when using video in a show was still considered to be quite naff. We had started using it with great reluctance, but it wasn't a great experience, and Bruce Springsteen didn't use the technology for years. These days video in all its forms is an intrinsic part of the live experience, but in the mid-'80s it was considered to be a particularly naff form of presentation, as though using it meant you were not somehow authentic. The Glass Spider Tour was being talked about as this great extravaganza, so I went to see it, in Belgium I think. Sadly it wasn't very good at all, and theatrically it was a failure. The reviewers couldn't bear to say that Bowie hadn't actually delivered, but it was a terrible show. There was a lot of disappointment.

MARTIN SCORSESE: Being a great fan of his work, the early '70s I think was what confirmed it for me. It all came together on the *Diamond Dogs* album, which I found myself listening to repeatedly, and the music particularly at that time was something that had a very, very strong influence on me. I sort of lived my life by this music. I loved the construction of the orchestration, so to speak, in every one of his pieces—through the use of guitars, the rhythms, a very different kind of approach to rather bland, mainstream rock. It was very different to that; it was unique in that it was a personal voice. His voice was kind of like a *chanteur*, you know, in "Time" and other pieces. And then there was the extraordinary rock piece, "Suffragette City," which just gave me so much inspiration. At that time all this music was there, the early Bruce Springsteen, the Rolling Stones, but a lot of it was leading to arena rock, which I didn't really admire that much. There was Neil Young, there were still aspects of the Band, of course there was Dylan. Bowie was something else entirely. I was surprised by the way he played and the kind of music he made. I got to see him at the Hollywood Bowl I think in 1974, which was extraordinary. I remember "Space Oddity" very strongly. I think he sort of levitated over the audience. It was quite something. I mean, it wasn't outlandish and it wasn't overly spectacular, but the song is very haunting. I tried years later to use "Space Oddity" in *The Departed*, but then it gave way to "Gimme Shelter." It's just the way the footage works. Whenever something doesn't work I use "Gimme Shelter!" But I didn't realize that! My team kept telling me, "Why do you always keep using 'Gimme Shelter'?!"

Anyway, in 1979 I become friends with Michael Powell, who made *The Red Shoes* amongst many other films. He came over to America, and met my editor Thelma Schoonmaker and they [eventually] got married. And so, at that time Michael and I were involved in a project called *13 Ways to Kill a Poet*, which was going to involve thirteen short films, with each filmmaker selecting a different poet. Francis Coppola was going to do one, I contacted Terry Gilliam, thought of Wim Wenders. Then I thought we should really look further out. I thought of David Bowie because of his records, and because of his videos for things like "Boys Keep

Swinging" and "Ashes to Ashes." Why couldn't he direct one? And so I got to speak to him on the phone. I called him and talked to him about this project, and suggested that he be a director on it. At the end of "Boys Keep Swinging" with the three women, or three guys in drag, the last woman comes out with the blond wig and suddenly, slowly walks towards the camera with a cane. I mean, this look on his face was quite extraordinary, and as it fades up she blows a kiss to the audience. I thought this had a command of visual style, and also, him being "the man who fell to Earth," he already had a command of the frame, the space, and his body language was extraordinary. So this, plus the visualizing I've seen in these rock videos, made me think why not suggest it, let's try something new. It's a short film, meaning that it'll be what they call an omnibus film, you know, and so we got to meet after that and he would come over to my apartment, downtown in a loft, and we'd have some dinners and talk about directing and talk about music.

David was intrigued by the project, but ultimately it couldn't come off, I couldn't pull everyone together. It was a good dream project, and in fact it's still something that we talk about a great deal. But these days, things are a little slower. I remember the phone call and I remember him coming over to the house, to the apartment, the loft. And the thing about him was, he was just a very disarming man with such power. What I mean is [he had] a kind of charismatic power, a beauty and extraordinary talent and genius at what he did. And you felt very comfortable with him at the same time. He asked a lot of questions, he was enthusiastic, and he was always kind of positive. So you know, I guess when the time came for *The Last Temptation of Christ* I immediately thought of David. It was a film that had started, been canceled, and was spoken about as a picture that would never get made. Eventually we found ourselves getting ready to shoot it in Morocco and of course I wanted a certain type of actor in the picture. I wanted to play against the traditional biblical epic, so between Willem Dafoe, Barbara Hershey, Harry Dean Stanton, Harvey Keitel, when the question came to who should play Pontius Pilate, I immediately thought of David. He was the first person I thought of. It was his charisma, his look, and ultimately the way he moved. When we started I had to have him keep still, as he was moving around a lot. He was meant to be a Roman—"No, you're Pontius Pilate, just stand there," I said, and then that gaze would appear. And that was it, that's what I wanted, that gaze as Willem Dafoe was sitting there as he was berating him. David only came down there for about three days or something, but he did it so well, he was so good.

He was trying to really give me what I needed, really trying hard. The film was extremely low budget and it was a rush, constantly fighting the weather, time, everybody's schedules; we were trying to make the film as if we were being chased. So when an actor would arrive, from another place, let's say, who hadn't been there for two months, they'd have to go into costume, and hair and makeup immediately. And so David arrived and I said hello to him in the morning. I was shooting this very difficult scene, supposedly in the Temple of Jerusalem, but we had no set, and it was extremely intense. I'm shooting and trying to get this scene done, and I'm sitting in my director's chair and there are some chairs behind me and suddenly I feel a tap on my shoulder and I turn around and there I was face-to-face with the ancient world, a being from the ancient world. I suddenly looked into the face of history. His face was right up close to me and he was smiling and his hair was done as Pontius Pilate, he was in his toga and his eyes of course, one was one color and the other another color. It was the most shocking, beautiful thing I had seen. This is the ancient world and it has come alive! He was an alien in the best sense of the word! That's my fondest memory of him. I was stunned; I couldn't speak . . . David? Yes! Let me see the toga! It was fantastic. That's why I wanted him to also stay a little still during the shoot because he became that world. He didn't have to show his authority by moving, he could just glare and speak, you see. We talked a lot about music, different kinds, including reggae, and we obviously talked about film, Oshima, *Merry Christmas, Mr. Lawrence.* He was very affable, pleasant, and always a gentleman, with a great sense of humor.

REEVES GABRELS (MUSICIAN): We met in 1987 when my then wife, Sara, who was a journalist, was working as a publicist for David while he was on tour. We'd sort of known each other for a couple of months because I was Sara's husband, and had an all-access backstage pass, but David thought I was a painter. Most of our conversations were about art. I had no real business being there, but we just talked about art.

I remember our first meeting was in his trailer watching *Fantasy Island* with the sound off, making up our own story line. He gave me a copy of *The Shock of the New* by Robert Hughes, which I had not read, and we would give each other little art books. It was only at the end of the tour that my wife gave him a tape I'd done. A few months after the tour finished, we got a call at home, in London. This guy, who I thought was pretending to be David, said he'd liked my tape, and as I thought it was a spoof I said, "Who the fuck is this?" he then started laughing and said, "We watched *Fantasy Island*!" He said that he thought I might be the guitarist he was looking for, and then we talked some more, about Jimi Hendrix, Cream, Led Zeppelin bootlegs, the Pixies, the music we were both into at the time. He rang back an hour later, asked me what I was doing that weekend and I said, "Nothing I can't change." So I went out to his house in Switzerland to work on an eight-minute version of "Look Back in Anger" he was doing for [contemporary dance troupe] La La La Human Steps. I suppose that was my test. I went for the weekend and stayed a month, and started writing for Tin Machine.

When you're twenty in this business, the temptations of the occupation tend to supersede the occupation itself, but when you're thirty, it's different, and I think he liked the fact that my wild guitar playing wasn't manifested in my personality. We got on. In the fifteen years we worked together we would tend to get apartments together when we were recording, and were never more than a hallway away from each other. In the studio he would take me out of my comfort zone, and say things like, "You really like that pedal, so try it without it . . ." I would say the same thing to him, when I thought he was basing too much of his lyrics on iambic pentameter. He talked about being unhappy with his two previous records, and the larger audience, and he didn't feel it represented who he really was. He felt trapped. We were having dinner in a Moroccan restaurant near his place in Switzerland, and I asked him if he had creative control. And he said that they basically had to put out what he gave them, so I suggested he start making records for himself again. I said it was all about his ego, and his ability to accept criticism for going left instead of right. So we just started writing. We wrote "Heaven's in Here," "Baby Universal," "Bus Stop," and some others. We kept trying to write two-chord rock songs and then failing by having to use a third chord. At that point this was a David Bowie record. Then David ran into Tony Sales at a Glass Spider wrap party, and called me to tell me to listen to Iggy Pop's *Lust for Life*—on which Tony and his brother Hunt played—as he said he'd found our new rhythm section. They had a lot of attitude. Very bossy, giving David a hard time about stuff. And then David came into the rehearsal studio one day and said that he didn't think this was going to be a David Bowie album, but a band album. And as we'd just recorded the song "Tin Machine," he suggested it as a band name. I thought it should be called White Noise, but David thought that was too excluding and quite possibly racist. He liked Tin Machine because Bad Company and the Monkees both had songs named after them. I was against the whole thing, as I'd had it with bands. But I was outvoted, and that's how we became a band. It didn't form so much as coagulated. I think it was a relief to be in a democracy for a while. I think he enjoyed it. I was just keen to work—give me a crumb of an idea and I would endeavor to turn it into something cool and brilliant and big. Songwriting is like trying to build a fire with straw and flint, you've got to all crowd around it and protect it from the wind, and collectively try and get it to catch. I was all about that. It was a fun atmosphere though. David was funny and Tony and Hunt were the sons of a famous comedian [Soupy Sales]. David and I went to the movies one day to see the Eddie Murphy movie *Coming to America*, and when we came out he said, "It's funnier in the studio."

The Sales brothers were loose cannons, and it was hard to do anything serious when they were around. I suggested that the songwriting credits remain the songwriting credits, but that we should split the publishing four ways, because things do evolve in the studio. We had a voting structure, and because the Sales brothers would probably vote together, I suggested that on any issue, David had two votes. We were a four-piece band with five votes. Matt Resnicoff, who was a senior editor at *Musician* magazine said, "Oh, I get it. You and David are like the left and right hand side of the brain, and Hunt and Tony are the two testicles."

Tin Machine taught me that rock and roll has to exist beneath the waist. David said at one point, "It's OK now in the studio, but just wait until we go public, and we step outside. When we're in the world of the press, don't be shocked. Because it's going to go all lopsided." He was aware of that. The first thing I saw when I went to visit him for the first time in Switzerland was his rejection letter from RCA when he had given them *Low*. He had had it framed. He knew it was going to be rough. He used to say that being famous was good for pulling rank, for getting free stuff and for getting a good table in a restaurant or tickets for a show. He told me when we started that he had already booked to do the *Sound+Vision* tour and that he would have to take a year off, but that he would come back to Tin Machine, which is what he did. In some respects you could say that we anticipated grunge. After the second album we put out a live album that was a limited edition—limited to what we sold.

KEVIN ARMSTRONG: Having worked with David on "Absolute Beginners," I got a call to go and work on an Iggy Pop record, another one that David was doing for him. He was his great benefactor. On *Blah Blah Blah* David was in the studio with a clipboard. He was the executive of that record because Jim didn't have a record deal at that time, and it was Bowie's attempt to give Iggy's career a lift.

JULIEN TEMPLE: We hung out a lot in the '80s, and spent quite a lot of time together in L.A. After the failure of *Absolute Beginners* I couldn't work in England anymore, as no one would give me financing, so I moved to L.A. to try and work on projects there. We saw a lot of each other there, and would have these big Sunday lunches. David seemed to be obsessed with L.A., with the seamier side of it, and loved telling me things he'd heard, things he'd either read or discovered. He had all these L.A. stories that he loved to tell. I stopped seeing him after he wanted me to direct a video, and as I couldn't do it I asked one of the young directors who worked for my production company to do it instead. Anyway, it didn't work out, and the relationship faltered, although he later became very active on email.

DAVE STEWART: We hung out a lot during the '80s, especially when we were in New York, which I think is where we first met—at a Big Audio Dynamite concert, at the Ritz. I was staying in Mick Jagger's brownstone at the time, and David would often come round for dinner. We were both in London at the end of the decade, and we were out somewhere and he asked if I wanted to go back to his flat and listen to his new record. He'd just recorded it and was obviously very enthusiastic about it. Once we were there we just started talking about music, especially Stax, the blues, and R&B, and he had an almost encyclopedic knowledge of the blues. I knew he knew a lot about soul music, but I had no idea he knew so much about the blues. He had obviously studied it. He always played his cards quite close to his chest, and I don't blame him, in most situations, but he had a tremendous sense of humor when he wasn't being guarded. He was sharp as a razor. He played me the Tin Machine songs a few months before they came out, which was a bit difficult, because they weren't actually that good. It was a bit like when a woman asks you how old you think she is, and you always try and take at least five years off. So when he asked me what I thought of them I had to be a bit more enthusiastic than I wanted to be. I suddenly had to be very diplomatic. Most artists are so sensitive and you can crush them in seconds. Bowie was the same. He only listened to the criticism. All the praise went by the wayside. It was in his nature. In that respect he was just like Damien Hirst. I think I told him I wasn't sure it was what he should be doing, and was perhaps less complimentary than I normally would have been. If you dig within it there are some good songs, but it's not a good record. He lost a few people with that record, and he certainly lost me. It was obvious he wanted to be in a band again, but the production, the sound, it wasn't where it should have been. We lost Bowie during this point.

TONY PARSONS: When my first marriage broke up, and I became a single parent, he was the only single parent that I knew. He carried that quite lightly, but a lot of our private conversations were about fatherhood. I know he was incredibly proud about "Joe" as he called him, and he must have got a PhD, because I can remember him saying to me, "My son's a doctor, I can't believe it." He was a role model for me as a single father, because I didn't know if I could do it, and it was completely unexpected to be this young, twenty-nine-year-old journalist suddenly bringing up a four-year-old kid by myself. And the only person I knew who had done it was David Bowie, whose son looked like my little mop-haired Muppet.

He phoned me from Heathrow once, I think he was going back to

Switzerland, just to have a chat, just to see how I was, just to touch base. And he had me on his side for life after that. He had a great capacity for kindness. I remember him playing keyboards for Iggy Pop, and thinking how low key he was about it. I knew Iggy Pop pretty well, and Iggy would have been a drooling junky in a gutter without David Bowie, he really would. And Lou Reed too. So he could transform careers, change lives. I think he had the genius of making you love him. But it didn't feel like hypnotizing chickens, it didn't feel like a cheap trick. It felt real, and I think he had a lot of empathy in him, and curiosity. So it wasn't manipulative, that "I want this person to be on my side, and I can get them to do that." I think he had a genuine love and interest in people. I think he saw surrounding himself with friends as a way of being grounded, connected with people. I think he did have that real fear of ending up like his brother. And he said that more than once, "People say, 'My family's mad,' and mine really were." He helped more people than anybody, like Lulu, Lou Reed, Iggy, Mott the Hoople. He did have this ability to insist, "I'm not a star at this moment." I remember being in the Ivy with him one Saturday night, and it was absolutely packed, and people were looking for famous people, were literally craning their necks to look around this diffident Englishman in a blue suit. They were looking past him in the hope of seeing [comedians] Ant & Dec or something. And he had that actor-like ability to play it cool when he wanted, to just disappear.

JULIEN TEMPLE: He didn't talk about his parents much, and there didn't appear to be much love lost between them. I remember he said once that they hadn't been there for him, but I think maybe he was slightly embarrassed about them in a way. He came from quite humble origins, and although he never played on this, and rarely wrote about it, when he sang John Lennon's "Working Class Hero" on the *Tin Machine* album he did it with such ferocity that you could tell it was sung with real emotion. Everything he had achieved in life he had achieved himself, and he slightly resented his parents for not being able to give him more of a start in life. He was extraordinarily well read, but then he was an autodidact. David really enjoyed his own mind, and he really enjoyed what he could do with it, really enjoyed the places it could take him and the things he could do with it when he got there.

DAVID BOWIE: Did I care that no one liked Tin Machine? I got my first real hatchet job on *Aladdin Sane* in 1973, so I've not really expected much else [since then]. With *Never Let Me Down* I knew that I wanted something I could tour with on a very ground roots level. I wanted something that would work well with a small band. So it had to logistically be a five-piece-band kind of music. I wrote small but energetically. I don't think I actually strayed any closer to the mainstream, I just think that my music [became] mainstream. I'd like to think of it that way. I think *Let's Dance* was probably the most commercial. But I don't think *Never Let Me Down* was intended to be inherently commercial. Otherwise I'd have been doing another *Let's Dance.* Hits are not something I've gone for either. Dylan, the Rolling Stones, myself, John Lennon, none of us really sold albums, far fewer albums than people would imagine. The big sellers were always bands like Foreigner, Heart, the kind of bands you couldn't put a face to, they always sold masses and masses. There are a lot of us out there who were maybe musically pretty important, but actually didn't sell vast amounts of albums. I was always quite happy with the amount I sold up until *Let's Dance*, and when *Let's Dance* happened I was delighted to say the least. That was the watershed.

HUGH PADGHAM: When we were recording with Tin Machine he took me out to dinner every night. He was so nice. I've read that he had a nasty side, and he certainly treated the Spiders quite shoddily, but I never saw that.

PAUL MCGUINNESS: I saw Tin Machine in Dublin, and I didn't like that very much. They played a bar called the Baggot Inn I think. They were very aggressive, a sort of avant-garde thrash metal band. I always got the impression he was somehow kept prisoner in the band by the Sales brothers, as he didn't seem to be enjoying it very much. I'm sure he wasn't a prisoner, and was no doubt completely in charge, but it didn't show, and the music was pretty terrible.

JOHN GIDDINGS: Tin Machine were doing a sound check at Wolverhampton Civic Hall and there were all these women quieting up outside waiting for the gig to start. The noise coming from the venue was terrible, as they were so loud, and they really only had one good song—"Bus Stop." They were even louder than the Ramones, and I eventually had to go and ask them to turn it down. David said that I was the only person who had *ever* asked him to turn his music down. It was the women I felt sorry for, as all they wanted to do was dance around their handbags to "Ziggy Stardust."

TONY PARSONS: I interviewed him when he was launching Tin Machine. I went to Dublin, and because the record company had made such a fuss about treating them like a band, I interviewed all the others first. Which meant that by the time I got to Bowie he was gagging to talk. Of course the Sales brothers, these tattooed thickos, didn't really have much to say for themselves, so it was a relief when Bowie took over.

HARVEY GOLDSMITH: I did a couple of Tin Machine dates, and he was just experimenting. He told me he knew people weren't going to like it, but he did it anyway. He knew it wasn't what everybody wanted, but he didn't care. And people certainly didn't like it.

NICK KENT: Tony Sales, the bass player of Tin Machine, got into a very bad car crash. He was in the hospital for ages, and really messed himself up. And he didn't have any medical insurance. He had over $100,000 worth of operations, and David Bowie paid the lot. He was generous, and it gives you an idea of what he was like. You hear a lot of scuttlebutt about Bowie, but this stuff is important. That was an act of kindness. Self-interest is the religion of the music business, but not with Bowie.

GEORGE UNDERWOOD: He paid for Mick Rock's heart bypass, which is something he obviously didn't broadcast.

MARIANNE FAITHFULL: We became friends again much later, when he came to Ireland and came to see me in Shell Cottage, and we had a lovely time. He appreciated the Weimar period. Otto Dix and George Grosz and all that . . . very decadent. This was during the time he was working with that funny band Tin Machine, that I thought were really terrible I must say. But it brought David to Ireland and I went to see him and I went to their gigs and everything, and we became friends again and it was very nice. He had got really healthy and he wasn't putting on any of the acts anymore, as far as I could see. I think because he'd made it, you know, he didn't need that rubbish. I understand that people want to sort of put things on and pretend to be this and pretend to be that and all the other, but it's not really what I like. That's all. But I don't think he would have reached the success he had without the act. I think he had to do all those funny things. He was a normal person by then, or reasonably normal anyway. He didn't look weird anymore. But I remember he talked about his brother. He was pretty upset, he felt bad about it.

TONY MCGEE: So in 1989 it was really good to see him again after six years. Of course, I respected his work as he was a perfectionist and never seemed to be satisfied. He loved his mind and he loved the capability of himself. And he loved the curiosity and the investigation. I really saw the humanist side of him at this point. David was preparing for the *Sound+Vision* tour and wanted to do some pictures at the Rainbow Theatre in Finsbury Park, where he'd once played as Ziggy. It was derelict at the time, and was full of down-and-out men. Tramps, people who drink on the street. There must have been a hundred of them in there when we started shooting. The noise and the flashes obviously attracted some attention, and I felt the presence of a few people and I thought it was just maybe the night watchman. And then suddenly I looked and there were about forty tramps who recognized David and started to heckle him and tease him. They referred to some of the photographs we had projected behind him, and one of them said, "Why is it that you are no longer as good-looking as those pictures behind you?" And he laughed and put his hand to his mouth and did this little mime. He charmed them all. He'd changed, though, and looked weathered. He didn't look as fresh as he had been before the Serious Moonlight Tour with the tanned face with blond hair. I think he may have somehow had a hard time during the time I hadn't seen him. He would stare off into the distance, but then he would snap out of it and play to the camera. He'd just drop his chin and then suddenly he was on. He took some pictures himself that day. I've never seen any photographs he took, but I bet he was good, as he knew everything about taking a picture, everything. That day Coco had told me that on no condition was I to go out with him later, but then at the end of the shoot he asked me what I was doing. When I told him I was going home he asked me to go out with him, "Just for one." So we went down to Café de Paris in Leicester Square. It was bedlam just getting him from the car to the door. People were just throwing themselves on him. We went inside and of course the guy running the club, Nick Fry—who used to be one of my assistants—sits us at the circular table literally as you go in just on the right, overlooking the dance floor. Bono and U2 arrived within half an hour, with the photographer Anton Corbijn. Then Leee John, the guy with Imagination. There was a whole crowd. And David was getting very much the worse for wear. I went outside and told the driver to get him out of there. He was gone. Drinking too much.

11

IT'S CONFUSING THESE DAYS

1990–1999

IMAN MOHAMED ABDULMAJID (MODEL, ENTREPRENEUR): I found my soul mate. I had no intention of getting married again, ever. No. And somebody in music? Never. Like a hole in the head . . . I was not ready for a relationship. Definitely I didn't want to get into a relationship with somebody like him. But as I always said: I fell in love with David Jones, I did not fall in love with David Bowie. I remember once we went out to dinner and the laces on my trainers came undone. And David was down on his knees in the middle of the street, tying them for me. I thought to myself, This one's a keeper. His actions spoke louder [than words]. We were dating for two weeks and I was coming from Paris to L.A. and at the airport, the doors open to the plane and I come out and I see all these people taking a picture of somebody. And he was standing there, flowers in hand, no security. He didn't care if anyone saw.

HANIF KUREISHI: He was really in love. I think this was the first time he'd ever *really* been in love. With Iman he was really committed to the relationship. In a way, the most interesting thing about his later life was that this Bromley boy was in love with a Muslim from Africa. She was a model, she was fashionable, she knew everybody, but ultimately she was from Africa. To us she was glamorous and all that but she spent years in Somalia, and that would have made her different to most people she would have known. So that seemed to me to be an extraordinary relationship. But he never talked about that.

However, I do remember her having a row with Salman Rushdie. I had a dinner for a novel I'd written, *The Black Album*, which was partly about Muslim fundamentalists. In those days you had these huge fucking launch dinners that would go on for hours and hours in places like the Ivy. At this one, Paul Smith was there, Bowie was there, Iman was there, and Rushdie was there. I put Rushdie and Iman next to each other thinking they would get along. And Iman got really shirty about *The Satanic Verses*. And that quite surprised me—I wish I'd remembered or written notes, because they really had a go at each other. I thought, Well she's a Muslim from Somalia, but she's also with a pop star who is one of the most liberated people you could imagine. So why would she have a go at someone for writing *The Satanic Verses*? I thought that was quite interesting, as she was obviously quite complex. I think that's the bit of him that people don't think to talk about.

BRIAN MOLKO (MUSICIAN): We used to joke about it in the band, we wanted to find out what pills Bowie was on. Because we wanted them too, because he seemed so happy. I think the stability he found with Iman was a major part of that. It was beautiful to watch them together. Iman has this regal presence about her, she glides into the room, but seeing them together was like seeing two teenagers in love. It's impossible not to lose your temper every now and again, when you're operating at such a high speed as he was at that time, but he seemed at peace and very comfortable in his own skin. Which was an amazing thing to achieve, because it's a kind of transcendence, really. And I know from firsthand experience that that's what you're seeking through alcohol and drugs. You're seeking transcendence. He found it somehow. He certainly kept a watchful eye on me. He recognized certain traits that I had, certain behaviors that I had. He would just mention it every now and again like, "I was worried about you that night—are you sure you're OK?" Avuncular in that sense. Looking back, I really appreciate that. There was no narcissism about David. Perhaps in the drug years, but not when I knew him. A narcissist makes every conversation, every exchange, about himself, but David was genuinely interested in other people, because I think he felt he still had a lot to learn.

HUGH PADGHAM: I saw him in New York shortly after he'd met Iman, and I remember the chat being unbelievably quick and succinct, because she was waiting in the office next door and he couldn't bear to be away from her for more than a few seconds. She was unbelievably beautiful, in this long fur coat wrapped around her.

JOHN GIDDINGS: Iman was really good for David, as she made him happy. You could see it in their eyes.

Iman Mohamed Abdulmajid, mononymously known as Iman ("faith" in Arabic), was born in July 1955 in Mogadishu, in Somalia. Her father was a diplomat and a former ambassador to Saudi Arabia, while her late mother was a gynecologist. Educated at boarding school in Egypt, she later studied political science at university in Kenya. When she was eighteen she was briefly married to a Somali hotel executive, before being discovered by the American photographer Peter Beard on the streets of Nairobi. Her first significant modeling assignment was for American Vogue *in 1976.*

PETER BEARD (PHOTOGRAPHER): I was driving down Standard Street in Nairobi—and this is the total truth, because we invented a more glamorous story for our mutual interests—with Kamante, Karen Blixen's ex-employee. Kamante and I were just going to have lunch. This was March of '75 in the usual stress and density of "Nairobbery," the most clogged-up, ex-colonial nightmare of all time. This amazing Somali girl was striding down the street, and I just said, "Kamante, look at that amazing sight, in the middle of Nairobbery." And he said, "Oh yeah, I've seen her before." She had the original Somali dress. Africans have not lost that ability to walk, which we have. So we parked our Land Rover and went into the New Stanley Hotel. And who should be walking into the New Stanley? I just went up to her and said, "I hope you're not going to let all these aesthetics go to waste. Don't you think we should just record some of it on film? Get you into the world of visual 'communication'?" Of course, like every African she was desperate to get out of Africa. So we had a nice conversation. And Wilhelmina [Cooper, the New York model agent] was a great friend of mine. So I could just nail her right into Wilhelmina's agency. Wilhelmina, sight-unseen, took Iman.

ANNA HARVEY (FORMER EDITOR AT BRITISH *VOGUE*): One became aware of Iman in the late '70s, when she started modeling for all the big houses. She was modeling first for Yves Saint Laurent, which in those days was quite a rarity. Back then you didn't have many women of color walking for the big designers. Beverly Johnson was the first black model on the cover of American *Vogue*, and that wasn't until 1974. This was the heyday of Saint Laurent, when he started having a more multicultural catwalk. There were various others, like Pat Cleveland, Billie Blair, Grace Jones, and Mounia, but for some reason Iman was the one who stood out. Saint Laurent liked striking black models, as they looked wonderful in his clothes, but because Iman was Somalian, she had a completely different look. Very refined. Quite European in a way. Aristocratic.

She was very dignified and was quite unlike any of the models at the time. She kept herself to herself, and was very proper. She wasn't aloof, just quiet. She had such presence, and had a peace about her. She wasn't demanding or too opinionated. Didn't have much conversation, but was very charming. She didn't gossip with the crew or the other models; she just got on with it. Her success certainly hadn't gone to her head, even though she was married to this very successful American basketball player, Spencer Haywood. Eric [a photographer] said that Iman was boldly ethnic, and made the other girls feel underprivileged not to be from Africa. She was actually quite inscrutable.

GEORGE UNDERWOOD: You'd never know who you would end up meeting when you went on holiday with David. You could be in Europe, or in Mustique, or the US, but you never knew who you were going to be with. He bought a boat once and invited us down to stay on it, and said he had a few people coming for lunch the next day. This was down in Cap d'Antibe. First on the boat was Michael Caine, then Robin Williams, Eric Idle, Steve Martin, and us. Michael Caine took one look at the boat and said, "I think I'm in the wrong business."

TOMMY HILFIGER: I first met David at a fashion function in New York, raising money for AIDS at the Armory Show. We sat next to each other and had a long talk. I'd just come back from Mustique, and we were chatting about the island, because he had just started to build his home there.

This was in 1989. It was called Mandalay—six acres, five bedrooms. Then a few years later, in the early '90s, just after the house was finished, he invited me for a New Year's Eve party. I was building my own house, and renting a house next to Mick Jagger's. David's home was magnificent, overlooking Britannia Bay. He had commissioned Arne Hasselqvist, a Swede who had also built houses for Mick and Princess Margaret. He also built my house. It was Balinesian and impeccable, and the interior was done by the Bali-based designer Linda Garland. Arne said David was the most meticulous person he'd ever met. Everything was done in deep, dark mahogany, with a lot of hand carving. All of the hand carvings were symmetrical, and all of the hinges on all of the doors were neatly lined up, the mosquito nets were all knotted in exactly the same way, it was almost OCD. On the night of the party, he and Iman answered the door, and they were dressed in '70s rock gear. They both had platforms on; he was wearing a bellbottom jumpsuit and an orange shag wig. The theme was disco. There was a DJ, a reggae band, a great night.

A year later we were both going down to Mustique at the same time, and I'd chartered a jet and asked David if he wanted to join me. I didn't realize he was afraid of flying, but he told me as we were in the car on the way to the airport. He actually said, "I'm really, *really* afraid of flying." He asked all these technical questions about the plane, and I could tell that he was nervous. So we boarded the aircraft, and he seemed OK until we took off, and he was holding on to the arm rests on the seat. He was almost white-knuckling it. But after we took off and went up into the air he was calm. It was a four-and-a-half-hour flight, so we got into a deep conversation. What I learned was at that time in his life, art was more important to him than music, not only as a collector but as an artist himself. He seemed obsessed with Charles Saatchi, and was quite interested in Damien Hirst. He knew art history like no one I had ever met. Rembrandt, Picasso, Basquiat, Haring, Miró, really informed. I thought I knew a little about contemporary art, but his knowledge of the Renaissance, of the Impressionists, of the art world in general, was incredibly impressive. He talked a lot about Warhol—Andy had taken me into his Factory in the '80s, and I was really impressed with him, so I knew him a little. I think David actually wanted to be Andy. He also told me that when he was living in New York in the '70s he was basically a recluse, holed up in his apartment on the Upper East Side, just creating art, for days at a time. I assume these were drug-fueled days, but when I was with him he was totally sober. He had an exhibition of his paintings around this time in Cork Street, in London, and I bought some of his art. I bought a series of five paintings—one is the moon, one is the stars, one is the sun, one is the earth, and one is death. It made me think that he had death on his mind for some reason. When I talked about music on that plane ride he said he never wanted to go back and play what he'd played before. He said, "That's the past." He wanted to move forward, and said that moving forward in life is more important than looking back. So he said he wanted to go into a studio with a bunch of talented musicians and just start playing. Unrehearsed, just play. He talked about Tin Machine too, and said he didn't care if they were popular or successful.

Spend any time on Mustique and you'll start to meet Bowie's ghost, whether it's in Basil's Bar, the waterfront dive bar where everyone on the island still congregates after dark (Bowie was a regular, and would occasionally get up to sing with whatever house band happened to be playing there; he would also refer to one of the house cocktails as a "Penis Colada"), or at the Cotton House, one of the island's two hotels, or indeed on one of the many beaches. When Bowie was on the island he tended to be extremely sociable, and even before he started coming with Iman, would spend his evenings carousing with the likes of Bryan Adams, Bryan Ferry, or Mick Jagger. He held parties, went to parties, and encouraged anyone he met to host one. He sang in the choir in the local Bamboo Church every Christmas, and even ventured out onto the ocean (he didn't learn to swim until 1980, and was never very confident in the water).

DAVID BOWIE: I went down to spend a couple of days with Mick and Jerry in their house [on Mustique], and while waiting for the boat—I was going to take a trip up and down the Caribbean and it never happened because the propeller fell out or something—I was stranded. And I just went scouting one day, having nothing better to do, there being little else to do there, I came across this area of land attached to Arne Hasselqvist's. And we talked about it, and I thought, Why not?

Arne was willing to sell, if the sister house to be built on the site matched in weight the house he'd built for himself. I could agree to that, but then what to do with it? I said to him, "Look, you've obviously been to the East, Arne. Have you ever been to Indonesia?" He'd had a romp through there, so he knew what I was talking about. He had an idea for the waters going into the pools and into the swimming pool. I wanted something as unlike the Caribbean as possible, because it's a fantasy island, Mustique. Everybody just builds a getaway from it all so they can get there and see the same people they see all around, but in a holiday situation.

BONO: In the early '90s he came to stay with us in Temple Hills in Dublin. Coco was saying, "Look, David's not great. He wants to stay the night, I'd rather he didn't. But look, if he insists on it I can't stop [him]. But don't worry if he turns up at the end of your bed in the middle of the night." And I was like, "What?" And she said, "Look, just whatever you do, don't be worried. He kind of goes on walkabout." Then I think she told me, "Whatever you do, just don't close the door on his bedroom." And of course I forgot to tell [my wife] Ali, and after the first breach, she was very sure she was closing the door! We had just had [our daughter] Jordan, and Ali was getting up to feed Jordan. And every time she'd get up, the door to Bowie's bedroom would be open, and she'd close it. So she'd seen he'd come. And she'd go in and see him and he'd still be there, with his little head sticking out of the bed. So she would close the door, then get up to feed Jordan and the door would be open again! So he was clearly walking around all night. But we were scared of visitation. But that stuff really enthused me to him, he was such a gorgeous guy. He was so slight. Before he stopped drinking, two beers and he was flying. So Ireland was not the right venue for him.

Another moment, he was over in Dublin and he called my friend Gavin Friday. And he said, "Gavin, are there any cool places to go out? What's this place the Docker? I've heard about it." And Gavin said, "That's where you know, U2 would go, it's round the corner from Windmill Lane, yeah we'd all kind of go there." And he said, "Yeah, I'd like to go to the Docker, can you pick me up?" So Gavin came to the hotel, and David said, "So where's your car?" and Gavin said, "You don't need a car, I came in a taxi." And David was like, "What?! How are we going to get there if we don't have a car?" And Gavin said, "Taxi!" So they went to the Docker pub, which is actually on the docks, because it's where dockers drink. It is not a themed bar. So he walked in thinking it would be lots of hipsters and whatever, and it's full of dockers! And he was like, "What is this! Is this where Bono hangs out all the time?" At this point, he was wearing an electric-blue suit. And he's dressed to go out. He's not low-key David, he's neon David coming to the Docker. And people are just like "Ahhh-hhh!" A while later, somebody shouts, "How do you know David Bowie is a queer?" And then he said, "Because he's with I-man!" So he had to be rescued and brought somewhere cooler. Which I don't think there was, in Dublin. We went to the Docker to get away from cool places.

When we relocated to Berlin—with his producer!—the homage couldn't have been more direct. And having the experience of playing him some of the results. I remember playing him "The Fly," and he said, "I think you should record it again." He didn't like the recording. And then it went to number one, and he said, "Oh, I got that wrong." I said, "No David, you didn't, it is messy. It could have been a more coherent piece of work, had we listened to you." He arrived on that occasion, as we were mixing *Achtung Baby*, dressed in a kind of naval uniform. We started laughing and we said, "What are you doing?" And he said, "I have a boat!" And we said he was playing at being a superstar. He didn't really like it. I met him later and he said [that period] had been a bit of a mistake. He was trying on different personas, and that for me is just so much more interesting as an artist than the otherworldliness. When he finally got one of those characters right and became it as a method actor would, you just thought, Wow, where did he come up with that from? The answer is, trying out lots of others along the way! And he really tried out lots of different David Bowies. That's sort of wonderful for other artists, I think that should be a real encouragement. He didn't arrive properly formed.

I have a theory about "David Bowie, the missing years," and it applies to all of us actually, not just David. People as brilliant as David Bowie are often creatures of a theme. So even though we think of them as completely out on their own, they depend on a phenomenon that Woody Allen calls osmosis. As high as his IQ was, he needed to stay around very bright people, to stay that luminous. And it's not actually written about a lot, but Woody Allen has written about it, which is to say that it might have been a mistake for him to live in Switzerland. And I did say, Look, David, you are where you eat. I think as much as he loved the physical beauty of Switzerland, I think he needed and depended on scenes, whether it was London, Berlin, or New York, finally. You can be as clever as you want to be, but it's the cleverness of the people around you that you sort of thrive on. So I think that was part of the problem, and I think he got a little lost and a little lonely. And it's a painful embarrassment for me now that he's gone, that I realized that on occasion I think I squandered an opportunity to know him more. He used to call me more. And I didn't realize what was going on. Now I think I understand he was quite lost in that period, and I think it went on for quite a while. By the time he sort of [retired] . . . you know I would email with him. Towards the end, occasionally he would write a response, but he wasn't that interested in my company over the last years. I felt that maybe if I had been more attentive when he needed that company, maybe I would have been a better friend. He could be fractious, and I think that brittleness came from real vulnerability. So I suppose what I'm saying to you is, I'm not sure I was sensitive or subtle enough to spot just how raw he was in those years that he felt estranged from a scene.

REEVES GABRELS: Tin Machine sort of disappeared. We didn't have a meeting about it, but it just collapsed. There were a few personality issues, and I think at one point David realized that he could just go back to being David Bowie. He didn't exactly say, "Fuck this, I'm going back to my other career . . ." but . . . after Tin Machine he got back together with Nile, because even though we sold something like two million records, we were a failure. I think there was some external pressure to do *Let's Dance 2*.

Tin Machine officially ended when Bowie shaved off the beard he had grown for the project. One night he had arranged to go out with Nick Rhodes, from Duran Duran. Rhodes joked that he didn't really want to go out with him if he was determined to keep his beard. "So it came off there, and then, in my sink," says Rhodes. "David shaved it off himself immediately. And that was the end of Tin Machine."

ADRIAN BELEW: I played guitar on the *Sound+Vision* tour, which David thought would be the last rendering of his hits, although it didn't turn out that way. Twenty-seven countries, 108 shows, and a lot of material. You get close on a tour of that length, we had a private plane for much of it, and you get into a kind of bubble. You're at breakfast, dinner, out at a museum, hanging out. When I first met him in 1978 he still had a buffer zone of people around him, but by 1990 he was far more comfortable with himself, he was much more of a down-to-earth person, if you can say that about him—for someone with such an eye for sophistication and art you can't really say he was down-to-earth, but he kind of was. On that particular tour he was one of the guys. However there was always an aura around him, and everything was first-class, both literally and metaphorically. You were made to feel as though you were part of something important and big, which you were. This was the highest level a touring musician can ever reach. For a couple of years afterwards we had an email relationship, and the thing I noticed was that he always responded immediately. He must have really loved his computer.

OLIVER JAMES: A friend of mine who was a coke dealer met Bowie in the early '90s and he hoovered up huge amounts of coke, so much that my friend, who is kind of an expert on this stuff, said that he must have been doing some other drugs to protect him from the effect. Because if you took that amount of coke in one go, it could potentially kill you. He must have had some other drugs in him before he took those drugs, because he was doing so much of them. This was just before Iman, of course.

ERDAL KIZILÇAY (GUITARIST): I was on the *Sound+Vision* tour, although I didn't love it. I don't think any of the band did, because we were hidden off the side of the stage. If you didn't know we were there, you couldn't tell from looking at the stage, as we were invisible and the band wasn't that important to the show. One night in Canada David walked across the stage during "Jean Genie" and started waving at me, and I thought he was beckoning me to walk towards him. So I started following him. Normally we wouldn't have done this because we were told to keep behind the screen, but David was calling me out so I went to follow him. Halfway through the song he threw his brand-new Gibson and smashed it onto the floor, and stormed off. And that was the end of the gig. Backstage, David took his shirt off, threw it at me and then screamed, "Erdal, take my shirt and next time why don't you sing in my place!" Then he left. So that night I decided to leave the tour. Half an hour later one of the security guys asked me to go and see David in his plane before it was due to take off. He said, "Erdal, I've spent eleven million fucking dollars on this show, and if I need a dancer I can find a better one than you. And if you're not happy you can just fuck off." I tried to explain it to him—that it was a mistake—but he wasn't interested. So the next day I called my manager and said I was going to finish the tour, but then David invited me to dinner in his suite that night, and we talked it out. Then we went out to a jazz club to see Courtney Pine and we never talked about it again. What we did talk about was the jazz album he was going to make next; he wanted to call it *Black Tie White Noise.* But it didn't turn out to be a jazz album at all.

TONY PARSONS: I didn't meet him properly until the late '80s, and then when *Arena* [magazine] were planning their huge Bowie special in 1992, 1993, I saw him a lot during a short period of time. *Arena* was really the dry run for the Victoria & Albert exhibition. I just found him fantastically easy to interview, and easy to be around. He had that social intelligence, which was quite unusual in a musician, because what social intelligence meant to most of the bands I'd interviewed was staying up all night taking drugs, drinking yourself into oblivion, and trying to have sex with some willing stranger in some miserable Holiday Inn in Philadelphia or Birmingham. But Bowie was different, maybe because we were both older by then. But it was never staged, it was never cozy, it was never dull. You'd go out for dinner and then he'd say, "Right, there's a couple of clubs I want to check out," and these were, like, little holes in the wall—here today, gone tomorrow places. But he had an endless curiosity about what was happening, because every artist is a cannibal, and you need to feed that music. So we would go out, and tour around in a limo. Coco would get out of the car and go to the door and say, "David Bowie is in that car right there," and it would be like the Red Sea being parted by Moses. He would be just charming to everybody, and people young enough to be his son or daughter would be happy to see him. And he was incredibly well mannered, the only musician I've ever met who's helped me into my coat, the only musician I've met who I've seen wearing a suit in the studio. It did feel to me as though he was clinging to normality. He realized that after the screaming madness of the mid-'70s, he needed to keep alive, to stay alive. So that was why he kept in touch with old friends, why he kept in contact with people you wouldn't necessarily think he would, school friends, people from way back, the guy that damaged his eye. He wanted to be surrounded by people—Antony Price, one of Duran Duran, whoever. It was what I imagine hanging out with David Niven was like.

He seemed to have very intense relationships for two or three years. My time was the early '90s, after that *Arena* thing, and he suggested to me that I could write the book on him, the big book, the autobiography. And he said, "But I want you to devote three years to it full-time." I was flattered with the idea of doing the book, but there was no way I could spend three years doing it. I mean *Man and Boy* didn't take me three years; there was no way that I was going to spend that on one book. I was also aware that you're in a court, really. His old friends would say to me, "You saw David at the weekend. I didn't even know he was in London." And it would become a thing that you had spent time with the great man and they hadn't known about it. I never really enjoyed that. I loved spending time with him, and I felt incredibly privileged and honored to have spent time with him, and it was fun, and it was interesting. But if you wanted to stay long term you had to be part of a court, and I wasn't interested. I think a lot of people had those two or three intense years, and then he just drifted away—he was geographically somewhere else, artistically somewhere else. And that's fine, that's fair enough.

KATHRYN FLETT (JOURNALIST AND FORMER EDITOR OF ARENA): I remember the day distinctly, as it was Bill Clinton's inauguration, January 20, 1993. We had breakfast in a rehearsal studio above a shop somewhere in Primrose Hill, in north London. We had been planning this mammoth issue of *Arena*, dedicated completely to David, and co-edited by him. Tony Parsons had already done his big interview, Charles Shaar Murray had filed his big think piece, and Robin Derrick had flown off to Switzerland to have a look at all the costumes Bowie had at his house. Bowie had basically opened up his address book, and contacted lots of friends, acquaintances, and musicians, and asked them all to accept our telephone calls and faxes. I said to David's PR, Alan Edwards, that it felt a bit odd to have commissioned all of this material and to be so closely involved and to not actually have met the great man. So Alan kindly set up a meeting, which was very nice of him. I remember what I was wearing because this was an important day for me; I was dressed head-to-toe in Jean-Paul Gaultier, and a hat, and David was wearing . . . a suit! Tony Parsons was there, as was Alan, and as soon as I walked in Bowie came up to me and said, "Hello, I'm David," just in case there was any doubt about the matter. I said, "Yes, you definitely are." He was blond and tanned, but not blond and tanned in an ironic way, like he had been during Serious Moonlight. He was the very model of handsomeness, and he looked how any forty-six-year-old man would love to look. His hair was faultless, and it almost came into the room before he did. He had perfect *"Heroes"* hair. Unsurprisingly he was incredibly charming, and you knew that he was giving you the David Bowie that you wanted. I got the sense that I was being given a performance that totally reflected my expectations. The experience was so perfect that after meeting him I never wanted to meet him again, just in case it wasn't quite as good as it had been the first time. He seemed like a boy from the 'burbs, not an "other." So we had our coffee and croissant, and we then started rifling through all these boxes of photographs that he had brought along, photos of his friends, family, recording sessions, holidays, the lot. He had so much ephemera it was extraordinary. He even had these electromagnetic pictures of his brain that he'd commissioned to show all the holes he'd created through his chronic cocaine abuse in the '70s. After about ninety minutes a courier arrived, with the contact sheets of the Nick Knight portraits David had commissioned for the cover of *Black Tie White Noise.* He showed them to me, and asked me to pick one. I said because of the new CD size of albums that you really needed as much eye contact as possible, like you do on a magazine. He was almost certainly just being polite, but he appeared to agree with me, and that was the image that went on the cover. I later found out that Nick Knight's idea was to have an image on the cover that was Bowie's face mirrored down the middle—so the front would be the two right sides of his face, and the back would have been the two left sides.

HUGH THOMSON (WRITER, DIRECTOR): In 1993 the BBC decided they were going to try and do the whole history of rock and roll over ten hours of television—*Dancing in the Street*—and spend a lot of money: five million quid, which in the early '90s was a lot of money, so they really planned it very carefully. For complicated reasons I ended up both producing the series and directing quite a few of the programs, so it became sort of my baby. I found myself in the position of going around and interviewing all the musicians, including Bowie. There was very much of a sense that to get this to work you had to get big names, and people would only agree to be interviewed if they knew that certain other people had been interviewed. We knew if we had Bowie then everyone else would follow. For the interview we ended up building him this very elaborate set that was modeled on the room at the end of *2001: A Space Odyssey*, a sort of mock Georgian room, very strange and unsettling. Having already talked to several other musicians for the series, I knew that Bowie did engage with you as though it was a genuine conversation. Charm can be a shallow commodity, but Bowie had that charm of genuine interest and engagement. He was a listener. During the interview he talked a lot about the anonymity of the suburbs, and about being able to then become whoever you wanted when you escaped them. He was an incredibly sophisticated and worldly and cosmopolitan person but quite often he reminded me of a smart sixth-form kid, the one who's masking his insecurities with a lot of knowing references. He was also surprisingly bitchy, particularly bitchy about Tony Visconti.

AVA CHERRY: I went to their engagement party in New York. At the time I was a sort of lightweight friend with Iman, not a deep friend, and we used to hang out. At the party she walked over to me from the middle of the room. And she goes, "Ava, look at this engagement ring that David just gave me." And I was like, "Oh, congratulations Iman, congratulations to both of you. I wish you all the happiness." I wondered why she did that but I think it was because she was aware that I was there first.

BRIAN ARIS: So this was April 1992. I'd met David at Live Aid, when I was shooting pictures backstage. Then Bob [Geldof] married Paula [Yates] and they asked me to do the wedding, at that time when magazines like *Hello* and *OK!* were beginning to sign up stars when they got married. David was one of the guests at the wedding, and so we met again. Then Alan Edwards, David's long-term PR, asked me to do David's wedding. The first thing he said was the problem we were going to have with the paps, as the wedding was going to be in Italy, in Florence, the home of the paps. My heart sank, because I was proud that no one had ever taken a rogue picture at any of the celebrity weddings I had done. There had already been a rumor that the wedding was going to be in Mustique, which had thrown a lot of people off, but that didn't last long. After a while everyone knew it was going to be in Italy. Everyone knew in Italy. The service was going to be at the St. James Episcopal Church, and Alan and I went over early to try and figure a way of keeping the photographers out. They had already married in a civil ceremony in Lausanne, but this was the big service. We had put small trees on the terrace of the villa where they were due to stay, but the church was the real problem. It faced a whole row of houses and apartments, so anyone with a long lens could get a picture. You just knew that every window would be full of long lenses. I suggested that the ideal way to protect the process was to drape the church, so that cars could drive underneath it. Which is what we did. We constructed a cabling system, and then dropped the drapes just as the car arrived. It was hysterical. All the paps were in place but they couldn't get any pictures. But as David and Iman left the church after the service, a flash went off. Back at the villa I went up to Alan and the first thing he said to me was, "There was a flash." So we got the seating plan and worked out where it came from, and who it was. It came from one of two aisles, and as we were looking at it, we both said the same name almost at once. Alan said we needed to tell David, so that's exactly what we did. We went upstairs, knocked on his bedroom door, and David came out in his dress trousers and said, "A flash went off." We told him who we thought it was, and to our horror he said, "Right, let's deal with it," and went off in search of the culprit. We weren't sure, and just hoped we had got the right person. We walked all the way through the reception, and eventually found the guy sitting on a coach. He still had his topcoat on, so we figured it was probably him. David strode over, held out his hand and said, "Camera. Now." There was silence, and he said it again: "Give me the camera, now." And the guy stood up and gave David the camera, who tore the film out and said, "Get out of my wedding." And that was that. There was also a policeman who had a camera, but the picture he took was meaningless, and only published in a local paper. It was a relatively small wedding. David's mother was obviously there, as was his son, Joe, who was best man. Iman's family were there, and the guests included Yoko Ono, Brian Eno,

Bono, Eric Idle—Joe's godfather—Thierry Mugler, who made David's suit. Geoff MacCormack read Psalm 121, and David's cousin Kristina read something from Corinthians. It was very intimate, a special wedding.

NILE RODGERS: I thought I probably would have been his first choice for *Tonight*, but that didn't happen. I didn't work with him again until Live Aid, where I did "Dancing in the Street" and then I did a film called *Cool World*. Then I produced *Black Tie White Noise*, his wedding album. He was really different on that record because it was David steering the ship. It was more his vision, whereas on *Let's Dance* he showed me his vision and allowed me to interpret it. With *Black Tie White Noise* it was more "This is what I want to do." When I played the solo on the song "Miracle Goodnight" he even told me how I should approach it, which was weird, because usually you let the artist play. He said, "Nile, I want you to play this solo as if the '50s never existed." No Blue Note, no Chuck Berry, no Little Richard, no James Brown. So I played like Les Paul.

KEVIN DAVIES (PHOTOGRAPHER): This time around it was all about the saxophone. That was the idea for the shoot. That was the concept—a black suit, an undone bow tie, and a saxophone. I was doing the press pictures for *Black Tie White Noise*, at Metro Studios in Clerkenwell, and it was a very tight brief. Any opportunity he had, he would talk to the younger people on the shoot. Makeup artist, hairdresser, stylist, asking them what clubs they went to, what they were listening to. He was absorbing it, like a sponge. Very good at making people feel relaxed. He seemed to respect people. Didn't act like a star in any way.

STERLING CAMPBELL (DRUMMER): It was a chance meeting. Dennis Davis lived in the same building as me, on the Upper West Side, and I passed him in the lobby and he gave me a ticket for a Bowie show he was doing later that day at Madison Square Garden. I was fourteen. This was the *"Heroes"* tour, 1978. I had been playing drums for about three years, and here was Bowie's drummer giving me a ticket. He was so kind. Back then the Garden was like the mecca, and you had to be good to play there. You had to be Led Zeppelin, you had to be Stevie Wonder, you had to be the Who, you had to be Elton John. It was no joke. The idea of knowing someone who was playing there just blew my mind. At the time the only David Bowie song I really knew was "Fame," although at the show he was covering everything he'd done up until that point. The show was amazing, as it taught me where you could go with music, what the possibilities were.

We lived in a very liberal, arts-orientated part of the city, and lots of musicians lived in the area, including Miles Davis. There were five drummers in my building. And people tolerated it! I went to school with the sons of jazz musicians, like Gil Evans and Ron Carter. Once I got the buzz after seeing David, I'm like, I wanna be over at Dennis's place all the time. I was really into music, and at that time I didn't have the skill set, but Dennis helped me. He gave me the jazz-oriented mind-set, and David eventually gave me the European aesthetic. David was the ultimate casting director, mixing all these styles together. I saw David in 1978 and he already looked like he was in the '80s. You had ambient, funk, guitars, everything. When I left the concert at Madison Square Garden that night it was like I'd just seen *Star Wars*. So I became a drummer. I got my first break with Cyndi Lauper, then played with Duran Duran, Soul Asylum, and then in 1991 I started working with David. And stayed working with him for over a decade. I met him through Nile, who I knew, who got me involved with *Black Tie White Noise*. He'd just met Iman, he was happy, very welcoming, very encouraging. But I was prepared, as I'd wanted to work with him for ages. Even though it wasn't a successful record, nothing he wrote sounded like anything else. Dennis did six records with David, and so did I. David loved New York drummers.

DAVID QUANTICK (JOURNALIST): In 1993 there was little reason to expect that David Bowie might make a decent record. He'd just given the world, unasked, the sludgy group rock of Tin Machine, which had done nothing to cleanse the listener's palate after his '80s solo albums, which reached their nadir with 1987's *Never Let Me Down*. But the release of *Black Tie White Noise*, which reunited Bowie with Nile Rodgers, changed all that. Now it seemed that Tin Machine had existed solely to wipe away any memory of what Bowie himself called his "Phil Collins albums." Job done, Bowie was now free to pick up where he'd left off with *Scary Monsters*, the first of his records to actively look back over his own career and consolidate its many sounds.

Black Tie refers to many aspects of Bowie's career. Rodgers provides a more considered sound than the crash and glitz of the pair's previous collaboration, *Let's Dance.* Mick Ronson, who'd not worked with Bowie for almost twenty years, played on a cover of Cream's "I Feel Free," an old Spiders staple (it was sadly their last recording together, as Ronson died of cancer soon after). Another song covered here, the Walker Brothers' "Nite Flights," is one that directly influenced Bowie's own work with Eno; and that work is also referenced in the instrumental opener "The Wedding," which is named in tribute to Bowie's own wedding that year. And while the title track (featuring rapper Al B. Sure!) considered the recent L.A. Riots, the darkly beautiful single "Jump They Say" was a more personal effort, Bowie expressing his feelings concerning the death of his half-brother Terry.

All of this could have been something of a mishmash were it not for Bowie's immense confidence (his vocals had never been better) and Rodgers's sympathetic production. As an album, it was both a critical and commercial success (number one in the UK). As a statement of the next stage of Bowie's career, it was perfect. The '90s would be a decade of change and experimentation for Bowie, and *Black Tie White Noise* was the first step on his new journey.

Not everyone was so enamored of "Jump They Say." Bowie's estranged aunt Pat called it "macabre and pathetic," accusing her nephew of using Terry's suicide "to put his record in the charts." The image of Bowie's face upset her terribly as it looked "just like Terry did when he became schizophrenic."

DANA GILLESPIE: I saw Ronno when he was diagnosed with cancer in 1992, and he was still saddened by the fact that he still hadn't reconnected with David. He made up for it by appearing with Ronno at Freddie Mercury's memorial concert, when he performed the Lord's Prayer, and for Ronno there was some redemption, but not much.

CHARLES SHAAR MURRAY: What a lovely man Ronno was. He was one of the three or four nicest people I've ever met in the music business. Utterly guileless. And when I say that he was guileless, I don't mean to say that he was stupid or naïve, but was just this totally straightforward, straight-shooting guy. In a sense it was a really dumb idea to launch Ronno as a solo artist when David stepped down from the Spiders, because Ronson had everything necessary to be a big star except one thing. He had the looks, he had enormous musical talent, he could sing, he could play, he had stage presence, but what he didn't have was ego. Ronno was always happiest, always most himself, when he was helping other people to realize their ideas. When they had the Spiders, Bowie shared the stage with Ronson in a way he never did with anyone else. It was really like a Mick and Keith, a Plant and Page, or Joe Strummer and Mick Jones. The fans considered that it was David and Mick. After that it was David and a bunch of musicians at the back of the stage. He never shared as much stage space with anybody else ever again.

HARVEY GOLDSMITH: I loved Mick Ronson, he was a very special guy, and I don't know why Bowie didn't do the tribute concert in 1993, after he died. When they were together they were like Mick Jagger and Keith Richards, so tight. Neither would ever talk about the other, and when you mentioned Bowie to Mick, or Mick to David, they would just clam up. Something obviously happened and it was obviously extremely deep. They never talked about the breakup, and they never talked to each other either. I spent weeks on the road with both of them, and whenever their names came up, nothing.

MOBY (MUSICIAN, DJ): [In 1993] I was over at his [Bowie's] house and he gave me a present, the greatest present anyone has ever given me: the fedora that he wore in *The Man Who Fell to Earth*. And on the inside of the brim it said: "To Moby, Love David." I felt like I'd been given the Holy Grail, because Bowie is my favorite artist of all time. A few weeks later, I'd been in this terrible bar and it closed and I invited three people back to my apartment. Anyway, people were smoking crack in the bathroom, and at six in the morning I took out this hat and I was showing it off, and in the morning it was gone . . . I remember thinking: Boy, I need to stop drinking.

HANIF KUREISHI: I first met David in 1993, for dinner. I'd briefly interviewed him for a magazine a few weeks earlier, but I asked Alan Yentob to set up dinner, as I wanted to ask him if we could use some of his music on the television adaptation of *The Buddha of Suburbia*, which we were just about to film. That was the plan. So off we went to the River Café in Hammersmith. And when I asked if we could use his tunes he said, "I thought you'd never ask." And what he actually wanted to do was write the soundtrack. So that was how we agreed to do it. Then we became mates. I'm sure everybody says this, but he was really charming. He went to a lot of trouble to be liked. I remember him saying to me—when you ring up a company, always remember the name of the secretary, because she's the one who's going to put you through in the future to X, Y, or Z. When I knew him he had got over all the bad stuff and didn't drink at all. We used to drink and get stoned in front of him, and it was hilarious. We used to behave badly and he was an impeccable gentleman. He could be a bit bitchy, a bit queeny if you got him going on certain subjects, and he liked to gossip. He obviously really liked to be liked and worked hard at being liked.

So we shot the film and then we went to Switzerland, to his little studio. He was bored out of his mind in Switzerland. He said the only person who used to come round was Roger Moore. And he said Roger Moore used to come round every fucking night. At first Roger Moore was really good fun, telling good stories about the Bond films. Then he'd come round and tell the same stories, night after night, but it was the law of diminishing returns, as each night the stories were a little less interesting. And Bowie used to dread this knock on the door, as it would be fucking Roger Moore. It was like a cartoon scene—Roger Moore and David Bowie sitting around talking about James Bond. [This was somewhat ironic, because when the Broccolis announced 1985's Bond film *A View to a Kill*, along with the inevitable return of Roger Moore as 007, they revealed that Bowie would be playing the villain Max Zorin. However, Bowie turned down the role, which was eventually played by Christopher Walken.] So then we showed him the material on the monitor and he played us some music. We were shitting ourselves because one of us had to tell this rock genius that the music wasn't quite right. I mean, how do you do this? He'd actually bothered to make it, which is more than he did for *The Man Who Fell to Earth*, but then we had to tell him it wasn't quite right. So we would sit around going, "You tell him," "No, you tell him." We spent a whole day with him going, "That's not right there. It's a good tune but it just doesn't fit there." So he went and started to work on it at night. And he would stay up all night. He didn't say, "Oh fuck you, that's what I've done." He went and redid the whole thing. He was really good about it and was really proud of it by the end. He didn't object at all. Then he said he wanted to write some songs for it, because he wanted to make some money out of it. "Because the BBC pays you shit I'm going to make an album." And he wrote "The Buddha of Suburbia," which I thought was a really great song.

After we worked on *The Buddha of Suburbia* he wanted me to adapt *Ziggy Stardust* as a musical. He'd been to see *Tommy* and he thought that Pete Townsend had what he called a gusher—you know, money just poured through your reservoir forever. And he thought he could do this with *Ziggy Stardust.* So I used to go to his hotel and we would sit there and he would walk around singing *Ziggy Stardust.* Walk around, go to the bathroom singing *Ziggy Stardust* along to the record. So I worked on that with him for a while. He didn't want it to be a sort of narrative. A pantomime. He wanted it to be really modern, really avant-garde. He didn't really quite know how to do that. So he got that guy in from La La La Human Steps. Very nice guy. But I don't think Bowie really knew what he wanted or what he was doing at that time. Rock stars go on, then go off, they're hot then they're cold. And then they're really into it and then he got really nervous and said this was going to be a disaster. He had a reputation to protect.

We started socializing with him quite a lot too. We had just had twins and he used to come around and see the kids. I was tremendously flattered. We writers just sit in the shed in our pajamas. So when a pop star turns up it's a completely different level of existence for us. Our rather miserable, unglamorous existence. He was like a proper person. Me and Tracy, my first wife, were rather obsessed with Paul McKenna at the time, and we used to go and see stage shows and we got him to do a book for Faber [where Kureishi was a consultant]. And Bowie was quite interested in him—he wanted to give up smoking. So we got Paul McKenna round to the house and Bowie came round with Iman. It was hilarious. Bowie said, "I'm not going to do this, this is ridiculous." So Iman said, "Oh, OK I'll do it." So McKenna hypnotized her first. Then hypnotized Bowie.

Then McKenna fucked off. Bowie woke up and said, "For fuck's sake go and get me some fags, please get me some fags." I said you go and get your own fags. He said I can't. I can't just walk along the street and buy cigarettes. I suddenly thought, My God, that's true. He can't go to the shop without people going, "Oh, there's David Bowie." I thought that's awful. So after he was hypnotized he went back on the fags. It was hilarious, with McKenna going, "You'll never smoke again blah, blah, blah."

He could meet anyone in London, so I used to go around with him to dinner parties and stuff. I remember having dinner with Eduardo Paolozzi with him. If he wanted to meet anybody, he would just ring them up and go round and see them. He was very curious and intelligent. He used to ring me up very late at night from Switzerland and he would talk for ages about serial killers. For some reason he got really obsessed with serial killers, because I think he was doing an album called *Outside*. He would talk for ages, interminably. Terrible monologues. When I say terrible I mean impossible to understand, and actually I think it was him talking to himself. And then that was it really. He did that to people. I'm sure you're aware that he did that to people. He just dropped them. And then moved on to somebody else, something else. And I understood that, it was fine. I was sorry about it because I really liked him. But I can see it's very difficult to stay friends with a rock star unless you're a rock star yourself.

COURTNEY LOVE (MUSICIAN): I was into Bowie earlier than *Ziggy Stardust*, probably around "Width of a Circle" time. I was young, but I was into it because I was into new wave and punk. I hadn't even come to Dublin or Liverpool or London yet, so this was probably around 1979. I also loved the Lou Reed record he did, *Transformer*. But then the *Low* and *"Heroes"* records were a bit obtuse to me. All of the guys who mentored me, Bono, Julian Cope, Ian McCulloch, they were hugely influenced by Bowie, so it made sense for me to be influenced by him too. He was obviously big in Britain but he was big in Portland, Oregon, too. He made up these rules, like, if you're going to be a rock star you've got to have a certain look. The look should change; the sound should change. Like he kind of came up with those parameters that Madonna followed. I couldn't relate to Madonna musically at all. I understood what she was doing. She had a look, she had a sound, and the sound changed. I understood that, but other than "La Isla Bonita" I honestly don't know her music. But I don't get the music part. But Bowie influenced me, what with each of the albums being operatic and having a theme—operatic mini opera and whatever. To be relevant again is the dream of anybody, especially if you've had success. But in fact after *Scary Monsters* it's just sort of not there, not for me. I know he fought back to try and be relevant again, but it was tough. But I wouldn't be around without him. He was David fucking Bowie, the best rock star I can think of.

It is a fucking mystery to me why Kurt covered "The Man Who Sold the World" on the MTV *Unplugged* album. I mean, he never played Bowie. I know that people would come up to Bowie and say it was cool he covered a Nirvana song, and that must have killed him. But I don't know how Kurt got into him. It's a fucking mystery because he had *Sabbath Bloody Sabbath*, Flipper, the Pistols, but he didn't seem to get Bowie the same way I got Bowie. When he covered that song I truly believe it was just a whim. You know, Kurt and I are in the house together, we're playing a continuum of music, and he gets on a plane and goes to New York and two days later he does a new unplugged "Man Who Sold the World"? I don't understand why he did that, because he wasn't listening to it at home. And he did it flawlessly. Was it just to be funny? Was he being ironic? I think it was actually a cry for help.

DAVID BOWIE: I wanted to create an installation with Brian Eno for the Flowers East show [in which forty pop celebrities exhibited works in order to raise money for an arts project in beleaguered Sarajevo], but in the end I just didn't have the time. Anyway, a little after this, Brian and I were sitting around wondering what we would be doing if we weren't musicians, thinking about the unlikeliest professions. We came up with these two characters, Davide and Briani, designers of bathroom accessories! This turned from a joke into the real thing, and I decided to try my hand at some wall coverings.

So I produced two designs. The first one was called "British Conflicts," featuring a charcoal and watercolor portrait of Lucian Freud inside a Damien Hirst–style box. The second was called "The Crouch," which is a charcoal drawing of a Minotaur. They're both superimposed over some generic Laura Ashley patterns. The kitsch stuff is Laura's. Conflicts was simply about the war of attrition between figurative and conceptual art in this country, between the modernists and the traditionalists, using Freud and Hirst as totems of the opposing camps. I think their combined entanglement helps diminish the importance of the argument. The Minotaur is just a representation of godlessness and paganism—a bull with a little brain—and is based on the exhibition I held at the Berkeley Square Gallery. Both prints represent an end of the century, a fin de siècle feeling, a comment on our harried attempt to make amends to the gods.

I chose wallpaper because of its status as something extremely incongruous, particularly in the world of art. I didn't completely lose my sense of irony, you know! I suppose I'm midway between high art and low art—I'm a mid-art populist and postmodernist Buddhist who is casually surfing his way through the chaos of the late twentieth century. Going for Laura Ashley was a shot in the dark, really, but then I asked myself who I would want to produce something like this, and they sprang to mind. It was a good working relationship, apart from the castration, that is. They erased the minotaur's genitals, which is the fourth time something like this had happened to me. I wasn't allowed to show my genitals on the inner sleeve of *Aladdin Sane*, nor on the cover of *Diamond Dogs*, nor on the cover of one of the Tin Machine LPs. I've been de-balled four times! It says a lot about Western attitudes towards male genitalia. I mean, breasts don't seem to be hacked off in the same cavalier fashion.

My art has little to do with trends, and nothing at all to do with style; in fact, it's almost the opposite. I've always been a bit of a Duchampist—in fact, when I was young I thought Duchamp was God—and I always reflected that in my music, so I think you can see that in my art too. There is painting, sculpture, installation—you name it, we've got it. I'm enormously proud of it, from the figurative pieces through to the more abstract conceptual stuff. I've always painted and recorded in parallel, since the very early '70s. I've made a point of it, and I've found that the problems I've encountered in my music can easily be solved by things which occur in my painting, and vice versa. It's very therapeutic in that way. I suppose that's why my music has always been so visual.

FERGUS GREER (PHOTOGRAPHER): I was commissioned to shoot him for the *Sunday Times* in 1995. Digitization, computer graphics, and Photoshop were all quite new, and so Laura Ashley had commissioned him to design a series of wallpaper. I couldn't believe how lucky I was. I worked as an assistant for Terence Donovan and Richard Avedon, but we'd never photographed anyone as important to me as David Bowie. He wanted to do it at his agent's terraced house in Fulham, and he turned up, by himself, with no assistants, wearing a turtleneck and a nice suit and simply said, "Hi, I'm David." While we were setting up he explained why he had got involved with the project, which was because he found it a new challenge creatively, working with computers, et cetera. He said he'd always wanted to be an artist, and he talked a lot about German Expressionism, but he said he'd turned to music because he thought he could make more money at it. He was what he was: a gentleman. Terence Donovan once told me that people with fame and money need to be intelligent, because it's really difficult. And it really struck me that Bowie was someone who had really been able to hold on to who he was, but at the same time sit with what he had become. Not that many people do it with such success. He wasn't remotely interested in letting me know that he was David Bowie. He didn't appear to use "professional deafness," which is what a lot of famous people do—pretending not to hear something when they obviously have. I photographed Margaret Thatcher once, and she definitely had it. Bowie was engaged. He didn't seem interested in having a huge entourage, because he enjoyed his freedom. When he was finished with me he just walked outside, hailed a cab, and went off to the Saatchi Gallery. He certainly had a youthful energy about him. He left having made all of us feel great, whereas a lot of celebrities leave situations like this having made you feel frustrated, diminished, and angry.

CLIVE LANGER: I was surprised by the fact he had a big collection of German Expressionist paintings. In fact, later I went to his own exhibition and bought one. I imagine he was influenced by the paintings he liked, and that he had a go at seeing what he could do. He must have been pleased by them because he exhibited them. I like Bob Dylan's too. I like artists who paint. They might be naïve, but they're full of attitude and expression.

MARK ELLEN: You get the impression a lot of pop stars are fairly conventional people making a huge effort to appear creative and eccentric in public. With David Bowie it seems the other way round—as if he's the owner of a genuinely rapid-fire, butterfly mind trying hard to adapt to our pedestrian pace. I interviewed him at a London gallery in October 1994, an exhibition of artwork by musicians to raise money for the War Child charity. Again, the entries from Kate Bush, George Michael, Paul McCartney, and the others were quite formal; Bowie's was a box of seventeen computer-modified drawings entitled *We Saw a Minotaur*—"illustrations for an imaginary play," he told me. Everything about him seemed unusual. He had a trim mustache and goatee and was smaller than I'd expected (he was five foot nine), and perilously thin in his severely belted white jeans and green-and-black check shirt. He still had his "English teeth," which were wonderfully crooked and characterful though he later had them expensively corrected. And he smiled all the time in a powerfully winning way, the evangelical grin of a man who believes passionately in his view of the world and wants you to see it the same way too (he once told a session musician to "play like a fried egg"). His mind was racing all the time, sparking ideas and thoughts and theories. Brian Eno was with him, and I asked him about working with Bowie. "Ideas arrive at such a speed," Eno said, "it's like watching a fast-motion film of a flower blossom."

ALAN EDWARDS: I spent thirty-five years working with David, from watching Tommy Cooper videos in the back of tour buses in the US—he would watch enormous amounts of comedy—to visiting Nelson Mandela with him in South Africa, organizing the trip to Somalia.

David got very involved with Iman's trip there. I recall one slightly surreal meeting where we went to the offices of *Newsnight*, at the old BBC in Shepherds Bush, and we ended up on the floor poring over maps of East Africa whilst discussing the potential trip with BBC reporter Robin Denselow. Staff wandered around being very "British" trying not to notice and act as if having a rock superstar and supermodel on the office floor was all perfectly normal.

He had a tremendous personal influence on me, but bizarrely the strongest memory I have of him, actually my fondest memory, is when we were in Rome in the early '90s. We were being given a personal tour of the Vatican, and we're going from room to room and David's got the peaked cap, and his mac, and he's totally unrecognizable—he told me once that the best way to get around London on the Tube without anyone recognizing you was to wear a cap and carry a Greek newspaper—and gradually David starts talking about the pictures himself. He's talking about Botticelli and he's going into the history of Medici, and he's going into extraordinary detail about the paintings and their provenance, and he's like the Pied Piper of Hamelin. So I look around and there is now a line of people behind us, and soon that line is full of fifty people or so, and they all think that David is the official tour guide. They have no idea who he is, they don't know that he's David Bowie, they're just listening to someone give them a history lesson.

David was definitely someone who every day woke up and wanted to learn things. He didn't go to university, so for him knowledge was something to treasure and strive for. He was completely self-taught and like all self-taught people he'd miss out a couple of bits, some of the obvious bits, but take you down kind of incredibly interesting roads you wouldn't have normally gone down. He had a huge effect on me, because he introduced me to so many things, so many people, so many things I otherwise wouldn't have engaged with. People think he was a fashion plate but he couldn't have cared less. He had great cheekbones and looked fabulous in everything he wore. I mean obviously there were stylists, great photographers, and you had people who were obsessive about helping him, but he did not stress over this stuff. He had an interest in fashion as a way of expressing himself, almost a theatrical presentation of his various personas. Obviously he had a fantastic eye and really understood and liked a good cut and decent fabric. I seem to remember him being especially interested in well-crafted shoes but he wasn't in any way a fashionista. It was something that came naturally to him but not something he obsessed about. On a personal level, he was mostly incredibly low key and relaxed in the way he dressed, often just jeans or a workman-shirt type of look. When we were in Australia on tour in the '80s I even did interviews for him. We sounded quite similar, so when he didn't want to do a radio interview, sometimes I would do it, and no one would ever cotton on. We were born within a mile of each other. He was a Buddhist; he didn't care about such things.

DAVID BOWIE: People accused me of dabbling in the art world, but it was more than dabbling. I started with small Arts and Crafts pieces, some

William Morris, some Wyndham Lewis Vorticism pieces. I suppose in the late '60s I was a bit of an amateur, and I sold the majority of my collection in the late '60s when I was poor, before all that stuff became fashionable. Then in the '70s, I started collecting German Expressionist work, people like Heckel and Schmidt-Rottluff. I joined the board of *Modern Painters* magazine, and my first commission was an interview I conducted with the French artist Balthus. The same month I also bought a painting by Peter Howson, an ex-soldier who was Britain's official Bosnian War artist. It depicted a rape, and was called *Croatian and Muslim.* I was initially going to buy two other pieces by him, but as soon as I heard that *Croatian and Muslim* was about to be bought by an American, I decided to step in. After all, it's a great picture. I think it was ridiculous that the painting wasn't shown [at the Imperial War Museum, which was showing a selection of Howson's work], but the irony is, that I gather it was defended by the women on the museum's committee. I suppose it's just like working for a record company; you finish something you're really pleased with, something which means something to you, and the record company turn around and say they can't use it. You are completely at their mercy. The pieces the museum chose I think are more conservative, but then David Bomberg had the same kind of trouble during the First World War. He was unfairly compared to cartoonists, but would you put down Hogarth because of his tendency to caricature? I think it's awfully churlish. I really do think that it is an exceptional portrayal of that particular world. This [was] a war not about bombs, but about genocide, about cruelty and humiliation, and that is what this picture portrays. I don't *like* it. I think that is a completely inappropriate word, but I do think it's very powerful, and, obviously, very important. Also, it's one of those paintings that really comes alive when you see it, because it's so vast. He comes from a long line of war painters, starting with Goya, Dix, Beckmann, Grosz. In fact his work is really quite similar to a lot of German Expressionism. *Croatian and Muslim* joins the list of great British war paintings, and it reflects the cruelty and fragmentation of the twentieth century.

WILLIAM BOYD (WRITER): The *Modern Painters* dinners were to decide future issues and their content. We would pitch our own ideas. Bowie did a certain amount of journalistic work, also, usually interviewing artists he admired or was interested in. I remember he did Balthus (a coup) and Tracey Emin (less of a coup). I remember I thought he looked amazingly good, in very good nick, for someone who'd taken such vast amounts of drugs over the years. He seemed in excellent health—hair, teeth, skin, all top-notch. He didn't drink alcohol but he was a ferocious chain smoker and consumer of espressos. I think he was viewed with some suspicion by the other art experts around the table—as if he was some kind of celeb gimmick to boost the magazine, somehow—so he was quite diffident and modest—aware of anything he said being analyzed—not in a hostile way, but as if he had somehow to present and prove his credentials. Bowie was an avid reader so we often talked about books. What do you think of X? Have you read the latest from Y? We didn't talk about music at all. He was present because he was interested in art.

He was dry—worldly, amused at things. He wasn't a comic in any sense, cracking jokes. He had a big and spontaneous laugh that used to erupt from time to time when he was amused. He wasn't self-absorbed at all. Very open, I would say. No sense of an anguished soul or tormented artist. He was just married to Iman at the time we met (I got to know her then, also) and you could sense the genuine happiness in that marriage. It made him very content, secure, and relaxed, I think. He was ill at ease with the other art experts—the professors, the eminent art critics, the gallerists, the philanthropists, the collectors, the visiting artists and architects who came to the dinners. I was ill at ease, also. We were both outsiders, in a way, amateurs amongst experts who made their living from fine art. The conversations were often very intellectual and highbrow. I had done a PhD at Oxford so knew that world and its mores. I could just about hold my own. David was an iconic rock star. Some of the stuffier, older professors were, I think, surprised to find him at the table—might only have been dimly aware of who he was. Not a situation Bowie would often find himself in! I sensed his unease, sometimes, almost a nervousness when he spoke and these eminences listened intently. At the first dinner he'd asked if he could bring a friend—for protection, I suppose, someone to talk to, a kind of shield. But he didn't. He came alone, but he was pretty much Daniel in the lions' den.

MATTHEW COLLINGS (ART CRITIC): Bowie seems to have started buying a lot of art in the late '80s and '90s, when he was isolated and bored, and living first in Switzerland then Bermuda as a tax exile. He drifted off it when his music got going again at the end of the decade. He bought things from the '70s to his death, but the '90s was the big period, and the style and look mostly revolved around Modern British. The quality is sometimes awesome, as with expressionism by Frank Auerbach, David Bomberg, and Leon Kossoff, and lyrical artists like Peter Lanyon and Alan Davie. There's also a fair bit of work in the collection where the quality isn't particularly high, but it still reflects the same interest in art that has a bit of expressive turbulence and usually comes round to figuration even if it's distorted. He hardly seems to have bought at all for status or social climbing reasons. It's not at all a collection that keeps up with anything. There's virtually no conceptual art—one or two token examples, without much weight. Hirst and Basquiat (two works by each artist), being glamorous names, are actually exceptions in the collection rather than the rule. (He also collected Memphis design.) Also in the '90s he made an attempt to be known as an artist himself, putting on a show at a self-help gallery in Cork Street, with a couple of sales to Saatchi.

His main source for buying was the Bernard Jacobson Gallery. He must have felt safe with Bernie. Rockers do get involved with buying art, of course. Eric Clapton, Mick Jagger, for example. But they tend to buy according to lists of blandly obvious market heavy hitters, provided by percentage-collecting consultants. The impetus is status-plus-investment. Bowie's collecting tendency was more simple enthusiasm. His collection reflects an awareness of art that's partly British '50s, and partly emotional or histrionic. There's very little irony. Paintings tend to be really painted; sculptures really sculpted. The hand-done is emphasized. He liked what could be seen straightaway to be romantic, not what could be seen to be smart.

Bowie started collecting seriously in the '90s, buying work by Jean-Michel Basquiat, Peter Lanyon, Ettore Sottsass, Damien Hirst, Gavin Evans, Harold Gilman, David Bomberg, and more. Beth Greenacre was hired to curate his collection at the turn of the century, and says that the work he bought formed a narrative around him. "He was an observer, and he was an historian," she says. "He really looked back at history to understand his current position, and that is what these artists were doing too." Kate Chertavian acted as an art consultant for him during the '90s: "His pictures describe him perfectly. What I got from the get-go was that it was very important for him to have untrammelled access to the artists. He loved talking to them. He didn't want any pomp and circumstance." Chertavian first met Bowie in 1993, when Iman walked into the gallery in which she was working, and showed her a scribble of a sculpture that her husband had drawn. Iman wanted to buy it for him, and Chertavian was blown away by the fact that "this beautiful, amazing couple gave gifts like that to each other." Having found the sculpture, Chertavian was hired, and became his eyes and ears at art fairs all over the world. She said he assembled his collection to "enjoy it, on a deep level. Collections can be a coat of armor, or an exploration. And he was a great collector."

DAMIEN HIRST (ARTIST): I remember telling him to come to the studio in old clothes, but he turned up in brand-new expensive clothes. He said he didn't have any old clothes but didn't mind getting paint on the new shit he was wearing. I loved that. [When I showed him how to make a spin painting] he took his watch off at one point and stuck it on the painting, but we spun it some more and it threw it across the studio and smashed it. He never even picked it up. Around the time we made the painting [1995] we were hanging out a lot and having these long conversations about what it meant to be an artist. What does an artwork say about an artist's personality? Is the person of the artist always present in a piece of art? I told him they [spin paintings] were like punk art to me and he thought about it for a little while and told me a story of where he said he was once going to a punk gig with his son in New York and his son came down wearing punk clothes and David had said to him, "Do I have to go out with you dressed like that?" Amazing that even David Bowie could react like that when confronted with the new.

TRACEY EMIN: I met him in 1996, in a Lebanese restaurant in West Kensington. I was with a group of people and someone leaned over and said, "Tracey I'm so sorry to interrupt but I'd like to say I really like what you do." And it was David Bowie. And I said, "Well, can I just say I really appreciate your work too?" And then we became friends. He had been and seen a show of mine in Toronto and really liked it. He had seen my work for real. He used to telephone me out of the blue, and so we largely kept in touch by phone calls. He was really into emails, but I couldn't email. Then a year later we went to Dublin, for me to interview him. Then every time I went to New York I would see him. When he was doing his tours I went to see him play, but mainly we kept in touch through emails and phone calls.

He absolutely loved art, and I think he would have preferred to have been an artist, than a musician. I used to say to him, "You are an artist—everything you do is art." But he thought visual art was different, on another level. I think if he had had a choice, it would have been visual art. But he didn't have a choice; he was too good a musician to be able to choose. He told me about meeting Andy Warhol and other artists and how it affected him and how he felt stupid in their company. He felt naïve in terms of creativity. He understood that they were true geniuses. That's what his benchmark was. He was so self-effacing and judgmental. That's what kept him at the top of his game. Especially when he was young, that's what kept pushing him. That's why he was unique, because he didn't sit around resting on his laurels. I saw his art, but I always thought his paintings were naïve in comparison to his music. What he did music-wise was so sophisticated compared to his easel work. But he had spent all his life doing music. It's like the Velvet Underground, they're not just musicians, they're artists, their music is art. David Bowie was an artist but with sound.

The surprising thing about him was how unaffected he was. He had a really puerile, stupid sense of humor and so the idea of David being really cool isn't true at all. He was very silly, and very slapstick and very open. No matter what ego he was, that wasn't what he used to get what he needed. He wasn't like, "I'm David Bowie." When we were in Ireland, we went to see the Book of Kells with my mum. We were queuing, and it was quite a long queue, and after a while this woman came up to him and said, "Mr. Bowie, Mr. Bowie, no need to queue, no need to queue!" So then everyone started looking. Because we had been queuing for about ten minutes and no one had realized. Then when we got inside, someone actually fainted because they couldn't believe it was him. He appeared to be completely unaffected by his fame. From a personal point of view, it's quite funny. He made me feel so equal in his company. I told him once that when I was young I vomited at the end of "Rock 'n' Roll Suicide" after drinking a bottle of sherry, and he said, "I also remember vomiting at the end of 'Rock 'n' Roll Suicide.' I remember vomiting at the end of quite a few songs."

When I got to know him he also started taking the piss out of me. He used to tell me I had such a huge ego. He once told me that the best way to travel in London anonymously is on public transport: all you have to do is wear a hat and read a Greek newspaper. He used to walk around London all the time when he was here, just like he did in New York. He came round to my house once and I was putting the curtains up. I was meant to be meeting him round the corner, and the doorbell rang. And I thought, Well, that can't be him because there would be a car. But it was him, and I said, "How did you get here?" and he said, "By Tube, you should try it sometime." When we were out people would often come up to him and say, "Has anyone told you you really look like David Bowie?" People would often ask him for his autograph, and he'd say, "I'll do it, but please promise me you'll give a pound to charity." I said I wouldn't know what to do if I'd met him when I was younger, and he said, "You'd say, 'Hello, my name is Tracey Emin.'" He was very sexy, also quite flirty. But with everybody. He was very physical.

MATTHEW COLLINGS: In April 1997 I had a book published by a new company formed by David Bowie called 21. The launch was at a club in New Burlington Street. I was in the middle of filming a TV series called *This Is Modern Art*. Because he was the glamorous host of the launch it was full of conventional-style press photographers and press and media people. It was the first time I met him. When we were introduced he said, "I've read everything you've written." I couldn't understand what he meant. Everything?

In those days I wrote a diary column for *Modern Painters*. Maybe he was referring to it. He was on the editorial board of the magazine. In my mind the book, *Blimey*, and the TV series *This Is Modern Art*, were each continuous with that column, whose purpose was anarchic comedy. Objective but understated reporting or chronicling was mixed with personal confession.

The evening included David reading aloud extracts from the book at the launch and then a dinner for about a dozen people at a restaurant off High Street Kensington. At the end he showed Emma Biggs [the London-based mosaic artist] and me a note Iman had just passed him that said, "Will you come home and sleep with me?"

I met him several times. One meeting was at his office in New York on the day of a double launch of a book by William Boyd and one by me. He said he didn't collect any conceptual art; instead if he was interested in something he had his assistants make up a version for him. At the launch that night we both read extracts from my new book, *It Hurts.* He gave me a good tip about inflection so a malicious joke sounded milder, because the subject of the story would be in the audience. The next day we were on *Charlie Rose.* Charlie introduced the TV audience to my books, pronouncing *Blimey* "Blimmie."

Sometimes David phoned up to chat. The first call was to report *Blimey*'s first thousand sales a few days after it came out. The last time I met him was at a recording studio. To get past the automated security system the man I was traveling with, Bernard Jacobson, one of the partners with David in the publishing company, who'd been selling art to him for many years, had to answer questions from a disembodied voice about who we were looking for. Bernie had been given a codename for David, but when he provided it the voice said there was no one here called that. Eventually without any formal or polite thing being said, the gate simply opened and we drove through. The place was a ranch-like setup in the Catskills. Iman waved from a balcony. A drummer had been flown in and was recording his track in the studio. David said it was great but it should be less splashy. He pointed out Tony Visconti: Tony gave us a friendly greeting. There was a framed photo of Little Richard. David said he had it at every recording session. He showed us the view over the hills. He said it looked like the dinosaur period, pre-man. I could easily believe it. I told him Emma and I had been painting. He said he'd been wondering if God existed.

TOMMY HILFIGER: When he started off with Iman he was absolutely so in love. He told me a makeup artist had introduced them. She became quite protective of him, because when he would go out in New York, it was like wildfire. "It's David Bowie, look, there's David Bowie . . ." It was like

Michael Jackson. In 1994 we were thinking of doing an ad campaign for the "H" collection, and we knew we had to do something very different. Being obsessed with music and musicians I thought that if I had a choice of anyone to be in the campaign it would be David and Iman, because you're talking rock royalty and fashion royalty. You're talking about two of the most beautiful creatures on Earth, with such respect and notoriety. So I called Bill Zysblat, his business manager, and he said he'd ask, but he wasn't really sure. I said just tell them that I will let them choose the photographer, the location, and even the publications I put the ads in. So it went back and forth—how long would the campaign run, what do the clothes look like, does it have to be in color? But it happened, in Amsterdam, with Ellen von Unwerth, and it was the first time they'd ever done anything like this together.

For a while we sporadically corresponded, and sent each other Christmas cards, while my oddest Bowie encounter happened on the phone. It was one of those dark, miserable winter weekday afternoons at the Sunday Times, *sometime around 1994, one of those days when you spent most of the afternoon longing to escape Wapping and drive back to civilization. Today was no different from any other: phones were ringing, faxes whirring, subeditors screaming for copy, and couriers were coming and going and losing packages as though the whole idea of losing packages was coming back into fashion. It was raining heavily outside, as it always was in Wapping, even when it was sunny everywhere else in London, and the hail hit the windows like furious fingers on industrial PC keyboards.*

My phone rang, I picked it up, and a more-than-familiar voice on the other end asked, "Hello, is that Peggy?" although in the retelling (and in the weeks afterwards I told this story a lot) I always imagined it more as "Hellooooo, is that Pigga-aay? This is your son David, the Cockernaaay in cyberspace," in the sort of Mockney drawl that has been used by everyone from Anthony Newley to Damon Albarn via Mick Jagger, but which had been honed to perfection by the chap on the other end of the line.

"Er, no, this is Dylan Jones. Is that David Bowie?"

It seems Bowie's mother had just moved, and as I'd only recently interviewed Bowie for the Sunday Times, *my number was on the same page as hers (her name was Jones, after all). Surprisingly, Bowie seemed as thrilled as I was flattered by this bizarre stroke of serendipity, and stayed on the phone for twenty minutes, as I frantically made explanatory hand gestures, threw hastily scribbled notes at my colleagues and mouthed* "IT'S DAVID BOWIE!" *to anyone passing through the office.*

Peggy's boy was gearing up for another of his purple patches—and at the time he really needed one—and over the next few years would produce many records as good as those he made in the '70s, when he was in his prime. The tin-pot Tin Machine had been thrown into the recycling bin (to be picked up by God-knows-whom), bouncing against the walls of a cast-iron box already full of the Glass Spider, the Laughing Gnome, the nightmare scarecrow of Labyrinth, *and that weird guy from the* Jazzin' for Blue Jean *video.*

"I've got to stop mucking about and start making records for myself rather than for other people," he told me on the phone that day. "Anyway, I better call my mum before I get round to that. . . ."

Next came Outside, *the most self-enraptured record he ever made.*

DAVID BOWIE: I might like *Young Americans*, but then there are a lot of people who just think that record was all about process and not about heart and soul. They'd be wrong, but I can't tell them that. You have to succumb to the wisdom of crowds. If people, my people, say that *Outside* is the best thing I've ever done, then I'm happy to go along with that.

ERDAL KIZILÇAY: The demos for *Outside* were really terrible, awful things. Brian Eno and David had worked on them before, up in David's ski-lodge near Gstaad, but when we got in the studio to make the record, the demos just didn't work because they weren't any good. Eno didn't appear to do anything at all, he just ordered us around and told us to jam, which is what we did. He played around on this toy synthesizer. All Brian ever said was, "Continue, continue . . ." We jammed and we jammed and the record is based on edited sections of our jams. David seemed to spend most of his time painting, until he put his vocals on right at the end.

CARLOS ALOMAR: The older he got, the more he wanted control over his arrangements. He started rejecting my suggestions. He wanted to adhere more and more to his demos. Fuck man, you want your records to sound like a demo? He just wanted more and more control. On the *Outside* album I didn't know what he wanted. I never met Robert Fripp; I never met half the guitar players on his records, as they were all overdubs, and now I was an overdub. I had to relinquish my role. That album was the classic example of experimentation. I actually really liked it. David's curiosity would not let him settle, and that unrest marked his trajectory throughout his life. His restlessness and curiosity was pretty necessary in order for him to be who he had to be. I don't know about how he grew up, or his introduction to jazz and R&B, but he had something within him that made him keep moving.

You compare his life with the regular man. The regular man is not afforded the musician's life. Look at a traveling minstrel, if you want, who does he answer to unless himself? He travels around and tries to get the stories of the moment, so he can revel in the fact that he's able to label the war or label the people in song, and in so doing, becomes a spokesman. If that's not David then what is it? You're taking a medieval form of expression and changing it and marketing it and allowing it to coincide with all the advents of all the technologies, and still there he is, traveling the world, trying to make heads or tails of everything so that the common man can understand what he's seen, or should I say so that the common man can experience something he will never live. David Bowie's life was something else. He was a pioneer who took the road untaken. Don't look on his life as a life, look at it as an odyssey. There's a reason why this word exists—it's not a journey, it is not an adventure, it's an odyssey, in itself imposing its will, its logic, its reasoning on the moment. I traveled with him for a while and I'm all the better for it.

BRIAN MOLKO: We owe it all to Morrissey. He was opening for David Bowie, and then one day he got on the tour bus and left his band behind and drove home to his mum's. We happened to have the same agent at the time, so when that happened he played David our demo. This happened before we had a deal, certainly before we had our first album out. I must have been about twenty-four or twenty-five. It did wonders for my ego. I was a little unstoppable after that. And on the strength of this demo, he asked us to fill Morrissey's shoes. This was towards the end of the *Outside* tour. So we toured with *Earthling*, and then *Heathen*. He took us under his wing, and we became one of his favorite support bands. We even opened up his fiftieth birthday party at Madison Square Garden, which was an incredible thing to do for a band who hadn't released their first album yet. I first met David backstage in an arena in Milan, at our first show. He turned out to be genuine and without pretension, and he continued to make time for us through the years. He would make a point of coming to speak to us before our show, at festivals we would eat together, and I kind of felt that during those five years I was in his orbit I gained an incredibly illustrious friend and a mentor. First of all he taught me that you don't have to be a dick, you know, just because you are who you are. He was incredibly generous with his time and incredibly polite with people, but not in a superficial way. The other thing, as a musician, when my tiny band joined his tour, he was playing a lot of his new music, he was beginning to work with Trent Reznor, and wasn't trying to rest on his laurels but trying to pull his music into the present and into the future. He said that the future comes to those who can see it coming.

JOHN GIDDINGS: David would occasionally get grumpy, but everyone gets grumpy. He was never angry, though. Even when Morrissey walked off his tour. David called him to try and get him to come back, but Morrissey wouldn't call him. Can you imagine anyone not returning David Bowie's phone call? I tried to sue Morrissey for the £20,000 I'd paid him, but then someone pointed out that no one had complained.

HANIF KUREISHI: I think he just knew what he was going to do and he was going to do [it] his own way and he wasn't that interested in other people's ideas. He took everything from everywhere but he certainly made it his own. But I thought he was a bit lost after *Black Tie White Noise*, around *Outside*. As if he wasn't quite sure what he was meant to be doing by then. What are pop stars of that age supposed to do? Who are you supposed to be? He spent a lot of time with me thinking about art, talking about painting. He'd gone back to that I guess. He'd got tired of being on the road. I remember him saying to me, "I can't understand how Mick Jagger can sing 'Brown Sugar' ever again. I can't understand how he can do that as I'd be bored out of my mind." So I think he lost it a bit.

REEVES GABRELS: I turned up a week before the *Outside* sessions with a few ideas, and then Brian came in, and Garson, and Sterling Campbell and Erdal and we just started jamming. But Brian isn't really an instrumentalist, and his instrument is his ideas, his opinion. We went out to dinner every night, but in the studio it was difficult. What we did is we improvised. Some say that Brian scripted these sessions, but that's not true.

David had got sober during the second Tin Machine album and adjusted some of habits, which on *Outside* meant that we were starting earlier in the day. But David was David throughout. There were just fewer hangover days. No hangover days, I should say.

STERLING CAMPBELL: *Outside* was a great record because it was very intimate. Every morning Brian would pick me up and we'd go and have breakfast together and then just jam and laugh all day. We were in Montreux. It was the off season, so we were up in the mountains, on Lake Geneva, and it was beautiful. We just made up whatever we wanted. David was just painting. He stood in the corner painting everyone while we just jammed. Every day. Five days a week. Brian was a funny guy, cracking us up, but when it came to business . . . We did these jams, using reel-to-reel tape, and then they'd just cut up the tape and keep the bits they liked. When we finally heard the record I couldn't remember any of it, because we had never heard it that way before. So then we had to learn the songs again when we went out on tour. That was crazy. One day, Brian printed up role-play characters for each of us, which we had to keep secret, and told us to play "in character." Mine was, "You are a musician at 'Asteroid,' a space-based club (currently in geostationary orbit 180 miles above the surface of the moon) catering mainly to the shaven, tattooed, and androgynous craft-maintenance staff who gather there at weekends . . ."

DAVID BOWIE: It was so good to be back with Eno, as we had achieved some wonderful things together. The record was utterly scary. Not only was it the most experimental thing I think I had ever been involved with, but I was very excited by it. Fundamentally it's a record about the end of the century.

SIMON SWEETMAN (BLOGGER): People talk about Bowie's phenomenal run of albums across the '70s, and it really is (almost all) great. So much of it is wonderful, sublime, so near to perfect. And depending where you stop on the scale you have the absolute cutoff of *Scary Monsters* or tolerance/appreciation for *Let's Dance*. From there it's usually agreed there's little of merit; little that is required/necessary. *Reality* wasn't really necessary. It's not at all terrible—but it's really a less successful rerun of *Heathen*. There might be Bowie fans out there prepared to make a case for *Black Tie White Noise*—and certainly it had (like almost all Bowie albums) some strong songs. There might also be people prepared to go in to bat for *Tonight* and *Never Let Me Down*. These people carry hand towels at all times and breathe through the mouth.

For me there's no question—the great underrated David Bowie album is 1995's *1. Outside*, a baffling and overreaching concept album that comes with liner-notes that are almost a novella detailing a sci-fi plot. *Outside* was to be the first in a series—hence *1. Outside*; it also carries the rather unwieldy (downright unnecessary) subtitle: *The Ritual Art-Murder of Baby Grace Blue: A non-linear Gothic Drama Hyper-Cycle.* [*sic*] Um, OK. This was to be part of a trilogy—then there was talk of five albums, even ten. There was just the one. And it tanked. I bought it—because I was a huge Bowie fan in 1995. Just a few weeks after buying it I found it for $5. I bought three more copies. I couldn't believe it was so cheap. I wanted to have it to give to people; to let them experience it.

I've never tired of *Outside*. It's still one of my favorite Bowie albums. It's less an album, more a musical version of a graphic novel. Funnily enough it seems to have gained some standing with time. The song "Hallo Spaceboy" was a live favorite, and "The Heart's Filthy Lesson" was a pretty decent hit as a single. In fact "Heart's Filthy Lesson" owes a great deal of its success to its inclusion in the hit film *Se7en*. Similarly, "I'm Deranged," also from *Outside*, was crucial on the soundtrack to *Lost Highway*. These moody, lurid films were perfect for the *Outside* material. Bowie's songs were perfect for those movies.

One of my favorite Bowie songs is "We Prick You," and I think the album's closing track, "Strangers When We Meet," is up there with the best of his stuff, too. Listening to *Outside* now I'm struck by the fact that it's rather dated in places and still quite futuristic-seeming (if not completely futuristic-*sounding*) in some other places. I remember, when it came out, thinking the same thing. Some of it was brash, gauche even. Some of it was transcendent. Importantly it's an album that *makes* you listen. It's a challenge.

GAIL ANN DORSEY (MUSICIAN): It was May 1995, and I was in England, at [Tears for Fears'] Roland Orzabal's house. I had been playing for them and we were just writing songs and hanging out in his recording studio in Bath. I thought this has to be a fluke, it can't be the real David Bowie. Then he said, "No, love, it's David." I think he was probably used to that reaction. So a six-week gig turned into a twenty-year association. I wasn't a huge fan beforehand, but he was an amazing artist. The way he would dress up and wear skirts . . . he wasn't just a rock and roll singer, not just a performer or a musician, for me it was his voice. I've also always thought, and still think, that he's the best rock vocalist ever. The Frank Sinatra of . . . hard to say what you'd call his music, I always thought he was the best singer out of all of those who were around, like Robert Plant and Elton John. He had such a great voice. "Win" from *Young Americans* is his best vocal performance—the delivery, the range. I like it I guess because I'm from Philadelphia. When you listen to "Wild Is the Wind," it's kinda like what he was, that kind of loneliness, a solitude. I'm a little bit that way too, quite insular, not very social and everything would affect me very strongly. The way he would sing "Wild Is the Wind," it was speaking to me from that place, someone who understood being isolated and a little bit afraid and lonely.

When we first met I was so, so nervous, and then he walked into the room and he was just so sweet, as he always was, he was always very gracious to everyone and made me feel at home instantly. He was very funny, very sassy, always a quick comeback with something. He was always in touch with popular culture, had papers from every city. I don't even know how he had so much time, and it was before the Internet was so intense. He always had his ear to the ground with music, art, fashion, always who and what is the latest thing. It was because he was interested in it, he wasn't trying to copy it, he just wanted to know what was going on. He would come into rehearsals with twelve-inch singles and vinyls that you'd get on Brick Lane and be like, "This is what's happening in London right now," and that's how *Earthling* came along.

He designed an outfit for me for the *Earthling* tour, a one-piece unicorn with a real horse's tail, a black tail that was attached to a harness almost like a flagpole. Who would have thought of that? He drew it in an airport when we were in eastern Europe, hanging around waiting for a small private plane and we were sitting around smoking cigarettes and he was drawing in his sketchbook and called me over and asked me to take a look. There was a drawing of a woman with devil horns and a horse tail, and said, "This is a cool look. What do you think?" Then I had the shoes made by a shoe-cobbler in Brixton, a little lady in a flat who could make shoes out of anything. They were like horse's feet and it would just go over the shoe like a clog. They just looked like a horse.

There were lots of moments in the studio when you saw his genius. He never wanted to do any of the old catalogue when we first started, he didn't want to do the hits. If he was going to have to, he wasn't going to do it the same way and instead make a new arrangement. What he would come up with we'd all be like, "Ooooh, why didn't I think of that?" So that's what I mean; he had an individual thumbprint, an ability to see something from so many different angles. He wasn't a dictator, though, and would welcome any suggestions. He wanted everyone to have their own personality, and he was very good at putting his team together, whether the band, or the art directors for the stage, the clothes or the hair; he always knew exactly the right people because he was so good at observing what other people could do.

At first I didn't know why he wanted me to be in the band. But I think he liked my singing voice, and I'm pretty easygoing, I'm very professional, I don't pry in people's business, I'm not [an] opportunist. I was always very conscious of his needs and his privacy and I guess in general I was easy to get along with. I'm not a huge reader, and he was miles ahead of me, but we'd talk a lot about films, and he introduced me to some interesting African American writers, like Ann Petry; he gave me a book of hers called *The Street*. He had an amazing collection of African American culture. Occasionally I would go with him and listen to his record collection, and he would play Little Richard. He would read all the time—AS Byatt, Margaret Drabble. He would read anywhere, anytime, on a plane, traveling in a bus, car, in an airport. Even in a studio, he might be reading a book but he'd also be listening and then pipe up occasionally.

Back then we dragged around all these books in our suitcases. We talked about TV programs, he loved Ricky Gervais, and that guy whose catchphrase was "Shut that door."

TOMMY HILFIGER: One day David told me he was going to sell his house in Mustique. He said he liked to move on in life. For a while they were going to move to Umbria. Before he left he rebuilt the fishermen's huts, which he didn't have to do. They were originally all without plumbing. He wanted to do something for the people on the island. He was loved on the island, as he treated everyone so well. He was humble and unassuming. Before he left we had one more Christmas in the bamboo church. I remember thinking it was magical that here we had Mick Jagger and David Bowie singing "O Come All Ye Faithful." Then in 1995 he sold his house to Felix Dennis, who made some changes to the house that were more Felix than David, including the huge sculpture of the mating turtles.

When Felix Dennis bought the Mustique house from Bowie, it came with most of its contents, at least most of the furniture. Apparently there was a painting that Iman wanted to keep, which had been included in the sale. David Cherry, who used to work for Felix, says that when Bowie asked Felix if he could have the painting back, Felix said, "Sure, if you buy the whole house with it."

ROBERT CHALMERS (JOURNALIST): I am by no means an expert on David Bowie. I never interviewed him, never met him, and I'm not familiar with all of his work. I only ever saw him live once. Despite being a tireless name-dropper, I have not mentioned the following incident to anybody on social media or elsewhere and I think it does offer some small insight into the man.

I was sitting at home one Sunday afternoon . . . it would have been around 1995 . . . when the phone rang. "Robert? It's David Bowie."

"Oh, really?" [This came in a period when Dylan Jones had called me on a couple of occasions successfully masquerading as a star who was eager to meet me, or more usually inflict grievous bodily harm].

"Yes."

"*The* David Bowie?" [The inanity of that remark is not lost on me.]

"Right, yes."

"Right, well just fuck off, Dylan, I told you I'd had enough of this after the Alex Higgins incident."

"Dylan?"

"Where did you get my number?"

"From Damien [Hirst]."

"OK 'David,' then, what's your date of birth?"

"January the eighth, 1947."

"Wait there."

[Pause while I consult *The Encyclopaedia of Rock and Pop*. I have a sudden queasy realization that this is not my Friend of a Thousand Voices but the creative genius behind *Station to Station* and *"Heroes."*]

"Oh shit. And you caught me [he had] listening to Morrissey."

[Good-natured laugh from him] "Well, it could have been much worse."

Damien Hirst had given David Bowie my number so that he could talk to me about a project that involved buying a Greek Island and, as I recall, placing the embalmed body of a human volunteer (yet to be found) at the heart of a labyrinth which they planned to construct. Oddly enough, I think this scheme came to nothing. What I remember is the good grace with which he accepted being told to go fuck himself in the course of a call he had no need to make, his generosity with his time, and his general sense of irony and good humor. I think I have only ever encountered two interviewees blessed both with an unusual level of self-regard, and a very likeable ability to laugh at themselves; the other, oddly enough, being Morrissey.

MARTIN SCORSESE: Whenever I think about David I think of Gershwin. Once in the '90s I was going to make a film about George Gershwin, and for whatever reasons we were never able to pull the film together. It just slipped away. Nevertheless one of the key characters was Fred Astaire, and once we got clearances from the Gershwin family, as to what was appropriate and what was not, they wanted some sort of consultation on actors. And once we got clearance from Mr. Astaire, who was alive at the time, he said the only person he would have portray him in a film was David Bowie. It figures. The dancing. The movement. You look at the thing he did with Mick Jagger on "Dancing in the Street." Also his face, his extraordinary charisma. And his figure, if you look at Fred Astaire, he had in his contract that you could only photograph him from head to toe. No close-ups of him dancing . . . he wanted to show how the whole body moved. So don't come into a close-up, you know. And he admired David so much.

PETER YORK: There was a period in the '90s when you'd be talking to people who were part of that envelope-stretching artistic community, and they'd say something like. "I'm doing this thing, but it's really difficult because David Bowie has taken an interest in it and I can't get rid of him." As if the oldest swinger in town was just about to descend on your studio and want to collaborate with you. If you were twentysomething, you might be tremendously flattered in the first instance, but then you think, How do I handle this one? I'd heard it often enough to make a little joke of it for myself. He was pursuing these things in a totally admirable way, he wasn't thinking, Oh bugger it, I'm going to become a company bourgeois, he was still interested in things. And that created this curious tension.

DAVID BAILEY: He was awful in the Warhol film [*Basquiat*] because he played him as camp, and Warhol was never really like that. At the time Bowie was obsessed with Basquiat, and for a while it was all he could talk about. Warhol was more low-key than that. Bowie was desperate to be taken seriously as an artist, although his paintings actually aren't bad; they're better than Paul McCartney's.

REEVES GABRELS: I had to teach Lou Reed how to play "Queen Bitch" for David's fiftieth birthday party, and unbeknownst to me David had set up a live feed so everyone else could hear. Lou predictably put me through the wringer, shouting at me, telling me all the things I was doing wrong, telling me I was playing in the wrong key, but after that he became like my mad old uncle. "Hey, call me any time, I don't sleep, I'm always up."

On the second Tin Machine tour I was listening to a lot of Nine Inch Nails, and I used to play that all the time. I played it at the back of the tour bus and everybody would go to the front. So as I was listening to industrial music, David was listening to drum 'n' bass. We used to argue a lot, as I used to like Underworld and he used to like Prodigy. Beatles and Stones, Oasis and Blur. By the time we started *Earthling* we had Pro Tools, so it became much easier to cut and paste and experiment. We were meant to be taking a break, but then David wanted to go back into the studio to work on material for *Earthling*, as musically there was so much going on. It only took two weeks to really put it together. We wanted to have the power of a rock band but introduce elements of drum 'n' bass and elements of what became electronica. I went to raves, took ecstasy, and the scales fell from my eyes and I saw what worked. We even played "Little Wonder" at his fiftieth birthday show. It wasn't really a drum 'n' bass record but that's what the press called it.

ANGUS MACKINNON: Really? Bowie is doing a jungle album three or four years after everyone else? Why?

DAVID BOWIE: I wanted variety on *Earthling*, industrial pop, drum 'n' bass, an aggression. Techno and electronica [reminded] me of the German music of the mid-'70s. My favorite song on the record is "I'm Afraid of Americans," which is an unusual type of song for me to write, as it's so literal, but I was sick of traveling the world and seeing a McDonald's everywhere I went. US culture can be so reductive.

Whether it's art, multimedia, dance, film, or any of the many collaborations I've done, I've always been told by the critics that I should stop it and get back to the day job. Yet those collaborations kept me alive. I see no harm in embracing the future, it's there to be embraced. I tend to immerse myself in things just to see how involved I can get before I get bored. I'm a contemporary person.

Growing old in this business is a really fascinating prospect because it's never been done before. I've still got an insatiable appetite, and either you've got to voice that excitement through your work or give up. I'm lucky in that I'm not hungry for the past, I don't have an appetite for how things were. I'm not going to spend the rest of my life bashing out those songs which make you remember when you first met your wife. I'm annoyed by indifference more than anything. For many years art and music were the only ways in which I could communicate with anybody, were the only ways I could express myself properly. They were my safety valves, if you like. I was always so shy, so awkward in social situations, that it was much easier for me to say what my pains were through the music. And if I'd met a stone wall I possibly would have been in a very bad place mentally. I don't much mind if I'm misinterpreted, because really I just want to be noticed. I could never sit in a garret and say the audience didn't matter. I also get accused of plagiarism, but although I've been influenced by so many people, I always acknowledge them. Those aren't the kind of secrets I keep.

I've never been especially flattered by awards. Doesn't matter if they're from the industry, your peers, the government. I'm not sure if you can really measure creativity in that way, not with any great sense of dignity anyway. I suppose for me as an artist it wasn't always just about expressing my work; I really wanted, more than anything else, to contribute in some way to the culture that I was living in. It just seemed like a challenge to move it a little bit towards the way I thought it might be interesting to go. I realized right from the beginning that you could actually affect the way people saw things in quite a major way. Every artist will say that they don't need validation, that we only ever need self-validation, but that's not true. You just have to work out what you believe in, who to listen to, and not to freak yourself out. Just get on with it! There is a hegemony that freaks out everyone in the artistic community, and if you create art then there is always a sense, a worry that the orthodoxy will reject you. And it's a difficult thing to cope with, even when your ego is telling you that what you are doing is beyond reproach.

Sometimes you saw the flinty side of him. Toward the end of 1996 I flew to New York for a playback of Earthling, *in front of Bowie himself. This is one of those situations that you really want to avoid with a musician or performer, as it's nigh on impossible to judge your own performance correctly, let alone theirs. All they want to hear is blind adulation, a litany of superlatives, and lots of applause. The last thing they want is honesty, not unless honesty masquerades as 100 percent approval, anyway. I remember him bouncing into the studio in a harried but charming way; he was a little blokey in his manner and his attire; he wore a black leather jacket, jeans, and carried a large tote. I'm not sure what could have been in it, but it seemed to suit his look. After a few minutes of pleasantries, in which he repeatedly said my name—the oldest trick in the book, but one he had learned at an early age from his father—we moved into the re-*

cording studio, and he asked an engineer to play the entire album. Loud. This is one of the tricks of the playback session, making sure that the volume is stadium-worthy—so loud that the music inevitably sounds important.

So the album started powerfully, with "Little Wonder," the drum 'n' bass song that drew most of the press attention at the time. After it had finished, I said something facile and enthusiastic—"Brilliant," probably—and then "Looking for Satellites" began, another song I liked, resulting in yet another superlative. The third song, "Battle for Britain (The Letter)" was even better (or so I thought at the time), making it possible for me to say I liked it more than the other two (I must have been out of my mind, as listening to it these days it sounds rather comical). Then, from "Seven Years in Tibet" onwards, I started sounding more circumspect, which was not what was required at all. I started saying things like, "Well, I like it, but I don't like it as much as the others. . . ." and "I can see what you're doing there. . . ." Stupidly I thought that on this occasion I was being summoned to offer some critical judgment, where all that was actually required was blind adoration. By the end of the playback, Bowie looked a little irritated, although I think I managed to bring him around by repeatedly saying that I thought that on the whole it was one of the best things he'd ever done (I know, I know, what was I thinking?). Stereogum *rated it his 17th best album, although I think they're being kind.*

KEVIN MAZUR (CONCERT PHOTOGRAPHER): He toured a lot in the '90s, and I mean a lot. The first time I shot him was the Serious Moonlight Tour, from the audience. I was just a fan then. Then I got a job at *Rolling Stone* and started doing it properly. I shot David dozens and dozens of times. I would always make sure I shot him in a flattering way, and made sure he was happy with the pictures. I never had a problem with offering people picture approval. When I was a young kid and just starting out, I took some photos of Robert De Niro when he was filming *The King of Comedy*. He came up to me, pushed me up against a trailer, and said, "Don't ever, ever take a fucking picture without asking." And he just walked away. But it taught me a lot. Bowie played in New York a lot, and I'm a New York photographer, and there was always something special about his concerts in the city. His best concerts were always at Madison Square Garden; there is something special about that venue, because of the way the roof is tied in with the cable system, so the floor actually moves. It bounces when people are moving, so you can actually feel the audience. It's my favorite venue—in my will it says I want half my ashes to be in the Great South Bay, and the other half I want dumped in the photo pit at Madison Square Garden. Elton John said it, David said it.

REEVES GABRELS: If you ask me what David's Rosebud was, I'd say Weetabix, about an hour before going to bed. I have this image of David sitting in a recording studio in various parts of the world, wearing cargo shorts, a short-sleeved shirt, and white athletic socks, one leg perched on the other, watching television and eating Weetabix.

DAVID PULLMAN (INVESTMENT BANKER): In 1997 David Bowie was thinking of selling his masters and as I was working with his business manager Bill Zysblat at the time, I thought it would be a much better idea to securitize the cash flows instead. David basically didn't want to sell his babies, so we thought of a way to capitalize on what he had already written. I came up with the idea to sell the rights to future royalties from his extensive body of work. Securitization is effectively a loan backed by the future payments, and in this case it seemed like the perfect thing to do. So these became the "Bowie Bonds," the first instance of a catalogue-tied financial instrument on Wall Street. Bowie Bonds were asset-backed securities of current and future revenues of the twenty-five albums and nearly three hundred songs that David recorded before 1990. When we started the deal, I asked what David earned a year, and his earnings were the amount you would expect a large corporation to earn in terms of revenue. I spent a while discussing all the detail with Bill, and then we went to meet David. We were in this office in midtown Manhattan, and within ten seconds he had got it. His initial response was, "Why haven't you started yet?"

He was savvy from the beginning. When he signed his recording deals, he took less up front, and was betting that his albums were assets that would be worth more later. Bowie's assets were worth more than $100 million at the time, and he had offers of that amount on the table from lots of people interested in his catalogue. But instead we issued the securities, which carried a 7.9 percent interest rate. Bowie Bonds began in 1997 as a stock of $55 million in $1,000-denominated bonds, underwritten by my firm, Fahnestock & Co. In order to get the deal off the ground, I had the bonds rated by the three credit agencies at the time, Moody's, Standard & Poor's, and Fitch. It was all good. We later did the same thing with lots of Motown artists, with James Brown, Ashford & Simpson, the Isley Brothers, and with Holland-Dozier-Holland, but it took David Bowie to do it first. The press understandably went crazy, and as soon as it was announced, he was on the cover of the *Financial Times*. He knew what was happening with the Internet, he knew how the industry was changing, and he knew the golden days were over. He later gave an interview to the *New York Times*, in which he said that absolute transformation of everything that we ever thought about music would take place within the next ten years, and nothing would be able to stop it. He said there was no point in pretending that it's not going to happen. He actually said that copyright wouldn't exist in the future. The quote was, "Music itself is going to become like running water or electricity." So the deal we did together was estate planning, thinking about the future. The reason it had never been done before is that no one had thought about it. The financial press took a lot of notice because it was such a landmark transaction. These were masterpieces with cash flows. The bonds liquidated in 2007 as originally planned, without default, and the rights to the income from the songs reverted back to him. Of course, as soon as the deal was done he started touring in earnest because he was now making for himself, rather than anyone else. Cover versions started flowing in too: Dr. Dre covered "Fame," which made millions, and Jakob Dylan and the Wallflowers covered "Heroes," and Microsoft had a big campaign with "Heroes." There were new streams of cash flow. David didn't second-guess people, and if he chose to work with you, he trusted you, He was adult and sophisticated. The other thing I realized about David was that all the people he chose to work with were all very bright. Attorneys, assistants, producers, musicians . . . and as far as the deal was concerned, he wasn't afraid to fail. You never forgot that you were dealing with a rock star, though, because whenever he came into the building for a meeting, *everyone* was working late. Everyone. Who wouldn't want to catch a glimpse of David Bowie?

DAVID BOWIE: [Bowie Bonds were] extremely successful. It was very solvent. My business partner came up with the idea and we both wondered why nobody had ever done it before. A few people have been able to do it, but the major obstacle in doing anything like that is that you've got to own your stuff, otherwise it's not going to work. A lot of writers have given away or lost control of their publishing, and you have to own your publishing to be able to do it. Nobody knew back in the day that publishing was where the money is. At first everyone thought it was concerts, then it was records, then it was licensing, and then it went back to gigs. But you can't really beat publishing, can't really beat owning all your stuff.

TONY MCGEE: You'd always get a cuddle if you bumped into him. He always asked how you were. The last time I saw him was in the '90s in New York. It was a busy room. I think he was amongst a group of artists—Larry Rivers, Julian Schnabel—that he was really comfortable with. He knew I was there, he'd said hello and it was fine. And he asked me what I was doing and if I was living in New York. But I knew it was over. He had the ability to just move on. I don't think it was anything intentionally bad or rude. It was more to do with his journey. He knew he had to get things done and he said excuse me my friend while I take care of business. That's all it was. I was never insulted by being so hot and then being dropped. People would ask me why I wasn't working with him anymore, and I'd say, "Don't be ridiculous. It's not part of it. You're part of a period."

He could be pissy, though, and would express his displeasure in particular ways. One method was keeping people waiting—not in the traditional celebrity way by keeping people hanging around in an anteroom as a variety of assistants make excuses about their nonappearance, but by doing it in front of them. More than once I saw him engaged in conversation with someone as a "notable" hove into view, and then simply carry on talking. I saw him do this once backstage at the Hammersmith Odeon: he was talking to a crime writer as two rather self-important film producers waltzed into the dressing room, expecting to be given the red-carpet treatment; but they had obviously annoyed Bowie, as he just kept talking to the writer—asking him seemingly extraneous questions about arcane plot points—while studiously ignoring his new guests. He didn't do this for thirty seconds, or a minute, he did it for nearly five minutes, an unnecessary and pointedly elongated period of time that not only told the producers he didn't think they were quite as important as they thought they were, it told everyone else too. Of course, when he finally allowed the crime writer to move on, he embraced the producers with open arms, treating them like long-lost relatives. But they had been told.

TONY OURSLER (ARTIST): My first actual contact with David was like a shock of energy, fully charged with the magic of media, music, and glamor. It was as if he had somehow bilocated between our world and one of myth and didn't fully exist in the same space as ordinary earthlings. Of course, this was all in my mind, and my reaction said much about the delusions of popular culture. Somehow this giant I'd been listening to and watching with such admiration was in my studio. It was hard to reconcile fantasy with flesh. Later, I would notice that this was a common effect of David's presence, sometimes with hilarious results. I remember seeing a Jasper Johns exhibition at MoMA with David, Iman, and the artist Linda Post. David sauntered through the show, busily discussing the art and holding forth like we were in a bubble, while the focus of everyone around us shifted from the art to him. Finally, as we were leaving the museum, a group of women surrounded David and began touching him, as if in a spontaneous frenzy of admiration.

This was in the late '90s, in the early stages of a friendship that lasted more than twenty years. At that time I was living in a hovel of a studio at 175 Ludlow Street, on the Lower East Side. During David's first visit, it took me at least an hour to calm down. I still remember fragments of our first conversations: we both agreed from experience that drugs are bad. While he was chain-smoking and sipping coffee, his thoughts ricocheted, much like his career, from music and film to books, art history, and comics, and back again. He was humble about his accomplishments (saying of his work, "One can pluck a few peppercorns from the shit"), and his humor was unforgettable, as was his deep laugh, often accompanied by a conspiratorial sideways grin. Friends asked me why he came to my studio, and at first I honestly didn't know. It took me a while to understand that he loved art, from discussing how it was made to seeing how artists lived and worked. And it turned out that David wanted to interject some of my work into his lexicon. Much of what we did together became very public—videos can be found on the Internet—but some has never been seen.

All artists want to be rock stars and all rock stars want to be artists. At least that's what I came to believe about the many performers who I discovered were closet painters. David's paintings and installations, which he knew would not be taken seriously, seemed different, though, as if for him the act of making them was part of a ritual engagement with the art world that extended to visiting studios and museums or reading about art history. Like his immersion in so many other forms, this fed his insatiable interest in the creative process, which in turn fed his projects in direct or indirect ways. He was private about his creative process, but I was able to glean more than a few insights over the years. David adored Jacqueline Humphries's work, and once, while he and I and Coco were visiting her studio, I noticed that David was staring, deep in thought, as we were all basking in the glare of Humphries's silver surfaces. I asked how he related to her compositions. His reply was immediate and revealing: "It's very similar to the way I think about constructing music. Overlapping patterns and layers scraped away to reveal other patterns." "Drawn or written out?" I asked. "I see them in my head," he replied.

As an artist, I've always been fascinated with, and jealous of, pop music's ability to take utterly banal material—chord progressions, submoronic lyrics—and imbue them with the ability to enrapture people. Sound directly enters the brain and evaporates, leaving only neuronal traces. Direct, simple, and free for the people, perhaps music is the greatest and most egalitarian art form. It's almost a perfect model, and like many others, I have often wondered whether art could unlock the same secret. Exactly when did poetry become subsumed by rock and roll? When was experimental film swallowed and digested by music videos? My generation of artists held a starry-eyed belief in the notion of crossing over; of leaving the elitism of the white cube for other media and venues: video, performance, audio, music. Previous generations of Brits had a similar notion—maybe the art world just hasn't recognized their work as art yet?

At one point after his heart attack, David went very quiet before reporting to me that he was reading approximately one book a day; he suggested I read one he loved that traced the fate of Oliver Cromwell's head, which had been cut off his disinterred body shortly after burial and traveled here and there. I am grateful to have had these kinds of discussions with David, and sometimes when he thought it had gotten too highbrow he would say with a smile, "It's only rock and roll." When I met him he was flirting with drum 'n' bass, wearing Alexander McQueen clothes onstage—what I think of as the late period. He was in his forties and already living with a huge and storied history. I remember people thinking he was old for a pop star, moving into the murky territory of adult entertainers. He was so disturbed by the endless questioning of his sexuality that he eventually avoided interviews, preferring his work to speak for itself.

WILLIAM BOYD: I wasn't surprised he went along with the *Nat Tate* hoax. Once the text had been written, and the photographs selected and the artworks "created," and was going to be published in the magazine, he came up with the idea to make it a book. He and a few other people had this small art publishing company called 21. He published a few art books (notably by Matt Collings) and he saw Nat Tate as an opportunity. He also offered to write the blurb—who would have turned that down?—and it was great, very clever. And he was the great instigator of the launch party at Jeff Koons's studio. It was his idea to read out extracts, deadpan, making no comment. So he was very much a key conspirator. Nat Tate was invented by me—and the hoax devised by me (I got Gore Vidal and John Richardson—both friends—involved)—but Bowie was a vital part of its launch and presentation to the world. And of course his participation in the hoax has had a huge effect on its survival and notoriety. The party was on April Fool's Day, 1998. Eighteen years later the Nat Tate story shows no sign at all of fizzling out. The book is still in print and selling. It's been translated into German, French, and Spanish. We've made three TV documentaries about Nat Tate. I sold a Nat Tate drawing at Sotheby's for £7,500—and so on. The Bowie connection is absolutely key to that longevity.

It was always phenomenally hard getting in touch with him. Maybe that was a rock-icon thing. I remember trying to reach him when he was in Switzerland, once. I had to write to a Mr. Mueller, who would then give me another address, and then I would write to another pseudonym at another address. He never told me where he was staying even though he owned a house in London. I never spoke to him on the phone. In later years—say, the last decade—it was the same. He became—as far as it applied to me, anyway—something of a recluse. And yet I was sufficiently part of his circle to be asked, by Iman, to contribute a message or a drawing for a scrapbook she was compiling for his sixtieth birthday. But he always kept the world at a real distance, I felt. A very, very private man.

He liked a spoof. When he appeared on the BBC's Comic Relief *in 1999, he made a film which involved him performing a parody called "Requiem for a Laughing Gnome": "Hello boys and girls, I'm David Bowie and I'm talking to you for* Comic Relief. *Tonight I thought I'd do something a little different, so I thought I'd play a new composition for you, that I think you may enjoy. It's called 'Requiem for a Laughing Gnome.' It's for recorder, and it has some choreography that I picked up from a Navajo Indian that I met last week [from] the Croydon chapter. It's in four movements, and I should probably begin with the first movement. Thank you." He then proceeds to play an awful recorder solo, followed by some shoe tapping. A sign flashes up: "THIS LASTS 4 HOURS." Bowie continues playing, and then, in the voice of puppeteer Harry Corbett, says, "Oh, put your clothes on, Sooty." Then, as Bowie starts playing again, another sign then crosses the screen: "We'll go on showing it if you don't call. . . . Please. . . . Please. PLEASE."*

FRANCIS WHATELY (BBC PRODUCER): In those days, in the late '90s, just before *Newsnight* there were two-minute films for fledgling directors about a painting from a recent exhibition in London or wherever it was, and they would get a florist, or a butcher, or a baker to talk about that painting—just a member of the public who might have something interesting to say. I was given a series of ten films on British sculpture. I thought this was a pretty tall order actually: to make two-minute films about British sculpture with members of the public and celebrities. So I faxed David Bowie and said, "Would you be interested in doing this?" And he phoned me immediately and said he would love to. We did a piece that he narrated on a sculpture by Richard Devereux, which was a stone in a wood in Hampshire and on the stone was written the word "Sacred." He created this rather beautiful poem about life and then put "Ian Fish" from *The Buddha of Suburbia* as the soundtrack to it. It was a very gentle, lyrical piece. Anyway he seemed very keen on this when it came out and we kept in touch.

He told me that he'd had an idea about doing something about British art and then it all went quiet. When it came around again I presented his idea to the BBC. And the BBC in their wisdom said, "I don't think so. We don't know who David Bowie is." So they rejected it. Then when I was making an *Omnibus* film on the art of Stanley Spencer, as I knew that he collected Spencer's work I asked him to get involved, and he ended up narrating it. I remember standing in the recording booth with him, somewhere near Times Square in New York. He was with his assistants, one of whom said to me, "You seem awfully nervous, Francis." And kept on saying, "You seem awfully nervous, Francis." Which made me much more nervous. Eventually David said to the assistant, "I would like you to stop saying Francis is nervous; if he wasn't nervous he wouldn't do a good job. Now, leave him alone." Which put me at ease and made me feel very good. During the recording he was talking about various members of the Slade School and he called the artist Percy Wyndham Lewis "Windham" Lewis. And I thought: Oh my goodness; can I really tell David Bowie he's pronounced the name incorrectly? But I thought I must and so I did. And I said, "David, I think his name is Wyndham Lewis." And he said, "Oh, all right, Francis, you're the boss." Which, again, helped the situation. He was very, very gentle, and easy, and respectful, and put me at my ease, like he does with everyone.

In 1998 Angelo Badalamenti received a phone call from the record company that was doing the Red Hot AIDS benefit albums. This year's concept, they said, would be called Red Hot + Rhapsody, and would be dedicated to the songs of George Gershwin. They were looking for collaborations and asked him if he would like to work with a singer. So Badalamenti said yes, and chose "A Foggy Day (In London Town)." He did a demo of the track, and did a guide vocal. He actually asked if he could sing on the finished track, but the record company demanded he use an actual singer. A short while later he is in the Edison Recording Studio on Forty-Sixth Street, in New York, working with Tim Booth from James.

The engineer says, "Angelo, there's a phone call for you."

"Who is it?"

"It's David Bowie."

Bowie says, "Angelo, I just heard this track. It is fantastic. This is for me. I gotta do this song. Please let me do the vocal on this song."

So Badalamenti obviously says yes, telling him how perfectly suited his voice is to the song.

The very next day, seven o'clock in the morning, Badalamenti is at home when the phone rings.

"Angelo, Angelo!"

"Yes, who is this?"

"This is Bono."

Bono says he's in a car, in Ireland, and even though he's insanely busy, on tour with U2, with ten thousand things to do, he's heard the track and he really, really wants to sing on it.

Badalementi says, "Bono, man, it would be great . . . but last night I committed with Bowie."

And Bono says, "Well . . . he sings good too."

REEVES GABRELS: I was doing some stuff for a solo album, which both David and Gary Oldman sing on, while at the same time David was also asked to write some music for the video game Omikron. Initially these things were going to feed into *Hours*, which I had envisioned as *Earthling Part 2*, but then David started thinking he wanted to do more of a singer-songwriter album, so as David had moved to Bermuda, I would go over and work on songs with him, just on acoustic guitar. It was also starting to feel that it might be time for me to move on.

DAVID BOWIE: When you're young you think that every day-to-day thing you do and say is sacred and important, and when you get older, you realize that one's actions in the scheme of things are virtually undetectable. Occasionally I've done things for the wrong reasons, but I would never blame anybody for manipulating me. I've made some gross mistakes, but fortunately they're all on my shoulders, so I've had nobody to blame but myself. I stopped having management and managers and all that kind of thing around 1977. We are just a species dependent on survival instincts, and that's how we build up our moralities, absolutes, and truths. Good and evil we have created ourselves because those two things help us survive as a unity and as a species. There is no basis that one is superior to the other, not at all. A lot of evil is just a series of dysfunctions. That is not a popular opinion, and it isn't something I'm going to get on my soapbox again and shout about, because the didactic element of entertainment begins to pall after a while. Ambition is a funny thing.

EARL SLICK: I would see him whenever he played in L.A., where I was living, but we didn't work together again until *Heathen*. In late 1999 I got the call again. He didn't know what condition I was in, so he asked me to audition, which I wasn't happy about. He was in a great state of mind though, the best I ever saw him. Throughout *Heathen* and *Reality* he was in such a good place. On the road he had such a blast, smiling all the day, I'd never seen him happier. We had a good run for about four years straight. We also did a record called *Toy*, which never came out, which was rerecorded versions of old songs. Great record. I think he was in between record deals and had contractual problems.

Toward the end of the '90s, I was invited to a dinner somewhere in north London. I'd just come back from a trip to New York and I'd got a call in the office asking me if I wanted to go to a small dinner the following evening being given by a very notable person. In truth what I actually wanted to do was go home and fall asleep in front of the TV, but the invitation was too tempting, so I accepted. The next night, having arrived bang on time, I saw three other guests, so there was just going to be the five of us (I know, to my cost, that often when you're invited to a "small" dinner, it can mean anything from 50 to 250 people). And it was fun, and actually quite real. Sometimes, when you're in the presence of a celeb, all they want to do is talk, and have you nod, laugh, and agree with their opinions. But this was a real conversation, and we discussed everything from politics and journalism to fashion and music, and obviously who was sleeping with whom. At one point the celeb gave me a hard time for some of the more combative writers I had hired, accusing me of just using journalists who were attack dogs—the accused being A. A. Gill, Boris Johnson, Rod Liddle, Piers Morgan, and Giles Coren, all of whom had been hired by me for GQ*—but I fought my corner, and felt all the better for it.*

But then the mood changed, and just as we were discussing one particular singer-songwriter's habit of ripping off other people (I can't actually remember who this was), our host started tearing into David Bowie. Big-time. "If you're talking about plagiarism then you have to mention David fucking Bowie," said our host. "He is such a rip-off artist. I know so many people whose ideas have been stolen by him, and I wouldn't have him anywhere near a recording studio. He's always called a magpie, but he's not, he's a fucking thief. The number of times I've heard other musicians, other artists, say that Bowie has stolen something of theirs, or called a producer they had mentioned they were thinking of working with, or designer, or a songwriter. He just can't be trusted." Soon this turned into a fantastically entertaining monologue, even though it soured the evening a bit.

DAVID BOWIE: I smoke like a chimney, but that's about it. I do Tylenol, but nothing else. I don't do *anything* anymore, I don't drink, I don't do drugs. I'm not a fitness freak, though, and I only really work out before I go on tour. The rest of the time I'm dreadful. I do virtually nothing. I walk about a bit, but that's about it. I'll drag my wife from museum to museum, and that's about the only exercise that I get. I'm an old bloke. Ha!

As for mortality, it's here, it's now. Martin Amis said that a man doesn't begin to feel mortal until his forties, but I disagree with Amis, actually. It's never occurred to me at any time in my life that my time could be anything but finite. Even as a young man I was always aware that death was the one absolute certainty about life. It didn't reduce my feeling of buoyancy, it pushed me into a kind of colossal, obsessive activity. I'm still like that. I work overtime. I tend to work on three or four projects at once, often in very different worlds. I usually find that one feeds the other. It almost feels like you're touching different parts of your brain. Nothing ever impedes. I never get confused.

I don't look too bad, and I don't feel too bad, if I'm honest. It's a genetic thing, a flesh-and-blood thing. My father's to blame. Considering what I've been through, I'm a lucky so-and-so. It's nauseating, I know, but I'm in love with my wife. I've still got my health and I love my job. So shoot me.

12

AS LONG AS THERE'S YOU

2000–2015

BAZ LUHRMANN (DIRECTOR): With the success of the previous films [*Romeo + Juliet* and *Strictly Ballroom*], I was in a position to make pretty much whatever I wanted—although I had to do some convincing to get *Moulin Rouge!* made. During the early *Moulin* writing sessions, I was once again working with my closest friend from school, the wonderful Craig Pearce. From the day we met, Craig and I shared a devotion to Bowie. We were great fans. When Craig and I were constructing the script, we imagined a character called Christian, a nineteenth-century poet, who keeps going off to Paris, rejecting his wealthy family, to become a bohemian in the underworld of nineteenth-century Montmartre. If Christian is gifted with song like Orpheus, it's because the underlying storytelling of *Moulin Rouge!* was Orphean. It's the spirit of the underworld. And when he sings or speaks poetry in the underworld, he must beguile its spirits. "The very rocks and stones rise up and follow him." So we started writing "poetry" for Christian, and (surprise, surprise) it was laughable. We settled on the unusual conceit that Christian, our Orpheus, would sing and channel popular contemporary music from the greats including Elton John and others. I didn't know Elton at all, but thankfully once I did he said, "Yes, this is a great idea, let's do it!" and he led the charge.

We were using many classics and were thrilled to be able to incorporate interpretations of two Bowie classics: "Diamond Dogs," which we worked on with Beck and Timbaland. And then the iconic "Heroes," which crescendos in the "Elephant Love Medley," sung by Ewan [McGregor] and Nicole [Kidman]. Eventually, we settled upon the idea of using "Nature Boy" as our principal narrative device. This was my chance to reach out to David Bowie, for indeed, all of *Moulin Rouge!* was truly influenced by Bowie and his creative sensibility. I was in the editorial room in Los Angeles one day and the phone rang: "Hi, Baz. It's David here." In my head it was all nerves: Uh, uh. OK. Right. Yes. That would be *David Bowie*?! Stay calm. Stay calm.

By this point in my career, I had worked and mixed somewhat with all manner of icons. But Bowie was different altogether. He was more than an icon. Bowie was such a profound part of my youth. Mine was a true, deep, and abiding fandom. So to hear his voice—which Craig and I used to mimic—was very disconcerting. David and I spoke quite briefly and he said, "It sounds like something I should get close to. Let's meet."

So I went to meet him at the Four Seasons in Los Angeles. Thankfully, David's longtime assistant, Coco, had obviously spent a large part of her life making people feel quite relaxed about being around him. And when he joined us, thankfully it seemed that he had spent a large part of his life making people feel quite relaxed about being around David Bowie as well. Bowie's imagery was so diverse, but essentially the characters are distant, alien-like, and you expect *him* to be alien-like. The thing I was not expecting was that he had an incredible social ease, and an active desire to put you at ease.

So I showed him my reel, which demonstrated how *Moulin Rouge!* would work, and explained, "What we're trying to do is decode the idea of the musical using the classical DNA of what a musical is, but transposed for this audience, in this time." He paused, his eyes kind of narrowed into that "David Bowie stare," and he began, "Well, from one decoder to another . . ." In fact, that "one decoder to another" moment was the moment where I finally thought, OK, I might be on the right track with *Moulin*.

David immediately got what *Moulin* needed to be. Then came the "Nature Boy" recording and he did this remarkable thing. He was in the studio with his longtime producer and collaborator Tony Visconti. They were in the middle of a session when David reached out to ask, "How do you want me to do the end?" David said he could do it one way—which is how most people would have done it—*or*, "do you want an operatic ending?" "Let's do both?" I said. So he did both and he did it [in] two takes: one take for each. That's all we needed. Each was vocally pristine. The best I've ever heard in my life. The operatic ending went on gloriously for what felt like ten minutes. Of course it was probably ten or fifteen seconds, but the vocal was such true opera in its purity, strength, and clarity.

KATE MOSS (MODEL): The first time I ever went to Glastonbury [in 2000] was because he was playing. I just went down there with my mum, Petrina Khashoggi, and Anita Pallenberg; it was a really random mix of people. We all jumped in my Range Rover, and we didn't have tickets, and I just thought we could all blag it when we got there, but obviously you can't do that! We were waiting at the gate, and I was shouting, "I need to speak to somebody that's in charge!" You know, doing one of those. Then Jools Holland drove out and saw me and just gave us all his passes, and so did everyone in his car. So we got in just in time to see David Bowie. And Anita Pallenberg made a little fire, and we were dancing around it, and that was the first time we saw him live. And that was my first Glastonbury.

HANIF KUREISHI: I remember how nervous he was at Glastonbury. His voice was failing, he had to do a gig the next day at the BBC, and he was really worried. I remember going out and standing at the side of the stage, and the sound was terrible and it was freezing. As soon as it was finished he rushed offstage, grabbed Duncan, and then got in the car and went straight to bed. He hated it. I thought this was a crazy way to make a living. I'd never seen so many people in my life as I did that night in the crowd at Glastonbury. It was incredible to me that someone could be so nervous, and yet still have the balls to go out there and make it all work. At this stage in his life he was worried that the young people might not like his records anymore. He felt insecure, and was obviously at a strange point in his life.

DAVID BOWIE: When the Twin Towers were attacked, I personally wasn't recording, I was up north, in Woodstock, in the album mines. Iman was there with our baby so, of course, psychologically it was unbelievably traumatic because I wasn't on the bloody spot. And it was all done by phone, until the phones were cut off. Oh man, I can't tell you how terribly scary that was. That was terrifying. Because the thing happened and I was talking to Iman, and she was saying, "Oh my God, a second one has gone in." Boom! And I said, "Get the fuck out of there: you're under attack." It was so obvious to me, as soon as the second one hit. It was like, Jesus Christ, they're being attacked. I said, "Get the pram, and just put all the essentials in it and get the hell out of there." She rushed up about fifteen, twenty blocks, just literally running with the pram, and then got to her friend's, because we're quite a way downtown. I said, "Call me when you get to a place of safety," and of course she never called back because all the lines were down. I thought, No, no, not now. Did she get out? And of course nobody knew anything. Nothing. And then all the roads were cut off. We couldn't drive into New York because the police had the city surrounded. You couldn't get in, you couldn't get out. It was really awful. In a way I suppose it was inevitable, especially with what's been happening politically. It's very easy to look at situations like these in a binary fashion, and the September 11 attacks encouraged us to look a little closer.

MARKUS KLINKO (PHOTOGRAPHER): It was the late spring of 2001 when I met Angelina Jolie's makeup artist, Paul Starr, on a shoot for *Interview* in New York. He asked if I'd ever worked with Iman, another client of his, and said he'd take my portfolio over to her house, just a few blocks down the street from my studio. The next day, Iman called me and said she wanted to meet and talk about a project. She'd been working on her first book, *I am Iman*, already had contributions from Helmut Newton and Steven Meisel, but wanted me to shoot the cover.

The session was successful. She wore dresses sent over by Alexander McQueen, and took on the role of a fierce warrior goddess. A couple of days later, she returned to the studio to look at the edits with me, and Bowie came along to help choose the cover. He was every bit as charismatic as you'd expect. David was very involved in the selection process and had a great eye for detail. During the editing session, he casually mentioned he might be working on a new album and that perhaps he would call me to talk about shooting the cover for it. That sounded a bit too good to be true, and I didn't get my hopes up. Meanwhile the events of 9/11 took place less than a mile from my studio, and for a while I forgot about the album cover. Yet, a few weeks after the tragedy, true to his word, Bowie called. He asked if I could come over to a Broadway recording studio and listen to some tracks, and so I went over the next day. I wandered around the studio to find Bowie and Tony Visconti in one of the anterooms, huddled over some tapes. After listening to the album together, we started talking about the shoot—he had many ideas and was very precise.

He was eager to get it all set up as quickly as possible, and when he returned the next day, he brought a series of early Man Ray images he was interested in referencing. He wanted to be styled in '40s suits and wanted to get into the character of a blind man. At that time, most of my work was very colorful, but he absolutely wanted black and white. At the shoot he knew exactly what poses and expressions to do in order to portray the character, and during the following weeks, often came by to edit the photos. One day, he stopped by while I was shooting a British *GQ* editorial with a lot of male and female models running around in towels and he said, "This reminds me of the '70s! And I remember nothing from the '70s . . ."

Heathen was released in 2002, and Bowie went on tour to promote the album. Around that time, I got a call from *GQ* in London, asking me to shoot David for their "Men of the Year" cover. Since Bowie was busy with the tour and was not available for a shoot within the deadline, a solution had to be found. So I called him up and asked if he would trust me with creating a series of photocompositions, using a body double and several wild wolves. He agreed, and gave me carte blanche to do what I liked. My agent called the modeling agencies, and I decided on a young guy who had Bowie's body shape. Next, I needed to find a bunch of wolves and get them to SoHo. Luckily, a prominent handler of wild animals for photo shoots was a huge Bowie fan and agreed to bring the beasts to New York. Our male model proved himself up to the job, and while he looked nothing like Bowie, was able to channel him through his body language. The images of David from the *Heathen* session and the shots of the body model and wolves were later combined by postproduction. Bowie was fascinated by the notion of authenticity, and loved the fact that the images were as imaginary as so many of his album covers: *Hunky Dory*, *Aladdin Sane*, *Pin Ups*, *Diamond Dogs*, *Heathen*—all were permutations of himself.

What you learned quite quickly about Bowie was his ability to focus. It was all about focus. He could look at a situation and gauge its importance and its repercussions like a man watching sand run out of an hourglass. He had no interest in random nature, only in events that could be co-opted or improved upon. In September 2002 we were holding our annual GQ *Men of the Year Awards at the Natural History Museum in South Kensington, a venue that had become renowned for its appalling acoustics. His award was a Legend Award, and the last to be presented that evening. I was waiting for him backstage when he turned up with Coco, Alan Edwards, and a couple of freelance security guys. He was dressed head-to-toe in Hedi Slimane, and looked marvelous. But his focus was not on the way he looked. He knew that he was due to walk out into the audience, hop up onstage, and collect his award from Stella McCartney. It had all been arranged, and he had known the details for months. And yet he couldn't hear a thing, couldn't hear what the host, Jonathan Ross, was saying onstage, couldn't gauge the tone of the audience, and was actually completely out of his comfort zone. As it got closer to the time he was due to walk out, he looked at me in panic. And not in a good way. Everything about him said,* Why have you put me in this position? I am about to walk into a room full of five hundred people—the great, the good, and the entitled—and I am without armor. I know nothing about what's on the other side of that door, and I don't like it. *Nevertheless, he walked out, collected his award, made an impassioned, funny speech, and then posed with Paul Smith, [the band] Travis, and Stella McCartney afterward. However, against the advice of Alan Edwards, he refused to have his photograph taken with another winner, Holly Valance, a young actress who had just embarked upon a surprisingly successful singing career. This was a mistake, as most of the papers the next day carried photographs of her rather than him. Focused to the end, he was furious.*

DAVID BOWIE: I would definitely put *Heathen* up there with some of the better work that I have done, for sure. *Heathen* I like. Although I think it would be easier to say that if the albums were consistently one style. It's the best album at doing what? It's not *Low*. So does that mean that *Low* is my best ever album? It's not like *Heathen*, and it's not like *Scary Monsters*, or *The Man Who Sold the World*. *Heathen* is much more a collection of songs, you know? It's more straightforward. It's verses and choruses and la-di-dah and I'll see you at the end. So would you compare it to *Hunky*

Dory? I don't actually think you could. I think they're chalk and cheese, but then I can probably say that about nearly every record I've ever made. I've made over twenty-five studio albums, and I think probably I've made two real stinkers in my time, and some not-bad albums, and some really good albums. I'm proud of what I've done. In fact, it's been a good ride.

RICKY GERVAIS (COMEDIAN): Well, first of all, he couldn't have really done any wrong when I met him, because he was already a hero. He'd been a hero since I was fifteen. The first time I met him, *The Office* had just broken, so I was invited to a VIP audience with David Bowie at the BBC, must have been about 2002. I'm there with my girlfriend, and we went to the green room afterwards. And Greg Dyke, then director general of the BBC, comes over and says, "You're a fan, aren't you?" "Yeah, I love Bowie." And he says, "Come and meet him." And I'm going, "No, no, no." And he says, "Come and meet him . . ." So I say OK, and so we're walking to see Bowie, and he goes, "Salman!" to Salman Rushdie, and so he joins us. So there's me, my girlfriend, Salman Rushdie, and Greg Dyke and we go down and meet David Bowie. He went, "Hello, Salman." And then I was introduced, and I was sort of thinking, It's fucking David Bowie!

The next night I'm out with my mate, and we're going down the pub and he says, "What did you do last night?" And I said, "Nothing." I mean, what could I say? "Oh yeah, I've just been hanging out with David Bowie, Salman Rushdie, and Greg Dyke?"

Then about a week later, I just bought *Aladdin Sane* again on CD. I think I was getting a second CD because it was scratched. I get home and I get an email from David Bowie. I'm nearly 100 percent sure he did not know who I was on the night, or cared, he was just polite, said, "Hello, Ricky." Afterwards he must have said, "Who's that?" and someone said, "Oh, he did a thing called *The Office*." And the email was just this. It just said, subject: The Office. "I watched, I laughed, what do I do now? DB." And I sent back, "That's weird, I just bought *Aladdin Sane* and then the composer emails me."

We became pen pals, and started exchanging funny emails about art and everything. When he came over to England, he invited me to dinner, "With some very old friends." So me and my girlfriend went along to this place in Richmond, and there was us, these people—David Bowie,

Richard E. Grant, Pete Townshend—all having dinner. The night before I'd been on Paul Merton's *Room 101* and they'd showed a clip of Seona Dancing, the New Romantic band I was in thirty years ago, which is me basically doing a Bowie impression. So at dinner the next night, David Bowie turns up and comes up to me and says, "Seems I owe you an apology. I saw you on TV last night and I think I've been ripping you off for the last thirty years." I went, "Yeah, all right, calm down, it wasn't just me, it was everyone else in 1983 ripping you off."

It was just really sweet, do you know what I mean? I remember asking about his work, or I think I told him once that he was my favorite and then never again. Then I plucked up the courage to ask him to be in *Extras*. I said, "I thought the joke would be that I bump into you and you're just really awful to me." I thought wouldn't it be funny if he was an asshole? He liked the idea and so I sent him the lyrics for "Little Fat Man." I then called him up and said, "Can you do something retro, like a 'Life on Mars?'–type thing." And he said, "Oh sure, I'll just knock out a quick fucking 'Life on Mars?' for you." I just started laughing, like, who am I to be telling Bowie what to do?

A few years later he was curating a festival for the High Line in New York, and he asked me to be the headline act at Madison Square Garden. I was a bit worried, so I said, "Have you seen my stand-up? Can I just do anything?" And he said, "You can do anything as long as it's delightfully offensive." What a thing to say. Delightfully offensive.

KATE MOSS: I had him up on my wall when I was about twelve. I think it was a birthday card from my dad actually, of him as the Thin White Duke, with short blond hair. The first song that really hit me was probably "Life on Mars?" because I think I thought I was the girl with the mousy brown hair. I thought it was about me, being a pain to my mum and dad, because I was young and modeling. It touched me because I thought it was my song. I did a shoot with Ellen von Unwerth in 2003, and they wanted me to interview him, and because I'm not a muso, I'm not one of those people who knows everything about David Bowie, I sat around with some friends and ripped up all these pieces of paper that had questions on them, and put them into this old top hat, and asked him to pick the questions out. He said that because you didn't have to save up for music anymore—like when he was young he would have to save up for ages and then send away for a record to be delivered—that music didn't mean as much anymore. I was saying that was not the case because I didn't have to save up to listen to "Life on Mars?" but I didn't know how much music could touch somebody like that. I even asked him if there was a moment when he thought he might have changed music forever. He said it was in this club [the Greyhound] in South London that I knew, in West Croydon in 1972. He was playing that night with Bryan Ferry and Brian Eno, and after everyone had left, David said that he and Eno were talking about existentialism. And he said that that's when everything changed, when his whole vibe of music changed. The interview was only meant to be an hour and I was there for five hours. His manager kept coming in from the studio and saying, "David, you've given them enough time now, if you want to go." And David kept saying, "No, we haven't had enough time yet. We haven't finished." And he wouldn't let me go. And I think the studio manager knew I was really hungover, and I was so desperate to get out. And I couldn't smoke and I couldn't drink. So I think he knew, like I was thinking, *Please let me go. Please let me go.* But he didn't let me!

On the shoot the day before I had got really overexcited because it was so amazing. I was naked, wrapped around his back, and he was straddling me, going, "You've got beautiful eyes." And I was just like, Oh my God David Bowie, David Bowie, David Bowie said that. And then all I said was, "Oh, you've got a beautiful eye!" I was so nervous that was all that could come out of my mouth. The nerves afterwards meant I just got really pissed. But then the next day I had to do the interview. I was in my element during the shoot as I was in my turf, but then so was he. It was really easy. He didn't make me feel uncomfortable at all. We got on with it. I don't know whose idea it was for me to be naked, but at that point in my career I think everyone asked me to get naked! I wore less clothes than clothes when I was modeling at that point. But he was very paternal. During the interview he started asking me questions. I remember him saying, "You drink, don't you? You're a 'nighty' girl" and [mentioning] all the anorexia stuff. I just didn't expect that at all. I was like, "You did drugs," and he was like, "Not really." He didn't admit to me that he had. He was being paternal. He wanted to take care of me. He sent me emails over the years which said, "Just want to know how you are, what you're doing. Are you behaving yourself?" I've got the Polaroid of me naked from that shoot, wrapped around the back of him. That's probably my favorite memory of him. That's my claim to fame. I can say, "Look at this!" It's on a shelf in my study.

STERLING CAMPBELL: David loved playing live but he hated touring. At one point on the final tour he talked about having a residency somewhere, so he didn't have to travel, but it never happened. The last tour was far too long. That surprised me at first. It was a big production and it needed to be long to pay for itself, but it was too long and he got very tired. The day he had his heart attack was surreal. You couldn't believe it was happening.

EARL SLICK: It's not true that the last tour was too long. I had a conversation with him about a month before the tour was over, and he pulled me aside and he said he didn't want to do yearlong tours anymore, for the next four or five years he wanted to do residencies. A week at Radio City. A week at the Shrine Auditorium in L.A. Whatever. Fucking great. Less traveling. Less wear and tear on our asses. I'm in. And then he had the heart attack. But the heart attack had nothing to do with the tour. Obviously he had a time bomb going on. First of all he wasn't even smoking. We'd both been sober for many years. So it wasn't drugs and alcohol. I spent every day with him and he ate well. And when I was out the back of the hotel smoking, he was in the gym. He was taking good care of himself.

MIKE GARSON: I think he loved the last tour. But it was way too long. The mistake was that after we finished the first leg, maybe nine months, we started doing the secondary cities in America, just to keep us going, and I don't think he wanted to do them. We should have just taken a few months off and then picked it up for the European shows. What happened is he got tired. He stopped smoking around 1999, and thank God he did, because he was always smoking. We were on the bus in 2002 or 2003, and he was very pissed off because the doctor had put him on cholesterol pills. He had a trainer and he was working out. He had a chef. And I said, "What, you don't think the last twenty-five, thirty years has taken a toll on your body?" Then seven months later we're onstage in Czechoslovakia and there's something wrong with David and he didn't look good at all. He stopped the show for a while but somehow finished it. Then two days later we're in Hamburg, and before we go on he told me that he had seen the president of Czechoslovakia's doctor and he had told him he'd had a muscle spasm. Then we went onstage and he had his heart attack, which put a stop to everything. And then he had these stents put in. He was overworked. I think we could have pulled it off had we not done all those smaller cities back in America. We had already had a guy fall to his death on the rig because he hadn't put his safety belt on. Things were already starting to go wrong. He was the mystery man and you never knew what was in his head, but it didn't look like he was going to come back and play live. We all had hope.

HARVEY GOLDSMITH: On his last tour, the *Reality* tour, in 2004, when he ended up having the heart attack, I'd actually seen him in L.A. a few months previously. He was doing a show in a theatre on Wilshire Boulevard called the Wiltern before he was going to play Anaheim. And I got a phone call to ask if I was coming down to see the show, and would I like to go backstage afterwards and see him. I spent about half an hour with him that night; he closed the door and wouldn't let anyone else in, and he started complaining about the tour. He said he wasn't enjoying it, said it was too long—it was 112 shows in all—and that he was dealing with bureaucrats. He said the tour had no soul. He asked me why I wasn't promoting it and I said I wasn't given the opportunity to pitch for it. But he was uncomfortable. I put those heart problems down to exhaustion.

BRIAN MOLKO: I was actually playing the festival, the last one, that he had to cancel because of the heart problem. After that he just wanted to go back to New York and see his daughter grow up. Then we entered the Christmas-card stage of our friendship. But that was cool. For me, I gleaned enough stardust from the man just by osmosis.

BEBE BUELL: When my daughter [Liv Tyler] got married to Royston Langdon from Spacehog, they did a concert on a rooftop—this was in 2003—and he came to support them. He loved to support young musicians and new music. He would quietly slip in. So there I am standing there with David, Todd, and Steven [Tyler], and my daughter. I remember standing with him on that rooftop, it was like a hundred degrees, and Spacehog were playing, but he had this beautiful smile on his face, and he loved the music, and I remember he leaned down and whispered in my ear, and he said, "Look, we're all still here!" And it brought tears to my eyes. It just did. You know when you feel that sense of community and sense of family. I know a lot of people in his life were ostracized and he had to get rid of people because their energy was very negative, and he couldn't keep that around him, and sometimes you have to make tough choices in life. Some people don't evolve; they remain drunk and high and don't evolve as humans. But David was very much about growing. He was very much about changing and learning and becoming a better man. That was very eminent in his last fifteen to twenty years. He was such a family man; he was very real. The bottom line—and I know this firsthand, because he told me this when we were young and crazy—was that all he ever wanted was true love.

DAVID BOWIE: Having a family leveled me out. I'll tell you what a lot of it is; it's moving from a life of action to one of a little more of contemplation. Initially every minute of your life has to count, and you have to be doing something. Possibly because both my parents had the same work ethic thing—you know, work as salvation, almost as salvation from what else was going on in their lives. The humanists' replacement for religion is what it's all about: Work really hard and somehow you'll either save yourself or you'll be immortal. Of course that's a total joke, a sham, and our progress is nothing. There may be progress in technology but there's no ethical progress whatsoever. We're still exactly the same immoral bastards that we were twenty thousand years ago. You start to feel that maybe there is no pattern there, that it's just one endless miasmic experience. And that's when it really gets very serious because then you have to start contemplating that there might be a situation where there is no God.

MOBY: In the year 2000, David Bowie moved in across the street from me in New York and we became very good friends. We went on tour together. We had Christmas together. It was remarkable but very disconcerting to be neighbors and very good friends with a man who was my favorite musician of all time! We would wave at each other from our balconies. I would go to the deli to buy soy milk and oats and he and Iman would be in there buying oranges and coffee. They were my neighborhood pals. It started to seem normal but at the back of my mind I never forgot the fact that David Bowie was a demigod and a genius and the best musician who will ever live.

DAVID LAUREN (EXECUTIVE VICE PRESIDENT, RALPH LAUREN ORGANIZATION): Around 2004 I met him at a big fashion event in New York with my mother and father. David was with his wife, and was the personification of elegance. I couldn't get over how shy he was, how quiet. He wasn't showy, didn't have an act, and seemed to be incredibly humble. He wasn't the least bit demonstrative, which in a rock star can be unusual. We talked a little at dinner, and he came across as someone who was very respectful, and who didn't especially want to hog the limelight. It was only a brief encounter but I think I got the measure of the man. He appeared to be such a lovely gentleman.

DAVID BOWIE: Fashion? Well, you see, the thing is, I'm not that interested in fashion. As long as I'm comfortable, that is. But I do know the importance of how a way of looking denotes your attitude about whatever it is you're supposed to be involved with. So for me, dressing is performance, simple as that. People have always thought I was obsessed with fashion and it's just not true. I'm fascinated by it, and I use it when I need to use it, but I don't obsess about it. Why would you! I like Ralph Lauren, have for years. It's chic but anonymous. It's luxury but you wouldn't know it unless you made a song and dance about it. Paul [Smith] is a great British designer, but I also like his attitude about himself. He's very modest and full of grace. There's something clunky about English fashion that I like. It's not as svelte as the Italians, only the English can wear it well.

KEANAN DUFFTY (FASHION DESIGNER): My work was always very influenced by Bowie, and when I moved from London to New York, everything I did in the runway area was very Bowie-esque. People were always encouraging me to work with him, so eventually I approached his business manager Bill Zysblat, initially with just ideas about doing T-shirts and merchandising for the tours, but possibly doing it with a bit more of a fashion aspect to it. Bill was going to get me together with David but he was in the middle of tour, with nine months to go, and then David had that heart issue, so his health interrupted everything. A little later, in 2006, I went back to Bill, having just made a deal with Cargo, the mass retailer, making collections for Target. I said it would be great to design a collection that was directly associated with David. The collections I had done were in six hundred stores, so this was big. I didn't expect to meet David, but Bill arranged for us to meet in his office on East Fifty-Seventh Street. Bill said we should meet to see if we got along, which from my side was a bizarre idea. So we kicked the tires of the idea. He turned up as David Jones, in a very lighthearted and jovial way. He was very demystifying. I'm sure he met so many people who have been so in awe of him over the years, that I think he developed this persona to deal with it. He'd worn some of my high-end stuff previously, but he didn't really know what Target was. He was very clear that he didn't want to be in any way identified as the designer, but he was talking about "if" we were going to do it, so he was obviously very decisive. After forty-five minutes we were doing it. The thing that struck me most was that he turned up wearing bad clothes. A dodgy sweatshirt, baggy trousers, beat-up old shoes. He actually said are we going to do shoes like these? At first I thought he might be fucking with me, intentionally being anti-fashion. He actually said, "I'm not interested in fashion particularly," which was quite a shock. Then I thought, Of course he's not fucking with me; he didn't care that much to mess around with someone's head. He's just turning up wearing regular clothes because he's off duty. He was very friendly. When I told him I was from Doncaster he said his dad was from there.

Then I went to Minneapolis, where Target is based, and made a presentation. I took all my Bowie albums and a little plastic portable record player. They were expecting mood boards and samples, and instead they got music. I said I want to bring a major rock star's collection to Target, and I'm not going to tell you who it is, I'm just going to show you. I put one of the albums on and they were aghast. "Oh my God! Bowie, Bowie!" Then they said, can you do this again because we have to bring the president! There were three different collections initially, one based on *Station to Station*, one on *Hunky Dory*, and another on Serious Moonlight, which was very sporty. One idea was the circuit-board print that he wore on the *Ziggy Stardust* cover. Bowie loved the ideas when I went back to him, and although he wasn't interested in designing anything, he seemed fascinated by the process. He obviously spent his entire career legacy building. I always think of Bowie as being very futuristic, but when I look back at everything he was always referencing past stuff. Just look at all the images from *"Heroes"* and *Aladdin Sane* hidden on the back of *Scary Monsters*.

Target went into overdrive, David gave us some unreleased material for a merchandising CD, and the whole thing was huge. They even concocted a holographic fashion show at Grand Central Station for the launch. Our final meeting was in David's own office on Lafayette Street, where we looked at the finished collection. The circuit-board print shirt hadn't made the cut, but David was adamant he wanted it included. Interestingly that was the only piece in the collection that didn't sell out. Everything else was gone in two weeks. He was moving on, anyway. By that time he was seeing so many other celebrity-driven collections going into the fashion marketplace he'd lost interest. The two things I learned about was firstly that he liked to surround himself with people he could trust—Tony Visconti, Bill, Earl Slick, Mike Garson, Coco. The other thing is how normal he was. Here was a guy who in the early part of his career was a relatively normal ex-mod who was trying to be arty and weird, and then he actually did become weird. And then he spent the end of his life trying to get back to being normal. He was striving to be a regular person. He even recorded in a studio near his apartment so he could go home for tea.

DAVID BOWIE: My past doesn't belong to anyone but me, although I am obviously respectful of people's relationship with it. I'm not much interested in my own mythology. It feels quite fabulous when you watch MTV and realize that someone is doing "me," but I don't want to go back myself, and I don't want to trawl through the archives. I've forgotten the number of times I've been asked to revive Ziggy as a musical; everybody sees money, they look at *Tommy*, and a lightbulb goes off in their heads. But I must admit I like reading about myself, and I even read my ex-wife's book. It's terrifying! The first time I ever read one [a biography by George Tremlett back in the early '70s] I didn't know whether to be angry or mystified, as there were so many inaccuracies. But as subsequent books kept coming out with all their own interpretations, I thought I'd quite like to put one out which incorporates all the inaccuracies, making this kind of truly fantastic creation. It could be my autobiography.

You can throw any amount of shit at me and it's really not going to have much effect, but when it starts to touch my family, then it's horrific. I never lectured Joe about sex or drugs or what he was going to do with his life. I didn't think it was my role. Ostensibly he's so much more mature and far more disciplined than I was at that age. He's very different in his ability to cope with relationships; he's much better at it than I ever was. He's had the same girlfriend for years, which is something that I could not have conceived of at that age. I was irresponsibly promiscuous. And he's never to my knowledge been involved in drugs. He doesn't drink and he doesn't smoke.

MICK ROCK: In New York he disappeared. He had had the strokes and was keeping himself to himself. He was just enjoying not talking to the press, and the less he talked the more we wanted to know. I teased him and said it was his Greta Garbo period. He laughed at that. At the time everyone thought he was dying, but he was just not doing anything. We would meet at his apartment on Lafayette and just go for a coffee. He always looked fine, he was just taking things quietly. He would say, "I just need a bit of downtime, Mick." He just wasn't interested in engaging. He'd been quite seriously ill, he'd stopped touring, and then all these rumors started about what was wrong with him. But the only thing wrong with him was that he simply wanted to disappear.

CHALKIE DAVIES: Before he moved downtown he had a place up by Lincoln Center. When you went in they gave you a little ticket, and you went to the elevator and they took you to the floor but there were no numbers on the doors for security reasons. Then you stepped into this beautifully decorated apartment, where the skirting boards all looked like Mondrians.

DAVID BOWIE: I did sit down with a couple of seriously talented guys, and we thrashed out a plan of what could happen with Ziggy as both a stage show and as another record, even though I had initially been wary about revisiting something which obviously still means so much to people. We endeavored to put a shape to it as a theatrical piece and actually it was a nonstarter. It just didn't come together in the way that I thought it might. The more I wrote into it, the smaller and smaller it just seemed to be. How something so iconic as Ziggy Stardust could end up being so reductive in my own hand, I don't know, but it did, it really did. And one of the guys actually posed the question, "Why are you doing this?" He said that it means a lot to people and why was I buggering around with it. My word, not his. Didn't I feel that by developing him, developing Ziggy, I would be closing up all the possibilities to the character? He said if I devised a formidable storyline, I'd probably be ruining everybody else's ideas about who Ziggy really is, or at least who he really is for them. We kind of got to the consensus that we would probably be doing the whole idea of Ziggy a disservice by nailing it in this way. I think its major strength is that there was such an ephemeral quality to the whole business, and it left so many options open for people to read into themselves. That was his valuable service to humanity: I'm Ziggy, use me. Which is what we all did. Even me!

TONY OURSLER: Once, while visiting the Rubin Museum of Art, David and I discussed Carl Jung's *The Red Book* in relation to Jung's alternative view of channeling characters while making art. That's a distinctly alternative view to Freud, and to my mind, Bowie's collection of personas offers just such a liberating trajectory, while also providing an alternative to the American cliché of rugged individualism and fixed "authentic" identity. I believe David relocated to the US in part as a reaction against the class system of the UK, and was surprised by the Puritanism he found here [in the US]. For him, self-invention was inherently futuristic, linked to the notion of a disposable self. His work implies seemingly endless possibilities at the same time that it deconstructs the mechanism of self-presentation. A few props come out of the closet, he puts on a little greasepaint and turns on a light or two; in this way, David offers infinite alternatives, inviting us all to join in the play. He is one of the rare artists whose work truly functions as a refuge for outsiders, and through a mysterious spontaneous combustion it gives birth to other artists too.

HANIF KUREISHI: Mark Adams worked for David, looking after his website, his box sets, general administrative stuff. I once did a reading from

The Buddha of Suburbia with Erdal; Lisa Ronson, Mick's daughter; Marc Almond; Glen Matlock; and some other Bowie people, in a club just off the Tottenham Court Road. And Mark was there, and when I asked him why, he said, "David likes to know what's going on." I thought that was fascinating.

OWEN PALLETT (MUSICIAN): In 2005 he invited Arcade Fire to play some shows with him, and then Bowie offered to take the band out for dinner. Most of the band had other plans, so it was literally me, Patrick, Win, Regine, Will, and Jenny having dinner at a place on Avenue A with Bowie and Coco. Me and Patrick were sitting across from Bowie, and Bowie and I hit it off insanely and talked about Mishima (Bowie was in Tokyo when Mishima died) and This Heat and all sorts of stuff. Patrick hit it off with Bowie too, [and] they talked mostly about fashion and furniture design. We talked about his smoking habit (he told me he'd quit just a year before he had his heart attack). He was wearing Creed Silver Mountain Water cologne. Which is wonderful but too ostentatious for anyone but Bowie to ever get away with. Bowie drank pomegranate juice, which was the new thing in 2005, and was delighted when they provided him with [a bottle of] POM. Every report I'd heard about "meeting Bowie" suggests that the guy was really good at meeting people and making them feel like a million bucks, but no words could really describe the man's complete generosity of spirit, intelligence, and charisma. Anyway, the next day we were all in rehearsals and Bowie saw me and said hello and looked around and said, "Where's Patrick?" Patrick had flown back to Toronto to get back to work at his job at the Power Plant. When I called Patrick on the break, Bowie tapped me on the shoulder and said, "Are you talking to Patrick? Can I say hello?" and I gave him the phone. Patrick spoke with Bowie for a while and when they hung up Patrick turned to his coworkers and said, "That was David Bowie. He just wanted to see how I was doing."

JAYNE COUNTY: I saw David a few years ago in a bar down in the East Village, and I made the mistake of bringing up Romy Haag [with whom David once had a relationship in Berlin]. David's face fell to the floor, as I think he was really gone on her at one time. There's some beautiful photos of them together up on Romy's wall in her flat in Berlin. I saw David much later at *Hedwig and the Angry Inch* in New York, which is basically a play that's a mishmash of a bunch of underground figures including me! David was with Iman and he was very nice, and called me Jayne and not Wayne. Although we bickered back and forth at each other for years, when we would run into each other we both became very nice and enjoyed talking together. He was like that.

MICHAEL WOLFF (JOURNALIST): I knew him in the context of schools in New York. That is, not as David Bowie or even all that much of a celebrity, but as a parent. As someone playing second fiddle to his kid. In that sense, he wasn't different from the bankers, restaurateurs, writers, CEOs, and other types of parents in private schools in Manhattan—rather curiously leveled places. I once sat next to him in a high school production of . . . I can't remember. But my son had the lead role and Bowie was very complimentary and seemed very excited to be sitting next to the father of the star. Even Iman and Bowie together, as striking as they undoubtedly were, still seemed in this context more like ordinary parents than icons. In fact, they'd mostly have to be pointed out to be noticed. They fit in. I think you can extend that to New York as a whole, or at least their particular neighborhood where, necessarily, you're often out on the street, just one of many familiar faces. We both lived in the East Village and it would not be uncommon to see him and exchange a smile and nod.

CHRISTOPHER NOLAN (DIRECTOR): As someone who was the biggest Bowie fan in the world, once I made that connection [that the real-life physicist Nikola Tesla, the man who develops the contraption that brings the rivalry of the magicians played by Hugh Jackman and Christian Bale to a head in his 2006 film *The Prestige*, was very close to the role Bowie played in *The Man Who Fell to Earth*], he seemed to be the only actor capable of playing the part. [But having decided on Bowie, the director realized that convincing his idol would prove rather difficult.] It was the only time I can ever remember trying again with an actor who passed on me. In total honesty, I told him if he didn't agree to do the part, I had no idea where I would go from there. I would say I begged him. I've never seen a crew respond to any movie star that way. But he was very gracious and understood the effect he had on people.

KEVIN MAZUR: I photographed his last concert in 2006. David had sung "Arnold Layne" and "Comfortably Numb" at the Royal Albert Hall that May, but his last public performance was at the Alicia Keys benefit at the Hammerstein Ballroom on Thirty-Fourth Street on November 9, for the Keep a Child Alive Black Ball. He sang "Wild Is the Wind," "Fantastic Voyage," and did a duet with Alicia on "Changes." It was a great show, but he looked a little heavy.

He was very protective of his daughter, Lexi, and hated her being photographed. He used to say, "I'm famous, but she's not famous, and they shouldn't be able to photograph her." He was so into his family. When Iman was about to have Lexi, David said, "You won't be seeing me much anymore . . ." After he had his heart attacks he was obviously recuperating, but after a while he wanted to start going out again. He didn't want photographers making a big deal of it, taking pictures of him on the street. So when he was ready, he called me and asked me to take some pictures of him back on the street, so I took all these pictures of him shopping in Chinatown, which took some of the heat off. The pictures went everywhere, and it worked, as nobody bothered him from then on. He liked the city for the same reason John Lennon did. He could blend right in. He was a very private person.

MIKE GARSON: I got called back for *Black Tie White Noise* and then did pretty much everything with him right through to the Alicia Keys gig. He always liked to have a guitarist with him, whether it was Reeves or this one or that one, and at one point he wanted me to move to New York. I would have loved to have played on those last two records, as I'm a New Yorker, but I was living in L.A. He didn't like me being out here, as he had had terrible experiences in L.A. But I had a wife, two children, grandchildren, and I couldn't move. I was willing to come in when he wanted me, but that wasn't quite enough. But then he'd done the same thing when Lexi was born, as he said he wasn't going to be touring. He said he wasn't there for Joe, so he was going to be there for his daughter. The Alicia Keys gig was his last ever performance. The sad thing about it was that there were lots of video people there who wanted to film it, but he said no. He was still gun-shy. He wanted to be anonymous. He had a little meat on him, and I thought he looked good, but he was self-conscious. That was probably the real reason he didn't want to be filmed. The same year he called me and asked me if I thought it was a good idea for him to go out on the road again. Much as I liked the idea of it, I said that he should only contemplate it if he was hearing it himself, and he obviously wasn't. I knew he wasn't hearing it. He told Sterling the same thing a year later. He was still very active on email, and just three months before he passed we were emailing back and forth about the Nina Simone documentary. Gary Oldman was another one—David used to Skype him every Sunday.

STERLING CAMPBELL: After the 2004 tour, we would go to a lot of concerts in New York together. We went to the first Arcade Fire show. He always wanted to see new bands, but then we went to see the Who together. Then he'd just turn up at the studio, out of nowhere. He was solitary, and we tended to leave him alone. He would just turn out unexpectedly. He had a big life and he was just disappearing. That happens to a lot of heavy people. After the heart attack he just wanted to lay low, bring up his family, stay out of the limelight. He was in legacy mode, with this huge downtown museum in his apartment. He was like the English gentleman, sitting in his room with his books and his chair and his knowledge. He was such a prodigious reader. He understood art, deeply. He had a deep understanding of film. He was a renaissance character. He didn't need to make records all the time. He could take on anyone. He could take on heads of state, he was so smart. He could take on Gore Vidal. He could take on William Buckley. With lipstick on. I saw him mad a few times, and he was so commanding. We had a few run-ins. But you listened, you took notice. He could play with you when he wanted to, but he would never take himself too seriously. When he was onstage he would turn it on. He would be in David Bowie mode.

BONO: We were building a space station, the biggest one on Earth, let alone anywhere else, so who would you want contextualizing that? It had to be David Bowie. We decided to use "Space Oddity" to introduce U2's *360°* show because firstly it would on a very basic level let the audience know that we were about to start, secondly because the song encapsulated the entire show itself, and thirdly because it was obviously a nod to the great man himself. It's our biggest tour ever and he [was] on it as much as we [were]. I always knew it was the song I wanted to introduce the show with. We'd always seen the stage as a space station, and I liked the idea of immediately setting the scene with the song. In some ways it reminded me a bit of "Space travels in my mind" from the Only Ones song "Another Girl Another Planet," a song that evokes travel, escape, and moving on. So. We're all here, where are we going to go? The most powerful throw-down in our set is in "Where the Streets Have No Name," and I sing, "*Wanna go there, wanna go there.*" It's all about travel, and that's what "Space Oddity" is about too. . . . We walked onto the stage like astronauts, with our hero playing around us. A hundred times! When the show was interrupted by the astronaut Mark Kelly from the International Space Station, he recites some of the lyrics from "Beautiful Day" but he also weaved in some words from "Space Oddity."

That moment in the middle of "Beautiful Day" when Mark Kelly comes forward in the International Space Station, and he comes to the camera, and he goes, "*Tell my wife I love her very much. She knows*"—only a tiny percentage of people we played that to realized that Mark Kelly's wife was Gabby Gifford, and she'd just been shot [in an assassination attempt]. And the poignancy of that moment, and walking out onto the U2 space station with one of the great story songs of all time, I'm very proud of that moment.

And the fucker didn't come! And I'm glad David never saw it live, or maybe he did, I'm not sure.

PAUL MCGUINNESS: Edge and I went to the NASA Space Center in Houston, which I thought would be an upbeat American military-industrial PR exercise, and the mood of the room was completely different. It was actually quite somber. That huge room where they all sit in front of those screens is where all of the missions have happened, has an incredibly serious, almost tragic atmosphere because it was in that room where they had all witnessed the missions that went wrong, and where *Challenger* blew up. This room was where so many people had died, it was a place where death was part of the process of working there. This was no place for levity. So there was a certain sense of decorum, of respect, of not wanting to abuse the room's status and dignity in any way. When we explained what we wanted to do with the International Space Station, which was to broadcast "Space Oddity" by David Bowie during a U2 show, they actually understood. They liked that. They knew that they were part of the culture, and David Bowie had the right resonance.

For the last seventeen years of his life Bowie lived mainly in Manhattan. He was like royalty in exile. After his heart attacks in 2004, and the subsequent operation, he mellowed out completely. It hit him hard, and so he moved down through the gears. A few years before his death he bought a property in upstate New York, near Woodstock, but the bulk of his time was spent in his apartment building on Lafayette Street, a former chocolate factory. The apartment had been designed by Jonathan Reed, and was a veritable library, housing almost as many books as the McNally Jackson bookshop he liked to visit on Prince Street, just round the corner. Here he tended to his daughter, Lexi, his website, his wife and—sporadically—his back catalogue. If you wandered around SoHo and NoHo you might have seen him, in his quilted black Belstaff jacket, his skinny jeans, workman's boots, and peaked cap, looking like a cross between a gamekeeper and Lou Reed circa 1966. Blending in with most everyone around him, he would be invisible. Unless you were looking for him, of course. On any day when the air was crisp and there was a chill between the buildings, you could see Manhattan's downtown quilted army out in force, drinking peppermint mochas, shopping for clothes, or simply convening with their smartphones. They all dressed in black quilted jackets, pea coats or puffas, with their collars pulled up, scarves tied in fat knots, and buttons tightly fastened. Oh, and they'd be wearing sunglasses too, just in case. You couldn't miss them: they'd be wearing black caps, and matching jeans, maybe with a pair of designer biker boots, or some hybrid trainers. Oh, and they'd be carrying a man bag of some description, and maybe walking a dog (a little black one, sporting its own quilted jacket). These men were anything between sixteen and sixty, and not only did they all look the same, they all looked like David Bowie. On one of his morning walks you could see him in the Strand on Broadway (his second favorite bookshop), and before it closed in 2013 (after forty-five years), he could be found in Bleecker Bob's in the Village, looking for old vinyl. He would stop for a latte at Bottega Falai, the Italian café and grocery, where he would regularly order the prosciutto di Parma sandwich. Or maybe he'd pick up some salad at the Dean & DeLuca on Broadway. In the first fifty years of his life, no one much cared where David Bowie lived—he was an itinerant rock star, after all, and appeared to enjoy his peripatetic life—yet as soon as he retired from public life, his whereabouts became of paramount importance. In New York, spotting Bowie became a spectator sport, until he started spending time out of the city, when it became a game of sleuth. His sixty-two-acre estate in Ulster County, a mountainous region along the Hudson River about one hundred miles north of Manhattan, was one of his most prized possessions. "He lived a relatively quiet existence up here, but that's exactly why New York City residents like the area," says Bill Sidoriak, a broker at Fleming Realty, which covers the Ulster County area.

COURTNEY LOVE: I lived in his building in Lafayette Street for two years, from 2011, and so we were neighbors for all that time. We had a doorman at the building named Bernard and he called up at about nine one morning and said, "Would you please turn your music down?" I play music very loud, but this was nine a.m. not p.m. I was playing *Rumours* by Fleetwood Mac and said, "Who could possibly object to *Rumours*?" And Bernard told me that the Bowie family had asked me to me turn it down. I was just like, "Don't Stop." I kept thinking did that offend him? Like, that's what offended David Bowie? Fleetwood Mac? I didn't see him much in the neighborhood but I knew he was ill. I heard he was ill from the streets and I didn't want to bother him. I'm not a stalker, I'm a good neighbor, or at least I thought I was until the music complaint. He had this attitude that if you don't want to be seen in New York, you're not, and that's true. He had a very invisible life, and would walk through the city and no one bothered him. I left a note and some flowers once—"Hello, I moved in!"—but I never got a response. The only person I know that communicated with him at that time was Trent Reznor, but basically he was too much of a sacred character to approach.

BEBE BUELL: He had his rituals. You know he loved to get up at five a.m. and go walking through Chinatown. That was his daily walk. He wanted to get out there and get his walk in before the streets got crazy and before he would be recognized.

So we know he was a gentleman and that he had an enormous capacity to charm. He had an innate ability to ingratiate himself, but also a completely expedient capacity to get information out of people as quickly as he could, before moving on. People liked David because he was famous, and then if they were admitted into his world—and frankly, famous people usually feel a lot happier around other famous people, rather than civilians—grew to like him because he was a genuinely likeable man.

He could also be a beast when he wanted to, something that comes naturally to anyone who has experienced a modicum of fame, let alone someone who was considered to be a cultural icon for nearly half a century. He was impatient, wouldn't suffer fools, and didn't like taking no for an answer. You don't possess his kind of quality control without being dogmatic about what you do, and without being harsh in your opinions of others. He was even critical of his friends, telling Bono that his Broadway Spider-Man: Turn Off the Dark *musical wasn't much good, and declining to collaborate on a Coldplay tune, having told Chris Martin that it wasn't a very good song. Quote unquote. He dropped people (often mid-collaboration), didn't return emails and telephone calls, fought fiercely with his record companies, and was occasionally imperious to staff. But then this sort of behavior is not unusual in the world of fame. What was different about Bowie was his extraordinary self-awareness. If he was acting like an asshole, he usually knew it. Which actually made his mood swings more chilling, because when the shutters came down—and I saw them come down a few times—you knew that he knew exactly what he was doing, and was doing it for a reason.*

BAZ LUHRMANN: Much later after this initial period of working together on *Moulin*, our friendship grew and I remember David coming round to our house in New York and visiting with Coco and his dogs. My daughter, nine, and my son, seven, did not know who he was. We had lots of interesting people come through our door, but in fact, my daughter finally got her dog because of David. We were having a meeting at the top of the house, in my studio, and my daughter was there petting David's dog—who coincidentally has the same different colored eyes as David—to get on with work, I motioned to Lily to go, but David said she could stay. My daughter kept petting the dog, and eventually David said, "Dogs really help kids give something to focus with." It was a small but really good lesson in disarming and relaxing those around him. Of course, after that, I let my daughter have a dog.

A public dinner with David and Iman was both relaxed and yet the whole restaurant would stop and people would come over and introduce themselves. But the conversation would jump from the pop culture to heavy politics. He was "avaristic" about reading, and was interested in everything from culture to art, politics, the humanities. Around that time he might've been working on *The Next Day*, although I wasn't aware of that; he just said he was writing and in passing he mentioned something we might do together, which I now profoundly regret I did not do. I think it is one of the great sadnesses of my life. As a much older and wiser man once said to me, "Generally, not always, you tend to regret the things you said no to more than the things you said yes to." And there was a moment there when David said, "Berlin, we should go to Berlin." And I was in the middle of something and I couldn't. He didn't really say let's actually absolutely do that. But it was put in a way where I could have seized upon it and have gone *OK, let's go.* So I think he was in a moment of self-examination. And of course what we got out of that was that next album, and the increasing realization of what was in his soul, in his heart and his mind, his creative journey, which was knowing that his life was finite but his legacy would not be. He had such a buoyant energy. Witty, dry, warm, all of those things, and yet, David Bowie.

ALAN YENTOB: After the heart scare he knew he was in a difficult place, and in the end he knew that this new life was good for him, because he was able bring up Lexi, spend time with Iman, and have a family life, which is something he hadn't really had before. He was again satisfying his imagination and his curiosity. During those days he was a voracious reader, and he'd just stay at home reading every day. He was always exploring new ideas and new themes, absorbing things. When *The Next Day* came out, you could tell that he had things to say because even during his hibernation he had been keeping his mind busy.

TONY VISCONTI: With *Heathen* he came in much more prepared than he used to be. *Heathen* and *Reality* were done within two years of each other. And that was 2001 and 2003. And then after that he just decided to take ten years off for his own personal reasons. He wasn't ill. That's when people were speculating—"Oh he's dying, he's got cancer." When in actual fact he was a picture of excellent health. He just wanted ten years off, to do nothing. To chill. Then when he felt like writing again, he phoned me out of the blue and said, "I think I've got an album," so we went in the next day. For *The Next Day* we had a team of about twenty people who had to keep it under wraps. So it was easy. We could phone around and discuss it between us, those that knew about it. If I had kept it a secret, just myself, it would have driven me crazy.

STERLING CAMPBELL: Then one day he decided he wanted to get back to work. We worked on *The Next Day* for two years, in this dingy little studio, in the basement. The drums were awful with a terrible, broken cymbal that didn't work. But it was a great experience. He really wanted to keep it under wraps, didn't want anyone to know that he was actually making a new record. Everything was so secret. But then we weren't going to tell anyone. If anyone had heard, it would have been awful. He was being real subtle about it. Very sophisticated. Just keeping it quiet until he was ready to release it. He wasn't in everyone's business. When the record came out, people kept asking me questions about him, which was crazy. All he wanted to do was put out a record. He was reinventing subtlety. Even in death.

TRACEY EMIN: When *The Next Day* came out I was called up by the *Sun* newspaper wanting me to review it. When I asked who had suggested it they said, "David Bowie." He knew everything that was going on. When I was on *Desert Island Discs*, and I had "Young Americans" as my number-one track, he sent me a note afterwards. Nothing slipped by him.

ALEXIS PETRIDIS (JOURNALIST): The astonishment that greeted the release of "Where Are We Now?," David Bowie's first single in a decade, seemed almost universal. The shock was not merely that Bowie—long since presumed retired—was back, with an album, *The Next Day*; it was that one of the biggest stars in the history of rock had managed to spend two years making a record without even a hint of rumor reaching the wider world. This in an age of camera phones and social media. "We haven't seen this before, a real legend dropping the announcement, the music, the photographs, everything in the blink of an eye," said Tim Ingham, editor of music industry magazine *Music Week*.

At least part of the reason Bowie was able to keep his comeback a secret until the last minute was down to the remarkably low-key nature of his business arrangements: a reaction, Tony Visconti suggested, to the early '70s, when Bowie's management company MainMan "had about forty-five people looking after him, or allegedly looking after him," an arrangement that ended in chaos and litigation. By the time of *The Next Day*, his New York office had a staff of one. He had no official manager, relying instead on his business manager Bill Zysblat, who began life as the Rolling Stones' tour accountant before joining Bowie in the early '80s, and his fiercely loyal PA, Coco. The latter is something of a legend in Bowie mythology and rumored to be the subject of his song "Never Let Me Down."

Even Rob Stringer, the president of the Sony Music Label Group and one of the most powerful men in the music industry, only became aware of *The Next Day*'s existence a month before it was released, when he was invited to the studio in New York to hear some tracks. "He came to the studio. He was thrilled. He said, 'What about the PR campaign?'" said Visconti. "And David said, 'There is no PR campaign. We're just going to drop it on January eighth. That's it.' It's such a simple idea, but Bowie came up with it."

By contrast, the people who actually worked on the album seemed not so much happy as desperate to talk about *The Next Day*. "I was on the cover of *Guitar Player* magazine," lamented Earl Slick. "It was the Christmas issue, the one you want to be on the cover of, the one that's on the newsstands twice as long. And I'm making a new Bowie album and I can't tell them anything. The only person I told was my manager." Visconti, who said he only finished work on the album a week before its release, also seemed delighted to be rid of two years of subterfuge, nondisclosure agreements, and, as he bluntly puts it, "bare-faced lies." He told only his partner and his children what was going on. "People would ask, 'What are you working on at the moment?' After a while, I started saying, 'Well, I'm working on a very big project but I can't tell you what it is.' That satisfied most people, but then a few people would say, 'It's Bowie, isn't it?' And I'd go, 'I can't tell you who it is, even if you said the person's name I can't say yes or no.' And they'd go, 'It's Bowie.' And I'd go, 'No, really it isn't.' I was a little uncomfortable with that, but it was the only way to do it."

Complete secrecy was a precondition from the start: early on, they were obliged to move studios after the owners allegedly leaked information about who was working there. "We told them to keep it a secret and they blew it within twenty-four hours. We hadn't even started the album but we got a phone call: 'Is it true you're making a record at such and such a studio?' We just denied everything. Even when we made the first demos, we were sworn to secrecy. The three musicians working on them—me, Sterling Campbell on drums, and Jerry Leonard on guitar—had to sign a nondisclosure agreement. It was unnecessary with the three of us; we were longtime Bowie people—if he'd just said keep it a secret and don't tell a soul, we would have done that without signing—but later on, as the crew on the album got bigger, the NDAs were necessary because we didn't know everyone that well. We got lucky with the studio, a place called the Magic Shop in SoHo. Normally there are interns at studios, but whenever we were there, they gave their interns time off. They didn't want them to witness it. When we were working there, they had a skeleton staff of two, which is not normal."

Even with security so strict that when Earl Slick first turned up to work on the album, not even his own roadie was allowed in the studio—"I told him to pick me up Tuesday at one p.m. and drop me off at the studio, but I said, they got guys to haul the gear in at the studio, you just sit in the truck"—Visconti seemed astonished that no one found out. "The evidence was there, but no one put all the pieces together. He was photographed near the studio. Over a year ago, he asked Robert Fripp to play on the album and Fripp put it on his blog, something like 'David Bowie's asked me to play on his album but I'm too busy' and no one believed it! If someone was actually monitoring all these leaks, they could have put it together."

JONATHAN BARNBROOK (GRAPHIC DESIGNER): He phoned me up and asked to come to my studio and to talk about some design work. I suppose it's a case of, he seeks out people to work with rather than they come to him. So he'd identified something interesting in our work: he'd seen the book I'd done with Damien Hirst in 1997, which I think caused a bit of interest in the art world. And he was quite good friends with Damien at the time, so that's the connection. He was looking for a designer for a book for Iman, which she wanted to be contemporary but didn't want it to be just a photobook, as it were. And from there it kind of developed into working on his album. I was always honest in the process of doing Iman's book; I was never sycophantic and I think he understood that I wouldn't sacrifice trying to do something that I thought was best for being a yes-man. And that's the way most projects develop when people try to do something with them and they get on very well. That creates an energy.

You know, a working relationship is a complex thing, and I wouldn't say we were best buddies and we hung out all the time. But for the ten years that he wasn't making records we would still chat, and the working process was a time full of jokes and insults, so we'd got to the level of informality where we could actually take the piss out of each other. Which takes a bit of courage! I think that's his saving grace, his humor, that's why he wasn't dead at thirty, because he actually re-appraised himself, evolved in his life to be something else other than Ziggy Stardust. That fame would have killed him.

He was never nasty, but he would be quite clear when he didn't think something was right. But there's a good way to say things and a bad way to say things, and he wasn't Donald Trump. But there were certain moments when he had a very strong idea about what he wanted to do, and it was my job to implement it. That happened with *Reality*, which I think was the least successful cover we did. None of the fans like it that much, and some think it's a bit busy. I think we could have tried harder with it, and I argued to do it in a different way. But with that one he had a very strong idea of exactly what he wanted it to be, and no matter how much I said we should do something else.

With *The Next Day*, he saw that there was something new here, and reassured me when I was worried that the idea would be misunderstood—with just the white square over the cover of *"Heroes."* There was quite a lot of discussion behind the scenes with the record company about that cover, because it was taking quite a big chance. It's confusing, it doesn't make sense. But I do think, of all the covers we did, it is the most unusual; it actually generated quite a lot of discussion. I think he said in the past that he's responsible for getting the best sort of work out of a lot of musicians, and I think he is responsible for getting the best work out of me.

I think [our best cover] has to be *The Next Day*, because it's quite an original idea, taking your own album cover and defacing it. I mean, it's been done before but not with regards to an artist who is always being compared to his past. We often discussed *Ziggy Stardust* and he said it would be dishonest to do an album like that now, because I'm not that twenty-three-year-old person. I'm fifty now. It was an acknowledgment of his history. And instead of going with the fans' expectation, it was a twisting of their expectation of a new image of David Bowie, which actually they put their hopes, fears, and pressures in. So it's about them rather than Bowie, often. That's why they didn't get this idea of a new cover. The most controversial reaction to *The Next Day* was that it looked like it could have taken five minutes to do. You just put a white square on the album cover. I'd send David some comments on Twitter and we'd laugh about them, and we'd talk about the good comments as well.

EARL SLICK: We mainly communicated by emails until *The Next Day.* But I didn't know he was recording *The Next Day.* He'd been in the studio for quite some time with other people, and he'd sworn everyone to secrecy. I came in at the very end. I was in New Jersey with a friend of mine, a surgeon, and we were driving in his Cobra sports car in the middle of a fancy-schmancy neighborhood, and the fucking car catches fire, and we barely got out before it blew up. The fire department are there, the police, the press, and it's only a matter of time before my name gets all over the fucking Internet. The next morning I get a call from David, after not hearing from him for quite a while, and he asks if I was OK, and then he asks me to come and play on the record. But I honestly think that if the car hadn't have blown up I wouldn't have been on that record. I wasn't in his mind.

TONY PARSONS: I wasn't very interested in the later music, although "Strangers When We Meet" is probably my favorite Bowie song. But I wasn't as engaged with his later music until he released "Where Are We Now?," which I thought was like hearing *Blood on the Tracks* for the first time, it was just outrageously, shockingly, movingly, incredibly personal, something torn from the heart.

There probably were fifty guitarists, fifty producers, fifty photographers, fifty journalists who think David liked them best. And that was his great ability, to make these massive great groups of people over many years feel like that—you're not alone. It wasn't just the wattage of his stardom, because all celebrities have a veneer of fame. . . . But Bowie had something special. He could connect with people, he could connect through his music, and he could connect one-on-one. And you never forgot it. And it was all there in "Where Are We Now?," an incredibly passionate record that was ultimately universal.

FLORIA SIGISMONDI (DIRECTOR): I first met David in 1997. My video for Marilyn Manson's "Beautiful People" had just come out and he had seen it and wanted to meet. I met him at the studio he was recording at in NYC. When he saw me he was taken aback, because I was wearing a leather aviator's cap and goggles and he had just watched a film where the main character was wearing the same outfit. It was a coincidence, but it meant something to him. We instantly connected and talked about art for five hours. He really trusted the creative process, so he let me do my thing. For example, he thought that being completely myself was the only way. I remember sitting in bed coming up with some "out there" ideas, thinking, wow this could be how I spend my life; expressing myself through my art. Because he allowed me to experiment and trusted me, I was able to form who I was without any kind of self-censorship. For the video "Little Wonder," I designed a suit for him with pointy shoulders and elbows. I had no idea whether he'd like it or even want to wear it, but I just went with it. As soon as he put it on he knew exactly what that character would do. He became different characters at the drop of a hat. He was fearless. A kid in a candy store.

I was obviously surprised when he got back in touch after his retirement. He called me on my cell and was very cryptic, wanting to fly me to New York, where he would tell me what he was up to. When I arrived, he played me "The Stars (Are Out Tonight)." I was so thrilled he was writing and recording music again. Very few people knew about it. I felt like I was about to be a part of a very special moment. I felt like everything was full of electricity around him. He was energized in a different way than he was in the '90s. He dealt with everything himself, schedules and due dates. He called me directly about these things; there was no one in between. Because of the secretive nature of the project we had all our meetings and fittings at my house and he really liked that.

He asked to do "The Next Day" video the same way. He felt very natural. I gave him the script that morning and he just embraced it so openly. I went into his trailer in between shots and his hands were busy working away on something as we talked. He handed it to me. It was a little origami bird. A symbolic gesture, I thought. He devoured art around him, he devoured literature and ideas. He'd seen it and done it all, but was able to remain open to see something new and beautiful in it. He was never jaded.

KIM JONES (FASHION DESIGNER): David had worn some [Louis] Vuitton in his video for "The Stars (Are Out Tonight)," the video with Tilda Swinton, so we approached him about being in one of our commercials. I thought he would work in the series that we had been doing at Vuitton, using the likes of Gorbachev and Keith Richards. Plus Bowie looked great in our clothes. He was receptive to the idea, so I went over to New York, to his studio, to meet him. He had these extraordinary piles of books, magazines, artifacts, reference material. Everything was in piles and categorized and immaculate. I loved the way he had every edition of *The Orton Diaries*, every foreign edition, every paperback, every hardback, everything. He had piles of Derek Jarman material, Derek Boshier drawings, photographs of outfits, sketches, drawings. He kept picking things up and showing them to me: "You should read this. . . . You'd love this. . . ." He knew where everything was. He said there was only one piece of clothing that had gone missing from his archive and he knew exactly who had taken it and when they had taken it. I noticed all his furniture was Memphis, but in natural wood—cherry, walnut—rather than color, so it looked extraordinary. The attention to detail was really something else, and something that very much appealed to my aesthetic. We appeared to get on because we both had a relationship with Lee [Alexander] McQueen, which led into talking about the commercials, about Vuitton, and how we might work together. Of course I was star-struck but it was lovely to be able to work with someone who operated at such a high level. He wasn't overbearing either, and was happy to discuss ideas rather than just be dogmatic. He was aware of not dressing too young. He wanted to be cool for his age, which I think is a nice thing. He didn't want to look like a peacock. He wanted to look real.

HANIF KUREISHI: I asked Eno if he'd seen the Bowie show at the V&A, and he said, "Yes, and he's got all my fucking gear there." Brian had been selling lots of his old equipment at auction and David had bought it all under another name. He said he'd gone to the V&A and seen all the stuff he'd sold! Bowie kept everything, had everything stored in a warehouse. Every pair of trousers, every notebook, every toothpick. That shows an incredible level of control.

As I walked through the David Bowie exhibition at the V&A on its opening night—oblivious to the great, the good, and the overly cantilevered around me—I came across something I'd never seen before. Like almost everyone else at the show, I considered myself an expert on all matters Bowie, but this was something that had never crossed my desk, so to speak: an appearance on Saturday Night Live *in 1979, performing "The Man Who Sold the World" in a ridiculously oversized suit, along with the experimental singer Klaus Nomi.*

I was immediately mesmerized and watched it three times before moving into the next room, to be confronted by hundreds of even more esoteric Bowie moments. As the curators said themselves, Bowie was a search engine before there were search engines. There was a dinner after the private view but like everyone else I talked to that night, I just wanted to go around the exhibition again and again, wallowing in my youth. (The denouement of the dinner was Tilda Swinton's speech, in which she said that Bowie had told her that when "Where Are We Now?" was released, he had finally got more press than the man who shares his birthday, Elvis.)

There was such a lot of hyperbole surrounding the V&A show that I assumed it couldn't live up to expectations. Yet it was easily as clever and as immersive as the "Postmodernism" show they'd held a couple of years previously. It was a proper multimedia extravaganza, and, for Bowie obsessives like me, probably the final word on the man (in a good way). Its title, David Bowie Is . . . *also managed to make sense of his fair-to-middling middle period, from* Never Let Me Down *through to* The Buddha of Suburbia, *when our Dave was struggling to come to terms with global success and had started trying to make records that "sounded like David Bowie."*

A friend of mine had dinner with Bowie in New York a few years before the V&A show and at that point he said he wasn't "feeling the music," wasn't in the mood to record again. But as his health improved, and as his inertia became debilitating, he started writing lyrics and recording again. The V&A show assisted in his reemergence, as did the small mountain of books, magazine covers, and newspaper articles that appeared after his "disappearance." So, was The Next Day *any good? It was hilarious to watch a bunch of fifty- and sixtysomething men who should have known better than to treat the record as though it were a new wheel or the missing testament. Great though this record was, if it had been released in 2005, those selfsame critics would have probably just said it was another fair-to-middling David Bowie record. Personally, I loved it, and with this album Bowie seemingly reinvented the art of the middle eight, meaning he obviously had a huge surfeit of tunes and wanted to squeeze them in somewhere. Yes, he could have made more of a statement if he had made a record with only eight songs on it, or produced an album of songs that all sounded like "Where Are We Now?," but in the end he opted for the route-one approach: that is, releasing an album of rather conventional David Bowie songs, including two—"Where Are We Now?" and "The Stars (Are Out Tonight)"—that are so damn good they should be included on any greatest hits albums of the future. And not just David Bowie's. (Bowie appeared in the video for "Where Are We Now?" wearing a* SONG OF NORWAY *T-shirt, a reference to the film that his ex-girlfriend Hermione went to make when she ended their relationship back in 1969.)*

VICTORIA BROACKES (CURATOR): From my perspective, I suppose I had developed the pop-culture genre at the V&A. We did a Kylie [Minogue] exhibition in 2007, but nothing on the scale of *David Bowie Is . . .* We had 270,000 visitors, and it went down very well. I think we were all a little bit concerned because the Kylie show wasn't supposed to be here, and we just inherited it. But I think that opened the door. We were thinking of doing an exhibition based around a single entertainer, and David Bowie was at the top of a very short list that included Elvis and Madonna.

GEOFFREY MARSH (CURATOR): This all came about because in the autumn of 2010 I was in Memphis in Tennessee trying to negotiate an exhibition about Elvis Presley. I went down to do a presentation to the team in Graceland and it all seemed it was going very well, and I came back to the UK and suddenly out of the blue the company that owned the rights to

Elvis was being sold and they decided they didn't want to get involved. So we had a gap in the program and we were wondering what to do. I spoke to a few people and then a short while later had a phone call from Bowie's office, and they asked if I knew that David had an archive.

VICTORIA BROACKES: We had no idea that he had an archive, but that's not the reason we pursued it. It was through talking to other people in the music business that we were introduced to his manager, Bill Zysblat, and Sandy, his archivist. We were here in the museum when Sandy said there was an archive, and she opened her computer and said, "It's this sort of thing." I remember my heart quickening and saying before leaving the room, "We *definitely* have to do this."

GEOFFREY MARSH: So Vicky and I went over in early 2011 and it was just this . . . enormous thing. One of the curious things about most performers is that they don't actually keep much stuff. They usually have their press cutting books because they are kept by their managers and publicists, but Bowie appeared to have kept everything. Sandy, his archivist, had been working on it for four years at that time, and she had also been buying up things from around the world from collectors. There were two fascinating things from day one. One was the extent of it all—when we visited the archive everything was brought out in pop-up boxes, with acid-free tissue and everything. When I saw all the costumes I looked at them and thought these can't be real because they were in such fantastic condition. There was all this other stuff, all these working drawings and sketches and thoughts and all the rest of it. Basically Bowie had archived his life, and because they had started turning it into a collection, thought they could maybe show it. David was obviously always interested in the art world, and he understood museums, understood how they work, understood curation. . . . And so in April 2011 we agreed to do it and basically had two years.

VICTORIA BROACKES: When we first went to New York to see the archives in person, obviously it was clear to us that Coco was in essence the gatekeeper. I think we rather naïvely believed we had been asked to do the show and therefore we were doing the show. So we went up there assuming we were doing the show. I think it was after we got started that we really realized that perhaps there'd been other people who'd been through this particular hoop before, and then fallen. So we went through the costumes, because we needed to know that there were enough of them, and then we started looking at everything on-screen. His team had already developed a number of storyboards, which I think communicated to us they were looking for a really imaginative approach. As with all things Bowie, if it was going to be done, it had to be done incredibly well. And I think that was actually one of the exciting things about working on the project. I felt that we were sort of pushed all the way on all sides. And there's clearly something very Bowie-ish about that.

The honest truth is that it wasn't until the objects arrived here in January 2013 that I really knew it was going to happen. We imagined it had his stamp of approval, but we were not aware how involved he was or how much he knew of exactly what we were doing. There was no reason to suggest it wasn't going to happen, but equally from experience when you're dealing with people with enormous clout and influence, if they don't want it to happen it won't happen. And it wasn't until the stuff appeared on site that I felt absolutely certain that it would happen.

GEOFFREY MARSH: I would say that eighty percent came from his archive, and we got the rest. Immediately I realized there was an issue, as this was a collection about David Bowie, and not David Jones, and there was nothing from his early life, and nothing about his family. There was also very little from the early '60s, which was a shame as I think a lot of that material, especially the early solo stuff, is very interesting. He had obviously spent a lot of time acquiring things, buying them back, but there was nothing about David Jones in it at all. . . . There were a few sketches of his parents, but it's an archive about a character and that's what was really odd about it—not odd, unique, in that it wasn't about the real person, it's about this construction. I've curated a lot of exhibitions, but with this one I don't think I ever got to the heart of it, the reason he did what he did, I could never get to what that was. Clearly somewhere around the age of ten he decided to become a star. Not a singer, not an actor, a star, and that's quite weird actually. This was in the late '50s, when celebrity culture, if it existed at all, was the Queen and the Duke of Edinburgh going round the Commonwealth and Laurence Olivier and Vivien Leigh and that sort of world. He loved American culture, and I know that Little Richard was hugely important. . . . But at that age he just decided to become a star. From then on it was about complete control, and he never did anything out of the blue. He was there from day one. At fifteen or sixteen he was trying to design sets that were better than the ones on the BBC!

There was also nothing about his brother in the archive, and having had personal experience of this, I think if you have weird siblings your reaction is slightly to put them in a box and define yourself as not that. A lot is made of the fact that David's parents got rid of Terry's room when he moved out, so he couldn't come back, but given how small the house was I'm not sure that was such a big deal.

VICTORIA BROACKES: We wanted it to be a bit like [the theatre company] Punchdrunk, very immersive, and they were already on board with that, they knew all about immersive theatre. But while we were constructing our themes, and developing the narrative and the actual production, time and time again we would be blown away by what Bowie had in his drawers in New York. Everything had been kept, everything had been catalogued and wrapped in plastic, or neatly slipped into plastic folders: the school drawings, early band costume designs, illustrations of the Kon-Rads, the Bowmen, little Ziggy cutouts, things that would make me say, "Oh my God." He had Post-it notes, and scribbles; he had kept literally everything. He had obviously done so much market research for the Ziggy concept. The other thing that I just thought was incredibly sweet was this sort of mileage chart of one of their very early tours, where clearly they were zigzagging across the country. It's just the idea of Bowie himself writing that out. Those things were just . . . you wouldn't expect those of anyone. We also fought to have the lipstick-blotted tissue included, even though we were worried about the press reaction: "Oh, for God's sake what is the V&A doing showing a lipstick-blotted tissue?" What was so odd was that he'd *kept* the lipstick-blotted tissue. For us this was a holy relic.

GEOFFREY MARSH: There were several hundred costumes, but we had to choose sixty. But which ones? It wasn't until the third trip that we decided that we weren't going to do it chronologically. The real interesting stuff was the unfinished stuff and of course a lot of it was felt tip pens and things which are a nightmare to exhibit because they fade so quickly. He initially said he wouldn't be involved, but then we could tell he was micromanaging it from behind a screen like the Wizard of Oz. When you requested to see something, and wrote a handwritten question, the answer that came back always looked as though Bowie had been responsible for it. You just knew that actually he read everything.

CHALKIE DAVIES: In meetings with the people from the V&A they weren't allowed to refer to him by name, he was referred to instead as "The artist." He pretended not to have anything to do with it, but he used to come in at eight o'clock in the morning and take a look. He was absolutely involved in everything, in a very meticulous way.

GEOFFREY MARSH: We worked largely off a sort of database, where literally everything was catalogued. With Elvis there is a big warehouse in Memphis that is just full of stuff, including television sets that Elvis had shot at with bullet holes through them. But with Bowie everything was in order. I kept saying to myself, don't curate this! Don't curate this! Just let Bowie speak because he is far more interesting than anything that you can say and what you're showing is the stuff that people have never seen.

We found out that he was coming to visit a few days beforehand, but I had already booked a holiday to Turkey. This is kind of weird, but I was kind of glad that I didn't actually meet him because of course he was not David Bowie, he was David Jones. I kept thinking of the situation like a zoo or going to the Grand Canyon. Have you seen it? Have you seen him? Everyone who really knew him said what an incredibly nice person he was and obviously he was very controlling and all those sort of things . . . and in some ways I prefer to have those sort of thoughts about him.

VICTORIA BROACKES: The only thing we weren't allowed to use was the original saxophone, because it was too precious to lend. I understand that. And the other thing which was a mystery was the dress. Somebody told us that Bowie had the man dress that he wore on the cover of *The Man Who Sold the World*. But they claimed they didn't have it. Anyway, I think there were 100,000 objects altogether.

He visited the exhibition when he flew into London for a holiday. He came on a secret morning visit. And I didn't talk about it while he was alive. But it seems now rather important. I met him here. We told no one at the museum except the director and the head of security. It was part of a family trip to Europe in the summer of 2013. I had taken many people around the exhibition, people such as Robert Redford for instance, but it was a massive deal taking him round. So of course I acted as normal as I could and he was as everybody said he always was—just totally charming, immediately keen to put you at your ease. It was made clear it was a family visit and I met him at the entrance to the museum, took him to the exhibition, said a few things about it, gave him the headphones, and then wandered around while they were going around it. Iman and Alexandra were there as well, and Alexandra had a friend with her. Coco was here, and a couple of other people. And they spent about an hour and a half in the exhibition. What can I say? He did say that it was awesome. I didn't get a photo with him though. Sad. We talked a little bit, but what do you talk to David Bowie about? I know everything about David Bowie, of course not everything, but I had been studying the subject in depth for years. I'd read every book and every article and every interview and everything else. And then you meet the man himself and of course you know nothing really. So what do you talk about? So making conversation I said that Earl Slick had been in the other day. I said that he'd kept his sunglasses on all the way through. And Bowie said, "Oh yeah, he's very rock and roll." So he was very friendly.

There is always an expectation that an exhibition will give you the truth, that it has all the secrets. But I think the whole business of pop is kind of based on something different. Is it based already on a kind of mythology. So it becomes harder still to uncover what happened. And Bowie himself quite liked people sometimes getting the wrong end of the stick. There was an assumption in the '60s that you had to kind of tell the truth, and many people were undone by that. And then entertainers and pop stars learned to be slightly vaguer.

TONY PARSONS: The V&A exhibition is the greatest exhibition I've ever seen. I was just absolutely overwhelmed by it and how much it meant. It was great because it was the only exhibition I've ever been to where the headphones weren't optional, you had to take the headphones, you had to put them on, you had to immerse yourself. Every one of his lives was there.

For me he really represented our generation—how the people who lived in the baby boom generation all had fathers who were very different men, and how we dealt not only with the chemical and sexual excesses of our age but how we came through that and raised children, and stayed alive when a lot of our friends didn't, and how we carried ourselves as men. He very much saw himself as an artist.

I think the exhibition just captured how important he'd been, it captured the changes he'd been through. And I was genuinely interested in what he had to say. What do we tell our children about drugs? What do we say to them when we've done it? He had a disastrous first marriage, and I was quite interested in how pragmatic and practical he was in getting it right the second time around. He represented so much of what has happened to those postwar generations, the drugs, the divorce, to crawl out from the wreckage of all that excess in the '70s, he was like point man for all of that. And it's just the greatest story, the greatest story in music, more than Elvis or John Lennon, because he got out there more, he got around the world more. He's the herald of a global age in a way that those earlier people weren't.

HARVEY GOLDSMITH: I used to have dinner with him in New York after he'd retired and he would never discuss coming back. He just didn't want to know. He said he was never going to make another record, wasn't going to tour, and was never going to do another interview. He was just going through this phase that he thought would last forever. He just didn't want to talk about it. He was having a home life and he wasn't interested in doing anything creatively. We were exchanging various emails about the V&A exhibition and I casually asked if he might be interested in doing one number at a charity event I was working on and he just shut me down: "No, I'm not working." It wasn't that he was shy; he just didn't want to be part of the madness. Even in the early days, he had his own little crowd, his own little scene. He kept away from the morass of what was happening elsewhere. He only wanted to discuss what he wanted to discuss.

Whatever he did was pure, he did it the way he wanted to do it, when he wanted to do it, and he didn't want to be tainted with anyone else's version of what he did.

The last time I saw him was at these Jeff Beck shows at the Iridium Jazz Club in New York that we'd organized as a tribute to Les Paul. This was 2010. He phoned me up and asked to come to the show, and we sat together throughout it. At dinner afterwards he said he didn't really like writing with people, but that he wanted to write with Jeff Beck. But it never happened, and he disappeared again.

IMAN MOHAMED ABDULMAJID: We flew in on the jet to Luton and every day we went and did different things and the press never knew. It's absurd, this idea that celebrities can't be anonymous. We even went to the London Eye. We queued separately, Lexi had a friend with her and they went with the bodyguard and then we all met on board. [David] took her to Beckenham. They went and took a photo outside the house he grew up in.

CHRIS STEIN: The last time I saw him was the summer of 2013, upstate. We were talking about Lou Reed, which was ironic in retrospect, as this was just after he had the liver transplant. We were saying how we were concerned about him and all that stuff.

DAVID BOWIE: If you're an artist then you measure everything by what you produce, because you have to. If you ask me whether or not I have fifteen good years left, or twenty or twenty-five, then I'm just going to think, What do I fill them with? But that's the thing. I wonder if it's worth filling them; I'm not so sure that there is any purpose, and that's the thing that really starts to confound me. Because it's contradictory. I don't do it with a sinking sense of negativity; I can actually feel quite content with the idea that nothing's important. But then I suppose I can only say that because I've banked a fair amount of creative endeavor.

The older I get the closer to God I should feel, but it's actually less and less. That's what I'm finding. I suppose this is the wrong thing to feel, as Graham Greene would definitely say. I don't know what Samuel Beckett would have said. I mean, I never really understood what he thought at the end. All I know is that his very last words were, "What a morning." I just think, Oh God, I hope I can come up with something like that: "Oh, what a morning!" When I had a stronger link with Buddhism, it was easy for me to think that there is a force rather than a God, and not to adopt a position on God; so it's not such an odd position for me to want to come to—but it sort of negates any spiritual life. This is all academic anyway, as at the moment I don't feel a keen sense of mortality. Of course I feel more vulnerable than I did when I was younger, but I don't feel like I'm rushing towards the end. That could all change tomorrow, though. Ha!

TOMMY HILFIGER: The last time I saw him was at another awards ceremony at Lincoln Center. I had a chat with him but he didn't seem himself. He didn't look well. This was 2012, or 2013. He looked frail.

If David Bowie's records gave a sense of premeditated enumeration (having a look around and then using whatever had just been gleaned and forcing it into a song), then "Sue (Or in a Season of Crime)," which was released at the end of 2014 to publicize the reverse-order three-CD retrospective, Nothing Has Changed, *was everything but. A collaboration with New York's Maria Schneider Orchestra (and produced by Tony Visconti), "Sue" was a heavily theatrical seven-minute free(ish)-form jazz workout, heavy on the brass and the drums, that—how many times did we say this in the first fifteen years of his career?—literally sounded like nothing he had recorded before. While it might have possessed the same foreboding as some of Bowie's Berlin recordings, it was principally postmodern noir, all Saul Bass, Weegee, and Edward Dmytryk. You could almost see Bowie turning up the collar of his oversized trench and pulling down his fedora, almost feel the rain bouncing off the sidewalk as the city turned black and white. And it was all the better for it. Yes, his vocals sounded closer to Scott Walker's than they ever had before, and being a murder ballad the lyrics referenced traditional tropes—a grave, a train, some weeds, and an X-ray—and it carried the obligatory "note," but stylistically it extended Bowie's repertoire dramatically. No longer reworking the once-difficult parts of his '70s work (exaggerated Cockney vocals, saxophone stabs, atonal power chords, and so on), Bowie was instead acknowledging the jazz he'd been introduced to by his brother, Terry, back in the '60s. He sounded like a man reborn, and someone who wasn't going to take karaoke lying down.*

KATE MOSS: I'd bump into him out and about at fashion dinners and parties in New York. He was friends with Lee McQueen, because he was designing for him. Then Iman, if I ever bumped into her, we'd always hang out. I love her. She was great, I'd see her out and about and she would come back to my house and we would end up having fun and drinking and dancing around. Then in 2014 he asked me to collect an award for him at the Brits, and that's when we started to have conversations again. And I said I'd only do it if I could wear something of his, because I'd worn all his clothes before for *Vogue*, and so he sent over two Hammersmith Odeon Ziggy Stardust outfits. His assistant gave me two different playsuits, and we pulled up the zip on one of them, and it was like a glove. It fit me like it was made for me, it was mental. And he asked me if it fitted and to send him a picture. When it was over I was like, "Oh no, now I don't have an excuse to talk to you again!" I was surprised he asked me. We weren't like friends, it's not like I could call him up and say, "Hi, David, what shall we do tonight?" but we had a bond. We had some sort of connection. He had such a great sense of humor, and I think we had such an immediate bond because we were both from South London. I've spoken to other people about it too, like Jools Holland, and Gary Oldman, because we're all from that part of London. We were both from Bromley.

DAVID BOWIE: I just know that death is inevitable. I don't really have much in terms of artistic ambitions for the future, I'm quite happy working on what I'm doing at present. When you're young you want to be a bit ice, you don't want to be like everyone else, you want to be bang on the money. But I'm not like that anymore, thankfully. I place a touching importance on each day having been worthwhile. I get up incredibly early, feeling really optimistic, and expect that day to be as good as I can possibly make it. Life is really interesting at the moment. But then I really don't remember being bored. I've been depressed plenty of times but I've never actually been bored. Looking out of a window and watching people is quite enough to keep me occupied for half an hour.

13

FOR IN FRONT OF THAT DOOR IS YOU

2016

RICKY GERVAIS: After his heart problem—"I was in a very dark place," he told me—I went to his flat downtown. The little concierge there said, "Oh, are you here to see Mr. Jones?" And I went, "Oh yeah, of course I'm here to see Mr. Jones. David Bowie doesn't actually exist, does he?" And we went in, and his apartment was beautiful, just *beautiful.* He asked if I wanted a coffee, and then when he reappeared from the kitchen he was shaking and fumbling as though he was really ill. He wasn't taking it at all seriously. There was this pewter, or steel, statue right in the middle of the floor. And he went, "Yeah, the artist was trying to do in 3-D what Picasso tried to do with 3-D in 2-D, but anyway my daughter likes to hit that with a hammer." So that's why we got on.

GAIL ANN DORSEY: I was never his best friend or anything. Artists have their own world, and I always remembered that I was hired and there to do a job. Jobs come and go. I've been in the business long enough to know that nothing lasts forever. I felt very close to him in terms of our working relationship, and there were times when I'd gone to his house, or gone to Christmas dinner, or gone to his apartment to listen to records, then I wouldn't see him for a while and we would email just to say hi. And then in the last year he sent me a few emails just to tell me that he loved me, quite out of the blue and I didn't know then that he was sick but I would respond and I would say, "Hey, I love you too." I'm so glad I took the time to tell him I was so grateful for his presence in my life, because he changed my life forever. He gave great gifts. One Christmas, he did a portrait of all the band members as Christmas gifts. He'd gone around with a Polaroid camera on the last day of the *Outside* tour, and snapped every band member and he did the paintings from those photos. They look like the cover of the *Outside* album, which is his own painting of himself. Very cool, very modern. I would guess everyone kept theirs. I'm never gonna sell mine, I can tell you that.

My fondest moment could have been any night, after any concert, just when the night is done, him coming over to me and just giving me a hug or giving me a kiss on the cheek or rubbing my head. It was just that thing of him being proud of me. He was very protective. The last time I saw him was October 2014, while I was making the Daphne Guinness record in New York, and David came to the studio to hang out, as he knew her, it was right around the corner from his house. It must have been right before his diagnosis, as he was fine, he looked fine, there was no sign of anything. I didn't see him for the next year or so, so it was all emails. I knew he was doing a new album and that it was secret. I always knew he wanted to do a jazz album, but I didn't think it was going to be what it turned out to be.

GEOFF MACCORMACK: My last significant communication was when I'd sent him some music by an American experimental band I was really excited about, and he sent me this message and I thought, That was a bit . . . slushy. But then I suppose he must have known he was ill. He said, "Geoff, your choice in music has always been on the money. Thank you for being my friend all these years and I miss you lots, now fuck off." So I wrote back, "Likewise pal, off and fuck," and he came back with "Mission accomplished."

GEORGE UNDERWOOD: "Toothbrush" was the last thing I actually said to David. When we were together, we had a real surreal sense of humor, and I think a lot of people felt excluded. They didn't know what was going on. People used to fuss and pamper him, but he was very down-to-earth. He was funny. Weirdly, when we only had landlines, I'd be just about to call him and I'd get through immediately as he was calling me. This happened a number of times. He used to call me Michael and I used to call him Robert, which are our middle names. We were on the top deck of a bus once when we were kids, and we both said at the same time, "Don't forget your toothbrush." And so for the next fifty years, whenever we wanted to remind ourselves of that, we said, "one-two-three toothbrush!" The last time I saw him we finished by saying, "Toothbrush." It was silly. Towards the end we always kept in contact by email. "Hello, Michael." If I emailed him, he'd always answer immediately.

PAUL MCCARTNEY: I spoke to Iman at the Met Ball, when Stella was co-hosting a few years ago. I saw Iman but I didn't see David, and she said, "Oh you should give him a ring, because he sort of sits in the house and doesn't do much." So I didn't think much more of it, but then probably about a year later I did give him a ring and I figured now that it would have been around the time he got his diagnosis. So we couldn't hook up, we were just going to have a cup of tea in New York, so it was very sad. We didn't work together, and the only thing we ever did was a concert in New York. We had dinner together—we were on a skiing holiday together, and he was there with Iggy Pop. So we had a great evening. I have a picture now of the two of us that I have on my computer.

GEOFF MACCORMACK: It was early in the morning and I was in my house in Southend and the phone rang. I missed it, but there was a message from Co [Coco] saying, "Hi, darling, I really need to speak to you." And I thought, That's bad. David must be really, really ill. I should come over. And then I saw the news. It was only when I spoke to George [Underwood] that I lost it.

While David was in London, showing his family the places he used to live, he called the theatrical producer Robert Fox, whom Bowie had known for forty years, asking him to tea. He went to meet him at his hotel and within minutes he told Fox he was going to write a musical based on the character Thomas Newton, from The Man Who Fell to Earth. *They discussed writers for him to work with, and Fox suggested the playwright Enda Walsh, whom he felt had all the right qualities to convey the story of a man from another planet stuck in New York, desperately trying to get home. In November 2014, Fox flew to New York for a preliminary workshop, where he expected to meet Bowie. Instead he was told to go to Bill Zysblat's office, where he spoke to Bowie via Skype, and where David told him that he was ill and undergoing a treatment that meant he wouldn't be able to attend in person. "It was shocking," says Fox. "He was feeling unwell but he wasn't making a fuss about it. He was about to start a new treatment that was quite experimental and that had had some success in other people. He felt optimistic about it being able to prolong his life, hopefully in the belief there would be better and newer treatments that would come along."*

TOMMY HILFIGER: He smoked so much. One time we were flying down to Mustique and the minute he stepped off the plane he lit up a cigarette. My son had come to meet us and I introduced them and he said, "You shouldn't smoke!" David started cackling and said, "You're so right!" and stubbed it out on the tarmac. But he never had a cigarette out of his hand. Liver cancer is usually the result of medication or drinking, but maybe his body had taken such a beating early on. I would have thought he would have died of lung cancer, as he was a terrible chain smoker.

TONY PARSONS: I always felt that if you smoked that much you usually died at sixty-two, and if you smoke as many cigarettes as David Bowie did then he should have died at sixty-two. That's the age that my father was, that's the age that Christopher Hitchens was when he died. Your body just packs up after that. So it's not a bad innings, and yet I was just devastated by it, I was choked by it, really choked by it. Strangely, I only met Mick Ronson once, and he was dying. He still looked like Jean Harlow, the blond guitar hero, but he had cancer. And he was dying.

MICK ROCK: I knew about the strokes, and I knew there had been a complication and he had had to go back in, but I didn't know he was as ill as he was. I know what he officially died of, but he died from smoking. When I look through my old photographs of David, he's got a cigarette in his hand in every other photograph. David had to give up smoking when he had the strokes, but the damage had already been done. Cigarettes had more to do with his death than you think.

In the summer of 2014, Bowie was having boxing lessons even though he was still on medication because of his heart problems. But then he was diagnosed with liver cancer, and a concentrated bout of chemotherapy ensued. It was a fight he would eventually lose. About a week before his death, and a few days before the release of Blackstar, *Bowie called Tony Visconti—via FaceTime—to say that he wanted to make "one more album." Bowie had been writing a fresh set of songs, and had demoed five of them, even though he was still undergoing chemotherapy. Apparently he had known since November that his cancer was terminal, but according to Visconti, he thought he had a lot more time left. "He thought that he'd have a few months, at least," says Visconti. "I don't know exactly, but he must've taken ill very quickly after that phone call." The producer says he first learned of Bowie's illness in early 2015, when he turned up for a* Blackstar *session "fresh from a chemo session, and he had no eyebrows, and he had no hair on his head. There was no way he could keep it a secret from the band." Again, according to Visconti, by November, the cancer had spread all over his body. Visconti says that when he first saw the* Blackstar *lyrics, he said to Bowie: "You canny bastard. You're writing a farewell album."*

AVA CHERRY: I was here in Chicago when I heard he'd passed. I was asleep. I let my phone tell me when different things are going on. It gives me alerts. It was four in the morning and I just kept hearing *ching ching ching*. And I was thinking, Who's calling me at four in the morning? And I look and I see all these Facebook people say I'm so sorry I'm crying I feel so depressed I don't think I can live and I was like, What? And they were like, David's dead. And I just started to cry. I couldn't believe it. I didn't realize that it was going on but here it was. When I first heard *Blackstar* I kept saying to myself, Why is this so dark? Why is it apocalyptic-sounding? Why is he grimacing and making faces and stuff? Now I understand. He didn't tell anyone except his immediate family that he was going through chemo for two years and that he was dying of cancer. And *Blackstar* is all about that and expressing his feelings about death. And I didn't know that.

CHRIS STEIN: It really is extraordinary that he made this last record in the full knowledge that it would be his last, his swansong. I guess some of the classical poets did things like that. It's a bit like Mishima, who committed public suicide, but that was a little sloppier, and didn't come out the way he intended it to.

TONY VISCONTI: The last album was hard to produce because I didn't know he was going to die. I only realized it was a parting gift when he passed away. Then I reviewed the lyrics and it hit me hard. I think he did have plans for another album, but the subject of death had always been strong with him, and he wrote a lot of songs about it. In a way he was obsessed with death. I know he loved Jacques Brel's "My Death," and he used to sing that live with his acoustic guitar all the time. And there are a few beautiful renditions of it. I think it is a theme for a lot of writers, like Woody Allen, who writes about death all the time but he's a comedian. David was just realistic about it.

All writers work their fears out in their writing. They have this privilege that most of us don't have, as writing and performing is a cathartic experience for them. I honestly think *Blackstar* is his best album, his magnum opus. He just got better and better. Some fans might disagree, as they might ask why he recorded "Sue" again, but I know he did it because he wanted to make a different version of it, with a completely different flavor to it. I was watching a master in action, a grandmaster. He really was amazing on this album—the songs were extremely well written and his vocals . . . I just couldn't believe how rich his voice sounded and how loud he was singing and how passionately he was singing. So I saw firsthand how this album was shaped over about nine months, and it just sounded so beautiful every time I heard it. It's melancholy rather than sad. Some bits are quite cheeky. It's kind of humorous.

Every time Bowie put out a new album, there were a lot people who hated it and then they ended up loving it. This happened because he broke his own rules, he broke his own mold. He just threw the old David Bowie away and created a new one for each album. People say why didn't he record "Rebel Rebel" again or why couldn't he write another "Space Oddity"? Because he'd done it, he didn't write the formula. So now if he hadn't passed away I think people would still be loving the album. You have to discard your beliefs of what you think David Bowie is going to write and just be open to the new things he puts out. But I've seen this with every album. With *Young Americans* you heard people saying that white people weren't meant to make soul, and with *Low* the record company almost rejected it because there weren't enough vocals on it. But everybody loves *Low*—that album gave birth to Gary Numan and a lot of other styles of British electronic music. He was a trailblazer but you didn't see it at first.

MIKE GARSON: What I couldn't tell anyone until he died was something he told me in the mid-'90s, and something that sat very heavily with me for twenty-one years. We were on the tour bus in 1995, somewhere in mid-America, one o'clock in the morning, and he told me that ten years earlier he had seen a psychic, and the psychic told him he would die at the age of sixty-nine or seventy, so it's almost as though he designed the end of his life that way. So the last eighteen months he had liver cancer, so he knew for a fact. But this was something he had known for over thirty years. I couldn't tell anyone. Who could I tell? So I just lived with this knowledge. Then, when I got the call, like everyone else I went into shock. Then I swear, ten seconds later, I think, Oh, that's what he told me.

TONY VISCONTI: I'd always be there from day one. I'd be on the thing right from the beginning. We always started every album with about two weeks of discussion—kicking ideas around, formulating what we were going to do. It was a procedure. Because it's very much like making a film—you have to plan it. So, before we even recorded one note of music, I was already totally prepared for what I was about to do and hear. Then you just dived in. From day to day the role changed. Some days I would do nothing. Other days I would do everything. It depended on what the song needed. It's not so much what I gave to David. It's what I gave to each song. Each song was like a baby. It had a life of its own. It needed special food. It couldn't drink milk. This baby loved pineapple, this baby didn't. It was really more about addressing the music and the songs. Sometimes it was giving him the confidence to go on and reassuring him that I was there for him and I would make sure everything went smoothly. Producers do everything nowadays and I'm one of the earlier producers who started that. David was much more proactive as a producer as well. He used to be a little more passive, just gave you the songs, the melodies. He often picked the band members. But then he started doing demos at home and being very specific about what he wanted. On *Blackstar*, he was playing a lot of instruments. But he played them at home and then was able to take them off of his home recorder. By the time he died he was just so much more intelligent and more experienced. And I wasn't going to hold him back at all.

ELTON JOHN (MUSICIAN, SINGER-SONGWRITER): David and I were not the best of friends towards the end. We started out being really good friends. We used to hang out together with Marc Bolan, going to gay clubs, but I think we just drifted apart. He once called me "rock and roll's token queen" in an interview with *Rolling Stone*, which I thought was a bit snooty. He wasn't my cup of tea. No, I wasn't his cup of tea. But the dignified way he handled his death, I mean, thank God. I knew he'd had a heart attack onstage in Berlin years ago, but not about the cancer. Everyone else, take note of this: Bowie couldn't have staged a better death. It was classy.

PAUL GORMAN: I guess my point is that he's too interesting to be turned into a sacred cow. It does him and his achievements a grave disservice. He could be terribly corny; part of that generational thing among Englishmen doing Goons voices with Brian Eno at the Château—shudder . . . he was great but not as great as everyone says he was. I mean, [*Guardian* columnist] Suzanne Moore said she's convinced that his death inaugurated a new phase for the world where Terrible Things happen because he was such a Good Person. Seriously. This is a grown person with, I assume, a mortgage, driving license, and adult responsibilities yet is peddling forced and otherwise unacceptable juvenilia dressed up as worthwhile comment. I followed him since 1973, had a brother who saw him at UFO, went to all the gigs, met and interviewed him, worked on the same War Child projects as him, so I am a fan . . . and yet . . . he was a shit to his mother, he was a shit to his manager who supported him through thick and thin, and he was a shit to numerous partners, including his first wife, whose contribution he meanly refused to acknowledge even unto death. He didn't pay UK taxes for forty years, he made execrable records during 1984–1995, often wore terrible clothes, stupid makeup and had rotten haircuts, definitely flirted with right-wing politics, and made silly statements on the subject . . . in other words, a normal, flawed human being. This absurd elevation—particularly by people I know wouldn't have known *Lodger* from *Tonight* before he died—needs puncturing.

ERIN KEANE (JOURNALIST): After David Bowie's death took us all by surprise, the tributes overwhelmed. Social-media feeds were filled, almost unanimously, with videos and links and memes praising the influential artist who seems to possess near-universal appeal—he made enough hits to feel populist, and yet remained sufficiently influential to exist on a forever-cool plane with his scant handful of equals. But in between the *Labyrinth* GIFs, the retrospectives, and moving tributes to his style and gender performance, a quiet pushback began online too. *Don't forget this part of the story*, the messages suggested, with links to this earlier interview shared: "I Lost My Virginity to David Bowie: Confessions of a '70s Groupie," in which Lori Mattix recounts her teenage days in the Los Angeles rock scene. Mattix had, in her own words, consensual sex with not only Bowie—at age fifteen—but with Jimmy Page as well. . . .

Mattix's narrative is troubling to read in the sober light of 2016. A girl loses her virginity to a man in a hotel room, and that same night has her first threesome with him and another teenage friend as well. There are drugs and alcohol everywhere. There is David Bowie's wife, Angie, banging on the door the next morning. There is the girl's mother, indifferent when she's not overtly approving of the conquests; her father, deceased. There is David Bowie's face Monday all over the Internet, fans moved to tears over his death. There is scant, if any, mention of that girl in those moving tributes. There is, even in 2016, the question of how appropriate it is to talk about her at all.

I believe Mattix when she says that she felt special in the company of these glamorous, powerful men, happy to let them decide how and when she'd have sex and with whom. At fifteen, at sixteen, at seventeen. Not because I agree—most people grow out of the idea that sex with a rock star is a goal to pursue—but because when you're young it's easy to believe that experience is the one currency you're allowed to hoard and never pay out. Because it's alluring to believe a woman is made from her chosen experiences, and aren't you already a woman at fourteen, at fifteen? Doesn't the world, goddamn it, let you know that every day? Our culture, too, makes it easy to simply accept Mattix was a girl who decided she knew what she wanted, and to let it go at that.

And wasn't it, as she says, "a different world"? *Oh, the '70s. Things were different then.* But they were not, really, no matter how many times we all collectively wish that to be true. If you can say with a straight face "Men don't have sex with young girls anymore"—well, good luck to you with that. What changes is this, only—which girls, which men, how and where it is allowed. What is more appropriate than making sure we don't forget this, ever, even at inconvenient times?

I believe Mattix when she says the sex with her rock-star partners was consensual on her behalf, and I also believe, for good reason, David Bowie and the others committed acts that are exploitative, and illegal. Age fifteen is young, no matter what, and *they* were the adults with all the power in this dynamic, and that is not what healthy, normal sexual relationships for teenagers look like. I also believe it's important to say this is different from the horrific decades' worth of rape allegations brought forth against Bill Cosby, and different from Roman Polanski's rape of a drugged girl. It is not the same as the lawsuits against R. Kelly over his alleged sexual abuse of young girls, though the conditions that made all of these stories possible stem from the same terrible old root: powerful men, young women, and a whole lot of people who looked the other way—or in the case of these teen groupies, even romanticized the tales. Say, wasn't *Almost Famous* great?

Does even talking about the story, now that he has died, taint Bowie's legacy, as some fear? What is any true legacy but complicated? If we feel guilty for talking about it, maybe we should explore where that guilt really comes from. I can believe that David Bowie might not have believed he violated anyone by having sex with Lori Mattix and whoever else, though of course I don't know his (or, for that matter, Jimmy Page's) heart, or even whether these events transpired at all the way Mattix says they did, although the tales have been out there long enough to be read as a generally accepted narrative of the times. It is not hard to believe Bowie likely understood at the time—without even having to acknowledge it—that he was simply availing himself of the sensory perks of his station. How was a girl any different from good dope, the best table, a forgiven room-service bill? They were an indulgence to finally grow out of, perhaps, like cocaine and cheeseburgers.

And it would seem as though she believes the same—she was availing herself of the pleasures available to her at the time, and she made her own decisions willingly and enjoyed herself with no major regrets. Should we demand she represent her experience any other way? If what we do is *believe women*, should we believe her? It is possible to believe her and to know objectively that it was wrong anyway, and to say so. Not for her or for Bowie, necessarily, but for other girls now who are absorbing how we talk about these stories, and all the girls yet to come.

EARL SLICK: In a lot of ways people thought they knew David, but they didn't. I did. We had a problem in common, a situation, our whole lives, and I understood him because of that. I don't even want to go there. It's something that we had in common, that we had talked about privately. And that's why I'm telling you this, because I've never told anybody. So in my own way I could understand what seemed to be the callous shit that he would do. The not calling you, or all of a sudden deciding you were going to be replaced by this guy or that guy. But that was David. You know, he never discussed his brother. With me it came up maybe a couple of times over the whole time I knew him, during certain conversations we had about a certain thing. And when it came up, it came up not at length at all. As far as his personal life was concerned, how he grew up, his mother, his brother, his family, it really wasn't anything he talked about at all. David was very, very, very private about that. Anything to do with his private life. The only thing I knew was that he did his own washing up and stuff. If there was a coffee cup that needed washing, instead of calling the maid in, he'd do it himself. On the bus he'd get all bitchy: "Slicky, this has got to be your cup! So clean it." He had no problems making coffee, washing up, but that's about as far as it went. I've felt very negative about David at times, but I loved the man to death. He wasn't a saint, but I miss him a lot.

NILE RODGERS: The last time I saw him was on film. I was being honored with an award and I wanted him to give it to me, but Iman was getting honored that exact same night, so of course he wasn't going to choose me over his wife, plus she was getting her award in San Francisco. So he made a film for me, which was really sweet. When I heard that he'd died I wasn't as shocked as some people were, even though I hadn't seen him for a long time. Because when he did the film for me I could see in his face that it wasn't the same. I would always call his office and ask him to come and perform "Let's Dance" with me if I was playing in the New York area, so I was in contact with him a lot. But the people who worked with him on the last record were very loyal. Sterling Campbell, who I introduced him to, didn't say a word to me.

STERLING CAMPBELL: I sent him a message when [the musical] *Lazarus* came out, congratulating him, and he just sent a message back: "Thanks Ster." That's what he called me, "Ster."

CANDY CLARK: I really regret not going to see *Lazarus.* I was going to go to the opening night, as I was really intrigued to see what he had done to the movie, and what he had done to Mary-Lou, my character in *The Man Who Fell to Earth.* I just put it off, and now I'll never be able to see it. I thought, he'd probably be happy to see me, I'd probably get a good seat. It's a valuable lesson: don't take anything for granted. When I saw pictures of him on opening night, standing there holding hands with the other actors, I thought he didn't look good. Either he's really, really tired or he's sick. He looked like he was in pain, and kinda yellow. Jaundiced. Dry. That should have been a clue.

ANGIE BOWIE: In the '70s he had a terrible fear of death, but then that goes hand in hand with the excessive paranoia that comes with excessive drug taking. He confided all about that with me. However, it wasn't a fear of death he spoke about. It was a fear of getting killed. It's a bit different. Getting cut down in your prime is different from dying. I don't think that was an issue. And he managed his departure—because he had some notice of what it was going to be—I think, with great grace and style. Because you can't just throw your hands up in the air and become morbid. He stayed busy and focused and left us with a huge inventory of art and activity in that final eighteen months, once he knew.

WENDY LEIGH: I do think it's fascinating that David died when Angie was sequestered in the *Big Brother* house. She obviously had this dilemma: Do I stay in and try and win the prize money, or do I go out and try and capitalize on David's death. I mean, she has dined out on him forever and ever and ever. That was delicious.

BONO: David called Jordan, my daughter, who was feeding when he stayed with us in Dublin, Pixie. He called her that because she was a tiny little bald head when he met her. She's an exceedingly clever girl, and she's had a very, very deep connection to David Bowie. Not related to the fact that he was going to be walking in any minute when her mother was feeding her. She was very evolved with her taste in music, and she's a bit of a music Nazi. I'm terrified of playing her stuff. But she's a big Bowie fan. And when *Blackstar* came out, we were walking over Killiney Hill, and we shared an earphone. I put it in one side and she did the other. And we listened to *Blackstar* together on this walk. And it was a very special moment between father and daughter, her hearing *Blackstar* for the first time, us hearing it for the first time together. And we loved it. And we were together a few weeks later, and I sent him a photograph of the two of us and told him the story I just told you. And it was his birthday. And I sent him a long, long email. And then a few days later [when] we got the news and with the devastation of losing somebody who all of us in the family loved, came the tiniest little morsel of comfort, which is that we actually did communicate with him on his birthday. I'm told he read it, but he did not reply.

MICK ROCK: My wife had gone to bed, and I had watched some TV, hung out with the cats, and crashed out on the sofa. The next day I turned on the TV, which is something I never do, so it must have been intuitive, and I saw my "Space Oddity" video, and I wondered why. I assumed it was some kind of follow-up to the release of *Blackstar.* And then I saw the tickertape along the bottom saying "David Bowie dead at 69." Tony Visconti said this, and I feel the same, that David wasn't thinking he was going when he went. The picture taken of him a few days before he died, he looked fine. I find it very difficult to look at the *Blackstar* video even now. To be so creative right up to the end, that's brave, that's special.

WILLIAM ORBIT (MUSICIAN, COMPOSER, RECORD PRODUCER): I had been eager to watch *The Last Panthers* after reading an online synopsis, impatient to get into the story, and had not known about the Bowie song ("Lazarus"). Subsequently I learned that it came from an album that was a final testimony, and I let it slip by, as my current mood and new projects weren't allowing room for the full acceptance of Bowie's departure from the world, nor was I in the right frame of mind for listening to his final message.

I suppose I thought it was a maudlin record, but it is anything but. The full song as it appears on the album had the signature sobbing, moaning Bowie moments that were amongst his huge range of vocal expressions—which went from Broadway musical to rock and roll ball-busting to intimate confession to primal scream—and it colored my first impression. This, and the brittle close harmony, unsettled me. In my experience, musicians generally have an optimistic view of life, and never more so than when actually creating music, preferring to hedge the reality of oblivion with the thought that people will say nice things about their work when they've gone, and thereby existentially remaining in play. All of the tracks on *Blackstar* twist and turn musically, especially the key. Most of the great David Bowie songs, as with most great pop songs generally, stick to one key, containing a basic set of related chords. This album does not have that consistency, to the point that there is even a multitude of spacial effects on his voice. I could also hear a deep commitment in the performances of all the musicians, especially Donny McCaslin's sax and Mark Guiliana, the drummer. They sound like a band who could play absolutely anything to its fullest. But the album feels like an open-ended gift to all of us who were gutted to learn of his death.

But it is not maudlin. I've always taken the word for granted, and so I looked it up, and it is the wrong word entirely. Just as it would be for Henry Purcell's "Dido's Lament." *Blackstar* is not "self-pitying" or "tearfully sentimental." This album has actually had a profound emotional effect on some people closest to me in my life. I take longer to respond to matters of the heart, but I get there. I'm getting there now as I journey back from that word. Let's put that word far away in the rearview mirror.

TONY VISCONTI: I think the music industry would get in David's way if he had been starting out now. I think David was ahead of his time and he had a very difficult time being signed back in the day. He started out writing songs for the West End, he tried folk music, he tried a lot of things. "Space Oddity" is what finally got him a singles deal rather than an album deal, and then he didn't really come out with a new hit single until *Ziggy Stardust*, so my point is the labels believed in him. Once he had shown that he managed to get one thing as a hit on the radio they didn't drop him, whereas nowadays anyone will do that. They just don't allow any experimental style artist to be signed, but we would have gone underground, we would have used the Internet and used all those tools. He would be true to himself. I would still be working with him. I only support geniuses, I'm afraid, people who are courageous and very intelligent. Those are the only people I work with.

KEN SCOTT: David would never get signed by a label today, as he wouldn't be given the chance to develop. He would have floundered, as he wouldn't have been supported. There is no way a record company could afford to nurture someone in the way that Bowie was nurtured all those years ago.

DAVE STEWART: Like a lot of people in the rock and roll bubble, he used to go on tour and take cocaine and go crazy, and was surrounded by lots of women who would throw themselves at him, and he was quite happy to take the opportunities . . . but when he met Iman he knew this was it. He changed immediately. You could see that something had happened in his brain, a lightbulb moment: *Oh, I can be loved by someone.* I think it was hard for many people to get their heads round the fact that he had domestic bliss. People liked him as a decadent rock god, not a man who was happy at home. But he desperately needed it. Personally I was enchanted by the dignified way in which he decided to go, and I'm fully expecting to see a video at some point where he is somewhere in heaven singing, "*Here am I sitting in a tin can . . .*" Nothing would surprise me. . . .

LINDSAY KEMP: He was splendid, a genius. I still love him. I never fall out of love. Once in love, always in love.

JOHAN RENCK (DIRECTOR): It became a project that had a lot of tears. It started very innocently. I was directing a television series called *The Last Panthers*, and when we started approaching the end of the shoot I decided that I wanted someone from my childhood to write the music for the opening credits. So we started looking around and someone suggested David Bowie, but it didn't even cross my mind because it was so unreachable and so unthinkable. So I just told her: "You don't even ask somebody like that." But she insisted, and a day after we approached him we got an answer saying that David was interested in the project. So I sent him a rough cut of the first episode, the script, and a mood board, and very shortly thereafter, he sent me a rough outline for the song that later became "Blackstar," but in a very different arrangement, in a very different shape and form. When I heard the piece I knew it was absolutely right, immediately. A couple of days later, he and Tony Visconti Skyped me from their studio—they're playing it to me and the two of them are sitting there like kids, looking eagerly at me and wondering what my response is going to be. Then I hear myself saying, "Well, I love it, but I do not like the guitar you have on top of it." And I'm thinking, "What the fuck am I doing?" Then I see David and Tony just look at each other and they stop nodding and they say, "OK, OK. We'll call you back in one hour with a different idea. Hang on." Then they just hung up. So I hung up and said to my wife, "What the fuck did I just do? I'm, like, producing David Bowie and Tony Visconti while they're in the studio. I'm an idiot." But at the same time, it was what I wanted. So, they called me back an hour later, and they're playing me a new version in which they'd replaced the guitar with a more string-like effect, or something slightly more droning. And I thought it was perfect.

A few weeks later I find myself in New York and I get an email from David: "Look, I've completed this song; do you want to come over and have a listen to it?" So I walked over to his office, which is just a couple of blocks away from my mine, and he puts on this CD and he puts a hand on my shoulder and says, "Mind you, it's ten minutes long." Then he plays me "Blackstar" and asks if I'd be interested in making a video for it.

Obviously from the get-go he was an extraordinarily nice man, charming, curious; he would listen as much as he would talk, he would be very gentlemanlike on all levels, and I took an immediate liking to him; I liked the human being that was David Bowie very much. So we started collaborating. He would send me random drawings, and I'd send drawings back to him. Then he'd send me some Luis Buñuel fake documentary about some strange Spanish village up in the mountains, and I would send him some old, obscure Russian film that I felt was interesting. The collaboration was amazing because it was a collaboration in its absolute truest form, like nothing I've ever had before. There's always egos, there's always people who need to prove a point, or people who need to prove their salary by commenting on stuff, rather than just saying, "This is good, let's just move on." This one had none of that; this one was just the way it should be. Then in the summer of 2015 I was in my country house in Sweden, moping around in my shorts, and he sends me a message saying that he needs to Skype me. So he comes up on Skype and says, "I have to tell you something. I have to tell you that I'm very ill and that I'm probably going to die." And it's one of the most absurd, bizarre moments I've ever experienced. I'm trying to put words to it now, but it's almost impossible to do that. And some stupid thing comes out of my mouth like, "What do you mean?" or "Are you joking?" because I couldn't even grasp it. And then he said, "I'm telling you this. I've been contemplating and I feel that I have to tell you this because I'm not sure I will be around to be in the video." And we're like two months from shooting the video. I'm saying, "What the fuck are you even saying? I've known you for my entire life pretty much and now I met you for a moment and now all of a sudden you're saying you're going to die?" It's like the most insane thing ever. So this is what he tells me and we speak about it a little bit and for a minute the conversation is pretty serious, but then he sort of says, "I've known this for a while and I'm in treatment." He explains everything to me, but from that moment, since I'm a very optimistic type of guy, my reasoning was always that he's going to be in treatment, he's going to fight this shit, it's going to be a battle, and then he's going to be fine and then it's all good. So, from the moment of him telling me I went onto the trajectory of pro-life on his behalf. But, to be honest, I don't think he told me only so I could figure out what to do on the practical level for the video, to find a replacement for him, I really think he told me because he wanted death to be a third collaborator in this video; he wanted death to be there as a presence in terms of formulating all the ideas and lying as a middle instigator for his thoughts as we went onwards. Because what I found out later, he knew he was ill enough to not make it, because of the nature of his cancer, but he never told me that.

When I went into the process of making the videos, I immediately sensed the reflective aspect of them. He had been around for so long, with such an enormously prolific career and I said to him early on, "The interesting thing here is we don't have to look outside your myth to look for references. Also, it's almost impossible to make a video with you without mirroring elements of your various iterations over the years." But I never thought they would be the last videos he ever made. Never did it cross my mind. I was even hoping we were going to do videos for other songs on the album. So, for me, there was nothing morbid about making them. Nothing suggested that he was ill over these seven months that we were working together, and the "Lazarus" video we shot in November, which was only pretty much a month and a half away from his passing, and he was as perky as ever. I later found out that during that week he had understood: It's over; we're going to end all treatment and you have a short time left to live. But there was nothing that ever came up between us.

He had told very, very few people about his illness; even people in his closest sphere around him didn't know. He told because he had to. Obviously his family knew, and obviously his close collaborators knew, and Coco, and [photographer] Jimmy King, and [business manager] Bill Zysblat. Our conversations would touch upon stuff that to some extent related to mortality and death. He would randomly text me or chat—and this is not me trying to say I was becoming besties with David Bowie; that's not at all what I'm saying. All I'm saying is that because of the information I sat on, there were conversations that he had with me that perhaps he didn't have with other people. I was sure that he was going to make it. He was so young physically and mentally and spiritually. He literally felt ten or fifteen years younger than his age—he was sixty-nine and he didn't look a day over fifty and some change, to be honest. And a big, warm smile that he always had and his honest, cheeriest eyes never revealed anything like a battle with death on the inside. Obviously in "Blackstar," death is present with this sort of wraith that is summoned within the video, and even in "Lazarus," obviously, death is present. But to me, the wraith was not death; it is more the illness that needs to be fought and dealt with to some extent, but it was not necessarily death.

"Blackstar" was an extraordinary piece of music—it's like an anthem. It's really my cup of tea: it's kind of dark, it's ominous, but it's also dreamy. It changes, it starts to be different colorings in the mid-part and all that. So I really loved it. I can tell you one thing though, within these songs, within the harmonies and within the lyrics, there are references to death on a lot of levels. And to me I didn't find that peculiar. "Lazarus" was not intended to be a requiem. When he came to me, he said, "I want to make a video for this song, but I just want to stick to a performance video." And I said, "Great. I already have an idea." And I drew a picture of him in bed with this weird sort of . . . To me, Lazarus means a man in bed—from the Bible—and that's what I wanted to say. It had nothing to do with Bowie being on his deathbed; I'm sure it did on his behalf, but for me it didn't. For me, it was about the man who rises from his bed and takes his bed and walks. So, when he died and I look at this video of this old man—he managed to look very old at the beginning of the video there—lying sort of struggling with his demons in the bed, it was like, Holy, fucking shit, what have I done? He had sent me these images from *Station to Station* with the black-and-white striped outfit and said, "What about if we reawaken this guy?" It was all his own myth. When we were shooting "Lazarus," he knew that he only had a month or two left of his life; we were sitting there, me and David and Jimmy King, who's his long-time collaborator, stylist, archivist, and all that kind of stuff. We're sitting watching the playback of the take we just did and one of us said—I don't remember who it was, to be honest, but I think it was Jimmy: "Hey David, wouldn't it be funny if you ended the video by going back into the closet." And David started giggling like mad: "Yeah, look, David Bowie has come back into the closet! Fuck yeah, we've got to do that. Let's do that right away." So we did this thing where he, sort of, reverses into the closet and closes the door and disappears. And it was just for fun; that's how that idea came up. And little did I know how extraordinarily powerful this was, to end the last video he ever did by him going into his own fucking coffin and closing the door and disappearing, for all eternity. Even at the very end of things, he would have a laugh and he would be audacious. He had an enormous loyalty to his fans. He would do things to please his fans, or to tease his fans: "They're going to question this. They won't know what this is about. They're going to have a lot of fun thinking about this," and so on and so forth. He was extraordinarily loving towards everybody who liked his music.

BRIAN ENO: David's death came as a complete surprise, as did nearly everything else about him. I feel a huge gap now. We knew each other for over forty years, in a friendship that was always tinged by echoes of [comic characters] Pete and Dud. Over the last few years—with him living in New York and me in London—our connection was by email. We signed off with invented names: some of his were Mr. Showbiz, Milton Keynes, Rhoda Borrocks, and the Duke of Ear. About a year ago we started talking about *Outside*—the last album we worked on together. We both liked that album a lot and felt that it had fallen through the cracks. We talked about revisiting it, taking it somewhere new. I was looking forward to that. I received an email from him [recently]. It was as funny as always, and as surreal, looping through word games and allusions and all the usual stuff we did. It ended with this sentence: "Thank you for our good times, Brian. They will never rot." And it was signed "Dawn." I realize now he was saying goodbye.

I was shown a copy of that last email, and while it would be intrusive to mention precisely what it said, it was a celebration of the pair's collaborations over the years, a litany of achievement; "We did all, that, Brian." The email quite quickly veered off into Pythonesque banter, with Bowie repeatedly writing "Bum, bum, bum, bum, bum . . ." (which is also German for Boom, boom, boom, boom, boom . . .)

FRANCIS WHATELY: In November 2015 he sent me an email. My daughter and his daughter were exactly the same age and I'd sometimes mentioned my errant daughter and the difficulties of bringing up a teenager. And he asked me how my family was, and I said, "Things aren't great." He said, and I'm paraphrasing: "I'm very happy with my lot. I'm very pleased with the new album. What more could any man ask for." Which I thought was a very strange thing to say, and I didn't really think more of it. He then said: "How are you and yours?" And I wrote back—and I know you're not meant to write back to David Bowie and actually tell him how you feel, but I did because the BBC were going through a round of redundancies again, in their infinite wisdom—and I said, "Well, the BBC are cutting 50 percent of the staff in my area, but perhaps it's time to move on." He wrote back about two days later and said, "If the BBC have any wisdom at all, they will give you a job for life." And that's the last I heard from him. I've worked at the BBC for over twenty years and interviewed Hillary

Clinton, academics, journalists, actors, and all sorts of very clever people. And I never met anyone as clever as him. I never met anyone with his star power; I never met anyone with his ability to put someone at their ease; I never met anyone who was as un-starry, actually.

How much he played on his own family's madness, I don't know. He might have played on it because it made him more romantic. People have told me that he had this great fear of going mad. I find that unlikely. I think he was a man very much in control of his own destiny and his own ability. Do I think he wrestled with the black dog? Yes, his music says it all. But do I think he ever thought he was going to go mad? No.

What I'm surprised about is the amount of people who worked with him for a short period who never heard from him again and who found it impossible then to get through the machine to get to him again. So I remember Jack Hofsiss, who directed *The Elephant Man*, who told me that he'd been trying to get through to David but couldn't get through the office. Did the messages get through to David? I don't know. Did his people not pass on the message? Did he feel that was a time in his life that was now over? I don't know. What I am surprised by though is the amount of people who appear to have been "rejected," in inverted commas, by him, who still remained incredibly fond of him and reluctant to say anything bad about him at all. He seemed to exert his charm well beyond their own personal sell-by dates.

KIM JONES: He was here for a real reason you know. I'm not at all religious, but some people are here for a reason, aren't they? It was awful when we heard that he'd died. On the Friday beforehand I had been with Kate Moss and we had done a happy birthday message for him and sent it to him, and then on the Monday I saw that he was dead. It was a shock because Kate and I had just that weekend been planning to ask him to do a special project together . . . it didn't seem real when I heard.

KATE MOSS: I cried a lot when he died. I was at home. I had just sent him a birthday message, because he would always send me an email on my birthday. So I put together a piece of paper that said Happy Birthday DB, and I did a film to "Mr. Bojangles" whilst holding the poster, and sent it. The next morning, it was really early morning, as I'd had a really late night and I was just going to bed. It was six o'clock. And my boyfriend told me what had happened. Because everything about the few days before had been about him. I'd even come home and watched the Hammersmith Odeon film on the projector. I've lost count of the number of times I've watched that concert. What made him so special was that he was just so not scared. He was so out there, and so free, and so himself and also not himself. That's a true artist, making himself into a walking piece of art. He took it to another level. It wasn't just about music, it was everything. It was his whole culture. I think a lot of people have a female side, but he just managed to not be frightened by it. He used it to his advantage in his music, his stage presence and in his looks. He had such good legs! And when you see him going across the stage in those boots, it's just heaven!

DORIAN LYNSKEY (JOURNALIST): News of David Bowie's death arrived like news of his surprise comeback, in the early hours of a bleak January morning. This time, however, a bulletin from Bowieworld made the morning even bleaker and the disbelief was horrific rather than magical. In our house, like so many others, it wrenched the day out of joint. My wife burst into tears, my oldest daughter sang "Life on Mars?," and I had the same reaction as if I had lost a friend or family member rather than a pop star: a stubborn, instinctive "No." In pop terms, Bowie's death was a hole in the sky; a disturbance in the Force. It's customary when a great musician dies to play some of their songs in tribute but we are always listening to Bowie, and to people inspired by Bowie; he's one of the elements that constitute the air that pop music breathes. The radio played "Space Oddity" but it could have played any of a couple of dozen peerless songs and they would have been no less representative.

Looking back, you can hardly believe how fast he moved. "I can look back on a song that I've just written and it means something entirely different now because of my new circumstances, new this or that," he said in 1972. Just look at him go. On Radio 4's *Today* program John Wilson said it was a fallacy to call Bowie a chameleon because chameleons blend in with their environment whereas Bowie reconfigured his environment. He had a voracious appetite for exciting developments in music, cinema, fashion, media, and visual art and the strength of vision to mold these whirling influences into records that were unmistakably David Bowie.

You could argue that a genius is someone whose extraordinary world hunger is equaled only by their capacity to harness it.

Bowie knew he had cancer all the time he was making *Blackstar* but he withheld the news. His final gift, to himself as well as us, was to allow this brilliant album to be received on its own merits, undistorted by a sense of finality and the sentimentality that comes with it. For just three days after its release, it sounded like someone racing forward rather than looking back and you could imagine that yet another new phase had begun. Now it transpires that he knew this would be his last record, which makes its fearless strangeness even more impressive.

Blackstar *was actually meant to be released in the last week of October, to escape the mass of "Best-Ofs" released at Christmas, although its release was held up because the video for "Lazarus" wasn't quite ready. This whole idea of releasing the album to coincide with his death was just morbid speculation. There was also a whole lot of disinformation concerning the secrecy of Bowie's illness, as the fundamental reason he didn't tell anyone was because he didn't want anyone to be upset. This was the reason he kept the seriousness of his situation secret from Sony, his record company; the whole team working on the record were so resolutely positive about its release—and genuinely giddy with excitement because of his new jazz direction ("a genuine sonic departure")—he didn't want to burst their bubble. This was typical. Bowie knew exactly what effect he had on people, and behaved accordingly. Which meant that he always tried to act normally, even though it was inevitably a heightened sense of normal. He knew that* Blackstar *would be an important album for him—at Sony they internally compared it favorably to* Low*—and he was as concerned about its marketing as he was about its predecessor,* The Next Day. *With that album he couldn't quite believe how Sony had managed to keep it such a secret, and was equally appalled when he found out certain people involved in the making of the record had started blabbing to the press. He didn't want there to be an excessive amount of noise, he just wanted it to be taken seriously. Remarkably, he read every review of* The Next Day, *every broadsheet thesis, every hastily scribbled blog. Everything. He was engaged but separate, obsessive about the world around him, and his role within it, but loath to engage. He really enjoyed being the Englishman in New York, being able to disappear at a moment's notice. He had no interest in being the custodian of his back catalogue, no interest at all in his past—one* *of the reasons why there were no boxed sets during his "retirement"—but was driven by contemporary culture. He always wanted to know what was going on. He would delve into medieval history, but you wouldn't catch him boning up on anything that had happened in his own past. Let the fans do that. One Sony executive remembers asking him why he spent so much time in the studio in the '70s, to which Bowie was disarmingly blunt: "It was the only way I could make any money. Every time I delivered an album I got paid. You didn't make any money from touring in those days." He was extremely proud of* Blackstar. *In a final missive to one of the somebodies at Sony he wrote, "Not bad for an old rocker."*

THOMAS DOLBY: I was in the States and saw the news on the BBC website. I wasn't very surprised, as I knew he had been sick. Michael Jackson once said to me, "When I die I want to go like Elvis, because the bigger the star the more disgusting the death." Bowie turned his death into a statement, which is just extraordinary.

DORIAN LYNSKEY: Enigma is not usually a renewable resource. Once you lose it, it's gone forever. In that respect, as in so many others, David Bowie is the exception. While it's foolish to assume any lyric from this master of masks and bluffs is autobiographical, Bowie liked to leave the possibility open, and if there's anything on ★ (aka *Blackstar*) that feels like a direct address to the listener, it's these lines from its final song: "*This is all I ever meant/That's the message that I sent/I can't give everything away.*" Bowie's unusual comeback, which began one night in 2013 with the bolt-from-the-blue announcement of his album *The Next Day*, was predicated on giving away as little as possible. Bowie could do whatever he liked and his choices were never predictable. He gave no interviews and played no live shows. He snubbed Danny Boyle's efforts to use his songs in a musical biopic while saying yes to a low-key musical stage show, *Lazarus*, the Sky Atlantic drama *The Last Panthers*, and, most improbably, a show based on *SpongeBob SquarePants*. We thought we had him figured out. We were wrong, and hooray for that.

Like *The Next Day*, *Blackstar* was recorded in secret and delivered to a record company expecting nothing. But while the previous album was a dance with his past, especially *Lodger* and *Scary Monsters*, *Blackstar* is what happens next. The retro allusions are fleeting: "Girl Loves Me" binges on Nadsat, the *Clockwork Orange* argot Bowie deployed on "Suffragette City"; a fiercer version of 2014's "Sue (Or in a Season of Crime)" recalls *Earthling*'s drum 'n' bass; that's about it. It is not half as daunting as reports originally suggested. These are strong songs, powerfully rendered. Each one creates its own distinct space. The title track, a new angle on Bowie's favorite word "star," is an art-rock tour de force with hints of Scott Walker and later Radiohead. "Lazarus," from the New York musical, is an opaque fable, by turns elegiac and throat-grabbingly intense. "'Tis a Pity She Was a Whore" and "Sue (Or in a Season of Crime)" are urgent experiments in rhythm and violence. "Dollar Days" and "I Can't Give Everything Away" hail from a parallel-universe version of Bowie's '80s, with thick synth chords and rampaging sax. Bowie's voice constantly changes, too, from a jaded croon to a spooked warble to a strangled squawk to a muttered threat. If there's a criticism, it's simply that seven songs are too few but they contain more new ideas than most artists, of any age, could manage in seventeen.

JONATHAN BARNBROOK: I didn't know David was ill when we were designing the cover for *Blackstar.* I didn't guess when I met him. And we talked about the theme of mortality but not in a personal sense, in a more universal sense. You can hear it on the record of course. So I was as surprised as anyone else when he died. I would have probably designed it differently had I known. But then I think I picked up on [it]—it's a black album, with a black life and a black label. I picked up on the emotion in the album and I think it's better that I didn't know. I think he didn't tell me because it was just more convenient and it made the working process easier.

For *Blackstar* I actually went to New York to meet him and to listen to the album with him; for the other ones it was generally emails of the music and just a quick discussion. We'd never directly talk about the actual meaning of the songs or often even the meaning of the album, and I think it was better that I just interpreted the emotional meaning of the album than think about what [the] actual songs were about. I'd tried to keep it abstract and I think he was quite happy to keep it abstract. There's so much visual noise on album covers these days so it's better to keep it really simple and make it stand out.

Actually it doesn't have any type on it, which made the record company very nervous, because normally you'd have "David Bowie" on it and a picture of him, and both elements had gone. We spoke about having a picture of him on the cover. And I said that this is not the kind of album where you should have a picture of you smiling on the front. He said I completely agree. So, I mean, he was coming at it from a different place. He didn't specifically ask for his name not to be on it, but the first thing I wanted to do for the album was to shorten it to "Bowie," because "David Bowie" jarred with the minimal nature of using the star instead of writing *Blackstar.* And we deliberately didn't tell people directly it was his name. So it's playing with things coming into focus, which is the same as music as an abstract thing. Music suggests things to people and they may not be right. David would often say, "What people see in my songs is far more interesting than what I actually put into them." The way people construct the story around the meaning of the lyrics, that was the thought for the *Blackstar*/Bowie name. Still people come up to me at lectures or tweet me and say, "What do these stars mean?" Or "I've just discovered that the stars mean Bowie." I think it's nice. Not everything needs to be explained. When I look at the stars I think of the first discussion we had, about black holes. They give you life and they will finally drag you back to your death. He talked about mortality and the universe and the star. There was also a discussion about the current political state of the world, and the way gender is moving around these days, and how that is related to the *Blackstar.* Not sure why, but he showed me quite a lot of drawings that he had done. And a lot of these provided the basis of the *Blackstar* video. Women with tails. That was a comment about gender. Strange non-female or non-male-specific characters.

Even right until the end he was not a negative person. His last few emails were very definite and strong about what we were going to do with the designs, how the album would be promoted, and that kind of thing. And the people from the "Lazarus" shoot which was shot not long before he died commented on what a positive presence he was that day. I don't think he was feeling sorry for himself.

PAUL SMITH: At the beginning of January I was curating our installation for London Collections Men at the Royal Academy, when I heard the news. I was re-creating my original Nottingham shop—which measured about ten by ten feet—and filling it with a variety of artifacts. There was a pile of vintage speedometers that inspired some of my watch designs; some examples of Frank Auerbach's work, which I made into scarves; an old-fashioned squeezebox, which was the inspiration for one of my leather concertina bags. Lots of stuff like that. So when we heard the news we also made the shop an homage to David. It felt like the right thing to do. We had just done the official T-shirts for *Blackstar.* He asked me to design them, and they came out at one minute past midnight on the eighth, the same day as the album. It was quite dark, and it had a hint of jazz as well, but it was superb.

There came a point, not long after his death, when it appeared that anyone and everyone felt they needed to express an opinion about Bowie. The memorializing and reminiscing became something of a rite of passage, almost as though you hadn't somehow fully engaged with the modern media maelstrom unless you had made public your thoughts about DB. Many recollections were based around the lightning-bolt moment when he had fallen into their lives, or around a particular interaction, which obviously was now encumbered with huge significance. Others still were Twitter-esque exclamations of grief, love, and respect. Martyn Ware, who was in both the Human League and Heaven 17, described a typical vignette: "I met Bowie in 1978 when he came to see the Human League [in a pub in Fulham]. I have a photo of it, amazingly—I couldn't believe someone took a photo of it. It was completely unannounced; we had no inkling he was coming, he and his entourage. The dressing room, to give you an idea, was like a cubbyhole, really; the ceiling and the floor were covered in graffiti. It had no door and, like all those places, it just smelled of beer and pee. For me, it was like Jesus stepping out of a medieval painting and walking into your front room. It was just bizarre, I couldn't comprehend it; I still can't quite comprehend it to this day, really. He was such a hero. And then, of course, no pressure at all, that was ten minutes before we were due to go onstage." Some, like Cyndi Lauper, simply applauded the fact that he managed to successfully and repeatedly fuse sound and vision: "Corporate people who don't understand performance art"—the suits—would say, "Your image is so big, I can't hear you sing." That's why we all looked to Bowie, because he was one of the first performance artists and he didn't give a rat's ass; he didn't say, "Oh, I think I won't dress up this time." You know, he just fucking looked at the image and the sound, and put them together. And some got him completely: "There was David, and there was Bowie," wrote the illustrator Edward Bell in a poem. "Schizophrenia was in the genes. He could be cold and ruthless; He could be charming, erudite, witty and extremely good company." Or, as Robyn Hitchcock said, "There was always something about Bowie in his day that was very triumphalist. He was always about powering through and getting there and making your way—as he himself once said: 'Very Capricorn.'" So many people had stumbled upon him in their early teens. "David Bowie was somebody who I loved when I was fourteen, when his career was just starting," said the novelist Nick Hornby. "We followed him every step of the way, and I think you can feel a lot of our own mortality in the shock of his death. We thought this generation was somehow immortal. But it shouldn't be shocking. Let's face it: It was a guy who was nearly seventy, and he died too soon, but he died roughly at an appropriate age—threescore years and ten, and all that. So in that way, it's even more stark than somebody who was shot or who died of a drug overdose."

The one voice that was absent from the chorus of approval belonged to Tony Defries, who as far as the media was concerned was absent without leave. Some said he was living in South Africa, others that he was living and working on the West Coast. His LinkedIn profile was fascinating: "A successful British entrepreneur and inventor. Currently working on commercializing a flexible electronic quantum battery powered entirely by human biophotons and light. This patent pending wearable clean technology will provide a constant supply of electricity for smartphones and other mobile devices. Quantum entangled renewable energy is a game changing technology that can help to make a zero emission sustainable future possible." The summary of his career cast him as assisting in the creation of independent record and publishing companies acquired by major conglomerates, as well as being the architect of deals enabling "photographers, illustrators, designers, songwriters, producers, performers and other creators to secure and retain valuable creative rights and benefit from ongoing revenue streams." His profile then goes on to reference his time with MainMan, which had once created "a unique management structure that combined movie studio dynamics with those of independent producers, record labels and music publishers. He made Bowie a superstar and launched the careers of Iggy Pop, Lou Reed,

Mick Ronson, Mott the Hoople, Luther Vandross and John Mellencamp." It obviously made no reference to the business troubles (offshore tax issues, copyright infringement) that blighted the latter part of his career.

I spent several months trying to track him down, and then, having eventually made contact, suddenly got an email from him. "Before considering any request I need details of your previous published work," he wrote, "and the length, scope, topic, specs, status, deal, terms, delivery and publication dates, territory, format medium and all other rights being sought for the proposed (oral as in written and spoken/audio or audiovisual) RH biography + list of people interviewed and their comments good or bad. Also need a copy of the bio so far that shows your overall approach and tone."

So we started corresponding, with me outlining exactly what I was attempting to do with the book, and encouraging him to speak to me; and with him parrying in kind, wary of what I was trying to do. Then, one day in November, he suggested we talk, and so planned a call for later that week. When we spoke—for an hour, off the record, on the phone between Johannesburg and London—we covered a lot of ground. Defries was passionate in his espousal of Bowie, and was at pains to describe the affection he continued to feel for him. He appeared to be completely at ease with the ramifications of their business dealings, and was adamant that none of David's success would have happened without him. We talked about how Defries had started tidying up Bowie's past, extricating him from various contracts that he felt were going to complicate matters going forward. He also talked at great length about his decision to sign with RCA, and the plan to turn Bowie into an Elvis-like figure, removed from public life, and—crucially—isolated from the media. He said he wanted Bowie to act like Hollywood royalty, which is why he hired two bodyguards to accompany him wherever he went, why he booked him into the biggest, grandest hotels, and why he kept him away from the press. Simply by encouraging him to think like a star, Bowie started acting like one—for instance when he went to see Elvis perform at Madison Square Garden in 1972, he came back to London demanding that Defries buy him hundreds of scarves, as he liked the way Elvis had something to throw at the crowd as a keepsake. After a while I began to feel as though I were listening to the proud parent of an occasionally wayward child, someone who had explained the rules during adolescence, and who was now both admonishing his boy for being so distrustful and also wallowing in his subsequent success. Because even Defries appeared to acknowledge that Bowie developed an uncanny, barometric ability to stay several steps ahead of those around him, a man who walked through the '70s looking like a perpetually changing magazine cover, rarely leaving his house or his dressing room without imagining a huge logo hovering somewhere above his head, like a birthday balloon or an alphabet blimp.

After our initial conversation, Defries and I stayed in touch, with me trying to cajole him into cooperating, and him suggesting various revenue-sharing possibilities—was I open to him contributing to the book as an assistant author, co-author, collaborator, or "in some other mutually determined designation or capacity"? Would I be interested in him promoting the book through him appearing on network TV and/or streaming programs, and would I be interested in interviewing him for GQ*? He wanted to know if I might be interested in using unpublished pictures of David from his archives, and generally wanted to see how we might be able to work together. This correspondence went on for over a month until it fizzled out due to our inability to agree terms. (His final salvo contained a request for $360,000 for his contribution, which I replied proved that he had a keen sense of humor.)*

MADONNA (SINGER): I never felt like I fit in growing up in Michigan. Like an oddball or a freak. I went to see him in concert at Cobo Arena in Detroit. It was the first concert I'd ever been to. I snuck out of the house with my girlfriend, wearing a cape. We got caught after and I was grounded for the summer. I didn't care. I already had many of his records and was so inspired by the way he played with gender confusion. He was both masculine and feminine, funny and serious, clever and wise. His lyrics were witty, ironic, and mysterious. At the time he was the Thin White Duke and he had mime artists onstage with him and very specific choreography, and I saw how he created a persona and used different art forms within the arena of rock and roll to create entertainment. His music was always inspiring, but seeing him live set me off on a journey that for me I hope will never end.

Bowie's last will and testament, which detailed how his estimated $230 million fortune was to be distributed, was officially filed in Manhattan Surrogate Court on Friday, January 29. He left the bulk to Iman, Lexi, and Duncan, but gave $2 million to Coco, along with all of his shares in a company called Opossum Inc. As the company was officially dissolved in 2008, after only five years *trading, it was thought to be either some sort of tax-efficient wheeze, or a cypher. Conspiracy theorists had a field day, alighting on the fact that the* Wikipedia *entry for "opossum" says, "When threatened or harmed, they will 'play possum,' mimicking the appearance and smell of a sick or dead animal."*

PAUL SMITH: He was the punctuation marks in so many people's lives, including mine. One night in the '90s, my wife and I had supper with him and Iman at Christie's in St. James. When we left to get the cabs, there was a big staircase and as David walked down it, he started singing, "*The party's over, it's time to call it a day,*" to [my wife] Pauline and I. She reminded me of that moment the morning he died, and we were both in tears.

AVA CHERRY: He did so much for black music. He campaigned to have Michael Jackson's videos on MTV; he was always fighting for those kind of rights. When he wanted to do *Young Americans* I took him to the Apollo, which is where he met Carlos. Richard Pryor was there, the Spinners . . . and of course when we did *Young Americans* he opened up a whole new market for himself, which was black people.

He showed everybody that it's not about whether you're gay or straight or you wear your hair green or blue or black or white. Be yourself. Project yourself as an artist, be yourself, be who you are. Don't let other people influence your muse and what you really need to be. He looked like a girl but he was still a man. When you're an artist you have to have a person who says it's OK to be yourself. Don't try to be someone else.

CHERRY VANILLA: I am in so much awe of him orchestrating his own death. Who does that? What an artist. The album, the theatre production, the photographs, I just thought, Bravo, David.

"I knew David at the very beginning and then bumped into him along the way," said the Kinks' Ray Davies. Thirty years after covering the band's "Where Have All the Good Times Gone" on Pin Ups, *Bowie invited Davies onstage for a 2003 Tibet benefit concert at Carnegie Hall. "We played 'Waterloo Sunset.' We took a verse each, and a bridge, but we said, 'How shall we do this?' After a long discussion, we decided we'd impersonate one another." Davies also had a "mad"*

idea of producing a musical based on the life and career of Dirk Bogarde, which would have starred Bowie. "But we never got round to it. I think he'd have been great." They became "quite good email friends," and two years before his death, Bowie wrote the sleeve notes to the compilation The Essential Kinks. *"I always feel David could have collaborated more. You listen to 'Heroes,' he had such a great feel for music. And a mischievous chap."*

LADY GAGA (SINGER): Well, the moment that I saw the *Aladdin Sane* cover for the first time, I was nineteen years old, and it just changed my perspective on everything. I remember I took the vinyl record out of the casing and I put it on my vinyl player—which was on my stovetop in my kitchen, because I was living in this really tiny apartment and I had my turntable on my stove. I started to dress more expressively. I started to go to the library and look through more art books. I took an art history class. I was playing with a band. I guess what I'm trying to tell you is, my friends and I in New York, we've lived a lifestyle of total immersion in music, fashion, art, and technology since we were kids—and this is because of him. I just would never be here, or have the philosophy that I have, if I didn't have someone to look up to that blew my mind so intensely. You know the way that Nile Rodgers talks about Coltrane, and the way that Coltrane makes him think about jazz? That's how David Bowie is for me. You meet or see a musician that has something that is of another planet, of another time, and it changes you forever. I believe everyone has that, don't you? That one thing you saw as a kid that made you go, "Oh, OK. Now I know who I am."

IVO VAN HOVE (DIRECTOR): He didn't call me. It was Robert Fox, the producer of *Lazarus*, who was a longtime good friend of David. He knew me, and said they didn't want a conventional Broadway musical director, but somebody a little bit more innovative, experimental, whatever, out of the box. Robert wrote me an email and I thought it was really like a joke, like, this is not real. So I left it there for a day or two. And when I replied, Robert called me immediately. He said, yes, Ivo, this is for real and then indeed I sat with David Bowie within three weeks after that, at a table in New York, in his office. Which was scary, but he was so nice, such a gentleman, so open, very well informed. He had seen a lot of productions of mine on the Internet. He even went to Lincoln Center because there are a few productions there in the library. He had seen it all. He was [so] well prepared for that meeting. [In the abstract], meeting David Bowie, I wouldn't know what to say, I would have been like a groupie, a stupid groupie. But knowing that I was going to work with him, the meeting was immediately at another level. [As for *Lazarus*], people want to see what they cannot see at home on the television, so I think that theatre is not only there for entertainment. People that buy tickets, that pay a lot of money, in the West End or on Broadway, they want to see something special, something they cannot see somewhere else.

BEN BRANTLEY (*NEW YORK TIMES* THEATRE CRITIC): There was a certain expectation surrounding *Lazarus*. Bowie himself was involved, Ivo van Hove had become the director of the moment, and Michael C. Hall was involved. I mean, it did seem a strange mirage of individual talent, but I think there was a certain amount of anticipation, even if I don't think anyone knew quite what to expect. Bowie was channeled beautifully in the play. It was interesting, because the singers did have that great heft that musical comedy or American musical voices have, but they also got his inflections. I didn't like it when they talked so much, but it was quite beautiful when they sang. The plot was a little bit thick, but it was gorgeous to look at and to listen to. It was very much in the science-fiction vocabulary—vampires, reincarnation—and for me it seemed almost collegiate. I mean, all you have to do is follow a few seasons of *Star Trek* and you'd follow most of the plot. But gosh it was so beautiful. When you look back and see it as a sort of valedictory piece, it does acquire another kind of gravity and eloquence.

Bowie was always sort of throwing around these autobiographical clues throughout his career. It was a sort of hide-and-seek thing. Throughout his career he had put out these various avatars of himself, more than any other famous person I can think of. They were populating the world on their own, long before Bowie died, and *Lazarus* sort of brought them all together because the different performers incarnate different aspects of the different Bowie characters. It's a little literal in parts, and I think like a lot of great art, Bowie's best when you don't dissect him too literally. But when you listen to the music, when it actually all comes together in some of those moments of performance, I think that it's a very worthy reflection of his work, and his preoccupation with fame, and it's an interesting comment on the legacy of fame and how it alienates. Because that was his most abiding persona, wasn't it? And this was the alien in the twilight of its life.

You could say that the first part of his career was devoted to work that acknowledged his fear of madness, and the second part reflected his mistrust of fame. But he did manage fame rather well by the end though, didn't he? I mean, obviously if you started the day with the cocaine breakfast, well, he really needed to get past that. But the way he walked among us in New York to the extent that he did was kind of extraordinary. He had a profound ambivalence about fame, which I think most famous people have, unless they're just absolute morons. The only way to be really famous in that way is to have no nervous system. Which means you can't be an artist. So it's a really double-edged gift. As much as anyone I can think of, he was able to have it both ways in the end, which is a certain privacy but also the sense that there was this creative horse still giving out signals, that he was this man from another planet. I mean, David Jones walked this Earth and the streets of New York and Soho but David Bowie was still whispering to us from another dimension and in other forms. I have such respect for people who have that degree of celebrity who can die privately. The only other person I can think of in recent years who pulled that off to the same extent was Nora Ephron, as no one knew she was sick. It means she got to leave in her own way, on her own terms, which is rare when you're that well known.

Bowie had an incredibly astute self-educated mind, and even though he had a lot of different artistic personas, they were all being fed by one very, very original sensibility. I think he does hold up to close scrutiny. Mystery is a great part of the artist's mystique, but I think if you look at the man you realize he was incredibly intelligent. Through all the years of muddle and excess, he was still seeing things, and there was a crystal unconsciousness always at work. He's a little like Warhol in that I think he's the other artist who predicted for our culture, what would come. I think they both identified the culture of celebrity and alienation of the twenty-first century. This makes them sound more trivial than they are, and I don't mean that, but I think they realized how the world would be hungry for those superficial images. An endless population or personas. I mean, obviously Kim Kardashian is not a great artist but David Bowie made her possible. I think he was as smart about fame as anyone I can think of. Who knew that the strange man with the strange eyes and the bad teeth would become a sex symbol? In the '60s he kept experimenting until he got it right, but he wasn't an obvious candidate for superstardom from day one. But then he became famous and did this Houdini act, and managed to escape it. He stage-managed the latter part of his public career as well as anyone I can think of.

JOEY SANTIAGO (MUSICIAN): We had the privilege and pleasure to meet him: He was humorous, humble, effortlessly genuine. He invited us to have dinner with him. [We] had Indian food. I sat next to him! He admired the way I played simple lines for the sake of the song. He paid for dinner and I had to peek at his credit card. Seemed like he wanted all to see that he is Davy Jones. He was Davy Jones that night. Glad we met one of the nicest human beings on the planet. He'll be the first man on Mars. RIP.

MICHELLE JASPERSON (BLOGGER): Speaking to people about how I've dealt with his passing, the first thing they say is "He's gone, but his music lives on." That might be considered adequate if you were making reference to one of the current pop-tartlets rising up through the ranks, but it doesn't even come close to someone of David Bowie's status and legacy. To those who were only paying attention in passing, he was a singer. From my perspective, though, he wasn't just a musician. He wasn't just a singer. He wasn't just someone who wrote and sang songs.

My love and admiration of David Bowie recognized and encompassed so much more than that, and this fact alone clearly demonstrates the monumental generational gap in entertainers of his vintage, in contrast to the artists who're currently clinging to their coveted spot on the iTunes chart. The reasons why I've always been attracted to David Bowie involves so much more than just "the music." It included what he valued and the integrity that he demonstrated. I admired his intellect and constant quest for knowledge. He had immense business savvy, which was demonstrated particularly well in the promotion of his final two studio albums—even, incredibly, while he was being treated for cancer. The promotion and release of *Blackstar* were carried out with incredible depth and forethought, despite the pain that he must've been experiencing. I dread to think of the energy that the planning of *Blackstar* must have consumed from a body that was gradually falling apart. In his personal life, he and his wife were smart enough to understand the difference between their personal and professional lives—Iman has often been quoted as saying that she was married to David Jones, not David Bowie. They weren't media whores constantly seeking attention and cameras—instead choosing to let the quality of their work speak for itself. David Robert Jones was honest, genuine, and real. Like all of us, he had his faults and his younger lifestyle choices were questionable, to say the least. But over the last twenty-five years of his life, after cleaning up his act, he became a role model unlike any other—full credit to Iman and his daughter, Alexandria, for forcing him make the necessary changes.

We've learned since we lost him that he refused collaborations with bands like Coldplay and the Red Hot Chili Peppers. His reasons for this will go to his metaphorical grave, but one can only assume that he simply didn't think they stacked up, or that they didn't present him with material worthy of his collaborative input. I love that about him. He had a standard that he was not willing to compromise, regardless of how it would reflect back on him. David Bowie wasn't motivated by commercial success or media attention, unlike the manufactured bullshit that currently dominates the radio waves. Throughout his career he maintained a certain benchmark of integrity and made sure he called the shots—and he was respected for it industry-wide. This was demonstrated in his ability to keep his cancer a complete secret from the world outside of his inner circle—the few people he confided in respected his request for privacy and confidence and kept the secret—something almost unachievable and unheard-of in our current age of instant digital worldwide communication and twenty-four-hour news cycles. Most artists are used and abused by their "hangers-on," the people that I unaffectionately refer to as "leeches." God knows you attract plenty of them when you have a high profile, and they all want something out of you. David Bowie shed as many of these people as possible in the final decade of his life. He valued education, privacy, health, and family. In the media interviews that he did prior to 2004, his intellect always shone through. After his heart attack in 2004, as is well publicized, he completely avoided all media and redirected his priorities. I'm a married thirtysomething living in the greater Wollongong region of NSW, Australia. I work full-time in customer service. Sometimes I enjoy writing. David Bowie was my biggest single influence in life—may he Rest in Peace.

Iggy Pop spent much of 2016 holding back a tide of grief, uncharacteristically staying away from the media, almost berating himself for being so upset. When he did occasionally surface, he was at pains to emphasize the difference between Iggy Pop and James Osterberg: "The art of survival is knowing just when to switch off the Iggy." He treasures his memories of his friend, eternally grateful to Bowie for (a) taking care of him when he was in a drug spiral, (b) teaching him how to behave around celebrities ("He explained to me how these guys ticked and how to deal with them"), and (c) introducing him to Europe. He was also sad that his friend never got to see him become a character in a LEGO video game: "I checked out some pictures of the LEGO version of myself and found them hilarious: LEGO jeans! LEGO hair! Bowie would have loved it."

DR. MARK TAUBERT (PALLIATIVE CARE CONSULTANT AT VELINDRE NHS TRUST, CARDIFF): A thank-you letter to David Bowie, January 15, 2016 . . .

Dear David,

Oh no, don't say it's true—whilst realisation of your death was sinking in during those grey, cold January days of 2016, many of us went on with our day jobs. At the beginning of that week I had a discussion with a hospital patient, facing the end of her life. We discussed your death and your music, and it got us talking about numerous weighty subjects, that are not always straightforward to discuss with someone facing their own demise. In fact, your story became a way for us to communicate very openly about death, something many doctors and nurses struggle to introduce as a topic of conversation. But before I delve further into the aforementioned exchange, I'd like to get a few other things off my chest, and I hope you don't find them a saddening bore.

Thank you for the '80s, when your *ChangesOneBowie* album provided us with hours of joyful listening, in particular on a trip from Darmstadt to Cologne and back. My friends and I will probably always associate "Diamond Dogs," "Rebel Rebel," "China Girl," and "Golden Years" with that particular time in our lives. Needless to say, we had a great time in Köln.

Thank you for Berlin, especially early on, when your songs provided some of the musical backdrop to what was happening in East and West Germany. I still have *"Helden"* on vinyl and played it again when I heard you had died (you'll be pleased to hear that *"Helden"* will also feature in our next Analogue Music Club in the Pilot pub in Penarth later this month). Some may associate David Hasselhoff with the fall of the wall and reunification; but many Germans probably wish that time had taken a cigarette and put it in Mr. Hasselhoff's mouth around that time, rather than hear "*I've been looking for freedom*" endlessly on the radio. For me that time in our history is soundtracked by "Heroes."

Thanks also on behalf of my friend Ifan, who went to one of your gigs in Cardiff. His sister Haf was on the doors that night and I heard a rumor that Ifan managed to sneak in for free (he says sorry!). You gave him and his mate a wave from the stage which will remain in his memory forever.

Thank you for "Lazarus" and *Blackstar*. I am a palliative care doctor, and what you have done in the time surrounding your death has had a profound effect on me and many people I work with. Your album is strewn with references, hints, and allusions. As always, you don't make interpretation all that easy, but perhaps that isn't the point. I have often heard how meticulous you were in your life. For me, the fact that your gentle death at home coincided so closely with the release of your album, with its goodbye message, in my mind is unlikely to be coincidence. All of this was carefully planned, to become a work of death art. The video of "Lazarus" is very deep and many of the scenes will mean different things to us all; for me it is about dealing with the past when you are faced with inevitable death.

Your death at home. Many people I talk to as part of my job think that death predominantly happens in hospitals, in very clinical settings, but I presume you chose home and planned this in some detail. This is one of our aims in palliative care, and your ability to achieve this may mean that others will see it as an option they would like fulfilled. The photos that emerged of you some days after your death were said to be from the last weeks of your life. I do not know whether this is correct, but I am certain that many of us would like to carry off a sharp suit in the same way that you did in those photos. You looked great, as always, and it seemed in direct defiance of all the scary monsters that the last weeks of life can be associated with.

For your symptom-control needs, you will presumably have had palliative care professionals advise on pain, nausea, vomiting, breathlessness, and I can imagine they did this well. I envisage that they also discussed any emotional anguish you may have had.

For your advance-care planning (i.e., planning health and care decisions prior to things getting worse and before becoming unable to express them), I am certain you will have had a lot of ideas, expectations, prior decisions, and stipulations. These may have been set out clearly in writing, near your bed at home, so that everyone who met you was clear on what you wanted, regardless of your ability to communicate. It is an area not just palliative care professionals, but in fact all healthcare workers, want to provide and improve, so that it is less likely that any sudden health incidents will automatically result in a blue-light ambulance emergency-room admission. Especially when people become unable to speak for themselves.

And I doubt that anyone will have given you cardiopulmonary resuscitation (CPR) in the last hours/days of your life, or even considered it. Regrettably, some patients who have not actively opted out of this treatment still receive it, by default. It involves physical, sometimes bone-breaking chest compressions, electric shocks, injections, and insertion of airways and is only successful in 1–2 percent of patients whose cancer has spread to other organs in their body. It is very likely that you asked your medical team to issue you with a Do Not Attempt Cardiopulmonary Resuscitation order. I can only imagine what it must have been like to discuss this, but you were once again a hero, or a "Held," even at this most challenging time of your life. And the professionals who saw you will have had good knowledge and skill in the provision of palliative and end-of-life care. Sadly, this essential part of training is not always available for junior healthcare professionals, including doctors and nurses, and is sometimes overlooked or under-prioritized by those who plan their education. I think if you were ever to return (as "Lazarus" did), you would be a firm advocate for good palliative care training being available everywhere.

So back to the conversation I had with the lady who had recently received the news that she had advanced cancer that had spread, and that she would probably not live much longer than a year or so. She talked about you and loved your music, but for some reason was not impressed by your Ziggy Stardust outfit (she was not sure whether you were a boy or a girl). She too, had memories of places and events for which you provided an idiosyncratic soundtrack. And then we talked about a good death, the dying moments and what these typically look like. And we talked about palliative care and how it can help. She told me about her mother's and her father's death, and that she wanted to be at home when things progressed, not in a hospital or emergency room, but that she'd happily transfer to the local hospice should her symptoms be too challenging to treat at home.

We both wondered who may have been around you when you took your last breath and whether anyone was holding your hand. I believe this was an aspect of the vision she had of her own dying moments that was of utmost importance to her, and you gave her a way of expressing this most personal longing to me, a relative stranger.

Thank you.

DAN FOX (AUTHOR): I had never before felt any sense of grief for a public figure, someone I've never met before, or a famous person. It's sad when you hear the news but I didn't feel a wellspring of grief or anything like that, but I felt oddly out of sorts that morning when I heard. I walked up to his apartment on Lafayette Street, just to see the crowds there, and on the way I bought some flowers from a local deli. I left them and I walked away.

When I was walking back to work part of me, the sort of rational part of my brain, just thought, That was a bit corny, that was a mawkish thing to do. Another part of my brain realized that those flowers weren't necessarily for this famous musician—they were actually for what he represented. [His] songs, which are songs about loneliness and feeling different, of course appealed to me as an arty adolescent—which doesn't make me special, that's what he did for millions of people. But it was a sense of cultural literacy that I also got through Bowie. He provided a model of autodidacticism where you could become culturally literate outside the academy. You could find out a lot about the world and other creative lives and projects through the prism of this particular musician. There are lots of bands and musicians that have done that, he's not necessarily unique in that regard, but he was certainly a significant one for me. I also think that a lot of the ways in which he comported himself as a creative person are really relevant to artists and the way they work. There's a sense of collaboration and community; he was someone who always celebrated working with other people. There's a sense of restlessness, of wanting to do lots of different things—for better or for worse—whether it's acting, writing, or painting as well as making music. There's a sense of knowing when to stop and take a break from things, to step back from the work you're making, and of changing things up to keep them interesting for yourself. There's having a sense of humor about yourself and self-deprecation, and just maintaining a sense of possibility, that there are other places in the world to go and explore.

PAUL MORLEY: We have all collaborated with the idea of David Bowie, according to when we had our first contact, when we first started to like him. We've all collaborated with creating the idea of David Bowie and I think having worked at that, on and off, for a period of time, it seems crazy to lose that impetus. What we need to do is keep reinforcing the idea of David Bowie as an important historical figure, more than just being a pop musician, or a rock musician, all of these kind of things, which tend to be reduced, but transfer him into history in a more significant manner. Bowie spent his life exploring what it meant to be not just an artist, but what it was to be a human being.

On the day that it happened, I got a lot of calls from broadcasters asking me to comment, and I realized that part of being the future of journalism is being a kind of professional mourner. It's a strange reduction in a way—that sentimentality, talking about a loss and missing something. I was getting the calls all day from an astounding amount of news organizations and I was determined not to do it; not least because I always found when I used to do that kind of thing and go on these live television programs and try and communicate what I felt, that you'd get forty seconds before being shunted on the way to weather. So, even though they acknowledged that they had to acknowledge the death of David Bowie, there was still a slight condescension, there was still a slight sense of: it's just a pop star. I ended up going on *Front Row* on Radio 4, but I was only given a minute, and was so frustrated by this that I went home and sobbed—not necessarily for the death of David Bowie, but more for my inability to really encapsulate as I wanted to what he really meant to me, what I felt about him. There might have been hundreds of books about David Bowie, but I had my own David Bowie and I like that history of David Bowie. And I figured that everything had changed because he'd died; the architecture, the geography of David Bowie had died; there was a new David Bowie in town and I wanted to write about that David Bowie.

He spanned the entire history of pop, from making music in a skiffle band as a teenager to ending it as this kind of abstract Internet internationalist who's using the Internet to transmit electronic signals around the world. No one else has managed to go from that to that. And within it, he's there and thereabouts as everything happens: as mod happens, as the British blues happens, as rock and roll happens, as albums happen, as singles happen, into the early '70s as glam happens. He's always there or thereabouts. Sometimes he's embedded in it; sometimes he's sort of on the outside but not being completely exiled by it. Punk doesn't exile him, because his sensibility somehow, unlike a Mick or a Rod or an Elton, doesn't get exploded and turned into something deeply uncool by punk. Artistically his sensibility is not really embedded in the genre. He's playing with genre, he's using genre, he's brilliant at using influences and then taking what's happening around him at the same time and updating it. Even when he was out of favor, he was aware of his out-of-favor-ness and he was exploiting that because to try not to be out of favor would have been deeply uncool.

He lived his life as someone who was working out what it is to be alive. From the very early stages of his life he was working out what it means to be a human being, and a lot of the information about how to decide what it is to be a human being came from his interest in music and art and poetry and books. That idea that you never really knew who he was is part of the great illusion, it's the wonderful conjuring trick, it's the great piece of show business; we're all looking at David Bowie and meanwhile he's over here being someone completely different. I always think that's why he loved Iman—because when he met her, she didn't know much about his music, didn't know much about him. He could be David Jones there; he didn't necessarily have to be David Bowie. He'd been David Bowie. . . . He'd been making up David Bowie from early doors. What's fascinating about his archive is he's the very first student of David Bowie. He's collecting stuff before he ever knows that he will be that famous, or that iconic. He's the first student of David Bowie and the last student of David Bowie and we're all just students that join in along the way and help him create the idea of David Bowie. It's this David Bowie that's fascinating, but it's definitely not David Jones.

I love this wonderful way that he pinned together, like no one else, an avant-garde sensibility with a middle-of-the-road showbiz sensibility: so over here, he's Marcel Duchamp, he's Roland Kirk, and he's John Coltrane; and over here, he's Judy Garland, and he's Elvis Presley, and he's Anthony Newley, and he's Shirley Bassey. He also made intellectual discovery seem glamorous, and that's incredibly important because ultimately that transcends it just being about fashion, or just being about music, or popular culture. It's about the greater reasons of being alive and trying to create something that is fairer, and better, and stranger, and more wonderful. He didn't make political statements—he was never a messenger—but embedded in these great sexy pop songs and this incredibly glamorous image, were incredibly important points about how to make life better, more wonderful, and less brutal. I think it's inevitable that we will feel really grateful in that sense because there's not many people who can do it in the way that he did it.

A few days into February, news spread that Blackstar *wasn't the sum total of his final recordings, and that there were a few songs that were finished—maybe even a whole album's worth—that might be released in the future. Conspiracy theorists, tired of creating ever more bizarre accounts of Bowie's own micro-*

management of his own death, started suggesting that the artist had recorded not one, but maybe several albums' worth of songs, records that were scheduled to appear at regular intervals after his death—singing from beyond the grave. Well, in October 2016, three unreleased tracks finally saw the light of day on the Lazarus *cast album, three songs written, recorded, and produced by Bowie at the same time as* Blackstar. *The record contained the cast and band of the original New York production performing their versions of the eighteen songs from the show (from "Life on Mars?," "All the Young Dudes," and "Heroes," through to "Valentine's Day," "Love Is Lost," and "Dirty Boys"),* Blackstar*'s "Lazarus" (which increasingly sounded like something The XX could have had a hand in), as well as the three new Bowie tracks. Coproduced by Bowie and Tony Visconti and recorded with Donny McCaslin and his quartet, the same band that played on* Blackstar, *these last three songs—"No Plan," "Killing a Little Time," and "When I Met You"—were predictably intriguing.*

"No Plan" was the standout, a genuine greatest hit that sounded like it came direct from the Scott Walker songbook, with vaporous traces of Dusty Springfield (although it was faintly reminiscent of the opening theme of Prometheus*). A ballad both mournful and uplifting, the version sung by cast member Sophia Anne Caruso actually sounded like a classic show tune, while Bowie's version is one of the most haunting things he's ever done. It's a beautiful song, and sounds almost as though it's covered in a buttery light. The words, too, while seeming to slip easily from Newton's lips, could quite easily have applied to Bowie's present and perennial disposition:* "There's no music here/I'm lost in streams of sound/Here am I nowhere now? No plan? . . . All the things that are my life/my moods, my beliefs, my designs/Me alone, Nothing to regret/This is no place, but here I am/This is not quite yet." *It almost sounded apostolic.*

The rest of the Lazarus *cast album was produced by the show's musical director Henry Hey, who had previously worked with Bowie on* The Next Day *and featured vocals from Michael C. Hall, Caruso, Cristin Milioti, Michael Esper, and other cast members backed by the seven-piece house band Hey assembled for the New York run. Extraordinarily, the album was recorded on January 11; when the musicians turned up at the studio, they were quietly told that Bowie had died the night before.*

MICHAEL C. HALL (ACTOR): The recording gave us a chance to actively do something productive that we knew was in sync with his wishes. It was very emotional and surreal. Doing the show was more challenging, realizing just how much David's enthusiasm for it had to do with its capacity to be a meditation on mortality and death.

Meeting him and singing his songs felt like more than a formality. David didn't come to see [me in] *Hedwig*—he was aware of my acting, but that was the first time he heard me sing. I did puddle on the floor when he left, for a second. The music doesn't operate the way it does in traditional musical theatre, in as much as it isn't always there to move the story forward. It can be atmospheric, but also provide a counterpoint. I know David didn't want to do a jukebox musical, and this is the furthest thing from it. He maintained a fascination with the [Newton] character. That theme of isolation and the interest in that embroidered interior world we all create runs through all his work.

DANNY FIELDS: When I visited Britain the month after David died, it was like a grief-stricken civilization. He was very great, and wonderful, but he was not God. He wasn't an Iggy or a Lou. All of those people who went to Brixton on the day he died and danced all night and fucked all night, they were torn apart because he liberated them. But they are all as good as David, all brilliant. People were saying that he set them free, and showed something to them about themselves. I thought that this was maybe his greatest achievement. It's not something he did; it's something people felt he had demonstrated. Each person said he made them acknowledge themself, their talents, their emotions, or maybe their sexuality. Each had a different example.

BAZ LUHRMANN: I would hazard a guess that someone who so constantly reinvents themselves, and is so restless and relentless in the search for story and culture and other worlds and other people and other ideas, someone who was so moving forward, that that movement has to come from something in one's childhood. He had a natural body intelligence. Mind intelligence yes, but also a body intelligence. A sensitivity to how he feels, and also how others feel. That you can't learn. Some giant intellectuals have tremendous computing energy, but no body intelligence at all. For those that have both, they have a sensitivity to the world around them. And that turned into this tremendous cultural engine.

Also, he created the world around him. It wasn't enough that he would create a character, he would have to change the world to suit that character. He would change the world around him to contextualize his character. So with Ziggy Stardust and the Spiders from Mars, wherever that went so too would the show go with him. He lived it. Then he would go on and do the Thin White Duke, and he lived it. He did a mash-up of all the English royalty or grand landed gentry and a sort of gothic figure. It was Byron-esque. That ability to make a cultural collage, to tear sheets from disparate culture and make something new out of it. I think it's interesting that the period that we've passed through and are living in now is one where cultural eclecticism is de rigueur; it defines the world around us, but it's also a world where we're comfortable exposing the mash-up, the montage, the eclecticism. We don't want to have to go over all the cracks in all the joining lines of the collage. That's why he was at the forefront and so important and so thought about in the modern era. It's a bit like hip-hop, which is at the end of the spectrum and also changed the world. I think those are two really great reference points. One was coming out of England and all the art schools, and one was coming out of the Bronx. They sort of cross over. I remember a period in which this whole hip-hop thing was happening and then David Bowie was shocking America with his whole theatrical collage. He's collaging theatrics, pop culture, and music, and in the Bronx young kids are collaging with records and images on the sides of trains, comic books, and superheroes, and everything around them. Even their dance moves are an assemblage of influences collaged together in something new. Just like Bowie, they were able to make something new out of a whole lot of references without trying to hide the joins.

I think genius is of course the rustiest word. It's like "cool," the easiest overused word and flung around. Genius to me, it's not like you're brilliant at everything, it's when you've got some crossed wires within you, that makes you relentlessly move towards something at such a high level that it stands above the rest of the regular playing field. David's internal energy, the intelligence in the eyes, you could tell that the mind was still looking and the heart still searching. Even towards the end, he was writing his own narrative. After he had a heart problem, which was very downplayed, I remember when he came to my house midway going to the studio at the top, I suddenly became conscious of this, but he refused to let it be seen. Always energetic, he would walk right up to the top of the stairs. So he refused to even consider that there might be an end to the journey. He dealt with that, I think, in the same way that he dealt with everything else. He was writing his own narrative. I mean obviously not the conclusive part of it. There are a lot of performers and artists who left immense visual, literal, or sonic thumbprints, but few of them affected the culture across the board. Just that kind of boundary smashing. He led a lot of young people from his generation to believe that there are just no boundaries, it's just expressing yourself. You can be music, cinema, performance, art, writing, it does not matter, it's how you mix it together to get something really expressive. It's either true and effective or it's not. He didn't just lead the charge, he lived the charge.

JOHAN RENCK: He didn't really [say goodbye], to be honest. And I spent some time being disappointed by that, because I didn't speak to him during the last week. I texted him on the Monday of that week—the following Friday was his birthday, was the release of his album and the "Lazarus" video—so I texted him on Monday and said, "We're all good for Friday," without any question or anything like that. And he didn't respond. Then on Thursday I sent him a birthday gift to his office—I found this really cool old book that I knew he would like. He didn't respond to that either. And then on the weekend I was like, Why the hell didn't he answer it? Then he passed away, which . . . I can't even go there. And a few days later I was like, Why wouldn't he have said goodbye? I felt, I mean, not hurt, to be honest; it took me not a long time at all to realize like, Stop being a fucking idiot. He said goodbye to the entire world through these videos and that was the goodbye to everybody out there who had a relationship to him. I was not in any position to ask for more [of a] goodbye than anybody else, of course not. So I realized that I got a fucking great goodbye from him because not only did I witness it, I was part of him, I was next to him, whilst he was constructing this goodbye. So to me it was like I got the same goodbye that everybody else got and I'm super fucking happy about it.

CARLOS ALOMAR: I was in a state of mourning for months. David was everything. Think ten years ago: who were you listening to? Well, they're gone. That fucking sucks. You were my star. I cried over the song. You said just what I wanted to say when I broke up. You were my all. And now you're gone. I love the fact that David's fans looked to him with anticipation, with acceptance, and glorify any change, even if they weren't able to go there with him. They understood that it was a needed change. And they would just wait until the next one came, when they would revisit him again and find them enhanced all over again. Our curiosity was what we were looking for in David. To make us look more curious, and not let us settle for the same old thing. There was one artist who was never able to be put in a box, and that was David. There's always got to be one. Every artist has a moment, but for an artist to be there more than once for you? Look, you were fourteen years old when you heard him, then you were twenty-four, thirty-four, forty-four, fifty-four, and he's still talking for you? Jesus Christ, who does that? I've got a lot of things to be grateful for, and one of those is knowing David Bowie.

FRANCIS WHATELY: He'd said throughout his life that it wasn't so much the getting old that he feared, but the dying. And from what I have learned, he was terrified of death. I think a lot of people are who have what he had, which is a very complicated relationship with a higher power, with a God, whatever we want to call it. Throughout his life he rejected formalized religion, but I think as he got older, he was ticking off the answers he wanted to be answered. He had that relationship with Buddhism, but his mother was a Roman Catholic. You can't get away from that. You can't get away from the fact that he was English and was brought up with Christianity to some degree as well. The fact that he wore a cross for most of his life; I think it possibly was more than simply a symbol. The fact that he protested that he believed very much in God, around the time of the Freddie Mercury concert. I think, like all of us, perhaps he was terrified at the end that that was it and that there was no afterlife. I think he rejected the simplicity of the modern cult of atheism among a lot of his peers. There are two Lazaruses in the Bible—and I think it's interesting that he chose the one who came back to life. I think everything was thought through and I do believe in that last album he was saying a lot of things that he hadn't said before and wanted the audience to read into it. I really do.

BAZ LUHRMANN: Through my wife, who has a close tie to the disease [schizophrenia] in her family, I've come to know a lot. And yes, if it's very present in your family, it's a reasonable summation to think that there'd be a degree of fear in the members of the family. Of course, kids develop mechanisms to deal with fear. That mechanism can be the use of the imagination. Now of course, it can manifest in violence and anger, but it also can trigger an escape into the imagination. So was David in his work dealing with this? Absolutely yes, not overtly but that environment that he grew up with and the presence of that in his life. I would proffer, as an outsider, and looking at David's life as a story, I would suggest that when his work isn't quite firing in the early stages that there comes a moment when he decides to self-medicate his fear and anxiety through his work. I'm guessing that there would've been a personal moment that none of us would know about. I certainly don't, and I'm guessing here, but some personal moment where he is alone, something is happening, and the fear and inside voices are being dealt with by going, "I'm going to create my way out of this and be someone and something else and guess what? My work happens to be such that I can do that in front of people." He goes into a chrysalis and comes out completely transformed; what's on the inside is suddenly shown on the outside but in the most fearless and expressive way. I think that's the moment at which the self-medication resulted in creative energy. It was a creative force. I really believe that. And not only do I believe it, I think it's actually a fairly classic pattern for particularly remarkable creative artists. I mean, go back to Alexander the Great. You'll see there's a fear in the childhood in the relationships growing up that is turned into moving energy.

FRANCIS WHATELY: When I was filming people for the documentary I made after his death, I asked them all at the end what they would have said to him if they'd been able to say goodbye, and they all said, "I love you, thank you," but mostly thank you for being a part of their lives.

Perhaps a final word should go to the midwife who delivered Bowie into the world in his parents' house in Stansfield Road in Brixton, in 1947. "This child," she said, "has been on this Earth before." His mother thought it "was rather an odd thing to say, but the midwife seemed quite adamant."

CHRONOLOGY

1947 David Robert Jones, son of Margaret Mary "Peggy" Jones (née Burns) and Haywood Stenton "John" Jones, is born on January 8 in Brixton, London.

1953 The Jones family moves to the London suburb of Bromley.

1961 Given a white, injection-molded acrylic Grafton saxophone with gold keys by his father for Christmas.

1962 George Underwood punches him in the eye on February 12.
Sees Little Richard perform at the Woolwich Granada on October 13.
First public performance, playing the saxophone for the Kon-Rads at the Bromley Tech PTS fete on June 16.

1964 Releases his first single, "Liza Jane," credited to Davie Jones with the King Bees, on June 5.
Appears properly on television for the first time (he appeared in the audience on *Juke Box Jury* on June 6), on the BBC's *Tonight* program, representing the Society for the Prevention of Cruelty to Long-Haired Men on November 12.

1965 Officially changes his name to David Bowie (principally to avoid any confusion with emerging star Davy Jones) on September 16.

1967 *David Bowie*, his first album, is released on June 1.

1969 "Space Oddity," which would become his first hit single, is released on July 11.
David's father passes away on August 5.
David Bowie, his second album (later rereleased as *Space Oddity*), is released on November 14.

1970 Marries Angela "Angie" Barnett at Bromley Register Office on March 19.

1971 *The Man Who Sold the World* is released on April 10.
His son, Duncan Zowie Haywood Jones, is born on May 30.
Hunky Dory is released on November 17.

1972 First concert on the *Ziggy Stardust* tour at the Borough Assembly Hall in Aylesbury on January 29.
The Rise and Fall of Ziggy Stardust and the Spiders from Mars is released on June 16.
Appears on *Top of the Pops* performing "Starman," a performance seen by approximately a quarter of the UK population, on July 6.

1973 *Aladdin Sane* is released on April 13.
Pin Ups is released on October 19.

1974 *Diamond Dogs* is released on May 24.

1975 *Young Americans* is released on March 7.

1976 *Station to Station* is released on January 23.
The Man Who Fell to Earth, directed by Nicolas Roeg, is released on March 18.

1977 *Low* is released on January 14.
"Heroes" is released on October 14.

1978 *Just a Gigolo* is released on November 16.

1979 *Lodger* is released on May 18.

1980 Divorces Angie Bowie in Switzerland on February 8.
Scary Monsters (and Super Creeps) is released on September 12.

1983 *Let's Dance* is released on April 14.
The Hunger is released on April 29.
Merry Christmas, Mr. Lawrence is released on August 25.

1984 *Tonight* is released on September 1.

1985 His schizophrenic half-brother, Terence "Terry" Guy Adair Burns (Rosenberg), commits suicide at Coulsdon South train station on January 16.
Performs at Live Aid at Wembley Stadium in front of 1.9 billion people via satellite on July 13.

1986 *Absolute Beginners* is released on April 4.
Labyrinth is released on June 27.

1987 *Never Let Me Down* is released on April 27.

1988 *The Last Temptation of Christ* is released on August 12.

1989 *Tin Machine* is released on May 23.

1991 *Tin Machine II* is released on September 2.

1992 Marries Iman Mohamed Abdulmajid in Lausanne on April 24.

1993 *Black Tie White Noise* is released on April 5.
The Buddha of Suburbia is released on November 8.

1995 *Outside* is released on September 26.

1997 *Earthling* is released on February 3.
Bowie Bonds announced on February 4.

1998 BowieNet launched on September 1.

1999 *Hours* is released on September 21.

2000 His daughter, Alexandria "Lexi" Zahra Jones, is born on August 15.

2001 His mother passes away on April 2.

2002 *Heathen* is released on June 11.

2003 *Reality* is released on September 16.

2004 Suffers the first of several heart attacks onstage at the Hurricane festival in Scheessel, Germany, on June 25.

2006 *The Prestige* is released on October 20.
Final public performance at New York's Hammerstein Ballroom (playing "Wild Is the Wind," "Fantastic Voyage," and "Changes") on November 9.

2013 *The Next Day* is released on March 8.
David Bowie Is . . . opens at the Victoria & Albert Museum in London on March 23.

2014 Makes final trip to the UK with his wife and daughter, visiting Brixton to see the home in Stansfield Road where he was born; Plaistow Grove in Bromley, where his family moved when he was six; and Foxgrove Road, in Beckenham, where he lived in 1969.

2016 *Blackstar* is released on January 8.
David dies in his apartment in Manhattan on January 10. He is cremated in New Jersey two days later.

DRAMATIS PERSONAE

Iman Mohamed Abdulmajid married David Bowie on April 24, 1992.

Carlos Alomar, guitarist, played on more Bowie albums than any other musician except pianist Mike Garson.

Kristina Amadeus is David's cousin.

David Arden is a music business manager who previously worked with ELO and is the son of the infamous "Al Capone of Pop," Don Arden.

Brian Aris photographed David and Iman's wedding.

Kevin Armstrong played guitar with Bowie at Live Aid.

Ron Asheton was the original guitarist in the Stooges.

David Bailey is a world-renowned photographer.

Jonathan Barnbrook designed the sleeves for *Heathen*, *Reality*, *The Next Day*, and *Blackstar*.

Toni Basil choreographed both the *Diamond Dogs* tour in 1974 and the Glass Spider Tour in 1987.

Peter Beard is the photographer who discovered Iman in Nairobi in 1975.

Adrian Belew worked with Bowie on the *"Heroes"* tour in 1978, *Lodger*, and the *Sound+Vision* tour in 1990.

Rodney Bingenheimer is the legendary mayor of Sunset Strip and escorted Bowie around Los Angeles in the early '70s.

Tony Blackburn was the presenter of *Top of the Pops* on July 6, 1972, when Bowie performed "Starman" with the Spiders from Mars.

Leee Black Childers was a writer, photographer, and MainMan mainstay.

Trevor Bolder was the bassist in the Spiders from Mars.

Bono is the lead singer of U2.

Angie Bowie was married to Bowie from 1970 to 1980.

Boy George was a teenage Bowie obsessive.

William Boyd wrote *Nat Tate: An American Artist 1928–1960.*

Ben Brantley is the chief theater critic of the *New York Times.*

Anne Briggs lived in Brixton in the 1950s.

Victoria Broackes was the cocurator of *David Bowie Is . . .* at the Victoria & Albert Museum.

Bebe Buell met Bowie on the 1972 tour, and went on to become a successful model and singer.

Sterling Campbell toured as a drummer with Bowie for fourteen years.

Josette Caruso met Bowie on the US *Ziggy Stardust* tour.

Robert Chalmers is a contributing editor of *GQ.*

Chris Charlesworth was a writer on *Melody Maker* before becoming an RCA publicist.

Ava Cherry sang on *Young Americans* and had a four-year relationship with Bowie.

Keith Christmas played guitar on the *Space Oddity* album.

Candy Clark starred in *The Man Who Fell to Earth.*

Nicholas Coleridge is the chairman of Condé Nast UK.

Matthew Collings is a British art critic, writer, broadcaster, and artist.

Mark Cooper is a producer at the BBC.

Jayne County is an artist and performer.

Roy Dalley was Bowie's neighbor in Beckenham.

Roger Daltrey is the lead singer of the Who.

Chalkie Davies photographed Bowie apparently giving a "Nazi" salute at Victoria Station in 1976.

Dennis Davies was Bowie's long-standing drummer.

Kevin Davies is the celebrated photographer.

Greg Davis worked in the wardrobe department on *Labyrinth.*

Justin de Villeneuve once managed Twiggy and photographed the cover of *Pin Ups.*

Robin Derrick is the creative director of Spring, having previously art directed *Vogue*, *Arena*, and *The Face.*

Bernard Doherty was the publicist for Live Aid.

Thomas Dolby played keyboard with Bowie at Live Aid.

Gail Ann Dorsey played bass with Bowie for twenty-one years, from 1995.

Sean Doyle is a journalist and film expert who edits the website *The Worst Albums Ever.*

Keanan Duffty designed a clothes collection with Bowie in the 2000s.

Brian Duffy photographed the cover of *Aladdin Sane.*

Paul Du Noyer is the former editor of *Q* and *Mojo.*

Alan Edwards is the chairman of the Outside Organization, and in a PR capacity represented David Bowie for over thirty years, and continues to do so.

Mark Ellen is the former editor of *Smash Hits*, *Q*, and *The Word.*

Tony Elliott is the chairman of *Time Out.*

Tracey Emin is one of the world's leading artists.

Brian Eno worked with Bowie intermittently from 1977 onward.

Marianne Faithfull appeared in *The 1980 Floor Show.*

Danny Fields signed and managed Iggy and the Stooges, signed MC5 and managed the Ramones, and worked in various roles with Jim Morrison, the Velvet Underground, and the Modern Lovers.

Mary Finnigan started the Beckenham Arts Lab.

Kathryn Flett is a journalist and former editor of *Arena.*

Arthur Fogel is chairman, Global Music, and president, Global Touring, of Live Nation.

Peter Frampton was a childhood friend and guitarist on the Glass Spider Tour.

Robert Fripp played with Bowie on *"Heroes"* and *Scary Monsters.*

Reeves Gabrels played guitar with Bowie for over a decade.

Ricky Gardiner played guitar on *Low* and *Lust for Life*, and is responsible for the riff on "The Passenger."

Mike Garson played piano for Bowie for over forty years.

Bob Geldof fronts the Boomtown Rats and famously initiated Live Aid.

Ricky Gervais is a comedian.

John Giddings is a concert promoter who worked with Bowie for over thirty years.

Dana Gillespie is a singer and former Bowie consort.

Bernard Glazier knew Bowie as a teenager.

Harvey Goldsmith is a promoter and co-instigator of Live Aid.

Glenn Goring was a member of Comus.

Paul Gorman is a journalist and cultural commentator.

Fergus Greer photographed Bowie in the early '90s.

Bob Harris is a DJ and broadcaster.

Deborah Harry sings with Blondie.

Anna Harvey is a former editor at British *Vogue*.

Jason Heller is a writer for *Pitchfork*.

Brian Henson is a puppeteer, director, producer, and the chairman of the Jim Henson Company.

David Hepworth is the author of *1971: Never a Dull Moment*.

Tommy Hilfiger is one of America's foremost fashion designers.

Damien Hirst was one of the original YBAs (Young British Artists).

Jack Hofsiss directed *The Elephant Man* on Broadway.

Tim Hollier played at the Three Tuns.

Jackie Homewood was a regular at the Three Tuns.

Glenn Hughes was a member of Deep Purple in the '70s.

Oliver James is a psychologist and author of *Upping Your Ziggy*.

Michelle Jasperson is a fan and blogger.

Elton John is one of the biggest entertainers in the world.

Allan Jones is a former editor of *Melody Maker* and *Uncut*.

Duncan Jones was born on May 30, 1971.

Kim Jones is a celebrated fashion designer.

Michael Kaplan is a journalist based in Brooklyn. He has written for *Details*, *Wired*, *Playboy*, and the *New York Times Magazine*.

Erin Keane is the culture editor of *Salon*.

Gary Kemp is an actor and the creative powerhouse behind Spandau Ballet.

Lindsay Kemp was instrumental in teaching Bowie to dance professionally.

Patsy Kensit starred in *Absolute Beginners*.

Nick Kent is one of the world's most revered rock journalists.

Erdal Kizilçay is a multi-instrumentalist who played on *When the Wind Blows*, *Never Let Me Down*, *The Buddha of Suburbia*, and *Outside*, as well as Iggy Pop's *Blah Blah Blah*.

Marcus Klinko photographed Bowie for *GQ*.

Hanif Kureishi wrote *The Buddha of Suburbia*, among other things.

Lady Gaga performed a Bowie tribute at the 2016 Grammys.

Clive Langer produced "Absolute Beginners" with Alan Winstanley.

David Lauren is chief innovation officer and vice chairman of the Ralph Lauren Organization.

Amanda Lear is a singer who dated Bowie for eighteen months in the mid-'70s.

Wendy Leigh was a Bowie biographer.

John Lennon recorded with Bowie in the '70s.

Bill Liesegang played with Bowie at the Beckenham Free Festival in 1969.

Courtney Love is an actress and singer, formerly with Hole.

Mary Lovett was a teenage friend, and formerly married to Peter Frampton.

Baz Luhrmann directed *Moulin Rouge!* as well as many other movies.

Dorian Lynskey is the music editor of *GQ*.

Geoff MacCormack knew Bowie from the age of seven until he died.

Angus MacKinnon is a journalist and critic who once worked for the *NME*.

Rory MacLean is a travel writer and an expert on Berlin.

Madonna picked up Bowie's torch of reinvention.

David Mallet directed the videos for "Boys Keep Swinging," "DJ," "Look Back in Anger," "Ashes to Ashes," "Fashion," "Wild is the Wind," "Let's Dance," "China Girl," "Loving the Alien," "Dancing in the Street," and "Hallo Spaceboy."

Geoffrey Marsh was the co-curator of *David Bowie Is . . .* at the Victoria & Albert Museum.

Harry Maslin co-produced *Young Americans* and *Station to Station*.

Lori Mattix was an infamous '70s groupie.

Brian May is the guitarist for Queen.

Paul Mayersberg wrote *The Man Who Fell to Earth* and *Merry Christmas, Mr. Lawrence*.

Kevin Mazur is principally a concert photographer, who worked with Bowie many times.

Paul McCartney is one of the greatest songwriters of his generation.

Tony McGee is a photographer.

Paul McGuinness is a film producer and the former long-term manager of U2.

Legs McNeil is a coauthor of the punk classic *Please Kill Me* and one of the founders of *Punk* magazine.

Pat Metheny worked with Bowie on "This Is Not America."

John Mitchinson is, among many other things, the head of research for the British TV show *QI* and a vice president of the Hay Festival.

Moby is a musician and DJ who toured with Bowie in 2002.

Brian Molko is the singer of Placebo.

Paul Morley wrote *The Age of Bowie*.

Giorgio Moroder produced the *Cat People* soundtrack.

Kate Moss is one of the most famous models in the world.

Mark Mothersbaugh is one of the co-founders of Devo.

Tiffany Murray is a writer and the author of *Diamond Star Halo*.

Simon Napier-Bell was the manager of T. Rex.

Kris Needs lobbied for Bowie to play Friars Aylesbury in 1971.

Christopher Nolan directed Bowie in the 2006 movie *The Prestige.*

Chris O'Leary runs the *Pushing Ahead of the Dame* website, and is the author of *Rebel Rebel.*

Terry O'Neill photographed Bowie countless times, most notably around the *Diamond Dogs* period.

William Orbit is a musician, composer, and producer.

Denis O'Regan first started photographing Bowie in 1972.

Tony Oursler is an artist who worked with Bowie on many projects, including the video for "Where Are We Now?"

Hugh Padgham produced *Tonight.*

Owen Pallett is a musician, composer, and arranger.

Tony Parsons is an author and journalist.

Guy Peellaert was the artist and illustrator who designed the *Diamond Dogs* sleeve.

Orson Peellaert is the custodian of his father Guy's estate.

Alexis Petridis is the music editor of the *Guardian.*

Roy Pike once owned a furniture shop in Beckenham.

Ken Pitt managed Bowie in the '60s.

Iggy Pop made four albums with Bowie.

Val Portelli went to Raglan Infants' School with Bowie.

Bill Prince is the deputy editor of *GQ.*

David Pullman is the investment banker who initiated Bowie Bonds.

David Quantick is a journalist and comedy writer.

Lou Reed was the beneficiary of Bowie's production on *Transformer.*

Paul Reeves is a childhood friend who later opened the Universal Witness on Fulham Road.

Johan Renck directed the videos for both "Blackstar" and "Lazarus."

Nick Rhodes is the keyboard player in Duran Duran.

Bruce Robb runs Cherokee Studios.

Tommy Roberts was the owner of City Lights Studio.

Mick Rock photographed David Bowie on and off for over forty years.

Nic Roeg is the director of *The Man Who Fell to Earth.*

Mick Ronson was David Bowie's arranger and lead guitarist during the Ziggy Stardust years.

Joey Santiago is the lead guitarist for the Pixies.

Jon Savage is the author of *England's Dreaming: Sex Pistols and Punk Rock*, *Teenage: The Creation of Youth Culture*, and *1966: The Year the Decade Exploded.*

Coco Schwab was Bowie's long-term assistant and gatekeeper.

Martin Scorsese directed *The Last Temptation of Christ.*

Ken Scott produced *Hunky Dory*, *The Rise and Fall of Ziggy Stardust and the Spiders from Mars*, and *Pin Ups.*

Tony Scott directed *The Hunger.*

Lee Scriven masterminded the documentary *Starman: Freddie Burretti—The Man Who Sewed the World.*

Charles Shaar Murray is an author and journalist who was once referred to as "David Bowie's representative on Earth."

Floria Sigismondi directed four videos for Bowie: "Little Wonder," "Dead Man Walking," "The Next Day," and "The Stars (Are Out Tonight)."

Nina Simone was the high priestess of soul.

Siouxsie Sioux is the lead singer of Siouxsie and the Banshees.

Earl Slick played guitar on six Bowie albums.

Sir Paul Smith is an internationally recognized fashion designer.

Chris Stein plays guitar with Blondie.

Dave Stewart is a writer, producer, performer, and one half of the Eurythmics.

Chris Sullivan is a journalist and DJ who once ran the Wag Club.

Simon Sweetman is a New Zealand music and arts writer—he blogs at offthetracks.co.nz and hosts an interview series at Sweetman Podcast.

Dr. Mark Taubert is a palliative care consultant at Velindre NHS Trust, Cardiff.

Julien Temple directed *Jazzin' for Blue Jean* and *Absolute Beginners.*

Neil Tennant is one half of the Pet Shop Boys.

Jeremy Thomas was the producer of *Merry Christmas, Mr. Lawrence.*

Hugh Thomson produced the ten-hour series *Dancing in the Street: A Rock and Roll History.*

George Underwood was one of David Bowie's oldest friends.

Midge Ure cowrote "Do They Know It's Christmas?"

Ivo van Hove directed *Lazarus* at the New York Theatre Workshop.

Luther Vandross was one of the vocalists on *Young Americans.*

Cherry Vanilla worked as a publicist for Bowie.

Tony Visconti produced thirteen David Bowie albums.

Rick Wakeman played keyboard on "Space Oddity" and "Life on Mars?"

Dave Walking is a photographer who used to live in Beckenham.

Martyn Ware was a founding member of the Human League and Heaven

17, and produced data sonifications of Bowie's albums for *David Bowie Is . . .* at the Victoria & Albert Museum.

Michael Watts was a *Melody Maker* journalist.

Iain R. Webb is a journalist, lecturer, and tutor.

Paul Weller is the Modfather.

Francis Whately is the producer of *Five Years.*

Steve Whitmire was a senior puppeteer on *Labyrinth.*

Michael Wolff was a neighbor of Bowie's in Manhattan.

Woody Woodmansey was the drummer in the Spiders from Mars.

Alan Yentob has been an executive at the BBC for over forty years.

Peter York is a connoisseur of urban tribes.

Richard Young is one of London's premier society photographers.

Roy Young played piano on *Young Americans* and *Low.*

Tony Zanetta was the "president" of MainMan.

Christopher Zara works for the *International Business Times.*

ABOUT THE AUTHOR

New York Times bestselling author Dylan Jones has written twenty books on subjects as diverse as music and politics and fashion and photography. He has been an editor at the *Observer*, the *Sunday Times*, *i-D*, *The Face*, and *Arena*, a columnist for the *Guardian* and the *Independent*, and is currently the editor in chief of *GQ*. He has won Magazine Editor of the Year eleven times, and been awarded the prestigious Mark Boxer Award, while his book on the former British Prime Minister, David Cameron, was shortlisted for the Channel 4 Political Book of the Year. He is a trustee of the Hay Festival, a board member of the British Fashion Council, and an advisory council member of the Norman Mailer Center. He was awarded an OBE in the Queen's Honours List in 2013. He lives in London and Powys with his family.